MORMON RELIGIOUS BELIEF has long been a mystery to outsiders, either dismissed as anomalous to the American religious tradition or extolled as the most genuine creation of the American religious imagination. This study presents the first extended analysis of Mormon theology to have been written against the backdrop of religion and popular culture in the early modern North Atlantic world, a context that permits the most coherent analysis of Mormon origins. John Brooke argues that Mormon doctrines of the mutuality of spirit and matter, of celestial marriage (in the nineteenth century, polygamous marriage), and of human deification can be understood only in light of the connections between the occult and the sectarian ideal of restoration forged among early modern religious radicals. Hermeticism, of which alchemy was the experimental practice, posited that humanity could regain the divine powers of Adam lost in the fall from Paradise; so too the prophet Joseph Smith promised the Mormon faithful that they would become "gods" through the restoration of ancient mysteries. Exploring the opposing forces of hermetic purity and danger – manifested in sectarian religion, magic, witchcraft beliefs, alchemy, Freemasonry, counterfeiting, and state formation – in the making of the Mormon church, the book closes with an overview of the transformation of Mormonism from the 1860s to the present.

9

0

The Refiner's Fire

The Refiner's Fire
The Making of Mormon Cosmology, 1644–1844

JOHN L. BROOKE

Tufts University

CAMBRIDGE
UNIVERSITY PRESS

Published by the Press Syndicate of the University of Cambridge
The Pitt Building, Trumpington Street, Cambridge CB2 1RP
40 West 20th Street, New York, NY 10011-4211, USA
10 Stamford Road, Oakleigh, Melbourne 3166, Australia

First published 1994
Reprinted 1996
First paperback edition 1996

Printed in the United States of America

Library of Congress Cataloging-in-Publication Data
Brooke, John L.
The refiner's fire : the making of Mormon cosmology, 1644–1844 /
John L. Brooke.
p.   cm.
Includes bibliographical references and index.
ISBN 0-521-34545-6
1. Mormon cosmology – History of doctrines – 19th century.
2. Occultism – Religious aspects – Mormon Church – History of
doctrines – 19th century.   3. Mormon Church – History – 19th century.
I. Title.
BX8643.C68B76   1994
230'.93'09 – dc20   93-37366
                                                              CIP

A catalog record for this book is available from the British Library.

ISBN 0-521-34545-6 Hardback
ISBN 0-521-56564-2 Paperback

Portions of Part III were previously published in " 'Of whole nations
being born in one day': Marriage, money and magic in the Mormon
cosmos, 1830–1846," *Social Science Information* (1991), Vol. 30,
No. 1. Reprinted with permission of Sage Publications Ltd.

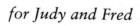

for Judy and Fred

Contents

Illustrations

Maps

Preface

This study began in May 1985, when the newspapers first published accounts of startling documentary discoveries touching on the history of Mormonism. Letters purported to have been written in the 1820s conjured up a fascinating picture of popular magic, treasure-hunting, and ancient, alchemical salamander symbolism among the peoples of the Burned-over District. Piquing my curiosity as a historian, these images perhaps triggered childhood memories, memories of after-school expeditions to dig for garnets, or of coming upon red efts, summer salamanders, scarlet with delicate orange spots, in the moist, mossy woods below Lenox Mountain.

Not unlike these red efts, which always managed to escape when brought home to makeshift terrariums, the Mormon salamander vaporized between October 1985 and June 1986, as a series of bombings and careful forensic proof of forgery demonstrated that the "White Salamander Letter" and a host of other newly "discovered" documents were the work of a master counterfeiter, Mark Hofmann. But in the interval the salamander opened up a new view of the origins of the Mormon religion. Though the Hofmann letters were forged, they were rooted in documented behavior; Joseph Smith was indeed deeply involved in the popular magic of treasure-divining in the 1820s, the decade when he claimed to have discovered golden plates buried in the earth and translated them into the *Book of Mormon*. And beyond this story of divining and prophecy lies the content of the Mormon theology itself, developed by Joseph Smith and associates such as Brigham Young, Heber C. Kimball, and Orson Pratt. Barely touched on in the *Book of Mormon*, this doctrine was compiled in official revelation, printed essays, and reported sermons between the establishment of the church in 1830 and a final florescence at Nauvoo, Illinois, in the early 1840s, with important amplification in Utah in the 1850s. Quite simply, there are striking parallels between the Mormon concepts of the coequality of matter and spirit, of the covenant of celestial marriage, and of an ultimate goal of human godhood and the philosophical traditions of alchemy and hermeticism, drawn from the ancient world and fused with Christianity in the Italian Renaissance. Mormonism and hermeticism both propose a distinct relationship between the visible and invisible worlds. The classical Mormon theology announced by Joseph Smith at Nauvoo in 1844 cast the Mormon faithful not in traditional Christian terms, supplicating divine favor, nor in the role of magicians, manipulating and coercing supernatural forces. Rather, Mormons were to expect, as hermetic perfectionists, to be coparticipants in divinity and to play a direct role in the supernatural cosmos of the invisible world.

This insight, which I have since happily found that many others have arrived at,[1] poses a series of methodological problems. First and foremost, it is not entirely clear how hermeticism might have been conveyed from late-sixteenth-century Europe to the New York countryside in the early nineteenth century. Second, and equally problematic, is the question of how to specify the role of hermeticism in relation to the many obviously Christian elements in Mormon theology.

This book is deeply indebted to the vast historiography on Mormonism, yet it departs from it in fundamental ways. Unlike the official histories and evangelical critiques, which both have their roots as early as the rise of Mormonism itself, this study is not intended to advance a cause or a polemic but arises from simple intellectual curiosity, perhaps an excess of curiosity. If I share some of the agnostic skepticism of Fawn Brodie, whose *No Man Knows My History*[2] raised such an outcry in Mormon circles, I am perhaps more willing to accept the personal sincerity of Joseph Smith's prophetic claim.

I also depart from at least one major strand in the more recent literature on Mormonism. During the 1950s and the 1960s functionalist theory began to take a broad and deep hold in our understanding of religious development in early-nineteenth-century America. Drawing on the work of Max Weber, Ernst Troeltsch, and H. Richard Niebuhr,[3] American historians began to interpret the religious movements of the Second Great Awakening in relation to social and economic transformation and the new political order of the young Republic. This functionalist perspective has been extremely productive in generating new understandings of the place of religion in the American past, but it also has had a deleterious effect, reinforcing a tendency toward chronological compartmentalization and discouraging attention to the content of religious belief and discourse.

Functionalist theory has had a particularly powerful and ironic impact on Mormon history. Starting in the 1960s, a central theme in the interpretation of Mormon origins has been that the new religion was a functional response to the social stress experienced by poor families in the northeastern countryside and frontier in the wake of the American Revolution.[4] Ironically, this was a theme that both secular and Mormon historians could agree upon. For non-Mormon historians, the rise of Mormonism was merely the most extreme example of a broad pattern that they were discovering across the entire Northeast during the Second Great Awakening, whereas Mormon historians could adopt this social-scientific interpretation without challenging the legitimacy of Joseph Smith's revelations, the central pillar of the Mormon church. Thus the functionalist emphasis on social stress subtly unified the historical examination of Mormon origins in ways that discouraged a serious examination of the content – and possibly earthly origins – of Mormon thought. This has created a gap in the literature that I hope this study will fill.

In some measure the functionalist school was working to overturn a prior interpretation advanced by Whitney Cross and David Brion Davis that rooted Mormonism in the culture of early New England.[5] In some cases the functionalist position has been virtually Turnerian, arguing with Tolstoy that Mormonism was the quintessential American religion, forged on the frontier without any debt to the Old World or to the religious culture of the colonies. Although my book is in some measure a restatement of the Cross and Davis thesis of cultural continuity, I must dissent from their rooting of Mormonism "in the Puritan culture of old New England."[6] Rather than running from the Puritanism brought to New England in the Great Migration, firmly situated in the Magisterial Reformation of Calvinist theology and a state-supported religion, Mormonism springs from the sectarian tradition of the Radical Reformation, in fact from its most extreme fringe. Ironically, in pressing their case against Cross and Davis, the functionalist historians have forged an important understanding of these Mormon roots in the Radical Reformation. Whereas some earlier work discussed Mormon theology solely in terms of the millennial beliefs current in evangelical Protestantism, a wave of important research since the late 1960s has pinpointed religious primitivism and especially the concept of restoration as critical to the Mormon message. The religious authority of the Mormon prophet rested not on a prediction of the end of time but on his announcement that his visions and revelations were the divine intervention required to restore the true church, a third dispensation that inaugurated the Kingdom of God on earth and superseded all previous dispensations as corrupted.[7]

Restoration may have reached dramatic manifestations in the New World, but it is incomprehensible without a consideration of its Old World roots. So, too, the rediscovery of Joseph Smith's fascination with popular magic in the 1820s has added yet another line of continuity with the Old World, as scholars have worked to understand and situate Smith's money-digging in the broadest possible context.[8] Such has been the premise of this study. Though the functionalist theory of social stress may well explain the potential for the emergence of a radical restorationist movement, and the potential for a response to such a message,[9] it cannot explain the theologically distinct message of the Mormon church or sufficiently explain the social origins of the converted membership. If biblical primitivism is a broad theme in American religious history, the Mormon claim of a revealed restoration ideal has few parallels, and the combination of temple ritual, polygamous marriage, three-tiered heavens, the coequality of spirit and matter, and promise of godhood is essentially unique.

Unless one rests one's argument on revelation, Jungian archetypes, or simple reinvention (all of which are of some importance to this problem), we have to ask from where these ideas came, we have to take seriously the problem of the transmission and reformulation of memory and of text. This has led me to a detailed reexamination of the interval separating Joseph Smith from the late Renaissance, guided and inspired by the work of Frances Yates, Carlo Ginzburg, Christopher Hill, and Jon Butler.[10] Joseph Smith's cosmology becomes comprehensible only when it is placed in a setting broader than that of antebellum America. Smith's Mormon cosmology is best understood when situated on an intellectual and theological *conjuncture* that reaches back not simply to a disorderly antebellum democracy or even to early New England but to the extreme perfectionism forged in the Radical Reformation from the fusion of Christianity with the ancient occult hermetic philosophy. The milieu of the antebellum American hinterlands can explain the context of the Mormon emergence but not the content of its cosmology. For this content we need to look beyond milieu to memory, to the diffuse and divergent trails of cultural continuity that prepared certain peoples – and a particular young man – for the building of a religious tradition that drew deeply from the most radical doctrines of early modern Europe's religious crucible.[11]

Quite obviously, this is not a traditional Mormon history, for I am not a Mormon historian. It is a selective reinterpretation of the founding story of Mormonism from 1796 to the 1850s in light of a reexamination of the relationships between religion and the occult in the early modern North Atlantic. Perhaps the image of an hourglass best captures the book's structure, with the various fragments of sectarian and hermetic culture passing through Joseph Smith's youthful consciousness to shape the classical Mormon cosmology. Thus Parts I and II widely examine the connections among magic, hermeticism, and radical religion in early modern Europe and early America, asking who were the people prepared for the Mormon message and what were the vectors of hermetic culture that they encountered. Here I write as a historian of early American society and religion, exploring little-known byways of popular culture in somewhat greater detail than might be given to them in other studies of Mormonism.[12] Part

I ventures a broad interpretation of the relationship between religious and occult belief in early America; Part II introduces a dyad of hermetic purity and danger – Freemasonry and counterfeiting – both of which I argue played formative roles in the rise of Mormonism. Part I and Part II each close with a chapter examining the experience of families of future Mormons in seventeenth- and eighteenth-century New England, Chapter 6 looking at the life of Smith's parents in turn-of-the-century Vermont. Part III opens with the narrow waist of the hourglass: Smith's early life in the Lake Ontario region, especially the circumstances surrounding the writing of the *Book of Mormon,* as he moved from conjurer to restorationist. Chapters 8 to 11 explore Smith's transformation from prophet to Christian-hermetic *magus,* with particular attention devoted to the various purities and dangers, hermetic and otherwise, that framed the rise of Mormonism. Chapter 12 briefly suggests how the Mormon church has gradually distanced itself from its hermetic origins since the 1850s.

Several caveats are in order. This book is fundamentally a presentation of the hermetic interpretation of Mormon origins, in relation to the prior cultural history of hermeticism in the early modern North Atlantic. This is not necessarily a well-rounded approach to early Mormonism. Hermeticism explains the more exotic features of the inner logic of Mormon theology, but given the secret nature of this inner logic before 1844, and its relative obscurity to this day, it may not necessarily explain the reasons for Mormonism's public appeal. Thus the latter half of the book is less a balanced history of Mormonism than a reconstruction of the intellectual life of Joseph Smith Jr. and the Mormon leadership in light of the hermetic tradition examined in the first half of the book. Here, however, other important dimensions of the Mormon story could not be excluded, and I explore the ways in which Joseph Smith's quest for hermetic divinity shaped perceptions of marriage and gender, the building of a separatist Mormon polity, and the dynamics of the prophetic personality.

My final caveat brings me to acknowledgments. Since I began this work a wealth of new studies bearing variously on Mormonism, hermeticism, and sectarian religion in the early modern North Atlantic have appeared, too numerous to list in full, which have made my work much easier and more productive. Among these, I should single out Michael Quinn's *Early Mormonism and the Magic World View.* Quinn and I come to somewhat different interpretations, but his study has been an invaluable guide and treasure-house of information.

After I intuited a hermetic–Mormon connection in 1985, I soon found that many others had been there before me. Thus in many places this book has more of the character of a synthesis than an original piece of research. Here I am very happy to thank Thomas L. Revere for the detailed research on the genealogy and local history of treasure-divining that he shared with me so generously over the years. Tom Revere also patiently introduced me to the role of Freemasonry in early Mormonism. He has been a friend and advisor whose help has contributed immeasurably to this book.

Over the past eight years a host of other people have helped me with research. Special thanks go to William Stokoe, whose family preserved Joseph Stafford's collection of books and manuscripts over two centuries, for welcoming me into his home to study them, and for donating these items to the Rhode Island Historical Society. I am also grateful to Thomas G. Alexander, Richard Anderson, Jeff Bach, Peter Benes, Wayne Bodle, Jon Butler, Drew Cayton, John Engstrom, Robert Filerup, Dean Jessee, Mark Mastromarini, George Mitten, Peter Onuf, Rosamund Rosenmeier, Randy Roth, Jan Shipps, Robert St. George, Alan Taylor, Linda Walker, and the late Wesley Walters for responding to my inquiries and sharing unpublished papers and material from their own research. Lou Masur helped to settle down the title. Among many institutional connections, I am very grateful for the efforts of Ronald Barney of the LDS Church Historical Department, James Folts of the New York State Archives, Greg Sanford and his staff at the Vermont State Archives, Gary Thompson, Elaine Morie, and Michael Hunter of Hobart/William Smith Libraries, and Anne Filiaci, Kathy Muzdakis, and Margaret McCaughey of the clerk's offices in Ontario, Monroe, and Livingston counties in the state of New York.

Tufts University's origins as a Universalist college and the helpful assistance of the staff have made Wessell Library a wonderful base for research and writing. I have also been fortunate to be able to use the comprehensive Mormon collections at the Widener Library, Harvard University, and at the Bancroft Library, University of California at Berkeley, the religious history collections at the Andover–Harvard Divinity School, and the excellent collections in Masonic history at the Museum of Our National Heritage. I have also used the collections at the LDS Church Historical Department, the LDS Family History Center, the Utah State Historical Society, the Marriott Library at the University of Utah, the Harold B. Lee Library at Brigham Young University, the New England Historic Genealogical Society, the Massachusetts State Archives, the Connecticut State Archives, and the Rhode Island Historical Society.

This project has been generously supported over the years. I am especially grateful to the American Council of Learned Societies and the Commonwealth Center at the College of William and Mary, both of which provided funding for a year of research and writing in 1990 and 1991. The Institute of Early American History and Culture provided a very collegial and productive place to work in the spring of 1991. A Tufts faculty sabbatical in the spring of 1993 provided me ample time to finish and revise the manuscript.

The first test that a research project undergoes is the scrutiny provided by public presentations. I am very much indebted for the opportunity to develop my ideas and my evidence – and for commentary and critique given free of charge – at a variety of such forums, including the Charles Warren Center Seminar, the Organization of American Historians, the University of Connecticut History Department Colloquium, the Colonial Society of Massachusetts paper series, Viola Sachs's Colloquia at the Maison des Sciences de l'Homme at the University of Paris, the Andover–Harvard Divinity School Church History Seminar, the Institute of Early American History and Culture Colloquium, the Commonwealth Center Colloquium, the Atlantic History Workshop at Johns Hopkins University, Michael Zuckerman's seminar at the University of Pennsylvania, and most recently the Dublin Seminar for New England Folklife. All of these occasions were extremely stimulating and provided much food for thought.

The second test is that of the manuscript itself. Over the years Barbara Dailey, Paul Goodman, David Hall, Steve Marrone, Larry Moore, and Marcus Rediker have read (and reread) various chapters at various stages; Jeff Bach and Clarence Spohn critiqued and improved my discussions of Ephrata. Most heroically, Frederick Balderston, Jon Butler, Tom Revere, Jan Shipps, Frank Smith, and Michael Zuckerman have all read the entire manuscript. The voluminous commentary all these readers have provided over the years would fill a volume of its own. Whatever virtues this book may have are due to their efforts; they bear no responsibilities for its many failings.

Finally, I come to an important group of people who really could not care less about this book. Sara, patient but not a little skeptical about the entire project, has kept me firmly grounded in reality. Matthew, a budding historian in his own right, has kept me busy with soccer and baseball. And perhaps Benjy has absorbed something of this story through some osmotic process. The day I began to write this preface he picked out a new T-shirt and shorts, emblazoned with a smiling salamander, green and purple with a bold red stripe.

PART I

A Prepared People

1

Dreams of the Primal Adam

[I]t shall be done unto them all things whatsoever my servant hath put upon them, in time and through all eternity; and shall be of full force when they are out of the world; and they shall pass the angels and the gods, which are set there, to their exaltation and glory in all things, as hath been sealed upon their heads, which glory shall be a fulness and a continuation of the seeds forever and ever.

Then shall they be gods, because they have no end; therefore shall they be from everlasting to everlasting, because they continue; then shall they be above all, because all things are subject to them. Then shall they be gods, because they have all power, and the angels are subject to them.

Revelation of Joseph Smith, the Mormon prophet, recorded July 12, 1843, at Nauvoo, Illinois[1]

THE STORY OF THE MORMONS, the Latter-day Saints, begins with Joseph Smith Jr. In the spring of 1829 this young man of twenty-four years announced a new dispensation to the peoples of the Burned-over District of the state of New York, a countryside recently settled by New England migrants and now swept by the fires of evangelical religion. Announcing that his revelations restored the primitive apostolic church and opened the Kingdom of God on earth, Smith claimed to have brought forth not simply a new church but a new dispensation, fully equivalent to the dispensations of Moses and Christ. Mormonism, in his vision, would some day sweep away all other faiths as the universal true religion.

The Mormon restoration had its own prophet, its own testament, its own sacred tabernacles. As a prophet, Smith claimed to be a vehicle of the continuing revelation of the "Word," opening a channel of divine power between the visible and invisible worlds. He laid claim to the authority of Enoch and Elijah, the biblical prophets who were carried bodily into heaven by divine power. This restoration was inaugurated with the miraculous writing of the *Book of Mormon,* translated by divine power from golden plates buried by the last survivor of an ancient people. The promise of this dispensation would be realized in sacred temples to be built in Ohio, Illinois, and finally Utah. Among the Mormons the Lord would come into his tabernacle, spiritualizing matter and materializing spirit.

3

In this divine presence, the Mormons would receive divine privilege. Claiming a power of continuing revelation in a new dispensation, Smith throughout the 1830s prophesied the granting of keys and the unfolding of mysteries to come. As all-out civil war closed in on the church in Illinois in the final year of his life, Smith specified these mysteries: the promise of a progressively perfect divinity to the Mormon faithful. Thus his revelation at Nauvoo promised the people of the Mormon Kingdom that if they were true to the ordinances and commandments of the church, "[t]hen shall they be gods." In announcing a new dispensation, in assuming the revelatory powers of a prophet, in blurring the lines between spirit and matter, and in promising godhood to the faithful, Smith defied not only the established and evangelical churches of the Second Great Awakening but even the most ardent contemporary advocates of the imminence of the millennium. In establishing the Mormon church, Joseph Smith staked out a claim to dispensational authority placing his Latter-day Saints at – and even beyond – the radical fringe of the Christian tradition.

These are the central themes of the Mormon story as it traditionally has been told. But we also know that the young Joseph Smith was a treasure-diviner, or money-digger. His discovery of the Golden Plates of the *Book of Mormon* was embedded in a culture of magical practice that drew upon a compound of popular lore of witchcraft, conjuring, counterfeiting, and alchemy. And we know that at Nauvoo Smith's announcement of the temple rituals carrying the Mormon promise of divinity came in the wake of his renewed interest in Freemasonry, which was just emerging from the stigma imposed by the Antimasonic furor over the murder of William Morgan that had swept the Burned-over District as Smith was composing the *Book of Mormon*. With different levels of system and coherence, both treasure-divining and Freemasonry were rooted in the philosophy of metallic transmutation and human perfection known broadly as hermeticism, and hermeticism was fundamental to the origins of the Mormon cosmology.

This book argues that Joseph Smith went through two critical transformations. He began his engagement with the supernatural as a village conjurer but transformed himself into a prophet of the "Word," announcing the opening of a new dispensation. Then, moving beyond his role as prophet and revelator, Smith transformed himself and the Mormon priesthood into Christian-hermetic *magi,* a role previously manifested in the medieval alchemist, the Renaissance hermetic philosopher, and the perfectionist sectarians of the Radical Reformation.

An adequate understanding of this evolving fusion of conjuring, restorationist prophecy, and hermetic perfectionism requires that we take a long view. Little in the religious and cultural history of Puritan New England prepares us for the combination of radical religion and magical influence that we find in Joseph Smith. Certainly this history will have to be reexamined, but we must begin with an exploration of Reformation Europe and revolutionary England, for here we will find the closest analogues, indeed critical antecedents, of the evolving identities of diviner, prophet, and *magus* assumed by Joseph Smith from the coming of the *Book of Mormon* in the hills of central New York to the framing of the Mormon Kingdom on the banks of the Mississippi.

The peoples of medieval and early modern Europe viewed earth and the cosmos as a hierarchy of visible and invisible worlds, of matter and of spirit, stretching from village streets and fields up to supernatural forces in the stars and beyond to a divinity in the heavens. The Reformation was a struggle for the definition of and control over this hierarchy of visible and invisible worlds. The outcome was the fragmentation of medieval theological unity under the Catholic church with the religious insurgency of the new Protestant churches and sects. But the rise of Protestantism was only one of a series of fault lines wracking the spiritual life of Reformation Europe, fault lines involving claims to divine immanence, the popular practices of magic, and the esoterica of hermetic divinization. Seen from this perspective, we can isolate four distinctly different spiritual authorities competing for popular allegiance in this struggle: church reformers, utopian prophets, cunning folk, and Christian-hermetic *magi*.

In many ways, the reforming clergy and laity of Protestantism and Catholicism shared a common agenda of regularity, order, and control. Although Protestants clearly led the assault on the form and spirit of medieval Christianity, they were closely followed by the Catholic reformers of the Counter-Reformation. Certainly Protestants, especially Calvinists, were far more thorough in their purging of Christianity: at its extreme, Protestant spiritual life was reduced to the believer, Bible in hand and lectured by preachers, facing in fearful isolation the uncertainties of predestination at the hands of an omnipotent God. But following the mid-sixteenth-century reforms of the Council of Trent, Counter-Reformation Catholicism reasserted papal authority, revitalized popular piety, and suppressed many of the irregularities and layers of sacred theater that had inspired the Protestant revolution in the first place.[2]

Protestant and Catholic reformers also shared a common antipathy for contrary and disorderly voices, most obviously those of prophetic, millenarian, and utopian radicals who challenged the spiritual hegemony and civil privilege that both parties struggled to assert. The medieval church had long struggled to suppress heretical movements such as the Albigensian Cathars, the Lollards, and the Taborites, and Catholics certainly viewed the rise of Protestantism in the same light. But the Protestants were divided similarly into two broad camps, reformers and radicals. The first, the Magisterial Reformation of Lutherans, Calvinists, and Anglicans, limited biblical primitivism to a restoration of Augustinian piety and retained a central place for predestination, a restricted human will, and the state's role in upholding a true faith. The advocates of a Radical Reformation, divided in northern Europe broadly between Anabaptists and Spirituals, rejected the state's role in a Christian commonwealth and advanced doctrines of a restoration of a pure apostolic church, free will and universal salvation, human powers of prophecy, and an impending millennium or new dispensation. The militancy of the Anabaptists of Münster and the perfectionism of the English revolutionary sects posed just as much of a threat to Protestant reformers as Protestantism itself posed for Catholicism. The lineage of the Latter-day Saints runs back to this Radical Reformation.[3]

Most fundamentally, Protestant and Catholic reformers worked to narrow the supernatural universe to the singular divinity of God, but they also set this essential goodness in opposition to an essential evil: Satan. A fear of the devil pervaded medieval Christianity and intensified in the later Middle Ages with mounting demographic, social, and political stresses. This fear of demonic power brought into focus a common Protestant and Catholic agenda: the isolation and elimination of another alternative authority on the spiritual landscape. This alternative authority, real and imagined, comprised the conjuring people and sorcerers – the witches – of medieval Europe.[4]

Protestant and Catholic theology declared that spiritual power would move in one direction and from one source between invisible and visible worlds. Divine providence would flow from above to below to determine the course of earthly events, and divine grace would flow from above to below to effect the heavenly salvation of mere mortals. In sharp contrast, a host of lay practitioners of magic claimed to be able to intervene in the heavens, to manipulate forces in the invisible world. These wise men and women, the cunning folk or white witches, offered their supernatural services to solve mundane personal problems, claiming to heal the sick, to divine the future, to cast spells, to control the weather, to find lost property and ancient treasure-hoards, and to protect against the devil and his minions, the sorcerers or black witches.[5]

The cunning folk, claiming to invoke beneficent spirits for beneficial ends, were the inheritors of the complex fusions of medieval piety, in which syncretisms of pagan practice and Christian belief, vernacular tradition and learned text, churchly magic and occult piety, had contributed to the initial and continuing spread of Christianity in early medieval Europe.[6] The sources of their magical knowledge were diverse, and a matter of some debate. Much of medieval magic ritual derived from pre-Christian sources, sometimes classical but more usually indigenous, or "barbarian."[7] Some historians see evidence for a deep stratum of folk cosmology dating to preclassical Indo-European sources, grading into a primal folk religion of healing, fertility, and domestic life carried by generations of women into the early modern era.[8]

Paradoxically, the Reformation saw something of a heightened demand for the services of the cunning folk, as people sought protection from evil forces of witchcraft in Protestant regions, where the traditional churchly magic of exorcism was abandoned.[9] But the comforts provided by the practitioners of white magic were anathema to the church, Catholic and Protestant, exposing the conjurers to deadly peril. For Catholics, white-magical practice was a usurpation of the powers of the priest; both Protestants and Catholics denounced witch magic as superstition and demonic collusion. For the devout Calvinist, both ecclesiastical and folk magic challenged the concept of a sovereign God whose divine providence determined all things. Magical practice of any sort was an effort to manipulate the spiritual, invisible world and thus involved a suspension of the Calvinist belief in the immutability of God's providence. White magic elevated mere men and women to the level of potent actors in spiritual affairs, actors who conceivably were in league with the devil. Throughout early modern Europe, and in early New England, the cunning folk were often accused of the very witchcraft they claimed to be guarding against.[10]

Whereas the people of the churches stood in awe of the invisible world, the cunning folk offered a practical but indirect manipulation of that cosmos, by means of often ancient magical practice. In an ambiguous affinity, the radical prophets offered a similar connection between the spiritual and the material: divine power would be manifested in direct revelation and the literal coming of the Kingdom of God. But a fourth spiritual archetype – with much less ambiguous affinities with the radical messages of prophecy and restoration – promised an even more fundamental departure: human participation in the cosmos as divine beings.

The mystical philosophies of alchemy, the Cabala, and more broadly the hermetic theology offered not only a view of the stars but a ladder up through them to the divine Godhead. The goal of the hermetic philosophy was to recover the divine power and perfection possessed by Adam before the Fall, and indeed before Creation. Just as the purification of the church by Protestants and Catholics isolated and demonized the cunning folk, so too the hermetic *magus* was expelled in the destruction of the medieval synthesis. When recombined in the Radical Reformation and the English

Revolution with currents of millenarian prophecy and a conviction of the imminence of the restored Kingdom of God, hermetic divinization posed a potent challenge to Christian orthodoxy. It also prefigured the cosmology constructed in the 1830s and 1840s by Joseph Smith, who was born in – if not of – a Calvinist culture and moved from the ranks of the cunning folk to the status of an Adamic *magus* as the prophet of the Mormon restoration. This chapter, and indeed the entire book, explores the particular affinities, latent and manifest, running between the religious culture of prophecy and restoration and the occult cultures of popular conjuring and esoteric hermeticism.

Since it is unfamiliar to many readers, and so central to this story, we need to examine briefly the history of hermeticism.[11] The origins of hermetic thought lay in Greco-Roman Egypt, where ancient metallurgical traditions were fused with Platonism, Gnosticism, and Egyptian theology. Passing from Islamic sources at the turn of the twelfth century, fragments of the hermetic philosophy emerged in medieval Europe in the form of alchemy.[12] These fragments contained a theory of material creation from ethereal vapors, rooted in a vision of a living, breathing earth and of necessary correspondences between material and spiritual entities. The alchemist believed that metals grew and changed within the earth from exhalations of philosopher's mercury and sulphur, derivations of watery vapor and earthly smoke. By means of a spiritual experimentalism requiring a strict sequence of distillations and sublimations, one might imitate and accelerate a natural process of metallic growth. At its core, hermetic alchemy offered the possibility of a mystical transmutation encompassing living metals and living mortals. The alchemist sought by laborious ritualized experiment to formulate a medicinal elixir, the philosopher's stone, which would transmute base metals into gold and would perfect mere mortals, giving them earthly immortality. The stone, also known as the quintessence or the *prima materia,* was the central element in an elaborate alchemical symbology of divine perfection, produced by alchemical marriage, the *coniunctio,* allegorized as the mating, fusion, death, and resurrection of philosophical sulphur and mercury, the sun and the moon, the alchemical King and Queen. In a complex, Christian-hermetic symbology, these opposed principles were described in terms of a host of dyadic pairings: light and dark, good and evil, male and female. The agent of their resolution was the divine flame of the "refiner's fire," or the Holy Ghost. The outcome of their resolution was the androgynous Adam, the manifestation of divine immortality.[13]

By the time of Albertus Magnus (1193–1280) and Roger Bacon (1214–

The alchemical marriage, as depicted in Daniel Stolcius, *Viridarium Chymicum* [Pleasure garden of chemistry] (London, 1624).
Courtesy of the Department of Special Collections, Memorial Library, University of Wisconsin–Madison-Wisconsin.

92), alchemical experimentation had spread widely in scholarly circles in Europe. Medieval alchemists had practical intentions, hoping, as Bacon put it, "to make the noble metals, and colours, and many other things," including "such things as are capable of prolonging human life for much longer periods than can be accomplished by nature."[14] Other medieval alchemists were less concerned about the "public good." With the spreading rumors of the alchemic promise of making gold by art came a host of "smoke-sellers" and "multipliers of metals." With an appropriately scholarly demeanor, a pretended knowledge of mystic secrets, and some impressive pieces of alchemic equipment, these "Geber's cooks" or "puffers" persuaded gullible kings, gentry, and villagers that, for a minimal investment of scarce coin, they could have gold beyond their dreams. From the age of Chaucer to that of Shakespeare the ragged chemical con man was an archetypal figure, proscribed by law in many European states. He would reappear in eighteenth-century America.[15]

Where the Middle Ages saw practical and fraudulent alchemists turn the available fragments of an ancient tradition to rather mundane purposes, the Renaissance brought the full articulation of hermetic philosophy, as lost ancient texts were suddenly discovered and translated. Hermetic philosophy, or, more precisely, theology, reached a powerful synthesis at the late-fifteenth-century court of the Medicis, as Florentine intellectuals turned their attention from civic humanism to an otherworldly occult philosophy. Two central figures, Marsilio Ficino (1433–99) and Giovanni Pico della Mirandola (1463–94), adapted ancient hermeticism and the more recent Judaic Cabala to Christian traditions of mysticism, prophecy, and natural magic in an intellectual system that would be widely influential throughout Europe for centuries to come.[16]

The hermetic revival began in 1463, when Cosimo de Medici ordered his court scholar Marsilio Ficino to set aside his translation of Plato and work on a collection of manuscripts acquired in Macedonia in 1460. These writings, the *Corpus Hermeticum,* were supposedly the revelations of a divine being, Hermes Trismegistus. Although the texts made it seem that Trismegistus was a predecessor of Moses, he was a creation of second- and third-century pagan Gnostics, a fusion of the Greek Hermes with the Egyptian Thoth. Though the French scholar Isaac Casaubon demonstrated their second-century origin in 1614, occult philosophers continued to read the hermetic texts as ancient revelation until the end of the seventeenth century.[17]

The most important book of the *Hermetica* was the "Pimander," which Ficino interpreted as an Egyptian precursor to the biblical book of Genesis. Ficino was impressed by their similarities, but there were critically important differences between the traditional Mosaic Genesis and this rediscovered (and supposedly older) "Egyptian Genesis."

First and foremost, where the Mosaic Genesis described a divine creation of matter from nothing, *creatio ex nihilo,* the *Hermetica* firmly posited a *creatio ex deo.* Matter came not from nothing but from God himself. Unlike Christian thought, which posed a fundamental opposition between elemental matter and divine spirit, the hermetic Genesis described a sequence of separations and divisions, as a light emanating from the primal divine intelligence divided into light and dark, transmuted into fire and water, out of which the elements were "separated" to form an ordered world. Divine spirit was thus the original primal matter, the alchemists' *prima materia,* from which sprang the entire universe. This fundamental hermetic concept of the eternal origins of matter would be of primary importance to the Mormon cosmology that Joseph Smith constructed in the 1830s.[18]

Just as matter derived from divinity, so too did humanity. The biblical Adam and Eve, attempting to approach God by eating of the Tree of Knowledge, are banished from the Garden. Conversely, the hermetic Adam is embraced by God and granted divine powers on a par with the Seven Governors, star demons, who have been sharing in the work of Creation. Where the biblical Adam's sin brought his Fall, the hermetic Adam voluntarily gave up his divine powers to take "up his abode in matter devoid of reason" to mate with a beautiful "Nature." After the birth of seven "prodigious" offspring, he changed from "life and light" to "soul and mind," and eventually, with his children, divided into male and female and inhabited the earth as humanity. Having lost divine "life," humanity could recover it by an understanding of these divine origins: "if then, being made of Life and Light, you learn to know that you are made of them, you will go back into Life and Light."[19] For the speculative alchemist, the primal divisions and separations of the hermetic Creation made up the central type for his "great work": the philosopher's stone, the hermaphroditic fusion of male sulphur and female mercury, was the analogue of the hermaphrodite Adam, the perfect man. The ultimate purpose of the hermetics was to restore the powers over the cosmos that "Primal Man" had lost at the Fall. As Peter French has put it:

> Hermeticism raised man from the status of a pious and awestruck observer of God's wonders and encouraged him to operate within his universe by using the powers of the cosmos to his own advantage. . . . Through his intellect man could perform marvelous feats – it was no longer man *under* God, but God *and* man.

The offspring of Adam were once again to be equal with God, imbued with cosmic supernatural powers in their status as "*magi*" or "astral men."[20]

The *Corpus Hermeticum,* made up of both these philosophical texts and a technical body of alchemical writings, composed the centerpiece of Renaissance hermeticism, but there were other important elements as well. Ficino built around the hermetic theme of the magus a natural magic of sympathetic music and astrological talismans, devoted to perfecting a harmony between the material world and the stars in the heavens.[21] His follower Pico della Mirandola reached up beyond the stars to divinity above when he incorporated into the hermetic system the Hebrew Cabala, learned from Jews fleeing the Spanish Inquisition in the 1480s. Meditation on language, letters, and numerals brought the Cabalist to hidden meanings in the sacred texts: literally, the discovery of the primal universal language lost at the Fall. By mystical trance and alchemical experiment Cabalists and hermeticists hoped to break free from the elemental sphere of the earth and ascend through the lesser celestial and supercelestial heavens of the planets, the stars, and the angels, to communicate directly with the divinity.[22]

Hermetic thought would provide the key to the secrets of the cosmos. It was at its core an optimistic, expansive philosophy, celebrating the potential divinity and power of humanity; as a central thread of the Renaissance, and then a critical vehicle in the emergence of modern science, hermeticism might well be interpreted as an important root of Western modernity.[23] It certainly should be distinguished from previous traditions of European mysticism. Like Renaissance hermeticism, medieval mystical heresies, such as that of Meister Eckhart (c. 1260–1327), invoked the pre-Creation and offered a return to unity in God, but, in sharp contrast, they were dualistic and pessimistic. The material world was flawed and evil, to be transcended by the mystical experience and ultimately to be escaped in a reunion with the Godhead. God was unknowable; rather than intelligence, a profound empty ignorance was the "negative way" to divinization. Rather than being continuous, matter and spirit were unalterably opposed. The Cathars shared this view of a dualism of matter and spirit, and sought to make themselves perfect by renouncing marriage, bringing upon themselves accusations of Manichaeism by their insistence that the visible world was evil and demonic.[24]

The Mormon cosmology constructed by Joseph Smith was as optimistic as Renaissance hermeticism and shared with it a startling number of common themes. As he was gathering his church in Fayette, New York, in December 1830, Smith announced that he had been given "the keys of the mystery of those things which have been sealed, even things which were from the foundation of the world."[25] The revelation of these "mysteries of the kingdom" commenced with Smith's revision of Genesis in the months following; in February 1832 he reproduced the three heavens of the Cabala and hermeticism in the three Mormon heavens, the telestial, terrestrial, and celestial kingdoms.[26] Both hermeticism and Mormonism celebrate the mutuality of spiritual and material worlds, precreated intelligences, free will, a divine Adam, a fortunate, sinless Fall, and the symbolism and religious efficacy of marriage and sexuality. And, as in hermeticism, Adam, "the father of all, prince of all, that ancient of days,"[27] would occupy a central position in the Mormon cosmology.

Reformation Calvinists would stand before their omnipotent God of wonders and sovereign will as sinful and totally powerless inheritors of Adam's original sin at the Fall. They might be made aware of the power of God through the divine providences that he sent down on their world, but they must wait in doubt or faith for redemption through an arbitrary distribution of divine grace. In stark contrast, hermeticism promised divine power to mortal man as *magus,* restored to the freedom of will and the powers of Adam in Paradise before the Fall. Hermeticism and Mormonism both rejected the doctrine of original sin and advocated the freedom of the human will: both were bearers of the "Pelagian heresy."[28] Three centuries after the height of the Renaissance, Mormonism echoed the hermetics – and explicitly rejected Calvinism – in its advocacy of universal salvation and the freedom of the will, its replacement of the doctrine of original sin with that of the fortunate Fall, and its denial of the efficacy of grace alone. In granting priestly powers "to seal up the Saints unto Eternal life,"[29] Joseph Smith gave the Mormon hierarchy the same authority that the hermetic alchemist assumed: human means to immortality, indeed divinity.

Just as the Mormon doctrine of deification thus had important Renaissance antecedents, Mormon restorationism, seeing the ancient church restored in a new age, had antecedents running back into the Middle Ages. The writings of the Calabrian abbott Joachim of Fiore (1135–1202) formatively shaped the dream of a restoration of the primitive church in a totally new dispensation. Joachim argued that the history of the world was shaped by the Trinity into the Age of the Father, beginning at Creation, the Age of the Son, beginning with the birth of Christ, and the Age of the Holy Spirit, which he saw beginning sometime between 1200 and 1260. The Age of the Spirit would be a new dispensation, an era of spiritual liberty and perfection, to be announced by the second coming of the prophet Elijah-Elias. Joachim's elaborate numerology of the Trinity, of the Old and New Testaments, and of the Seven Seals of Revelation would attract the Renaissance hermeticists, who wove his prophetic system into their magical Christianity. In the thirteenth and fourteenth centuries Joachim's three dispensations could be assimilated into orthodox Catholicism, often by those attempting to reform the church from within, principally the Franciscans, and those who hoped for a divinely ordained ruler, a world emperor or an angelic pope, to save Europe from fourteenth-century chaos.[30] However, except among the apocalyptic Taborites, who rose to bloody glory in 1419 in Bohemia, there were few dispensational beliefs on the order of Joachim's among the proto-Protestant movements that sought to restore a biblical church: the Waldensians, the Lollards, and the mainstream Hussites.[31] Similarly, with the exception of the Cathars of southern France,[32] the late medieval dissenters were little influenced by the medieval mystics. Though medieval European mysticism emerged at roughly the same time as the practical hermeticism of medieval alchemy, there was no particular relationship between the two. During the Reformation, among small but important groups of radicals and spiritualists, the doctrines of dispensational restorationism and hermetic divinization began to interweave.

Conditions for such a fusion were optimal in the early sixteenth century, as the Protestant assault on the Roman church immediately followed the dissemination of the Florentine synthesis of Christian hermeticism. The two new traditions had a common impulse. If the Protestant impulse was broadly primitivist, seeking to return to first principles, so too was the hermetic impulse, with the obvious difference that the latter drove its quest for primal origins much farther back into antiquity.

But the impact of hermeticism on the Protestant Reformation was highly selective. It was among the radicals – not the magisterial reformers – that the ideas of Adamic, paradisial restoration and hermetic perfectionism emerged. And only a minority of the radicals were caught up in hermetic doctrine; it was the Spiritual thinkers who took these ideas the farthest, whereas Anabaptists settled for achieving the ideal of restoring the apostolic church.

The Anabaptist tradition, and its disastrous extreme manifestation in millennial New Jerusalem in the city of Münster, are important to the story, bearing close comparison to nineteenth-century Mormon polity and sociology. The sixteenth-century Anabaptists were perhaps the archetype of the Radical Reformation, and their tenets of believer's baptism, exclusive separatism, and restoration of the primitive church became the hallmarks of sectarian Protestantism in the North Atlantic. On the other hand, the Münsterites' prophesying, rebellion against the state, communal economy, millennial "Kingdom," and polygamous marriage have suggested comparisons with the Mormons.[33] At its origins, Anabaptist theology also had a central place for Adamic restoration, positing Christ as a heavenly pearl, the Melchizedek, and the Second Adam, saving humanity and opening a new age, the Kingdom of God, restoring the freedom of will enjoyed by Adam in Paradise.[34] Anabaptists were not, however, directly influenced by Renaissance hermeticism, and as they moved into their militant and then pacifist phases, paradisial doctrines were muted and crowded aside. When the Anabaptist militants gathered at Münster in 1534, the model shifted from Paradise to the Israel of David, Solomon, the Maccabees, and the Book of Daniel, legitimating a theocratic monarchy, warrior-saints, a community of goods, and polygamous marriage. This New Jerusalem was put to the sword in 1535, and the survivors, trying to build the pure church under the multiple threats of the Magisterial Reformation, resurgent Catholicism, religious warfare, and devastating witch purges, lowered their sights from chiliasm and dispensationalism to the quietist pure community.[35]

The isolated Spiritualists were freer to advocate a more radical restitution – and to dabble in the perfectionism of the Christian-hermetic *magus*. Renaissance hermeticism had made its way into German intellectual life in the late fifteenth century by way of Johann Reuchlin (1455–1522) and Heinrich Cornelius Agrippa (called Agrippa von Nettesheim; 1486–1535), the author of a massive compendium of intellectual magic, *De Occulta Philosophia*, published in 1533.[36] A hermetic spiritualism also spread among a scattering of German thinkers, the most significant of whom was Philip Bombast von Hohenheim, better known as Paracelsus (1493–1541). The son of an alchemical physician, Paracelsus traveled through Europe, working among miners and the urban poor, curing diseases, abetting popular rebellions, and composing a mystical and medical alchemy that would have a powerful influence for over a century to come. Drawing on medieval mystics, the Cabala, Ficino's magical system, as well as traditional alchemy and astrology, he approached his role as physician-*magus* with the hope of curing the whole person, working on the imagination as well as the body. Drawing directly from the hermetic texts, he described Creation as the separation of the elements from the *prima materia*, the "*mysterium magnum*." For Paracelsus, as for other contemporary hermeticists, spirit and matter were derived from the same eternal source and connected in a fundamental unity. In this creation *ex deo*, this equation of spirit and matter, Paracelsus anticipated the core of Mormon cosmology, as did his Joachimite hope that an Age of Spirit would commence with the second coming of Elijah in the guise of an alchemical "Elias *Artista*."[37]

In his travels Paracelsus met Caspar Schwenkfeld (1489–1561), a leading dispensationalist who advocated a universal redemption of "all creatures" by a Second Adam, who would deify the human soul and restore it to paradisial free will. He also encountered another important, if solitary, Spiritualist, Sebastian Franck (1499–1542). Differing from Schwenkfeld in believing that the soul never lost the divine image of Adam, Franck studied the work of Reuchlin, wrote a paraphrase of Agrippa's *Vanitate Scientiarum*, and claimed that the writings of Plato, Plotinus, and Hermes Trismegistus "had spoken to him more clearly than Moses did."[38]

Schwenkfeld, Paracelsus, and Franck, all born in the 1480s or 1490s, came of age with the Reformation. Influenced in varying degrees by medieval mysticism and the Renaissance hermeticism transmitted by Reuchlin and Agrippa, they collectively announced a cosmology of a new spiritual age, in which humanity would be divinized by the restoration of Adam's paradisial powers. In contrast to the tenets of limited human will, innate

depravity, and original sin central to the Magisterial Reformation, these
ideas provided the basis for doctrines of free will and universal salvation.
Four parallel streams linked this generation with the climax of the hermetic Radical Reformation – the religious sects of revolutionary England –
and framed continuities that would stretch down to the eighteenth-
century revival of the hermetic occult, the ground upon which Joseph
Smith built the Mormon cosmology.

The first stream continued the development of hermetic restorationism
among German Spiritualists, first by Valentine Weigel (1533–88) and then
by Jacob Boehme (1575–1624), the Radical Reformation's most influential theologian of a hermetic perfectionism. A shepherd, shoemaker, and
linen draper, Boehme had a mystical "illumination" around the year 1600,
following years of meditation upon the writings of Schwenkfeld, Franck,
and Weigel. Fusing together strands of thought running from the medieval
mystics, from the hermetic Renaissance through Paracelsus, and from the
paradisial traditions of the radical Spiritualists, Boehme's theology borrowed the Seven Governors and an androgynous divine Adam from
Hermes's "Pimander," and principles of philosophical sulphur, mercury,
and salt from Paracelsus. At the center of his thinking was a pattern of
dialectical interaction between opposites, emanating from and leading
back toward a primal perfection. As in the "Pimander," creation was *ex
deo*, or more precisely from the undifferentiated primal unity, separating
into opposites. Adamic divinity also comprised the perfect balance of
opposing qualities, light and dark, male and female. Again as in the "Pimander," the androgynous Adam's first love was a Heavenly Nature, the
Virgin Sophia, and Adam fell twice, first in division into male and female,
and then out of the Garden. Boehme's foundation in Lutheranism conditioned the optimism of the hermetic tradition: humanity was only passive
and there would be no hope of a universal restoration of primal perfection. However, translated into English during the revolutionary years between 1644 and 1662, his writings would have a wide impact for the next
two centuries on German and English pietists, the theosophy of Emmanuel Swedenborg, the fabrication of high-degree Freemasonry, and the
revival of the occult in the late eighteenth century.[39]

Three other streams running from the early sixteenth century were
unrelated to that leading to Boehme, though they may well have had
points of contact among themselves. Even if they were not connected, the
Family of Love, John Dee's hermeticism, and the Rosicrucian mentality all
helped to move the traditions of Adamic divinization from the Continent
across the Channel in the half century before the English Revolution.

The Family of Love emerged around 1540 in the Netherlands around
Henrick Niclaes (1502–c. 1580), a merchant born in Münster who

claimed to be a prophet of a new Joachimite dispensation, a "begodded man" in whom God could "tabernacle." By 1565 Niclaes had institutionalized his vision of personal divinization in a highly organized underground sect, the House of Love, that involved a hierarchy of priesthoods corresponding to degrees of perfection or divinization. Niclaes himself was the "Oldest Elder in the Holy Understanding," followed by twenty-four Old Elders, Seraphims, or Archbishops, and by five layers of priesthoods, including the majority of the initiated members, men and women, who were called "Priests of the Pleasure Garden of the Lord." Rooted among a prosperous and intellectual mercantile class in the Low Country, Familism spread by the 1560s to mercantile circles in London and to East Anglia, where it took hold among more humble sorts, many illiterate, particularly transient artisans.[40]

The English Familists do not appear to have been directly influenced by hermeticism until the 1620s, but they may have had earlier hermetic sympathizers. England's premier occult philosopher of the sixteenth century, John Dee (1527–1608), interacted with Dutch Familists in London who were part of a wider Familist connection among printers in the Low Country.[41] It was in great part through Dee's efforts that Renaissance hermeticism made its way into England during the sixteenth century. A leading intellectual in Elizabethan England, Dee pursued the hermetic goals of attaining a total knowledge of the workings of the universe, a knowledge that was locked up in the primal language lost with Adam at the fall from Paradise and that was accessible only through the Cabala, alchemy, astrology, Joachimite prophecy, and the wider hermetic philosophy. These priorities shaped his work in mathematics, optics, and science, as well as his millenarian justification for empire. In this effort, Dee was a primary architect of the English nationalist cult that emerged under Elizabeth. But after 1583 Dee sought patronage on the Continent, and here, it has been argued, he laid the groundwork for Rosicrucianism, the international hermetic movement that would formatively influence Freemasonry.[42]

Rosicrucianism emerged in the form of manifestos published in Cassel in 1614 and 1615 after the death of Rudolph II, in the context of fears that the Catholic Hapsburgs would assume the throne in Prague and suppress a Protestant tradition running back to the Hussites. Hopes resting on Frederick, Elector of the Palatine, and his English wife, Elizabeth, daughter of James I, were dashed when the Hapsburgs set off the Thirty Years' War, devastating German Protestantism. In the last years of peace, a furor over the Rosicrucian manifestos swept through Europe. Fusing the hermetic allegory with the style of chapbook romances, the manifestos announced the existence of a secret brotherhood of occult philosophers, the

The Mountain of the Adepts, depicting the alchemical stages as steps to perfection. From Steffen Michelspacher, *Cabala, Speculum, Artis et Naturae, in Alchemia* (Augsburg, 1667).

followers of Christian Rosencreutz, a mystic figure who supposedly had lived in the late fourteenth century and would reemerge periodically to advance a "Universal and General Reformation of the whole wide world." One of the Rosicrucian texts, called *The Chemical Wedding of Christian Rosencreutz,* by John Valentine Andreae, was intended to invest the marriage of German Frederick and English Elizabeth with mystical and apocalyptical implications and to provide a millennial ideology of Protestant alliance against the Catholic Hapsburgs. Supposedly, tablets bearing secret inscriptions had been found in Rosencreutz's tomb in 1604, restoring the brotherhood's lore of occult knowledge to save a Europe in crisis. The date was important: Paracelsus had predicted that the prophet Elijah, as the alchemical Elias *Artista,* would return in 1602, and between 1602 and 1604 in hermetic circles throughout Europe there were hopeful rumors that a mysterious wandering alchemist was demonstrating a perfect transmutation. A Joachimite new dispensation, a return to Adam's paradisial powers, was at hand, if one could contact the "Brothers RC" and gain access to this knowledge of the ancient mysteries. The Rosicrucian tale of the vault-tomb containing occult knowledge that would reveal the ancient Adamic mysteries would be an important theme in eighteenth-century Masonic mythology, and there is increasing agreement that the Rosicrucian hoax was one of the important elements in the emergence of Freemasonry.[43] In turn, we shall see, the Rosicrucian–Masonic mythology of sacred texts buried in underground vaults had a formative influence on the young Joseph Smith.

It was in seventeenth-century England that the most powerful and popular manifestations of the fusion of prophecy and hermetic divinization developed, standing both as the culmination of the Radical Reformation and as the immediate precursor of critical themes in popular religion of the early American colonies. The English revolutionary sects achieved a vernacular form of the Christian-hermetic *magus* having direct analogues to the dispensationalism and divinization that two centuries later framed the Mormon cosmology. And beyond analogue here we may indeed find antecedent. The revolutionary sects had a selective but important influence on much of the religious culture inherited by the sectarian peoples of the American colonies, peoples who, we shall see, were particularly prepared for Joseph Smith's restoration. For these reasons the world of the English Revolution requires extended examination.

The decades before and of the English Revolution saw a ferment of intellectual and millenarian thought, drawing on the hermetic and Rosicrucian currents of the later Renaissance. The millennial kingdom

and a restored Paradise were powerful models for a society to be transformed in a "Great Instauration." Jan Comenius (1592–1670) and Samuel Hartlib (1600–62) and their associates in the Rosicrucian-like "Spiritual Brotherhood" and "Invisible College," including John Dury, Robert
Boyle, and Gabriel Plattes, proposed plans for universal education, based
on the hermetic ideal of "pansophia," to be articulated in a system of
public colleges, academies, and local schools. Plans for reform of agricul-
ture, the mechanical crafts, law, and medicine circulated in profusion. On
the eve of the Civil War, in 1641, Plattes brought these ideas together in a
plan for a utopian "Kingdom of Macaria," in which popular knowledge
was as central as popular property-holding was to James Harrington's
"Commonwealth of Oceana" two decades later. And such ideas were
available in print at the popular level for the first time; the lapse of royal
censorship and licensing allowed "an unprecedented torrent" of vernacular printing. The annual publication of scientific texts expanded dramatically in the 1650s, doubling in mathematics and agricultural reform,
and at least tripling in medicine. As Charles Webster puts it, paraphrasing
John Milton, the English people were about to enter a new age, and to
"recover the intellectual attributes sacrificed by Adam at the Fall."[44]

The quest for improving knowledge led the English to Continental
sources that had never been translated from Latin or German. Editions of
Paracelsus's writings began to appear in print in 1650, followed by those
of his disciples Jan Baptista van Helmont and Johann Rudolph Glauber.[45]
These works were read both as chemical treatise and as spiritual revelation, side by side with translations of Jacob Boehme's writings, selections
of which began to appear in 1645, after a capsule biography in 1644. In
1647 work began on a comprehensive translation of Boehme's works,
completed in 1661. Some, like the radical John Webster, saw the key to the
primal universal language in Boehme's cosmology of unifying signatures
and correspondences between visible and invisible worlds, continuing the
search for the secret code to the cosmos that had consumed Ficino and
Dee. It was in this climate that George Starkey, a Paracelsian doctor
recently returned from New England, could write in an alchemical tract
that the prophet "Elias *Artista* is already born, and glorious things already
predicted of the City of God."[46]

The works of other Continental Spiritualists and occultists – Weigel,
Agrippa, Niclaes, Franck, Eckhart – also made their way into English
print in these years.[47] Many of these were translations made by John
Everard (1582?–1641?), an Anglican minister in London who turned to
Spiritualism in the 1620s. Reaching further back, Everard translated the
central text of the hermetic tradition, the "Divine Pimander" of Hermes
Trismegistus, which was published in 1650, nine years after his death.[48]

Along with these great Continental sources, the hermetic writings of Roger Bacon and John Dee appeared for the first time, along with the contemporary works of Elias Ashmole and Thomas Vaughn. And a large group of occult polemicists, astrologers, and occult medical practitioners, led by William Lilly and Nicholas Culpeper, put their own writings into print in the form of pamphlets, almanacs, and popular handbooks.[49]

This flood of occult publications brought the ideals of the "Great Instauration" to a broad popular audience and became the means by which a new, alternative system of knowledge began to emerge in the late 1640s. Astrology emerged as a quasi religion outside clerical control; William Lilly drew up horoscopes for the triumph of the Parliamentary armies and editorialized in his popular almanacs for the success of the Commonwealth. Medicine was another arena in which the occult sciences lent themselves to popular purposes. The traditional Galenist methods of doctoring were expensive and were tightly controlled by the College of Physicians; the chemical preparations advocated by Paracelsians were relatively cheap, and their recipes were publicized in a host of vernacular publications. Conceptions of the supernatural also underlay popular uses of astrology and demonic exorcism to treat mental illness. Occult knowledge and hermeticism were becoming vehicles of popular empowerment, breaking down old monopolies of intellectual authority and privilege.[50]

Though Samuel Hartlib and some of his circle continued to be enthusiastic about a popular hermeticism through the 1650s, they grew increasingly isolated from many of their peers, as alchemy and astrology came to be associated with the more radical forces in society, and in the early 1650s intellectuals like Robert Boyle, once a part of Hartlib's circle, retreated into the universities.[51] These intellectuals left the field to two familiar groups, the inheritors of the Calvinist Magisterial Reformation, the Presbyterians and Independents, and the inheritors of the Spiritualist and Anabaptist Radical Reformation, the Seekers and a proliferation of sectarian movements. It was among the latter, denounced as "rosycross wolves which turn divinity into fancies," infused with a "Familistical-Levelling-Magical Temper," that the ideas of restorationism, divinization, and hermeticism were carried to their furthest synthesis in the English-speaking world, before the appearance of Joseph Smith on a distant frontier.[52]

The roots of radical sectarianism were diverse and intertangled. They drew upon ancient separatist impulses inherited from fifteenth- and sixteenth-century Lollardry, ingrained in certain cloth-working districts and forest regions. These native roots were complemented by older Continental influences shaping the Baptist and Familist traditions, each now a century old in England.[53] And most immediately, the sectarians drew upon the explosion of Continental influences suddenly available in the 1640s through the efforts of men like John Everard.

Everard was a leading figure among a broad group called the Seekers, individuals who hoped for a new dispensation, the coming of the New Jerusalem. Never organized, except in occasional meetings of like-minded persons, the Seekers collectively shaped many of the major doctrines of the sects that followed. Everard, with Giles Randall and John Portage, can be seen as a bridge linking the Familist movement and Continental mysticism to the Seekers and the revolutionary sects. Early in the 1640s Randall and Portage preached the Familist ideas of a new dispensation and human deification, with a new emphasis on hermetic themes drawn from Boehme and other Continental sources. Randall argued that the indwelling of the Holy Ghost would allow a person to gain universal knowledge. Less concerned with the prospect of a literal New Jerusalem, Everard preached a mystical individualism informed by Familist doctrines of divinization and by a deep immersion in alchemical hermeticism.[54]

Where Everard focused on a hermeticized divinization, other Seekers were centrally concerned with the coming of a new dispensation, in great part because they lived through the era of the Civil War, as Everard did not.[55] An influential group, many of them chaplains in Cromwell's New Model Army, they spoke of the coming of a new age in the terms of Joachimite categories of imminent divine revelation and the Three Ages, prefiguring Joseph Smith's dispensationalism and heavenly cosmology. Among these, John Saltmarsh wrote in *Sparkles of Glory* that history would break into three dispensations of "Law, Gospel and Spirit, or of letter, graces and God, or of the first, second and third heavens"; in *Smoke in the Temple* he wrote of "a time and fulnes for the Spirit and for the later pure spiritual dispensations, as there was formerly for the first dispensations."[56]

The English Seekers followed the path laid out by Caspar Schwenkfeld: those expecting the restoration of the Kingdom of God must set aside all gospel ordinances and wait quietly for a sign of divine intervention. But many others captivated by the idea of a new divine order could not wait and began to take action. Doctrines of a third dispensation or the New Jerusalem led in two directions in the next decade: toward the mysticism of the Fifth Monarchists, Muggletonians, and Quakers and toward the secular rationalism of the Levelers and Diggers.[57] Although rooted in the radical religious milieu, the Levelers channeled their hopes for a new age into the political arena. The Diggers advocated a similarly secular utopia, manifested in the agricultural commune established on the Surrey commons in 1649, but their program was grounded in powerful hermetic imagery.

Gerald Winstanley, a failed merchant-tailor and recently a herdsman, conceived the Digger plan in a mystic trance. As would James Harrington, the republican utopian, Winstanley placed the problem of land as property and the source of sustenance at the center of his vision, but his vision was fundamentally shaped by an optimistic hermeticism. The Fall of Adam had brought not only original sin but private property and the state, mutually reinforcing and oppressive hierarchies. Winstanley's new age would restore Adamic innocence and equality; the vehicle was the hermetic ideal of universal divine reason, infused in humanity by God at the day of judgment. Judgment Day would bring an alchemical transmutation of earth and humanity into a new age, a restored Eden. God, in the form of an alchemical Sun, would burn away the impurities of the fallen condition, destroy the evil "serpent-seed," and bring the seed of human righteousness to perfection and universal reason in the condition of a Second Adam. Winstanley's construct echoes those of Boehme, Paracelsus, and the "Pimander" of the *Hermetica:* in a dialectic of opposites, or an alchemical marriage and consummation, a male sun would act upon a female earth to bring forth a perfect being. And as in the hermetic cosmology, God was equated with both reason and matter; creation was not *ex nihilo* but from preexisting and eternal elements. Again, there is a prefiguring of the Mormon cosmos in Digger rhetoric, and of the Mormon United Order in the Digger communitarian plan for a new society.[58]

The assorted people who came to be known as Ranters shared with Winstanley a radical pantheism: God, reason, and matter were all one. They differed from Winstanley in that they assumed that the new age of spiritual liberty had arrived and that, as extensions of pervasive divinity, they were perfect, sinless beings, freed from all legal and moral constraint.[59] As Ranter Lawrence Clarkson put it, "Sin hath its conception only in the imagination. . . . Which act soever is done by thee in light and love, is light and lovely, though it be that act called adultery." Apparently, Clarkson took these ideas literally, making love with assorted women throughout his travels up and down the country. Some supposed Ranters, such as John Robins and William Franklin, went so far as to claim to be gods. Emerging among roving artisans and laboring people, Ranters fused mysticism with the disorderly culture of the taverns and the open road; like Winstanley, they advocated a community of goods.[60] This fusion of mystical and secular antinomianism would reappear within decades in the American colonies, with formative implications for Mormonism.

Winstanley allegorized a new age of spirit, and Ranters lived in it. The Fifth Monarchists sought to bring on the temporal Kingdom of God, a theocratic dictatorship of the saints. The most militantly restorationist of the revolutionary sects, their inspiration was not hermetic mysticism.

Drawn from Baptist and Congregationalist meetings, the Fifth Monarchist program reflected this conservative Puritan background. Rather than a universal enlightenment, they looked forward to a society governed by the predestined elect, ruling as kings or nobles under the terms of the Mosaic law. They sought not a return to Paradise but the founding of the godly Monarchy prophesied in the Book of Daniel, a typology popular among both the chiliast Münster Anabaptists and the Latter-day Saints at Nauvoo and in early Utah.[61] In the years of defeat following the Stuart Restoration, their commitment to the Mosaic law drew many Fifth Monarchists into the Sabbatarian movement, also soon to move across the Atlantic.[62]

The frustrated activism of the Fifth Monarchists was one response to the reversal of the tide of revolution in the early 1650s; the mystical quietism of the Muggletonians and the Quakers was another. Accommodating their doctrine to the force of civil authority in Protectorate and Restoration, the Muggletonians and Quakers, with the Fifth Monarchists-turned-Sabbatarians, would be the only organized survivors of revolutionary radicalism. If the Quakers were to be distinguished by their numbers and by their reach into the American colonies, the Muggletonians were distinguished by their extreme interpretation of the hermetic-Joachimite tradition.

Most fundamentally, the Muggletonians believed in a new dispensation. Rather than a future prospect, it had already arrived: a "Commission of the Spirit" had been revealed to two London tailors, John Reeves and Lodowick Muggleton, in February 1652. They were the Two Last Witnesses of Revelation 11:3, given a revelation to announce the opening of Joachim's Third Age. Reeves's *A Divine Looking Glass* was the sacred text for the new dispensation. Opposing the militant advocacy of the coming Kingdom of the Fifth Monarchists, the Muggletonians shared a broad set of hermetic doctrines with the Seekers, Winstanley, and the Ranters, though giving each a unique twist. They believed in a primal materialism: creation had come from the substance of God. But they rejected the hermetic pantheism of a pervasive divinity: their God was a finite being about "five foot high," complete with bodily parts. Where other sects preached a universal salvation or divinization, the Muggletonians were predestinarian; the touchstone of election was belief in Muggletonian doctrine. Here they introduced a theme developed by Winstanley and rooted in Boehme's hermeticism, that of the "two seeds." Good and evil forces rested in the sexual events of Genesis: the good seed of the "blessed Israelites" was the product of the union of Adam and Eve, and the bad seed of the "cursed Canaanites" was the product of Eve's seduction by the devil. Descending among the separate peoples of Adam and Cain, the two seeds had been mixed by the intermarriage of these two lineages, and caused good and evil behavior in humanity. But rather than elevating reason, as Winstanley did, Muggletonian belief made it the mark of the devil's seed, with faith the mark of Adam's seed. Belief in Muggletonian prophecy was a sufficient sign of a preponderance of Adam's seed, and thus election. Organized among a loose group of small merchants and artisans in the Midlands and the south of England, Muggletonianism survived in a small way into the twentieth century.[63] It would have interesting echoes among the sectarians of eighteenth-century southeast Connecticut, the region from which Joseph Smith's mother came, and in the texts and ethos of the Mormon church.

The Quakers inherited the world of the radical sects. Beginning in the north of England in 1652, by 1660 they had gathered perhaps 40,000 people into their meetings. Quakerism became the refuge of many – perhaps most – of those who, during the revolutionary years, had seen the possibility of a religion of equals, universally saved by their recognition of a pervasive, internalized divinity.[64] The sum of Quakerism lies in the Inner Light, the presence of the divine in the human soul. This inner divinity was "the coming of Christ in the spirit to save his people from sin": it was an internalized millennium, a new dispensation superseding all church ordinances and sacred texts. The revelations, or "openings," that came to George Fox in 1647 provided the central inspiration for Quakerism, but the evidence suggests to many historians that Familist doctrines of divinization and Jacob Boehme's and John Everard's writings were important in shaping the ground for both Fox's vision and the reception of his message.[65]

The very dimensions of early Quakerism and its antiauthoritarian strain meant that diverse interpretations and influences were at work. If the coming of the Inner Light brought an internal millennium, James Nayler in 1656 acted it out in a very external way, riding into Bristol dressed as Christ, and with a following of worshiping women. One Quaker went so far as to claim to be "above St. Peter & equal with god." George Fox himself may have hoped that he could achieve perfection and a hermetic "unity with the creation." He was reputed to have worked as many as one hundred and fifty miracle healings of lunatics and exorcisms of the bewitched. His healing powers rested in his claim of having been "renewed into the image of God by Christ Jesus, to the state of Adam, which he was in before he fell," exactly the aspiration of the hermetic *magus*. And the very name of "Quaker" derived from the tremors and shaking that ran through the early meetings, "outward manifestations of the inward workings of the power of God."[66]

The radical sects, in sum, briefly realized the promise of divine perfection and of an optimistic participation in the cosmos, synthesized in the Renaissance figure of the Christian-hermetic *magus*. Prophets, *magi*, and even conjurers shared a common field of supernatural belief, a field of manifest affinities and latent coincidences. These relationships produced theological positions, such as those we have been exploring, but they also framed popular experiences in ways that we can only occasionally glimpse.

The experience of Lawrence Clarkson suggests that the impulses of traditional conjuring, solitary hermetic mysticism, and dispensational authority may have flared up at distinct phases in the lives of people open to the broader possibility of communication between the visible and invisible worlds. Born in Preston, Lancashire, in 1615, Clarkson moved through the entire spectrum of reforming and radical movements. Joining Puritan groups in his youth, he passed from Presbyterianism through a brush with antinomianism into preaching to Particular Baptists by 1644. Accused of baptizing naked women, he was drawn into Seekerism in 1645. Apparently he was involved in Leveler agitation and possibly the Digger movement over the next few years; by 1649 he was calling himself a Ranter and by his own admission living freely with women who came his way. Imprisoned by a Parliamentary commission in 1650, Clarkson joined the Muggletonians sometime between 1656 and 1658. In the intervening years, he joined the ranks of the cunning folk, as he described in *The Lost Sheep found*:

> I came forth from prison and then took my journey with my wife . . . into *Cambridgeshire* . . . where I still continued my Ranting principle with a high hand. . . . I attempted the art of Astrology and Physick, which in a short time I gained, and therewith traveled up and down *Cambridgeshire* and *Essex* . . . , improving my skill to the utmost. . . . I had many clients, yet could not be there with contented, but aspired to the art of Magick, so finding some of Doctor *Wards* and *Wollerds* Manuscripts, I improved my genius to fetch Goods back that were stolen, yea to raise spirits, and fetch treasure out of the earth[.] [W]ith many such diabolical actions . . . , monies I gained, and was up and down looked on as a dangerous man, that the ignorant and religious people was afraid to come near me, yet this I may say, and speak the truth, that I have cured many desperate Diseases.

Succeeding in exorcising a bewitched woman, Clarkson was "puffed up" in spirit and "several times attempted to raise the devil." This failing he fell into spiritual reverie. The eternal creation was not that of Adam but "a Creation before him. . . . I understood that which was life in man, went into that infinite Bulk and Bigness, so called God, as a drop into the Ocean, and the body rotted in the grave, and for ever so to remain."[67] This language had a long history among hermetic sectarians, and it would reappear among American perfectionists in the centuries to come.

If Calvinism and the occult were opposites within the same field of visible and invisible worlds, the radical sects and the occult were almost contiguous, sharing overlapping audiences and overlapping cosmologies. Calvinism posited a cosmos where forces moved from the invisible to the visible world, at the will of an all-powerful deity. The radical sects and the practitioners of the popular occult posited a cosmos in which humanity in the visible world might in some way manipulate or participate in the invisible world. For sectarian leaders the occult was too close for comfort. Where many individual members might, like Clarkson, move easily between the orbits of the sects, the cunning folk, and the hermetic *magi,* the sectarian leadership – particularly of the Quakers and Muggletonians who survived the Restoration – increasingly had to draw firm lines of demarcation between sect and the occult. Sectarian leaders rarely acknowledged their debt to Jacob Boehme and the hermetic tradition, and they were often vehemently hostile to practices and beliefs of the cunning folk and the astrologers.[68]

In this boundary maintenance, the surviving sects were simply acting in the interests of self-preservation, for the Restoration brought a powerful ideological reaction. The explosive growth of the Quakers in the late 1650s may have been critical in building popular acceptance of a return of the Stuart monarchy.[69] Fears of the sectarian uses of hermeticism and the occult had broken the unanimity of the revolutionary Instauration in the 1640s, and the Restoration brought moderate and conservative intellectual figures out of their isolation in the universities, first to support the Crown and then to build an ideological bulwark against the radical sects. Restoration science attempted to incorporate the occult notion of a hierarchy of spheres into a theory of inert, dead matter ordered and motivated by entirely separate and all-determining divine will. This intellectual system, based on a metaphor of power emanating from a remote divinity, would help to shore up a fragile world so recently "turned upside down." The ultimate result would be the Newtonian enlightenment: a description of an ordered cosmos set into motion by a beneficent and distant God who no longer intervened in its workings.[70]

The decades of the "world turned upside down" brought a synthesis of traditions that had histories stretching deep into the medieval and ancient worlds. For a few brief years a host of radical, transformative, mystical ideas were passionately advocated and debated, and then, for the most part, set aside. They would survive in corners of Restoration and Hanoverian England, to be revitalized by a rising tide of pietism that prepared many in the English Midlands for the nineteenth-century Mormon message, carried by "common men from America." These ideas – fertilized by a parallel German perfectionism – also persisted in strategic pockets in the American colonies. And, as we have already seen and as several scholars have noted, the ideas brought together by the radical sects in the English Revolution reappeared in strikingly similar form almost two hundred years later at the hands of Joseph Smith.[71]

None of the seventeenth-century sects anticipated the totality of the Mormon cosmology, but, taken collectively, there are some remarkable similarities. Lawrence Clarkson, divining for treasure, looks a lot like the young Joseph Smith. Smith also looks a lot like John Reeves and Lodowick Muggleton, the prophets bearing a new text announcing a new dispensation. So too, we can see echoes of George Starkey's announcement of the birth of the prophet Elias in the visions of Elias and Elijah received by Joseph Smith and Oliver Cowdery in the Kirtland temple. Smith's church would militantly advance the cause of the Kingdom of God just as had the Fifth Monarchists. Something of the antinomian behavior of the Ranters, including their spiritual wifery, and the biblical polygamy of the Münster Anabaptists (and of John Milton) would be repeated among the Mormons. The "two seeds" of the Muggletonians and their descent from Adam and Cain would have an echo in the saga of the Nephites and the Lamanites in the *Book of Mormon*. Winstanley's communal economy would be reproduced in Smith's United Order of Enoch. The hermetic quest for the natural Adamic language of universal knowledge would be repeated in Smith's fascination with ancient languages and in the Mormon gift of speaking in tongues. Mormon prophets and priests would receive visions and revelations and have powers of healing and exorcism like those of the early Quaker leaders. The finite God of the Muggletonians would be reproduced in the Mormons' similarly finite God, as would be the hermetic reverence for Adam, the *magus*-man. The Mormon equation of spirit and matter, their vision of a living earth, and their doctrine of pre-Creation spiritual existence echoed the hermetic cosmology in its many forms. So too, there would be hints of a Mormon conception of an androgynous God, simultaneously male and female, replicating a central hermetic doctrine. Mormon baptism for the dead would reproduce the Spiritualist doctrine of the Christianity of the Old Testament prophets. The Mormon cosmos would include three heavens, and the Mormon faithful would rise as gods to the highest heaven, reproducing the doctrines of universal salvation and divinization that ran through many of the movements influenced directly or indirectly by the writings of Boehme, Paracelsus, and Hermes. Mormon divinization would be achieved by the "sealing powers of Elijah" restored to the Mormon priesthood, powers that, like the sacred experiments of the al-chemical *magus,* put divine grace into human hands. And like the Quakers and Muggletonians, the Mormon leadership in Utah would la-bor long and hard to establish and to maintain a firm boundary between their theology and the story of occult influences deeply embedded in their early history.

Are these relationships spanning centuries simply analogues, revealing but essentially unconnected? The reigning interpretations of Mormonism would force this conclusion. On the one hand, the Mormon believer would argue that Smith's was simply the most perfect of a sequence of revelations of a restored church. Conversely, the functionalist social scien-tist might argue that similar convictions of revelation emerge from analo-gous experiences of social upheaval.

But these answers are inadequate, because they fail to engage with history, experience, and memory. If social disorder may explain the form of religious movements, it cannot explain their content. The Mormon theology and cosmology were not simply products of "freedom's fer-ment" in a new land. Recoverable trails of popular experience and endur-ing, revitalized texts – the focus of the following chapters – suggest that the hermetic dispensationalism of important elements in the Radical Re-formation was not merely analogous with but antecedent to the theology framed by Joseph Smith centuries later on a distant frontier.

2

The True Spiritual Seed

The family of Smiths held Joseph Jr. in high estimation on account of some supernatural power, which he was supposed to possess. This power he pretended to have received through the medium of a stone of peculiar quality. The stone was placed in a hat, in such a manner as to exclude all light, except that which emanated from the stone itself. The light of the stone, he pretended, enabled him to see anything he wished. Accordingly he discovered ghosts, infernal spirits, mountains of gold and silver, and many other invaluable treasures deposited in the earth. He would often tell his neighbors of his wonderful discoveries, and urge them to embark on the money-digging business.
                    Joseph Capron, Manchester, Ontario County, New York,
                                                    November 8, 1833[1]

IN THE YEARS BEFORE HIS ASSASSINATION in 1844, Joseph Smith, the prophet and seer of the Church of Jesus Christ of Latter-day Saints, revealed to his people the mysteries of the Kingdom of God. Fulfilling the dream of paradisial hermeticism, the Mormon faithful, by the sealing powers of Elijah, would become gods, carried up in an endless progression to the highest kingdoms of glory.

This American realization of the hermetic theology was rooted in a very different hermetic experience. For at least five years in the mid-1820s, and possibly for many years thereafter, Joseph Smith was deeply involved in occult divination. From 1822, when he discovered a seer-stone in Willard Chase's well, through 1827, when he renounced "glass-looking" in a dramatic confrontation with his father-in-law, Isaac Hale, Smith was known for his powers with the seer-stone. He could see unknown things, locating his neighbors' lost possessions and stolen goods and advising groups of money-diggers on the location of buried treasure, hidden mines, and salt deposits.[2]

Joseph Smith was only one of many occult practitioners who worked with seer-stones and divining rods across the landscape in the half-century following the American Revolution. Throughout the postrevolutionary Northeast, the unsettled economic and religious conditions of the 1780s and 1790s drew hundreds of people into "money-digging companies" in a futile search for an easy way to wealth. Recently, historians have documented the extent of the treasure-hunting tradition in the Palmyra neighborhood, the Burned-over District, and throughout the Northeast: Smith was not unique in his belief in occult divination. Legends of treasures buried by Spaniards and pirates, even the wording of colonial charters, contributed to a fascination with precious metals. Diviners located metallic treasures with stones and rods and then attempted to overpower guardian spirits by casting magic circles and invoking astrological influences.[3]

Woven into the fabric of these divining cults were connotations and fragments running back to medieval alchemy and Renaissance hermeticism. One of the central themes in the treasure-hunting sagas was the volatility of precious metal: chests of money "bloom" to the surface of the earth only to fall away when the diggers utter a sound or violate a ritual practice. Joseph Smith Sr., father of the Mormon prophet, told his Palmyra neighbor Peter Ingersoll that "the best time for digging money was in the heat of the summer, when the heat of the sun caused the chests of money to rise to the top of the ground." Smith also claimed that the chests were ruined by the summer sun when they reached the surface, the heat transmuting them into "large stones on the top of the ground." More usually, such chests would disappear into the earth from which they had risen, controlled by spirits that resisted the money-diggers' efforts; Joshua Stafford recalled Joseph Smith showing him "a piece of wood which he said he took from a box of money" that had slipped away; far into the nineteenth century Brigham Young recounted the story of Mormons Porter Rockwell and Martin Harris breaking off a corner of a chest as it sank into a money-diggers' pit.[4] These volatile treasures reflected a continuing, if truncated, belief in the hermetic concept of metallic growth. The spirits and enchantments guarding the treasures seem to be rooted in a residual belief in the spiritual powers inherent in metals, beliefs that in the German tradition were personified in gnomes and mine spirits.

Accounts of divining often incorporated references to very specific knowledge of alchemy and the transmutation of metals. Ransford Rogers, a fraudulent diviner who operated up and down the new states in the 1780s and 1790s, "had a pretended copious knowledge in chemistry, and could raise and dispel good and evil spirits." A sect of New Israelites emerged briefly in Rutland County, Vermont, between 1799 and 1802, claiming descent from ancient Jewish tribes and divining for both revelations and buried treasure. According to an early account, they claimed to have

> inspired power, with which to cure all sorts of diseases – intuitive knowledge of lost or stolen goods, and ability to discover the

hidden treasures of the earth, as well as the more convenient talent
of transmuting ordinary substances into the precious metals.

Mercury, or quicksilver, that most volatile of metals and a central alchemical emblem, went into the construction of ever more complex divining
rods, as in the celebrated case of the "Old Rodsman" in the Ohio country
in the mid-1820s, whose divining rod incorporated "a young heifer's horn
. . . filled with quicksilver, oil of amber, and dragon's blood" mounted on
a whale bone pivot.[5]

Like great alchemic mystics, the treasure-hunting diviners had to be in a
state of grace, spiritually pure, to achieve a gnostic control over volatile
metals.[6] The account of the Old Rodsman suggests that residual alchemical ideas could have a more profound religious quality, harking back to
the language once used by the Ranter Lawrence Clarkson. The Old Rodsman "had a natural turn for physic," treating the sick with Thompsonian
herbal remedies and his jug of "Hot stuff," but he sought out more expert
advice when it came to judging the qualities of the ores he discovered with
his divining rod. On one expedition far up a tributary of the Ohio he was
"accompanied by B. Devoe, a good judge of ores, and a thorough profi-
ciency in the mysterious science of alchimy, at which he had experimented
for several years." Several years later, after a long trek up into the Big
Sandy–Clinch River country of the Tennessee–North Carolina border
region in search of a lost silver mine, the Rodsman brought hundreds of
pounds of ore to be tested by another man "who had considerable skill in
metallurgy, having worked several years at alchimy, the transmutation of
metals, and the discovery of the philosopher's stone." Building a secret
furnace, they charged several crucibles with the ore, whose "obstinacy . . .
bid defiance to the skill of the alchimist." Despite the failure of his alchemic adept, the Rodsman retained a basic faith in the alchemical
scheme. A Universalist in belief, he had a strikingly material conception of
the universal perfectibility of humanity.

> He compared the soul of a vile man at death to a puddle of fetid,
> putrid water. However putrid it might be, he said the particles of
> vapor which rose from it, were pure and sweet, forming the clouds
> and nice clear rainwater. Thus . . . the souls of the wicked at death
> would be cleansed, and ascend to Heaven in a purified state.[7]

Far out on the Ohio frontier a metallic diviner had absorbed some of the
lessons of the ancient alchemical tradition: his scheme of salvation incorporated the concepts of putrification, sublimation, and distillation central
to the alchemical cycle of experiments that would lead to the philosopher's
stone. Expressed in language akin to that of Lawrence Clarkson, the
seventeenth-century mystic, the Rodsman's construct anticipated the

Mormon doctrine of blood atonement, preached in Salt Lake in the 1850s by Brigham Young and Heber C. Kimball.

The postrevolutionary diviners, near-contemporaries of Joseph Smith, conjure up images of the great alchemists of the seventeenth century. Here we have echoes of the grand tradition of alchemy, the experimental search for the philosopher's stone, the quintessence of life, promising for the sincere mystic gnostic transmutation of the soul and for the practical puffer the profane transmutation of base metals into gold. Emerging from this metallurgical divining, Mormonism would articulate the deepest purposes of hermetic divinization in a theology framed in Ohio in the 1830s and announced in 1843–4 at Nauvoo, Illinois.

We are faced with a series of problems. We need to define as precisely as possible how and why occult practices of divining and the systematic theology of hermetic perfectionism last seen in seventeenth-century Europe reemerged in the nineteenth-century American world of Joseph Smith. We also need to examine the relationships and affinities that connected magical practice and hermetic perfection with the dispensational restorationism that was such a central part of Joseph Smith's cosmology. And most specifically, we need to know more definitively who were the prepared people in the American settlements: who could accommodate both magical practice and religious devotion, who were prepared for the supernaturalist fusion of hermetic authority and millenarian restorationism that Joseph Smith would begin to preach in 1830. In short, we need to map the social and cultural geography of the intersection of religion and the hermetic occult in early America.

In some measure, many people were prepared for the Mormon message by the stresses and dislocations of postrevolutionary America. But we may also reasonably assume a transfer of occult practices and hermetic perfectionism to the New World from the Old, a transfer carried both on the streams of migration that peopled early America and on the tides of print culture that washed across the Atlantic. This chapter focuses on the first of these dimensions, the raising of a prepared people in the American colonies. For the purposes of understanding Mormon origins, this story may be confined to very specific peoples and religious experiences in the northern colonies.

The people drawn to the announcement of a Mormon restoration in the 1830s, living in scattered localities across New England or recently settled in the raw farm country of western New York and northeastern Ohio, came from families deeply rooted in the Protestant cultures of the North Atlantic, shaped in the European Reformation and carried to the northern colonies of British North America. Most Mormon converts, but not all, were from the New England states, often the children of families that had left the older coastal regions of Massachusetts, Rhode Island, and Connecticut in the decades before and after the Revolution to settle, in one or more steps, in New Hampshire, Vermont, New York, and Ohio. Others came from families rooted in the lower Hudson and Delaware valleys who joined the New England diaspora into New York's Burned-over District and Ohio's Western Reserve.[8]

We may conceive of the formation of the colonial cultures that framed these people's lives in terms of two broad movements of population across the Atlantic, divided by the decades of the English Revolution. From 1620 to the early 1640s, small numbers of English Separatists and then a Great Migration of Puritans, nonseparating Congregationalists, typically in families and occasionally as covenanted communities, took up lands around Massachusetts Bay from Plymouth to Cape Ann, with small outlying settlements in the Connecticut Valley and New Hampshire. This migration dwindled during the years of the English Revolution, and when movement was renewed after the Stuart Restoration it drew new peoples to new regions. This post-1660 migration brought English Quakers and German sectarians to the new Mid-Atlantic provinces, particularly Pennsylvania after 1682, and a small but important flow of people into New England. These two waves of migration brought with them very different configurations of religious and magical belief.

The hermetic occult was only a minor, muted undercurrent in the culture of the peoples arriving with the Puritan Great Migration of the 1630s. Puritan orthodoxy in New England shared in the basic tenets of the Magisterial Reformation: predestination, limited human will, an omnipotent deity, and the duty of the state to uphold the true church. Rejecting both dispensationalism and magical intervention, New England orthodoxy in no way anticipated the central features of Mormon theology or cosmology.[9]

It was with their biblical primitivism that English Puritans had their closest connections with the Radical Reformation. Sharing something of the minority status of the Continental Anabaptists, English Puritans also shared with these groups the faith that they could restore the primitive purity of the apostolic church.[10] At its heart, the ideal of biblical primitivism posited that only the elect could hold the keys to church authority, the right and the ability to claim title to the apostolic succession. For many English Puritans in the late 1620s, such a true church could only be realized in the New World, far from the authority of king and bishops. In New England they would establish an imitation of "the first Plantation of the Primitive Church," with full "liberty and purity of ordinances."[11]

But this was biblical primitivism, not full-blown dispensationalism, and after midcentury even this primitivism would be compromised. With the decline of popular willingness to make public statements of conversion experience and with the continuing need to gather as many as possible into the fold of church discipline and protection, the adoption of the Half Way Covenant in the 1670s introduced human innovations that undermined any claims to a pure primitivism.[12] The ministerial jeremiads that began in the 1660s and 1670s, holding up the first generation as the exemplars of the pure church, similarly crowded aside the model of the primitive apostolic church. If the first-generation settlers came to New England in search of the primitive church, the second-generation ministers seemed to claim that they had indeed restored it.[13] The identification of the New World with a restored church would have important ramifications for the history of American biblical primitivism. But the later generations' acceptance of the myth of a Puritan restoration led to complacency in the New England countryside, not a general demand for a new dispensation. Subsequent advocates of a biblical restoration would start by rejecting the legitimacy of the achievements of the early Puritans of Massachusetts Bay.[14]

The ideals of biblical restoration pointed backward to a prior time of purity; millennial ideas pointed forward to a point of transformation. As public affairs in England reached a crisis point around 1640, millennialism began to take hold in New England, anticipated by John Cotton's sermons on the Canticles, first delivered even before he left England in 1633. John Eliot centered his mission to the Indians at Natick in the millennial scheme, particularly after Thomas Thorowgood published his *Jews in America* in 1650, which promoted the idea that the Indians were the descendants of the Lost Tribes, whose conversion would be a critical step in the advance to the Second Coming. Eliot also incorporated his millennial thinking about the Indians into his utopian vision, *The Christian Commonwealth*, written in 1650 but not published until the height of the Fifth Monarchy agitation in London in 1659.[15]

But, all in all, millennialism did not strike an enduring chord in Puritan Massachusetts Bay. Cotton and Eliot were clearly at the militant edge of the consensus in the 1640s and 1650s, and the list of their fellow millennialist writers was never very long. Cotton died in 1652, and with the Stuart Restoration Eliot's millennial fervor fell outside the consensus. His *Christian Commonwealth* was banned by the General Court in 1661, and Eliot was required to write a renunciation. Even at its height, the millennialism espoused by Cotton and Eliot was by no means that of the Münster Anabaptists. James F. Maclear concedes that "apocalyptic radicalism was indeed less pervasive in conservative Massachusetts than in revolutionary English religion" and that only "a few American Puritans brought a modest contribution to the millennial politics of Cromwellian England."[16] Certainly this was no fertile source for Mormon dispensationalism.

For very different reasons, magical practice and belief were even more attenuated in orthodox New England. The established Calvinist doctrine of an all-powerful divinity left no sanctioned room for human manipulation of supernatural power, and the Puritans inherited a century-long tradition of the suppression of magic. This is not to say that the window between the visible and the invisible worlds was decisively shut: miraculous wonders and miracles demonstrated for ministry and laity alike the presence of divine power, and prayer was offered in the hope of channeling that power.[17] On the Puritan fringes, where the Calvinist certainties were inscrutable, unbearable, or simply ambiguous, people mobilized a fragmentary knowledge of folk magic – especially to divine one's future in this world and the next. But for the majority of the orthodox, magic was not an option, leaving them open to abiding fears of the threat of witchcraft's malefic harms. Paradoxically, it was the complex fusion of the lore of wonders, the denial of sanctioned magic, and a popular fear of witchcraft that combined to shape the devastating Salem witch trials of 1692.[18]

Beyond ministerial supernaturalism and the popular occult lay the hermetic tradition itself, which was transferred to early New England in qualified circumstances, hedged in by the imperatives of magisterial Calvinism. Led by John Winthrop Jr. a small group of intellectuals immersed in late Renaissance culture brought to New England the practical hermeticism of the Hartlib circle and the Great Instauration. Both Winthrop and his associate Robert Childe were physicians trained in the chemical Paracelsian tradition, and both threw their scientific knowledge into efforts to develop mineral resources in New England, experimenting with saltworks, prospecting for lead graphite, and establishing ironworks in 1643 at Braintree and 1648 at Saugus.[19] Winthrop maintained contacts with a wide circle of men with similar hermetic interests, corresponding with the likes of Samuel Hartlib in England and sending books and encouragement to Jonathan Brewster Jr., a trader on the Pequot coast at what would become New London, Connecticut, who was attempting to distill the "red elixer."[20]

Beyond the realm of a practical hermeticism, Winthrop seems to have flirted with its mystical dimensions. He amassed a huge library of alchemical literature, which included manuscripts that had once belonged to Dr. John Dee, acquired through Winthrop's friendship with Dee's son Arthur.[21] He and Childe were friends and mentors of George Starkey, who returned to England in the cause of alchemical reform, and they were interested in the Rosicrucian mysteries; Childe wrote to Winthrop in 1648 that he had seen letters "from ye *Fratres* R C" announcing the birth of the alchemical prophet Elias *Artista*. Childe also had great respect for Richard Leader, the ironmaster at Saugus. "Skill[ed] in mynes and tryall of metalls," Leader had, Child wrote to Winthrop in 1650, "more curious books than I, especially about Divinity business."[22]

There were other, scattered seventeenth-century intellectuals who drew upon the hermetic tradition in different ways. Anne Bradstreet of Andover filled her early poems with the mystical symbolism of regeneration in Renaissance alchemy.[23] Edward Taylor, the minister in Westfield, Massachusetts, at the end of the seventeenth century, also made use of alchemical symbolism in his devotional poetry; he kept a copy of Bradstreet's poems on his shelf.[24] Cotton Mather also toyed with the hermetic tradition, calling prayer a "spiritual alchemy" and corresponding with the members of the Royal Society and Continental Pietists on the material qualities of "the Plastic Spirit permeating the World" and governing the visible world.[25]

Clearly, however, these intellectuals lived in an isolated world. Winthrop's alchemy was so secretive that it has only recently been rediscovered. Few New England ministers followed Mather into the Royal Society; Robert Calef's reaction to Mather's theories was dismissive: "A plastic spirit. What foreign word is that."[26] Bradstreet's poetry was published in London in 1650 and in Boston in 1678; Taylor's was never published. Clearly the work of these poets was fundamentally private and devotional, divorced from public discourse and controversy.[27] From the 1680s to the 1720s Harvard undergraduates were exposed to the outlines of alchemical transmutation in the *Compendium Physicae*, written by an English exile, Charles Morton, minister at Charlestown from 1686. In all probability there was a broad familiarity among the educated in New England with alchemical, perhaps hermetic ideas, but they could have made little more than a minor dent in the popular imagination; no programmatic vision could emerge from the occultism of the Puritan intellectuals, walled in by the Calvinist priorities of their class and culture.[28]

The Puritan quest for a primitive biblical church in early Massachusetts simply left no room for alternative, more radical views. The authorities in Massachusetts Bay were uncompromising in suppressing sectarian separatism, radical doctrines of restoration, and spiritist interpretations of the relationship between God and humanity. During the 1630s they exiled a series of dissenters, and through the 1650s struggled to maintain by force a barrier against the radical influences emanating from the changing circumstances of a revolutionary England, to the extreme of burning sectarian pamphlets on the Boston docks.[29] Where the radical sects provided a means by which a hermetic occult might reach a broad audience in revolutionary England, the deflecting of sectarianism shut off the Puritan laity in New England from these influences. And for both the orthodox and the early dissenters there was the critical matter of the timing of their migration.[30] Alchemical and hermetic ideas exploded into vernacular print in the 1640s and 1650s, but in the 1630s they circulated only in foreign-language imprints, in manuscripts, and through the preaching of a few men like John Everard. Popular exposure to hermeticism was simply not part of the formative experience of English people migrating to New England before 1645. And the potential for a mass exposure to hermetic ideas declined precipitously with the onset of the Civil War. By 1645 the flow of migration to New England had slowed considerably, and the best estimates indicate that immigration was an insignificant source of population growth in New England until well after the American Revolution.[31]

In sum, there is very little to suggest that the hermetic occult could ever have been deeply rooted in the experience of the common people of the Puritan Great Migration. Thus we arrive at a paradox: although a majority of early Mormons were indeed drawn from New England families, there is little evidence that the hermeticism and dispensationalism of Mormon theology could have been derived from the classic Puritan experience. The conclusion must be that if the Adamic restorationism and hermetic perfectionism of the Radical Reformation and the English Revolution made their way to the Mormon restoration, they must have taken a different route than that through Puritan culture in orthodox New England.[32]

Hermetic perfectionism, Adamic restoration, and popular magic arrived in full form not with the Puritan migration to New England but with the migration of the survivors of the Radical Reformation to the Mid-Atlantic. The rising tide of Catholic absolutism in the mid–seventeenth century, decisive in France, challenged in Britain, devastating in middle Europe, shook the Magisterial Reformation, but it shattered the Radical Reformation into fragments. Over the last decades of the century, the radical tradition took new shape: separatism, primitivism, spiritualism, and perfectionism persisted in isolated regions and reemerged in new movements. This second Radical Reformation generally accommodated itself to the realities of a triumphant absolutism, but it also looked across the Atlantic in hopes of a final "Peaceable Kingdom." In the migrations of Quakers, Baptists, Pietists, and perfectionists, coming primarily to the new provinces of Pennsylvania and the Jerseys, and swelling to greater and greater numbers between the 1650s and 1730s, the Radical traditions of Adamic restoration and hermetic divinization were definitively brought to the New World.

Quakers were in the 1650s the first major wave of radical sectarians to come, initially to the West Indies, and then to New England. Violently suppressed in magisterial Massachusetts in the years following 1656, Quakers began to settle on Long Island and in East Jersey in the 1660s, there joined in the 1670s and 1680s by English, Scottish, and Welsh Quakers and Baptists. Trickling into Maryland and Virginia, after 1682 Quakers poured into Pennsylvania and West Jersey along the Delaware River.[33] On the Delaware, English dissenters had been preceded by a Dutch Mennonite communal colony in 1663. Twenty years later, with the founding of Pennsylvania, German Mennonites and French Protestant mystics, the Labadists, led a host of radical sectarians from the war-ravaged Continent, including Moravians and Schwenkfelders, surviving fragments of groups formed at the height of the Reformation.[34]

These sects and others were caught up in various manifestations of Pietism, the late-seventeenth-century revival of German spiritualism that had its roots in the Christian mysticism of Johann Arndt (1555–1621), Jacob Boehme, and the medieval Johann Tauler, as well as in strains of English and Dutch piety. Reacting to the social chaos and religious torpor of a war-ravaged Germany, late-seventeenth-century Pietism was forged in the writings of Philip Jacob Spener (1635–1705) and institutionalized at the hands of August Hermann Francke (1663–1727). Influenced by contemporary millennialism and Cabalism, and by the earlier mystics, Spener developed in *Pia Desideria* themes of heart piety and spiritual intensity that helped to carry the radical traditions of perfectionism and universal salvation into the eighteenth century. Bypassing the rational orthodoxy of the ministry, he appealed to the laity as "a chosen race, a royal priesthood, a holy nation, God's own people" (1 Peter 2:9). While one wing of the Pietist movement was established under Prussian patronage at the University of Halle, another was rooted in a disparate cluster of sects and societies re-creating much of the perfectionist fervor of the Radical Reformation. Among these were the Baptist Schwarzenau Brethren (some later known as the Dunkard Brethren), who formed in 1708 and began to move to Pennsylvania in 1719, and the German Philadelphians, influenced by English Boehmists John Pordage and Jane Leade, who had an important role in transferring hermetic mysticism into the eighteenth century.[35] Most broadly, the rise of Pietism can be seen as the beginning of the transatlantic revival that became the Great Awakening in the American colonies and the "Methodist Revolution" in England.[36]

The peoples of these transplanted Protestant sects, the inheritors of the traditions and texts of the Radical Reformation, constituted a deep reservoir of occult practices and perfectionist doctrines. Both as analogue and as source, the culture of these sectarian peoples brings us much closer to the language and cosmos of nineteenth-century Mormonism than New England Puritanism ever could. And as we shall see in the Mormon story, occultism could be central to the teaching and experience of the sects, or it could be very much at odds.

Among the Quakers, sect and occult were by this time clearly at odds. By the 1680s the era of Fox's miracles and Nayler's dispensationalism was well over, and under the guiding hand of William Penn, who had one foot in the meeting and the other in the king's court, Quakerism was defining its boundaries as it moved toward institutional stability. As in England, occult ideas persisting from the 1650s had to be suppressed. In 1688 Quaker Daniel Leeds was expelled by the Philadelphia Meeting for publishing the work of Jacob Boehme and of the English mystic George Wither. After his expulsion, Leeds continued to produce almanacs with quotes from "Hermes Trismegistus," material from the Civil War astrologer William Lilly, and advocacy of hermetic, astrological, and herbal medicine. Another Pennsylvania Quaker, Benjamin Lay, quoted at length from "The Divine Pymander" of Hermes in 1737. In the 1690s evidence of magical practice impelled meetings in Pennsylvania and New Jersey to condemn any Quakers "who, professing the art of astrology, have undertaken to give answers and astrological judgments concerning persons and things." Later still, in 1723 and 1802 the Philadelphia Yearly Meeting also condemned the "Art or Skill" of divining for lost and stolen objects.[37] Hermeticism was even manifested in the Keithian schism of 1692. George Keith had come under the influence of hermetic Cabalist Francis M. Van Helmont in the 1670s, and through a developing interest in the Cabala began to move away from the Quaker equation of Christ and the Inner Light. Disowned by the London Yearly Meeting in 1694 after disrupting Pennsylvania Quakers, Keith returned to Anglicanism. But during these years, he was briefly allied with Henry Bernard Koster, a German preacher, mystic, and Cabalist who drew off Quakers in the Delaware Valley to form the region's first Baptist churches.[38]

Koster had emerged from a very different occult connection: the Chapter of Perfection, or Society of the Woman in the Wilderness. Formed by Johann Jacob Zimmerman among Lutheran Pietists, they were led to Pennsylvania by Johann Kelpius, settling in 1694 on the Wissahickon Creek in Germantown. Kelpius's followers placed hermeticism at the center of their certainty of the imminent restoration of the Kingdom of God. Framed by Pietism and influenced by the Philadelphians, who had continued to elaborate Jacob Boehme's mysticism, they hoped to be the catalyst for a universal transformation on the general model of the

Rosicrucian Brotherhood. They held a Joachimite three-stage theory of sacred history and spiritual progression: passing through the "barren wilderness" and the "fruitful wilderness," they now expected a "wilderness of the elect of God," the state of mystical perfection. They lived as hermits along the Wissahickon and practiced a fusion of Lutheran liturgy and Rosicrucian ritual in a log tabernacle built true to the compass and forty feet square. From the roof of the tabernacle, set high on a ridge overlooking the creek, they kept track of the stars through a telescope. Continuing the hermetic quest, they contemplated the Cabala and worked alchemical stills and crucibles to distill the philosopher's stone. Kelpius corresponded with Philadelphians in Europe and others in the colonies, from Virginia to Long Island to Rhode Island. His 1699 letter to Steven Mumfort, a Seventh-Day Baptist in Newport, Rhode Island, captures a sense of the Chapter's hermetic millenarianism. Kelpius trusted that Mumfort shared his hopes of seeing

> that happy day, which when its new Earth swallows all that fore-mentioned Floud and where its glorious Sun causeth all other Stars and Phoenomena to disappear, no Night succeeds it, but that Night is swallowed up in ye Day, Darkness into Light, Death into Life, Judgement into Victory, Justice into Mercy, all imperfect metals into Gold, and Gold itself is refined seven times, all Churches and Virgins comprised into the one Dove (Cant. 6,9), then all the Sons of God will shout for joy as they did at the Beginning, when God was all in all, as he will be all in all, when the End hath found its Beginning. Amen! Halleluiah!

Ecumenical in their quest for perfection, the Chapter also reached out to the German and English settlers around them; Koster preached in German and English, gradually abandoning the sect, while Kelpius worked to improve education of the local children, to provide herbal medicine, to arbitrate disputes, as well as to cast horoscopes and to divine for water and metals.[39]

Kelpius died in 1708, and by then the Chapter of Perfection had begun to come apart, but it shaped a continuing fascination with universal restoration, the occult, and hermeticism among the Pennsylvania Germans. After moving away from the Chapter and influencing the Keithian schism, Koster formed "the True Church of Philadelphia or Brotherly Love" in Plymouth, Pennsylvania, in 1697, and returned to Germany in 1699.[40] As waves of sectarian Germans entered the province, a few joined the Labadist commune, which survived into the 1720s. Others formed new sects. Between 1719 and 1727 a sect of the Newborn had a brief life in the Oley Valley before joining the German Baptists (Moravians). Inspired by Matthias Bauman's vision that he had been "translated" to heaven like the prophet Enoch, the Newborns abandoned Bible, sacraments, matrimony, and sin, convinced that they had entered a restored Paradise. Bauman captured his divinization in language that echoed centuries of hopes for Adamic perfection: "As Adam was before the fall, so I have become, and even firmer." Another group, called the New Mooners, emerged during the Great Awakening, led by a grandson of Johann Zimmerman, the founder of the Chapter of Perfection.[41] But the most important and influential of these sects emerged in the late 1720s and early 1730s. The utopian community at Ephrata flourished for forty years, and the last celibates at Ephrata died after the turn of the century. It had continuing influences reaching far into the nineteenth century, and in some measure anticipated Mormon polity and cosmology.

Ephrata was forged in a synthesis of German communal, Pietist, and hermetic-mystical traditions brought together first by Conrad Beissel (1691–1768). Growing up in a region ravaged by French armies, Beissel as a young man moved through various secret groups of Inspirationists, Philadelphians, and German Baptists, absorbing Pietist, Boehmist, Rosicrucian, hermetic, and millenarian traditions and espousing a monastic celibacy. Planning to join Kelpius's Chapter, Beissel arrived in Germantown in 1720. Finding the Chapter reduced to two hermits, he served a weaver's apprenticeship among the newly arriving Dunkers and then joined in forming a congregation of Brethren in the isolated Conestoga Valley. By the late 1720s Beissel had taken up the solitary life, gradually gathering a group of followers out of the Brethren, which in 1732 coalesced into a celibate colony shaped fundamentally by Boehmist mysticism.[42]

At the core of Beissel's Ephrata lay the gnostic "wooing" of the Virgin Sophia, elaborated by Jacob Boehme a century before. Like the alchemical search for the philosopher's stone, the worship of the Virgin Sophia would lead to a gnostic union with God. With antecedents running through Boehme to the "Pimander," Beissel's theology revolved around an alchemical construction of a sexually androgynous God, composed of tinctures of male fire and female wisdom. Divided with the Fall of Adam into male and female, humanity could be restored to its original whole, as in alchemical marriage, or *coniunctio*. In the words of a 1765 translation of Beissel's writing, the marriage of "*male-life or fire*" with "*Sophianic and celestial femalety*" was "the foundation of the *restitution of all things.*"[43]

The rhetoric and ritual of alchemical perfection and "restitution" were taken to different extremes. Beissel's hermetic piety required a repudiation of human sexuality in a severe monastic regime of physical labor and mystical prayer rituals similar to those observed by the Chapter of Perfection on the Wissahickon. In the summer of 1734 one brother attempted to

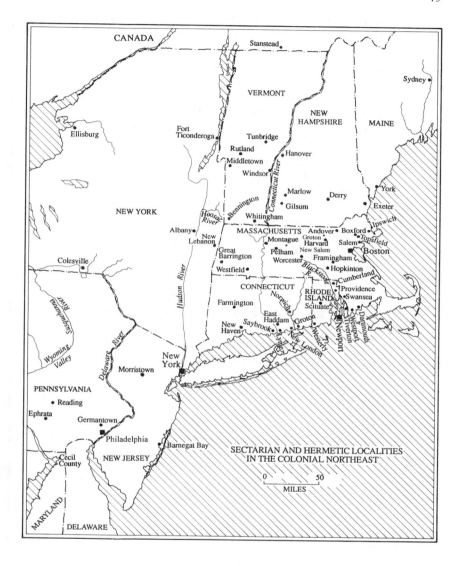

SECTARIAN AND HERMETIC LOCALITIES
IN THE COLONIAL NORTHEAST

0   50

MILES

subsist in the woods solely on acorns, as the oak was sacred in Rosicrucian tradition; alchemical experiments were carried on in the 1760s, and perhaps before. The cloister's hymns, famed throughout the region, were, according to the official chronicles, "entirely prophetic, and treated the restoration of the image of Adam before his division, of the heavenly virginity, [and] the priesthood of the Melchizedek."[44] According to a nineteenth-century account, the Melchizedek was actually restored in 1740, when three members of a Zionitic Brotherhood, Israel Eckerlin (the Prior Onesimus), Peter Miller, and Conrad Weiser, were consecrated as priests and "admitted to the ancient Order of Melchizedek." Apparently this was the priesthood that Beissel called the "sacradotal lineage." As the leading brother among the Zionitic Brethren, and perhaps as a Melchizedek priest, Israel Eckerlin was allowed to wear "an especial dress" when performing baptisms, a robe with "a clever breast-plate" sewn upon it.[45] Both a priestly breastplate and the order of the Melchizedek would reappear ninety years later in the Mormon restoration.

By 1744 Israel Eckerlin had lost a struggle to dominate the cloister and would soon travel to both the northern and southern colonies, with various company and in interesting circumstances, as we shall see. But his rise and fall coincided with the surging of popular piety in the Great Awakening, and the innovations inaugurated by Eckerlin and his brothers had echoes in the practices of lay Germans in the area for decades to come. As extreme as they were, the Ephrata celibates were not isolated from the German population surrounding them. While the celibate Solitaries lived the monastic life, there were affiliated Ephrata Householders who provided a conduit to the sects and to the church people. Some occult and mystic influences spread out, though in attenuated form, among the Pennsylvania Germans, mingling with their own inclinations toward popular magic.[46] Thus, when the Zionitic Brotherhood introduced baptism for the dead by proxy, the practice spread among the local Germans, surviving into the 1840s. Beliefs drawn from the alchemical worldview found expression in popular faith in chemical nostrums; one such preparation imported from Germany, known as the "Gold Tincture" or the "Elixir Dulcis," was widely used before the Revolution and remained in use down to the 1850s.[47] The highwater mark of religious hermeticism in the American colonies, and perhaps the entire post-Reformation era, the utopian perfectionism of the Ephrata cloister would have powerful echoes a century later among the Mormons.

Between the extremes of the magisterial Calvinism of the New England Puritans and the hermetic perfection of the German sectarians at Ephrata lay an important middle ground, literally a conduit between New England and the Mid-Atlantic. The sectarian peoples of southeastern New England, curiously neglected in recent historiography, played an important role in the transferal of the Radical Reformation to the New World. They are absolutely critical to our understanding of the hermetic inheritance of nineteenth-century Mormonism. With their own connections running back to the radical experience of the English Revolution, the New England sectarians were receptive to the systematic hermetic perfection of the German sectarians; certainly they were themselves the reservoir of a great proportion of the fragments of occult belief and practice floating around seventeenth- and eighteenth-century New England. Among their number, as we shall see, were ancestors of both Joseph Smith and Brigham Young, as well as quite a number of other Mormon forebears.

The first bearers of the Radical Reformation to New England advanced both extreme restorationism and paradisial universalism – making them both important antecedents of the Mormon theology and anathema to the Puritan state at Massachusetts Bay. Roger Williams, Anne Hutchinson, and Samuel Gorton all challenged magisterial orthodoxy in the early decades, and all would be exiled to the wilds of the Narragansett region, where the religious pluralism of Rhode Island and the Providence Plantations would be a beacon to radical sectarians throughout the Atlantic world.

Between his arrival in 1631 and the early 1640s, Roger Williams moved from an extreme biblical primitivism to the full-blown spiritualist Seeker-ism of a Caspar Schwenkfeld or a William Erbury. Williams rejected the common English Puritan typology of an Old Testament Israel. The Christian dispensation had superseded that of Israel, severing the civil and the religious spheres. Rejecting the slightest hint of compromise with a corrupt English church and state, Williams refused to join the Boston church unless the members rejected their former communion in English parishes; in Salem in 1633 he urged as apostolic imitation that women be veiled in church, and then he assailed the charter itself, arguing that the acceptance of the land patent from the king was itself corrupt.

Established on his own patent at Providence Plantations, Williams's ideas crystallized in a way that would differentiate him not only from Puritan orthodoxy but also from later Quaker spiritualism, and in a way that would anticipate the restorationism of Joseph Smith two centuries later. Rejecting Catholic tradition and the Anglican reformation as apostasy, Williams argued that there had been no true Christian church since Christianity had first been established as a state religion under Constantine. Rather than a Congregational covenant or Baptist rebaptizing, the authority for ministry and ordinances in a Christian church could only come from divine revelation. This would be a third dispensation: "There is a Time of purity and Primitive Sincerity, there is a time of Transgression and Apostacy, there is a time of the coming out of the Babilonian Apostacy and Wilderness." This would be an age of spirit; in this *"restauration of Zion . . . it may please the Lord againe to . . . powre forth those fiery streames againe of Tongues and Prophecie."* Williams's Seekerism clearly anticipated Mormon dispensationalism.[48]

Williams's challenge to Massachusetts was followed by that of Anne Hutchinson, who settled with her husband in Boston in 1634 and soon built a following behind her radical message that only the infusion of divine grace was sufficient for salvation; works were not only meaningless but infringed on the power of an all-determining Calvinist God. Accused of heresy, Hutchinson's final mistake was to claim to know "by an immediate revelation" through "the voice of [God's] own spirit to my soul" that the Massachusetts ministers lay under a covenant of works rather than grace.[49] Banished to Rhode Island, Hutchinson was welcomed by Roger Williams. By 1642 she had moved on to Seeker doctrines: John Winthrop wrote that she and her following not only "denied all magistracy" but "maintained that there were no churches since those founded by the apostles" and that there could be none until the Second Coming.[50] A year later she was dead, killed by Indians at Pelham Bay on Long Island.

If Anne Hutchinson's radicalism was thus truncated, that of Samuel Gorton evolved into New England's most direct connection to the spiritual mysticism of the English Revolution. As with Anne Hutchinson, there is no clear story of his early formative influences in England, though he – like Lawrence Clarkson and Gerald Winstanley – came from Lancashire. Gorton's theology was strikingly similar to the paradisial universalism of the Familists and earlier Continental mystics. Advancing, like Williams, a Christ-centered theology, Gorton argued that "Christ was incarnate when Adam was made after God's image." As Adam's seed, all humanity were heirs to divine perfection; there was, Gorton argued, an "equal nearness of the divine spirit to both the sinner and the saint." Such a circumstance destroyed all need for church ordinances. His near-pantheist universalism was more radically expressed in his injunction to "goe and preach the Gospell in every creature." This divinization put Gorton and his followers into a new dispensation and beyond sin: one Gortonist claimed in 1640 to have been "free from Original sin and from actual also for a year and a half." Holding themselves outside the confines of human law, the Gortonists were accused of advocating spiritual wifery and a community of goods; certainly they closely paralleled the English Diggers and the Ranters.[51] Arrested by Massachusetts authorities in 1643, Gorton returned to London in 1644, mingling with English radicals until moving on to Rhode Island in 1648, where he led a small and declining group of followers till his death in 1677.[52]

These individual radicals would be followed by more organized sectarians in the decades to come. Quaker missionaries, welcomed to Rhode Island, carried their gospel into Massachusetts in 1656, to face death for their convictions before a few meetings took hold in Boston and in towns to the north. Baptist dissenters emerging in the 1640s formed a church in Boston in 1663 and a scattered presence in the Merrimack Valley.[53]

Despite the drama of Baptist and Quaker efforts in the old Massachusetts Bay counties, the real core of New England dissent centered in Rhode Island and stretched east and west along the coast of southeastern New England. Baptists were established by the early 1640s in Newport and Providence, sending off sister churches and dividing into General Baptists (noted for their Arminian and universalist theology), Particular Baptists (ardent Calvinists), and Seventh-Day Baptists (advocates of strict Old Testament Sabbatarianism, which they shared with the German Brethren). The Rhode Island Baptists also provided a fertile field for Quaker conversion, and Rhode Island soon became the center of Quakerism, first for all of the colonies and then for the region north of New Jersey and Pennsylvania.[54] With Quaker outriders on the inner Cape and on the islands of Martha's Vineyard and Nantucket, and Baptist outriders up the Blackstone River valley, Rhode Island remained the core of a dissenter heartland in New England that, on the eve of the Great Awakening, stretched along the southeast coast from southern Bristol County in Massachusetts west to New London and Lyme in Connecticut. With the "outriders," this region in 1740 encompassed twenty-one of the twenty-eight Baptist churches in New England and eight of the thirteen Quaker Monthly Meetings. The Baptist churches in Rhode Island, Connecticut, and the Bristol County towns of Swansea and Tiverton bore the impress of the seventeenth-century radicals and biblical primitivists: fifteen of these churches followed the Sixth Principle of the laying on of hands and the Arminian theology of the General Baptists, and three followed the Mosaic law of the Seventh Day.[55]

This sectarian world maintained direct and ongoing connections with the English radical tradition, leaving open a conduit along which the hermetic theology might flow. John Clarke, the founder of the First Baptist Church in Newport, had been active in Fifth Monarchist politics in the mid-1650s, and this church attracted a Sabbatarian emissary, Steven Mumfort, sent directly from the Restoration era Sabbatarian circles in London still recovering from the drama of Venner's Fifth Monarchist insurgency of 1661. Joined by Thomas Ward, formerly an officer in the New Model Army, Mumfort drew off the Seventh-Day Baptist meeting in a 1671 secession from the Providence Baptists. Clarke's Fifth Monarchism may have provided an entry for Sabbatarian sentiment, but David Katz has suggested that a broader set of circumstances attracted Sabbatarians to Newport, specifically the simultaneous movement of Quakers and Jews from Barbados to Newport. Quakers, Fifth Monarchists, and Sabbatarians all had hopes of converting Jews to Christianity. On their part, the early Newport Jews may have affiliated with a very early Masonic lodge; Masonic mythology, Katz argues, provided connections between Judaic history and the hermetic–Cabalist tradition.[56]

One has to wonder who else was moving along the sea routes linking London, the West Indies, and Rhode Island in the 1660s. Barbados and Jamaica were noted for religious toleration, and they were the refuge and dumping ground for sectarians escaping or transported from Restoration England, among them Familists, Ranters, and possibly Levelers and Diggers. New Model Army soldiers served among the buccaneers in the 1671 raid on Panama, and transported soldiers, among them Fifth Monarchists and Muggletonians, were raising trouble in the Chesapeake.[57] Quaker missionaries encountered perfectionist Ranters, later manifested as "Young Quakers," "New Quakers," or "Singing Quakers," around Oyster Bay on Long Island and in Rhode Island in 1672, and into the next decade they were to be found as far afield as Plymouth Colony and the Chesapeake. Presumably these were locals, not in-migrants, yet there may well have been a West Indian leaven among them.[58] Such radical connections had lasting results in Connecticut, where the Rogerenes were simultaneously the last of the English revolutionary sects and the first of the indigenous American perfectionist sects, in a line that would run quite directly to the Mormons.

Having joined the Newport Seventh-Day Baptist Church in 1674, a group from New London, Connecticut, led by John Rogers withdrew in 1677. As one historian has put it, the Rogerenes were both "influenced by sectarian ideas emanating from England" and "the first indigenous American sect."[59] They were remarkably durable, cohering as sectarian communities in New London and nearby Groton into the nineteenth century, with outlying families scattered through the region and down into New Jersey. In a pantheism echoing Winstanley and the Ranters, the Rogerenes saw all days as equally holy and rejected any concept of a sacred Sabbath, incurring the wrath of the law for working on Sundays as well as disrupting orthodox services. Regarding themselves a form of Quakers, they adopted a pacifist doctrine and rejected both hired ministers and any oaths as unscriptural, as well as vocal prayer unless it was inspired by direct revelation. In 1678 John Rogers began practicing faith healing, praying over the sick and anointing them with oil. He died in 1721 tending the sick during a smallpox epidemic in Boston.[60]

Rogerene doctrine had very close affinities with radical beliefs in circulation since the Reformation. John Rogers announced a universal salvation based upon Christ's atonement: the sentence for Adam's transgression in the Garden "extended no farther than the first death" of the body. Adam in the Garden had eaten of the Tree of Knowledge, but Christ was a Second Adam, giving "access to the Tree of Life." The Second Adam brought not only "free pardon" for all sin but perfection: "the sinner is enabled [to?] live in the perfect Obedience of that Light or Knowledge of good and evil." According to Peter Pratt, a onetime Rogerene, Rogers preached that the "Gradual Work" of mortification of lusts "lands a Man in a State of Perfection" from which he "cannot fall." In language that paralleled Muggletonian thought, Rogers also preached a doctrine of the two seeds of Adam, "two nations, and two manners of people," descended from Cain and Abel, and linked respectively with the Tree of Knowledge and the Tree of Life. This doctrine of the two seeds was a central theme in English Muggletonian thought, and it would reappear, I shall suggest, in the form of Lamanites and Nephites in Joseph Smith's *Book of Mormon* over a century later.[61]

The spiritual powers claimed by the Rogerenes bring us again to the affinities between perfectionist dissent and supernatural practice. Scholars repeatedly have pointed to the instances in which the orthodox suspected religious dissenters of witchcraft.[62] Conversely, a few important dissenters in England doubted the reality of witchcraft: John Webster and Lodowick Muggleton disputed the Cambridge Platonists' claim that witchcraft could be detected.[63] But it is also clear that in witchcraft detection and accusation, New England sectarians could give as good as they got. At Salem, at least as many Quakers and their relations made accusations as were accused; the most notable among the Quaker accusers were Thomas Maule, Samuel Shattuck, and Joseph Pope.[64] And dissenters were not without the magical defenses against witchcraft that the Calvinist clergy sought to suppress. Thomas Maule had attended a meeting of Quakers in New Hampshire in 1682 where the house was apparently assaulted by spiritual forces, particularly stones thrown down the chimney. The assembled delegates, including the governor and deputy governor of West Jersey and Rhode Island, resorted to the occult defense of boiling bent needles in a pot of urine, to no avail. Samuel Shattuck, another Salem Quaker, had attempted to assault Bridget Bishop and Mary Parker by occult means, convinced that they had harmed his children. In 1694 in New London, Rogerene Bathsheba Fox, a sister of John Rogers, put witch's puppets in the meetinghouse in the midst of conflict between the Rogerenes and the orthodox community.[65] And diagnostically, where – as Richard Godbeer notes – the other New England colonies adopted statutes against witchcraft that were "biblically inspired and followed theological principles," the law against witchcraft in Rhode Island rested on the English statute of 1604. This law made no reference to the devil, and – in Keith Thomas's estimation – "left a loophole for magicians," who could claim to be dealing with good spirits rather than "evil" ones.[66] Magic in sectarian Rhode Island was not necessarily in "the Devil's Dominion."

The fate of the occult in the eighteenth century is a much discussed topic, complicated by evidence that points to persistence and decline. Certainly a basal "folklorized occult" persisted among the people of ordinary farming and artisanal households throughout early America. Almanacs continued to carry the man of signs and detailed astrological charts, and witchcraft beliefs continued to have a hold on popular imagination. Rather than being feared, witches were now threatened by a variety of easy remedies, such as twisting a branch of witch hazel or shooting a silver button or a copper coin at a cat. People in many parts of New England still had available scraps and fragments of magical protection from unseen harm.[67]

But scholarly efforts have come up with relatively few examples of magical practitioners in New England between the era of the Salem witch trials and the Revolution. Some could be found in coastal towns, providing predictive services to the maritime trades, but the evidence suggests that cunning folk and occult practitioners could best survive in the dissenting environment in and around Rhode Island.[68] Shielded from the harassment of a Calvinist ministry, the cunning folk here thrived well into the eighteenth century, fed on the mystical dimensions of antinomianism, Gortonism, Quakerism, and Sabbatarianism, and the Arminian universalism of General and Sixth Principle Baptists. This seems to explain why, when a child was lost in northern Worcester County, Massachusetts, in 1755, one of the search party had to journey forty miles south to Scituate, Rhode Island, to consult "a Wise-Man," a blacksmith named Williams Wood. Writing of the occult in 1773, the Reverend Ezra Stiles found that "[i]n general the System is broken up, the Vessel of Sorcery shipwreckt, and only some shattered planks and pieces disjoyned floating and scattered on the Ocean of . . . human Activity and Bustle." Noting that "it subsists among some Almanack Makers and Fortune Tellers," he could think of only two of the cunning folk. Granny Morgan, living in Newport, dabbled in "hocus-pocus" and divining with pin-stuck urine cakes. And there was "Mr. Stafford of Tiverton lately dead," who, Stiles wrote, "was wont to tell where lost things might be found and what day, hour and minute was fortunate for vessels to sail."[69]

The life of Joseph Stafford provides the most detailed view available for an understanding of the relationship of sectarian religion and the occult in eighteenth-century New England, and – usefully for our purposes – his descendants would be among the money-diggers associated with Joseph Smith in the Burned-over District.

Stafford came from a family who arrived in the colonies relatively late, well outside the orbit of Puritan orthodoxy, settling first in Mai,.e in 1649 and in the 1680s removing to Tiverton, a Baptist and Quaker town transferred from Massachusetts to Rhode Island in 1746. Born around 1700, Joseph Stafford was a Rhode Island justice of the peace and doctor as well as almanac-writer and fortune-teller. It is impossible to say exactly which sect he adhered to, but there were Staffords among the Quakers, and in 1778 his brothers Abraham and David were attending the Sixth Principle Baptist church located on the Tiverton–Dartmouth line.[70]

Something of this religious environment shaped Joseph Stafford's earliest almanacs, the 1737 and 1738 issues of *The Rhode Island Almanack,* published in Newport by Anne Franklin, widow of Benjamin Franklin's older brother James. Unlike that of the Franklins, Stafford's filler in 1737 and 1738 was explicitly religious, and reflected a sensibility nurtured on spiritual certainties rather than Calvinist fears. For April 1737 there was this gentle reminder, suggesting Quaker sensibilities: "What Pains men take to fit their Land to bring the Grain, But the true Spiritual Seed makes the greatest Gain." A year later there was a similar message: "The plowman guides his Plow with all his care and Skill, So does the Spirit guide all true Believers still." In 1739 Anne Franklin began putting out her own almanac, and for the next seven years Stafford carried his work to Boston for publication. In 1740 he described himself as "A Lover of the Truth," and by 1744 he was boldly calling himself "A Student of Astronomy and Astrology."[71]

Such is the published corpus of Joseph Stafford, but much more evidence of his life and practice has survived in a collection of books and manuscript fragments held in the family for two centuries.[72] Reflecting his role as a country physician, his collection was dominated by English medical texts, twenty volumes in all, dating from 1653 to 1757, comprising a comprehensive sample of medical opinion over this century. Numerous slips of paper with notations, page numbers, and transcribed formulas suggest that Stafford had a busy practice. Some of these notes suggest the intersection of magical and medical purposes. One hints at the hermetic ritual of transmutation. In a section on tinctures in R. James's 1752 *English Dispensary,* there is a slip with a Latin phrase repeated twice, translated on the reverse as "to make New Bodies out of old shapes." Beyond his formal medical texts, Stafford also had copies of *Aristotle's Masterpiece, Aristotle's Problems,* and *Aristotle's Last Legacy,*

Fortune written by Joseph Stafford, Tiverton, Rhode Island.
Courtesy of the Rhode Island Historical Society.

the classic texts in early American occult medicine and sexual advice.[73] Most important, his 1685 edition of William Salmon's *Synopsis Medicinae* included illustrated sections on the drawing up and interpreting of "judicative figures," and apparently he consulted these pages in preparing horoscopes for his neighbors. Fragments of these "figures" survive scattered among the texts as bookmarks. Among these slips is a blessing (see above) protecting a woman either from occult harm or from an accusation of witchcraft. Finally, another cluster of slips is dated to 1767 and 1768, five years before his death in 1773. In February 1768 Stafford wrote a figure for a Samuel Russell, noting "for A sea Voyag if safe & has not paid." Seven months later he wrote another for Keziah Davis "for the party[?] desired," perhaps a fortune for the outcome of a courtship. The most interesting of these slips, written in the shaking hand of an elderly man, shows that Stafford had hopes of finding buried treasure.

> December the 12 day 1767
> Joseph Stafford for treasuers
> hid by one wing in Sandwitch
> And 2 question by Beziah
> hammon for treasures hid by
> Indians . . .

Another slip notes money paid to Abraham Stafford in 1768 for "digging," perhaps in the search for Mr. Wing's treasure in Sandwich, a Quaker town forty-five miles to the east on Cape Cod.

Joseph and Abraham Stafford probably found nothing at Sandwich, and their brother David's children and the descendants of other Tiverton families were still looking for treasure a half-century later after they had taken up land in the Quaker settlement of Farmington, New York. And here they knew another family of money-diggers, the family of Joseph and Lucy Mack Smith, arriving from Vermont in 1816. It would be among such people of the postrevolutionary migrations that the occult search for treasure reached epidemic proportions.

The story of Joseph Stafford brings us back to the "Old Rodsman" of the Ohio Valley. According to the account of his life in the "History of the Divining Rod," the Rodsman was born in 1775 in the Westport section of Dartmouth, Massachusetts, a neighborhood immediately adjacent to Tiverton on the east and known as the "devil's pocket hole" and "prolific in witch stories." The Rodsman emigrated first in 1797 to the town of Sydney in Kennebec County, Maine, and then in 1813 to western New York, arriving in Marietta, Ohio, in 1816.[74] Research by Mormon historian Thomas L. Revere indicates that the Rodsman was a man named Stephen Davis, born in Westport in 1777. There were a number of Davises among the Seventh-Day Baptists in Rhode Island and New Jersey; as was the Rodsman they were descendants of Welsh immigrants. Davis was apparently related to Aron Davis, an early preacher in the Sixth Principle Baptist church attended by Joseph Stafford's brothers Abraham and David in the 1770s; the Keziah Davis for whom Stafford wrote a fortune in 1768 might have been an aunt or a cousin. And when the Rodsman moved west from Maine in 1813, his first stop was in Palmyra, New York, adjacent to Farmington, where David Stafford's son Joshua had settled around 1800, and adjacent to Manchester, where the Smith family would settle on Stafford Road.[75]

The alchemical universalism of Stephen Davis, as we may safely call the "Old Rodsman," was thus very much derived from the world of Joseph Stafford, a world compounded of magical belief and the Arminian theology passed down from the seventeenth-century General Baptists and Sabbatarians. Similar circumstances also characterized the origins of at least one other noted postrevolutionary diviner, Ransford Rogers. Born in the New London area, Ransford was still a minor when his father, Joseph Rogers, died in 1763. Joseph was a great-nephew of John Rogers, the Rogerene founder, and of Bathsheba Fox, who put witch's puppets in the

New London meetinghouse in 1694. He may have named his youngest
son for Mary Ransford, John Rogers's common-law wife.[76]

The career of Ransford Rogers leads us back to the primary center of
the occult in eighteenth-century America: the sectarian Mid-Atlantic. Old
enough to be mustered into a Colchester company of the Connecticut Line
in May of 1775, Rogers may have served in the Mid-Atlantic, perhaps
near Morristown, New Jersey, where in the late 1780s, impersonating
"the spirit of a just man" and distributing magic powders, he conned the
locals into paying for his services as a diviner and a conjurer. A decade
later, after spending time in the southern states, Rogers played the same
confidence game in York County in central Pennsylvania, and still later in
Exeter, New Hampshire, from whence he departed for Philadelphia with
several hundred dollars. In York County he teamed up with a Dr. Dady, a
former Hessian soldier, tricking a community into conjuring for treasure
by means of magic circles and expensive elixir powders.[77]

The Mid-Atlantic and German connection appears in other accounts of
treasure-divining,[78] and German metallurgical knowledge, running back
to Agrippa and Paracelsus, was a central theme in the continuing efforts to
discover and exploit minerals. Throughout the seventeenth and eighteenth
centuries, mines were as obsessively sought as was treasure after the Revolution. The ruling gentries of early New England and the Chesapeake were
obsessed with mines, and as Wayne Bodle has discovered, in the eighteenth century waves of mine-hunting fever spread like religious revivals
through the colonies.[79] First in the 1720s and again in the 1750s, both
entrepreneurial speculators and hundreds of "ramblers," "peering fellow[s]," and "mine-hunters" scoured the woods with total disregard for
the claims of equally interested proprietors. As one Pennsylvania proprietor complained, there were only "whispers" of discoveries by these metallurgical interlopers: "in these cases of discoveries – like ye adepts in
Chemistry, all are very secret."[80] William Byrd II wrote in 1733 of south-
side Virginia that "there's a bad distemper rag[ing] in those parts that
grows very epidemical. The people are all mine-mad and, neglecting to
make corn, starve their families in hopes to live in great plenty hereafter."
Byrd's description would have applied equally well to any one of the
divining episodes in the early Republic.[81]

In Bodle's estimation, the hunt for mines in the 1720s "embedded the
notion of mines more firmly into the American consciousness than it had
perhaps been since the mid-seventeenth century." The mine hunting constituted "a kind of Elizabethan revival," reeducating people in "arcane
Elizabethan understandings about the nature of ore development and
distribution."[82] The best sources for these "arcane understandings" were
Germans with proven – or assumed – skills. During the second mining

boom, in 1754, people in Worcester, Massachusetts, had hopes of mining a vein of silver; a "cunning German" who "pretended to knowledge of the occult sciences as well as skill in the art of deception" was hired to pursue the work. He departed for Philadelphia when the funds were used up and as people began to see "that stone and iron could not be transmuted into gold."[83] But in the course of these mining enthusiasms, non-Germans among the colonial populations began to reeducate themselves in the rudiments of the hermetic system, presenting themselves as miners and smelters, and providing an important channel of dissemination of Renaissance traditions in eighteenth-century America.[84] Similarly, the unprecedented wartime intermingling of peoples during the Revolution may have brought fragments of hermetic knowledge into New England from the Mid-Atlantic.

But such contacts had long been a tradition along the Sabbatarian axis linking southeast New England with southeast Pennsylvania. A series of letters and visitations, beginning with Kelpius's letter to Steven Mumfort in 1699, marked the relationship. Kelpius's authority as a mediator followed his alchemic-millenarian letter to Mumfort, and over the next few years, delegations of Seventh-Day Baptists and Rogerenes traveled south from Rhode Island and Connecticut to have Kelpius resolve church disputes. They were followed by William Davis, a Welsh Baptist converted by Koster, who moved between Sabbatarian congregations in Pennsylvania, Rhode Island, and New Jersey between 1710 and 1745.[85]

Two decades after John Rogers's death, the New London Rogerenes and the Rhode Island Seventh-Day Baptists received a return visit from the Pennsylvanian Sabbatarians. In the fall of 1744 two of the Eckerlin brothers, Israel and Samuel, with Alexander Mack Jr. and Peter Miller, began a pilgrimage that took them through Sabbatarian settlements in Germantown and in New Jersey, and then by boat to New London. Here they visited with the Rogerenes, with whom they are said to have discussed "abstruse theological mysteries" and, according to the Ephrata chronicles, caused a great stir in this "fruitful garden of God" among "the many converted souls . . . who were commonly called 'New Lights.' "[86]

The influence of the Rogerenes, to say nothing of wandering German mystics, on the course of the Great Awakening in southeast New England is difficult – and probably impossible – to unravel. All we can say is that there are interesting parallels between the perfectionism of these radical Sabbatarians and that of a scattering of sects that emerged in southeast New England during and after the Awakening. So, too, the role of the occult in some of these groups points again to its particular affinity with perfectionist sectarianism.

In particular, perfectionist tendencies emerged among Separates in several towns in eastern Connecticut and in and near the Blackstone Valley in northern Rhode Island and Massachusetts. The Mansfield, Connecticut, Separates wrote in their confession that their election, "humbling us by Gospel Grace[,] has made us Partakers of the Divine Nature, which being added to Christ's taking the Humane Nature makes up the Union between Christ and our Souls." In 1747 the orthodox ministers of Windham County united in condemning this confession, calling it "little short of the Blasphemy of *Jacob Bekman* [Boehme], our being *godded* with GOD, and *christed* with Christ." But claims of immortalism had already begun to spread among the Separates: in 1746 in Windham one group announced that they "were perfect and immortal; and one of them declared he was Christ."[87]

Counting themselves to be perfect in holiness, immortal, and even divine, some claimed the right of "spiritual wifery," a term to be applied to Mormon polygamy a century later. Among these were the Wards and Finneys of Cumberland, Rhode Island, whose notoriety reached down to the 1770s to influence Jemima Wilkinson's celibate Universal Friends. In 1749 Molly Ward abandoned her husband and took up with Solomon Finney as her spiritual husband. Finney's brother John later baptized his father and others on a personal conviction of perfection; in 1751 he declared for "the new covenant or a spiritual union" of marriage, declaring "that Christians ought to marry in the church without any regard to Babylon, as he called rulers in the State." Spiritual wifery spread among the Immortalists of the Blackstone Valley towns of Grafton, Upton, and Hopkinton, Massachusetts, and even among the Separate and Baptist churches. In 1765 Baptist leader Isaac Backus complained that some among the Attleboro Baptists had "been ensnared this year with antinomian notions so as not to be content with their own wives."[88]

Just as the Blackstone Valley Immortalists anticipated Mormon plural marriage, they also anticipated Mormon divinization. Initially scattered in towns throughout the region, the Immortalists coalesced into two followings, one around Shadrack Ireland in Harvard, Massachusetts, which gravitated to the Shakers after Ireland's death in 1778, and another around a Nat Smith in Hopkinton, Massachusetts. Ireland claimed to be immortal, and Smith claimed to be God himself, according to an account written in 1793 by Ezra Stiles.

> Nat Smith proceeded to assume & declare himself to be the Most High God & wore a cap with the word GOD inscribed on its front. His Great Chair was a Holy Chair & none but himself must sit in it. He had a number of Adorers & Worshippers, who continue to this day [1793] to believe he was the Great God.[89]

Stiles's account is confirmed in a long account from a Mormon source. Living for over a century in Hopkinton, the family of the prophet Brigham Young brushed up against Smith's Immortalists more than once. Born in 1787 in Hopkinton, Brigham's sister Fanny Young Murray in 1845 could write from memory to her brother Phinehas about this "strange society of people."

> They were and are the greatest wonder to everybody that knows them, of any people that ever came under my observation. They always had a God of their own, and they came in succession; when one died, another took his place. I was at the funeral of one of these Gods, when I was about eleven years old [1798]. But none saw the dead God, neither had they a prayer or any thing of the kind in their house. [T]hey were entirely by themselves, were very rich, kept their own [sacra?]ment every Sunday to the house of their God, but whether or no they worshiped him, was more than any one knew, as they kept close doors, and none but their own company were ever admitted into their meetings.[90]

A thread of treasure-divining moved through at least one of the Immortalist circles. Solomon Prentice Jr., son of the Immortalist Sarah Prentice, who lived with Ireland as his spiritual wife, moved to the Carolinas after the Revolution, where he was reputed to have "searched for Capt. Kidd's treasure." Similarly, Sarah's cousin, Nathaniel Sartell of Groton, was also drawn into the occult hunt for treasure in the 1780s, with a similar lack of success.[91]

Treasure-divining was a central dimension of the radical perfectionism of the New Israelite movement, which emerged in Rutland County, Vermont, at the end of the 1790s and which would have direct links to early Mormonism. The New Israelites had roots in the broad orbit of sectarian dissent in southeast New England. The leader of the cult, Nathaniel Wood, had emigrated in the early 1780s from Newent Parish in Norwich, Connecticut, to Bennington, Vermont, where his brother Ebenezer had settled in 1761, and then moved on with his family to Middletown, in western Rutland County. Perhaps influenced by Rogerene missionaries, who disrupted Sunday worship in Norwich in 1725 and 1763, the Newent Separates "tolerated some serious errors," including a perfectionist immortalism that led to spiritual wifery, in an echo of the Gortonists and Ranters of the previous century.[92] Associated with the Newent Separates after the Awakening, Nathaniel Wood may have been among a group of Separates who rejoined the orthodox church in Newent in 1770. If so, he would have listened to the Reverend Joel Benedict, whose belief that Hebrew was "the language of the angels" might have shaped Wood's subsequent visions of a New Jerusalem. Benedict was dismissed by the Newent church in 1782, and in that year the Woods began to arrive in Middletown. Aspiring to be the minister of the local Congregationalist church, Nathaniel Wood quarreled with the church until he was excommunicated in 1789. He then began preaching to small meetings that evolved into the New Israelite sect.[93]

The beliefs of the New Israelites brought together magical practice and biblical restorationism in ways not seen since Ephrata and the English revolutionary sects. After his excommunication, Nathaniel Wood prophesied "special acts of Providence" and claimed powers of revelation. Claiming literal descent from the Lost Tribes of Israel and to be living in a special dispensation, his family and followers began work on a temple and divined for gold "to pave the streets of the New Jerusalem." Their expectations that a *"Destroying Angel"* would bring down earthquakes and plagues on the "gentiles" so alarmed the town that on the appointed night (January 14, 1802) the militia turned out under arms. When the Apocalypse failed to materialize, the Woods removed west to Ellisburg, in St. Lawrence County, New York. Their story was much entangled with the formative origins of Mormonism.[94]

Quite simply, the peoples of the Radical tradition were well prepared for the Mormon message. On the sectarian coast running from Cape Cod through Rhode Island to the Connecticut River, a New England people lived outside the pale of Puritan orthodoxy. Here a religious history of Arminianism and spiritist universalism, a predisposition for the occult, continuities running back to the sects of the English Revolution, and connections running south to the hermetic mystics of the Mid-Atlantic all worked to forge a culture that anticipated much of the Mormon restoration.

3

Something of Our Ancestors

Brother and Sisters, Cousins, Nephews and Nieces and all who are
before me as such. I rejoice that I am connected with you, as there
are three branches here, descendants of Father Phinehas, and
Mother Susannah Goddard Howe. It might be interesting for me
to speak as I am the oldest – I will communicate something of our
ancestors to the Great Grand Children. Concerning my Great
Grand Father Goddard I will give you a little history of his character as well as others of our ancestors, for some of you have to be
baptized for some who are dead and worthy of it.

Elder John Haven, at a meeting of the Haven, Young, and Richards
families, formerly of Hopkinton, Massachusetts, at Nauvoo, Illinois,
January 8, 1845[1]

HISTORIANS LONG HAVE AGREED that the conditions of life in the
turmoil of postrevolutionary America, both in the commercial-
farming districts of the Burned-over District and in the hardscrabble mid-
western frontier, explain the emergence of the Church of Jesus Christ of
Latter-day Saints. In this interpretation, the appeal of a message of prophecy, restoration, and eventually divinization stemmed from the uniquely
disordered conditions of the early-nineteenth-century frontier and of a
rapidly democratizing society. People found refuge from a disordered
world in the authoritative pronouncements of the prophet Joseph Smith.[2]

Certainly, Mormonism was fundamentally shaped by the environment
in which it emerged, and the particular circumstances of time and place
must be kept clearly in view. But the Mormon cosmology, and the predisposition to accept that cosmology, were both equally shaped by strands
of culture inherited from the past, particularly from the era of the Radical
Reformation, filtered through family tradition, the printed page, and the
ebb and flow of cultural interchange across the eighteenth-century North
Atlantic world. Certainly the Mormons themselves were self-conscious of
these memories, real and imaged, and they centered their religion on a
cosmic hierarchy of familial connections stretching backward and forward through eternity. Thus John Haven lectured the children of his
Hopkinton cousinry at Nauvoo, children who were to be baptized in the
place of long-dead ancestors.[3]

Kinship provided these Mormon families with a well of vertical continuity with memory and deep history; it also established dimensions of milieu – some of the parameters of horizontal affiliation that shaped the boundaries of culture among these people. Perhaps extended kinship was less important among early New Englanders than it was among people of the colonial South,[4] but it certainly was an important frame for experience and worldview. Neighborhood life, church affiliation, military service, and even transatlantic migration were each situated in a "complex network of kinship," along which information flowed and traditions were perpetuated.[5] By necessity, kinship is central to our story; kinship is often the only social relation that can be reconstructed for the usually very obscure people we will encounter here.[6] And occasionally we have their own voices testifying to the durability of kinship ties, as among the Hopkinton families meeting at Mormon Nauvoo in 1845, or in the words of Joseph Bill, an eighteenth-century counterfeiter whose life we shall consider in a later chapter. A Connecticut man who had lived for decades in the Mid-Atlantic and southern backcountry, Bill in 1770 "came to Wyoming, on Susquehanna, where I found several of my relations, but we did not know each other till I told them my name; then they remembered that they had heard their fathers speak of me."[7] Uncovering the paths of familial experience shaping the situation, predisposition, and memory of the early Mormon converts provides a powerful perspective on the Mormon emergence, clarifying its connections to the sectarian and hermetic traditions.

Some of these familial experiences and memories were relatively recent. The immediate antecedent to Mormon conviction for many lay in the explosive emergence of new religions – what Stephen Marini calls the revolutionary sects – during and after the American Revolution. A popular alienation from Calvinist orthodoxy and, beyond that, hopes for universal salvation and dispensational restoration in the 1780s and 1790s were manifested most importantly in the rise of the Methodists, the Universalists, the Shakers, the Freewill Baptists, and the Christian Connection of Alexander Campbell and Elias Smith.[8]

An important body of the early Mormon leadership was grounded in these new vehicles of the now ancient radical tradition, first and foremost the Smith family itself. Joseph Smith's mother, Lucy Mack, moved from church to church searching for the true religion, while his father refused to join any denomination. The prophet's grandfather Asael Smith helped to form a Universalist Society in Tunbridge, Vermont, in the 1790s and advised his children to beware any formal creeds. Moving along a different religious current, Brigham Young's parents joined the Methodists before they left Hopkinton, Massachusetts, in 1800; in Whitingham, Vermont, they affiliated with the Reformed Methodists, a biblical primitivist group that practiced baptism by immersion, faith healing, and the laying on of hands. Others among the early Mormons who had been Methodists included Hosea Stout, Emma Hale, who married Joseph Smith in 1827, and Joseph Smith himself, who admitted in his "History" to having been "somewhat partial to the Methodist Sect."[9]

The Kimballs, who intermarried with the Youngs in Mendon, New York, followed a third path. James Kimball, born in Bradford, Massachusetts, moved to New Hampshire during the Revolution; then in the 1780s the family joined the Shaker community at Enfield, New Hampshire, only to withdraw and move to northern Vermont in 1796. His grandson, Heber C. Kimball, one of the key Mormon leaders to the end of the nineteenth century, stood among a group of neighbors in 1827 to witness a vast army marching in the sky, interpreted as a millennial sign.[10]

Parley P. Pratt, a Campbellite preacher who became another leader among the early Mormons, had a similar vision. Passing through the Lebanon Valley in eastern New York after addressing the Shakers at New Lebanon, Pratt saw in cloud formations a Masonic square and compass, which he interpreted as a "marvelous . . . sign of the coming of the Son of Man." While Parley Pratt moved from the Baptists to the Campbellites, Pratt's brother, Orson, and their father, Jared, like Asael Smith, refused to join any denomination, until Orson was convinced to join the Mormons. Newell Knight awaited the restoration before he was converted by Joseph Smith; his father had left Oakham, Massachusetts, as a Universalist. Wilford Woodruff, who joined the Mormons in Rhode Island in 1833, had been convinced by an "old prophet" named Robert Mason to avoid the churches and await the restoration. And a host of important early Mormons, including Parley Pratt, Edward Partridge, Lyman Wight, Newell K. Whitney, and John Murdock, were members of Sidney Rigdon's splinter Campbellite congregation in Mentor, Ohio, which was converted en masse to Mormonism in late 1830.[11]

This primitivist predisposition among early Mormon converts has been explained by the specific conditions of life in early-nineteenth-century America, most importantly the experience of sectarian pluralism coupled with economic stress. Some historians have seen the early Mormons, descended from old New England stock, consciously re-creating the certainties and unities of Puritan orthodoxy, with its seemingly theocratic polity, its corporate form, and its biblical primitivism. For a dispossessed people, Mormonism might provide a return to the certainties of the New England tradition.[12]

But, as I have stressed in the previous chapter, Mormon restoration and proto-Mormon primitivism were not a return to but a rejection of the Puritan tradition. In awaiting a literal restoration of the true church these seekers were moving decisively into the ranks of the radicals. Puritanism's return to biblical forms was only in imitation of the apostolic church. Even in the early seventeenth century the New England churches had no tolerance for radical aspirations for a literal restoration of the ancient church or for the opening of a new dispensation, a new age of spirit, in which the power of visions and miracles would be restored.[13] It was this boundary between biblical primitivism and literalist restoration that separated Mormon convert Sidney Rigdon from his former ally Alexander Campbell, the founder of the Disciples of Christ. Campbell objected to Rigdon's demands that a restoration of "the ancient order of things" necessarily meant that "supernatural gifts and miracles ought to be restored." Campbell held – in concert with mainline theology – that such spiritual powers had been lost irrevocably since the age of the apostles.[14] The primal Mormon impulse for the restoration of a spiritual Kingdom of God, in which men would hold supernatural powers, lay well outside the confines of Puritan orthodoxy.

However, where the religious experience of some Mormon families involved an alienation from Puritan or Calvinist orthodoxy, that of many others did not. The histories of fifty-three important Mormon families that can be traced to their point of immigration suggest that Mormon conversion was not typically based in classical Puritan experience. Many of the proto-Mormon families arrived after the Great Migration, and these and others were often rooted in deep histories of religious dissent.[15]

Among these fifty-three Mormon families, twenty-seven arrived in New England before 1650, in the era of the Great Migration. Of these, seven families settled in the sectarian southeast running from Cape Cod to New London. Few in absolute terms, these proto-Mormon families settling in southeastern New England were roughly twice as numerous relative to the total population in 1650 as those settling in the orthodox core of New England.[16] Families settling in orthodox regions, such as the Smiths, the Kimballs, the Whitneys, the Wights, and the Partridges, would have to go through a process of alienation from Puritan orthodoxy, but those proto-Mormon families in the sectarian southeast of New England would have already made that step.

Among the families coming to the southeast, the family of Martin Harris, an important early convert in Palmyra, had an ancient lineage of sectarian dissent. Thomas and William Harris had arrived in Boston from Wales in 1635; Separatists, they were banished with Roger Williams to Rhode Island, where their Quaker descendants lived in Smithfield. Passing through the Quaker town of Easton in the Hoosac Valley of New York (adjacent to southern Vermont), where Martin was born in 1783, the Harrises were some of the earliest settlers of Palmyra.[17] The Hoosac Valley was a focus of Baptist and Quaker settlement from Rhode Island at the end of the eighteenth century. Various Stafford families were here in 1790 and 1800, before joining a stream of Hoosac Valley Quakers resettling in Farmington, in Ontario County in western New York. Among the Hoosac Valley's sectarians, the gospel of a new dispensation was preached by Eliot Ward of Pittstown, New York, in the 1820s; one wonders whether he was connected to the Wards among the Rhode Island perfectionists of the 1750s.[18]

Another sectarian odyssey took the Culver family, some of whom would be baptized into Mormonism in 1830, from Massachusetts to Connecticut in 1653, and from there to New Jersey. The Culvers were among the leaders in forming the first Baptist church in Groton, Connecticut, and by the 1720s they had joined the Rogerenes. Persecuted in Groton, they were among the Rogerene families who removed to Morris County and Barnegat Bay in New Jersey. From New Jersey they visited the Ephrata cloister and in 1744 they hosted the Ephrata pilgrims on their way north. Living in Morris County, one of the Culver families must have heard something of the occult exploits of Ransford Rogers in Morristown forty years later, before they removed to New York's Susquehanna country in 1788. And on the Susquehanna the Culvers' Rogerene inheritance reasserted itself. In 1791 Nathan Culver had a dream of being guided through heaven and hell by Christ, who stood before him with "a bright shining light around him, which appeared brighter than the sun." After Culver drowned in the river that spring, his vision was published in five separate printings by 1795; thirty-five years later his nephew Aaron was one of the first Mormon converts among the celebrated Colesville Branch.[19]

Sectarians composed a small but interesting cluster among those proto-Mormon families arriving with the Great Migration; another, larger group did not arrive until well after this migration was over. Fifteen families in our proto-Mormon sample arrived in New England between 1650 and the 1730s. Among them were the Beebes, early settlers of New London and later numbering among the Rogerenes. William Cahoon, ancestor of Reynolds Cahoon, an important Mormon leader at Nauvoo and Utah, arrived in the 1650s as a Scottish prisoner of war and was sold into indentures before settling in the Baptist town of Swansea, Massachusetts. He was killed in the Narragansett attack in 1675.[20] William Young, Brigham Young's great-grandfather, arrived in Boston around 1712; a supporter of Boston's Presbyterian church, he married into a network of

West Country fishing families in New Hampshire and Maine – a group notorious for their hostility to orthodox Puritanism.[21] A few of these late-settling proto-Mormon families were refugees from the English Revolution. Benedict Pulsipher arrived in Salem sometime in the 1660s, having – according to tradition – changed his name from Pulford to escape Charles II's agents. Similarly, John Mack, the paternal ancestor of Joseph Smith's mother, Lucy Mack, changed his name on leaving Scotland in the 1660s. Another of Brigham Young's maternal ancestors, William Goddard, was the son of a Parliamentarian dispossessed at Charles II's return to the throne in 1660. Burned out by the Great Fire in London in 1665, William Goddard settled in Watertown, Massachusetts. His son Edward, remembered a century later by Elder John Haven as "Great Grand Father Goddard," rose to prominence in Framingham, where he led separations from the established church in 1732 and 1746.[22]

The post-1650 arrivals in this sample of fifty-three proto-Mormon families included seven families who settled in the pluralistic Mid-Atlantic colonies. Three were German, including the Whitmers, who lived for some time near the Ephrata cloister before moving to Seneca County, New York, around 1805, where they would number among the witnesses to Joseph Smith's miracles. Two others were of Dutch extraction, and two others were Quakers, including the Rich family, who lived for a century in West Nottingham, Cecil County, Maryland, in a county where the Labadist commune had been established in 1683, and in a township where there had been a Seventh-Day Baptist church since the days of the Keithian schism.[23] Finally, four of this sample of fifty-three families were themselves immigrants from England and Ireland, converted by Mormon missionaries before or after their emigration. Among these, William Clayton grew up in Penwortham and Preston, Lancashire, once a hotbed of the radical tradition.[24]

The definitive study of the religious origins of the earliest Mormon converts has yet to be attempted, and such a study may well overturn the tentative conclusions one can draw from this limited exploration. But these conclusions are worth summarizing: overall, among fifty-three Mormon families traced to their origins, only twenty can be said to have been exposed to the classic Puritanism of the Great Migration and to have abandoned that tradition for the new sects and the ideal of a literal restoration after the American Revolution. All of the other thirty-three families, by virtue of their settlement in sectarian southeastern New England or the Mid-Atlantic or their late arrival in the New World, would not have had any exposure to early New England Puritan orthodoxy. Scattered evidence suggests that many of them were indeed exposed in some way to sectarian alternatives. This sample suggests that, rather than an aftershock of the Puritanism of the Great Migration, we might better think of Mormonism as an aftershock of the Radical Reformation. Such indeed was the opinion of a German Reformed minister who witnessed the emergence of the church in central New York and wrote in 1830 that "[m]ost of their present adherents were apparently General Baptists."[25]

This is not to suggest that these families transmitted a hermetic culture intact from the seventeenth-century sects to nineteenth-century Mormonism. Rather, Mormon converts were drawn from a peculiarly prepared people, families that often had long stood outside the mainstream of New England orthodoxy. These family histories established a cumulative experience of sectarian inclinations, supernatural practice, and continuing migration that together shaped a predisposition to Mormon conversion in the 1830s. And the Mormon fascination with kinship and family history suggests that historians ought not to neglect such familial continuities in attempting to understand Mormon origins.

With this opening perspective established, this chapter will explore Mormon origins in New England from the 1630s to 1800 in some detail, examining specifically the experiences of the families of the two Mormon founders, Joseph Smith and Brigham Young. This will also be an exploration of the communities from which they emerged – Topsfield, in Essex County, Massachusetts; Hopkinton and Framingham, in the Blackstone Valley in Massachusetts; and Lyme and East Haddam, in the New London region of Connecticut – looking carefully at the themes of witchcraft fears, folk metallurgy, and sectarian dissent. We will discover no full articulation of Mormon restoration and hermetic divinization, but the experiences of these families in their communities tell us much about the intellectual and social preconditions for the framing of Mormon doctrine.

Robert Smith arrived in Boston in 1638, just months after Anne Hutchinson's banishment to Rhode Island. Only twelve years old, Robert had had no mature encounter with Laudian persecution or English Puritanism. Without a family other than a brother, who soon disappeared, his early exposure to Puritanism in New England came through the filter of either indentured servitude or an apprenticeship. After working as a tailor in Boston for some years, he married Mary French of Ipswich in the mid-1650s and established himself in Boxford in 1661. Mary was a member of the Topsfield church by 1684, but Robert Smith never joined the church. By 1693, when he had his will drawn up as he lay dying, Robert Smith enjoyed substantial yeoman circumstances, leaving three hundred acres to three of his sons. His son Samuel, Joseph Smith's great-great-grandfather, would move to neighboring Topsfield in 1693, where the family would remain for almost a century, before emigrating during the revolutionary years to New Hampshire and Vermont, and after the Cold Summer of 1816 to Palmyra in the Burned-over District of central New York.[26]

Two episodes dramatically set off the story of the Smiths in Essex County. In the spring of 1692, at the height of the Salem witchcraft trials, Samuel Smith testified to the occult powers of his aunt by marriage, Mary Easty, one of the three daughters of William Towne of Topsfield who were accused of witchcraft in 1692. On the evidence of Samuel Smith, Margaret Redington, and several of the "afflicted girls," Mary Towne Easty was hanged on September 22, 1692. A century later, in 1796, Samuel's grandson Asael Smith wrote a warm and friendly letter from Tunbridge, Vermont, to Jacob Towne Jr. in Topsfield, a great-great-great-nephew of Mary Easty, thanking him "with joy and gratitude" for a recent letter and sending his regards to Jacob's parents.[27] A long saga of community turmoil and reconciliation stood between these two events.

The Smiths and the Townes had been on very intimate terms during the 1680s. Though the Smiths lived in Boxford, miles from the Townes in south Topsfield, all three marriages among Robert Smith's children in the 1680s were with members of the Towne family.[28] But these cordial relations were shattered in 1692 when Samuel Smith of Boxford appeared at the Salem court and testified at the trial of Mary Easty, the aunt of three of his brothers-in-law. One night five years previously Smith had been "to[o] Rude in discorse" at the Easty house, probably at the wedding supper for his sister Amy, and Mary Easty had warned him he "might Rue it hereafter." Riding past a stone wall later that night he had "Received a little blow to my shoulder with I know not what and the stone wall rattled very much which affrighted me my horse was also affrighted very much but I cannot give the reson of it." Margaret Redington testified that during an illness three years earlier Goody Easty had vanished into thin air after offering her a piece of meat "not fete for the doges." On this evidence and that relating to the afflicted girls, several of them Putnams, Mary Towne Easty was hanged on September 22, 1692.[29]

Samuel Smith's testimony against Mary Easty, a striking violation of the family relationship established in the marriages of three of his sisters, was clearly a dramatic turning point in the relations between Smiths and Townes. With the exception of one marriage in 1732, after which the couple removed to Kennebunkport, Maine, there would be no significant associations between the Smiths and the Townes for seventy years. Abandoning the Towne family with this accusation, the Smiths moved decisively into the orbit of the Gould family, the largest landholders in the town of Topsfield and cousins of the Putnams of Salem Village, who led the accusations against the Townes in 1692.

In August 1693, eight months after the end of the Salem trials, Robert Smith had his last will and testament drawn up as he lay on his deathbed. His wife, Mary, and son Samuel were named executors, and the will was witnessed by his brother-in-law John French and by Captain John Gould. The conditions of Robert Smith's will may suggest approval of Samuel's accusation of Mary Towne Easty. Robert left Samuel, his third son, with one hundred acres of land, while he cut off his eldest son, Thomas, with six pounds.[30]

Samuel's one hundred acres were situated on the line between Boxford and north Topsfield, making him a neighbor of the Goulds, and the Smith–Gould connection would continue for decades. After witnessing Robert's will in August 1693, Captain John Gould inventoried the estate that September. John Gould II witnessed a further accounting of this estate in 1720 and was the executor of Samuel Smith's estate when he died in 1748; the three witnesses of Samuel Smith II's will in 1767 were all Goulds. In the intervening years there had been at least three Smith–Gould marriages, including two between Samuel Smith II and two first cousins, both named Priscilla Gould, in 1734 and 1745.[31]

The Smith family's decided shift in affiliation from the Townes to the Goulds is a strong indication that Samuel's accusation of Mary Easty was no passing whim. His fear of occult powers was embedded deeply in a context of kinship, behind which there may have been bitter anxieties over property. And in shifting from Townes to Goulds, the Smiths were taking a step that had powerful political implications within the microcosm of Topsfield. Formed in 1648 from "the village at the new medowes at Ipswich," Topsfield was wracked by intense conflict at regular intervals from the 1660s to the 1740s, conflict that invariably pitted the Goulds and families in their kinship circle with the Townes and their orbit. From the 1660s to the 1680s, the Goulds advanced the cause of the Puritan Commonwealth, while the Townes supported the Stuart authorities. In 1692 the Townes and their allied families were the target of witchcraft accusations, typically brought by Gould allies. In 1739 a shooting accident during militia training brought the two sides into court, and then the Great Awakening pitted the Goulds as ardent New Lights against the Townes as Old Lights. Twice, in 1692 and in 1746, the bitter and public quarrels between the two "parties" had to be reconciled in public meetings.[32] The witchcraft accusations of 1692 were only one episode in a pattern of endemic conflict that would be forgotten only in the drama of the midcentury wars.

A similar confrontation between "parties" set the stage for another incident of occult warfare involving the Goddard family, forebears of the

Mormon Youngs. The bewitchment and exorcism of the household of Ebenezer and Sybell Goddard apparently occurred in 1759, and the story was distantly remembered among the Mormons in the 1840s. The story also centered on a perfectionist cult, many of whose features anticipated nineteenth-century Mormonism.

The context for this episode encompassed a history of strife between Separates and Immortalists in Framingham and Hopkinton, Massachusetts, well south of Essex County in the Blackstone Valley. In 1724 Elder Joseph Haven was dismissed from the Framingham church to form a church in the new town of Hopkinton, and in 1732 Edward Goddard led a group of his neighbors on the Framingham–Hopkinton line to join this Hopkinton church, which accepted them without the usual letters of dismissal. The families were connected for the next century: in 1760 Joseph Haven would marry as his second wife Edward Goddard's widowed daughter, and in the 1830s the Havens would join the Youngs in the Mormon church. Goddard and many of his neighbors later returned to the Framingham church, but in 1746, toward the end of the Great Awakening, Edward Goddard led another secession in Framingham, this time to form a Separate church on strict Calvinist principles. This church survived about thirteen years, collapsing at the end of 1759, five years after Edward Goddard's death, with many of its members recombining to form a Baptist church.[33]

Just over the town line in Hopkinton, the Awakening spawned another sectarian group: the Immortalists gathered around their "God," Nat Smith, still remembered almost a century later in the Young family. The exposure of a proto-Mormon family to a band of eighteenth-century perfectionists is alone interesting enough, but beyond this simple proximity lay a history of conflict leading to a story of demonic possession. Some of this conflict involved Joseph Haven's church in Hopkinton: Ezra Stiles described an episode in which the Immortalists had walked "around Hopkinton Meet[in]gh[ouse] sound[in]g with Ramshorns & and denounc[in]g its downfall, in vain."[34] But there may also have been bad feelings between the Immortalists and Edward Goddard's Framingham Separates. Nat Smith was apparently Nathaniel Smith, born in 1712 in Ipswich, the brother of a Dorothy Smith Singletary, whose husband, Ebenezer, was a member of Goddard's church.[35] Bad feelings over "sheepstealing" may have been compounded by proximity: Edward Goddard's land, inherited in 1754 by his son Ebenezer, lay across the town line from that of the Smiths. Potential conflict became overt when, according to Fanny Young Murray's account, "old Nat Smith, their God," challenged Ebenezer Goddard's right to administer the estate of a widow whose property lay "somewhere on the outskirts of his domains." Goddard ignored Smith's threats; strange things soon began to occur in his household.[36]

First, all of Goddard's papers that were "of any consequence to him" disappeared from a locked desk to be found at the bottom of the well, though none of them got wet. Strict Calvinists and "not much inclined to the marvelous," the Goddards "concluded to say nothing about it, and let it all go as it was impossible to account for in any rational way." Next Sybell Goddard found the milk spoiled by a silver spoon "filled with the most horrible filth." Suspicion turned on a young slave boy, and when the milk was again spoiled, he was whipped severely. Kept under close surveillance, the boy nonetheless continued to disrupt the household economy, until one morning one of the girl's caps fell from his apron and – "cut smoothly in two" by some unknown means – half of it flew up the chimney and disappeared. With this, Sybell Goddard began to suspect supernatural powers at work and the boy, now forgiven, revealed

> that a little bird came every day and whispered in his ear, that if he did not do what it told him to, he should be killed that night. It also told him if he told anybody what made him do it, he should be killed; but said he tried to tell his master, when he whipped him so, but could not.

With occult power now apparent to all, their troubles continued. Soon after, the family books were found covering the oven fire; Fanny Young Murray claimed to remember having read books scorched in this fire, "where the edge of the leaves were burned a little, and some spots burned in onto the reading." Still later, the bed clothing of infant twins came down the oven chimney to be spoiled in the fire; Sybell ran and "found her babies naked, as she expected." The family began to fear that supernatural forces "were likely to destroy everything they had . . .; there seemed to be a kind of despairing consternation upon them."[37]

By this time the tribulations of the Goddard household were common knowledge. "Many went to see the wonders that were daily exhibited – It was noised through the whole country, it was the topic of conversation in every house both public and private; but nobody could do them any good." Finally the decision was made "to try what virtue would be found in fasting and prayer." Sixteen ministers were called together at the house, "the most devout and holy men they could find." After three days and two nights of fasting and prayer, one of the preachers took the lead in prayer and exorcised the house.

> He could not be denied, he plead with the Lord as a man would plead for life; that he would break the power of the destroyer, that he would rebuke him, and command him to leave that house and family forever. Towards night, on the third day, when he was

pouring out his soul with such fervour, and they were all united
with him, in a moment there seemed to be shock through the
whole house, not of distress or sorrow, but of joy and assurance
that there was a God in the heavens, who can be penetrated with
the cries of his children, and who was not slow to answer the
prayers of those that put their trust in him. From that hour, not a
thing of the kind ever took place in their house or anywhere about
them.[38]

This encounter with the occult powers of the "destroyer" was not
without its repercussions. These events seem to have taken place in the
summer and fall of 1759. The Framingham Separate church collapsed that
October, and in February of 1760 Ebenezer Goddard sold his land in
Framingham to remove to the frontier town of Atholl. Two years later he
was dead.[39] Not only was the Goddards' religious and household life
disrupted, but their view of the invisible world was transformed. Perhaps
they might have learned something of malefic power from Ebenezer Singletary, one of the Framingham Separates and a great-nephew of Jonathan
Singletary, bewitched by Jon Godfrey in the Ipswich jail in 1663.[40] If the
elder Goddards were "not much inclined to the marvelous" before the
household's bewitchment, one of their daughters would be remembered
decades later for her certainty of the connection between visible and invisible worlds.

The family meeting at Nauvoo in January 1845 brought together
Hopkinton families – Youngs, Richards, Havens – descended from the
Goddards through Susannah Goddard Howe, a daughter of Ebenezer and
Sybell Goddard, who was about seventeen years old in 1759, and who
lived until 1837. Elder John Haven, great grandson of Elder Joseph
Haven, had particularly vivid memories of Susannah Howe.

> I married Mother Howe's daughter Betsy and I knew Mother
> Howe's views of religion. She agreed with me in religious senti-
> ments. Mother Howe was one of the finest of women. She did not
> speak much, but when she did, you knew her heart. In her opin-
> ions on religion there was some difference with the sects of the
> present day; she believ[e]d that Jacob's ladder was not yet broken
> and that angels still continued to ascend and descend. It was a
> delight to be with her and to hear her talk. You are all descendants
> from the Goddards – and she was a Goddard.[41]

This seems to have been the residual influence of the bewitchment of the
Goddards, apparently by Nat Smith, the Immortalist god. Susannah Goddard Howe was remembered as a woman of distinct belief, convinced that
spirit and matter were inseparably connected, the central tenet of the
Mormon cosmology. Given the collapse of the Framingham Separate

church, one wonders how much the larger Goddard clan was influenced in later years by the Immortalists, who brazenly rejected the restraints of material existence, routinely divinizing their leaders. As Fanny Young's letter indicates, the Youngs were very much aware of the Immortalists in the late 1790s, just before they removed to the southern Vermont frontier. Certainly these encounters were of great significance for a family who would soon declare for the spiritual powers of the Reformed Methodists.

Such belief in the power of spirit in the material world was manifest in many of the early Mormon families and in the communities through which they moved. In some instances spirit acted in the world to bring visions, as for Parley Pratt, the Kimballs, and Joseph Smith's mother's family, the Macks, as we shall see. In other instances, as among the Goddards, spirit apparently acted to bring misfortune. Although the legal prosecution of witchcraft ended in 1692, ordinary folk throughout the eighteenth century continued to protect themselves from witchcraft with countervailing white magic. In 1746 the church in Salem Village took action against those people dabbling in white magic who had "resorted to a woman of very ill reputation, pretending to the art of divination or fortune telling." In Topsfield, belief in witchcraft persisted into the 1830s. People in Whitingham, Vermont, where the Youngs settled briefly after leaving Hopkinton, suspected a local woman of being a witch. The local historians of Derry and Gilsum, New Hampshire, towns where the Smiths and the Macks would live in the late eighteenth century, recorded a widespread tradition of magical practice to ward off bewitchment: placing Bibles on churns to protect butter from bewitchment, casting invalids' blood in the fire, twisting witch hazel branches, and shooting spirits with silver buttons or copper coins. These magical rituals must have had the same constituency as occult practices of faith healing by church elders, attempts to raise the dead, efforts to bake bread from stones through prayer, all recorded for Gilsum. So, too, the divining and treasure-hunting cults that sprang up throughout the New England hinterland between the 1780s and the 1830s would have drawn on this same constituency.[42]

Besides the Goddards, many of the central families in the Mormon emergence were described as being very much attuned to the supernatural powers of witchcraft. Pomeroy Tucker described Martin Harris as believing "in dreams, ghosts, hobgoblins, 'special providences,' terrestrial visits of angels, [and] the interposition of 'devils' to afflict sinful men." According to the German Reformed minister in Fayette, writing in 1830, the Whitmer family were "gullible to the highest degree and even believe in witches." Hiram Page, another early Mormon convert, was fascinated with seer-stones and was "likewise full of superstition." The Smith family were similarly described by Fayette Lapham, who claimed to have interviewed them in 1830. "Joseph Smith, Sr., we soon learned from his own lips, was a firm believer in witchcraft and other supernatural things, and had brought up his family in the same belief."[43]

As a treasure-seer, Joseph Smith was clearly a practitioner of white magic in the mid-1820s. Dark rumors circulated in Harmony, Pennsylvania, that "he had bewitched" his beautiful bride, Emma Hale. But the event that sealed Joseph's reputation as a charismatic prophet was his miraculous exorcism of Newell Knight, who claimed to be possessed by the devil when he fell into a wild fit one evening early in 1830. Ultimately, fears of witchcraft and magical powers over spirit and matter were enshrined in the sacred Mormon texts. According to a revelation of September 1832, Mormon priests of the restored Melchizedek order were to have miraculous powers analogous to white magic. They could withstand poison, make the blind see, the dumb speak, and the deaf hear; they were to "heal the sick" and to "cast out devils." Smith also condemned black magic. Witches and sorcerers were to be "cut off," to "have part in the lake of fire and brimstone," to "inherit" the third "telestial" heaven.[44]

Through the eighteenth century many of the families that in the 1820s and 1830s would be drawn to the Mormon restoration lived with a powerful sense of the reciprocal relationship between the visible and invisible worlds. Long after they were abandoned by the learned and confined by folkloric ridicule and sacramental routine for much of the orthodox laity, the powers of the spirit remained an omnipresent reality for certain families. This perception of human manipulation of spirit and matter was not simply rooted in primitive magical beliefs. The Bible offered ample evidence of the evil powers of sorcerers and the healing, protective powers of godly men, and the proto-Mormon families were certainly immersed in the language and the promise of the Bible. A biblical literalism would have provided a bulwark of certainty in the face of a broader culture in which the powers of the spirit were seen in progressively more metaphoric terms.[45]

Fear of witchcraft composed one field shaping occult and spiritual belief for certain proto-Mormon families. Metallurgy composed another, opening directly onto the world of alchemy and hermeticism.

In a few cases this knowledge was bound up in an alchemical revival of the 1780s. In early 1789 Dr. Aeneas Munson reported to Ezra Stiles that an alchemical transmutation had been performed in Wallingford, Connecticut, the previous December by a Dr. Ebenezer Cahoon. A few weeks later Samuel Woodruff, a Yale graduate in law practice in Wallingford, brought a sample of transmuted metal from Cahoon's experiments. Both Cahoon and Woodruff would have kin connections among the Mormons. Born in Rhode Island in 1763, Ebenezer Cahoon was the uncle of Reynolds Cahoon, who was born in New York's sectarian Hoosac Valley at Cambridge in 1790 and went on to become one of the leading Nauvoo and Utah Mormons. Samuel Woodruff, born in the Southington Parish of Farmington, Connecticut, was a distant cousin to Wilford Woodruff, who eventually served as the president and prophet of the Mormon church.[46] Similarly, Willard Richards, a Hopkinton cousin of the Youngs and Havens, would be one of a number of Thompsonian doctors among the Mormons and during the 1820s had toured New England with an "Electro-Chemistry" show.[47]

These encounters stemmed from a broader renewal of the occult in the late eighteenth century, which we shall consider in the next chapter. But the Smiths themselves encountered alchemical culture that derived from much earlier sources. Despite its very limited impact in Puritan New England, the Smiths in the century between the 1690s and the 1790s were successively situated in two kinship networks that would have exposed them to fragments of hermetic alchemy.

When they moved into the orbit of the powerful Gould family after the witchcraft trials of 1692, the Smiths were building closer relationships with families that had long been involved in the ironworks established in 1668 in their neighborhood in Boxford. Built on John Gould's land under the patronage of Simon Bradstreet of Andover, husband of the alchemical poet Anne Bradstreet, these ironworks may have been an aspect of the broader Gould concern for colonial autonomy, manifested most obviously in their hostility to the Andros government; certainly they represented an effort to gain wealth through the metallurgical tradition. In any event, no member of the Towne family was involved in this ironworking project, and at least seven, and perhaps nine, of the fifteen known proprietors were members of accusing families in 1692, including Nathaniel and John Putnam of Salem Village. As Paul Boyer and Stephen Nissenbaum have argued concerning the Putnams, the failure of the ironworks in 1680 may have intensified the general sense of insecurity and declension that played such a role in moving particular families to bring witchcraft accusations in 1692.[48]

The Smiths had other connections with the ironworks. In 1694 Samuel Smith's brother Ephraim married Mary Ramsdell, whose father, John, had come to Boxford in 1668 to work at the bloomery; in 1698 John Ramsdell would witness a bond in Robert Smith's probate proceedings. The connection between the two families seems to have gone back into the 1670s, because in 1673 Robert Smith and John Ramsdell had gotten up a petition with Edmund Bridges, a blacksmith, protesting the reassignment of certain families from Topsfield to Rowley for tax purposes.[49]

A family of artisans, the Smiths were exposed to the language and culture of the metallurgical tradition in their connections with these ironworking families. Robert Smith had been a tailor and possibly a house framer; his son Samuel was a carpenter. Samuel's grandson Asael was a cooper, a trade he handed on to Joseph Smith Sr., who turned to well digging in his years in New York State.[50] Ironworkers of Plymouth County believed that iron ore grew in bogs, and such beliefs in the "organick" nature of metals also must have circulated among the Essex County ironworking families. So, too, the thwarted dream of wealth from the Boxford ironworks could easily have been a bitter topic of conversation in the Smith–Gould connection, and the ancient vision of the endless growth of metallic ores a continuing source of inspiration for such dreams.[51]

In the decades following the Great Awakening, the Smiths would turn back to the network of the Towne family, and again there is good reason to believe that metallurgical traditions again loomed large in their familial experience.

This move toward the Townes was anticipated by the Smiths' indifference to the Awakening. Whereas the Gould family, with whom they were so strongly linked through the 1740s, was powerfully influenced by the revivals, not one Smith joined the church during the Awakening in any capacity. Following the example of Robert Smith, who never joined the church, none of the Topsfield heads of household among Joseph Smith's ancestors (Samuel I, Samuel II, and Asael), ever moved beyond "halfway" membership in the Topsfield church.[52] Ultimately, this resistance to the Calvinist revivalism of the Awakening anticipated Asael Smith's turn to Universalism, which would lead to the hostility to revival churches harbored by the two Josephs in Palmyra in the 1820s. Only marginally rooted in the Puritanism of the Great Migration, by the Awakening the Smiths stood among the town's "horseshed Christians," as David Hall has so precisely termed those who hung back from a total commitment to the theology of the Calvinist church.[53]

After 1748 the Smith–Gould relationship continued only for the older generation;[54] the younger Smiths again began to associate with families within the Towne orbit. Two marriages between Smiths and Townes in 1760 mark the end of the feud.[55]

The new Smith–Towne relationship seems to have been rooted in bonds forged in service in the provincial troops during the French and Indian War. In 1757 and 1758 Samuel III served as a corporal in a company at Lake George that included two brothers of his future bride. One of these

Towne brothers would be killed in action and the other severely wounded in a failed assault on Ticonderoga; he was saved from scalping only because a friend pulled a felled tree over him before joining the retreat. Corporal Samuel Smith III married the wounded man's sister Rebecca at the close of the war in 1760. The new Smith–Towne friendship may explain how Samuel's brother Asael learned the cooper's trade. Of the nine coopers in Topsfield known to have worked before Asael, eight were Townes or from families associated with the Townes. Asael turned sixteen in 1760, and an indenture with one of these craftsmen might well have been part of the sealing of a new family alliance.56

Most importantly, their new relationship with the Townes again brought the Smiths into contact with the metallurgical tradition. Several families among the Towne connection owned and worked a mine of copper-bearing ore in south Topsfield, and here another connection with alchemy and the Renaissance occult tradition can be established.

The Topsfield copper-bearing lands had been discovered in the 1640s by Governor John Endicott. Endicott brought in Richard Leader, superintendent of the Saugus ironworks, to try the quality of the ore, and Endicott may have consulted John Winthrop Jr., who had interests in Topsfield.57 But these copper deposits were never developed in the seventeenth century, in part because of a bitter land feud between Endicott and the first Zaccheus Gould. Interest in these lots was revived in the second half of the eighteenth century. Between the 1760s and the 1790s a flurry of speculative buying and selling of copper-bearing lands and attempts to establish productive mine shafts involved an important group of people: Townes, Cummings, Porters, and Herricks. All of these families had taken Royalist positions in the post-Restoration era and, with one exception, had been on the accused side in 1692 and had stood together in the disputes of the 1730s and 1740s. Three of these families were also closely associated with the Smith family. Besides the marriages with the Townes, Thomas Porter and Henry Herrick had witnessed Samuel Smith II's will in 1767. In 1784 Thomas Porter's nephew sold the upper mine lot to his neighbor Nehemiah Herrick, a first cousin of Samuel Smith III's company commander at Lake George and a distant cousin of the Herrick who signed the will in 1767. Although they were not neighbors, the Smiths had connections with these south Topsfield households who were seeking to make their fortunes in mining and metallurgy.58

Both Asael Smith and his son Joseph, the father of Joseph the prophet, would have spent their formative years under the spell cast by these copper lands. Even if Asael had not learned coopering among the Towne-orbit households of south Topsfield in the 1760s, he would have heard something of what was described in 1771 as "a certain shaft or Mine Hole which is commonly known by the name of Towne's Copper Mine." Asael's son Joseph, with his sons, would make his living a half-century later digging wells; the Smith family knowledge of underground workings may well have begun at this "Mine Hole" in south Topsfield.

Asael had married and moved to New Hampshire by 1772, but he brought his family back to Topsfield after his father's death. Between 1786 and 1791 he worked to pay off the debts on his father's estate, debts stemming in part from serious losses ensuing from the collapse of the Continental dollar. The 1780s were years of great turmoil and ideological transformation for a people emerging from national revolution, and the decade left a mark on personal lives and mentalities that would be felt for generations to come. Across Massachusetts the political economy of public and private debt led many to march as Regulators in Shays's Rebellion. These were also years when theological alternatives to Congregational orthodoxy began to penetrate areas previously immune to sectarian dissent, including Essex County. John Murray, an English preacher influenced by Wesley and distantly by German Pietism, served as chaplain to the Rhode Island Brigade early in the Revolution before forming New England's first Universalist church in 1779 in Gloucester, near Topsfield on Cape Anne. It seems likely that Asael Smith adopted his Universalist inclinations during the 1780s.[59] There were also growing Masonic influences in the region. During the 1770s six Masonic lodges had been formed in Essex County; Porters and Putnams were members of the United States Lodge in Danvers, and Henry Herrick, who witnessed Asael's father's will in 1767, was elected Master of Beverley's Amity Lodge in 1786.[60]

Asael's son Joseph Smith Sr. was at a particularly impressionable period during these tumultuous years: born in 1771 he was between the ages of fifteen and twenty when the family was living in Topsfield. Given his later fascination with divining and employment as a well digger, one has to wonder how much he knew of the Towne's copper mine. Interest in the copper lots reached what may have approached a speculative fever: rights of ownership and use changed hands at least seven times between 1772 and 1795. The legal language of the deeds must have been repeated in local conversation and gossip: they conveyed rights to "all and Singular mines, mine ore, and other Hidden Treasures of the Earth lying in . . . certain lot[s] of land." Joseph, with his son Joseph Jr., signed a mining covenant with similar language in the Susquehanna Valley thirty years later. There may well have been speculation and experiments with occult methods of divining the location of ore beds in Topsfield, perhaps with rods such as those reported in the treasure-hunting in Exeter, New Hampshire, Middletown, Vermont, and by Joseph the prophet in central New York. And following the excitement over copper lands in these years in Topsfield, copper ore was discovered in the final years of the eighteenth century in Strafford, Vermont, adjacent to the town of Tunbridge, where Asael Smith moved his family in 1791, and soon after throughout the nearby towns. Copper ore seemed to be everywhere the Smiths turned.[61]

If Asael or Joseph Sr. did indeed work at the "Towne's Copper Mine," he would have been exposed to a stream of very knowledgeable visitors. Though the Townes sold the lower lot to Edmund Quincy, a furnace proprietor in Stoughtonham, in 1772, they continued to "Labor . . . in the mine" during the early years of the Revolution, and their surviving correspondence with Quincy is very revealing. In 1777 Quincy wrote to Joseph Towne that an Israel Freeman was "willing to separate the ore that is got up." Freeman was planning to visit the mine to "make Tryal of what he can do with the different parts of the Ore" and was of the opinion that the ore "that lays upermost must be a good deal Sun burnt but that underneath will yield well." Thus the Townes and their associates operated under the assumption that metal, and specifically copper ore, grew in the earth, perhaps from seed, stimulated by the heat of the sun. They would have known the outlines of related theories of metallic transmutation, such as the thesis of the "organick" origins of bog iron, and the more complex alchemical theory of the separation and recombination of sulphur and mercury, summarized in Charles Morton's *Compendium,* rooted in the Aristotelian vision of earthly exhalations, spiritual breaths, condensing progressively into more pure and perfect metallic forms.[62]

An adolescent in Topsfield in the 1780s, Joseph Smith Sr. would use this alchemical language of sunburnt rocks and growing metals three decades later in Palmyra. The evidence strongly suggests that the Smith family's interest in divining, treasure-hunting, and mining so evident in the 1820s had its origins in their last years in Topsfield, building on an already established predisposition toward metallurgy and the occult dating back to the seventeenth century. Against this background, a dramatic passage in Asael Smith's letter from Tunbridge of 1796 takes on added significance. Writing to Jacob Towne Jr., Asael expressed his militant Universalism in a paraphrase of the Book of Daniel that must have had powerful resonances for those involved in the copper lands – and with references that had once carried powerful connotations of hermetic restoration:

> And now I believe that the stone is now cut out of the mountain without hands, spoken of by Daniel, and has smitten the image upon his feet, by which the iron, the clay, the brass, the silver and the gold – viz., all monarchical and ecclesiastical tyranny – will be broken to pieces an[d] become as chaff of the summer threshing floor. The wind shall carry them all away that there should be no place found for them.

This language anticipated that of the *Book of Mormon,* just as the Smiths' exposure to white magic and metallurgy in seventeenth- and eighteenth-century Topsfield anticipated Joseph Smith's behavior and belief in the Burned-over District in the 1820s.[63]

In Essex County the Smiths were overcome by fears of the malefic power of witches and they were exposed to the hermetic culture of metallurgy; in Framingham and Hopkinton the Goddards and the Youngs felt malefic power emanating from a cult of perfectionists. To complete this tour of the interpenetration of the visible and invisible worlds among the most important proto-Mormon families, we need to turn to the experience of Joseph Smith's mother's family, the Macks. Settling in the broader orbit of the Rogerenes, the Macks would carry their religious belief into the spiritual realms of visions, healings, and the quest for a new dispensation well before Joseph Smith Sr. married Lucy Mack in Tunbridge, Vermont, in 1796.

The founder of the family, John Mack, arrived in New England in 1669 at the age of sixteen, hailing from the Scottish town of Inverness. Again, like Robert Smith, we must assume that John Mack served an indenture or an apprenticeship. It is also interesting that he gravitated to a sectarian environment. In 1681 John Mack married Sarah Bagley in Salisbury, Massachusetts, just south of Hampton, New Hampshire, where Stephen Batchelor had established his Husbandmen, and where Quaker sentiments voiced in the 1660s anticipated the forming of a Monthly Meeting by 1705.[64] In 1692 his father-in-law, Orlando Bagley, was deputized as constable to arrest Susannah Martin on witchcraft charges, but John Mack had moved his family to Concord by 1684, and in 1696 moved on to Lyme, Connecticut.[65]

When they arrived in Lyme the Mack family included six children, the eldest about thirteen, and six more would arrive by 1706. Lyme was a place where the older proprietary families held the advantage, and prospects were bleak for most newcomers.[66] The town was still thinly settled, but the land was very stony and hilly, and the Macks arrived too late to gain a proprietorship. John Mack was granted an inhabitancy in July 1702, six weeks after the distribution of lots in the last division of Lyme's common lands.[67]

Mack died at sixty-eight in 1721, and his sons did not fare well in the decades following. The eldest, John Jr., thirty-nine at his father's death, moved away from farming into the retail trade, selling dry goods brought in from Boston. Taken ill quite suddenly, he died in 1734. His younger brother Ebenezer had inherited the family farm and had – in the memory of his son Solomon – a "large property and lived in good style" until he suffered a sudden financial disaster in the late 1730s. Though he did not die until 1777, Ebenezer Mack's family was dispersed among neighboring households, including four-year-old Solomon Mack, the maternal grandfather of Joseph Smith, the Mormon prophet. Solomon's cousin Ebenezer Mack (son of John Jr.), who would become the Baptist minister in east Lyme, chose a rich landowner in north Lyme, Samuel Selden, as his own guardian, and it is possible that Solomon too worked in this household until he enlisted in the provincial forces in 1755 to take part in the fighting on Lake Champlain. Over the next several years Solomon Mack alternated between service with the army and farming in Lyme. In 1759 he married Lydia Gates of the Millington District of East Haddam, and in 1762 they joined the streams of migrants moving up the Connecticut River to settle first in Marlow and then in Gilsum, New Hampshire, where they would live among people from Lyme and people who would figure in the later story of the emergence of Mormonism.[68]

These, then, are the outlines of the Mack family experience in Lyme. It is possible that John Mack, a Scottish immigrant apparently of dissenting inclinations, with no necessary commitment to the brand of Puritan orthodoxy in Massachusetts Bay, was attracted to Lyme because of the unorthodox reputation of its religious culture. If late immigrants were less likely to have had Puritan motivations, Lyme and its mother town of Saybrook would have been especially attractive. Saybrook was founded in 1635 by John Winthrop Jr. without the Puritan requirement of a settled minister or an established church, which was not organized until 1646. Lyme was even more aberrant. Settled in 1666 and set off from Saybrook in 1670, Lyme had regular preaching by Moses Noyes but no incorporated church until 1693, a circumstance that, as one historian has put it, "may have been unique" in seventeenth-century Connecticut.[69]

As we have seen, Saybrook and Lyme constituted the western flank of a region stretching from the lower Connecticut River to Cape Cod where sectarian dissent challenged and often supplanted Puritan orthodoxy. In southeast Connecticut itself, sectarianism began in the 1670s, with the rise of the Seventh-Day Baptists in New London, the secession of the Rogerenes, and the itinerancies of the Singing Quakers. By the 1720s Sixth Principle Baptist churches had been formed in Groton and New London, with a branch in Saybrook, and Rogerene sentiments and households were spreading from their center at New London into Groton, east Lyme, Saybrook, Colchester, and Lebanon.[70] The Great Awakening would bring even greater religious complexity to southeast Connecticut, with Separate churches hiving off from the establishment and Baptist meetings emerging from these, all in an environment intensified by James

Davenport's violent revivalism in New London.[71] And scattered through the region there were reminders of a radical religious tradition stretching back into the Reformation and the English Revolution. The New London Rogers family was descended from the martyr John Rogers, burned at the stake in 1560; the martyr's Bible was said to have been carried like a talisman to America, and passed down through Rogers's kin among the Westerly, Rhode Island, Sabbatarians. Valentine Wightman, who ministered to the Groton Sixth Principle Baptists while remaining on good terms with the Rogerenes, was descended from Edward Wightman, who went to his execution in 1612 in full expectation of the coming of the prophet Elias and a new dispensation. In New London, the Sixth Principle Baptists had connections to both the Rogerenes and to Gortonism. Sharing a meetinghouse with the Rogerenes until building their Pepper-Box Church in 1754, the New London Sixth Principle Baptists were led by Stephen Gorton, descended from Samuel Gorton of Warwick and a son-in-law of James Rogers of New London.[72]

The 1740s saw the visit of the Ephrata pilgrims and there were other strands of hermetic culture here as well. John Brewster, the trader at New London in the 1650s, corresponded with John Winthrop Jr. on his efforts to distill the "red elixir," and legends survived far into the eighteenth century about Winthrop himself. As late as 1787 Ezra Stiles recorded such a story about a mountain in East Haddam, "the Place to which Gov. Winthrop . . . used to resort with his Servant; and after spend[in]g three Weeks in the Woods of this Mountain in roast[in]g Ores & assaying Metals & casting gold Rings, he used to return home to N[ew] London with plenty of Gold."[73] And in 1797 one Isaac Walden was reported to have sponsored the republication of Muggletonian founder John Reeves's *A Transcendent Spiritual Treatise.* Walden, a contemporary of Solomon Mack, had joined the Rogerenes after harrowing experiences in the Canadian campaigns of the early 1760s; in 1797 he was described as a basket maker and devout Muggletonian, living on Carter's Island north of New London.[74]

It was this regional culture, pervasively colored by sectarian controversy, highlighted by Rogerene spiritism and Davenport's enthusiasm, in which the Mack family lived for six decades before joining the migration up the Connecticut River to New Hampshire. John Mack Sr. expressed his own hostility to the Congregational "standing order" in twice refusing to serve as a collector of the established minister's rate.[75] The Macks were not immune to economic aspiration, as suggested by John Mack Jr.'s venture in trade and manifested in Solomon Mack's lifelong neglect of religion as he tried "to lay up treasures in this world."[76] But when Solomon was converted in 1811, it was in a family tradition of visionary experience, a tradition nurtured in the sectarian environment of southeast Connecticut.

On February 13, 1721, John Mack Sr. scrawled his signature on his last will and testament, distributing his worldly goods and, in the manner of English dissenters, announcing that he died "in hope of a joyful resurrection at the last day [illegible] justified in Christ Jesus."[77] Three weeks before, John Mack Jr. had signed another document, the petition of eighteen inhabitants that a separate parish be set off in north Lyme. One of the men witnessing his father's will, Jasper Griffing, also signed the parish petition. In 1724 the north Lyme petition was granted, and then the Macks and the Griffings and their neighbors had to contend with efforts to make another division, to encompass sections of Lyme and East Haddam along the Connecticut River, finally granted in 1742.[78] North Lyme was the Third Parish in Lyme and followed the establishment of a Second Parish in east Lyme by only a few years; HadLyme Parish made a fourth division, and a fifth was created in 1764 from parts of east and north Lyme and New London.[79] Never a place deeply committed to the Puritan church tradition, religious unity in Lyme was breaking down in the 1720s, as people living on the edges of the town attempted to balance their interest in local worship with the costs of taxation, a contest that had men walking the roads with surveying chains.

As were the Macks, the Griffings were from non-English origins, and these two families would maintain their alliance in the religious contests that wracked Lyme over the next decades. Jasper Griffing's father had arrived in New England from Wales in 1670 and made his way (like John Mack Sr.) through Essex County, to Long Island, and eventually to Lyme, where he too was admitted to the privileges of inhabitancy just after Lyme's final land division.[80] In 1743, the year that James Davenport gathered the New London Separates and his New Light school, the "Shepherd's Tent," on a wharf in the Thames River to burn the texts and symbols of Puritan orthodoxy, Griffings and one of the Macks signed a petition for a Separate Society in North Lyme.[81] Macks and Griffings were also among the signers of Solomon Paine's 1748 petition to the General Assembly, signed by 332 "Separates or Independents."[82] Separate meetings formed in each of Lyme's three older parishes. The north Lyme Separates, led by Daniel Miner, formed the Grassy Hill Church, the Separates in the First Parish followed John Fuller, and the east Lyme Separates followed Ebenezer Mack, son of John Jr. and Solomon's first cousin. By the 1760s, in Ezra Stiles's estimate, roughly a third of the town attended these dissenting meetings, with the greater adherence in the east and the north Lyme parishes. These churches would be inclusive in their membership, accepting both "sprinkled" Separates and those advocating adult

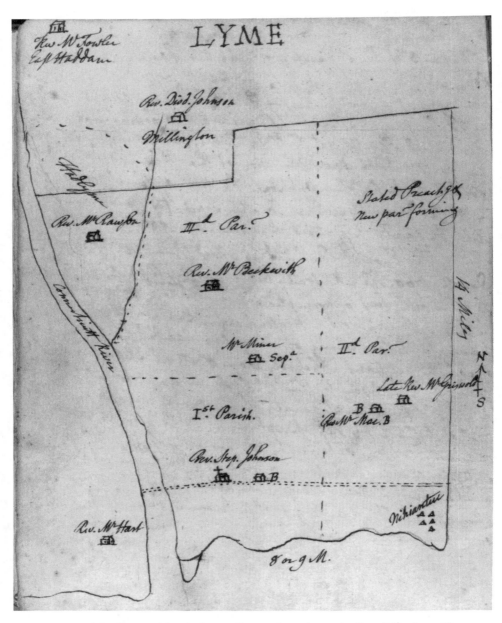

A map of the four parishes in Lyme, Connecticut, drawn by Ezra Stiles in 1768.
Courtesy of the Beinecke Rare Book and Manuscript Library, Yale University.

immersion in "Catholic Communion." Ebenezer Mack's church adopted open communion in 1752; by the late 1760s, Mack, ordained as a Separate in 1749, could no longer "build and commune" with those who would not accept the closed-communion form being advanced by Isaac Backus. Resigning from the church, he joined the flow of migration to the north, joining his younger cousin Solomon Mack in Marlow, New Hampshire.[83]

During the years of revival and church building, Solomon Mack was growing up on the farm of a master who, he wrote in 1811, never spoke "at all on the subject of religion." Solomon emerged from his service "totally ignorant of divine revelation or anything appertaining to the Christian religion."[84] His experiences over the next half-decade were equally unsuited for religious training. From this godless house Solomon entered the army in September 1755, serving for eight and a half months. Buying a farm in Lyme and two teams of oxen, he carried supplies for the army until 1758, when he set up a sutler's shop at Crown Point.[85] Apparently the dramas of the Great Awakening and its immediate aftermath passed him by, though later in life his family would be settled among people whose religious sentiments were shaped in great part by Ebenezer Mack's Baptist church. However, Solomon Mack's children, among them Joseph Smith's mother, Lucy, would be most influenced by their mother, Lydia Gates.

Solomon Mack married Lydia Gates of East Haddam in January 1759, presumably on a brief visit from Crown Point. Lying to the north of Lyme on the eastern shore of the Connecticut River, East Haddam had been settled in 1670 as an extension of the town of Haddam, and the Gates family had been a leading family since settlement. Arriving in Hartford in 1651 as a young man, Captain George Gates had been one of the earliest settlers east of the river in the 1670s and one of the founding members of the East Haddam church in 1704. His grandson Daniel Gates, Lydia's father, played a similar leading role in Millington Parish, formed in 1733 in the southeast corner of the town. A tanner and "a man of wealth," Daniel Gates served as selectman and deacon of the Millington church.[86] Lydia's mother was Lydia Fuller, from a family settling in East Haddam from Barnstable on Cape Cod in the 1690s who were greatly intermarried with the Gates.[87]

Compared with the religious contentions in Lyme, the Millington church was rather quiet. Apparently the church was New Light in tendency, for when its minister, Timothy Symmes, wandered off in 1740 as a radical New Light itinerant the Millington people waited three years before dismissing him. For several decades before the Revolution, however, the church was divided by a controversy involving a group known as the

"Old Fathers and Dissenters of New England," a group of Anglican lay readers led by the family of Jonathan Beebe, originally of New London, who in 1704 was the first to settle in the Millington District.[88]

Judging by church membership, the Fuller and Gates families were not swept by religious fervor. Other than Deacon Daniel Gates, no other Gates or related Fuller appears to have joined the church in the decades between the Awakening and July 1762, when Lydia Gates Mack was received into communion before departing for Marlow.[89] But here the lack of church membership in these families may not have meant a lack of piety. In Richard Bushman's assessment, Lydia Gates Mack "imparted faith to her children, but she did not give them a church." Growing up on the New Hampshire frontier and then after 1777 for some years in Montague, Massachusetts, the children's religious sensibilities were shaped by the family prayers conducted by Lydia. Lucy Mack Smith's detailed auto-biography does not mention a church in relation to the family until 1791.[90]

Rather than church centered, the children's religious experience was intensely familial and individual. Jason Mack, Lucy's oldest brother and an uncle of Joseph Smith Jr., by the age of sixteen "became what was then called a *Seeker.*" Harking back to the perfectionists of the Awakening, the Seekers of the English Revolution, Roger Williams in the Rhode Island wilderness, and hermetic radicals of the Continental Reformation, Jason believed "that by prayer and faith the gifts of the Gospel, that were enjoyed by the ancient disciples of Christ, might be attained, [and] he labored almost incessantly to convert others to the same faith." By the end of the Revolution, at the age of twenty, Jason was a lay preacher; after 1800 he led a communal society in the New Brunswick interior. In 1835 Jason wrote to his brother that for over a decade he had "seen the greatest manifestations of the power of God in healing the sick."[91]

Jason's sister Lovisa also claimed to have experienced such powers. Around 1791, after two years of incapacitating illness, Lovisa surprised her sister Lovina in announcing that "the Lord has healed me, both soul and body." Rising from her sickbed, Lovisa described her healing vision to a meeting in the local church a few days later:

> I seemed to be borne away to the world of spirits, where I saw the Saviour, as through a veil, which appeared to me about as thick as a spider's web, and he told me that I must return again to warn the people to prepare for death . . . and that if I would do this, my life should be prolonged.[92]

Twenty years later visions had become a family tradition. Solomon Mack was converted to religious faith in 1811 after days of anxiety were followed by the experience of flashes of light "as bright as fire" and a voice in the night calling his name. And over the previous decade, first Lucy Mack and then her husband, Joseph Smith Sr., had a series of dreams and visions that anticipated those that their son Joseph would experience at Palmyra, New York, in the 1820s.[93]

If the sectarian environment of coastal Connecticut had shaped this visionary familial spiritualism, we can also trace a number of paths by which Rogerene influences in particular might have reached these families. The north Lyme parish petitioners and Separates included a nephew of John Rogers, the founding Rogerene, and two cousins of a Rogerene outliver in neighboring Colchester. Solomon Mack's brother Elisha married into one of these Rogerene-connected families. In east Lyme, a branch of Valentine Wightman's Sixth Principle Baptist church was disrupted by Rogerene beliefs in the 1730s, and such sentiments might well have lingered among the people attending Ebenezer Mack's open-communion Baptist church. In 1733 Ebenezer's father, John Mack Jr., married a widow, Abigail Fox Davis, the niece of Rogerenes Samuel and Bathsheba Fox. Thus the Macks themselves had several direct connections to Rogerene perfectionism.[94]

It is entirely possible, of course, that these Lyme families may have had profoundly hostile opinions of the Rogerenes, as we may assume that the Goddards and Youngs had toward the Hopkinton Immortalists. In East Haddam, the closest link to the Rogerenes was among the Beebes, but Jonathan Beebe (whose brothers Samuel and William were a Rogerene and a Sabbatarian) clearly distanced himself from the Rogerene stronghold in New London by settling in Millington in 1704.[95] This family's subsequent Anglicanism suggests a continuing antipathy to perfectionism, though this stance had its sectarian undertones.

Two ministerial families in Lyme would have had bitter memories of John Rogers. John Rogers, like other perfectionists, had a complex marital history. In 1670, four years before he began to doubt Congregationalism, he had married Elizabeth Griswold of Lyme. When Rogers withdrew from the New London church and was baptized by the Seventh-Day Baptists, Elizabeth was convinced by her family to leave him, and through their powerful connections the Griswolds obtained a divorce without his consent. After twenty-five years of celibacy, Rogers took up with his servant girl, Mary Ransford, and announced their marriage in county court, but he rejected the authority of civil government over his marital relations, because it had taken his first wife from him against his will. After she bore him two children in a common-law marriage, Rogers sent Mary to Block Island in 1710, apparently because of continuing civil harassment, and in 1714 was married by a Rhode Island magistrate to a third wife, Sarah Cole, a Singing Quaker from Long Island.[96] These particulars of Rogers's life were detailed in 1725 in a tract titled *The Prey Taken by the Strong*, written by Peter Pratt of Lyme, the son of Elizabeth Griswold Rogers by her second marriage. When Pratt's father died in 1688, Elizabeth married Matthew Beckwith. Thus, by virtue of her birth and various marriages, Elizabeth was the aunt of the Reverend George Griswold, the orthodox minister in the east Lyme parish, who married Solomon Mack's parents in 1728, and she was the step grandmother of the Reverend George Beckwith, the orthodox minister in the north parish, who witnessed John Mack Jr.'s will in 1734. She was also related to another family of Beckwiths, noted Baptist preachers, who were affiliated with Ebenezer Mack's church in east Lyme and who emigrated to Marlow, New Hampshire, in the 1760s.[97]

Without more direct testimony, these connections are difficult to assess. What does seem clear, however, is that – like the Goddards and Youngs in Framingham – the Macks, the Gates, and the Fullers lived in a social environment where a sect of perfectionists would have been a topic of heated conversation. Even if they were alarmed by Rogerene doctrine and practice, they would have known something of it, and we may venture that a certain fascination followed on that alarm. An imperfect knowledge of perfectionist doctrine was more than no knowledge at all, and Peter Pratt's diatribe against the Rogerenes included a rather clear accounting of their belief. Suffice it to say that there are striking affinities of religious style between Rogerene spiritism and the Seekerism, faith healing, and visions that the Mack family contributed to the Mormon emergence.

We can only speculate on the roots of the visionary tradition among the families of Lydia Gates and Solomon Mack, but we are on firmer ground when we look more broadly at eighteenth-century Lyme and East Haddam as a hearth of nineteenth-century radical perfectionism. Elias Smith, one of the founders of the Christian movement, was born in east Lyme in 1769, where his father, Stephen Smith, had signed a 1766 Baptist petition with Ebenezer Mack. Moving with his family to Woodstock, Vermont, in 1783, Smith had a vision of "the Lamb upon Mount Zion" and a burning light in the woods before he joined the Baptist church in 1789. After ministering to the Baptist church in Woburn, Massachusetts, Smith withdrew to establish a branch of the primitivist Christians in 1803 and then turned to Universalism in 1818.[98] Mack's Baptist church produced at least one Mormon family, the Gees, intermarried with the Macks and with members of this church. Beyond the Mack connection, the towns of southeast Connecticut produced a number of Mormon converts: Beebes and Culvers from New London and Groton, the Pratts of Saybrook, and

Orson Spencer, whose family moved from East Haddam to West Stock-bridge, Massachusetts, where they were Baptists when he joined the Mormons in 1839.[99] The maternal family of the prophet Joseph Smith was part of a broader stream linking the sectarian world of southeast Connecticut to nineteenth-century Mormonism.

If perforce speculative in places, this exploration of proto-Mormon families in early New England takes us onto rarely explored terrain. The Smiths of Topsfield stand out in their assault on kin ties in the witchcraft drama of 1692, their exposure to alchemical metallurgy among the Topsfield copper miners, and their progressive alienation from orthodoxy. The Youngs and the Goddards were drawn from the thin stream of post-Restoration migration into Puritan New England; their encounter with the spiritual powers of the Blackstone Immortalists is a fascinating precursor to the spiritual claims of the Reformed Methodists, treasure-diviners, and eventually the Mormon priesthoods. The Mack family, also drawn from the post-Restoration migrations and not the core of Puritan orthodoxy, were exposed in Lyme and East Haddam to a religious culture of spiritual sectarianism that anticipated the visionary tradition among the Macks and the Smiths.

In sum, the experiences of these families all indicate that a cluster of attributes shaped the Mormon background. These families were relatively poor and from obscure origins. They often descended from families who arrived well after the Great Migration, a circumstance that made them both socially and religiously marginal. Often their late arrival made it difficult to build a landed competency, making them among the first to look for new lands on the eighteenth-century frontiers. And that same late arrival meant that such families were not rooted in the religious climate that forged New England orthodoxy, and that they were at least exposed to the religious turmoil of England in the 1650s, with its fusion of sectarian fervor and the hermetic occult. Thus many of those drawn to the Mormon restoration had long been a prepared people. Strands of culture and religious affinity ran through lines of kinship and community to form a predisposition to wonders and powers of the spirit.

This material needs to be put into perspective, however. All of these experiences formed a general background to the Mormon emergence, but they were simply that, scattered experiences among scattered peoples. Mormonism bore affinities to seventeenth-century hermetic culture, but it was not simply inherited by some cultural genetics. In the wake of the Revolution two specific circumstances would provide a focus for these diffuse strands of culture running back into the past. These scattered peoples began to congregate in new frontier settlements, and in this new environment they encountered another vector of continuity, a revived and reconfigured hermeticism forging fields of purity and danger that would fundamentally shape the Mormon experience.

PART II

Hermetic Purity
and Hermetic Danger

4

A Urim Spiritual

We have received some pressious things through the Prophet on the preasthood that would cause your Soul to rejoice. I can not give them to you on paper fore they are not to be riten. . . . We have established a Lodge here of Masons since we obtained a Charter. . . . Br. Joseph [Smith] and Sidny [Rigdon] was the first that was received into the Lodg. . . . [T]hare is a similarity of [Mormon] preas hood in Masonry. Bro. Joseph ses Masonry was taken from preasthood but has become degenerated. But menny things are perfect.

Heber C. Kimball to Parley P. Pratt, Nauvoo, Illinois, June 17, 1842

We have the true Masonry. The Masonry of today is received from the apostacy which took place in the days of Solomon and David. They have now and then a thing that is correct, but we have the real thing.

Heber C. Kimball at Salt Lake City, Utah, November 9, 1858[1]

MORMON THEOLOGY AND MORMON CONVERSION rested in great measure on the accumulated traditions and predispositions of prepared peoples, traditions and predispositions shaped in great measure by familial connections and oral culture. But they also rested on more contemporary experiences with eighteenth-century reformulations of hermeticism, experiences shaped by influences coming from the broader culture, influences that were often carried by the culture of text and print. On the one hand, the rise of Freemasonry over the eighteenth century, compounded by the Romantic revival of the occult in the 1780s and 1790s and fused with a renewed millenarianism and dispensationalism, carried the promise of the restoration of ancient truths and even Adamic powers. These influences, borne on a proliferation of secret societies and textual reformulations of Renaissance and Reformation hermeticism, may be seen as a sphere of hermetic purity in a broader field of hermetic culture. This chapter quickly examines their emergence and potential lines of transmission to the world of the divining cults of postrevolutionary America.

Nonetheless, just as Renaissance hermeticism was a big tent, encompassing mystical philosophers and smoke-selling puffers, eighteenth-century hermetic purities were balanced by hermetic dangers. These dangers involved the "projection" of currency, in particular by the shadowy networks of counterfeiters operating throughout the eighteenth-century colonies and the early Republic. These are the subject of the next chapter. Hermetic perfectionism and fraudulent money-making stood at the extremes in a broad field of hermetic purities and dangers. This cultural field impinged on many Americans in the early Republic, but it achieved a prismatic focus among the prepared peoples of the radical tradition. Just as philosophical sulphur and mercury fused to become the alchemical quintessence, first the divining cults and then the Mormon restoration were forged in the opposing action of hermetic purities and dangers.[2]

Chapter 6 explores this prism of preparation, purity, and danger in the new, postrevolutionary settlements in central Vermont, where Joseph Smith Sr. and Lucy Mack met, were married, and began to raise their family. Part III reinterprets the formative story of Mormonism as it moved from the Ontario country to the Great Salt Lake in terms of this dialectic of hermetic purity and danger. Here we need to outline the themes of the broader hermetic revival, manifested in alchemy, Freemasonry, and the rise of new prophets of a hermetic dispensation, renewing the radical search for Adamic perfection and the radical affinity for magical practice.

When Judge Samuel Danforth died in 1777, the Reverend Ezra Stiles of Newport, Rhode Island, noted in his diary that the judge had "believed the Philosopher's Stone a Reality . . . [and] was deeply studied in the writings of the Adepts."[3] The same was rumored of Stiles himself, who provides a useful point of entry to both the survival and the revival of alchemy and hermeticism in eighteenth-century New England.

The Congregational minister in Newport from 1755 to 1778 and president of Yale to his death in 1795, Stiles was very interested in the Cabala, in great part deriving from his friendships in the Jewish community in Newport. Although he ranked Danforth among a small group of practicing alchemists, Stiles denied that his own occasional writings "respecting the Rosacrucian Philosophy" implied any deep hermetic knowledge or belief. "I am not versed in the Books of the Adepts," he protested, and "I have no practical Knowl[edge] of the Matter: the few ideas I have about it are only imaginary, conjectural, & speculative." But like John Winthrop Jr., whom he described as "an Adept, in intimate Correspond[ence] with Sir Knelm Digby and first chemical and philosophical characters of the last century," Stiles kept a close watch on the prospects for mining in the coastal Connecticut towns. He also discussed alchemical experimentation with two friends from the late 1780s to his death in 1795. One was Dr. Aeneas Munson, a noted doctor in New Haven, of whom we have already heard and will consider further. Stiles's other alchemical acquaintance was the Reverend Samuel West, who like Danforth apparently actively worked to distill the philosopher's stone. A liberal "protagonist of free will," Samuel West was from 1760 to 1803 the minister of the established church in Dartmouth, Massachusetts, hard by Tiverton and Westport, home to other men of magic whom we have already considered, Joseph Stafford and Stephen Davis.[4]

The social circumstances of Stiles's alchemical circle thus indicates that the inheritance of seventeenth-century occultism could move beyond the dissenting orbit on the tolerant southeast coast of New England. But Stiles's diary, as well as the late-eighteenth-century context, requires that we consider newer sources of hermetic philosophy making their way across the Atlantic. By the 1780s Freemasonry had been organized for decades in England, on the Continent, and in the American colonies. Stiles dined with the lodge of Freemasons in New Haven on several occasions in the 1770s and 1790s; in 1784 he wrote approvingly of their growth in the new nation as well as in Europe. He also was aware of more esoteric developments. Stiles had long been reading the Gnostic texts of the Pseudo-Dionysius, and in 1788 and 1795 he also read from the writings of Emmanuel Swedenborg, the hermetic prophet who in 1770 announced the opening of a new dispensation. And Stiles even took the trouble in 1786 to write a letter to "the Arabian Count Cagliostro," a European sensation who was reputed to have the philosopher's stone and whose Egyptian Rite of Freemasonry combined hypnosis, divining, and transmutation, with a veneer of Egyptian hermeticism.[5]

Stiles's occult dabblings point to a broader eighteenth-century context for the transmission of the hermetic occult. If the treasure-diviners of the early Republic drew upon a German lore of magic and metals, and perhaps upon a thin vein of alchemical analogy and practice running from English radical traditions, a revitalized hermeticism was flowing from an increasingly dense network of Masonic orders and from a broader revival of the occult that was beginning to shape the Romantic and Gothic sensibility. Fused with Christian primitivism, a Masonic millenarianism marked one position in the radical currents sweeping through the Atlantic world in the 1790s. It was woven into the fabric of many of the divining cults, and it provided an essential grounding for the language of the Mormon restoration.

The origins and growth of Freemasonry and the explosion of a revived religious occult in the late eighteenth century are topics of immense complexity. The following will only sketch the main lines of their development, paying close attention to their roots in earlier hermetic traditions, the most significant intellectual fault lines, and their transatlantic diffusion.

Setting aside any claims to antiquity, Masonic origins can be traced to medieval guilds of stonemasons, whose institutions, rituals, and reputation for ancient secrets began to attract gentleman intellectuals over the course of the seventeenth century. By the eighteenth century "speculative" Freemasons, for whom the lodges were the vehicle of a fraternal enlightenment, had long since supplanted the operative Masons, for whom the lodges were an ancient center of labor power and craft authority. The process of this transformation is still quite obscure, but several scholars have argued that it was in the broader environment of late Renaissance hermeticism, fueled by rumors of a Rosicrucian brotherhood and secret networks of Familist mystics, that some began to seek out the Masonic guilds, said to maintain stores of ancient manuscripts on mathematics and geometry passed down from the Greeks and from the building of Solomon's temple. David Stephenson has argued that the emergence of speculative Freemasonry began in lowland Scotland in the late sixteenth century and only tentatively spread into England in the last half of the seventeenth century.[6]

The modern history of Freemasonry formally begins with the establishment of the London Grand Lodge in 1717. If the radical sects interpreted hermeticism in revolutionary ways, English Freemasonry was organized as a vehicle for perpetuating Hanoverian hegemony. And here, it must be stressed, hermetic lore receded into the background, superseded by Enlightenment rationalism. English Freemasonry reflected the broader currents of intellectual change that characterized the half-century following the Restoration. The English Grand Lodge was organized by one of the key figures in London's moderate Enlightenment, Jean Theophile Desaguiliers, a Huguenot refugee who absorbed the sanitized Newtonianism at Oxford and became a leading figure in the Royal Society after 1714.[7] Although leading English intellectuals were caught up in the hermetic millennialism of the 1640s, they backed away from its associations with sectarian occultism in the 1650s. With the formation of the Royal Society in 1661, they pursued a hierarchical view of nature that would allow for divine intervention from the invisible to the visible world. Humanity and matter were simply inert substances, acted on by a divine force. By the eighteenth century that divine force had been reduced to a rational plan at Creation: Newton without his alchemy. In sum, the Freemasonry of the eighteenth-century London Grand Lodge was fundamentally a bastion of Enlightenment deism.[8]

Such was not the case, however, in other strains of Freemasonry that emerged in the decades to follow. Reacting to both its Hanoverian connections and its deistic theology, a Scottish Jacobite exile living in France named Andrew Michael Ramsay forged a very different Freemasonry in the 1730s, compounded of hermetic theology and Christian millenarianism. As a young man in Edinburgh and London, Ramsay (1686–1743) had passed through the gamut of Protestant belief, including membership in the Philadelphian Society and encounters with the French Camisard prophets. Ramsay was a contemporary of Conrad Beissel, who a few years later moved through the same circles in Germany, on his way toward building the Ephrata commune in Pennsylvania. Moving to Holland in 1710, Ramsay saw in Catholic quietism the same possibilities for a nonsectarian, universal, mystical religion that previous generations had seen in Familism and the Rosicrucian brotherhood. Converting to Catholicism in 1715, Ramsay drew upon the Rosicrucian texts, Boehme, and quietist mysticism to arrive at a new hermetic religion. His *Travels of Cyrus*, published in 1727, quoted from the entire corpus of hermeticism, and bypassed the problem of its Egyptian origins (demonstrated a century ago) by locating the *hermetica* in ancient China. Ramsay's *Travels of Cyrus* and his subsequent *Philosophical Principles* made up renewed, and influential, efforts to legitimize hermetic thought, including universal salvation for preexistent souls, and to connect it with Judeo-Christian revelation and Newton's concept (abandoned by mechanical rationalists) of a divine "pure aether," an "exceedingly subtle SPIRIT" that governed the working of the natural world.[9]

Ramsay was a key figure in the emergence of Freemasonry in France in the 1730s. A member of the household of the Stuart pretender, Ramsay was connected to aristocratic French circles, and he conjured up a knightly mythology of Masonic origins that ran through the medieval Templars to Scottish lodges. From these beginnings, Freemasonry in France and throughout continental Europe evolved into a proliferation of competing institutions and rituals in the decades following Ramsay's death in 1743, broadly denominated as following a "Scottish Rite," in deference to Ramsay's influence and the legends of the Scottish refuge of the medieval Templars.[10] As the century progressed these Continental Masonic orders increasingly fused hermeticism with millenarian, apocalyptical implications. They were one manifestation of a Romantic, even revolutionary, reaction to the Enlightenment.

After Ramsay, the resurgence of a religious hermeticism in eighteenth-century Europe was grounded in the thought of Emmanuel Swedenborg

(1688–1772). An aristocratic Swedish mining engineer, Swedenborg after 1721 immersed himself in alchemy, the Cabala, and the works of Jacob Boehme, moving through occult circles in Europe, including the Moravian community in London, as he began to compose a set of mystical writings that became the basis for his Church of the New Jerusalem. His writings centered on a description of a spiritual world as a psychological state parallel to lived reality. Most would become aware of the spiritual state at death, but the initiated might experience it in mystical trances. At first, life in the world of spirit, which was composed of three heavens, would have continuities with human experience, but then it would develop into a fully spiritual existence, with evolving, gendered, spiritual personalities associating in angelic societies, and – most controversially – enjoying conjugal love with various partners throughout eternity. In the years just before his death in 1772, Swedenborg decided that his teaching was divine revelation superseding the Bible and existing church doctrine, and he declared in typical Joachimite manner that a new dispensation had begun on June 19, 1770, with the completion of his last work, *The True Christian Religion*.[11]

Swedenborg's teachings spread in England in the 1770s and 1780s, attracting a small but growing following who responded to its fusion of hermeticism and dispensational promise. In France and Germany Swedenborgianism competed with the sudden popularity of Franz Anton Mesmer, an Austrian "doctor" who captured the popular imagination just before the French Revolution with his reputed ability to channel and control a supposed harmonic fluid pervading the physical world. Hailed as a "new Paracelsus," Mesmer, like Ramsay and Swedenborg, was borrowing from the hermetic tradition of the previous centuries.[12] On the Continent, Swedenborgian ideas moved among the occult Masonic orders, including a Masonic Rite of Perfection that had been created in 1754 in the same Stuart circles in which Ramsay had moved. Composed of ' twenty-five degrees, later expanded to thirty-three in the Ancient and Accepted Scottish Rite, the Rite of Perfection included one of the so-called apocalyptic degrees, the Knight of the East and the West, which drew on both Ramsay's Templarism and the temple-building mythology at the heart of Masonry. The Rite of Perfection also included the most highly elaborated hermetic degree in the Masonic repertoire, the Knight of the Sun.[13]

This degree was written by a former Benedictine monk, Dom Antoine Joseph Pernetty (1716–1800), who was converted to Swedenborgian mysticism in the 1760s. In 1779 Pernetty formed the Avignon Society, the most extreme among mystical Masonic groups in advancing a doctrine of an impending millenarian regeneration of humanity, when the true, unitary church would be restored. Formed in Berlin, in an epicenter of influences coming from hermeticism, Hebrew Sabbatarianism, and the apocalyptical aspirations of the Polish count Grabianka to become king of Poland and a second Solomon in Jerusalem, the society announced its vision to a convention of occultists in Paris in 1784 and settled in Avignon in 1785. Here it had influences that reached into the English-speaking world, attracting several English Swedenborgian millenarians who a few years later became followers of the prophet Richard Brothers. In the midst of threats of war in 1794, Brothers, a former naval officer living in London, pronounced himself the "Prince and Prophet of the Hebrews" and predicted the coming of the Kingdom of God and the return of visible and "invisible" Hebrews to a New Jerusalem to be rebuilt in the Holy Land. Confined as insane, Brothers would lose some of his following to Joanna Southcott, "the woman clothed with the sun," who carried the renewed English tradition of the restoration of the Kingdom of God, dormant since the 1650s, into the nineteenth century.[14]

This, then, is an outline of a few of the leading dimensions of the late-eighteenth-century occult revival. In an odd and interesting twist, the very institution that was created to co-opt the hermetic tradition and turn it to the uses of the Hanoverian establishment – the London Grand Lodge – contributed indirectly to the revival of the radical millenarian tradition in England.

These ideas did ultimately contribute to the framing of the Mormon dispensation in the 1840s, but their impact on the world of the divining cults of the 1780s and 1790s is more difficult to assess. When they did begin to circulate along the coast and into the backcountry of revolutionary America, it was probably in spite of – rather than necessarily because of – the spread of lodge Freemasonry.

American Freemasonry was initially established under warrants from the London Grand Lodge, and its culture and ritual reflected the Enlightenment thinking of its English founders. Before the Revolution, Freemasonry was accessible only in the few small seaport towns and for the gentry of the southern Tidewater. Though it spread rapidly among the officers of the Continental line during the Revolution, Freemasonry did not begin to be a widespread popular movement until the 1790s. Occasionally suggestions of spiritualism and the occult emerge from the culture of the lodge Freemasonry, such as a Massachusetts woman's "Masonic Vision," a Saint John's Day sermon on the jewels of the biblical Urim and Thummim, or the publication in Philadelphia of the "Rites and Mysteries of the Oriental Freemasons."[15] On balance, given their grounding in the rationalism of the London Grand Lodge, the ordinary symbolic lodges, granting only the first three degrees of Entered Apprentice, Fellow Craft, and Master Mason, could only harbor the potential for occult interests, but not their realization.[16]

If not coming directly from the Masonic lodges, scattered themes from the European occult revival did appear in the early Republic. A host of occult publications began to appear in the 1780s and 1790s, some published in the United States and many more in England. Among the American publications were editions of *Aristotle's Masterpiece*, the *Book of Knowledge* by the apocryphal Erra Pater, and *The Complete Fortune Teller*; important contemporary English occult texts included Ebenezer Sibley's *A New and Complete Illustration of the Occult Sciences*, Francis Barrett's *The Magus*, John Heydon's *Astrology*, Herman Kirchenhoffer's *Book of Fate*, and William Lilly's *Christian Astrology*. Many of these English imprints, as well as earlier works, were available in American lending libraries and bookshops.[17] When Stiles received copies of Swedenborg's writings in 1788 they were probably a *Summary View*, published in Philadelphia in 1787; those he received in 1794 might have been any one of several full-scale editions published in Boston and Philadelphia between 1792 and 1794, followed by further editions published in the next two years. Similarly, Michael Ramsay's *Travels of Cyrus* was republished in New Jersey and in Boston in 1793 and 1795.[18]

A variety of circumstances suggest that occult and hermetic knowledge spread via the profusion of new personal contacts with the Continent during and after the Revolution. One possible conduit of hermetic information may have been the Hessian troops serving in the British forces during the Revolutionary War or the French troops aiding the Americans. French prisoners of war garrisoned in English "parole towns" in the 1760s and during the Napoleonic Wars established lodges that contributed to the spread of the high Continental degrees with Britain itself. In 1777 General Charles Rainsford, known to have devoted his entire life to high-degree Freemasonry and the hermetic occult, was in charge of shipping Hessian troops from The Hague to the British command in North America.[19] During the 1780s, hints and rumors about Mesmer's theories of universal fluid and animal magnetism appeared in newspaper accounts and traveler's reports, though both Thomas Jefferson and Benjamin Franklin, then in Paris, attempted to ensure that Mesmerism did not corrupt the new Republic. It was not until the 1830s that Mesmerism became widely and reasonably fully known in America.[20] Swedenborgianism as a religious movement arrived in 1784, when James Glenn lectured on the subject at Boston's Green Dragon Tavern, a Masonic gathering place. Over the next two decades small groups of Swedenborgians emerged in or near Boston, Philadelphia, and Baltimore, for the most part among a well-educated and wealthy circle. The Boston audience for Swedenborg would eventually include Ralph Waldo Emerson and similarly transcendentally inclined Unitarians. Though Swedenborgian texts appeared in very unlikely places, including the knapsack of an Ohio peddler named John Chapman – the legendary Johnny Appleseed – it would be difficult to argue that they were widely known among the rural peoples of the early Republic.[21]

Other, more ephemeral writings drawing upon Masonic and millennial themes appealed to a much broader audience. The rise of revolutionary France, its dramatic confrontation with the British-led alliance, and its ramifications in American politics inspired a wave of militantly pro-French sentiment and shaped an audience eager for premillennial predictions and prophecies. Among these, the prophecies of London's "Prince and Prophet of the Hebrews," Richard Brothers, were widely read in at least eleven American editions published from 1795 to 1797 in Philadelphia, New London, Worcester, West Springfield, and Albany, where it was put out by Freemason Thomas Webb. In Connecticut, the Reverend David Austin translated visions and a growing mental instability into a series of published sermons and treatises on millennial and Masonic themes during the 1790s, literally obsessed with the notion that the "Millennial Door" was opening.[22]

Many of these prophecies focused on legendary artifacts. Brothers's followers from the Masonic Avignon Society had accepted him as a true prophet based on prophecies popularly ascribed to Christopher Love, an English Presbyterian executed for conspiring against Cromwell in 1651. Love's *Prophecies,* which included references to an engraved pillar of brass erected by the patriarch Seth and the prophet Enoch before the Flood, were printed in at least twenty editions at presses throughout New England and the other northeastern states from 1791 to 1800. Another apocryphal writing, the anonymous *Remarkable Prophecy,* was associated with Love's predictions; it was claimed to be a transcription of an engraved stone recently discovered in Paris, supposedly buried for six hundred years. The stone's predictions of premillennial destruction and description of the millennial state, where the "remnant of all nations [were] to be of one religion," would have appealed to restorationists of many eras. These stories were reinforced by a reference in the popular *Works of Flavius Josephus* to Seth constructing pillars of brick and stone to preserve from fire and water knowledge of "the heavenly bodies and their order."[23]

These stones and pillars had parallels in a new Masonic ritual, the Royal Arch, which rapidly gained popularity in the United States from the late 1790s. The Royal Arch degree was rooted in a schism in British Freemasonry that had emerged in the 1740s, when a group of provincial lodges

Symbolism of the arch and temple veil used in the ritual of the Masonic Royal Arch chapters. From Jeremy Cross, *The True Masonic Chart, or Hieroglyphic Monitor* (New Haven, 1819).
Courtesy of the Livingston Masonic Library and Museum, Grand Lodge, F. & A.M., of the State of New York.

declared themselves the "Ancient Rite" and decried the London Grand Lodge as a debased "Modern" version. In great part this was a class-based schism, with artisans and small shopkeepers resenting the pretensions of the aristocrats who controlled the London Grand Lodge. The Ancient Masons claimed that the London Grand Lodge had changed Masonic history in abandoning some of the material connecting the order to Old Testament times. But the Ancients made innovations of their own, adding a fourth degree, the Royal Arch, to the three basic degrees of Entered Apprentice, Fellow Craft, and Master Mason. At the center of the Royal Arch tradition lay a myth of mysteries surviving from the time of the prophet Enoch. According to this myth Enoch, following a vision, had built an underground temple constructed of nine superimposed arches, hiding a triangular gold plate engraved with "ineffable characters" revealed in the dream. Two pillars, one of marble engraved with the secrets of the arched temple and one of brass engraved with "the principles of the liberal arts, particularly masonry," were erected outside the temple to withstand the Flood. Thousands of years later, architects assisting Solomon, while building a similar vault, discovered Enoch's arched temple and the mysteries on the gold triangle were restored.[24]

Invented by Andrew Michael Ramsay, the Royal Arch theme of ancient mysteries, purportedly dating back to Adam, rediscovered in vaulted caves, clearly drew upon the Rosicrucian legend. In the Rosicrucian story, the discovery of buried texts bearing the wisdom of the ancients would aid in the dawning of the millennium. The Royal Arch ritual was quite explicit about restoration, not only of ancient mysteries but of ancient priesthoods. In wording essentially replicated in Mormon doctrine, the high priest in the Royal Arch was to be "a priest forever after the order of Melchizedec," the Old Testament priesthood that commanded spiritual powers.[25] The Royal Arch discovery of lost texts and mysteries, however, was not couched explicitly in millennial terms; reading from the popular millennial tracts available in the 1790s, Love's *Prophecies,* the anonymous *Remarkable Prophecy,* or the *Works of Flavius Josephus,* contemporaries would have drawn their own prophetic implications from the Royal Arch myth. The Royal Arch myth of the prophet Enoch and sacred caverns also made a formative impression on Joseph Smith in the 1820s, a topic to be discussed in due course.[26]

The ultimate Masonic myth was, of course, that of the restoration of the paradisial powers of Adam. Sophisticated hermetic knowledge was a central part of the French Rite of Perfection. Carried from Paris to Santo Domingo in the West Indies in 1763, the Rite of Perfection was adopted by local gentry in and around Albany, New York, in 1767. The membership of this group was closed to all but a very small cluster of elite families, who before the Revolution had knowledge of only the first fourteen degrees, and in the 1840s twenty-one, none of these the hermetic Knight of the Sun.[27]

After the Revolution Lodges of Perfection were established in seaport towns, where it had particular appeal among French refugees, German immigrants, and Jewish families with West Indian connections. However, the diffusion of the higher degrees was complicated by the attacks on the so-called Bavarian Illuminati initiated by the Reverend Jedediah Morse and other northern Federalists in 1798, who sought to prove that a Masonic conspiracy lay behind the French Revolution, the Jacobin "international," and implicitly Jeffersonian Republicanism.[28] It was not until after 1800, with the beginning of itinerant lecturing and "degree peddling," first by "roving deputies" of the Scottish Rite Council in Charleston, South Carolina, and later by New Hampshire–born Jeremy Cross, that the higher degrees began to move out of the port cities into the rural districts. This process began earlier in the new plantation regions of the deep South and did not reach the rural North and Northwest until after 1816.[29] In 1829 the language of these degrees would become available for broader audiences in David Bernard's Antimasonic exposé, *Light on Masonry,* but in the 1790s the language of Masonic hermeticism was still a very secret matter.[30]

Nonetheless, the inquiring Freemason could find hints of the hermetic promises of Freemasonry scattered through Masonic publications. Masonic manuals wrote of Adam as a perfect being, conversing with God, and a master of the "mysteries of Nature," with Masonry the secret system transferring this primal knowledge of the universe.[31] In Thomas Webb's popular *Freemason's Monitor,* the initiates into the first degree were told that Masonic government and ritual "corresponded with those of the Egyptian philosophers," who, not willing "to expose their mysteries to vulgar eyes," had disguised them behind "signs and symbols which they communicated to their Magi alone."[32] The apocryphal medieval letter by a "John Leland" published in some of these manuals listed among Masonic secrets the universal language, "the art of changes" (the transmutation of metals), and "the art of becoming good and perfect without the helpings of fear and hope." Such language would suggest, to those inclined to read between the lines, that Freemasonry was a magical road to Adamic perfection. And if the details of the higher hermetic degrees were shrouded in secrecy, publications such as Webb's *Freemason's Monitor* gave tempting glimpses of their rituals, such as the meetings of the Lodge of Perfection in "a subterraneous vault, painted red, and adorned with many colors."[33]

For those so inclined, such descriptions would have provided fertile ground for efforts to realize the restoration of ancient mysteries. Such apparently were the aspirations of a millenarian church located in or near Cincinnati at the turn of the century. Calling itself the "Halcyon Church of Christ," this church announced in two publications in 1801 that it held the key to "the deep mysteries of the ancient theology": the "Urim or Halcyon Cabala." In their definition, the Cabala was the "secret" and "holy science" once known to "the most ancient Jewish divines"; the church's "Urim spiritual" contained "the true divine science by which truth shall again be restored to the world and error be defeated." The millennium would bring the "ushering in of the pure Halcyon church and divine government."[34] Similar language would reappear among the Mormons at Nauvoo in the 1840s.

In the light of the occult millenarianism of the 1790s, the New Israelite cult in Middletown, Vermont, an exact contemporary of the Halcyon church, takes on a different coloration. Certainly the Woods, the leaders of this cult, had roots in eastern Connecticut's perfectionist culture, but their claims to Israelite descent and to powers of hermetic transmutation and divining also suggest the influence of the millenarian–prophetic culture of the 1790s. According to one account, at the climax of the New Israelite drama, when destroying angels were supposed to bring on the apocalypse, there were two skirmishes between the town militia and "six

Rodsmen, fantastically dressed, and equipped" with swords – a suggestion of the elaborate costuming that was beginning to take hold in Masonic ritual.[35]

There are other connections between the occult revival and the divining
cults, connections that begin to turn our attention from hermetic purity
toward hermetic danger. In one account of Ransford Rogers's exploits in
Exeter, New Hampshire, in the late 1790s, his name is spelled "Rainsford," a tantalizing association with the hermetical General Rainsford.[36]
In the various descriptions of Luman Walter, the conjurer reputed to have
taught Joseph Smith the arts of divining in the 1820s, it is difficult to
separate fact from fancy. Brigham Young, speaking in the 1850s,
described a fortune-teller in the Lake Ontario region as "a man of profound learning. He had put himself in possession of all the learning in the
States, – had been to France, Germany, Italy, and through the world." This
may have been Luman Walter, described by a hostile source in 1884 as "a
drunken vagabond . . . who had been a physician in Europe," where he
had learned "the secret of Mesmerism or animal magnetism." Perhaps
Luman Walter was in fact an adept with European training; Michael
Quinn suggests that a man named "L. Walter" did in fact return from
Europe to New York in 1821. Another description written with tongue-
in-check by an Obadiah Dogberry in 1830 had Walter known for his
command of "strange books." But the book he used was not an obscure
occult text but "an old copy of Caesar's [Cicero's] *Orations,* in the Latin
language, out of which he read long and loud to his credulous hearers,
uttering at the same time an unintelligible jargon."[37]

Yet another account of the Vermont New Israelites brings us directly
into the realm of hermetic danger. Riding his circuit through Rutland
County, Methodist preacher Laban Clark was told by a lay brother that
the cult's divining rods could collect and raise up from the earth "vast
quantit[ies]" of gold and silver, sufficient "to pave the streets of the New
Jerusalem." But he was surprised to find that the gold appeared in both
"its native state [and] in currency." On further inquiry he was told that
among the cult's adherents there was indeed a man "who understood
refining gold" and who kept "himself secreted in the woods." This adept
was a man named Justis Winchell, once a Hessian soldier in Burgoyne's
army, who had taken up land in neighboring Hebron, New York, in the
1780s. By this account, then, the New Israelite sect was simply an elaborate screen for a counterfeiting operation.[38]

There is, then, room for multiple interpretations of the revitalized hermetic culture of the early Republic. The late-eighteenth-century revival of
the hermetic occult and its diffusion to America intersected with the rise of
intense millenarian aspirations, and these framed a powerful affinity be-

tween Masonic mythology and Christian restorationism. This connection may be termed a field of hermetic purity, informed by powerful and sincere spiritual seeking.

But the diviners of the early Republic found this connection a fertile field for offering the temptation of treasures in the earth. And the descriptions of Luman Walter, Ransford Rogers, Justis Winchell, and the New Israelites bring us to another perspective, the suspicion that the cunning folk of the seventeenth century had become the conning men of the nineteenth century, adopting the cover of the hermetic revival. Here we need to explore yet another neglected alchemical byway in the popular culture of eighteenth-century America, a world of hermetic dangers standing linked to the purities of Masonic restorationism.

5

Alchymical Experiments

> Very many persons in the society have asserted that while the
> money fever raged at Kirtland, the leaders of the [Mormon]
> church and others were, more or less, engaged in purchasing and
> circulating Bogas money or counterfeit coin; and a good evidence
> that the report is not without foundation is that each of these
> contending parties accuses the other of this crime.
>
> Reed Peck, Quincy, Illinois, September 18, 1839[1]

THE REVITALIZED HERMETICISM of the late-eighteenth-century
Atlantic world, borne on a Romantic fascination with the occult and
on the rise of Freemasonry, carried millenarian themes of the restoration
of ancient truths, even the restoration of the powers of the primal Adam.
Drawing both upon the magical and perfectionist predispositions of those
people inheriting the traditions of the Radical Reformation and upon this
revived current of hermetic restorationism, the treasure-divining cults of
the early Republic stood in a field of spiritual purity, connected to hopes
and dreams for a perfect glory. But the divining cults were also fundamentally focused on the discovery of wealth, and they clearly harbored conning men of many descriptions. Quite simply, divining occupied an ambiguous position in the broader field of hermetic purities and dangers. These
hermetic dangers involved money in all its various forms and all its shades
of legitimacy, and the deceptions that people practiced in the name of
money. The connections between money and hermeticism, legitimate and
spurious, already had a long and tangled history by 1830, and they would
play a powerful role in the story of the Mormon emergence.

Certainly building on medieval and Renaissance language, the radical
sectarians of the English Revolution advanced hermetic interpretations of
money and value. In the new dispensation, alchemy would make money
obsolete, bringing an abundance of wealth to the common people. Mary
Cary Rand, a Fifth Monarchist with alchemical interests, predicted that
"gold would shortly be commonly made." George Starkey himself, writing in 1645, predicted that with alchemy "money will be as dross" in the

new age. "These things will accompany our so long expected and so suddenly approaching redemption," he wrote in language anticipating Nathaniel Wood on the Vermont frontier a century and half later. Money, "that prop of the antichristian Beast will be dashed in pieces . . . [and] the new Jerusalem shall abound with gold in the streets."[2]

Rand and Starkey may be ranked among the radical mystics, but the practical hermeticists in Samuel Hartlib's circle were very interested in the questions of money and its supply. Hartlib's friend Gabriel Plattes wrote on metallurgy and alchemy; one of his essays was republished in Philadelphia in 1784. Hartlib himself was immersed in projects for agricultural improvement, and this seems to have shaped his ideas about banking, ideas that had a powerful impact on the colonies. Writing in a tradition of seventeenth-century economic thought that envisioned money as a commodity of extrinsic value, determined by demand in trade and in investment, Hartlib published a plan for a bank based on land mortgages in 1653. Over the next several years, Hartlib communicated with John Winthrop Jr. on the subject of a land bank, and by 1661 Winthrop was fully informed of Hartlib's concept, when he put it before the Royal Society, where it generated little interest.[3]

Winthrop soon abandoned his plans for a land bank, moving on to speculate in the Indian lands lying to the north of New London. But his ideas were revived in the 1680s and eventually informed the provincial emissions of paper money that began in the 1690s and the short-lived Massachusetts Land Bank of 1740. It is particularly interesting that two of the leading hermetic philosophers of the Puritan Instauration, Hartlib and Winthrop, should be a part of the "liberal" tradition of seventeenth-century economic thought that saw monetary value as a mutable and transformative commodity, expanding and contracting like a living organism in response to economic demand – and at the commands of an interventionist commonwealth. This dynamic theory of money as a commodity would be challenged by John Locke's assertion of an immutable, intrinsic value of silver and gold, determined for all time in the state of society preceding the formation of governments. Just as Newtonian science and the corpuscularism of the Royal Society placed the domain of spirit beyond the power of human manipulation, Locke demanded that currency be an absolute, beyond the influence of any government or other human agent. With the recoinage of 1696, Locke's immutable currency would stand for centuries to protect the interests of the propertied. And, just as Newton and the Restoration scientists were attempting to contain the radical sects, Locke was targeting the economic thought of the broader hermetic Instauration. Suppressed in Restoration and Georgian England, these two impulses would reemerge in very interesting combinations in the eighteenth-century colonies.[4]

Whether from hermetic connotations of banking surviving from the seventeenth century or from the fragmentary exposure to alchemical categories received by those influenced by the Harvard curriculum at the turn of the century (specifically in Charles Morton's *Compendium*), alchemical metaphors erupted at intervals in the Massachusetts currency debates. In the hands of Paul Dudley, defending hard currency in 1714, hermetic connotations were deployed to disparage a land bank scheme. As was the alchemical work, the bank was a "projection," and its "projectors" were attempting to create value in currency where none had resided before, overturning the natural order as defined by Locke. "If this be not the *Philosopher's Stone*," Dudley complained, "there is not such thing in the world." Seven years later the Reverend John Wise of Ipswich, writing in ardent support of a land bank as "Amicus Patriae," turned the metaphor on its head. The bank would be a vehicle of economic growth, putting the energies of an imaginative people to work. In strikingly spiritist language for an orthodox minister, Wise was certain that "we carry as much of the *Lapis Aurificus* or *Philosophers Stone* in our heads, and can turn other matter into Silver and Gold by the Power of thought as soon as any other People, or else I must own I have not yet Learnt the Character of my Country."[5]

Many among the colonial gentry, drawing on seventeenth-century thought, hoped to use the state as an alchemical alembic, fueling prosperity by the transmutation of authority into value. Others took this transmutation upon themselves. Our examination of alchemical and hermetic ideas takes on a new dimension if we go beyond popular occult beliefs and hermetic millenarianism to examine the murky – but particularly well documented – world of counterfeiting.

If divining drew upon alchemical concepts of volatile metals and promised a spiritual way to wealth, counterfeiting had more obvious roots in alchemy and offered a similarly flawed dream of riches and treasure. Counterfeiting, in its medieval and early modern manifestations, represented a low tradition of alchemical experimentation. While mystical alchemists toiled at their crucibles in hopes of achieving gnosis in the distillation of the philosopher's stone, legions of more practical adepts sought a more prosaic and immediate return: the transmutation of base metals into precious. Transmutation failing, the adept might become a puffer or smoke-seller, swindling gullible audiences both high and low. From here it was but a short step to the arts of clipping, coining, washing, and engraving that made up the mysteries – the deceptions – of counterfeiting. If we widen our definition of alchemy to include counterfeiting, the ranks and the chronology of the alchemical tradition are extended mightily. Literally thousands of men and women in the cash-poor colonies and early Republic were caught up in the dream of miraculously easy wealth, casting and coloring coins, engraving plates, striking bills, and passing bad currency for highly structured and remarkably persistent gangs of counterfeiters.[6] And counterfeiting bore complex affinities, real and imagined, to witchcraft, perfectionist dissent, and the divining cults. Hermetic purities were thus corrupted by hermetic dangers. These problems require careful examination.

In the spring of 1773 Joseph Bill Packer and four other men lay under sentence of death in the Albany County jail, convicted of coining Spanish milled dollars and sundry notes at a secret location, a cave in Great Barrington, Massachusetts, for use in the Indian trade. Joseph Bill Packer was the engraver for the gang, and since the 1740s he had been providing such services for "a line of money makers" stretching from Massachusetts to North Carolina. He was born Joseph Bill in Groton, Connecticut, in 1720; Packer was his mother's maiden name and one of his many aliases. Several of his cousins were also caught up in the "compulsive addiction" of the counterfeiting trade; Joseph Bill was also a second cousin once removed of Samuel Bill, who would marry Joseph Smith's aunt Lydia Mack in 1786.[7]

Awaiting execution in the Albany jail, Joseph Bill and his fellow prisoners did not rest idle. They had escaped from other lockups, and in their final days and hours they made a series of dramatic escape attempts, holding off the sheriff and his men with a smuggled bottle of gunpowder before they were finally brought to the gallows. But Joseph Bill had other means at his disposal, and in sending an account of his *Life and Travels* to the Albany press he pinned his hopes for pardon on the public's growing fascination for picaresque adventure. This account, selective though it is, gives us a fascinating perspective on the livelihood and worldview of a criminal of some notoriety, a livelihood and worldview that revolved around chemical knowledge and alchemic experimentation.[8]

Opening with an account of his youth, Bill spoke of his lifelong admiration "of the operations of nature" and of his constant "enquiring into any thing that [he] thought an arcanum," a difficult and perhaps occult mystery. First, Bill described his life in Virginia and North Carolina, where he headed after abruptly leaving southeastern Connecticut in 1742. Here he began a career as a country doctor. "The principal part of my business," he wrote, "was curing cancers; of this art I may justly call myself master."

Bill also played a role in the feverish hunt for mines that consumed many in the Chesapeake. He understood "the separation of metals, and was often called upon to examine minerals"; in particular he had worked "upon copper and lead ore" at the Bird-Chiswell mines on the New River in far western Virginia, beyond the Dan River region, where in 1733 William Byrd II complained that the people were "all mine-mad, neglecting to make corn."9 Passing over his counterfeiting exploits in the northern colonies between 1747 and 1751, Bill claimed to have served briefly as a schoolmaster among Quakers at Opechem Creek in the upper Shenandoah and, with the outbreak of war in 1755, seven years as a surgeon's mate at Fort Augusta on the Pennsylvania frontier. His movements for the next several years were left rather vague in his account, but he may well have operated under the name of Joseph Billings, counterfeiting money in southeast Pennsylvania and Maryland. In 1770 he moved north, and, as he wrote, "anxious to improve myself by philosophical studies, naturally inclined to learning, and remarkably inquisitive about the secrets of nature," he set up a series of workshops in the Hudson Valley and the eastern Connecticut border region with stills and glassware acquired in New York City. Here he "prepared medicines" and tried to "carry on" what he called "my chymical process." In the cold of one winter season he "embraced the opportunity to transcribe my philosophy book." And in a conversation with a Dr. Smith at a tavern in Dutchess County, Bill defined this "chymical process" more precisely:

> Among other things our conversation turned upon the transmutation of metals, the Doctor told me that he was a master of that art, but that his extensive practice of physick would not permit him to prosecute his discoveries in alchymy. I informed him that I intended to begin a course of experiments if I could get a convenient place to carry on the process.

Dr. Smith recommended that he might find a place at a Captain Hard's in New Milford, Connecticut, who "had for several years been carrying on operations of that nature." While living in New Milford, Bill was asked to engrave a plate for a ten-shilling note, which he claimed to have refused, "being then engaged in philosophical studies." However, at the gallows in Albany in 1773 he boasted of having engraved "plates in North-Carolina, Virginia, Pennsylvania, and the Jersies."10

Here, then, was a man for whom a knowledge of the hermetic tradition opened a host of opportunities. Joseph Bill was a metallurgist, a healer, a teacher, and a counterfeiter. Whether or not he actually pursued the dream of alchemic philosophy is a moot point. What is significant is that Bill had knowledge of the tradition and, at the very least, used the mystique of the alchemist as a cover for his counterfeiting activities.

Joseph Bill was not alone in combining interests in counterfeiting, alchemy, and medicine. In 1764 Joseph Williams and John Davenport were arrested for having passed counterfeited Spanish cobs at the house of Dr. Aeneas Munson in New Haven, the noted alchemic experimenter who often conferred with Ezra Stiles. Perhaps it was merely a coincidence that counterfeiters should congregate at Munson's house, but in 1792 Stiles recorded a visit from Munson where the alchemical prowess of a Dr. Prentice was the topic of conversation. Apparently Prentice could "fix Mercury," an important part of the alchemical work, and could "pretty freely & openly make Projection [the transmutation of metals], and says he cares Nothing for Money." But Prentice also "had been cropt and been in Simsbury Mines," the Connecticut State Prison. The traditional punishment in New England for counterfeiting was to have an ear cropped off; apparently Prentice "cared" enough for money to have dabbled in the forbidden craft.[11] In another interesting hermetic connection, Dudley Bradstreet Jr. of Suncook, New Hampshire, was arrested with a gang of counterfeiters in Andover, Massachusetts, in 1738. He was the grandson of Anne Bradstreet, the great seventeenth-century hermetic poet, whose work was rooted directly in late Renaissance culture.[12]

The connections between the technology of counterfeiting and those of metallurgy, chemistry, and alchemy suggest that it bore a relation to the mining enthusiasms of the 1720s and 1750s. Metalsmiths of various kinds were involved in coining money or in cutting the plates from which paper counterfeits were struck. Others involved were chemists or apothecaries, who made regular use of the alchemist's stock of chemicals. Various accounts describe how base-metal coins were "glazed over with quick silver," using closely guarded formulas for alloys. Counterfeiting recipes for coining dating from late-seventeenth-century Lancashire – and from 1772 in Connecticut – prescribed "sal ammoniac" (ammonium chloride) to color coins; this chemical had been a key material in the alchemist's stock for centuries.[13] Others among the counterfeiting fraternity who would have been familiar with the chemical tradition were the many real and fraudulent physicians who turned to counterfeiting in the eighteenth century.[14] A host of conning men, with pretensions to learning and a gentleman's style, moved across the countryside, providing a ready source of cheap but fraudulent currency and, apparently, a reservoir of arcane knowledge of the old scientific traditions.

In short, counterfeiters drew upon a wide knowledge of chemistry and metallurgy intersecting with the old alchemical tradition. This was a knowledge common in the criminal underworld; forgers, con artists, and pickpockets had long had an acquaintance with methods of making the fraudulent seem real, methods that to the uninitiated might appear magical. Colonial counterfeiters often bought horses and oxen with their bad money, animals that might be stolen, an endeavor that required an understanding of dying hair and falsifying brands. And in England since the late Middle Ages the usually itinerant fraudulent alchemist, or puffer, had operated on the fringes of this underworld, claiming possession of the philosopher's stone and offering for a price to work his magic or divulge his secret. Edward Kelly, alchemist and scryer for Dr. John Dee in the late sixteenth century, was pilloried and had his ears cropped for forgery in his native Lancaster. More recently, Count Cagliostro, the alchemist who in the 1780s captivated Paris and Europe and attracted the attention of Ezra Stiles, had started out as Joseph Balsamo, a Sicilian forger and counterfeiter. Even if the Renaissance puffer did have alchemical skills, he was concerned solely with the transmutation of base metals into gold rather than a search for mystical perfection. "To the serious alchemist," as Charles Nicholl has summed it up in his study of the alchemical influences on Shakespeare, "these various smoke-sellers, counterfeiters and coiners were simply those 'lewd persons' through whom 'the worthy science of Alchemie is come in such disdain.'"[15]

The *Memoirs* of Stephen Burroughs provide a dramatic account of alchemical "smoke-selling" and counterfeiting in late-eighteenth-century New England. Burroughs himself became a famous counterfeiter in the early nineteenth century, flooding New England and New York with counterfeit bank notes from a secret location in Ontario. In 1784, while living in Pelham, Massachusetts, Burroughs and his friend "Lysander" learned of a "wonderful transmuter of metals" named Phillips living with the noted "money-maker" Glazier Wheeler nearby in New Salem. Arranging a visit, they were given what seemed to be "proofs of his skill." Putting into a crucible a half ounce of copper and a concealed object wrapped in paper, Phillips produced a boiling reaction lasting for ten minutes, when the material "settled down into a clear beautiful metal which, . . . poured off and cooled, was good silver, [withstanding] the trial by aqua-fortis." They repeated the experiment several times, each time stirring the crucible with a different rod of iron or wood. Convinced that Phillips had mastered the secret of transmuting copper into silver, Burroughs and his friend laid plans for transmutation on a grand scale off the New Hampshire coast on Sable Island. And in the fashion of the occult mining companies of the era, a "writing was made and signed by all parties, for our regulation in prosecuting said purpose."[16]

It was not until several months later, and after a complex series of adventures, that Burroughs and Lysander discovered that they had been deceived. The tips of the rods had contained hidden deposits of silver, an ancient puffer's trick.[17] Lysander and Burroughs would not be put off from their dream of quick wealth, and they then proposed to contract with Glazier Wheeler for counterfeit Spanish milled dollars. But the "business" required certain "drugs proper for carrying it forward," and going down to Springfield, Burroughs was arrested for trying to pass one of Wheeler's coins. Burroughs, Wheeler, and several other men from the east Hampshire hill towns were convicted of forging or passing Spanish milled dollars by the Supreme Judicial Court in 1785 and 1786. The promise of miraculous wealth through alchemic transmutation had led to counterfeiting and prison.[18]

If the writings of Joseph Bill and Stephen Burroughs demonstrate the connections between counterfeiting and alchemy, those of other counterfeiters lead us to connotations of witchcraft. Karl Marx is reputed to have once noted that European societies stopped burning witches when they began hanging coiners.[19] The evidence from the eighteenth-century colonies puts some empirical flesh on this interesting, if perhaps apocryphal, observation. Manipulating matter to deceive honest people, coiners and counterfeiters in the eighteenth-century colonies seem to have occupied a place in the popular imagination not far removed from that once held by witches and sorcerers.

Suggestions of demonic possession or witchlike powers emerge first from language attributed to counterfeiters themselves. Owen Sullivan, an Irish engraver who had organized counterfeiters all over the northern colonies before being hanged in New York City in 1756, wrote in his confession of being possessed by spirits for several nights as a youth: "I was called by an evil Spirit by my Christian name; John, John, John." The men drawn into passing bad money also used the language of supernatural power to describe counterfeiting as a way of life and the engravers and printers who led the gangs. In 1748 a Connecticut counterfeiter petitioned for a pardon, claiming that he had been "bewitched" and "seduced" into uttering false bills of credit. John Smith, imprisoned with Joseph Bill in 1773, spoke of his counterfeiting days in North Carolina, his marriage into a good family in New England, and his relapse into the craft. "I lived very well a while but having that itching desire for gain, sought out that Witch of Endor, which now proves my overthrow." Referring to the diviner and necromancer who summoned up the spirit of Samuel for Saul, this "Witch of Endor" was either Joseph Bill, the engraver for the "Albany County Gang," or the seductive enticement of easy money.[20]

Perhaps the mystique of the alchemic *magus* that Joseph Bill seems to have cultivated was the root of the suspicions of sorcery. But such a mystique could also adhere in seemingly magical feats of mechanical ability. Burroughs was particularly impressed by Phillips, the New Salem puffer, who, though he had lost an arm, was "very ingenuous in executing mechanical undertakings" and a master of all parts of the "coining art"; when they were languishing in the Northampton jail, he would demonstrate a Houdini-like capacity for escape. The public ascribed these exploits to Burroughs and, assuming that "the devil had assisted" him, flocked to the jail "for a discovery of matters unknown to themselves; as things lost, stolen, etc."[21] More importantly, however, personal powers of persuasion and deception might raise fears of "bewitchment." Samuel Ford, the leader of the Morris County gang in the early 1770s, was described as "an artful Fellow – with the Serious and Grave, can put on the Face of Seriousness, Religion, and Gravity, and with the Gay, can behave with as much Levity as any one." In Burroughs's description, Phillips was "plausible in conversation" and "had the entire command of his feelings, so that his countenance or actions never betrayed his inward sensations, persevering in any undertaking, perfidious subtle, and designing; [he was] a rank coward, yet possessing the happiest abilities of imitating courage of any man I ever saw."[22] Burroughs was a good judge of such matters, for at the time he was making a living posing as an orthodox minister, preaching to the people of Pelham, Massachusetts, with the help of old sermons he had stolen from his father. In later years Burroughs would mockingly claim that "the Pelhamites" had invoked the spirits but had "received no answer, by Urim nor Thummim, by voices nor dreams."[23] A petition for pardon presented to the Vermont legislature in 1810 by John Niles, recently convicted of counterfeiting, directed similar language at Burroughs himself, complaining of the "peculiar seductive language" and "insidious intrigues of this artful and unprincipled man." Imitation, deception, seduction, persuasion: in addition to uncanny chemical and mechanical abilities, the counterfeiting masters seem to have had control of voice, word, and gesture, by which they manipulated their associates and victims by inexplicable means. They were, in the eyes of their contemporaries, masters of natural magic.[24]

Of course, these intimations of supernatural means of deception and seduction were connected to a broader ritual language of crime and confession. Thus the association of counterfeiting with witchcraft was an external one, merging with a broader linkage between crime and sin as the Devil's work, and particularly evident in official pronouncements, which charged the accused with "not having the fear of God before his eyes but being moved and seduced by the instigation of the Devil." Similar formulas appear in criminal confessions. Herman Rosencrantz, hanged for counterfeiting in Philadelphia in 1770, wrote that he "gave [himself] over to an uneasy and restless mind, with an undue desire of gaining riches;

which disposition, pushed on by the enemy of my soul, has been a means of downfall." John Cartwright, hanged at Poughkeepsie for horsestealing in the same year, used this formula, speaking of falling into evil company, among whom "the Devil is always at work."[25]

But imputations of witchcraft must have gone beyond simple formulas. For very good reasons, the counterfeiters were associated in the popular mind with the wild places feared as the sanctuaries of demonic Indians, witches, and Tories. To hide their operations the counterfeiting gangs met like witch covens, deep in the woods and swamps, and their shops were often located in hidden caves. Into the twentieth century caves throughout western Massachusetts – in Goshen, Woronoco, Adams, Hancock, Lanesborough, Great Barrington – were known as "Counterfeiter's Cave." Owen Sullivan's "Dover Money Club" operated out of a hillside cave deep in a wooded swamp, and Sullivan himself was arrested in a false cellar specially fitted with its own forge.[26]

The wilderness thus sheltered illicit gain associated with occult means, a threatening source of fraudulent value that would undermine the true value of the products of honest labor. For households abiding within the law, and living with the constant threat of being passed false bills, the counterfeiter's arts were a literal *maleficium*. Fraught with occult connotations, the counterfeiter, unlike the witch, could do real harm to household welfare. It is suggestive that in eighteenth-century belief witches could be killed with silver buttons or copper pennies: real value would destroy the false. The punishment of cutting off counterfeiters' ears common in New England may have been popularly associated with a well-known countercharm for bewitched animals; the ritual burning of counterfeit bills in New Hampshire may have implied a connection with earlier punishments for witches. And like the accusers at Salem as interpreted by Paul Boyer and Stephen Nissenbaum, ordinary folk in the eighteenth century often wondered how certain individuals had arrived so rapidly at a state of wealth and plenty. Here suspicions of counterfeiting might have developed in parallel with suspicions of witchcraft, as in cases such as that of General Stephen Moulton of Hampton, New Hampshire, who, as John Demos relates, was rumored to have gained his great wealth by cheating the "Great Deceiver."[27]

Beyond the *maleficium* of the village witch lay the demonic compact, the satanic and heretical plot to destroy a society. The execution sermon for a counterfeiter hanged at Poughkeepsie, New York, in 1758 was redolent with the connotations of wide-reaching demonic conspiracy that had overwhelmed the region around Salem, Massachusetts, in 1692. In almost frenzied language, the Reverend Chauncy Graham argued that some men committed overt crimes of violence and property against individuals, and others chose "to act more covertly . . . carrying on a Trade of over-reaching, cozening, cheating, extortion and defrauding in their dealings." But still others – the counterfeiters –

> take a more expeditious method . . . to become rich, by ruining whole Provinces and Colonies; aiming, by one fatal stab, to let out the very Heart's Blood of Communities. . . . Of this kind ar، our money-Makers, a Brood of Vipers, that are eating out the Bowels of Provinces and Colonies . . . [by] their devilish Craft and Cunning.

Graham went on to link counterfeiters with highwaymen and pirates in "almost ruining the trading interests" of the province. In a society plagued with overwhelming currency problems, counterfeiters were easily seen as in league with the "Great Deceiver."[28] The image of a secret conspiracy against society was often imputed to the counterfeiters, in a few instances with some justification. The authorities were convinced that the "Albany County Gang" had "a Deep Laid Plan for to have the several Governments Ruined in their Commerce," and the Tory counterfeiters who operated between New York City and the backwoods of New Hampshire during the Revolution clearly had this intent. One of the editors of Stephen Burroughs's *Memoirs* wrote in 1812 that Burroughs "openly declares war against the stockholders of banks, and the community at large," and he was said to have sent a cartoon to the leading Boston bankers from his Canadian hideout subscribed "Death or Botany Bay."[29]

If counterfeiting was associated with alchemical magic and implicitly seen as a form of secular witchcraft, these connotations drew upon a long history. Reformation era witch-hunting, perhaps more in rhetoric than in prosecution, had targeted magical practice as demonic collusion. The cunning folk, astrologers, alchemists, and hermetic philosophers were agents of the devil according to many scholarly witch-hunters; ordinary people found them at least suspect. In both England and New England the village cunning folk and healers – and those who frequented them – stood in some risk of accusation of witchcraft. In addition, the charge of witchcraft in seventeenth-century New England was often leveled at those accused of heresy; among these were Anne Hutchinson and some of the early Quakers. And just as the counterfeiter's punishment of having an ear cut off echoed the countercharm for bewitched animals, it also echoed the 1658 Massachusetts decree that Quakers have their right ears cut off. Witchcraft, heresy, and counterfeiting formed a triptych in popular imagination and in the law.[30]

Contemporary European practitioners of alchemy and hermeticism were also suspected of entering into demonic compacts. In seventeenth-century England, orthodox scholars from William Perkins to Joseph Glanvill and Henry More strove mightily to condemn as witches the cunning folk, astrologers, Paracelsian physicians, and, especially, the hermetic sectaries for conspiring with the devil. On the Continent, similar concerns were raised about the purported Rosicrucians. In New England, Cotton Mather went so far as to equate the devil and the alchemist: "If chymists can make their Aurum fulminens, what strange things may this infernal chymist effect?" Sectarian hermeticism was defended from charges of witchcraft by John Webster, once condemned for a "Familistical-Levelling-Magical Temper," and by Lodowick Muggleton, one of the few sectarians to survive the Restoration.[31] A passing acquaintance with the orthodox position in these seventeenth-century debates could only have prejudiced eighteenth-century colonists against alchemists and folk healers. Such views would have contributed to popular imputations of *maleficia* and demonic compacts to the very real operations of the money-makers. If the white magic of cunning folk and alchemists could be turned into black magic, then the deceptive arts of the counterfeiter, arts rooted in alchemical experiment and secret, "occult" knowledge, could be as well.

A stereotype of the counterfeiter as a heretical witch or a hermetic sectarian can thus be constructed from surviving evidence, looking at the counterfeiter through the eyes of the fearful observer. A rather different view, but with some surprising points of intersection, can also be constructed from biographical evidence on the counterfeiters. They were men alienated from communions that were themselves separated from the structure of church and state that continued to shape New England society.

   With surprising consistency, counterfeiters can be found on the fringes of sectarian communities. They seem to have been particularly frequent in Quaker neighborhoods: Joseph Bill's sojourn as a schoolmaster for the Quakers at Opechem Creek in the Virginia upcountry was a symptom of a much wider pattern. Joseph Boyce, the engraver for a gang in Salem, Massachusetts, was born into an old Quaker family, and at least seven other Essex counterfeiters, and especially those from Salem, were from the Quaker orbit. Quakers in Rhode Island were involved in money-making, and a series of gangs operating in the Oblong region on the eastern edge of New York Province were intermingled with Quaker communities. Leaving Essex County ahead of the law, Boyce and other Salem counterfeiters moved first to Mendon, Massachusetts, and then to the Quaker area of the Oblong and were involved in a number of counterfeiting operations in the 1740s and 1750s. At Quaker Hill in the Oblong, a number of men with Quaker surnames testified against various counterfeiters in 1745, but later retracted their testimony; others were indicted. In all likelihood these men entangled with counterfeiting were lapsed Quakers, dropped from the meetings, but still linked by kinship and neighborhood.[32]

In southern Connecticut and western Massachusetts counterfeiters were affiliated with Separates and Separate Baptists. Joseph Bill's family moved between Groton, the location of a branch of the Rogerene sect, and North Preston, overrun by Separates. Bill's counterfeiting cousin Solomon was a member of the Strict Congregational Church in Middletown; when one of his passers, Jedediah Ashcraft of Groton, was arrested in 1749, Park Avery, a preacher for a local Separate meeting, helped pay his surety. Across western Massachusetts men from Baptist communities in Charlton, Sturbridge, Ashfield, Conway, and Leverett were accused of counterfeiting in the 1770s and 1780s, though at least one of these accusations, that of Elder Chiliab Smith of Ashfield, was part of a broader effort by the county elite to discredit the Baptists. One of the counterfeiting doctors, Augustus Parker, was connected to Universalism. His father, Isaiah Parker, had been the pastor of the small Baptist church in Harvard, Massachusetts, before 1804, when he took up the Universalist "doctrine of the salvation of all men."[33] And Stephen Burroughs came from a family immersed in religious controversy. The original Burroughs had arrived in Connecticut from Bermuda in 1695, and his family would not conform to orthodoxy. Stephen's father, the Reverend Eden Burroughs, had already left one church in Connecticut before he separated from another in Hanover, New Hampshire; and Stephen's aunt had married into a sectarian family that moved from the Congregationalists to the Baptists and then to the Universalists.[34]

Counterfeiting cropped up with similar regularity among New England's perfectionist antinomians. Samuel Fox II of New London, son of Bathsheba Fox of the witch's puppets, nephew of John Rogers, the Rogerene founder, and a distant cousin of Ransford the con man, was arrested and convicted for passing false bills in 1739. Among the Cumberland, Rhode Island, perfectionists, who practiced gifts of baptism and spiritual wifery, John Finney Jr. turned to counterfeiting in the aftermath of the Awakening in 1753; forty years later his nephew Appollus Finney was convicted in Vermont for counterfeiting the bills of the Bank of the United States. Up the Blackstone River, Solomon Prentice of Grafton, son of Sarah Prentice, the spiritual wife of Shadrack Ireland, moved to North Carolina after being arrested for counterfeiting in 1773. One wonders whether he was the Dr. Prentice whose powers of "projection" Stiles and Munson discussed in 1792. And thirty years later some of the leading followers of another Cumberland perfectionist, Jemima Wilkinson, were drawn from Quaker families in Rhode Island and Pennsylvania that had dabbled in the trade in bad money. Most notably, Judge William Potter supported Jemima Wilkinson with money and a safe refuge at his farm in Little Rest. From 1739 to 1742 Potter's brother John had led a counterfeiting operation that had included Benjamin Boyce of Salem and Jemima Wilkinson's cousin Benjamin of Scituate, Rhode Island. A second set of counterfeiters was operating at nearby Tower Hill in the 1760s. And yet another connection brings us full circle. Among Jemima's followers in Philadelphia was a retired Quaker druggist named Christopher Marshall; in 1751 Marshall too had been convicted of counterfeiting. Marshall had long been exposed to the hermetic tradition, as he was a friend of Peter Miller, one of the four Sabbatarian pilgrims who journeyed from Ephrata to New London in 1744.[35]

Counterfeiters also intersected with the myriad small religious movements that bubbled up in late-eighteenth-century Vermont. Coming into the Coos country of the upper Connecticut River in New Hampshire in 1762, Glazier Wheeler "fell in with Samuel Sleeper," a Quaker preacher from Hampton on the coast, and sledded Sleeper's family and household goods over the late spring snows into the new settlement. Over the next several years Wheeler would become famous as the "money-maker of Cohass [Coos]," providing stamps, plates, and milling machines for gangs of counterfeiters throughout the northern colonies. Promised the right to preach in the Coos settlements, Sleeper was set aside for an orthodox minister, whom Sleeper and a follower harassed with cries of "Thou lies, friend," and "False doctrines" and "glorious truths!" Spurned and suppressed by the people, they crossed the Connecticut River into Vermont, where they tried to fast for forty days in a mountainside cave.[36] In a similar episode, a Peter Saunders was arrested in Albany in 1789 for passing bad coin: he had come down through Vermont from Canada, "[a]like prepared to act the saint and the villain, at one house preach[ing] the gospel of Christ (as he says), with much vociferation and fervor, at the next with unsanctified hands, . . . distribut[ing] his counterfeits among the ignorant and the unwary."[37]

Counterfeiters thus tended to cluster around the edges of the dissenting meetings and sects that emerged across New England in the aftermath of the Great Awakening. Others were even more disassociated from the orthodox mainstream. Some, like Owen Sullivan and Thomas Lynstead, came directly from the British Isles, on a thin stream of indentured servants and mariners that continued to trickle into the region, to say nothing of convicts transported to the Chesapeake. Others were simply alienated from society, whether "of an unsocial, refractory disposition" or driven by "a spirit of Revenge."[38]

Another mode of alienation was apparently rooted in recent history. One place where counterfeiters were particularly active in the eighteenth century was Essex County, Massachusetts, especially in the years of the greatest controversy over currency, 1738–45.[39] For the most part, these Essex counterfeiters were involved in trades rather than farming.[40] But the most interesting dimension of the Essex County counterfeiters was their association with persons accused of witchcraft in 1692.

Of the 41 accused counterfeiters and their 28 sureties, 20 can be linked by kinship with the 376 persons involved in the 1692 trials, either as accusers or as accused. These twenty links between the witch trials and counterfeiting were not evenly distributed; 65 percent (13/20) of them were linked to the accused witches, who made up only 38 percent (141/376) of the 1692 total.[41] In Salem and Lynn, counterfeiters included a great-nephew and a great-grandson of Rebecca Towne Nurse. The former, Joseph Very, who would become involved in the Oblong gangs with Joseph Boyce, was also a great-nephew of John Proctor and a grandson of Thomas Farrar of Lynn. The witchcraft–counterfeiting connection was particularly strong in Andover, where it included the Fryes, the Parkers, the Wrights, and – most importantly – the Bradstreets.

Three generations of Bradstreets pose a telling continuum. Anne Bradstreet, the hermetic poet, died in 1672. Twenty years later two of her sons, John and Dudley, with Dudley's wife, Anne, fled to New Hampshire to escape accusations of witchcraft. And forty-six years later, Dudley Bradstreet Jr., an innkeeper in Suncook, New Hampshire, was arrested in the roundup of the Andover gang of counterfeiters.[42]

Such family ties suggest that one enduring result of the witch trials was a profound alienation from society. The divisions caused by witchcraft accusations ran very deep, estranging once cordial families far into the eighteenth century. It is not impossible to imagine a sense of profound injustice translated into a familial tradition of separation and dis-association – ultimately to be manifested in counterfeiting conspiracies. In the case of the Bradstreets, high hermeticism may have suggested witch-craft; in turn familial humiliation may have given rise to "a spirit of Revenge."

Counterfeiters did not, of course, act alone. The spreading of counterfeits required a sophisticated gang structure; the engraver might sell his plates to a group of printers, who in turn might take into their scheme a number of passers. And there is some evidence that counterfeiters enjoyed wide-spread support in backcountry regions, where they may have provided the only available paper currency. Like highway robbery and piracy, "money-making" could have connotations of "social banditry." A New York justice of the peace pursuing members of the Albany County Gang into Vermont in 1772 wrote to Governor Tyron that his own constables had let the suspects escape and asked bitterly, "What can a Justice do when the whole Country combines against him?"[43]

If at times the counterfeiters had a "whole Country" behind them, it was because they provided a necessary function, a function connected to the seventeenth-century intersection of hermeticism and economic theory. Quite simply, counterfeiters provided a source of cash in a cash-poor economy. Just as the banking schemes inaugurated by Samuel Hartlib and John Winthrop Jr. drew upon the metaphor of hermetic projection, so too the counterfeiter offered the prospect of the growth of value. One New Hampshire counterfeiter expressed a prevailing sentiment when he argued that "it was no hurt for a man to make money provided it would pass in the treasury and was not known to be bad by the common people." The justification for counterfeiting offered by Burroughs's associate Lysander went so far as to invoke the commodity theory of value. Bills of credit were inherently valueless, "good for nothing; but the moment mankind agree to put a value on them, as representing property, they become of as great consequence as silver and gold." Precious stones and metals were only valued because of an implicit agreement based on their scarcity: "Gold and silver are made use of for convenience . . . as the representation of property." Property and its monetary representation ought to be kept in balance, and given the "undue shortage of cash" in the 1780s, whoever "contributes, really, to increase the quantity of cash does not only himself, but likewise the community, an essential benefit."[44]

But here, of course, Lysander went beyond the seventeenth-century commodity theorists, for it would be the counterfeiter, not the commonwealth, who would make the decision to enlarge the supply of circulating currency. And, in reality, that decision would not involve a neighborhood but individuals alone and in temporary association in money-making gangs. Though not without connotations of social banditry, and implications of commodity theory, our best model for counterfeiting is that of a secular antinomianism. As Lysander himself admitted, the counterfeiters were taking the law into their own hands. In his view, "the law speaks in general terms," and thus "general principles must direct us in our interpretation of the law." John Finney, one of the Cumberland perfectionists, was more direct; rejecting the authority of "Babylon" to govern in baptism and marriage, he extended his individual authority to currency. Its broader association with dissent, spiritual wifery, and immortalism suggests that counterfeiting, the "projection" of monetary value in violation of mere human law, was a secular equivalent of the antinomian perfectionism of these eighteenth-century sects.

One can speculate, as well, about more distant connections. Might colonial counterfeiting be derived from what Christopher Hill calls "the experience of defeat"? Given their circulation on the sectarian fringe, and in some cases their post-Restoration origins, the counterfeiters could have been one dimension of the collapse of the English Revolution and the suppression of the radical sects. Eric Hobsbawm suggests that robber bands in eighteenth-century Germany "provided a refuge for libertinist and antinomian sectarians, such as the survivors of central-European anabaptism." Hill points to this observation in asking whether the buccaneers and pirates of the late-seventeenth-century Caribbean could be seen as refugees from the Restoration: transported and escaped political radicals and sectarians.[45] Burroughs's origins in Bermuda, the maritime origins of some of the counterfeiters, and their frequent use of the coasting trade all point to the possibility of a West Indian connection. Barbados in particular was the origin of numbers of poor freed servants coming to the mainland at the end of the century, possibly bearers of traditions of antinomian Ranting and alchemical coining, certainly outside the mainstream of the mainland colonies. But even without such a seventeenth-century connection, it does seem reasonable to view the eighteenth-century colonial counterfeiters as laws unto themselves, acting out the antinomianism that was often only latent among the perfectionist sects.

Divining, alchemy, and counterfeiting formed a hermetic triad in popular culture, in effect the poor man's bank. Divining was a spiritual means to a material end; alchemy was a material means to a spiritual end. Counterfeiting was strictly material in both ends and means, but it was often enveloped in connotations of occult power. All three were species of the miraculous, situated on points along a gradient from sincere spirituality to pure fraud, a gradient of hermetic purity and danger. And both counterfeiting and divining were associated with the splintering of religious unity throughout greater New England in the postrevolutionary decades, a splintering that – in the case of the New Israelites – could lead to perfectionist restorationism having connections and resonances running back to the sectaries of the English Revolution, the Separates of the Great Awakening, and the mystical, apocalyptical Freemasonry of contemporary Europe.

But the counterfeiter lurking among the New Israelites in Middletown, Vermont, poses something of a problem: were divining cults simply fronts for counterfeiting rings? One other case might suggest as much. In 1804 in

Canaan township in the Kennebec Valley in Maine, a Daniel Lambert and his sons drew an entire community into an occult treasure-hunting craze, all to hide another counterfeiting scheme.[46]

Scattered shreds of evidence suggest that there were particular hotspots of occult metallurgy across the northern states in the decades following the Revolution. In 1786, on the Massachusetts border at Whitingham, Vermont, a prominent landholder named Silas Hamilton kept a diary account of the treasure dreams of over forty people, the meetings of mine companies, and an elaborate ritual procedure for locating treasure involving steel rods, hen's blood mixed with hog dung, and magic circles. Many of the towns mentioned in this diary harbored rings of counterfeiters.[47] Other notable locations where divining intersected with deep-rooted traditions of counterfeiting include northern Middlesex County, Massachusetts, in and around the towns of Groton and Harvard, and Morristown, New Jersey, the scene of Ransford Rogers's exploits.[48]

The relationship between counterfeiting and divining can be roughly quantified for Vermont. The Vermont State Archives contain a body of petitions dating from the 1790s to the 1830s from groups of individuals from fifty-four towns requesting pardons and restoration of citizenship for specific counterfeiters or remission of bonds sworn for convicted coiners. These petitions provide a rough index of the locations where counterfeiters had considerable community support. In addition, the distribution of twenty-six Vermont towns where there are records, however sketchy, of divining and treasure-hunting episodes provides an approximate cultural geography of divining. By these measures, counterfeiting and divining were not perfectly associated in early Vermont. Counterfeiting petitions were quite widely distributed, and fewer than half of the towns producing these petitions, and towns adjacent to such towns, were located in divining localities. Conversely, practically all of the towns in divining localities were the source, or adjacent to the source, of a petition about a counterfeiter. In brief, counterfeiting was widely distributed, but divining occurred _almost exclusively_ in counterfeiting localities. Similarly, counterfeiting was better associated with divining than was the presence of Methodists, Freewill Baptists, Universalists, and Masonic lodges and chapters, though Freemasonry came in second, ahead of the perfectionist churches. Thus the appeal of divining, a spiritual hunt for treasure, was dependent upon – and perhaps a reaction to – the presence of counterfeiters.[49]

There was a significant geographic consistency between counterfeiting and divining, but what was the relationship between the two? The accounts of the New Israelites and the diviner–counterfeiters of the Kennebec region suggest that divining might often be a front for counterfeiting operations, providing a plausible explanation for sudden wealth, but a certain distance lay precisely in this plausibility. Counterfeiters could hide their false coin in the excitement of occult divination for treasure because people in certain backcountry places found such a way to wealth believable. However, although they were eager to accept the idea of buried treasure, they were more resistant to the simple expedient of passing counterfeits. Thus, in Middletown, a Brother Done was "alarmed" to hear from Laban Clark that there was "counterfeiting going on" among the New Israelites, but only at his wife's insistence would he allow the Methodist preacher to burn his divining rod.[50]

A naive enthusiasm for magical practice could easily expose a community to the stratagems of a confidence man. Counterfeiting itself was something of an occult con game, especially when it played upon residual beliefs about alchemical transmutation. Such was the case when Stephen Burroughs was duped by Phillips the transmuter in 1785. A similar con game led to the conviction of another group of men across the Connecticut Valley in the towns along the Deerfield River in 1789. They had been drawn in by "a set of sharpers" who had offered to double their money, changing $500 into $1,000, and who had sold them formulas for "transmuting copper into silver" and "silver into gold." A similar multiplication scheme came to trial in Windsor County, Vermont, in 1800; another surfaced in Wilkes-Barre, Pennsylvania, in 1811. However, although the transmutative counterfeiters in both New Salem and Deerfield River emerged in the heart of the region covered by Silas Hamilton's 1786 diary, only one man was involved in both treasure tales and counterfeiting.[51] Overall, the evidence suggests that divining and counterfeiting occurred among *different* groups of people living in the same localities.

The life of Obadiah Wheeler of Rutland, Vermont, suggests a mutually exclusive, and perhaps adversarial, relationship. Two divining episodes occurred in late-eighteenth-century Rutland, one involving an expedition to New Haven and the other based on dreams about a local man murdered during the Revolution. In the later case, Obadiah Wheeler had dreams in which his murdered uncle told him the location of buried treasure, which would be Wheeler's after the performance of several ritual tasks. Wheeler could not or would not perform the required tasks, which included crossing the Atlantic. Other men, hearing of the dream, hired a skilled diviner from over the mountains in Ludlow, who cast magic circles and wielded divining rods loaded with quicksilver, only to have the treasure sink down into the earth. Roughly a decade later, in 1810, Obadiah Wheeler would be in trouble with the law regarding his bond for Abel Platt, who had been convicted of passing counterfeit bank notes. Among five men in Rutland associated with the treasure-hunting episode, Wheeler was the only one to sign an 1811 petition for the restoration of Platt's rights of citizenship. Obadiah Wheeler, the dreamer, who had the most to gain from breaking the guardian spirit's spell, would consort with counterfeiters rather than divining wizards.[52]

The sequence of events in Morris County, New Jersey, may typify the relationship between divining and counterfeiting. New Jersey's one known episode of divining, orchestrated by Ransford Rogers in 1788, took place in a town and a county that had been overrun with counterfeiters in the 1740s and again early in the 1770s. Involving mutual assistance among noted families and the connivance of justices of the peace, constables, and a church deacon, the counterfeiting conspiracies must have created a paranoiac sense of anxiety and distrust.

The establishment of a copper-penny mint in Morristown in 1786 also may have fed local speculation on the creation of wealth. But people in Morristown in the 1780s were also gripped by a powerful "assurance in witchcraft": several young women "had been harassed . . . by witches for a long time," and "the generality were apprehensive of witches riding them." They were thus "predisposed for the reception of marvelous curiosities." These curiosities took the form of "money deposited in the bowels of the earth, at Schooler's Mountain, with an enchantment upon it." Determined to break the spell controlling these riches, certain people determined to find "a man that could work miracles." Their efforts were answered by the appearance of Ransford Rogers. Assembling a group of treasure-seekers near the site of the copper-penny mint, Rogers and several confederates disguised as spirits used sleight of hand, ritual powdered bone dust wrapped in paper, and controlled explosions to extract hundreds of dollars in gold and silver from their followers, mostly "honest, judicious, simple church members" drawn from the Presbyterians. Here we may suggest what may have been a more general sequence: the operations of counterfeiters created an environment of anxiety about deception by mysterious powers and a fascination with easy wealth, both of which in turn fed witchcraft beliefs and treasure fantasies.[53]

Thus, if the evidence for a counterfeiter operating in the midst of the New Israelite diviners suggests that the two were identical, this evidence suggests a much more complicated relationship. It seems much more likely that divining and counterfeiting were mutually interactive but opposed and perhaps hostile, two distinct options within the single cultural arena, an arena defined by the critical conjunction of metallurgical knowledge and occult belief against the general background of the cash-poor backcountry, especially in the decades immediately following the Revolution, when hopes of material advancement far outstripped opportunities.[54] Locked in opposition, counterfeiting and divining were drastically different symptoms of a common affinity for the mysteries of volatile metals and sudden wealth, parallel but opposed within a single cultural arena of hermetic purity and danger.

But it is best not to draw the line too sharply. When viewed simultaneously, through a somewhat functionalist lens, the two seem quite distinct. But when viewed in long sequence, the culture of counterfeiting seems to have contributed centrally to the divining cults. While most of those drawn into the money-digging companies were sincere in their occult beliefs, many of the conjurers who presided over their rituals were clearly con men; some must have known something of coining. It is impossible to avoid the conclusion that the con man Ransford Rogers, with his "copious knowledge of chemistry," must have been acquainted with the secrets of counterfeiting. One is reminded of his contemporary, Dr. Prentice, who "freely & openly [made] Projection" – the transmutation of metals – and who also had been cropped as a counterfeiter. One is also reminded of a third Connecticut man, "Dr." Joseph Bill, who had spent so much time in the Mid-Atlantic and the South.

Joseph Bill's career, in particular, indicates how the master counterfeiter mediated between the seventeenth-century occult and the early national diviners. If we take at face value his account of his *Life and Travels,* Bill was a student of obscure, arcane knowledge, he was skilled in chemical processes, he had some success as a physician dispensing medicines in the southern backcountry and as an army surgeon, and he took the time to maintain a "philosophy book." If we fill in some of the blank spaces in his chronicle, we find him engraving plates for counterfeit notes in New Jersey, New England, and New York between 1747 and 1751. Assuming that he worked in the 1760s as Joseph Billings, we find him in 1762 living at the house of Frederick Weiser in or near Reading, Pennsylvania, working ostensibly as a printer but also engaged in counterfeiting three-pound notes. When he was arrested in February 1763, Bill claimed that Weiser was involved, and he "thought it hard a poor man should suffer for a crime in which rich men were equally concerned"; a Herman Rosencrantz definitely was an accomplice.[55]

To say nothing of the occult connotations of Rosencrantz's name, Bill's association with Frederick Weiser leads us into a tangled interweaving of sectarian pietism and hermetic occultism. His father, Conrad Weiser, and brother and sister had been celibate followers at Beissel's Ephrata. Conrad Weiser was anointed a Melchizedek priest with the title of "Enoch"; after he left the cloister, he was the agent in the town of Reading for alchemical medicines imported from Halle, the center of Prussian Pietism.[56] Such elixirs were certainly part of Joseph Bill's medical kit as he wandered about, curing cancers, separating metals, and engraving counterfeits. Certainly they were the model for the "mineral dulcimer elixer" that Ransford Rogers and the Hessian Dr. Dady advertised in York County, Pennsylvania, in 1797 as a means of conjuring spirits.[57]

Bill's association with Frederick Weiser leads us to a reconsideration of the world in which he moved during his various travels. He had grown up in Groton, Connecticut, in the orbit of the Rogerenes, leaving for Virginia in the early 1740s, perhaps along the same coastal route that the Ephrata pilgrims – the Eckerlin brothers, Peter Miller, and Alexander Mack – took on their journey north in the fall of 1744. On their way through New Jersey the Ephrata pilgrims passed through the Sabbatarian community at Barnegat Bay. The Connecticut Rogerene families here had originally settled in Morristown, and in 1748 they returned, taking up land on the same Schooler's Mountain where forty years later Ransford Rogers, a Rogerene descendant, would lead the Presbyterians on a futile search for buried treasure. In September 1745, soon after their pilgrimage to the New England Sabbatarians, the Eckerlins set out for the lower Shenandoah Valley, establishing a hermit village named Mahanaim on the New River, a few miles north of the Bird-Chiswell mines, where Joseph Bill was engaged to "separate metals." Here one of the Eckerlin brothers took up trapping, while another became a "quack doctor." Five years later they returned to Ephrata and, then, with new recruits, established settlements on the Monongahela River and on the Cheat River at Dunkard's Bottom south of present Pittsburgh. Two Ephrata brethren who joined the Eckerlins at Dunkard's Bottom previously had settled in 1752 on Massanutten Mountain just south of Opechem Creek, where Joseph Bill taught school among the Quakers sometime between 1751 and 1755. They remained until the church people in the valley began to suspect them of "spying, counterfeiting, and holding secret celebrations of the Roman mass."[58]

It is thus very suggestive that the highly mobile Joseph Bill, a chemical doctor, philosopher, and counterfeiter, should have passed through Weiser's house and, apparently, much more of the German orbit of pietism and hermeticism, particularly that dominated by the Eckerlin brothers. If so, he was not the only con artist to work the edges of the Ephrata community. In 1747, William Young, a Philadelphia "trickster," joined the cloister only to run up £200 in debts and then abscond. Another complex fraud involved an English convert named Israel Seymour, who set up a parallel community on French Creek before fleeing to South Carolina in the early 1750s after defrauding several families of the noncelibate Ephrata Householders. Within a few years a wave of monetary and hermetic occultism hit Ephrata. In January 1761 a series of spirits appeared to Elizabeth Beeler in the Virginia settlements, claiming to be the ghosts of her husband's former wives. Demanding that their children receive fair treatment, the spirits revealed the location of hidden bills and coins throughout the house. The spirits were calmed only by a late-night ritual in the Saal at Ephrata, presided over by Conrad Beissel. In 1762, Catherine Hummer, the wife of a Dunker preacher settled to the west of the Susquehanna, had visions and spiritual revelations that continued to 1765, attracting great crowds of believers. Similarly at Ephrata in 1762 a new member established an alchemical laboratory somewhere near the cloister, where he attempted to distill the red tincture and the philosopher's stone.[59] One wonders whether Joseph Bill was aware of these hermetic endeavors at Ephrata as he toiled over his engraving at Frederick Weiser's house. It would also be interesting to know the identity of a "vagabond doctor" who caused such strife among the Massanutten Sabbatarians when he was allowed to live in Samuel Eckerlin's house in 1767.[60]

In sum, it seems that from the mid–eighteenth century such detached conning men, living on the edges of sectarian communities, collected a smattering of archaic hermetical knowledge for their personal collections of professional "secrets." The shreds and fragments of the alchemic philosophy preserved by hermetic wizards like Joseph Bill, Solomon Prentice, and Ransford Rogers, deployed in occult con artistry, quack-doctoring, and the projection of counterfeit notes and coin, determined much of the ground upon which the postrevolutionary cult of divining would emerge.

We are left with a paradox. The occult concepts that would inform divining in postrevolutionary New England were in great measure rooted in the counterfeiters' experiences in sectarian communities where the hermetic traditions were preserved from the seventeenth century. But the treasure-divining that exploded after the Revolution seems to have been a spiritual defense against the temptation to engage in the counterfeit trade.

By and large, the early national diviners were not counterfeiters. The two occupied the same social world, and to a great degree the impetus to divine for treasure, with its language of volatile metals, must have been rooted in the lure and lore of counterfeiting. Diviners clearly had the opportunity to take the plunge into counterfeiting, yet they chose an occult way to wealth. However much in vain – and perhaps silly – divining would not harm the community and required an intense belief in the sympathy of the natural and the supernatural.

Divining may be interpreted as a defensive reaction to the threats and temptations of counterfeiting, a spiritual alternative to secular fraud and deceit. But they were part of a common culture, the opposite sides of the same debased alchemical coin, simultaneously interpenetrating and antagonistic. If counterfeiting threatened demonic temptation and destruction, it also provided a window, however hazy and dusty, onto the grand alchemical tradition that had crumbled under the advance of science in the twilight of the seventeenth century. Divining and counterfeiting perpetuated the medieval distinction between the mystical philosopher and the fraudulent puffer, one searching for a spiritual control of matter and for a Gnostic transcendence of earthly realities by white magical practice, the other producing deception and fraud, with dark implications of evil and black magic. And beyond divining, itself compromised by the search for easy wealth, lay the revitalized millenarian hermeticism, with its dream of ancient theology and the powers of the primal Adam. Restoration, divining, counterfeiting: these were a volatile triptych framing fields of purity and danger within a broader hermetic culture. The early history of the Mormon church would be entangled on the complex and ambiguous boundaries dividing these multiple hermetic purities and dangers.

6

I Was Born in Sharon

I was born in Sharon, Vermont, in 1805, where the first quarter of my life grew with the growth and strengthened with the strength of that "first-born" State of the "united Thirteen." . . . I appeal to the "Green Mountain boys" of my native State to rise to the majesty of virtuous freemen, and by all honorable means help to bring Missouri to the bar of justice. If there is one whisper from the spirit of Ethan Allen, or a gleam from the shade of General Stark, let it mingle with our sense of honor and fire our bosoms for the cause of suffering innocence.

> Joseph Smith's "Appeal to the Green Mountain Boys," November 29, 1843, to be distributed throughout New York State and Vermont by Parley P. Pratt[1]

THE TOWNS OF CENTRAL VERMONT were the immediate hearth of Joseph Smith's Mormon church. The Smiths of Topsfield were predisposed to witchcraft beliefs and metallurgical dreams; the Macks of Lyme lived in a religious milieu of visions, healing miracles, and sectarian perfectionism. The marriage in 1796 of Joseph Smith Sr. and Lucy Mack in Tunbridge, Vermont, brought both streams of familial culture into a single household. So, too, the northern frontier attracted many other people from the dissenting, sectarian communities of older New England, people at odds with orthodoxy, people sharing a deep-rooted affinity for works of wonder. And here this prepared people encountered the full force of the late-eighteenth-century reformulations of the hermetic tradition. Long before the 1820s the Smiths were caught up in the dialectic of spiritual mystery and secular fraud framed in the hostile symbiosis of divining and counterfeiting and in the diffusion of Masonic culture in an era of sectarian fervor and profound millenarian expectation. The specific circumstances of the popular experience of religion and the occult in postrevolutionary Vermont provided a pivot between past and future, the loom upon which the specific fabric of the Mormon cosmology began to be woven from strands of culture and predisposition running deep into the past.

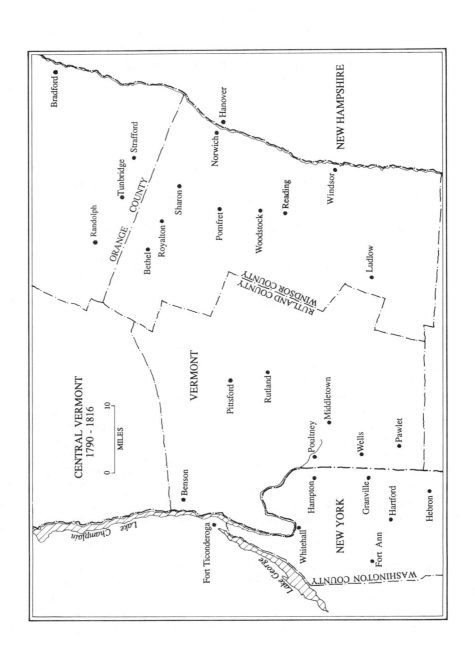

In 1791 Asael Smith moved his family from Topsfield to Orange County in east-central Vermont, where he purchased land in Tunbridge Gore, unincorporated land lying between the towns of Tunbridge and Royalton, eventually totaling four hundred acres. Solomon Mack's son Stephen settled in Tunbridge in 1793 and invited his sister Lucy to visit him after Lovisa died in 1794. Two years later, on January 24, 1796, Joseph Smith Sr. and Lucy Mack were married, and with the assistance of their families began six years of householding in Tunbridge. In 1799, having moved back and forth between Marlow, Gilsum, and Montague, Solomon and Lydia Mack also settled in Tunbridge.[2]

Having just left a Topsfield ringing with talk of "copper-lots," life in eastern Vermont brought the Smiths into yet another New England region where mining for precious metals occupied many people's attention. In 1793, two years after the Smiths' move to Tunbridge, iron sulphate ore was discovered in great quantities in a belt of towns running north from adjacent Strafford through Vershire and Corinth. People in Vershire began also to look for copper, following – in the words of a mid-nineteenth-century antiquarian – the Welsh adage that "mundic always rides a good horse." Forming themselves into a Farmer's Company, they dug and found copper sulphate, described as having a "bright golden yellow appearance." In south Strafford the deposits would be exploited by a group of Boston-based entrepreneurs, who were incorporated as the Vermont Mineral Factory Company in 1809. Hopes were high that lands in neighboring Thetford, Norwich, and Sharon would also be ore bearing, and lots were bought and sold in a speculative atmosphere that must have reminded Asael Smith of the copper mines in Topsfield. In any event, the mining fever ran high in the region where Asael and his son Joseph established households in the 1790s.[3]

These years also saw a crystallizing of religious belief for Asael and Joseph Smith. In December 1797, with Joseph's brother Jesse and fourteen others, they signed off from the town to form a Universalist Society.[4] The Smiths' Universalism probably ran back to their years in Topsfield, but they were joining a rising wave of religious perfectionism that was making the hill towns of northern New England as much a center of radical religion as southeast New England had been in the previous century.

Originally settled by New Light Congregationalists and Baptists, Vermont was one of the prime fields for the explosion of the perfectionist churches and sects of the early Republic. New England Universalism was just spreading into Vermont in the 1790s, carried by the itinerancy of Massachusetts and New Hampshire preachers, as was the gospel of the Freewill Baptists. Methodism, spreading up from the Mid-Atlantic, was established in six circuits in Vermont in 1800, a year when a thousand people flocked to a Methodist revival in Vershire, adjacent to Tunbridge. By the 1830s, when Mormon missionaries began to move through Vermont, there were Freewill Baptist meetings in more than fifty towns, Methodist circuits based in at least seventy towns, and Universalists in over eighty towns. Widely distributed, these meetings tended to be located in the hilly interior towns rather than the more prosperous valley localities.[5] Elias Smith, son of Baptists from Lyme and the founder of the New England branch of the restorationist Christian Connection, had his youthful visions of the Lamb on the Mount in Woodstock, south of Tunbridge; by 1809 agents of his *Herald of Gospel Liberty* were situated in Woodstock and in Randolph and Bradford, hard by Tunbridge in Orange County. In 1817 a bearded prophet dressed in a bearskin, Isaac Bullard, swept through Woodstock, gathering a band of pilgrims who followed him west into New York and eventually on to Missouri.[6] By 1793 the Shakers were gathered in a community to the east in Enfield, New Hampshire, but perhaps they could not compete with this dense perfectionism, because their presence in early Vermont was confined to only a few outlying families. Perhaps it is only coincidental, but these few Vermont Shakers were situated in hotbeds of perfectionism, where sectarian movements emerged throughout the first half of the nineteenth century. In the 1790s Guilford, in the southeast adjacent to Massachusetts, was the center of a sect called the Dorrellites, led by former British soldier, William Dorrell, who was convinced of his powers of prophecy and immortality. In the 1840s the towns of Brattleboro and Putney to the north would be the site of the first of the perfectionist communities formed by John Humphrey Noyes to explore the virtues of "complex marriage." To the northwest in Rutland County, a Shaker family in Pittsford would have witnessed the rise and fall of two millenarian uprisings in the nearby towns of Poultney and Middletown, where in 1800 the New Israelites prophesied the Last Days and hunted for treasure, and where William Miller lived for many years before again announcing the advent of the end times in 1843. One of these Pittsford Shakers, Leman Copley, joined the Mormons briefly in Ohio in the early 1830s. Institutional or episodic, perfectionism and millennialism in Vermont were planted in very fertile soil, and in a tradition that had direct continuities with the similar movements of prerevolutionary Rhode Island and the greater Blackstone Valley.[7]

This perfectionist culture may have emboldened Asael Smith to commit his own beliefs to paper. In 1799 he wrote a long letter to his family that articulated his belief in universal salvation. Urging them to look to "the hidden man of the heart" rather than to "outward formalities," Asael was certain that "God is just to all, and his tender mercies are over all his works . . . there is no respect of persons with God, who will have all mankind to be saved and come to the knowledge of truth."[8] And, as we have seen, Asael's perfectionism had alchemical and hermetic analogues. Several years earlier, just before the marriage of Joseph and Lucy, Asael had written his letter to Jacob Towne in Topsfield. Sending his greetings to friends and acquaintances, Asael drew language from Nebuchadnezzar's dream in the Book of Daniel: "I believe that the stone is now cut out of the mountain without hands, spoken of by Daniel, and has smitten the image upon his feet." This language had once been deployed by radical English sectarians and was soon to be taken up again in his grandson's Church of Latter-day Saints; in the 1790s it could be found in the English prophet Richard Brothers's *Revealed Knowledge,* where the stone signified the restored Kingdom of God, soon to destroy all other kingdoms, as Asael hoped the stone would destroy "all monarchical and ecclesiastical tyranny."[9] The Masonic-millenarian connotations of Brothers's tracts, along with those of Christopher Love's writings and the anonymous *Remarkable Prophecy,* all circulating in New England in the 1790s, could well have shaped Asael's writing, complementing the alchemical connotations that this passage would have had for a family still in communication with the Townes, once owners of the Topsfield copper lots.[10]

This Masonic millenarianism also seems to have shaped the hermeticism and restorationism of the New Israelite cult of Middletown, led by the Wood family, recently moved from Norwich, Connecticut. One nineteenth-century account places Joseph Smith Sr. himself among the New Israelites. If true, it would have taken him about fifty miles from his young family in Tunbridge. In any event, Joseph would boast in the 1830s in Ohio that his divining career had begun decades before in Vermont.[11] The other Mormon connection with the New Israelites noted in this account is much more certain. William Cowdery Jr., the father of Oliver Cowdery, who would be Joseph Smith Jr.'s closest associate in the early years of the Mormon church, was connected to the New Israelites when he lived in Wells, Vermont, providing a room in his house for the counterfeiter Winchell. William Cowdery apparently learned to divine during these years, and his son Oliver carried with him to Palmyra and Harmony the power of the divining rod, which Joseph Smith spoke of in revelation as Oliver's "gift of working the rod."[12]

The story of the relationship between Joseph Smith Jr. and Oliver Cowdery is one of the central elements of early Mormon history. On April 5, 1829, twenty-three-year-old Oliver Cowdery presented himself to Joseph Smith in Harmony, Pennsylvania, and two days later replaced Martin Harris as the scribe for the translation of the *Book of Mormon.*

That May Joseph and Oliver experienced a vision in the woods at Harmony that restored to them the "keys" to the Priesthood of Aaron. For the next eight years Cowdery would be one of Smith's closest confidants.[13] According to Mormon tradition, Cowdery learned of Joseph's work when he boarded with the Smiths in the winter of 1828–9, while working as a schoolteacher in Palmyra, New York. But, as Mormon historians rarely note, this was not a chance relationship but an old connection, running back to Poultney and Tunbridge, Vermont, and to East Haddam, Connecticut.

Oliver Cowdery's great-grandfather Nathaniel moved his family in the 1720s from Charlestown to Hadley and Montague in the Connecticut Valley, and then down the river to East Haddam, where he was paying taxes by 1737. In 1761 he signed a protest against rebuilding the Millington Parish meetinghouse; two of his sons were married in Millington Parish in 1756 and 1760, where Solomon Mack married Lydia Gates in 1759. William Cowdery, Oliver's grandfather, married in 1760, joined the Millington church in 1763, and migrated to Reading, Vermont, south of Tunbridge in Windsor County, in 1786, where he was noted as a lay preacher. William Cowdery Jr., Oliver's father, married Rebecca Fuller, Lydia Gates's second cousin, and settled to the west in Wells, Rutland County, Vermont, by 1788. Other Cowderies settled to the east in Orange County. Between 1785 and 1790 two of Nathaniel Cowdery's sons, Jabez and Jacob, settled in Tunbridge. Both were physicians, and Jabez's wife, Ruth, was also a healer, who achieved "marvelous" cures. These Cowdery relations may have provided a connection between Joseph Smith Sr. and William Cowdery Jr. later in the decade when the New Israelites offered another species of the "marvelous." Certainly William Cowdery was drawn to the Ontario country of western New York at roughly the same time as the Smiths. In 1810 he and his family were living on Lake Ontario north of Palmyra, and after returning to Middletown Springs by 1814, the Cowderies were living in Arcadia, just east of Palmyra, in 1830.[14]

Oliver's father was not the first of the Cowderies to be drawn to Ontario County, for in the mid-1790s his uncle Dr. Jacob Cowdery disappeared, leaving his family in Tunbridge. A "great hunter," he ventured out to Canandaigua in western New York, married a second, bigamous, wife, had a son, and then returned to Tunbridge seven years later. This experiment in plural marriage may have reminded some – particularly his wife Mary Beckwith – of John Rogers of New London. It would have an echo in the covenant of celestial marriage inaugurated by Joseph Smith at Nauvoo some forty-five years later.[15]

The experience of the Smiths in Vermont was colored by perfectionist sectarianism and hermeticism; it was shaped by a growing impoverishment. The years following the end of the New Israelite episode were filled with particular misfortune for the young family of Joseph and Lucy Smith, the prophet's parents. After six years of farming in Tunbridge, the family moved to the bustling center of Randolph in the spring of 1802, where Joseph set himself up as a merchant, operating with $1,800 in goods on credit from Boston merchants. Hoping to turn a quick profit, he speculated in ginseng root for the China trade, taking a load to New York himself to avoid paying a partner. His earnings were stolen by a Royalton merchant who sailed with the ship to China and then fled to Canada when his fraud was discovered. Unable to meet their debts, Joseph and Lucy were forced to sell their farm in Tunbridge to cover their debts in Boston.[16]

This financial disaster struck a blow from which the Smiths would never recover. Instead of the stable, propertied independence that they had briefly enjoyed, they would be condemned to constant movement and tenancy over the next fifteen years, as the family grew larger and larger. Bitterness over fraud, deceit, and the threat of "secret combinations" would run though the formative Mormon text, the *Book of Mormon,* and through Lucy Mack Smith's biography of her son the prophet. Such bitterness lay behind Joseph's 1831 revelation at Kirtland that it was "forbidden to get into debt to thine enemies." Ultimately, the Mormon effort to establish an autarchic economy, first embodied in the Law of Consecration of February 1831, was an effort to separate the just from the iniquitous dealings of the world.[17] These concerns lay rooted in a long experience with economic failure and suspicion of fraud running back for decades into the eighteenth century, and coming to a climax for the Smiths in the ginseng swindle. The Smiths' failure to achieve an independent competency, interwoven with anxieties over illegitimate ways to wealth and perceptions of satanic power, would combine with traditions of hermeticism and restoration to shape the emergence of the Mormon church.

Moving from Randolph back to Tunbridge after the ginseng disaster in 1802, the Smiths moved on to Royalton for a few months sometime in 1804 and then moved to Sharon, where Joseph Jr. was born in December 1805. For the next eleven years the family would sink further and further into debt and tenancy, until the Cold Summer of 1816 pushed them out of the Upper Valley of Vermont onto the rolling hills of Ontario County, New York.[18]

The Smiths' misfortunes came as a coda to those of their parents. Solomon Mack, in particular, wrote of his life as a train of misery and bad luck in his *Narrative.* After a childhood indentured to a "gold-worshiping" master who failed to give him an education, Solomon Mack encountered a host of tribulations. In various ventures on land and sea, he gained and lost large tracts of land through accidents and injuries, and he lost cargoes of goods in perilous sea voyages to Nova Scotia. After one postrevolutionary voyage with his son Jason, he returned to find his family turned out of their house and property, and Jason's girlfriend married, convinced by a forged letter that they had perished at sea.[19] Once in Vermont, Solomon Mack was again reduced to poverty, this time for putting up bail money "for a number of people" who absconded, leaving him in debt to the state.[20] The Smiths of Topsfield fared better only in that their misfortunes started later, in the 1780s rather than in the 1730s. But the events of the 1780s were clearly very traumatic for Asael Smith and his family, as they were for many others. Both Asael and his father, Samuel, "lost considerably in the downfall of Continental paper," and Asael spent the late 1780s in Topsfield paying the debts left after his father's death in 1786, before moving to Tunbridge in 1791.[21]

These families also had troubling encounters with the counterfeiting underworld. Solomon Mack may have known of Joseph Bill, who had been born in neighboring Groton in 1720 in a similarly dissenting family, and who was well along in his career of counterfeiting by the time Mack came of age. Among other grueling adventures in the Champlain campaigns, Solomon marched in 1758 with Robert Rogers on a dangerous reconnaisance to Fort Ann. Here he was surrounded by counterfeiters, for Rogers had been arrested for counterfeiting with Owen Sullivan in New Hampshire in 1755 and freed from a trial on the condition that he raise a company of Rangers for the northern war; several of his officers and men had been arrested with him in New Hampshire. Taken sick in the winter of 1756, Solomon Mack was "carried to Albany in a wagon, where I saw five men hung at one time." Rogers's partner Owen Sullivan was hanged in New York in 1756, and Joseph Bill was one of five men sentenced to hang in Albany in 1773. Did Solomon Mack confuse these events when he sat down to write his life story in 1810 at the age of seventy-six?[22] Joseph Bill was posthumously related to the Macks by a 1786 marriage, but counterfeiting struck somewhat closer in the arrest of Lydia Gates Mack's cousin Stephen Gates for counterfeiting in 1773.[23]

From the 1760s through the 1780s, Solomon Mack's family lived in Connecticut Valley towns – Marlow and Gilsum, New Hampshire, and Montague, Massachusetts – that were surrounded by continuing counterfeiting activity. In the late 1760s Glazier Wheeler, the "money-maker known throughout New England," plied his trade at the head of a wide-ranging gang in Westmoreland, New Hampshire, and during the early years of the Revolution a network of Tory counterfeiters included families in Marlow and the adjacent towns of Alstead, Stoddard, and Keene. In the 1780s the valley buzzed with stories of the continuing operations of Glazier Wheeler, who "wrought openly for months . . . in New Salem" high in the hills above Montague, where the Macks lived from 1777 to the early 1790s.[24] The Smiths of Topsfield apparently avoided any entanglement with the Essex County gangs of the 1740s, but when they moved to Dunbarton, New Hampshire, in the 1770s they were exposed to the threat of Tory counterfeiters. The townspeople petitioned the legislature in 1779 that the presence of the families of Tory exiles threatened them with the "danger of receiving counterfeit money, and every evil attending *Spys, Lurking Villains, & Cut Throats, & Murderers.*"[25]

Counterfeiting was also well established in the Upper Valley of Vermont when the Smiths and the Macks settled there in the 1790s. Tunbridge lay in Orange County, the Vermont side of the greater Coos region, long a base for counterfeiters. Glazier Wheeler had operated across the river in Haverhill in the 1760s, and Stephen Burroughs grew up just downriver at Hanover. The years following the discovery of the copper deposits – and the settlement of the Smiths in adjacent Tunbridge – saw a number of counterfeiters arrested in these towns. In February 1795, a Seba Beebe of Pomfret was sentenced by the state supreme court to "have his right ear cut off" and to be branded on the forehead with a "C" for passing Spanish milled dollars in Strafford. Two years later two other groups of counterfeiters were arrested in the nearby towns of Norwich and Bradford.[26]

Did this outbreak of coining have a Burroughs connection? Stephen Burroughs lived at his father's house in Hanover, New Hampshire, from the fall of 1795 through the spring of 1799, when he departed for Canada and began his career as a large-scale counterfeiter. The Windsor County court records suggest that counterfeiting subsided in the region around 1800, just after Burroughs's departure.[27]

Circumstances of kinship and settlement connected the Mack family with this counterfeiting world. After his conviction and ear-cropping, Seba Beebe, originally from Lyme, Connecticut, moved his family to the Canadian border town of Stanstead, Quebec, establishing a neighborhood called Beebe, which extended south into the Vermont town of Derby. Here his family was joined by other migrants from Lyme, coming by way of Marlow, New Hampshire, including a cousin married to a daughter of the Reverend Ebenezer Mack of Lyme. Over the next decade Stanstead would be the headquarters of Stephen Burroughs and his company of counterfeiters.[28]

A second cycle of counterfeiting, running from 1804 to 1809, brought a deluge of counterfeit bills from Stephen Burroughs's Stanstead workshop as well as from more local sources. Royalton, where the Smiths were living, was an early target, as were the towns in the immediate neighborhood.[29] Joseph Smith Sr. was drawn into the counterfeiters' web, certainly as a victim, and possibly as an accomplice.

Among the forty-six counterfeiting cases heard at the Windsor County Supreme Court between 1804 and 1809, sixteen involved Royalton and Sharon, where the Smiths lived at various times, and the adjacent towns of Pomfret, Bethel, and Strafford.[30] Joseph Smith was involved in at least two and perhaps three counterfeiting cases in these years. In the clearest of these cases, a Beniah Woodward was convicted of passing on April 1, 1807, a counterfeit ten-dollar bill upon the New York State Bank to Joseph Smith of Royalton, a town where Smith is known to have lived, though – according to his wife's account – the family was living in Sharon at the time. Fawn Brodie has argued that Joseph Sr. also was passed counterfeit bills by Abner Hayes of Woodstock on April 13, 1807, though the court records describe Smith as being "of Bethel," just west of Royalton.

The most controversial case involved a George Downer of Sharon, who was convicted in 1807 of having passed two counterfeit bills in Sharon the previous spring. Daniel Woodward, apparently a descendant of Beniah, wrote in 1870 that "Joseph Smith, Sr., was, at times, engaged in hunting for Captain Kidd's buried treasure; and he also became implicated with one Jack Downing, in counterfeiting money, but turned state's evidence, and escaped the penalty." Apparently referring to the George Downer trial, this would suggest that Joseph Sr. had been "seduced" by the counterfeiter gang, briefly succumbing to the temptation of easy money, which many thousands in his circumstances had done in the previous three-quarters of a century. Historians, including Fawn Brodie, have rejected this Woodward evidence as biased, but they have neglected to mention that the Windsor court record included a petition by Downer to have his conviction overturned. Downer complained:

> First, that the only evidence against the respondent in the prosecution was the uncorroborated Testimony of one who was an acknowledged accomplice, which was insufficient in Law to found said Verdict upon. Secondly That the Testimony of said witness did not relate to facts generally but to the Confessions made by the respondent to the witness.

If Downer meant Joseph Smith Sr. in this reference, then Woodward apparently was grounding his claim on some basis in fact. The evidence for Smith being involved in counterfeiting is at least as good, if not better, than the evidence for his involvement in the New Israelite movement.[31]

These years saw the Smith family constantly on the move, according to Lucy Mack Smith's history. Joseph the prophet was born in Sharon in

1805, and the next son, Samuel H. Smith, was born in Tunbridge in 1808. From there the family moved back to Royalton, where two more sons were born in 1810 and 1811. If Joseph Sr. did fall into counterfeiting in 1807, it was only one of a number of ways in which the family confronted their misfortunes. Joseph Sr. apparently took to drinking, a compulsion he was not able to shake until the formation of the Mormon church two decades later.32 But the Smiths had other, more spiritual resources to draw upon, resources that played a pivotal role in the shaping of early Mormonism.

Asael Smith, with his sons Joseph and Jesse, had helped to form the Universalist Society in Tunbridge in 1797, but in the years following, the men of the Smith family argued vehemently against joining any denomination. In 1803, as Joseph Sr.'s commercial venture in Randolph was dissolving, Lucy was stricken with what was diagnosed as consumption and in the depths of her illness had a converting vision of the voice of God, rather like that of her sister Lovisa. Revivalism among local Methodists drew her into a Methodist meeting, and Joseph, in a moment of weakness, attended with her. Asael and Jesse argued furiously with Joseph for this capitulation to evangelicalism, and according to Lucy Smith's earliest account, Asael went so far as to throw "Tom Paine's *Age of Reason* into the house and angrily bade him read it until he believed it." Though Lucy continued to feel the pull of the mainstream churches, the Smiths would remain outside the fold of the church while they lived in Vermont.33

The Smith's spiritual world did not include organized religion, but it did apparently include treasure-divining. During the Mormons' Kirtland, Ohio, years, Joseph Sr. would claim to have been divining for treasure for thirty years, presumably since the first decade of the century. If he did join the New Israelite movement, it was before setting up in trade in Randolph and before his failed venture in ginseng. Divining was one way to wealth, commerce was another, and Joseph Sr. apparently tried them in quick succession at the turn of the century. Years later, both he and his son Joseph would be immersed in the lure of divining in the Palmyra region, and in the 1830s, as the Mormon church faced financial crisis in Kirtland, Joseph Jr. turned first to divining and then to banking.

Of course, one might well ask why Joseph Smith Sr. would have ventured fifty miles away from home, west over the Green Mountains, to divine for treasure with the New Israelites in years that saw the birth of his two eldest children, Alvin in 1798 and Hyrum in 1800. There is no convincing answer to this question, but there was a history of connections between the Tunbridge area where the Smiths lived and the west Rutland County towns where the New Israelites emerged. One of these connections was the Cowdery family, who had households settled in both Tunbridge and Wells, where they were involved with the New Israelites. The Macks had a long-standing connection with the region just west of Wells and Poultney in New York State, in the lee of Lake Champlain in central Washington County. At Fort Ann, two townships to the west, Solomon Mack had fought against the Indians with Rogers's Rangers in 1758, and in Granville, between Fort Ann and Wells, he had lost a 1,600-acre grant of land in the early 1760s. This family history might have drawn Joseph to the lower reaches of the Champlain Valley, and there are hints of ongoing connections. Contact between the Smiths and the Woods may have been revived decades later, for Joseph Smith Jr. spoke of a gold bar in a cave in Watertown, Jefferson County, New York, near Ellisburg, where the Woods emigrated after the collapse of the New Israelite cult.[34] Isaac Hale and Elizabeth Lewis, parents of Emma Hale, who married Joseph in 1827, made up another connection in west Rutland County. They had lived in Wells, were married there in 1790 before leaving for Harmony, Pennsylvania, and left considerable kin connections in this divining town.[35]

Finally, from the 1790s on, the Smith family was exposed to Masonic influences, and Freemasonry formed an important link between Tunbridge and west Rutland County, between the Smiths and the Cowderies, and between the millenarianism of the 1790s and the culture of early Mormonism. The Grand Lodge of Vermont was organized in 1794, and in 1798 it chartered its fifteenth lodge in the town of Randolph, where Joseph and Lucy Smith settled in 1802. Joseph might have joined this lodge, but membership lists are unavailable. A "Joseph Smith" did join the Ontario Lodge in Canandaigua, New York, in December 1817, a year after the Smiths moved west, and Joseph's second son, Hyrum, was a member of the Mount Moriah Lodge in Palmyra during the 1820s. None of this proves a Masonic affiliation in Vermont for Joseph Smith Sr. but among officers of the Federal Lodge in Randolph there was at least one close relation of the Smiths. John C. Waller, who married Joseph's sister Priscilla in 1796, was the lodge's Senior Warden in 1804; and a John Smith serving as Senior Warden in 1813 may have been another of Joseph's siblings.[36]

The Masonic history of west Rutland County, the New Israelite territory, is somewhat more complex. Here Masonic groups were chartered by New York organizations, reflecting New York's former authority in western Vermont and the social relations spanning the New York–Vermont border in the southern Champlain Valley. The first lodges in the area were formed between 1793 and 1796 at Hampton and Granville, New York, and in Rutland and Pawlet, Vermont; these lodges probably attracted members from the nearby New Israelite towns of Poultney, Wells, and Middletown. They were ordinary symbolic, or "blue," lodges, offering initiation into the three degrees of Entered Apprentice, Fellow Craft, and Master Mason of English Freemasonry. They were soon followed by the lodges and chapters of the Royal Arch, which took the aspiring Mason through his first steps toward the hermetic culture of the higher degrees. Mark Masters lodges, some of which were later upgraded into Royal Arch chapters, were formed by the New York Grand Chapter around 1800 in Granville and in Rutland and Poultney. An unchartered Mark Masters lodge operated in Pawlet between 1797 and 1799 and was warranted in 1805 by the new Vermont Grand Chapter. The concentration of Masonic institutions in the southern Champlain Valley towns did not go unopposed. Even though there would be no lodge in the town until 1807, the Congregational church in Poultney was thrown into turmoil by the Masonic affiliation of its minister, Ithamar Hibbard, as was a Baptist church in nearby Hartford, New York. The minister of the Poultney church in the 1820s, Ethan Smith, was an ardent Antimason. Until 1807, however, there were no blue lodges in Poultney or in the other towns where the New Israelites once divined for treasure and awaited the millennium. But on October 6, 1807, the Grand Lodge of Vermont chartered the Rainbow Lodge and the Morning Star Lodge in the New Israelite towns of Middletown and Poultney. On the same day the Grand Lodge granted a charter to the Rising Sun Lodge in Royalton where Joseph and Lucy Smith were living with their young family on a farm rented from Solomon Mack.[37]

The records of these three lodges are not available, so a detailed examination of membership is impossible. It is, nevertheless, striking that the petitions for these lodges, located in the towns so central to the proto-Mormon experience in Vermont, were all brought forward in the Grand Lodge on the same day. Although we cannot determine the details of the Masonic dynamics connecting Royalton with the New Israelite region, the records of the Grand Lodge and the Grand Chapter indicate that Freemasonry was very important to the Cowdery family, another important link between the New Israelites and early Mormonism. Stephen Cowdery (born 1791), the older brother of the Mormon Oliver Cowdery, was suspended from the Rainbow Lodge in Middletown in 1816 and expelled in 1817. Stephen may have been something of a black sheep in a Masonic family. His father, William Cowdery, born in East Haddam, Connecticut, in 1765, and his older brother, Warren A. Cowdery (born 1788), later to be a leading Mormon, were members of the Royal Arch Mark Masters lodge in Pawlet. William Cowdery served in the Pawlet lodge as Master Overseer in 1805 and Junior Warden in 1807 and 1809. It is not unlikely that William Cowdery was introduced to even more rarefied levels of Masonic ritual when Jeremy Cross, a traveling Masonic promoter, established a Council of the Cryptic Rite in Poultney sometime around 1817.[38]

The Cowdery family history is thus very revealing. At the turn of the century William Cowdery was deeply involved in the New Israelite movement, boarding Winchell, the counterfeiter at the center of the story, by one account; three decades later his son, Oliver Cowdery, bearing a divining "rod of nature," would serve as Joseph Smith's scribe in the translation of the *Book of Mormon*.[39] Between these two episodes, the men of the Cowdery family were immersed in high-degree Freemasonry, certainly the Royal Arch, possibly the Cryptic Rite.

In this case, then, high-degree Masonry seems to have served as a refuge for disappointed millenarians. In another, it would be a stepping stone to millenarianism. William Miller, the founder of the Millerites, was born to Baptist parents in Pittsfield, Massachusetts, and grew up in Hampton, New York, just west of Poultney, Vermont. Settling in Poultney in 1803, he associated with men who "were deeply affected with skeptical principles and deistical theories," beliefs "that would pass with the world as philosophical, pure, and sublime." Joining the Freemasons, Miller was accepted into the local Mark Masters lodge in 1810 and two years later was appointed Overseer. Converted by his Baptist uncle and grandfather after serving in the War of 1812, Miller embarked on a close study of the Scriptures. In the decades following, Miller would hear his own "Midnight Cry" and lead a great following to expect the end of the earth in 1843 and 1844 (exactly as the New Israelites of Poultney had in 1800), in the same years that Joseph Smith Jr. was putting the final touches on the new Mormon cosmology at Nauvoo.[40]

There were other elements to this complex tangle of Freemasonry and millenarianism in the New Israelite towns. In 1823 Ethan Smith, the Antimasonic Congregational minister in Poultney, published a text entitled *View of the Hebrews, or the Tribes of Israel in America*. As had Richard Brothers, the English prophet of the 1790s, Ethan Smith emphasized that the millennium and the restoration of the Kingdom of God depended on the return of the Jews to Jerusalem. In particular, the fulfillment of ancient prophecy required the return of the Ten Lost Tribes to Israel. On the basis of a report of a parchment book found in Pittsfield, Massachusetts (William Miller's birthplace), and stories of metal artifacts and plates recovered from Indian burial mounds in western New York and Ohio, Ethan Smith was convinced that the American Indian peoples were the Lost Tribes. The same general idea would stand at the center of Joseph Smith's *Book of Mormon*, and it seems clear that Oliver Cowdery was familiar with Ethan Smith's book when he joined Joseph Smith in translating the *Book of Mormon* in 1827.[41]

Ethan Smith drew upon an orthodox Congregational culture for his millennial views, but millennialism had much wider connections, including the mythology of lost texts and mysterious artifacts embraced by the ritual culture of Royal Arch Freemasonry. Ethan Smith himself was opposed to Freemasonry, but his Masonic neighbors easily might have identified the lost prophetic artifacts of Masonic legend with lost books or metallic plates describing Indian origins in terms of the Lost Tribes of Israel.[42]

The mysteries of the higher degrees – both those described and those inferred – constituted a fertile field reinforcing the connection between divining impulses and millenarianism and perfectionism. All of these themes, and that of counterfeiting, would play critical roles in the emergence of Mormonism.

Just as did the perfectionist sectarianism of the early Republic, divining and Freemasonry appear repeatedly in the histories of other early Mormon families besides the Smiths and the Cowderies. The family of Josiah Stowell, who would hire Smith to divine for a silver mine in the Susquehanna Valley in 1825, had lived in Guilford, Vermont, in 1785 and 1786, precisely the years when Silas Hamilton recorded the mining activities of four Guilford men in his journal of treasure dreams and diggings, and just prior to the rise of the Dorrellites in the same locality. The Pecks, a leading family among those converted to Mormonism in Colesville, New York, in 1830, were also from Guilford. Brigham Young, who apparently believed in the divining stories for his entire life, was born in 1801 in Hamilton's town of Whitingham, just west of Guilford. Newell K. Whitney was born just north of these towns in Marlborough, Vermont, in 1795. Brigham Young and Heber C. Kimball would be given rods by Joseph Smith as signs of their faithful apostlehood; on a number of occasions Kimball received answers "by the rod" to questions posed in prayer.[43] And dozens of men who converted to Mormonism in the 1830s had been Freemasons before the rise of Antimasonry; when Joseph Smith established a lodge at Nauvoo, Illinois, in 1842, more than thirty former Masons were available to form the charter membership. Among them, Heber C. Kimball had joined the Milner Lodge in Victor, New York, in 1825, and in 1826 he had petitioned for admission to the Royal Arch Chapter in Canandaigua, just before Antimasonry shut down the lodges in the Burned-over District; thirty years later Kimball would speak of Mormon temple ritual in terms of a Masonic restorationism, claiming Mormonism was "the true Masonry."[44] Masonic imagery could capture the imaginations of non-Masons, as in Parley Pratt's 1830 vision of a Masonic square and compass above the hills of the New Lebanon Valley in eastern New York.[45]

A mass of evidence thus suggests that the various manifestations of a popular hermeticism – Freemasonry, divining, and counterfeiting – played an important role in shaping the cultural experience of future Mormons in the hill towns of early Vermont. We also know, however, that these future Mormons were attracted to perfectionist Christian religion. Which, we might ask, was more important?

An answer, however imperfect, may be gleaned from a quantitative analysis of the hermetic and sectarian influences apparently at work in the various towns in Vermont where 123 Mormon converts were born: the presence of Freewill Baptist, Methodist, and Universalist churches or meetings and of Masonic lodges and chapters; the records of petitions for convicted counterfeiters; and local histories of divining. Obviously a host of problems plague such an analysis, and it would be vastly preferable to know in detail the personal histories of individuals. However, if not taken too seriously, the results of this exercise are quite suggestive.

First, the best single relationship between the towns of Mormon origin and these six characteristics conforms with previous investigations of the religious background of Mormon converts. Vermont towns with Methodist circuits in 1835 were the most likely to produce Mormons. The particular salience of Methodist background for the first American converts to Mormonism has been noted by various historians and has been demonstrated for those people converted in Britain in the 1840s, where it was the largest category of prior religious affiliation.[46]

But, strong as it was, this relationship between Mormon origins and Methodist meetings was only marginally stronger than that with towns producing petitions for counterfeiters, or with Masonic lodges, Royal Arch chapters, Freewill Baptist meetings, or even histories of divining. Most importantly, it was the *combination* of sectarian and hermetic influences in a given town that was best correlated with Mormon conversion; conversely, those towns showing the *absence of either* and particularly the *absence of both* had a very low likelihood of producing Mormon converts. Any sectarian–hermetic combination of Methodists, Freewill Baptists, Masonic societies, and counterfeiting petitions correlated with Mormon conversion. The combination of divining, Freemasonry, and Mormon conversion was a relative rarity, but the four towns where this combination pertained – Milton, Poultney, Rutland, and Rockingham – together produced fifteen converts, the largest concentration of Mormon conversion of any category in this analysis. Tunbridge, Royalton, and nearby towns in Orange and Windsor counties producing Mormon converts were notable for their combination of hermetic and sectarian influences, whereas the towns around Poultney in Rutland County accounted for most of the localities where two hermetic influences converged.

Although any interpretation of these patterns must remain tentative, they do suggest that the emergence of Mormon belief among Vermont-born converts was closely associated with exposure to the tangle of hermetic culture with sectarian perfectionism. Clearly, sectarian origins do not tell the entire story of the preconditions to Mormon conversion. Rather, the attraction to Christian perfection was interlocked and continuous with the fields of purity and danger in the popular culture of contemporary hermeticism. This intersection of sectarian and hermetic purity and danger only becomes more important as the Mormon story moves west from Vermont into New York, Ohio, Illinois, Utah, and California.

What then of the Smiths? Joseph Smith Sr., moving his family from one hardscrabble situation to another, was certainly too poor to have been a Freemason in good standing. His Masonic education would have come from hearsay, kin ties to Freemasons, Masonic manuals, and his fascination with the related hermetic "field" of occult divining, if not also from his brush with counterfeiting. But he was clearly committed to the ideal of "restoration" circulating in various eddies – Masonic and Christian-perfectionist – in the Upper Valley of Vermont. The winter of 1810–11 saw a revival in the towns around Royalton, and Grandfather Solomon Mack was converted, apparently to evangelical Calvinism, and denounced Universalism; religious fervor suffused his *Narrative,* which he published sometime in the following year.[47] On his part, Joseph Sr. "became much excited upon the subject of religion," but he stood firm against organized evangelism. According to one account of the 1840s, he "contended" for an unequivocal restoration of the primitive church, "for the ancient order, as established by our Lord and Savior Jesus Christ and his Apostles."[48] Apparently, he also began to have dreams that reinforced this position, dreams that we shall consider in relation to the text of the *Book of Mormon.* Such sentiments were not uncommon in the Royalton neighborhoods; another son of Royalton, Orestes Brownson, was warned in 1815 by an old woman to avoid all churches except that persisting from apostolic times.[49]

The Smiths may have been captivated by visions of restoration, but they had little free time or leisure, for these were years of unremitting movement and affliction. Moving across the Connecticut River to Lebanon, New Hampshire, two children – including Joseph Jr. – almost died of typhus, and their recovery was ascribed to miraculous powers. The Smith family circumstances were lower than they had ever been, and tenancy in Norwich, Vermont, in 1814 promised only more of the same. Then three successive years of crop failure, culminating in the Cold Summer of 1816, brought the family to a crisis. The solution would lie in the stream of emigration flowing out of the New England hills and across the rolling country of New York's Burned-over District. Here the Smiths would produce a prophet forged in the cross-pressures of hermetic purity and danger, offering a refuge for Christian and Masonic restorationists in an Antimasonic age.[50]

PART III

The Mormon Dispensation

7

Secret Combinations and Slippery Treasures in the Land of Zarahemla

[A]nd Ammaron said unto me . . . when ye are about twenty and four years old . . . go to the land Antum, unto a hill which shall be called Shim; and there I have deposited unto the Lord all the sacred engravings concerning this people. And behold, ye shall take the plates of Nephi unto yourself, and the remainder shall ye leave in the place where they are; and ye shall engrave on the plates of Nephi all the things that ye have observed concerning this people. And I, Mormon, being a descendant of Nephi, (and my father's name was Mormon) I remembered the things which Ammaron commanded me. And it came to pass that I, being eleven years old, was carried by my father into the land southward, even to the land of Zarahemla.

The Book of Mormon[1]

THE SMITHS' MOVE TO PALMYRA began in the summer of 1816, when Joseph Sr. departed on a trip west to Ontario County.[2] Lucy and the family followed the next winter, but their journey was not made without yet more encounters with fraud and deceit. Having thought that she had cleared their debts in Norwich, Lucy was confronted by creditors whose books showed outstanding balances, and on the road through Utica their teamster attempted to steal their team of horses. Once in Palmyra the family set up a small "cake and beer shop" and began to make a living peddling pies, boiled eggs, gingerbread, root beer, and hand-painted oilcloth table-coverings and by working as day laborers in gardens, shops, and farms in the vicinity of the growing town. By 1818 they had accumulated sufficient cash to begin making payments on a hundred-acre farm several miles south of town over the line in east Farmington, soon to be incorporated as the town of Manchester.[3]

Despite these setbacks and small beginnings, emigration ushered in a nine-year period of relative calm and stability for the Smiths. The Manchester farm gave the Smiths their first hopes of independent competency since their early days in Tunbridge, and in this setting Joseph Smith Jr. came of age. But if their life was more stable, it was not without its troubles and pressures. Joseph's experience with religion and the occult was shaped in great part by a continuing conflict over religion between his father and mother, and by the pressing need for income to pay the farm mortgage. There were other familial stresses. Joseph's eldest brother, Alvin, died suddenly in 1823, done in, the family feared, by a doctor's mismedication. A year later there were rumors that his body had been stolen, and the family had to exhume his body, a gruesome process. And there seem to have been tensions among the surviving brothers: on one occasion someone fired a shot at Joseph, and his brother William carried a grudge against him for decades. The *Book of Mormon* itself would be filled with violent fraternal struggle.[4] It was in these circumstances, around 1825, that the hermetic-restorationist dialectic of purity and danger – of divining, Freemasonry, and counterfeiting – reemerged in the history of the Smith family, formatively shaping the story of Mormon origins.

In 1824, as commerce began to move on the Erie Canal, religious revival struck Palmyra and Manchester, reopening deep divisions within the Smith household. Lucy Mack Smith, long searching for a stable church environment, settled on the Presbyterian church, joining with three of her children, Hyrum, Samuel, and Sophronia. But Joseph sided with his father, attending briefly but then staying away. Apparently Joseph Sr. was having dreams of finding spiritual peace in a meetinghouse, suggesting that it was time to join a church. But he bore ill will toward the Presbyterian minister, who had implied that his oldest son, Alvin, was doomed to hell for not attending church before his death in 1823.[5] According to several accounts Joseph Jr. caught "the spark of Methodism" during the revival summer of 1824, attending "the camp meeting away down in the woods, on the Vienna Road" east of Palmyra village. He wanted to "feel and shout like the rest" and became what was described as "a very passable exhorter in evening meetings." But Joseph Sr. was still opposed to the evangelical churches, and his son accommodated to his opinion. Without the reinforcement that the patriarch Asael had provided in Vermont, however, he was unable to dissuade his wife from remaining with the Presbyterians.[6]

One point of harmony in the Smith family's religious culture, however, lay in the area of dreams and visions. Both Joseph Sr. and Lucy experienced dreams filled with religious symbolism in the decades after 1800, in a family tradition that stretched back to the Macks' life in Montague and probably back to the perfectionist environment of East Haddam. Exactly when Joseph Jr. began to have visions is a point of intense debate, of critical importance to questions about prophetic legitimacy and authority.

Smith wrote his first descriptions of early visionary experiences in his 1832 manuscript history of his life. He wrote that between the ages of twelve and fifteen (1817 and 1820) he "pondered many things in my heart concerning the situation of the world" and came to the position that his father espoused: "by searching the scriptures I found that mankind did not come unto the Lord but that they had apostatised [sic] from the true and living faith." This conclusion was confirmed in a dream or vision: "in the 16th year of my age a pillar of light above the brightness of the sun at noon day" filled him with "the spirit of god" and told him that "the world lieth in sin."[7] This was the controversial First Vision, which stands as the primal authority for the Mormon dispensation. What is certain is that Joseph Jr. followed his father's path, interpreting his dreams as admonitions to avoid the organized denominations. It is also certain that his vision was not taken very seriously by other members of his family, because his mother and three of her children remained in good standing with the Presbyterians through 1828.[8]

In addition to working the family farm and probably helping in the cooper shop, a trade handed down among the Smiths from Topsfield days, Joseph joined his older brothers in working as a seasonal laborer, harvesting crops, building fences, and digging wells to build a cash reserve to cover the farm mortgage. This round of labor took him out of the household to neighbors, to adjacent towns, and to more distant places; it brought him into new relationships with other households and with shifting gangs of young men working the seasonal circuit. With that of his father, the influence of his peers and employers shaped Joseph's fascination with divining for hidden things.[9]

Joseph Smith's reputation as a diviner emerged in a culture of historically rooted magical practice filled with some very familiar names and traditions. The Smiths lived on Stafford Street in northwest Manchester, named for relatives of Joseph Stafford, the Tiverton almanac writer, doctor, and fortune-teller. Descended from Joseph Stafford's brother David, these families had brought the divining culture when they settled in this Quaker area around the turn of the century. The Staffords formed one of several circles of money-diggers that dug in the hills of northern Ontario County; Joshua Stafford had a seer-stone "which looked like a white marble and had a hole through the center."[10] The Chase family also had deep roots in early dissent, coming from a Quaker tradition running back through Tiverton, Swansea, and Cape Cod to Stephen Batchelor's Husbandmen. Sally Chase had a seer-stone of green glass that she used to divine for money – and to search for the Golden Plates after Joseph announced their discovery.[11]

Joseph Smith learned divining lore from his father and also from Luman Walter, who lived to the north in the town of Sodus. Walter arrived in Ontario County some time after August of 1818, when he escaped from jail in Hillsborough County, New Hampshire, having been convicted of a charge of "imposing himself upon the credulity of people in this vicinity, by a pretended knowledge of magic, palmistry, conjuration, &c." Described as a "clairvoyant" in a family history, Walter was notorious in Ontario County during the 1820s as a "conjuror." Like the Youngs and Macks, the first American Walter was a post-Restoration immigrant, arriving in Salem in 1679, and the family moved from northwest Connecticut to Vermont around 1800. Just as Joseph Stafford combined the occult with medicine and handed his knowledge down to subsequent generations, medical knowledge ran in this family, which included an Indian herbalist and a Thompsonian botanical doctor. The magical orbit of the Smith family in Ontario County was thus filled with influences running back to the various sectarian-occult traditions of the late-seventeenth-century migrations.[12]

Joseph Smith Jr. used three seer-stones during his divining years. He apparently found the first of these, described as "a whitish opaque stone," in September 1819, by borrowing Sally Chase's green glass; he found his favorite stone, a brown one, while he and his brothers were digging a well for the Chases in 1822. Sometime after 1825, while in the Susquehanna Valley, he was given a green stone by one Jack Belcher, a diviner and salt digger.[13] There are many accounts of Joseph Jr.'s gift with the seer-stone. In one story, Smith himself described his discovery of his first, white stone in mystical, even Masonic, terms. Looking in Sally Chase's glass, he saw the stone a hundred and fifty miles away, buried under a tree. "It soon became luminous, and dazzled his eyes, and after a short time it became as intense as the mid-day sun." Digging up the stone after an arduous journey, Smith related that he "placed it in his hat, and discovered that time, place, and distance were annihilated; that all intervening obstacles were removed, and that he possessed one of the attributes of Deity, an All-Seeing Eye." If the stone gave Joseph the "second sight," perhaps bordering on the divine powers of the hermetic *magus,* this sight was put to mundane purposes. Pomeroy Tucker wrote that Joseph used the stone for fortune-telling and divining for stolen property; Martin Harris described Joseph's divining for a lost pin in a pile of wooden shavings, with the stone and his face buried in "an old white hat." William Stafford recounted going with the Smiths to dig for "two or three kegs of gold and silver" near their farmhouse; while Joseph Sr. laid out the ritual circles of hazel

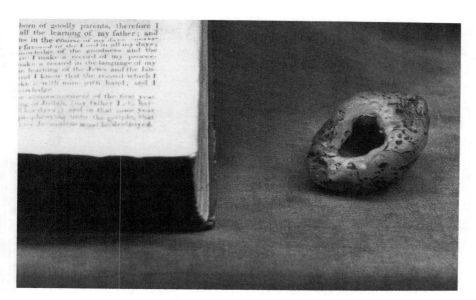

Joseph Smith's green seer-stone.
Courtesy of Princeton University Library.

sticks and the central steel rod, muttered appropriate incantations, and "enjoined" the crew to silence, Joseph Jr. remained in the house, "looking in his stone and watching the motions of the evil spirit."[14] By 1825 a well-defined group of participants in the Smiths' money-digging ventures had emerged. According to Martin Harris, "There was a company there in that neighborhood, who were digging for money supposed to have been hidden by the ancients. . . . They dug for money in Manchester, Palmyra, also in Pennsylvania, and in other places." Peter Ingersoll claimed that he "had frequent invitations to join their company, but always declined being one of their number." But on one occasion he did join in working the mineral rod with Joseph Sr., being "at leisure" while his oxen were feeding. When the elder Smith challenged him for his skepticism, Ingersoll "thought it best to conceal my feelings, preferring to appear the dupe of credulity, than to expose myself to his resentment." Family and neighborhood and broader peer group provided the recruits and an audience with varying levels of belief.[15]

It was in the context of money-digging that Joseph Smith received a second vision, this time from a spirit informing him of the sacred plates buried in the Hill Cumorah. Joseph recounted his vision of the plates to his money-digging friends, who would be known to the public as the

"Gold Bible Company," just as the early Mormon converts of 1830–1 would be called the followers of the "Gold Bible speculation."[16]

Although Joseph told the money-diggers about the plates, he went alone to receive them. According to Willard Chase's account, on September 22, 1823, Joseph Smith put on black clothes and rode to the hill on "a black horse with a switch tail." Finding and opening the stone box holding the Golden Plates, he encountered "something like a toad, which soon assumed the appearance of a man, and struck him on the side of the head." Denied possession of the plates, he was told to return in a year's time. When Smith began to write his personal history in 1832 the framework of money-digging was still a part of his recollection. In this account, the spirit kept the plates in punishment because Smith "had been tempted of the advisary and saught the Plates to obtain riches and kept not the commandment that I should have an eye single to the glory of God." Though he returned every year on the same day to the Hill Cumorah to attempt to gain the treasure, it would not be until September 1827, after his marriage to Emma Hale, that Joseph Smith would recover the plates that he would claim to be the source for the *Book of Mormon*.[17]

Well before 1827 there was an important – and familiar – turn in the family's fortunes and Joseph's life. In the fall of 1825 the Smiths were again threatened with the loss of their property when the carpenter building their house obtained rights to the title from the local land agent and tried to evict them. In this crisis the Smiths turned to trusted sectarian neighbors. An old Quaker farmer was willing to help but had no cash, but Lemuel Durfee Sr., a Quaker whose family once had been neighbors of the Staffords in Tiverton, bailed them out, purchasing the farm and allowing them to stay on as tenants.[18]

That October Joseph Jr. moved a hundred miles southeast to the Susquehanna River valley, where his skills with the seer-stone brought him work with a farmer and miller in South Bainbridge, Josiah Stowell (once of Guilford, Vermont), who hoped to find a storied silver mine supposedly discovered centuries before by wandering Spaniards. Smith would spend a good part of the next four and a half years in the Susquehanna Valley, in Colesville and South Bainbridge on the New York side and in Harmony on the Pennsylvania side. For his part in Stowell's magical excavations Joseph was brought before a local justice of the peace in Bainbridge in March 1826 and convicted of disturbing the peace as a "glass-looker," "a disorderly person and an Impostor."[19] The annual pilgrimage to the Hill Cumorah brought him back to Manchester in September 1826, and in the following January Isaac Hale's opposition to Joseph's secret marriage to Emma Hale brought him back to Manchester from Harmony for the better part of 1827. Taking Emma with him to the Hill Cumorah at the

The Mormon Hill.

The Hill Cumorah, Manchester, New York, depicted in John W. Barber, *Historical Collections of the State of New York . . .* (New York, 1845). Courtesy of Harvard University Libraries.

stroke of midnight on the morning of September 22, 1827, Joseph found what he claimed were golden plates inscribed with records of ancient peoples in America. From these plates he would "translate" the *Book of Mormon,* with the help of an "interpreter" – the jewels of the biblical Urim and Thummim used by Israelite priests to divine the future – that he claimed to have found with the plates.[20]

Decades ago Fawn Brodie noted that the *Book of Mormon* can be read in part as a veiled autobiography. Particularly in its latter sections, we can see Smith reflecting upon the scene of his coming of age in the 1820s, turning the Lake Ontario countryside into a sacred landscape and painting himself into the picture as the creator of the plates that he claimed to discover in 1827.[21] Thus the hero Mormon, who had been told of ancient plates buried in a certain hill, is taken by his father, Mormon, at the age of eleven to "the land of Zarahemla . . . by the waters of Sidon," just as Joseph, son of Joseph, had been taken by his father to Ontario County, by the waters of Lake Ontario. In the wake of a war, perhaps an allegory of the ongoing conflict among the Protestant denominations, the young Mormon, "being fifteen years of age and being somewhat of a sober mind . . . was visited of the Lord and tasted of the goodness of Jesus," a clear parallel to Joseph's First Vision. As Joseph was to claim of himself, Mormon "did endeavour to preach unto this people, but my mouth was shut, and I was forbidden that I should preach unto them." As wars and calamities assail the Nephites, Mormon recovers the sacred plates from the hill of Shim. And finally, the climax of the story is reached on an oddly pointed hill two miles south of the Smith homestead in Manchester, as narrated by Mormon:

> And it came to pass that we did march forth to the land of Cumorah, and we did pitch our tents round about the hill Cumorah. . . . I made this record out of the plates of Nephi, and hid up in the hill Cumorah all the records which had been entrusted to me by the hand of the Lord.[22]

Thus, on the eve of the destruction of the Nephites by the Lamanites, the plates were hidden by the hero Mormon for Joseph Smith to recover fifteen hundred years later.

In the fall of 1827 this sacred translation was two years away, but people scattered through the neighborhood and region knew of his boasts of finding a "Gold Bible." Crowds came to the Smith homestead demanding to see the plates. Conjurors – including Sally Chase with her green glass and another diviner brought in from sixty miles away – tried to locate the plates by the stone. As Martin Harris recalled, "The money diggers claimed that they had as much right to the plates as Joseph had, as they were in company together. They claimed that Joseph had been a traitor, and had appropriated that which belonged to them." With the ominous threat of a mobbing hanging over them, Joseph and Emma headed out of Manchester on a late October night for her father's house in Harmony, with the precious plates buried in a barrel of beans.[23]

Once in Harmony, Joseph and Emma would suffer the curiosity and scorn of her family and neighbors as they set up house in a dependency of the Hales, prepared for winter, and slowly began the "translation" of the plates. This process would take place in several stages, with Joseph sitting behind a curtain with the supposed plates and interpreters or out in the open with only his seer-stone, dictating to a series of different scribes. Emma Hale filled this role for several weeks, and Martin Harris took over between April and June of 1828. Harris almost derailed the entire project when he took the completed 116 pages of manuscript, comprising the Book of Lehi, to Palmyra to prove to his wife the worthiness of the project. She promptly threw the manuscript into the hearth fire. After about six months of delay, Joseph and Emma took up the translation the next winter, beginning where the Mormon story had ended in the destroyed manuscript, at about 130 B.C. In April 1829, Oliver Cowdery arrived in Harmony with his own gift of divining, and he and Joseph took the *Book of Mormon* story down to the climactic battle between the Nephites and Lamanites at the Hill Cumorah in A.D. 385. In May, after a series of revelations, Joseph and Oliver were baptized into the Priesthood of Aaron by John the Baptist, appearing in a vision. Moving north to the

Whitmer farm in Fayette, Seneca County, in June, Joseph and Oliver wrote the first two books of the *Book of Mormon,* covering the first 450 years of Mormon history and replacing the destroyed manuscript. While the book was at the printers in Palmyra, Joseph began to take on the role of a religious prophet, receiving visions and revelations, baptizing his key followers, and inspiring eleven witnesses to sign affidavits that they had seen and held the Golden Plates. In April 1830 the church was formally established in Fayette, and the institutional history of Mormonism began.[24]

Such is the outline of the formative story of Mormonism. This story was deeply entangled in the popular hermeticism of the divining culture, but this entanglement went beyond Joseph Smith's early experiences as treasure-seer. The accounts of the discovery of the plates, the language and narrative structure of the *Book of Mormon* itself, and contemporary circumstances in Ontario County all point to a wider hermetic influence.

Freemasonry provides a point of entry into this very complex story. As it had been in Vermont, Masonic fraternity was a dominant feature of the cultural landscape in Joseph Smith's Ontario County. The Ontario Lodge at Canandaigua had been formed in 1792, and the Mount Moriah Lodge at Palmyra, which Joseph's brother Hyrum joined, dated to 1804. Ten miles to the west in the town of Victor, Heber C. Kimball was a member of the Milner Lodge, formed in 1818, and in 1816 a lodge was formed in Manchester village, five miles south of the Smith homesite. All told, the thirty-six towns of old Ontario County (before its division in 1821) contained twenty-six lodges and seven Royal Arch chapters, one of each located in Canandaigua and Palmyra.[25]

This dense network of lodges and chapters helps explain the Masonic symbolism that runs through the story of the discovery of the Golden Plates. Most obviously, the story of their discovery in a stone vault on a hilltop echoed the Enoch myth of Royal Arch Freemasonry, in which the prophet Enoch, instructed by a vision, preserved the Masonic mysteries by carving them on a golden plate that he placed in an arched stone vault marked with pillars, to be rediscovered by Solomon.[26] In the years to come the prophet Enoch would play a central role in Smith's emerging cosmology. Smith's story of his discoveries got more elaborate with time, and in June 1829 he promised Oliver Cowdery, David Whitmer, and Martin Harris that they would see not only the plates but other marvelous artifacts: the Urim and Thummim attached to a priestly breastplate, the "sword of Laban," and "miraculous directors." Oliver Cowdery and Lucy Mack Smith later described three or four small pillars holding up the plates. All of these artifacts had Masonic analogues. Swords were carried in the Templar rituals, and the third, or Master Mason, degree told a story of a sword being used to behead a sleeping enemy, as the sword of Laban was used in the *Book of Mormon*. The Royal Arch priests wore breastplates covered with symbolic jewels, and a version of the Royal Arch myth told of three Masons finding a translating "key" in the Ark of the Covenant, analogous to the Urim and Thummim. Smith claimed to have worn the priestly breastplate with the Urim and Thummim attached while he translated a part of the *Book of Mormon*. Smith's directors were modeled on metal balls attached to the top of Enoch's pillars; these balls were engraved with maps and acted as mystic oracles.[27]

Smith's sources for these Masonic symbols were close at hand. Most obviously, Oliver Cowdery would have been a source, given that his father and brother were Royal Arch initiates; one Palmyra resident remembered Oliver as "no church member and a Mason."[28] But there were earlier influences, including the Masonic Smith relatives in Vermont and Hyrum Smith, a member of the Mount Moriah Lodge in Palmyra. A comment by Lucy Mack Smith in her manuscript written in the 1840s, protesting that the family did not abandon all household labor to try "to win the faculty of Abrac, drawing magic circles, or sooth-saying," suggests a familiarity with Masonic manuals: the "faculty of Abrac" was among the supposed Masonic mysteries.[29] Among the money-digging clans there was at least one contemporary connection with Royal Arch Freemasonry; Sally Chase's brother Durfee Chase was a member of the Palmyra Royal Arch chapter until he was expelled for "unmasonic conduct" in 1825.[30] Given the subsequent history of William Morgan, the Antimasonic martyr, one wonders whether this conduct involved the divulging of the ritual secrets of the Royal Arch to the money-digging circles.

Such secrets included the ritual setting of the degree of the Knights of the Ninth Arch, associated with the Enoch tale. This setting was to be "a most secret place," preferably "a vault under ground" with a trapdoor above, replicating the entry into Enoch's arched temple vault. Underground vaults and caves had powerful and ambiguous connotations in late-eighteenth-century popular culture. Among New Englanders, since well before the Revolution, caves had been associated with counterfeiting rings, and during the war they had been refuges for Tories. They were also an important element in a Gothic–Romantic culture available to young people of the early Republic. Titles such as *The Cavern of Death: A Moral Tale* and *Haunted Cavern: A Caladonian Tale,* which could be purchased in the upper Connecticut Valley in the 1790s, featured turgid plots of romantic love, murder, and spectral ghosts.[31] If Freemasonry, building on themes running back to the Rosicrucians, made caves places of mystery and purity, other themes running through contemporary culture made them places of mystery and danger. And anyone familiar with the Bible would have associated caves with places of refuge, burial, and the revelations of the prophet Elijah.[32]

Not only did Joseph Smith claim to find golden plates and Masonic artifacts in a stone vault atop the Hill Cumorah, but he and the money-diggers dug a long tunnel into Miner's Hill, three miles to the north and a mile from the Smith homesite. Several oral accounts referred to this man-made cave, claiming that "the Mormons dug into the hill" for a distance of forty feet in search of golden furniture left by ancient peoples, and that they covered the entrance with a wooden door. Brigham Young placed the cave at the Hill Cumorah and claimed that Smith and Cowdery had found "many wagon loads" of golden plates piled up in a subterranean room, with the sword of Laban hanging on the wall. There were rumors that Smith had translated the plates in this cave rather than at Harmony or Fayette, and according to Christopher Stafford, "some people surmised it was intended for counterfeiting." Such a cave, carved out of dense clay with picks and shovels, would not have been impossible for a family of well-diggers whose experience may have run back to the Towne's copper mine in Topsfield.[33]

With all of these occult and hermetic influences on the Smith family experience, it is not surprising that a culture of metalworking and hints of the alchemical worldview found their way into the language of the *Book of Mormon*, and metallurgical themes go far beyond simple references to plates of gold and brass.

The story of the *Book of Mormon* begins with the flight of the family of a worthy Israelite, Lehi, from a doomed Jerusalem to a western promised land. The bulk of the text then details the division of the family into virtuous Nephites and corrupt Lamanites and the long and bloody history of conflict between these houses and with shadowy Gadianton Bands, culminating in the final slaughter of the Nephites by the Lamanites. Throughout the book histories and prophecies are engraved on brass and golden plates; Smith claimed to have recovered at the Hill Cumorah only the last set of records, written by the lone Nephite survivor, Mormon.

As the story unfolds, metalworking proper emerges as a primary concern for Nephi as he builds a ship to convey his people to the New World. With divine instruction he made "a bellows wherewith to blow the fire" and "tools of the ore which [he] did molten from the rock." Arriving in "the land of promise" Nephi's band found "all manner of ore, both of gold, and of silver, and of copper"; their first commandment was "to make plates of ore . . . [to] engraven upon them the record of my people." When the Nephites were separated from the Lamanites, the latter cursed with a "skin of blackness" for their "iniquity," the hero Nephi "did teach my people to build buildings, and to work in all manner of wood, and of iron, and of copper, and of brass, and of steel, and of gold, and of silver, and of precious ores, which were in great abundance." Subsequently, at regular intervals in the narration of the cyclical rise and fall of societies, Smith described peoples waxing prosperous with a litany of precious metal and the means by which it was acquired: "they did dig it out of the earth. . . . they did cast up mighty heaps of earth to get ore, of gold, and of silver, and of iron, and of copper," and "there were also curious workmen, who did work all kinds of ore and did refine it; and thus they did become rich." Joseph Smith was fascinated with the technology of metalworking.[34]

Several words rooted in this metalworking language stand out as particularly important given their sacred contexts and connotations. The first of these is "refine": the Nephites refined ore, and the evil King Riplakish had "his fine gold . . . refined in prison." These were simple references to the processes of extracting metal from ore, also conveyed in the term "molten," and of enhancing the purity of gold. The term took on metaphoric qualities when the missionary Amulek told the people that "if ye do not remember to be charitable, ye are as dross, which the refiners do cast out, (it being of no worth) and is trodden under foot of men."[35]

But the more powerful metaphor conveyed by the language of "refining" involved the Lord's power and fire. The plates engraved after landing in the "land of promise" included the Lord's commitment to his covenanted people, loosely based on Isaiah 48:10: "I have refined thee, I have chosen thee in the furnace of affliction." In the Third Book of Nephi Smith borrowed an equally powerful verse from the Book of Malachi, comparing Jesus Christ to "a refiner's fire," who would "sit as a refiner and a purifier of silver [to] purify the sons of Levi, and purge them as gold and silver that they may offer unto the Lord an offering in righteousness."[36] Refine, purify, purge: throughout the *Book of Mormon* and Smith's subsequent revelations, codified as the *Doctrine and Covenants,* these terms and others convey the consuming and transforming power of the Lord, particularly his fire. Among the dozens of references to fire, the fire of judgment and the millennial firestorm are perhaps the most common: the Lord will "destroy the wicked by fire," "the world shall be burned with fire." But the chosen people would pass through these fires, purified and refined. A vast array of terms describes the people of the Lord and the nature of perfection and heaven as pure, bright, chastened, cleansed, and white.

"Furnace" is a second metalworking term with sacred connotations in the *Book of Mormon.* The people refined by the Lord survived the fires of the furnace. On three occasions Smith referred to Nephite disciples, including the character of Mormon, as "cast . . . into furnaces of fire and . . . [coming] forth receiving no harm." In another context he stated that "the life of King Noah shall be valued even as a garment in a hot furnace"; in another the heroes Nephi and Lehi "were encircled about as if by fire."[37] In an 1835 account of his First Vision, Smith related seeing two figures emerging from a "pillar of flame, which was spread all around and yet nothing consumed." The image of a human cast into the fire of a furnace was a common metaphor among the people attracted to Joseph Smith. In 1830, when Smith was brought to trial for a second time in South Bainbridge, one follower exulted in biblical language from the Book of Daniel that Smith "came out like the three children from the furnace, without the smell of fire upon his garments." By extension, all the Nephites – and ultimately all faithful latter-day Mormons – would pass through the divine furnace, surviving and purified by the refiner's fire to pass into the celestial kingdom. As Smith put it in a revelation of 1830, echoing the biblical injunction of John the Baptist, after baptism by water "cometh the baptism of fire and the Holy Ghost."[38] A central image in Utah folklore would be that of the "Three Nephites," spirits who would appear in human form to perform miracles, heal the sick, and testify to the Mormon gospel.[39]

Fire, refining, and the furnace had long been symbols connecting experimental alchemy with Christian themes of salvation, perfection, and the millennium. As Carl Jung demonstrated at length, "alchemical symbolism is steeped in ecclesiastical allegory," and Smith and the medieval alchemists used many of the same biblical images. A spiritual metallurgy, the alchemist's work was driven by the "philosopher's fire," often termed in biblical typology "the refiner's fire." This fire was a manifestation of the Holy Ghost, the divine fire symbolized by the sun, which turned elements into gold and by which "man, who before was dead, is made a living soul." For alchemists, the key figure in Daniel's parable of the three children in the furnace was a fourth person, who emerged from the furnace fires "like the Son of God." Alchemic literature often called the philosopher's stone the "three and one," the four figures in the parable representing the four elements, with the fourth figure being a symbol both of fire and of "the spirit concealed in matter" so central to alchemical purposes.[40] Magical white stones that appear at various points in the *Book of Mormon* echo the symbolism of the philosopher's stone. *The Pearl of Great Price,* the title of a collection of Smith's writings from the 1830s, similarly had ancient mystical and alchemical connotations. Most fundamental to the fusion of alchemy with Christianity was the parallel drawn between the philosopher's stone and Christ. The critical stage in the alchemical work was a fusion of elements in the furnace, followed by their "death" and "resurrection," the resulting stone having a Christ-like perfection, a source of immortality. Smith used analogous language, borrowed from Genesis 49:24, when he called Christ the "good shepherd . . . , the stone of Israel."[41]

The Smith family lore contained a number of such biblical–alchemical symbols, beginning with Asael Smith's language from the Book of Daniel about "the stone . . . cut out of the mountain without hands." Joseph Smith Sr. and Lucy Mack Smith were more oriented toward the Book of Genesis and the symbolism of the Tree of Life. In hermetic thinking the Tree of Life stood for the alchemical work of transmutation to perfection, and it was sometimes linked to the story in Daniel of the three boys in the furnace, who were given fruit from the Tree.[42] One of Lucy's early dreams equated two trees with her husband and his brother Jesse, who rejected the Mormon restoration. Joseph's tree was "surrounded with a bright belt, that shown like burnished gold, but far more brilliantly," and waved in a gentle breeze that she interpreted as "the breath of heaven"; Jesse's tree "was not surrounded with the belt of light as the former, and it stood erect and fixed as a pillar of marble."[43] These paired trees – one animated and alive, the other frozen as in death – echoed the paired Tree of Life and Tree of Knowledge planted in the Garden of Eden.[44]

Joseph Sr. had two dreams that, taken together, illustrated the dangers of the Tree of Knowledge and the blessings of the Tree of Life. In one dream he traveled through a barren land to find a box that would give him "wisdom and understanding," and upon opening the lid, "all manner of beasts, horned cattle, and roaring animals rose up on every side in the most threatening manner possible." This was Pandora's Box or, by implication, Eve's temptation to eat of the Tree of Knowledge, leading to the Fall from the Garden of Eden. In another, he saw a beautiful tree in a pleasant valley bearing "a kind of fruit, in shape much like a chestnut burr, and as white as snow." The interior was "of dazzling whiteness" and "delicious beyond description." As Joseph and his family sat eating this fruit, they saw a "spacious building" at the opposite end of the valley, representing the "Babylon" of competing sects.[45] True to the ideal of restoration, in language with decided hermetic implications, the Smiths stood with the Tree of Life and the promise of paradisial immortality, with the world of the competing sects in the distance, perhaps assembled around the death-dealing Tree of Knowledge.

These dreams were reproduced early in the *Book of Mormon*. Like Joseph Sr., the patriarch Lehi has a vision of eating white fruit from a tree, counterposed to crowds of people in a "spacious building." Lehi's vision was followed by similar visions experienced by his virtuous son, Nephi, including specific interpretations that "this thing which our father saw in a dream . . . was a representation of the tree of life."[46] It seems immaterial to ask whether the parents' dreams or the language of the *Book of Mormon* came first. What is important is that these formative Mormon texts revolved around symbols of perfectionism that had deeply hermetic connotations. The Mormon search for the fruit of the Tree of Life – described as the keys to the Lord's mysteries – would culminate in Nauvoo, when the adoption of temple endowments promised the hermetic divinization to which generations of radical restorationists had aspired.[47]

If the *Book of Mormon* eventually led to a promise of hermetic divinization, this was not its central, manifest theme. More obviously, the central themes of the book revolve around the depiction of the American Indians as transplanted Israelites. This idea had a long history in the millennial Protestant tradition. English millenarian Joseph Mede had posited in 1634 that the Indians were led to the New World by the devil as his chosen people; by 1650 Thomas Thorowgood was writing of them as the Lost Tribes, inspiring John Eliot's missionary work among the Natick Indians. In 1775 and 1816 the writings of James Adair and Elias Boudinot revived the thesis of Israelite origins, and Ethan Smith's *View of the Hebrews*, published in Poultney in 1823, attempted to confront the problem of the lack of recorded evidence, a flaw in the Israelite theory that Joseph Smith's *Book of Mormon* resolved.[48] If Smith's Nephites and Lamanites were not the Lost Tribes but the descendants of a later band of Israelite emigrants, nevertheless the story of the *Book of Mormon* provided a satisfactory answer to settlers' questions about the burial mounds scattered across New York State and the Ohio Valley. The treasure-diviners dug through these sites, and many of their seer-stones were in fact polished-stone implements made by Native Americans of the so-called Woodland period.[49] For the Smiths, the people buried in the mounds were the "ancients," who had hidden treasures protected by spirits in the hills around Palmyra and Manchester. There was a history here too. Cotton Mather, although skeptical of Israelite origins for Native America, was fascinated with the discovery of mastodon bones at Claverack on the Hudson River. In 1712 he wrote to the Royal Society that these bones provided evidence of a race of "antedeluvian GIANTS" who had walked with their heads in the clouds, called the "Nephilim" in Jewish tradition.[50]

There were contemporary and local sources for many of these ideas. The Palmyra *Herald* and the Wayne *Sentinel* carried stories throughout the 1820s speculating on Indian origins and describing finds in Indian burials throughout the trans-Appalachian interior. Elias Boudinot and Sylvester Larned, the latter a minister in contact with Ethan Smith of Poultney, both lectured in the area around 1820. The Smiths apparently had their own version of the Pittsfield parchment story, telling Peter Inger-soll of a book discovered in a tree in Canada that recorded the pre-Columbian history of America. A competing money-digging gang in Rochester had accounts of ancient conflicts very similar to those of Smith's Nephites and Lamanites. These money-diggers heard tales that ancient pygmies had hidden "great stores of gold and precious stones" in "great vaults" buried in the hills to protect them from a race of giant enemies. Accounts of violent primeval giants could be found in the text of the "Book of Enoch," an ancient manuscript discovered in Ethiopia in 1773 and published in English in 1821. Alternatively, such ideas might have had a more indigenous origin. In 1807, devastated by an epidemic, the Seneca Iroquois of the Allegheny River, a hundred miles to the south-west, dug huge pits in an unsuccessful effort to kill a subterranean mon-ster thought to be the cause of the disease. This failing, their prophet, Handsome Lake, turned to witchcraft accusation.[51]

Joseph Smith's transplanted Israelites were a very violent people, and his book is in great part a record of endless warfare, epochal struggles of good versus evil. Throughout the *Book of Mormon,* and especially the latter half, the Nephites struggle to survive both the onslaughts of Lamanites and Gadianton Bands and their own cyclical declension from virtue to corruption. This theme of dyadic conflict between opposing forces of good and evil requires our close attention, especially in light of the autobiographical qualities of much of the *Book of Mormon,* and in light of the broader problem of hermetic purity and danger.

Just as the landscape of Ontario County and Joseph's idealized coming of age were immortalized in the *Book of Mormon,* so too were a pair of dramas involving hermetic culture that unfolded during Joseph's final years in his father's household. If the Smiths saw in Freemasonry a means to knowledge that would lead to the restoration of divine mysteries, their faith would have been undermined by a wrenching schism in the ranks of New York Freemasonry in the early 1820s, with implications of worldly corruption only reinforced by the murder of William Morgan in 1826 and the furor over a judicial conspiracy in the year following. And, immersed in the world of treasure-divining, the Smiths in the early 1820s would once again brush up against the threat of counterfeiting they had encoun-tered in Vermont. When viewed against these contemporary hermetic dramas and in light of Masonic mythology, the conflict between good and evil that occupies so much of the *Book of Mormon* can be read in terms of a contest between hermetic purity and danger, between diviners and counterfeiters, and between pure, "primitive" Freemasons and corrupt, "spurious" Freemasons.

I have suggested that divining and counterfeiting were symbiotic yet opposed elements in a common popular hermetic culture rooted variously in sectarian magic, the high occult, and common crime. Divining cults offered a quick way to wealth for those who feared the "witchcraft" of counterfeiting. More formally and explicitly, the foundation myths of Freemasonry, as they were being popularized in the 1820s, offered a similar dyadic model of hermetic purity and danger. Before we can look at the contemporary hermetic dramas and their implications for the composition of the *Book of Mormon,* we need to look briefly at these foundation myths.

This version of Masonic mythology embedded the tale of Enoch burying engraved texts of the mysteries in an arched vault, to be discovered by Solomon, in a long history of dyadic segmentation and declension. At the heart of all Masonic mythology lay the divine Adam in the Garden of Eden, "in direct communication with God and the angels" and in "a state of perfection." With the Fall, Adam lost his divine immortality, but he retained "a perfect recollection of that speculative science which is now termed Masonry," the central principle of which "was to preserve alive in men's minds the true knowledge of God." From Adam's sons Seth and Cain descended two races of men, good and evil, carrying pure and spurious versions of Masonic knowledge. Not unlike Smith's Nephites in the *Book of Mormon,* the virtuous Sethites suffered declension and merged with the Cainites, mixing together pure and spurious Masonry. The pure Masonic tradition was preserved from the Flood by Enoch, who buried the mysteries in his arched vault before being taken bodily up to heaven, and by Noah, who alone with his family was saved from the Flood. But once again there was declension and schism, and Noah's son Ham became the new progenitor of spurious, Cainite Masonry, which became even more deeply entrenched after the dispersion at the Tower of Babel. A debased tradition of pure Masonry was passed down from Noah to Solomon, to be revitalized with the discovery of Enoch's buried plates in the arched vault. Following Solomon, pure, "primitive" Masonry was a secret tradition, theoretically transmitted through the medieval guilds, whereas the spurious tradition survived as the pagan mysteries. Masonic orders founded in eighteenth-century France and Germany developed various versions of this theme of schism and transmission, creating a profusion of conflicting rites and degrees, each order in some way promising to be the true source of an "antediluvian" purity.[52]

In the 1820s the outlines of this struggle were available in *The Antiquities of Freemasonry,* published in London in 1823 by George Oliver, an

Anglican minister and noted Masonic authority. The idea of ancient Masonic schisms had been discussed by Michael Ramsay a century before, and the theological writings of both Ramsay and Emmanuel Swedenborg, who shared a formative role in the mythology of the higher Masonic degrees, emphasized the theme of human declension from a paradisial state of perfection.[53] The Masonic mythology of schism had its parallels – and probably its roots – in earlier Judaic, hermetic, and sectarian thought. The Cabalist "Book of Raziel" detailed a similar patriarchal line of transmission of divine mysteries from Adam to Seth, Enoch, Noah, and Solomon. Conversely, other traditions had a chain of transmission of black magic as taught by Satan to Cain and descending through Ham. Among the English sectarians, the Muggletonians in the 1650s developed the doctrine of the "two seeds": the seed of Adam being virtuous and the seed of Cain (from Eve) being evil. These "seeds" became mixed in subsequent epochs, but Reeves and Muggleton claimed the power to recognize the preponderance of the seed of Cain in an individual, and to pronounce damnation. The Rogerenes of New London espoused the doctrine of the two seeds, conflating the story of Cain and Abel with an ancient mystical belief in two Adams: the Adam of the Fall, identified with the Tree of Knowledge, and a second Adam, identified with Christ and the Tree of Life. In John Rogers's words, "the seeds of these two *Adams* are two nations, and two manners of people, and the elder shall serve the younger." Like the Muggletonians, the Rogerenes (according to Peter Pratt) preached that the two seeds were blended in a "mixture of spirits," each vying with the other in the human soul. Sectarian or Masonic, the tradition of the two seeds provided a powerful tool for interpreting cosmic and sacred history.[54]

There is very good evidence that the two-seed tradition, specifically in its Masonic manifestation, played a significant role in Joseph Smith's later thinking. Just as he identifies himself with his heroic figure Mormon, who buried the plates in the Hill Cumorah before the slaughter of the Nephites, Smith announced in 1832 that he himself was the prophet Enoch. (Finding the plates, of course, also made him a latter-day Solomon.) When he wrote his revision of Genesis, his Book of Moses, starting in the summer of 1830, he added passages to the biblical text in which Adam's "pure and undefiled" language and "Priesthood" were passed to Seth and his progeny, and Enoch was shown "the seed of Adam" and "the seed of Cain."[55] His revelations restoring the biblical priesthood of the Melchizedek in the early 1830s included similar passages on the passing of the priesthood from Adam through Enoch to Solomon down a long line of patriarchs, as Masonic mythology proposed.[56] And in the eyes of his family and his closest followers, Smith's endowment rituals of 1842–3, the foundation of a new Mormonism promising a progression into godhood for the faithful, signaled the restoration of the hermetic promise of a pure Gnostic Freemasonry. Lost to the world since the days of Adam, Enoch, and Solomon, the pure tradition had been restored by the heroic treasure-hunting of Joseph the Prophet.

As of 1825, these developments lay well in the future, but this trajectory toward hermetic divinization brings into focus the fugitive evidence of a Smith family fascination with the intersection of Freemasonry and restoration. Theoretically, for those so inclined, Masonic knowledge came down from Adam, Noah, and the ancient prophets in an uninterrupted chain. But the continuity of that chain was put into doubt by an imperfect history of the ancient schisms. For those of restorationist opinions, the question of the nature of the true Freemasonry would have been acute: hermetic perfection was difficult to distinguish from hermetic danger. Perhaps Joseph Smith Sr. avoided joining the Masons, as he avoided the Christian sects, for fear of the threat of schismatic corruption. Such anxieties would have been amply reinforced by contemporary Masonic schisms in New York State in the 1820s.

For a fraternity that placed such a premium on union and unanimity, Freemasonry was notorious for its quarrels and differences. English Freemasonry had been divided from the 1730s to 1813 between London (or Modern) and Ancient rituals, the latter influenced in some measure by the very different Masonic culture that developed in continental Europe.[57] Similar schisms in New York Freemasonry were aggravated by the patronage of competing political chieftains. From 1807 to 1827 the elite Rite of Perfection, in which hermetic beliefs were most fully articulated, was divided into competing councils led by Governors De Witt Clinton and Daniel D. Tompkins. Struggling for preeminence in the old Jeffersonian coalition in New York from 1813 through the early 1820s, Clinton and Tompkins also served as Grand Masters of the Grand Lodge, from 1806 to 1820 and 1820 to 1822 respectively. In 1823, after several years of discontent aggravated by political factionalism, the Grand Lodge split into City and Country factions, in a schism driven by power and money. The western lodges complained that they had no voice in the Grand Lodge affairs conducted in New York City, and they met in Canandaigua in 1821 to plan a restructuring of the governance of the Grand Lodge. The city lodges complained about the salaries paid to three Grand Visitors established by Clinton in 1814; the Grand Visitor from the New York City area asked only minimal compensation, but the two Visitors from the north and west asked for over $1,000 a year. One of these men, Joseph Enos of Canandaigua, was eventually accused of embezzling Grand Lodge funds, but in the interval his election as Grand Master precipitated the secession of the City lodges. Members of Enos's Canandaigua lodge, led by Nicholas G. Cheesborough, who himself was elected to office in the "Country" Grand Lodge in 1825, were directly implicated in the assassination of William Morgan, who in September 1826 was preparing to print the ritual secrets of the symbolic and Royal Arch Masons. Concerns that Morgan was going to expose corruption among the Country Grand Lodge leadership may well explain his death.[58]

Thus the Morgan controversy followed hard upon, and was interwoven with, a Masonic schism and scandal that ran from the beginning of the decade. Between 1828 and 1830 most of the region's lodges halted their meetings and turned in their charters, but anxieties about the internal corruption of Masonic institutions well predated the subsequent fears about their corrupting influences on civil society. Many Freemasons were alienated from Grand Lodge authority during this division. Of over 350 lodges on the Grand Lodge register in 1823, 27 lodges affiliated themselves with the City Grand Lodge and roughly 110 attended the Country Grand Lodge meeting in 1824, leaving over 200 lodges that sat out the controversy. In particular, Joseph Enos's suspect character seems to have turned many lodges away from the Country Grand Lodge. Those who took Masonic "theology" very seriously would have seen an undermining of the fraternity by the affairs of a corrupt world, and such a perception would have been reinforced in the winter of 1826–7 with the murder of William Morgan.

Potentially, then, there were some among these alienated Freemasons open to a new way into the "ancient mysteries," such as that offered by Joseph Smith. Some of these alienated Masons did find their way into the Mormon church. William W. Phelps had been a Master Mason before the Morgan affair; in 1828 he signed a declaration of a convention of "Seceding Masons" and began publishing the Antimasonic *Ontario Phoenix* in Canandaigua. Phelps did not join the Nauvoo Lodge in 1842, but eleven other former New York Masons did; nine had been members of lodges that stayed away from the Country Grand Lodge meeting in 1824.[59] And if Joseph Smith and his family were drawn to the mystical dimension of Freemasonry, the *Book of Mormon* provides plenty of evidence of his alienation from its worldly dimensions.

A very important subtheme in the *Book of Mormon*, bound up with categories of treasure, magic, and sorcery that so fascinated Joseph Smith, involves secret combinations of robbers and murderers, the Gadianton Bands. For a significant section of the *Book of Mormon* these secret combinations present a far greater threat to the righteous Nephites than the savage Lamanites, who ultimately destroy them. These Gadianton

Bands have long been seen as a reflection of Antimasonic concerns about corrupting secret societies.

There are undeniable parallels between these bands of robbers and murderers and the popular images of the Masonic fraternity. David Persuitte and Dan Vogel have enumerated these parallels: secrecy, claims of ancient origins, similarities between names, the lambskin apron, "secret signs," and "their oaths, that they would protect and preserve one another in whatsoever difficult circumstances they should be placed, that they should not suffer for their murders." To these one might add the description of the "Gadianton robbers filling the judgment-seats – having usurped the power and authority of the land . . . doing no justice unto the children of men." Similarly, according to Nephite prophecy, the *Book of Mormon* would appear "in a day when the blood of saints shall cry unto the Lord, because of secret combinations," whose members were led "around by the neck with a flaxen cord" by the devil. Scholars have pointed to the similarity between the name "Mormon" and that of William Morgan and to the parallels between Nicholas Cheesborough's name and those of "Zeezrom," "Cezoram," and "Seezorum," respectively a corrupt lawyer, a robber leader, and a judge elected by robbers. Among the early Mormon leaders, Martin Harris as well as William W. Phelps were noted Antimasons. Martin Harris was elected to an Antimasonic committee for Palmyra by the Wayne County Antimasonic convention in October 1827; he was quoted in Ohio in 1831 as announcing that the *Book of Mormon* was the "Antimasonic Bible." Joseph would take more than a passing interest in William Morgan's widow, marrying her as his first recognized plural wife in 1838.[60]

On the other hand, Richard Bushman has pointed out dimensions of the Gadianton Bands that do not match a Masonic model. Bushman notes the absence of parallels with elaborate Masonic degrees and initiation rituals, or obvious parallels with Morgan's murder. Similarly, he points out that the Gadianton Bands were not one continuous society but a series of groups that episodically emerge to plunder and pillage the righteous and are then destroyed, only to reemerge at a later date among a different people.[61]

One interpretation of the disputed Masonic connotations of the Gadianton Bands is that Joseph Smith bore contradictory feelings about Freemasonry: he condemned the spurious tradition, while embracing the pure tradition. The Gadiantons were ascribed all of the evil qualities of the worldly Masonic institutions, while they were denied other more positive qualities – the inherent ritual and mythology of the order. Smith's controversy was not with the fundamental ideals of Freemasonry, which offered an approach to ancient mysteries, but with the corruption of those ideals by degenerate contemporaries.

We should not lose sight of the possibility of a conflation of contemporary "secret combinations" – and hermetic dangers – in Smith's imagination. The January 1827 newspaper accounts of the sitting of the Court of Oyer and Terminer at Canandaigua listed the light sentences given Morgan's kidnappers above the convictions and acquittals of several men on charges of counterfeiting and forgery.[62] Counterfeiters were described in the newspapers in ways that anticipated both Antimasonic rhetoric and Smith's accounts of the Gadianton Bands. Canandaigua's *Ontario Repository and Freeman* noted the arrest of a John Forbes in early 1824 in a sarcastic manner that played on a vague sense of identity between criminal and political conspiracy. In their words, Forbes had been

> present with fifteen other delegates, at a *Caucus* of the *craft* recently held in this vicinity, for the purpose of choosing officers and *"conserting measures for preserving the prosperity and harmony of the family."* The object of this *caucus* was, it seems, to defraud the people of their *money* – that of most others is to defraud them of their *rights*.[63]

The delegates to the Antimasonic convention in Albany in 1829 were more direct: they flatly charged that the "numerous gangs of counterfeiters who have so frequently flooded the state . . . were almost wholly composed of Free-Masons." "It is no longer a mystery," the convention charged, "how they so frequently eluded the ministers of justice, or escaped through the meshes of the law."[64] If Joseph Smith aspired to the authority of a restored, pure, primitive Freemasonry, contemporary counterfeiters and murdering schismatic Freemasons and the ancient Gadianton Bands of the *Book of Mormon* all would have been species of corrupt, spurious Masonry descended from Cain.

There is ample reason to see the counterfeiters as an important model for the Gadianton Bands, in combination with spurious Freemasonry. The robbers' episodic rise and fall in the *Book of Mormon* echoed the similar cyclical pattern of counterfeiting; both would emerge to prey upon the people's wealth and would be suppressed by force only to rise again. But, like the counterfeiters, the Gadiantons often escaped: "they took their flight out of the land, by a secret way, into the wilderness"; "the secret combinations . . . established in the more settled parts of the land, . . . were not known to those who were at the head of government; therefore they were not destroyed out of the land." Official corruption might play a role: judges would let "the guilty and the wicked go unpunished because of their money."[65]

The counterfeiting connotations of the Gadianton Bands become all the more apparent when we examine the extensive counterfeiting rings in the towns around Manchester and Palmyra in the early 1820s. And these counterfeiting gangs put the divining endeavors of the Smith family in a very different light. The plates that Joseph claimed to have discovered in the Hill Cumorah were a fantastic alternative to counterfeiting. Rather than multiplying false coin, Joseph would multiply sacred texts in search of the true path to perfection.

The Erie Canal was completed through the Palmyra region in 1822, and the entire canal opened in 1825. The economic activity generated by this reconfiguration of the landscape probably explains the particular focus of counterfeiting activity in the Ontario County region in the early 1820s. Whatever the explanation, Joseph's last years in Manchester coincided with a grand confrontation between counterfeiting and the law.

The register of convicts entering Auburn State Prison provides us with an index of counterfeiting activity in the Burned-over District from 1817 through 1830.[66] Relative to population, two regions stand out as particular hotspots for counterfeiting, as measured by convictions for counterfeiting and passing counterfeit money. The most prominent was the Niagara frontier, where Niagara and Erie counties, with less than 4 percent of the population of the Burned-over District, accounted for almost 20 percent of the counterfeiting convictions between 1817 and 1825. Here the proximity to the source of supply in Canada created a situation like that in northern Vermont, where Stephen Burroughs and others dumped floods of counterfeits from secret Canadian printshops.

The second most significant focus of counterfeiting in the Burned-over District was in the countryside immediately surrounding the Smith homestead: the greater Ontario County region. Specifically, the Ontario and Monroe county courts convicted eighteen persons on indictments of counterfeiting between 1821 and 1825; with roughly 15 percent of the region's population, these two counties accounted for more than 30 percent of the counterfeiting convictions. The mid-1820s clearly saw a crisis situation, with the number of counterfeiting convictions climbing to a peak in 1824 and 1825 and then dropping off sharply, suggesting that the counterfeiting organizations had been broken or driven underground.

The newspapsrs noted the ebb and flow of these cases with considerable detail, warning the public about the circulation of bad bills, noting convictions, and providing lurid accounts of arrests and confessions. In particular, they described in great detail the operation and disruption of at least three distinct gangs operating in Ontario and Wayne counties in 1824 and 1825. In early February 1824, the papers were full of accounts of the conviction for counterfeiting of Rufus and Dudley Smith (no relation to the Mormon Smiths) at Canandaigua and of the evidence that they had brought against a woman who was operating what was called a "Branch Bank of the counterfeiting establishment" to the east in Geneva, with $1,600 in bad bills "sent out from Canada" hidden in an iron keg in her cellar.[67] The second ring was much closer to the Smith world in northwest Manchester. The Geneva *Gazette* had the following to report on February 25, 1824, under the heading of "More counterfeiters":

> Another nest of these villains has been discovered in the town of Farmington. John Forbes, who formerly resided in the east part of Farmington has been arrested in Geneseo, as one of the gang, and on consideration of being admitted to bail, has disclosed the names of his confederates and the place of their retreat, which was at the house of a Mrs. Butler in Farmington. At this repository were found dies for counterfeiting dollars and half dollars, and receipts and chemical preparations for altering bills. The company consists of 15, none of which have yet been apprehended. Forbes says the bills were procured from Canada, at a place called Slab Village. The coins are extremely well executed, but are lighter than the genuine. Some of the bills are also well executed.[68]

The base of this Forbes–Butler gang in east Farmington must have been quite near the Smith homestead in northwest Manchester. In March 1825 the Wayne *Sentinel* reported a third ring of counterfeiters located in west Macedon, on the Monroe County line, perhaps seven or eight miles from the Smith farm. "They had been suspected of dealing in this trash for several years, but they managed in evading the eye of the public, until an honest neighbor was imposed upon." Suspicions focused on an innkeeper named Abraham Salisbury, and a search disclosed "a small wooden box containing $115 in counterfeit bank notes . . . concealed in a hollow tree near [his] house."[69]

The people tried in the Ontario and Monroe county courts seem to have been the passers for the most part, not the inner circle of these gangs. Abraham Salisbury was jailed but never convicted of passing counterfeit money, though other men brought before the county courts in Palmyra and Rochester in 1824 and 1825 may have been his accomplices. Similarly, the leaders of the Forbes–Butler gang also seem to have escaped. A George Butler and a James Carr, tried and acquitted of counterfeiting in Canandaigua in July 1823, may have been connected with this group. Similarly, John G. Forbes Jr., indicted in Geneseo in 1824 (the John Forbes cited in the Geneva *Gazette*), also got off lightly. Accused of passing a forged ten-dollar note upon the Bank of Utica in Geneseo in December 1823, Forbes was convicted by the Livingston County Court of Oyer and Terminer on June 29, 1824, sent to Auburn State Prison, and pardoned on

July 7. Though the newspapers cite Forbes as formerly residing in east Farmington, this was only a temporary location. He had been born in Manlius, near Syracuse, in 1803; his father, John G. Forbes Sr., was a prominent lawyer, militia colonel, and Bucktail politician in Onondaga County, moving from Manlius to Salina in the early 1820s and to the growing city of Syracuse in the 1830s. His powerful political connections go a long way toward explaining his son's rapid pardon.[70]

After decades of such exposure throughout New England, in moving to the Palmyra region the Smiths once again were surrounded by shadowy and menacing webs of counterfeiting. At least one firsthand account of their early days in Palmyra describes them again as victims. Pomeroy Tucker wrote that during the years of the Smith's proprietorship of the cake and beer shop in Palmyra village, "the boys of those by-gone times used to delight in obtaining the valuable goods entrusted to Joseph's clerkship, in exchange for worthless pewter imitation two-shilling pieces." Tucker also claimed that Joseph read Stephen Burroughs's *Memoirs* during these formative years. The Smiths seem to have known something of the material culture of counterfeiting, for Abigail Harris was told by the elder Smiths that with the Golden Plates Joseph had found "the vessel in which the gold was melted from which the plates were made, and also the machine with which they were rolled," fantastic analogues to the crucibles and rolling mills necessary for coining and printing.[71]

The Smiths may have been tempted to pass money for these local gangs, but the evidence suggests that, like many others throughout the postrevolutionary northern backcountry, they turned to divining for treasure as a spiritual alternative to the temptation to counterfeit. The counterfeiters and their passers, particularly those involved in the Butler–Forbes ring in east Farmington, maintained an insidious presence in the immediate neighborhood. James Carr and George Butler, acquitted in 1823, were from Palmyra and Phelps respectively, towns immediately adjacent to Manchester. Witnesses testifying for and against them fell into two geographic clusters, one of which suggests the impact of this counterfeiting group in the Smiths' locality and the second of which points to an important connection to the Syracuse area. The larger group was composed of people from towns adjacent to or near Manchester: eight from Palmyra, Farmington, Phelps, and Canandaigua, and five from Lyons, Seneca, and Perinton.[72]

These details are not unimportant, for among the witnesses for Carr and Butler were two men with connections to the Smiths' circle of money-diggers in Manchester and Palmyra. Thomas Ingersoll and Stiles Stafford testified on behalf of George Butler and James Carr in July 1823. Stiles, or Tyle, Stafford was the grandson of David Stafford and a cousin of the

Stafford diviners in Palmyra.[73] The Ingersolls are more difficult to pin down, but Thomas Ingersoll was either a brother or a third cousin of Peter Ingersoll, whom the Smiths had tried to recruit into their money-digging club.[74]

Thus some of the money-digging crowd had connections among the counterfeiters operating in east Farmington and along the canal or with others who found their way before the county courts for a range of serious crimes. These connections may help explain Joseph's efforts to extricate himself from the money-digging company. Martin Harris recalled in 1859 that "Joseph said the angel told him that he must quit the money-diggers. That there were wicked men among them. He must have no more to do with them."[75] And, as Richard Bushman has pointed out, one account of Joseph's March 1826 trial in South Bainbridge quotes his father as saying "that both he and his son were mortified that this wonderful power which God had so miraculously given him should be used only in search of filthy lucre, or its equivalent in earthly treasures."[76]

The question remains why Joseph suddenly decided to go to the Susquehanna country, a hundred miles from home, just as his family was facing a major crisis concerning their farm mortgage. The standard explanation has been that he was going to help pay off the annual payment by divining for Josiah Stowell, but surely work was available closer to home. His two subsequent moves, in January and November 1827, were closely connected to personal crises, marriage and the recovery of the plates. His sudden move to the Susquehanna coincided with the wave of counterfeiting – hermetic danger – in the Manchester region. One motive for his departure may well have been to avoid the "wicked men" on the fringes of the money-digging company, men who had connections with the world of counterfeiting. Given Joseph Sr.'s brush with this world in Vermont in 1807, it seems likely that Joseph Sr. was the critical influence, sending his son out of the way of temptation down into the Susquehanna country on a quixotic divining mission, into a region that had seen little counterfeiting activity for several years. In any event, during the last two years of Joseph's life in his father's household, a dramatic confrontation between counterfeiting and the law swept through his immediate neighborhood.

New York Antimasons, meeting in convention in 1829, detected a connection between counterfeiting and Freemasonry, and such a connection can be read in Smith's description of the Gadianton Bands in the *Book of Mormon*. These robber bands appear throughout the latter half of the *Book of Mormon*, from the Book of Helaman through the Book of Mormon, playing a central role in the great cycles of Mormon history described there. Each of these cycles displays similar themes: the prosperity and corruption of the people, the rise and fall of a "secret combination" of Gadianton robbers, and the preaching of a prophet. Interwoven with these elements are subthemes that bear a striking relationship to traditional meanings associated with counterfeiting, divining, and their root-metaphor of alchemy: slippery, volatile treasures, witchcraft and sorcery, and fiery furnaces. The reiteration of these themes in three narrative cycles suggests that Joseph Smith's emerging theological system was shaped by a perception of evil Masonic counterfeiters, who literally played the puffer to his philosophical alchemist in search of perfection.

The Book of Helaman begins with the Nephites in disarray, divided over the succession to the rank of chief judge in 52 B.C. In this context the secret combinations first emerge, and Gadianton, "who was exceedingly expert in many words, and also in his craft," rose to become their leader. "Pride of their hearts, because of their riches," leads the Nephites into corruption, and two prophets arise to urge them back to their faith. Here Smith introduces a theme that his grandfather Solomon Mack had developed in his *Narrative*, the distinction between spiritual treasures "laid up in heaven" and carnal treasures laid up on earth. The prophets urge the people to "lay up for yourselves a treasure in heaven, yea which is eternal, and which fadeth not away . . . that precious gift of eternal life." Thrown into prison by the Lamanites, Nephi and Lehi are "encircled about with a pillar of fire, [which] . . . burned them not."[77]

Convinced by the prophets to live in peace, the Nephites and Lamanites prospered, in "an exceeding plenty of gold, and of silver, and of all manner of precious metals," until the Gadianton Bands reemerged to plunder the land and "infest the mountains and the wilderness." Once again conditions were ripe for a prophet, and in 6 B.C. Samuel the Lamanite came into the land of Zarahemla to prophesy the destruction of the Nephites. The theme of spiritual treasures is repeated, with an explicit contrast with those laid up upon – or within – the earth. Unless they repented, the Lord would bring destruction to the people and "a curse shall come upon the land. . . . whoso shall hide up treasures in the earth shall find them again no more, because of the great curse of the land, save he be a righteous man, and shall hide it up unto the Lord." As Smith has Samuel the Lamanite develop his exhortation, the language evokes that of the early national diviner grappling with unseen spirits moving chests of money through the earth: "behold the time cometh that he curseth your riches, that they become slippery, that ye cannot hold them. . . . yea we have hid up our treasures and they have slipped away from us, because of the curse of the land."[78]

Samuel also predicts the coming of Christ and sets the stage for the next epic cycle. In the next book, the Third Book of Nephi, signs of Christ's imminent arrival abound, and as the afflictive element, the Gadianton Bands reemerge to "do much slaughter among the people." The Nephites and the Lamanites unite to defeat the robbers, they prosper and divide, and the stage is set for an apocalyptic coming of Christ to the New World in A.D. 34. Christ preaches to the people for twenty chapters, and again the treasure theme is repeated, the people being told to "lay not up treasures upon earth, where moth and rust doth corrupt and thieves break through and steal." Several chapters later occur two of the rare references to magic or witchcraft in the *Book of Mormon*. Christ says he will "cut off witchcrafts out of my land, and thou shalt have no more soothsayers"; several verses later the condemnation is extended to "all lyings and deceivings"; several chapters later Christ will "be a swift witness against the sorcerers." (The first association of these categories occurs in the first chapter of the Book of Alma, where Smith describes the unchurched as indulging "themselves in sorceries, . . . lying, thieving, robbing, . . . and all manner of wickedness.") Finally, there was the language of fire. Christ foretold the second coming of the prophet Elijah – the harbinger of the end times – and closed his sermon with an account of the millennium, when "he should come in his glory, . . . [when] the elements should burn with fervent heat, the earth should be wrapt together as a scroll, and the heavens and the earth should pass away." Then there are the usual furnace scenes; three Nephite disciples are anointed to "never taste death" and, persecuted by unbelievers, "thrice they were cast into a furnace, and received no harm."[79]

The final cycle of Nephite history unfolds in the Fourth Book of Nephi and the Book of Mormon, beginning around A.D. 200.[80] After over a century of peace and harmony, the people wax prosperous and they harden their hearts against religion; the requisite saintly disciples survive being cast "into furnaces of fire," and around A.D. 250 "the wicked part of the people began again to build up the secret oaths and combinations of Gadianton . . . and it came to pass that the robbers of Gadianton did spread all over the face of the land." Decades of violence and evil pass and the stage is set for the final contest between the Nephites and the Lamanites. At this point, at the beginning of the Book of Mormon, Smith's personal history intersects with sacred Mormon history in a very interesting way. Mormon, son of Mormon, is taken at the age of eleven to the land of Zarahemla, "by the waters of Sidon." At age fifteen he is visited by the Lord, but he is rejected by the people: "I was forbidden that I should preach unto them, because of the hardness of their hearts; and because of the hardness of their hearts the land was cursed for their sake."[81]

If Smith was making an analogy to his own life in the early 1820s, the next verses, compacting the themes of robbery, slippery treasures, and witchcraft as never before, had an unmistakable meaning: the simultaneous emergence of counterfeiting and the spurious Masonry of the corrupt Country Grand Lodge in the early 1820s was an affliction on the people, the consequence of their rejection of Joseph Smith as a preacher of the gospel.

> Lamanites, did infest the land, insomuch that the inhabitants thereof began to hide up their treasures in the earth; and they became slippery, because the Lord had cursed the land, that they could not hold them or retain them again. And it came to pass that there were sorceries, and witchcrafts, and magics; and the power of the evil one was wrought upon all the face of the land.

Several verses later the language was repeated with reference to a date that would be roughly analogous to 1825.

> And it came to pass that the Nephites began to repent of their iniquity, and began to cry even as had been prophesied by Samuel the prophet; for behold no man could keep that which was his own, for the thieves, and the robbers, and the murderers, and the magic art, and the witchcraft which was in the land.[82]

These three verses include five of the eight explicit references to witchcraft, magic, or sorcery in the *Book of Mormon,* and the other three references, noted above, are also linked to the theme of robbery. If Joseph modeled the robbing Gadianton Bands upon the contemporary counterfeiting gangs, it seems reasonable to suggest that he had inherited the image of the counterfeiter as witch, which I have suggested ran as an undercurrent in the popular culture of eighteenth-century New England. The counterfeiter's "magic art" was a species of black magic and a source of evil; his bad coins and bills were literally "slippery treasure." Conversely, the Smiths described the virtuous Nephites in language redolent of alchemy. Joseph Smith Sr. told Rosewell Nichols "that gold and silver was once as plenty as the stones in the field are now – that the ancients, half of them melted the ore and made the gold and silver, while the other half buried it deeper in the earth, which accounted for these hills."[83] The ancients who buried their treasures in the earth correspond to the backsliding Nephites: throughout the final sections of the *Book of Mormon* their earthly treasures are cursed by the Lord, and in the final narrative cycle they are subject to the depredations of robbers and witchcraft. But in this daydream, the righteous ancients, like the alchemist, refined ore into silver and gold.

If we read as disguised autobiography the passages in the *Book of Mormon* describing the afflictions following the rejection of Mormon, we have Joseph Smith beginning the process of revising and amplifying the story of his early years, as he dictated the *Book of Mormon* to Oliver Cowdery in 1829 in Harmony. His being rejected as a prophet, or being scorned as a diviner, had brought down plagues of witchlike counterfeiters and spurious Masons upon greater Ontario County, an affliction from the Lord.

As the prophet and seer of a new dispensation, Joseph Smith would work within the lines of affinity connecting the religion of a true, restored church with human spiritual powers one step removed from white magic. Following his father and mother, and his grandfather Solomon, Joseph would uphold the miraculous. His visions of God, Christ, and angelic spirits and the translation of the *Book of Mormon* from the Golden Plates through the medium of the Urim and Thummim were the latter-day miracles that established his dispensational authority. Like his great-grandfather Samuel Smith in Topsfield and the preacher at the Goddard's house in Hopkinton, Joseph would act against satanic power by assuming priestly spiritual powers long since renounced by mainstream Protestants. Smith's magic acted to defend the pure from the dangerous. His seer-stone was a white-magical defense against crime; as he developed his reputation as a diviner, Joseph had looked to the stone to locate stolen goods. Similarly, the plates and interpreter-stone called Gazelem described in the Book of Alma would shine light upon darkness, exposing "the mysteries, and their works of darkness, and secret works" of evil men. Although he never mentions them by name, Smith had declared an occult war on the witchlike art of the counterfeiters.[84]

We can begin to outline an evolutionary sequence in the Smith family's thinking, as they gradually redefined the boundary between hermetic purity and danger, moving it from that separating divining and counterfeiting to a new boundary separating the sacred and the profane. Joseph Sr. may well have fallen to the seductive temptations of counterfeiting in Vermont; his commitment to divining may have been fueled by this encounter. Turning from false coin to fantastic volatile treasures in the earth, the Smiths found them inaccessible, protected by evil spirits from the diviners' rituals. If "slippery treasures" were the false coin and bills of the counterfeiters, they were also the chests of money that Smith and the money-diggers worked in vain to control. In chasing after these elusive chests of money, the Smiths were also lusting after the carnal treasures "laid up in the earth" by backsliding Nephites. Sometime between 1825 and 1826 they began to turn away from the futile search for these slippery treasures in the earth to contemplate treasures in heaven, as Solomon Mack had urged upon the family two decades before in his *Narrative*.[85] Declaring eternal enmity with witchlike counterfeiters, Joseph Smith abandoned divining for prophecy.[86] Rather than multiplying filthy lucre, he would reveal sacred mysteries.

This shifting boundary was also entangled with the Masonic mythology of the transmittal of mysteries from Adam to Seth and his posterity, repeatedly threatened by backsliding or corruption by the "seed of Cain." As did divining, Freemasonry lost legitimacy in the mid-1820s; with the schism in the Grand Lodge and the murder of William Morgan, the contemporary lodges traded the aura of sacred mystery for the obvious signs of corruption. We may posit a set of correspondences in Smith's imagination, a line of hermetic dangers including witchlike counterfeiters, combinations of spurious Freemasons, ancient and contemporary, and the various forces of evil in the *Book of Mormon*. (Among the dangers condemned in the *Book of Mormon,* it must be added, was that of marrying multiple wives in polygamous relationships.)[87] We can also posit another set of correspondences, a line of hermetic purity including virtuous Nephites, pure, primitive Freemasonry, and the alchemist in search of the path to heavenly perfection. Between the purity of the Kingdom and the dangers of the world, Joseph Smith constructed a clear and unmistakable boundary.

Joseph Smith told Oliver Cowdery in three revelations in the spring of 1829 that the Mormon path to purity led to "mysteries which are great and marvelous." A year and a half later he announced to his newly formed church at Fayette, New York, that he alone, Joseph Smith, the prophet, had received "the keys of the mysteries, and the revelations which are sealed."[88] Over the next fourteen years, in an epic saga leading to Ohio, Missouri, and western Illinois, these keys would be used to gradually explain continuing revelations and unseal ancient mysteries.

The story of the revealing of the Mormon mysteries thus is complicated by its formative influences, both distant and more immediate. The Mormon path toward hermetic purity was built on streams of culture running from the past, streams often interlaced with currents of hermetic danger. But, as this chapter has tried to suggest, it was also a path pioneered by one man. Joseph Smith wrote himself into the drama of the *Book of Mormon,* and he would be the driving force in the formative epoch of the Mormon church. These autobiographical qualities bring us to a perplexing problem, a problem perhaps beyond the limits of historical interpretation: the inner life of the prophet. Indeed, in Jan Shipps's words, there is a "prophet puzzle," an "enigma," at the "core" of Mormon history.[89]

Traditionally historians have relied upon Smith's inner life as the critical explanation of the emergence of Mormonism. Devout Mormons can only accept the orthodox story of a young man, wrestling with questions of faith, receiving visions and revelations from a divinity. Secular historians, hostile or sympathetic, have noted the contemporary influences on the *Book of Mormon*. But since Fawn Brodie they generally have assumed that the content of Mormon theology was rooted in Smith's fertile imagination.[90] The present project, following many leads in the literature, has assumed that there was some ordered cultural material for this imagination to work upon, a grist of long-term preparation running back into the seventeenth century and of a more short-term reformulation of the affinities between hermetic perfection and dispensational restoration dating from the late eighteenth century.

But our problem is that this imagination was not simply an empty box, into which received culture was poured and out of which flowed the Mormon religion. Defining the structure of this imagination, the psychology of the prophetic situation, is a difficult task. The most important psychological analysis of Joseph Smith, that of Fawn Brodie, has as many problems as it has insights. Pointing to the evidence for stress and discord within the Smith family – particularly among the brothers – Brodie noted their striking parallels with the endemic conflicts structuring the *Book of Mormon*. In her interpretation, the *Book of Mormon* was an elaborate projection in which Joseph Smith "was working out unconscious conflicts over his own identity." Brodie suggests that Smith was suffering from a psychotic, divided personality similar to those of a range of notorious impostors, caught between fraudulence and reality.[91]

We need not assume a necessary connection between psychosis and the prophetic impulse. A prophet succeeds in his quest by building on a shared culture with a prepared audience, in a sort of interactive performance or theater.[92] Quite obviously, Joseph Smith succeeded in sharing his vision with a large and attentive audience, and by all accounts he was a gregarious, playful character. On the other hand, many among the early Mormons would later turn away from Smith's performance, dissenting from his testimony and rejecting him as a false prophet. And the evidence seems incontrovertible that Joseph Smith's imagination and personality were driven by a series of overlapping, opposed dualities, dualities that involved virtue and corruption, purity and danger, and that may well have been rooted in something approaching the identity crisis sketched out by Fawn Brodie.

There were, certainly, very different opinions as to which side of this opposition Smith belonged on. Whereas he identified himself with the forces of virtue in the *Book of Mormon* and announced himself as a prophet, popular sentiment in New York condemned Smith as a "blasphemer" and a fraud, a counterfeiter of sacred texts. Compounding the complication, Smith was operating with tricky symbolic tools. In his *Haymow Sermon* the great counterfeiter Stephen Burroughs had mocked the Pelhamites who resorted to the Urim and Thummim,[93] and Smith echoed but reversed Burroughs's implication in his account of the translation of the plates. Similarly, the sacred Golden Plates themselves echoed but reversed the connotation of the base copper plates upon which Burroughs rolled his "silk" – the quintessential "slippery treasure" – in his secret Canadian workshop. Hermetic danger lurked close to Smith's sacred enterprise; thus he marked the boundary in clear and certain terms. While some of the people of Ontario County condemned him as an impostor, Joseph presented himself as the Nephite, the prophet of the coming Kingdom, the vehicle for the restoration of ancient mysteries, against the profane world of scoffers, corrupt Freemasons, and evil counterfeiters.

Two points stand out: Joseph Smith viewed the world in a series of connected but antagonistic opposites, and he was drawn to alchemical and hermetic practices and metaphors. Although we are entering very dangerous waters, the psychological archetypes that Carl Jung saw in hermetic alchemy offer a useful interpretive perspective on the inner life of Joseph Smith.

Late in his life Jung began to argue that the medieval practice of philosophical alchemy was an unconscious projection of the psychic struggles of the alchemists themselves. The alchemical mysteries of material dissolution, opposition, and reintegration were for Jung mystical renderings of the processes of personality formation, in which the end was the whole, integrated self, symbolized in the philosopher's stone. The *coniunctio*, the alchemical marriage, resolved the opposition of sulphur and mercury, light and dark, high and low, fire and water, male and female, heaven and earth, the alchemical Sun and Moon, the alchemical King and Queen, just as a process of psychological healing resolved conscious and unconscious oppositions in the human psyche.[94]

Although I am very skeptical about a theory of universal archetypes, Jung's thesis provides a very useful frame of reference, if not an explanation, for the hermetic connotations of the early life of Joseph Smith and the coming forth of the *Book of Mormon*. Realizing all the pitfalls, one can suggest that Joseph Smith was unconsciously attracted to the broader hermetic culture because its basic categories resonated with his psychic situation, providing order in a life beset with familial conflict.[95]

Jung's model of psychic and alchemical oppositions requires a resolution: the achievement of union, wholeness, and completion in the *con-iunctio*.[96] It has been proposed that the canonical 1838 version of Joseph Smith's story of the visions, translation, baptism, and announcement of the Kingdom captures this resolution of opposites. In this analysis, the literary structure of the 1838 record gradually resolves the oppositions of light and dark, high and low, and heaven and earth in its account of Smith's visions, money-digging, recovery and translation of the Golden Plates, and baptism by John the Baptist. At the outset, the young Joseph, still immersed in the low, dark world, is blinded by the high, bright light of God and Christ. Gradually, as Smith framed the text and institutions of the new dispensation, this distance is overcome, darkness is balanced with light, and the Kingdom is realized separate from the world. Within the bounds of this Kingdom Smith and Cowdery can meet and converse face-to-face with John the Baptist. Here, separate from the corrupt world, the traditional boundaries between natural and supernatural, indeed between humanity and God, are set aside in a fundamental theological resolution.[97]

In the broader history of the church, such a resolution was not approached for many years, until the public announcement of the classic Mormon theology at Nauvoo in the early 1840s. Baptism for the dead, the doctrines of unity of spirit and matter and the progression of humanity to divinity, and the doctrines and practices of celestial and plural marriage were all part of the forging of the Mormon Kingdom's "whole and complete and perfect union."[98]

In effect, the greater Mormon emergence can be visualized as a meta-alchemical experience running from opposition to union, an experience shaped and driven by the personality of Joseph Smith. Having achieved a personal and theological resolution by 1844, it might be said that Smith's life was complete and that he willingly accepted martyrdom at Carthage.

But the theological resolution at Nauvoo permitted the erasing of the boundaries between purity and danger so elaborately constructed in the 1820s. In New York, the boundary between the Kingdom and the corrupt world was defined in great measure by the boundary dividing the hermetic opposites that Smith had inherited through the divining tradition from the early modern past. Thus at the founding of the church the boundary between hermetic purity and danger and the boundary between the church and the world coincided, each mutually reinforcing. But by 1844, and indeed by the latter half of the 1830s, these two boundaries no longer coincided. Those divinely appointed to lead the Kingdom of God on earth could violate the conventional boundary between purity and danger with impunity, for it no longer applied to them, as they were not of the world. In effect Smith articulated his personal psychic and religious oppositions in terms of the duality in hermetic culture, and then achieved a resolution by transcending them as a prophet of a new dispensation. This resolution was unacceptable to many among the Mormons, who abandoned the church in dissent and apostasy, and to the mass of public opinion in the United States, with implications running far into the future.

8

The Mysteries Defined

> They are they who are the church of the Firstborn. They are they
> into whose hands that Father has given all things – They are they
> who are priests and kings, who have received of his fulness, and of
> his glory; And are priests of the Most High, after the order of
> Melchizedek, which was after the order of Enoch, which was after
> the order of the Only Begotten Son. Wherefore, as it is written,
> they are gods, even the sons of God –
>
> Vision of Joseph Smith and Sidney Rigdon at Hiram, Ohio,
> February 16, 1832[1]

IN THE SPRING OF 1830 Joseph Smith offered himself to the people
of the Burned-over District as a prophet of a new dispensation. He was
restoring not only the true church but the age of miracles, an age that
orthodox religion assumed lay closed in the antiquity of the prophets. In
this assertion, Smith not only placed himself in the same posture toward
orthodoxy taken by earlier radical and hermetic sectarians but began to
replicate the core of their doctrine. Mormonism powerfully rearticulated
the fusion of hermetic divinization and millenarian restoration first forged
in the fires of the Radical Reformation and the English Revolution.

The restoration of a miraculous connection between heaven and earth,
between spirit and matter, was the most powerful attraction drawing
adherents to Smith's new church. But miraculous, spiritual powers were a
dangerous commodity, constantly in danger of slipping out of control.
The first nine years of the history of the Mormon church brought important doctrinal developments, as Joseph Smith began to institutionalize the
Mormon path to the divine mysteries. It also brought explosive episodes
of conflict and dissent, as people attracted to a church of miracles demanded the right to directly experience the numinous connection between
spirit and matter. During the 1830s, periods of relative calm and doctrinal
development were twice disrupted by strife – reminiscent of the dyadic
conflicts of Nephites and Lamanites in the *Book of Mormon* – ending in
the near dissolution of the Mormon movement in Missouri in 1839.

This chapter and the next detail the emergence of Mormon doctrine
over this decade, looking in sequence at what may be called purities and
dangers, against the background of the political strife buffeting the new

church. The following two chapters carry the story through a final cycle of doctrinal construction, again moving from purity to danger, with the framing of a classic Mormon cosmology of plural marriage and ritual divinization at Nauvoo, Illinois, between 1841 and the Mormon exodus for the Great Basin in 1846.

The miraculous was very much on Joseph Smith's mind in the final months of the transcribing of the *Book of Mormon*. In the Third Book of Nephi Christ is described as a master alchemist in powerful imagery drawn from the Book of Malachi: "Like a refiner's fire," he would "purify the sons of Levi, and purge them as gold and silver."[2] After the climactic battle at the ·Hill Cumorah, the surviving prophet, Moroni, spoke in similar language of the righteous surviving "the fiery furnace" and the final day when "the elements shall melt with fervent heat." He also spoke of "a God of miracles" continuing to act in palpable ways in the world. "And who shall say that Jesus Christ did not do many mighty miracles? . . . And if there were miracles wrought then, why has God ceased to be a God of miracles and yet be an unchangeable Being?" Smith's God conformed to a uniformitarian principle; his powers in the present day were no different than in distant antiquity. And one of his powers was that of acting through human intermediaries. As promised in the biblical Book of Mark, righteous believers would "cast out devils" and "speak with new tongues"; they would "take up serpents" and "lay hands on the sick."[3]

The miraculous was also central in Joseph Smith's imagination when, on March 26, 1830, between notices of state lotteries, bank payments, and canal tolls, he advertised the *Book of Mormon* in the Wayne *Sentinel*. The book was "written by way of commandment, and also by the spirit of Prophecy and Revelation"; it was "to show unto the remnant of the House of Israel how great things the Lord hath done for their fathers; and that they may know the covenants of the Lord, that they are not cast off forever." The Lord spoke through the *Book of Mormon*.[4]

This God of miracles would set the immediate agenda for the early Mormon church. News of miraculous events spurred conversion among a distinctly prepared people, hungering for a religion of immanent divine presence. The first miracle was the witnessing of the Golden Plates, the Urim and Thummim, the sword of Laban, and the directors that Smith had found in the Hill Cumorah. In June 1829 Joseph Smith and Oliver Cowdery moved from Pennsylvania to the town of Fayette in Seneca County, where on the Whitmer family farm they finished translating the *Book of Mormon*. During this summer Smith saw the necessity of sharing his charisma with a selection of his growing audience. The first witnesses were Oliver Cowdery, David Whitmer, and Martin Harris. After fervent prayer, Cowdery and Whitmer believed they saw an angel descend on a light bearing the plates, and confirming the authenticity of their translation. Harris did not claim to have had the vision but accepted that Smith had seen the angel. Several days later eight men, four Whitmer brothers and their brother-in-law Hiram Page, with Joseph Smith Sr. and his sons Hyrum and Samuel, were shown the plates, which they "did handle with our hands." "Seen and hefted," the plates were taken up to heaven by an angel.[5]

The account of Smith's visions and the revelations of the *Book of Mormon,* supported by the testimony of the witnesses, worked to bring conversions in the Whitmers' circle in Fayette and among the money-digging families in Manchester. These early believers assembled at the Whitmers' farm on April 6, 1830, to participate in the formal organization of the church. Joseph Smith and Oliver Cowdery had baptized each other in the Susquehanna River in May 1829; they and other Smiths, the Whitmers, Martin Harris, and Orrin Porter Rockwell, a close friend of Joseph's among the money-diggers, were baptized on April 6, followed by a dozen others on subsequent Sundays.[6]

Another miracle would bring conversions in Colesville, on the Susquehanna River, when Joseph Smith returned the next month to the scene of his divining adventures of 1826. Gathering prayer meetings at Joseph Knight's, Smith's preaching had a powerful effect on Knight's son Newell. Under the stress of these meetings, Newell "began to feel uneasy" and, returning to his house, fell into convulsions. "His visage and limbs were distorted and twisted in every shape and appearance possible to imagine; and finally he was caught up off the floor and tossed about most fearfully." Smith was called to "cast the devil out of him," which immediately happened; Newell later testified in court that he saw the devil leave him, "a spiritual sight and spiritually discerned." With this miraculous exorcism Newell began to have visions; he and many witnesses claimed that he was levitated by "the Spirit of the Lord" off the floor to the beams of the dwelling house. Many in the Knight neighborhood – including Aaron Culver, nephew of the visionary Nathan – were converted to the new faith in the following days and weeks.[7]

The exorcism and levitation of Newell Knight would be the first of many miraculous manifestations of divine power in Mormon lore.[8] The core of Smith's message was that of a restoration, but Smith was restoring not simply the apostolic church but the spiritual powers of ancient prophets to men acting as divine agents in a Kingdom of God. Smith's God was a God of miracles, but so too were his agents, his priests, men of miracles. Spiritual power descended from the heavens, but it was directed through divinely anointed humans, bearing powers not far removed from the diviner's touch. Here the supernatural powers of the pre-Reformation Catholic church – and the Muggletonian prophets – were being restored, conditioning and deflecting the power of the Calvinist God of the orthodox churches. In the years to come this conditioning of divine power would be amplified greatly, as Mormon priests assumed higher and higher powers.

A church of miracles attracted a particular kind of convert. As in Vermont, hermetic culture provided an important background for the New York converts. More than half came from towns with Masonic lodges or divining histories, and about a third came from towns with Methodist societies.[9] Unlike in Vermont, settlement in Seneca County from Pennsylvania meant that the large body of converts from Fayette (at least twenty-one people) were exposed to Pennsylvania German culture, institutionalized in four German churches, including the Zion church that the Whitmers had attended.[10] Diedrich Willers, the minister of this church, noted that the Whitmers had moved between German Reformed services and the Mennonites, Methodists, and Baptists. In a summary of the Mormon converts – who were calling themselves "The True Followers of Christ" – he noted that most "were apparently General Baptists," a comment that carries us back to the sectarian axis linking southeast New England and southeast Pennsylvania.[11] This may have been more of a broad disposition rather than an institutional presence in the Burned-over District, but the General Baptist notion of a universal redemption comported well with subsequent Mormon doctrine.

As we have seen, many of the Mormon converts had long been involved in the magical spiritualism of divining and exposed to belief in witchcraft. Certainly they were hostile to the Calvinist doctrine of election and to the doctrine of original sin advanced by Calvinists and Methodists alike. They often came from families of "Seekers" spinning off from sectarian communities, refusing to accept the authority and legitimacy of existing denominations, hopeful for the restoration of the "ancient order of things." Often they came from experiences of poverty and hardship, finding release and empowerment in a message of millenarian restoration and in a church where there would be no educated and salaried ministry.[12] Smith's visions, his translated text, his witnesses, and his miracles all provided the seal of prophetic authority.[13] Many of these early followers, however, had quite different visions of the restoration than did the prophet, visions much closer to biblical sources than Smith's divergences.[14] Such converts would not be easy for a young prophet to control. His followers were not content to leave spiritual power in his hands alone; they demanded the right to touch the world of spirit. For the

Joseph Smith Jr., a nineteenth-century portrait.
Courtesy of the Utah State Historical Society.

next decade Smith would have to struggle with his people over his authority and the terms of a broader sharing of charismatic power.[15]

The first explicit challenge came in July 1830, when Oliver Cowdery and the Whitmers objected that one of his revelations governing admission to baptism contradicted the *Book of Mormon* and came close to the orthodox requirement of relating an experience of grace to a minister. By the following September Cowdery and the Whitmers were beginning to accept revelations made by Hiram Page through the use of a seer-stone and written out on "a roll of papers." But if anyone with a seer-stone could claim the power of revelation, the church was doomed to chaos and dissolution. At a conference called later that month, with Newell Knight at his side, Smith questioned Page's authority to receive revelation and managed to assert his own supreme authority. After considerable debate, the conference announced that Smith alone was "to receive and write Revelations and Commandments for this Church." The vote was confirmed by a revelation that God had given Smith "the keys to the mysteries, and the revelations which are sealed." Page renounced his stone, just as Smith had set aside his stone, and all claims to the Urim and Thummim, a year before. Rather than from magic artifacts, revelation would rise from prophetic authority. With this break with the popular magic of Mormon beginnings, an authority structure began to take shape in the church.[16]

At the same time, Smith announced new doctrines that served to deflect attention from the challenge of the seer-stone dissenters. A few days before the conference he produced a powerfully worded revelation on the imminence of the millennium, a revelation that ended with the comforting universalist note that children were innocent of original sin. Within months he would totally abandon the doctrine of original sin, contradicting passages in the *Book of Mormon*.[17] But in the fall of 1830 the millennial thrust was most important, establishing the westward dynamic of Mormon history for decades to come: the restored kingdom was their refuge from a coming millennial destruction.[18] The July revelation on the "keys to the mysteries" also ordered Oliver Cowdery and Hiram Page, later replaced by David Whitmer, to begin a western missionary journey to convert the Lamanites (the Indians) and it announced that the millennial city of Zion, the New Jerusalem, would be built "on the borders by the Lamanites."[19]

The journey of the western missionaries would open a new chapter in Mormon history, that centering on Kirtland, Ohio. The missionaries set out in October, with western Missouri as their intended goal. But on the

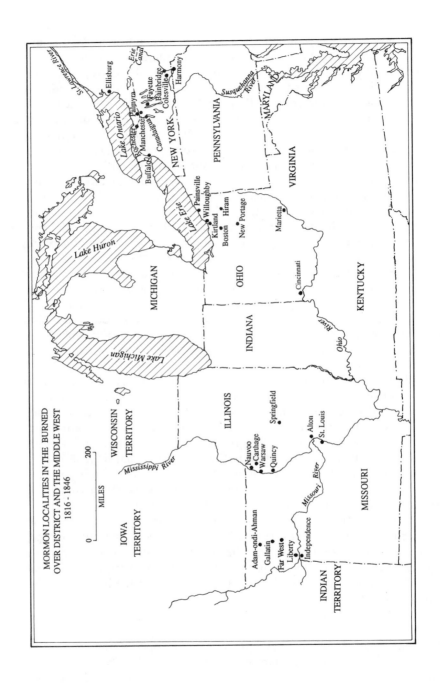

MORMON LOCALITIES IN THE BURNED
OVER DISTRICT AND THE MIDDLE WEST
1816 - 1846

way they were diverted to northeast Ohio, where one of the missionaries, Parley Pratt, knew they would find a prepared people. Pratt, born in a Baptist neighborhood in Canaan, New York, had spent several years in the frontier settlements, in search of work, a competency, and the true primitive gospel. Settling in Ohio, he found this gospel in the summer of 1829 in the preaching of Sidney Rigdon of Mentor. Once a Baptist preacher, and then a Campbellite restorationist, Rigdon broke with Alexander Campbell in the fall of 1830, holding that a restoration involved not only the apostolic church but "supernatural gifts and miracles." In August 1830 Pratt had journeyed east and had been converted by the Mormon bible; three months later he led the missionaries back to Mentor to see Rigdon. Impressed by their announcement of the miracles of the Mormon emergence, Rigdon visited the Smith household in Manchester, New York, that December and was converted. With anti-Mormon sentiment rising in New York, Rigdon offered the opportunity to move the Mormon communities west to Ohio, where he had established his former Campbellite following into a communal society based in Mentor and Kirtland. The following January the first westward Mormon exodus began.[20]

The conversion of Sidney Rigdon was of critical importance to the new movement. Rigdon became a close associate of Smith, and he offered both a field of hundreds of potential converts among the restorationists of Ohio's Western Reserve and property upon which to build a new start. The new start began almost immediately, with the emigration of the New York Saints to Ohio and the conversion of many of Rigdon's followers. Once again Smith faced challenges to his monopoly over charismatic power. During the spring of 1831 many among the new Ohio converts experienced spiritual events, seeing "wonderful lights in the air and on the ground," falling into fits, speaking in tongues, and claiming revelations and visions. In May 1831 Smith was able to suppress these "false spirits" with a new revelation, but the problem of an orderly sharing of charisma remained to be solved.[21]

The eventual success of Mormonism lay in the embedding of a shared charisma in the institutional fabric of the church. Joseph Smith would not maintain an absolute monopoly over spiritual power but rather doled it out in an evolving system of inclusive priesthoods, governed by an increasingly elaborate hierarchy. Church institutions began to take shape in 1829 and grew in complexity over the early 1830s both as membership grew and as Smith negotiated his way through a series of political crises. In May 1829, when John the Baptist appeared to Smith and Cowdery, they received divine appointments as First and Second Elders of the new church. Smith's authority as Seer and Revelator was announced in April 1830 and confirmed in September. In February and March 1831, Smith issued a series of revelations that began to establish sacramental and institutional structures, including the collective economy called the United Order of Enoch, or the Law of Consecration. The following January Smith was named President of the High Priesthood, and in March 1833 a First Presidency was established, including the president and two counselors. Stake councils were established in Kirtland and in Missouri in 1834, in a reorganization that saw the suspension of the communal United Order. The Council of Twelve Apostles was established in February 1835, and a month later a Quorum of Seventies was organized.[22]

These various offices met both the governance needs of the church and the political requirements of sharing responsibility with an often unruly band of leading followers. As did the collective economy of the United Order, this hierarchy of offices had parallels in other millenarian groups such as the Ephrata celibates and the Shakers, for whom collective order represented life in the Kingdom of God. Hierarchy and collectivity had been features of the millennialist sects of the Radical Reformation, most notably the Münster Anabaptists.[23] But the most interesting parallel was with the priestly hierarchy of the sixteenth-century Familists' House of Love, in which an Oldest Elder in Holy Understanding presided over ranks of Old Elders, Priests of the Throne of God, and four orders of lesser priests, the lowest of which included the entire membership.[24] In the Mormon hierarchy, this lowest, most inclusive rank was the Aaronic Priesthood, through which the Mormon believer would pass before entering the more powerful and charismatic Priesthood of Melchizedek. Institutionalizing the anticlericalism of his following, Smith established the ideal of universal priesthood among the believing men of the church, sharing charismatic power and organizational responsibility while retaining prophetic authority.

After their mutual baptism in May 1829 Joseph Smith and Oliver Cowdery claimed that John the Baptist had conferred on them the Levitical, or Aaronic, Priesthood. Conferred on "every worthy male member," eventually starting with boys of twelve years of age, these offices provided the semblance of an equalitarian order for white males in the church. Ranked as deacons, teachers, and priests, the Aaronic Priesthood held "the keys of the ministering of angels"; they were to watch over the church, teach the gospel, and perform baptisms.[25]

Some doubt exists as to the conception of this Aaronic Priesthood in the early years, and even more doubt exists about the timing of the announcement of the higher Melchizedek Priesthood. Smith claimed that the restoration of the Melchizedek was announced in May 1829 by the appearance of the archangels Peter, James, and John, following the type of Christ's vision of Moses and Elias. But the first references to these angels in Mormon texts did not come until 1835, and it appears that the high priesthood was not actually established until June 1831, as Smith was building his authority over the Kirtland settlements.26

If the high priesthood was not actually a reality before the summer of 1831, it certainly was implied in Smith's revelations. For the next fifteen years the key to the attraction of early Mormonism – and to the survival of Smith as a prophet – lay in his promises of the future revelation of the secret workings of God's Kingdom. In ten revelations issued between the summer of 1828 and February 1831, Smith promised that "the mysteries of God shall be unfolded," leading to "eternal life." In January 1831 he tied this promise to the call to "gather a righteous people" in Ohio: it was in "this cause I gave unto you the commandment that ye should go to the Ohio; and there I will give unto you my law; and there you shall be endowed with power from on high."27

On June 3, 1831, at a General Conference in Kirtland, twenty-three men were ordained into the high priesthood, which that November was identified with the biblical Priesthood of Melchizedek. Where the Aaronic Priesthood was limited to "outward ordinances," the Melchizedek Priesthood would hold "the key to the mysteries of the kingdom, even the key of the knowledge of God." Unlike the lower priesthood, the high priests were to "administer in spiritual things," in a specific sharing of spiritual power with the prophet.28

This diffusion of spiritual powers coincided with more miraculous events. Sometime during the summer of 1831 Smith succeeded in healing the lame arm of an elderly Mrs. Mary Johnson, whose family soon joined the church. And at the June 3 Kirtland conference, when "false spirits" stopped the voices of several of his new high priests, Smith drove them out, though according to one account he then failed in efforts to heal a crippled hand and a lame leg and to revive a child from death.29 The high priests would be capable of "wonderful works" of exorcism, faith-healing, resistance to poisons, and handling snakes. Certainly the high priests used these powers: Newell Knight – before and after his ordination – drove out evil spirits and healed the sick, and missionaries in northern Vermont and New York drew converts with stories of their healing powers.30

Such healing powers clearly had biblical antecedents (specifically in Christ's address to his apostles) that would have been familiar to primitivists searching the Bible for signs and miracles.31 But the greatest powers of the high priesthood lay in their sharing in the "keys to the mysteries," previously granted only to Joseph the Prophet. Smith first articulated these powers in October 1831, at a General Conference meeting in Orange, Ohio. "The order of the High-priesthood," he announced at the

Orange conference, "is that they have power given them to seal up the Saints unto Eternal Life." He repeated this language in a revelation the next month. In effect, Mormon high priests were given the authority to grant salvation through a ritual – an authority that orthodox Christians reserved to God, working through grace.[32] This idea of an earthly sealing was first introduced in the *Book of Mormon,* when Nephi was granted powers of salvation and damnation: "Whatsoever ye shall seal on earth shall be sealed in heaven; and whatsoever ye shall loose on earth shall be loosed in heaven."[33]

Here, then, was a fundamental theological departure, clearly inspired by the experience of magic. The Mormon high priests would in effect be *magi,* with powers extending up from the visible world on earth to the invisible world of the heavens, controlling and delimiting the power of a God whom the Calvinist tradition had made omnipotent. The next step, an even more fundamental departure, would be to join that limited God in divinity. Hinting at this promise in the early 1830s, Smith would not establish this path to divinization until 1843, at Nauvoo, Illinois. But the groundwork for this departure was laid in Ohio in a description of a new cosmos emerging in parallel with the new priesthood. Both had common roots reaching back into the hermetic tradition of the primal divine Adam.

The Old Testament Priesthood of the Melchizedek, endowed with great, *magus*-like powers and identified with Christ in the Book of Hebrews, was not unique to the emerging Mormon theology. Ninety years before the high priesthood ceremony at Kirtland in 1831, the celibate choirs at Ephrata sang of the restoration of the Melchizedek, as well as the unity of the primal Adam. More recently Shaker Benjamin Youngs, in his 1808 *Testimony of Christ's Second Coming,* had invoked the Melchizedek order in his account of a hermaphrodite Christ, and in 1824 George Rapp of the German Harmonist Society settled in southern Ohio and saw in the Melchizedek the model for millennial, communitarian selflessness. In 1840 Orestes Brownson, another son of Royalton, Vermont, in his second essay on the "Laboring Classes," demanded the replacement of human priesthoods with a divinely ordained "order of Melchizedec." Six years later Brownson's brother Oran joined the Mormons.[34]

But the most widely diffused use of the Melchizedek was in the ritual of Royal Arch Freemasonry, which, as we have already seen, was of great significance in the framing of early Mormonism. In the ceremonies installing the High Priests of the Royal Arch, the Masonic manuals uniformly borrowed from Hebrews 5:6 to tell the candidate that "thou art a Priest forever, after the order of Melchizedec."[35] Just as the Royal Arch tale of

Enoch's treasures appears to have had a formative influence on Smith's account of the discovery of the Golden Plates, so too, this mythology had powerful resonances in the new Mormon cosmology sketched between 1830 and 1833, in over a hundred revelations and a revision of the biblical Book of Genesis. A spiritually powerful high priesthood, a concern for a primal language, and a plan for the construction of temples were the underpinnings of this cosmic system, the realization that the Mormon faithful would be "endowed with power from on high."

The central statements of this cosmology were first laid out in Smith's revision of Genesis, the Book of Moses, and in revelations on the priesthood and temples. Smith wrote his revision of Genesis between June 1830 and February 1831, and his key revelations date from November 1831 to May 1833. From December 1830 Smith worked closely with Sidney Rigdon, the former Campbellite, who served as his scribe and confidant. Rigdon, renowned throughout the Western Reserve for his command of the Bible, was thought to have had a decisive influence on Smith in these years. (Rigdon had Masonic connections of his own, becoming a Mason later in life. His cousins Thomas and John Rigdon were both Campbellite ministers and Thomas was a Royal Arch Mason.)[36] David Whitmer, later a dissenter, claimed that Rigdon "soon worked himself deep into Brother Joseph's affections," and that it was at his "instigation" that the high priesthood was adopted. Perhaps that was so, but certainly Smith had the idea of the Melchizedek Priesthood in mind at least since the summer of 1829, when he – with Oliver Cowdery – wrote the priesthood into the Book of Alma.[37]

Many of the most important sections of the Book of Moses were written before Rigdon arrived in New York in December 1830, but Rigdon was with Smith when he wrote passages that had direct analogues to the mythology of a pure primitive Freemasonry. In the sixth and seventh chapters of the Book of Moses the prophet Enoch had a long vision of the days of Adam and of the future. Adam was described as having been "after the order of him who was without beginning of days or end of years, from all eternity to all eternity." This was the order of Melchizedek, as identified with Christ; this connection of Adam with Christ had long been an important dimension of radical universalism. Looking into the future, Enoch was shown the "seed of Adam" and the "seed of Cain," echoing hermetic and Masonic references to the two seeds.[38] And at the beginning of the sixth chapter of Moses, the descendants of Seth began to keep "a book of remembrance" written in "the language of Adam," which was equated with the priesthood: "And by them their children were taught to read and write, having a language which was pure and undefiled. Now this same Priesthood, which was in the beginning, shall be in the end of the world also."[39] The book of remembrance, written in the primal "language of Adam," in this account was passed down to the prophet Enoch; in September 1832 Smith claimed to have heard the "pure Adamic language" for the first time, when Brigham Young spoke in tongues at their first meeting. That same September Smith traced by revelation the lineage of the priesthood back from the sons of Moses to Melchizedek, Noah, Enoch, Abel, and eventually to "Adam, the first man."[40]

Thus, with Rigdon at his side, Smith added themes to the Genesis story that were directly analogous to Masonic myths describing priestly genealogies running back to Adam. The references to Adamic language were equally important, pointing to another critical link with the intellectual world of seventeenth-century hermeticism. At the core of the magic beliefs about correspondences lay the dream of a universal language, capturing the signature or inner essence of all things, understandable to all people if the key to its grammar could be discovered. The inspiration for ideas about this language lay in the second chapter of Genesis (repeated verbatim in the third chapter of Smith's Moses) where Adam gave names to the animals that God paraded before him.[41] Preserved after the Adamic exile from Eden, this language had been lost at the Tower of Babel. Cabalists and hermetic philosophers hoped to recover this natural, or Adamic, language through magical manipulations of Hebrew letters and Egyptian hieroglyphics. In the world of the English revolutionary Instauration, Jan Comenius and Samuel Hartlib, following Francis Bacon, led the search for a universal language. In the wake of the revolutionary epoch, John Webster's hope that Jacob Boehme's mysticism would provide the key to the universal language was scorned by men of science connected with the Royal Society. And – just as it became the repository of other fragments of hermetic lore – eighteenth-century Freemasonry was reputed to be hiding the secrets of this "universal language." Closer at hand, newspapers in Palmyra in 1819 and 1823 reported efforts to translate hieroglyphic inscriptions found on rocks in Pompey, New York, east along the Erie Canal in Onondaga County, and in Dighton, in Massachusetts's Bristol County.[42]

From 1827 into the 1840s, Joseph Smith was vitally interested in ancient languages. The Golden Plates were supposed to have been covered with ancient writing, which Smith translated into the published *Book of Mormon;* at the end of the Book of Mormon, Smith identified this language as a "reformed Egyptian," which had been "handed down and altered" among the Nephites.[43] This passage was written in the summer of 1829, over a year after Smith had sent Martin Harris all the way to New York City to consult with two learned professors, Samuel L. Mitchell and

Charles Anthon, on the origins of a list of figures that Smith had copied from the plates. As one historian has argued, the failure of these famous scholars, and the success of an unschooled Smith, in translating these supposed ancient records with his seer-stone and the Urim and Thummim, fulfilled a prophecy in Isaiah.[44] Magical implements were critical to the translation process because the ancient language had been "altered"; they were described as God's "means for the interpretation" of the "reformed Egyptian."[45] These concerns with language were repeated in the subsequent Book of Ether, where the family of Jared escapes from the destruction of the Tower of Babel with their primal language "not confounded." Later in the story God "confounded" their written language but left interpreter-stones so that men of spirit might eventually decode their engraved plates.[46] Similarly, in his advertisement in the Wayne *Sentinel* in March 1830, Smith emphasized that the *Book of Mormon* included this record of the Jaredites, "scattered at the time the Lord confounded the language of the people when they were building a tower to get to Heaven." This attention to sacred language resonated among the converted Ohio restorationists in the spring of 1831. In common with both earlier perfectionists and later Mormons, some of them spoke "in tongues," while others claimed to see gold, lighted letters, written by angels, showering down on the fields around Kirtland.[47]

These, then, were the broader connotations and contexts for Smith's attention to a "pure and undefiled" language of Adam in his revelation of Enoch, written out in the winter of 1830 to 1831. The concept of an Adamic language was central to the hermetic quest for perfect knowledge, it was the essence of the pure Freemasonry handed down from Adam, and it was certainly on Joseph Smith's mind throughout this period. Quite simply, the Adamic language was the royal road to perfection, the "key to the mysteries." Equated with the priesthood in Moses 6:6–7, the Adamic language was given ecclesiastical form in the priestly order of the Melchizedek.

Language was a central theme in Smith's emerging theology, and so too were temples. The restored Kingdom would not only save the Adamic language, but it would have a temple, rebuilt at a revealed location on the type of Solomon's temple, the Hebrew house of the Lord. Here the boundary between spirit and matter, heaven and earth, would be definitively transcended: "the glory of God" would "fill the house."[48] God would materialize among his saints in his tabernacle, achieving the union of all things that the Mormon Kingdom promised. By 1831 the Old Testament priesthoods of Aaron and Melchizedek had been restored; now a temple was needed to provide an architectural and ritual focus for their authority. And, just as these priesthoods had Masonic equivalents, the most widely available contemporary source for the typology of Solomon's temple was Freemasonry, founded according to legend at the building of the ancient temple.[49]

The typology of the Hebrew temple was well established in Smith's mind from the period of the translation of the *Book of Mormon*. Early in the *Book of Mormon* the hero Nephi built a temple in the New World "after the manner of the temple of Solomon." It was at this temple, in the "land of Bountiful," that Christ appeared after his Resurrection, and such a house of the Lord would be the site of the Second Coming.[50] Throughout the *Book of Mormon* the Nephites gathered at this temple, and in early revelations in the winter of 1830–1, Smith reminded his people that God would come "suddenly to my temple." And in the Book of Moses, written at roughly the same time, Smith revised Genesis to have the prophet Enoch build a city of Zion, a "city of holiness," which was entirely "taken up to heaven."[51]

Temples would be the material locus of divinity, the numinous conduit linking the visible and invisible worlds, in Mormon ritual and theology. Eventually the temple would be the place for the ordinances and endowments of divinization, but in 1831 the temple was viewed in apocalyptic terms. Rebuilding the temple of Nephi and the city of Enoch would fulfill prophecy and advance the Second Coming.[52] To that end, and in the interest of maintaining the momentum of his movement, Smith announced in the summer of 1831 that the city and the temple would be rebuilt in Jackson County in western Missouri, near the town of Independence. Joining the band of New York Saints led by Newell Knight, recently emigrated from Colesville to Missouri in July 1831, Smith appointed Sidney Rigdon to find a site for the temple, and then presided over its dedication.[53] This Missouri settlement would be known as Zion. For years Smith had been fascinated with the prophet Enoch; his discovery of the Golden Plates echoed the Masonic tale of Enoch, his revision of Genesis had revolved centrally around Enoch, and now he hoped to rebuild Enoch's city. Finally, when he set up the collective United Order of Enoch in March 1832, he adopted Enoch as his ritual identity. Under such authority in June 1833 he wrote a description for the building of the city of Zion, with a four-square plan to accommodate as many as twenty thousand people, with twenty-four temples.[54]

Smith's plans for temples and the city of Zion were interwoven with his evolving description of the Mormon cosmos. At the same time that Zion was identified with Enoch, Smith also began to speak of its connection with Adam. Independence was to be the location of Enoch's city, because it had once been Paradise itself. From this Garden of Eden, centrally located in the North American continent, Adam had been expelled to

"Adam ondi Ahman," where he gathered his posterity, and from where Noah had sailed his ark to Palestine during the Flood.[55] Thus three waves of Old World immigrants – Jaredites, Nephites, and Euro-Americans – had come to the New World in search of Paradise. Smith had found Paradise, and the twenty-four temples in his city there were to be assigned to six ranks in the two orders of priesthood and to the presiding presidency and bishops.[56] Quite literally, the priesthoods would be an ascending ladder, gradually attaining the ritual keys that would open the mysteries to restore the people to Paradise. If Smith did not attempt to define these rituals in the early 1830s, he did define the structure of the cosmos to which these mysteries led. This cosmos would be more fully elaborated in the 1840s, and the keys to its entry defined. The origins of this cosmos take us back to the world of early modern hermeticism.

Six months after dedicating the Independence temple site with the Colesville Saints, Joseph Smith and Sidney Rigdon were living in Hiram, Ohio, revising the Bible. Here, in February 1832, as they were retranslating the Book of John, they had a vision together that totally transformed orthodox notions of the cosmos.[57]

Rather than a traditional Christian heaven and hell, there would be three kingdoms in the Mormon cosmos; rather than a single divinity, there would be in the Mormon cosmos a hierarchical pantheon of gods. Arranged in a strict hierarchy, and designated for very different populations, each order of heaven would have its particular "glory." Drawing on language from First Corinthians, these degrees of glory were equated with the stars, the moon, and the sun.[58] At the bottom there was the telestial world, a heaven of a very limited glory reserved for "they who are liars, and sorcerers, and adulterers, and whoremongers." In a further revelation announced the following December, Smith qualified the threat of damnation in this lowest, telestial world: those "abid[ing] the law" of each heaven would receive a certain degree of "glory" and "fulness." In Fawn Brodie's estimation, this revelation was "a long step toward Universalism." Except for the "sons of perdition," who accepted and then rejected the "Holy Spirit," all of mankind would find a place in one of the Mormon heavens.[59] But the critical distinction lay between simple salvation and divine exaltation. Above the telestial kingdom was the terrestrial, for the non-Mormon just, "they who receive of the presence of the Son, but not of the fulness of the Father."[60] At the top lay the celestial kingdom: "the glory of the celestial . . . excels in all things." This ultimate heaven would be inherited by "they who are the church of the Firstborn," who were "priests of the Most High, after the order of the Melchizedek, which was after the order of Enoch, which was after the order of the Only Begotten Son." Raised to the celestial kingdom, the Mormon Priesthood of the Melchizedek would rank as gods.

> Wherefore, as it is written, they are gods, even the sons of God –
> Wherefore, all things are theirs, whether life or death, or things present, or things to come, all are theirs and they are Christ's, and Christ is God's. And they shall overcome all things.[61]

Smith's theology thus promised a radical departure from traditional Protestant Christianity. The Mormon cosmos announced universal salvation for humanity and promised divinity to the Mormon faithful. Human salvation and Mormon divinity would be structured in a radically new configuration of the invisible world, three ascending kingdoms replacing the duality of heaven and hell.

This challenge to traditional Christianity was not easy to swallow. Many in the Mormon ranks resisted the new doctrine, and in this resistance lay the seeds of later dissent. Some seceded from the church in the spring of 1832, and a month after they had their vision, Smith and Rigdon were attacked by a mob in Hiram, including the Johnson brothers, with whose family they had been staying. This mobbing was not directly related to the Smith–Rigdon vision, but that vision did nothing to deter the rioters, and it took months of exhortation before doubts about the new revelation began to subside.[62]

These doubts about the Hiram vision focused on its most highly elaborated element, the restructuring of the invisible world into three kingdoms, telestial, terrestrial, and celestial. Smith's promise of divinity did not receive the same attention; perhaps it was more oblique, and it was based on canonical language in the Bible, specifically in the Book of Psalms and the Gospel of St. John.[63] But the three Mormon heavens would ultimately only provide the backdrop for Mormon godhood, which gradually would emerge as the central theme of the new theology. It would be here that Mormonism would offer the same restoration of the godlike powers of the primal Adam that hermeticism offered as the reward to the true adept. This doctrine of eventual divinity would not be fully spelled out to the Mormon rank and file until April 1844, in Joseph Smith's funeral oration for King Follett, following two years of doctrinal and ritual development among the Nauvoo Mormon elite that incontrovertibly demonstrates the hermetic contributions to Mormon theology. But the hermeticism of the Nauvoo theology was anticipated by and grounded upon the early revelations in Ohio, that at Hiram in 1832 and another at Kirtland in 1833.

Smith's 1833 Kirtland revelation came at a juncture of great stress and turmoil. Finding the Missouri settlement threatened by armed attack by hostile opponents in April 1832, Smith abandoned hopes for a quick establishment of a unified Mormon stronghold on the frontier. He turned his attention to Kirtland, declaring it a "Stake" of the Mormon tent, and began to take measures to strengthen it, which by the spring of 1833 included the construction of a temple.[64] The Ohio Mormons were scattered through towns around Kirtland, and Smith proposed to bring them together in a new city established on the hilltop farm of Frederick G. Williams, a recent convert who would rise to high position in the church. After a very slow start, work began on a new temple at the center of the site on May 4, 1833, and two days later Smith issued another doctrinally central revelation.

The language of the February 1832 Smith–Rigdon vision at Hiram had equated Adam (the "Firstborn") and Christ (the "Only Begotten Son"). In the May 1833 Kirtland revelation, this equation became a fused Adam–Christ figure (again the "Beloved Son" and the "Firstborn") appearing in a vision to Saint John.[65] This Adam–Christ figure announced himself to be "the Firstborn" and all of his descendants to be "the church of the Firstborn." Most importantly, both he and his descendants "were in the beginning with the Father." These phrases became the core of the Mormon doctrine of preexistent souls: human spirits were not created but eternal, coexistent with the divinity.[66] This doctrine of a pre-Creation existence was reinforced several verses later.

> Man was also in the beginning with God. Intelligence, or the light of truth, was not created or made, neither indeed can be. All truth is independent in that sphere in which God has placed it, to act for itself, as all intelligence also; otherwise there is no existence.[67]

Human spirits had coexisted with God as a primal intelligence for eternity, rather than being created from nothing at a biblical beginning. This spirit was integrally connected to matter, the elements, and this connection was at the epicenter of the Mormon project of temple building.

> For man is spirit. The elements are eternal, and spirit and element, inseparably connected, receive a fulness of joy. And when separated, man cannot receive a fulness of joy. The elements are the tabernacle of God; yea, man is the tabernacle of God, even temples; and whatsoever temple is defiled, God shall destroy that temple. The glory of God is intelligence, or in other words, light and truth.[68]

Ten years later he would restate this thesis more plainly, as he sketched out the doctrinal basis for the covenant of celestial marriage, or polygamy: "There is no such thing as immaterial matter. All Spirit is matter, but it is more fine or pure."[69]

These doctrines were anticipated in Smith's Book of Moses, in which he describes two creations, one spiritual and one material. God had "created all things . . . spiritually, before they were naturally upon the face of the earth."[70] But the Kirtland revelation was more developed than the Book of Moses: in one a God was still creating both spiritual and material things; in the other, spirit and matter were both eternal substances, present through eternity and at "the Beginning."

Thus, by the spring of 1833, Joseph Smith had arrived at the most critical themes of hermetic theology. Clearly he had been influenced by hermetic culture throughout his life, but with the Hiram and Kirtland revelations he arrived at the essence of the hermetic divergence from orthodox Christianity. All things were dually spiritual and material, a concept that would have emerged naturally from an immersion in divining magic, where stones grew alchemically into silver and gold, to be buried in the ground and protected by volatile spirits. God had not created the world and humanity from nothing, *ex nihilo,* but from preexisting substances. If the new Mormon creation story did not quite match the hermetic ideal of *creatio ex deo,* creation from a division of divinity itself, it came quite close, arriving at a *creatio ex materia,* certainly within the conceptual bounds of the hermetic notion of a *prima materia.* In an exaggeration of hermeticism, humans were turned into gods, and God's power was diminished from infinite to finite. Spirit and matter were pervasively linked rather than divided by a chasm negotiated only by grace and atonement.[71]

In effect, Smith had arrived at the outlines of the Egyptian Genesis of the "Pimander," the central text of the *Corpus Hermeticum.* Both versions of Genesis diverged fundamentally from the Mosaic Genesis in positing a harmony between matter and spirit – and the restoration of divine powers to humanity. And they both centered on the mediating figure of Adam and his fortunate Fall.

Orthodox Christianity in one form or another interpreted Adam as the source of all evil in the human condition – his original sin in eating of the Tree of Knowledge brought sin, sorrow, and death to successive generations. But in Mormon theology Adam was the revered "father of all, prince of all, the ancient of days"; he was the archangel Michael.[72] As in the "Pimander," his Fall from Paradise was – if not voluntary – then fortunate. The Hermetic Adam by his own choice leaves heaven to mate with Nature. Given this Fall, the spiritually aware of later generations might recover the knowledge and powers of their inherited divine essences, as descendants of Adam.[73] Similarly, Smith had changed the story of the Fall in his biblical revision in 1830: it was both fortunate and forgiven. Spelling out a hint of the future coming of Christ (Genesis 3:15),

Smith introduces the promise of Christ's redemption with the Fall from Paradise. Smith has Adam and Eve offer animal sacrifices to God; an angel tells them that this is a "similitude of the sacrifice of the Only Begotten of the Father." Then "the Only Begotten of the Father" (Christ) in the form of the Holy Ghost envelops Adam, telling him that he and all humanity will be redeemed. Adam and Eve rejoice in their fortunate Fall, Adam "because of my transgression my eyes are opened, and in this life I shall have joy, and again in the flesh I shall see God," Eve because "were it not for our transgression we should never have seed, and never should have known good and evil."[74]

The Mormon Fall is fortunate, and it was forgiven. The Lord reminds Adam that "I have forgiven thee thy transgression in the Garden of Eden." Eventually Adam is baptized, in which he "was born of the spirit, . . . quickened in the inner man," made one of the order of Melchizedek, and made "a son of God" – with the promise of the same for all his posterity. In effect, Christ's atonement for Adam's original sin begins not at Calvary but in Genesis: the children of Adam were free of original sin, "whole from the foundation of the world."[75] In his 1833 Kirtland temple revelation, Smith reiterated this theme of a liberation from original sin. "Every spirit of man was innocent in the beginning; and God having redeemed man from the fall, men became again, in their infant state, innocent before God."[76]

The obvious corollary to such a theology of a limited God and an innocent humanity, untouched by primal sin and progressing toward divinity, was the devaluation of the doctrine of grace. Mormonism was indeed moving in this direction. In its final form the Mormon doctrine of salvation made the gift of grace through faith in Christ's atonement a *necessary* condition for salvation but not a *sufficient* condition. Salvation – admitting all but the "sons of perdition" to at least the lowest, telestial kingdom – was made possible by divine grace and Christ's sacrificial atonement and earned by personal merit. But mere salvation, offered to all humanity, was not the ultimate Mormon priority. Exaltation to godhood in the celestial kingdom would be fundamentally based on merit, rooted in a firm advocacy of moral free will. The faithful Mormon, inheriting an innocent condition from Adam, was to remain sin free – and to obey the sacred ordinances of the church.[77] This obedience to law – not the free gift of grace – would be the deciding factor in the soul's entry into the celestial kingdom. And Mormon ordinances were to be administered by the Priesthood of Melchizedek, who Smith announced in October 1831 had "power given them to seal up the Saints unto Eternal life."[78]

The changing language of the revelations in the *Doctrine and Covenants* provides a rather precise view of the shifting ground of Mormon theology. From 1828 to 1833, the classic Christian categories of grace, atonement, justification, and election appeared in the revelations. After 1833 they all but disappear, superseded by a new vocabulary – "fulness," ordinance, seal, and bind – that began to appear in the revelations in 1830. In particular, the last appearance of the doctrine of grace, in the 1833 Kirtland temple revelation, connected it with the evocative term "fulness." As had Christ, the faithful would "receive grace from grace" until they received "a fulness": the complete perfection of divine immortality.[79] But after introducing this suggestion of a growth toward exaltation, Joseph Smith subsumed the Christian ideals of grace and atonement under a new theology of priestly ordinances granting degrees of divinity.[80]

By 1833, then, Joseph Smith had arrived at the outlines of the essence of hermetic theology, most easily summarized in terms of the Egyptian Genesis, with its optimistic, fortunate Fall of the divine Adam from Paradise setting the stage for a universal salvation, the restitution of all things, including Adam's paradisial status. Exactly how he arrived there, the central problem of this study, is not quite so clear. Smith's Egyptian Genesis – if we can call it that – was incomplete, and a composite; he did not have a copy of the *Corpus Hermeticum* at hand. Rather, Smith arrived at an approximation of many of its fundamental points by a process of reassembling scattered doctrines available in dissenting and hermetic sources, fused and extended by what Mormons would call revelation – and by what others would call a very powerful imagination.

First and foremost, Mormon doctrines rejecting the inheritance of original sin and celebrating free will were broadly shared among the rising sects. Stephen Marini has described the variants of a similar doctrine of a fortunate Fall among Freewill Baptists, Universalists, and Shakers. Postrevolutionary sectarians rejected Calvinist theories of predestined election and reinterpreted Genesis in ways that eliminated the transmission of primal sin to Adam's posterity. Solidly rooted in New Light theology, the postrevolutionary radical sects had more distant moorings in Continental pietism, which in turn had drawn inspiration from the early-seventeenth-century hermetic spiritualism of Johann Arndt and Jacob Boehme. Like Joseph Smith, the Rogerenes, and the sixteenth-century spiritualists of the Radical Reformation, touched by hermetic thought, the revolutionary sects interpreted Christ as a Second Adam or had him intervene with his atonement at the Fall, guaranteeing universal salvation from the beginning of time.[81] In this abandonment of original sin, the sects and the Mormons stood in distinct contrast to the American Methodist church, which, though rejecting the Calvinist doctrine of election, retained a central place for original sin, passed down as a "seed" or primal condition from Adam and Eve.[82]

But Smith's theology went far beyond the universalism of the revolutionary sects to announce an invisible world structured by three heavens, the potential for divinity, the pre-Creation existence of eternal spirits, and their material nature. Much of this doctrine must be ascribed to a personal predisposition toward a hermetic interpretation of the "mysteries." The culture of treasure-diving in which Smith was immersed in the 1820s, grafted onto his parents' inclination toward witchcraft fears and visionary experiences and reinforced by a popular knowledge of Masonic "secrets," provided the solid groundwork for the development of such a theology. Perhaps, fused with a comprehensive command of the biblical Scriptures, this groundwork in popular hermeticism provided a sufficient framework to shape the new theology as conceived in May 1833.

There were, however, texts written in the broader hermetic-theological tradition circulating in contemporary print culture. Various contemporary theological dictionaries contained capsule summaries of doctrines of materialism and preexistence, for example, noting connections with the Cabala.[83] Robert Paul has shown the similarities between the material pantheon of heavenly spheres and the progression of spiritual intelligences described in the theological astronomies of Thomas Chalmers and Thomas Dick and the cosmic orders that appear in Smith's Book of Moses and Book of Abraham. Certainly the writing of Thomas Dick was influenced by a strain of hermetic materialism running from seventeenth-century science, and Dick was being quoted in Mormon newspapers by 1836. Recently Paul has suggested that language in Thomas Paine's *Age of Reason* might have been the source of Smith's thinking on the plurality of worlds.[84]

Michael Quinn has noted that the idea of three heavens, or degrees of glory, was available in Emmanuel Swedenborg's cosmic system, in which three heavens – topped by a "celestial kingdom" – were associated with the sun, the moon, and the stars. Swedenborgian theology, shaped by Paracelsus and Jacob Boehme, provided one direct connection to the high hermetic tradition, and its system of a triad of heavens reflected a wide range of occult influences. Swedenborg's cosmos was summarized in various short texts available in Palmyra, and translations of his original texts would not have been too difficult to locate in the 1830s. Swedenborg, like the postrevolutionary radical sects, rejected the concept of original sin, and even rejected the concept of atonement; salvation was universal and guaranteed, dependent only on merit. His elaborate theories of the correspondences between spiritual and material worlds incorporated a kind of material preexistence, where pre-Creation spirits were replaced with brute pre-Adamites that were slowly transformed by divine emanations into a perfect Adamic race in Paradise, from whence they fell. Sometime in the late 1830s Joseph Smith is reported to have admitted his knowledge of Swedenborg, telling a Mormon convert from Swedenborgianism that "Emanuel Swedenborg had a view of things to come, but for daily food he perished."[85]

Smith's use of the term "intelligence" for the uncreated spiritual material – a central hermetic theme running back literally to the "Pimander" – could have come from Thomas Dick or Emmanuel Swedenborg, but it could also have come from Andrew Michael Ramsay. Certainly Ramsay would have been an excellent source for the concept of a spiritual preexistence.

Shaped by the hermetic culture of the Philadelphian Society, as was his contemporary Conrad Beissel of Ephrata, Andrew Ramsay became both the theoretician of high-degree Freemasonry and an ardent defender of revealed religion. In two long texts, Ramsay attempted – in classic Masonic fashion – to demonstrate the compatibility of Christian revelation and ancient mystery religions. The first, *The Travels of Cyrus,* was published in 1738 and republished in Boston and New Jersey in the 1790s, and was available to the Smiths at a library in Manchester, New York, and before that at a bookstore in Hanover, New Hampshire. Ramsay's *Travels* described the fictional conversations of King Cyrus of Persia with a host of ancient *magi* and theologians, from Egyptian priests who told him of Hermes Trismegistus, to Zoroaster and Pythagoras, and to Eleazer and Daniel at the court of Nebuchadnezzar in Babylon. Along the way Cyrus learns about the primal ether and solid matter, the alchemical secrets of the "occult sciences," the primal fallen angel Typhon, who "broke through the egg of the world" to spread evil and death, and Hermes Trismegistus's concealing of "the mysteries of religion under hieroglyphics and allegories." From Eleazer he learns a theory of preexistence, in which lesser fallen angels are reincarnated in human bodies, which "were all shut up in that of Adam." Eleazer also describes the Messiah, "the head, and conductor of all intelligent natures, the first-born of all creatures," whose body serves as a tabernacle – "a portion of matter" – for the divinity. In his own summation of his work, Ramsay announced the hermetic doctrine that "Mankind are all but one family of an immense republic of intelligences of which God is the common father." Each soul "is as a ray of light separated from its source," enduring a mortal existence until "it becomes like a subtle vapour reascending to the superior regions from whence it fell." Ramsay's posthumously published *The Philosophical Principles of Natural and Revealed Religion* includes long discussions of the ethereal fluid, of two Creations (spiritual and material), and of the scriptural basis of a doctrine of spiritual preexistence.[86]

These sophisticated texts from the eighteenth-century resynthesis of the hermetic tradition could have contributed to Smith's new cosmology. There are some hints in the evidence, however, suggesting that it was Sidney Rigdon, and not Joseph Smith, who was more conversant with such texts.

Smith, although certainly possessed of great powers of intellect and persuasion, did not have unlimited resources at his command in the 1820s. His family was poor and struggling, without much money to spare on expensive volumes of theology. None of the Smiths or their circle were members of the Manchester Library, so it is unlikely that they could have used its resources.[87] Rigdon, on the other hand, was a sophisticated biblical scholar and had a wide experience in theological questions. He had debated Alexander Campbell, and he knew the details of the communal order of Harmonists, a German hermetic sect settled in western Pennsylvania, whose leader, George Rapp, was a practicing alchemical philosopher. It was Rigdon who quoted Thomas Dick on material heavens in 1836.[88] And on a number of critical theological points, including the Fall, predestination, the role of grace, and the account of the millennium, Smith's position in the *Book of Mormon* differed significantly from that developed between 1831 and 1833 in the *Doctrine and Covenants*.[89]

With the arrival of Rigdon late in 1830 there seems to be a subtle change in the focus of the revelations, with the "mysteries" being fleshed out with detail about priesthoods and temples, and a new language of sealing, binding, purity, and "fulness" becoming more and more pronounced. It may be simple coincidence, but it is interesting that it was the Kirtland converts, and not the New York Saints, who saw golden letters falling from the hands of angels, suggesting that ideas about the Cabala may have circulated in Rigdon's "Family."[90] As of 1830, if anyone had read Andrew Michael Ramsay's *The Philosophical Principles* (published in Glasgow), with its detailed defense of the doctrines of preexistence and of an ethereal fluid as the essence of life, it would have been Rigdon and not Smith. It is very interesting that it was Parley Pratt, the conduit between Smith and Rigdon, who in his *Key to the Science of Theology*, first published in 1855, used the language of a "spiritual fluid," a "heavenly fluid," or a "holy fluid" to describe the "essence" of spirit diffused among the elements, giving them "life, light, power, and principle." The references to "life and light" resonate with passages in the Gospel of John, but they also have a hermetic history running back to the "Pimander," and much of Pratt's text is strikingly similar to Ramsay's language, both in the *The Philosophical Principles* and in *The Travels of Cyrus*. Of course, by 1855, popular Mesmerism had swept across the United States, and Pratt could have been drawing on that tradition, as strongly suggested in his reference to the "modern magnetic term" of "communication." But Pratt had dwelt on the conquest of Babylon by King Cyrus of Persia in his millennial tract *A Voice of Warning,* and in his *Autobiography* he announced that "the characters of a Daniel and a Cyrus were wonderfully blended" in the prophet Joseph Smith.[91]

Certainly Joseph Smith was predisposed to a hermetic interpretation of sacred history and processes from his boyhood in New York's Ontario County. But it may well be that David Whitmer was not far off when he complained that it was Rigdon who provided much of the marrow of the mysteries "sealed . . . from the foundation of the world" that Smith began to unfold in the early 1830s.[92]

In less than three years, between September 1830 and May 1833, an outpouring of revelation framed the broad scheme of the Mormon restoration. Mormons were endowed with the assurance of being sealed to eternal life by spiritually powerful priesthoods, they were offered the promise of the opening of the keys to ancient sacred mysteries, they were given a new map of the invisible world, and they were ordered to build the literal meeting place of God and humanity. They were also promised the hermetic dream of divinity and given a sketch of a hermetic conception of the origins and future of the earth and the universe. Priesthoods, announcements of keys, kingdoms, and temples: these were the stuff of Mormonism in the early 1830s. Human divinity, and its hermetic sources, was a much more obscure area, easily overlooked by the Mormon rank and file. A series of factors mitigated against the ordinary Mormon having a full conception of the new theological directions that Joseph Smith and Sidney Rigdon were exploring. First, much of the new doctrine was not widely available: the Kirtland revelation was not published until 1835 and the Book of Moses was not published until 1851. And second, despite the experience in treasure-hunting and Freemasonry of many early Mormons, their frame of reference was overwhelmingly traditional and biblical. The hermetic implications of his theology may not even have been clear to Smith himself in 1833. And the rush of events overwhelmed any coherent presentation of doctrine. Particularly over the next five and a half years, the pace of new revelation would slow, as Joseph Smith and the young church struggled to survive in the face of external hostility and internal dispute, and as the boundaries between purity and danger began to collapse.

9

Temples, Wives, Bogus-Making, and War

Elijah the prophet, who was taken to heaven without tasting death, stood before us and said: Behold, the time has fully come, which was spoken of by the mouth of Malachi – testifying that he [Elijah] should be sent, before the great and dreadful day of the Lord come – To turn the hearts of the fathers to the children, and the children to the fathers, lest the whole earth be smitten with a curse – Therefore, the keys of this dispensation are committed into your hands; and by this ye may know that the great and dreadful day of the Lord is near, even at the doors.

Joseph Smith's and Oliver Cowdery's vision of
Elijah in the Kirtland temple, April 3, 1836[1]

THE HISTORY OF THE LATTER-DAY SAINTS between the summer of 1833 and the fall of 1839 is one of hubris and affliction. Mobs and militias in Ohio and Missouri threatened the church, but so did the strenuous but erratic efforts made by the prophet to institutionalize his authority and his new theology, and so did the response that those efforts engendered among some of his earliest followers. In sum, without a drastically different political framework, the cosmology and polity of the Mormon experiment were simply too absolutist to survive challenges from within or without.[2] It would not be until internal dissent was silenced and external hostility was held at a distance, first at Nauvoo and then in the Great Basin, that Mormon theology and society could be established on its prophet's own terms.

Until that establishment could be provisionally fixed, roughly in the decade before the Civil War, Mormon history was shaped by cycles of doctrinal development, prophetic legitimacy, and political crisis. One such cycle was completed in January 1831, when the New York Mormons emigrated to Ohio, escaping growing harassment in the Burned-over District. The summer of 1833 stood at the height of a second cycle, which rapidly descended into a trough of crisis and armed conflict.

On July 23, 1833, the cornerstones of the temple were laid in Kirtland; three days previously the Mormons in Independence, Missouri, were threatened by a mob, and their press was destroyed. That November both Mormons and Missourians were killed in a series of skirmishes, and the Mormon position in Jackson County was clearly untenable. Abandoning both Zion and their improved property, the Missouri Mormons took refuge to the north in Clay County or trekked back to Kirtland.³ Things were only marginally better in Ohio. There were threats of mob action and, one night in January 1834, cannons were fired over Kirtland. Several days later a citizens committee hired Doctor Philastus Hurlburt, a Mormon apostate, to gather information to undermine the church, resulting in the publication later that year of the first major anti-Mormon history, *Mormonism Unvailed*.⁴ That February the church formed a high council to oversee its affairs, which authorized an armed militia, "Zion's Camp," to march on Missouri to recapture the ancient site of Paradise and the lost properties of the Mormon settlers. Starting out in May, the "Camp" never had sufficient numbers or the promised support of the Missouri governor. The march ended that July in malarial fevers, a negotiated truce, and an ignominious withdrawal.⁵

The defeat of Zion's Camp would have serious repercussions in the years to come, as a rising body of dissenters rejected Mormonism's new militarism.⁶ Most immediately, in the summer and fall of 1834, Smith faced direct threats to his prophetic authority. People began to doubt the *Book of Mormon* and accused him of false prophecy. In response he launched a campaign of new institutional structures and theological promises. Twelve apostles, assisted by a quorum of seventy elders, would be chosen to spread the Mormon gospel throughout the world. The people were exhorted to redouble their work on the Kirtland temple, and they were reminded of the promise of a spiritual endowment "from on high." The Twelve and the Seventy were chosen from the veterans of Zion's Camp, who were gathered in a weeklong conference in February 1835, and the following September plans were made to form an "Army of Israel" to eventually restore the Mormon "Land of Zion" in Missouri.⁷

The two years from the conference of February 1835 to the collapse of the Kirtland Bank in March 1837 constituted the height of a third cycle of early Mormon history, a period of stability and doctrinal development equivalent to the church's emergence in New York and the early years in Kirtland. If not free of stress, these were relatively peaceful years, as internal dissent was mollified and external threats mitigated. During these years Joseph Smith had the freedom – the luxury – to experiment with various ways of institutionalizing his sacred order. He plunged into his search for the primal Adamic language, he dabbled in plural marriage, he endowed a temple, and he coined money. The boundary between purity and danger – so vigorously constructed in New York – began to blur, if not collapse, during these years in Ohio.

On July 3, 1835, the world of ancient Egypt came virtually to Joseph Smith's doorstep. A traveling showman named Michael Chandler arrived in Kirtland with a cargo of Egyptian mummies and papyrus scrolls, hoping that Smith could translate the scrolls as he had translated the *Book of Mormon*. Members of the church bought the bundle of artifacts, and they went on display in the Smith household in the center of Kirtland. Looking over the papyrus documents, Smith announced that they were writings of the biblical Abraham and Joseph.[8]

These documents rekindled Smith's interest in ancient languages. For several months he struggled to compose a grammar of Egyptian hieroglyphics. By November of 1835 he had fallen back on his powers of intuitive translation.[9] The product was the Book of Abraham, eventually published as Mormon doctrine in 1842. In effect, the Book of Abraham was another revision of Genesis, expanding on points made in the Book of Moses. Using an Urim and Thummim and talking with God, Abraham saw a vast hierarchy of greater and lesser stars in the heavens, ruled by greater and lesser eternal intelligences. The "great and noble" among these intelligences cooperated with the Lord in the Creation story, as "Gods" they "organized and formed the heavens and the earth" from preexistent matter. In effect, these "great and noble" intelligences played the role of the Seven Governors in the Egyptian Genesis of the "Pimander." But in an ironic twist that reflected Smith's growing commitment to Jacksonian democracy more than his conscious or unconscious replication of an ancient hermeticism, his genealogy of spiritual knowledge excluded blacks and Egyptians, as the descendants of Ham, from "the right of Priesthood." Until the original Chandler papyruses were discovered in 1967 and proven to be simple funerary inscriptions, the Book of Abraham stood as the scriptural basis of Mormon racism.[10]

Smith's translation of these papyrus records was formatively influenced by another venture into ancient languages in November 1835. On November 2 Smith and several elders went to hear a lecture "on the theory and practice of physic" delivered by Dr. Daniel Piexotto at a new medical college in Willoughby, Ohio. Smith may well have had matters of ancient languages on his mind, for Piexotto was a Jew from a learned family, who conceivably could have taught Hebrew to the Mormon elders. But Piexotto would not serve as the Mormon's Hebrew teacher, and Smith immediately commissioned Oliver Cowdery to travel to New York City to consult with Jewish scholars and to buy Hebrew-language texts. The next

January Hebrew classes were launched by Joshua Seixas, a Jewish scholar
from a rabbinical family long established in New York and Providence,
who was then teaching at a nearby seminary. Under Seixas's direction, the
elders studied Hebrew for two months at the missionary school, formed in
1833 after a revelation that Smith described as "plucked from the tree of
Paradise." A few of the elders advanced so far as to receive instructor's
certificates. A transliteration of the Hebrew word for eternal, "gnolaum,"
was written into the Book of Abraham, and a literal translation of
"Eloheem" as plural provided legitimacy for Smith's plurality of gods at
the Creation. But Smith's ultimate motive in studying Hebrew may well
have been to learn what had long been thought to be the "pure Adamic
language." There is no evidence that Seixas instructed the Mormon elders
in the secrets of the Cabala, but later Mormon leaders hailed Seixas's
Hebrew instruction at Kirtland "as an auxiliary to divine illumination."[11]

In the same months of the summer and fall of 1835 in which he was
experimenting with ancient languages, feeding an interest running back to
1827, Smith began to experiment with unorthodox sexual and marital
relationships, a departure that would culminate at Nauvoo in the Mormon doctrine of polygamous "celestial marriage." The first steps in the
evolution of this doctrine involved incipient Mormon state building, Old
Testament legitimation, and probably hermetic medicine.

On November 24, 1835, Joseph Smith challenged Ohio law in marrying
his old friend Newell Knight, recently widowed, to Lydia G. Bailey. Specifically prohibited from performing the marriage ceremony by the local
county court, Smith brushed aside a state-licensed church elder to perform the rites of marriage between Newell and Lydia himself. She was not
divorced from her non-Mormon husband, so this technically bigamous
marriage also challenged a broader moral code. Newell Knight wrote in
his journal that Smith had said:

> I have done it by the authority of the holy priesthood and the
> Gentile law has no power to call me to account for it. It is my
> religious privilege, and even the Congress of the United States has
> no power to make a law that would abridge the rights of my
> religion.

Lydia Knight remembered him saying, "Our Elders have been wronged
and prosecuted for marrying without a license. The Lord God of Israel has
given me authority to unite the people in the holy bonds of matrimony."
Over the next two months Joseph Smith performed five more illegal marriages, and at one he spoke of the "ancient order of marriage" – an early
and veiled reference to the idea of plural, polygamous marriage that
would become a secret cornerstone of Mormon faith in the early 1840s.[12]
Here he was asserting the power of his Melchizedek Priesthood and connecting it with Adamic origins. He wrote in his diary on November 24

that "marriage was an institution of heaven, instituted in the garden of Eden; that it was necessary it should be solemnized by the authority of the everlasting Priesthood." Unlike Protestant ministers, Mormon priests would have both spiritual powers and primary authority over marriage.[13]

Smith's public step of asserting the marital authority of the Mormon priesthood in November 1835 was very much entwined with the legitimacy conveyed by ancient languages. On November 20, four days before the Knight–Bailey marriage, Oliver Cowdery returned from New York with a load of Hebrew grammar books, and on November 21 Smith and the elders' school decided to extend their search for a teacher, as Piexotto "was not qualified to give us the knowledge we wish to acquire." On the twenty-third, Smith studied Hebrew and on the morning of the twenty-fourth "translated some of the Egyptian records," as he had on the nineteenth, before going out to marry Newell Knight as "instituted in the Garden of Eden."[14] Another impetus may have been the visit of Robert Matthews, or Matthias, alias "Joshua the Jewish Prophet," on November 8–10. Over the previous years Matthews had become notorious in New York City for his millennial prophecies and revelations on spiritual wifery.[15]

Priestly control over marriage – and defiance of civil authority – were steps toward a new Mormon order of marriage that Smith had been mulling over for years. The roots of Smith's concept of plural marriage lay in his early efforts at translating the Old Testament, and in his particular interest in the sections of Genesis describing and justifying patriarchal polygamy, completed in February and March of 1831.[16] The models for a plurality of wives would be the ancients Abraham, Isaac, and Jacob, who had taken concubines and fathered a host of children. As for temples and the primal language, the logic of restoration rested on Old Testament authority, with the Latter-day Saints literally reestablishing the circumstances of the ancient Israelites. In the church's first years the Mormons considered themselves gentiles taking up the ancient covenant, but by the end of 1832 (perhaps because missions among the "Lamanite" Indians were failing) they began to declare themselves the literal descendants of the Israelites, as the Vermont New Israelites had done three decades before. In November W. W. Phelps published an essay entitled the "Tribe of Joseph," arguing that the descendants of Joseph and his son Ephraim, "mixed among the nations," were gathering in the west to await the coming of Zion. In December Smith announced by revelation that the priesthood was "continued through the lineage of your fathers . . . [and] must needs remain through you and your lineage until the restoration of all things." That January Smith anointed his father, old Joseph Sr., as Patriarch of the Church, since he was "the oldest man of the blood of Joseph or of the seed of Abraham." The Patriarch then began to confirm the membership into that bloodline by giving "patriarchal blessings" to the Saints, promising good fortune to them and their "posterity," who were and would be "of the seed of Israel."[17]

Ultimately, however, Smith's vision of celestial marriage would not be based solely in Old Testament patriarchy but would replicate the hermetic concept of divinization through the *coniunctio,* the alchemical marriage. Obedience to the celestial covenant and the procreation of children in polygamous marriages on earth and in heaven would push the patriarch into higher and higher ranks of a divine pantheon of gods. But nothing in the Bible suggested that polygamy, or even obedience to covenant, would turn the faithful into gods. Thus it is worthwhile to explore some of the points at which hermetic knowledge – that window onto human divinity – intersected with contemporary notions of sexuality and reproduction.

Such a consideration of hermetic influences takes us back to Smith's life in New York. Smith's marriage to Emma Hale in January 1827 was the critical turning point in his early life, for in that year he put aside his association with the money-diggers (some of them associated with circles of counterfeiters), recovered the Golden Plates from the Hill Cumorah, and prepared to write a major religious work. In June 1828 Emma almost died in childbirth, and they lost their first child, named Alvin, "still-born and very much deformed." In April 1831 Emma gave birth again, only to have her twins, Thaddeus and Louisa, die soon after. Conceiving and giving birth were obviously overwhelming problems for Joseph and Emma.[18]

In the early 1840s at Nauvoo Smith would have the advice and council of John C. Bennett on such matters. Bennett was a doctor who specialized in obstetrics and who, coincidentally, was the president of Piexotto's Willoughby Medical College for several months at the end of 1834.[19] But in the late 1820s Joseph and Emma would have had only local doctoring – and the ancient lore preserved in contemporary sexual manuals. The most popular of these manuals, *Aristotle's Masterpiece,* first published as early as the sixteenth century, went through at least thirty-two American editions between 1766 and 1831, and one historian has argued that it "may be viewed as a trustworthy index of popular knowledge of and attitudes toward sex and gynecology in America for the period 1760–1840."[20] The popularity of Thompsonian medicine – its steambaths and purges of hot cayenne manifesting a broader revolt against orthodox medicine – with Joseph Smith, Brigham Young, and many other early Mormons is another hint that Smith might well have known the ancient lore in the popular manuals.[21]

The language of sexual generation and growth so powerful in alchemy and metallurgy had particularly accessible parallels in these manuals, which threw together Aristotelian, Galenic, and Paracelsian systems with wild abandon. Nicholas Culpeper's *Pharmacopoeia*, published in London in 1653 and republished in Boston in 1720, began with "an Astrologo Physical Discourse of the Humane Virtues in the Body of Man" and continued with recipes for a wide array of herbals and oils, advising the reader that "your best way to [de]still Chymical Oyls is to learn of an alchimist." The 1796 edition of *Aristotle's Masterpiece* included an astrological discourse similar to Culpeper's, as well as an account of "the secrets of generation" that described the male sperm as the "active principle, or efficient cause of the faetus," and the female egg as the "passive principle . . . endued with a plastic of vegetative virtue." A 1792 edition of *Aristotle's Book of Problems* added the categories of heat, color, and hierarchy of process. In a catechism at least two centuries old, the manual instructed that the seed "tis white in man by reason of his great heat and quick digestion, because rarified in the testicles; but a woman's is red because tis the superfluity of the second digestion . . . or else . . . because the terms [menstrual flow] corrupt undigested blood, and hath its colour." This edition also included a discourse on the power of the mother's imagination in shaping or marking the child: "The imagination is above the forming power, and therefore the child born followeth the imagination."[22] The "forming power" of the imagination suggests the Mormon fascination with a mutuality between spirit and matter, and the belief that mothers could "mark babies" was common among nineteenth-century Mormons.[23]

There is nothing particularly original in suggesting that the years between 1827 and 1830 were a period of fundamental transition for Joseph Smith, but the probability that he was reading these ancient sexual advice manuals puts this period of transition into quite a different light. If Joseph Smith had been exposed to these manuals in the 1820s, they might well have contributed to the sexual structure of his divine order. Their quality of authoritative text would have provided intellectual legitimacy for concepts that would be central underpinnings of Mormon doctrine. They also point to further layers of meaning in the image of the Nephite disciple emerging from the refining fire of the furnace.

With its alchemical analogues, this symbol takes on new force against the backdrop of the popular lore of sexual generation when the original biblical text is considered. In the original text of Daniel's dream, this figure in the fire was also associated with the three children in the furnace. Was the Nephite disciple a "child in the furnace," and by analogy a baby in the uterus? Again, the chronology is all-important. Joseph obtained the Golden Plates only after seeing in his seer-stone that he must be accompanied by Emma. This took place on September 22, 1827, eight months after their marriage on January 18, 1827, and nine months before the birth and death of their son Alvin on June 15, 1828. In at least one account, Joseph had high aspirations for this child, telling his wife's kin in Harmony that "the Book of Plates could not be opened under penalty of death by any other person but his first-born, which was to be male."[24]

These links between Joseph's problematic procreative intercourse with Emma, the Nephite in the furnace, and the rudimentary origins of his sexual divine order can only be speculative. The color symbolism of the advice manuals, analogous to, though the reverse of, the sequence of colors in alchemical symbolism, might have played a shaping role here. The white race of Nephites and the white male seed of *Aristotle's Book of Problems* were to be the progenitors of endless generations of Mormon elect who would propel the prophet Joseph through the limitless progression of the celestial kingdom.

Reflecting its Jacksonian environment, Mormon society was structured by hierarchies of race and sex. The *Book of Mormon* made the white race morally superior to the red, and the Book of Abraham subordinated blacks; polygamous celestial marriage was merely an amplification of Mormon patriarchy subordinating women. These hierarchies of white over red and black and male over female were fused in an ancient theory of sexual "generation" in the popular advice manuals. This configuration was also evident in Smith's revelation of July 1831, where he announced that Mormon men would "in time" take wives among the Indians, "that their posterity may become white, delightsome, and just."[25] Bound up in a sexual theory of "eternal progression" shaped by hermetic alchemy, parallel hierarchies of race and sex played a critical role in Smith's divine order and millennial plan.

Such hermetic thoughts about sexuality and marriage may have shaped Smith's move into spiritual wifery. Smith's initial revelation on plural marriage is said to have come in 1831, as he was "translating" chapters of the Old Testament. But, reputedly, he and Martin Harris had claimed in the summer of 1830 that "adultery was no crime"; Smith was accused of attempting to seduce a local girl that summer in Harmony. Sometime in 1831, and again in 1834, Smith supposedly told a very young Mary Elizabeth Rollins that she "was the first woman God commanded him to take as a plural wife." In 1832 the Johnson brothers joined in the riot against Smith, apparently because they thought he was involved with their sister, Nancy Marinda Johnson. Both of these women eventually became Joseph's plural wives. Among the non-Mormons in Ohio there were suspicions that the community of property dictated in the Law of Consecration included wives. In 1835 Smith took two steps that carried the seeds of the polygamous system. That summer, as he began attempting to decipher the

Chandler papyruses, he had his first extramarital affair, with a servant girl named Fanny Alger, who subsequently was taken to be the first of Smith's forty-odd plural wives. Caught in the act, literally, Smith had violent confrontations with Emma Hale Smith and Oliver Cowdery, who from that date became progressively disillusioned with his old friend.[26] And that November Smith married Newell Knight and Lydia Bailey.

There were simultaneously implications of antinomianism and state building in Smith's marital behavior in 1835. Testimony dating from 1843 suggests that Smith saw himself subject to no human law. Accused of "licentious conduct" with women in several families, Smith was said to have declared that "he was God's prophet . . . and that he could do whatever he chose to do, therefore the Church had no right to call into question anything he did."[27] As religious perfectionists for centuries had claimed – or were reputed to have claimed – Smith was subject only to a higher law. His stance was quite similar to that of John Finney of Cumberland, Rhode Island, who, eighty years before, had asserted "that Christians ought to marry in the church without any regard to Babylon, as he called the rulers of the state." Certainly his position echoed that of religious radicals of the Reformation and the English Revolution, as well as contemporary perfectionists like John Humphrey Noyes's Oneida community and the Cochranites, who had disrupted Maine's Saco Valley two decades before.[28] One of the principal articles of excommunication brought against Oliver Cowdery in the summer of 1838 was that he had sought "to destroy the character" of Joseph Smith "by falsely insinuating that he was guilty of adultry."[29] But if the partners had entered into secret plural marriages, such relationships would not be adulterous. As John Finney – and Emmanuel Swedenborg – had claimed, marriage should be a "new covenant or a spiritual union"; spiritual marriages would not end at death but continue in heaven to eternity. Smith's innovation – not unlike the Anabaptists at Münster or John Milton in revolutionary England – was to argue from Old Testament authority for plural marriages.[30]

Here, clearly, the moral boundary separating purity and danger was being breached, if not erased. The *Book of Mormon* had condemned polygamy as a "wicked practice," a "whoredom," "abominable in the sight of the Lord," and the Smith–Rigdon revelation of 1832 had consigned "liars, and sorcerers, and adulterers" to eternal flames, or at least to the lowest, telestial kingdom.[31] But this may have been language covering unsuppressible impulses, for in 1830 and 1831 we have the first rumors that Smith was thinking about setting aside – renegotiating – this conventional moral boundary. Bound up in this renegotiation were other boundaries. The *Book of Mormon* had depicted the Lamanites as the essence of evil, but in proposing to his men in Missouri that they might "take unto you wives of the Lamanites and Nephites," meaning the Indians,[32] Smith was transcending conventional racial boundaries and his own boundary constructed between the symbols of purity and danger. The coming of the Kingdom, and Joseph's central place as prophet, were forging a sense of union and resolution that was melting away earlier distinctions. The dimensions of sacred communication and sacred space would be unified by the restored Adamic language and the restored temple of Solomon. Now an even more powerful metaphor – one of marital and sexual union – was beginning to shape the Mormon Kingdom. Here again the Jungian model of an alchemical archetype of the psychological resolution of oppositions, of the achievement of self in the *coniunctio* of symbolic sulphur and mercury, provides a useful conceptual device, if not a scientific explanation.

The building of the Kingdom also lent itself to political dangers. To assert primary spiritual authority over marriage was to challenge the secular power of civil government. And just as he was moving to assert sacred control over marriage, Smith was holding meetings in Kirtland to form an "Army of Israel" – "the Lord's Host" – to recapture Zion in Missouri. Reestablishing the military structure of Zion's Camp, and eventually evolving into the Danites and the Nauvoo Legion, this military force, as one historian has put it, "achieved one of the important prerequisites of a nation-state."[33] Here, then, was one of the logics of an antinomian rejection of civil authority: such a movement would either collapse under the force of state power, separate and minimize contact with a corrupt world, or impose on that world a revolutionary theocracy based on a fundamental higher law. Driven by an absolute sense of its unique restoration of a Kingdom of God, Mormonism was moving in the last of these directions by the fall of 1835.[34]

Smith's assault on conventional boundaries was not uncontested. The seeds of apostasy had been planted and were sprouting. The inclusive charismatic ritualism of the Kirtland temple dedication in April 1836 was required by the tensions growing among the Kirtland Mormons, tensions set off by the failed march of Zion's Camp and reignited by the Alger affair. In choosing Oliver Cowdery to receive visions of God and the prophets, Smith was passing over Sidney Rigdon, with whom he had shared revelations in 1832. In choosing Cowdery to share this pinnacle of a sacred performance, Smith distributed prophetic charisma to shore up his unstable church polity – and to reincorporate a potential dissenter into his sacred Kingdom plan.

The Kirtland temple, photographed in 1904.
Courtesy of the Utah State Historical Society.

The Kirtland temple was in the final stages of construction in January 1836, and complete enough for Joshua Seixas to teach his Hebrew classes in one of the third-floor attic rooms. Eventually, the entire second floor was devoted to the elders' school. The third floor was set aside for administrative offices, and the first floor was elaborately designed for church meetings. At each end of the room nine pulpits ranked in three layers were reserved for the Melchizedek and Aaronic priesthood leaders. The interior detail was a richly carved Greek Revival, and the columns and piers hid rope-and-tackle systems that controlled cloth "veils" that could be unrolled from the ceiling to cover either set of pulpits or to divide the room into four compartments. Such compartment dividers had parallels in Quaker meetinghouses, but the pulpit veils had their contemporary analogues in Royal Arch Masonic symbolism and had legendary origins in the veils in Solomon's temple.[35]

The temple was finished in March 1836, two months after the six illegal marriages were performed, and Seixas taught his classes right up to the day before its dedication began. During these same months, in preparation for the dedication, Smith gathered his elders and instructed them in new ceremonies: the anointing with oil and the laying on of hands, which he had decided to adopt after a winter of Bible study, and a "sealing" of blessings. The men of the hierarchy, initiated into these rituals in the long attic rooms of the new temple, testified "that they were filled with the Holy Ghost, which was like fire in their bones," and fell into visions and prophecy. Smith had visions of Adam and Abraham, and of his brother Alvin in the celestial kingdom. This experience inspired a revelation that would inform the practice of baptism for the dead, begun six years later at Nauvoo.[36]

The temple was formally dedicated in a week of ceremony and ritual between March 27 and April 3, reaching climaxes on the two Sundays. The events of that week confirmed to the faithful that the temple was no simple meetinghouse but the sacred, numinous conduit of spiritual communication between humanity and the divine. On the first Sunday afternoon Smith was received as a prophet and seer by the congregation, and he exhorted the men to help prophecy the future. At one point the sound of "a mighty rushing wind" filled the meeting. Smith wrote in his journal:

> All the congregation simultaneously arose, being moved upon by
> an invisible power; many began to speak in tongues and prophesy;
> others saw glorious visions; and I beheld the Temple was filled
> with angels, which fact I declared to the congregation.

People in the surrounding neighborhood claimed to have seen a pillar of fire on the temple, perhaps the effect of the sparkling of the ground glass mixed into the temple's plaster coating. These ecstatic meetings, with ritual anointings and washings, continued through the week, reaching another high point on Sunday, April 3. Late that afternoon Joseph Smith and Oliver Cowdery disappeared behind the veil covering the Melchizedek pulpits at the west end of the temple. When they reappeared they reported more visions. They had seen "the Lord standing upon the breast-work of the pulpit, before us; and under his feet was a paved work of pure gold, in color like amber." Confirming the Mormon tabernacle, the Lord "accepted this house." He would "manifest myself to my people in mercy in this house . . . [and] appear unto my servants and speak unto them with mine own voice." Following this divine vision Smith and Cowdery received the "keys of the gathering of Israel" from the prophet Moses and the keys of the "dispensation of the gospel of Abraham" from the prophet Elias, invoked centuries before by Paracelsus and George Starkey as "Elias *Artista.*" Last to appear was Elias's Old Testament manifestation Elijah – the biblical prophet who, like Enoch, had been "translated" directly to heaven. Elijah repeated the prophecy of Malachi that he would return before judgment day "to turn the hearts of the fathers to the children and the children to the fathers, lest the whole earth be smitten with a curse." The ritual means to this ultimate covenant of union, the content of these keys to the mysteries – baptism for the dead and the divinizing powers of the Melchizedek Priesthood – would be spelled out at Nauvoo seven years later.[37]

The Kirtland temple dedication stands as a critical watershed between early Mormonism and the theological doctrine framed at Nauvoo. By this time the classic terminology of Protestant Christianity – grace, atonement, justification – had long since dropped out of the language of Smith's revelations. Where the original Mormonism of the *Book of Mormon* combined old with new, the Mormonism of the Kirtland temple was a fundamentally different religious tradition. This new religious tradition had been articulated in language, but with the temple dedication it was articulated in social and theological process. It brought into focus the Mormon departure from simple biblical primitivism. The Reforming impulse "to live ancient lives," carried to early America, had been replaced by an absolutist theocracy advancing the Kingdom of God toward a radical hermetic cosmos. The abandonment of biblical primitivism – and the collapsing boundaries between purity and danger – would shape the rise of dissent in the years following.

Ultimately the rituals and visions dedicating the Kirtland temple were not sufficient to hold the church together in the face of a mounting series of internal disputes. The Alger affair, the failure of the 1834 march of Zion's Camp, and hostility to theological innovations all contributed to the collapse of the Kirtland Mormon community by the end of 1837. So, too, did an explosion of credit buying, monetary speculation, and the rise and collapse of the illegal Kirtland Bank.

If the year before the temple dedication saw important theological developments, the year following was dominated by the question of money. The Mormon population at Kirtland was expanding rapidly, and the converts were by and large very poor. Mormon property holding could not keep up with the expansion in numbers, and non-Mormons would not hire Mormons in the area's mills and shops. The construction of the temple functioned as a public relief project of sorts, busying many of the underemployed faithful for almost three years, financed by tithing and subscription. But the commercial ventures of the church were based on borrowed capital, and by 1836 the financial structure of the Mormon communities in Ohio and Illinois was stretched to the breaking point, with old debts coming due and new debts being incurred as the church purchased supplies in the east on credit.[38]

Under these pressures, Smith reverted to the occult, ignoring a boundary established in 1830 in the crisis over Hiram Page's use of a seer-stone. Although divining for treasure was forbidden among the rank-and-file Mormons, it was apparently suitable for the prophet. In August 1836 Smith, Sidney Rigdon, Oliver Cowdery, and a small group of elders appeared in Salem, Massachusetts, hard by the ancestral town of Topsfield, and spent several weeks attempting to find treasure reported to have been hidden in an old house on Union Street. This effort failed, but Smith, his brother Hyrum, and Oliver Cowdery were able to obtain new lines of credit in the east.[39]

Whereas borrowing would perpetuate dependence on the world, banking would clear these debts and generate a wave of prosperity. With these ideas in mind, Smith and Rigdon in November conceived of the Kirtland Safety Society Bank Company, which went into operation the following January, with the authority of divine revelation but not a state charter. The Mormon leadership had great plans for this institution. Backed only by land mortgages in Kirtland it was to have a capitalization of $4 million. The bank would (in words attributed to Joseph Smith) "like Aaron's rod . . . swallow up all other Banks . . . and grow and flourish and spread from the rivers to the ends of the earth, and survive when all others should be laid in ruins." With "the greatest of all institutions on EARTH" (the bank) behind them, and reputedly boxes of lead shot covered with a layer of coin in the treasury to convince the skeptical, the Kirtland Mormons were soon awash with money, and "the spirit of speculation" swept the community.[40] In a dream of transmutation through banking that, among New Englanders, ran back to the land bank plans of 1720–40 and before that to banking proposals of the 1660s, Mormons assumed that their paper wealth would multiply and remultiply under their prophet's blessing.

The alchemical connotations of the Kirtland Bank paled by comparison with other ventures in the Ohio Valley in these years. Two years before, in September 1834, Stephen Davis, the "Old Rodsman," had ventured south into the Big Sandy country of western Virginia to divine for silver and had brought back ores to be smelted by an alchemist in Marietta. In the previous year a splinter faction of the Harmonists at Phillipsburg in western Pennsylvania had hopes that their leader, a German charlatan named Count Leon, would use his claim to the philosopher's stone to produce enough alchemical gold to finance their migration to the west. The count failed, finding "the Rocks in the Ohio hills forty years too young to produce the expected quantity of the precious metals." One of his followers, Jacob Zundell, joined the Mormons at Kirtland in 1836.[41]

The state of Ohio had a rather different alchemy in mind when they viewed the Kirtland Bank. Oliver Cowdery succeeded in obtaining engraving plates for the bank notes in Philadelphia, but Orson Hyde failed to obtain a bank charter, the legislature having already decided to curtail wildcat banking. Not to be deterred, Smith changed the name of the bank to the Kirtland Safety Society Anti-Banking Company, stamping the bills with the extra letters, and went into business. By March Smith and Rigdon, the cashier and president respectively, were in court for operating an illegal bank and were fined $1,000. Three months later the bank was still issuing notes, and in late June Rigdon again was brought into court "for making spurious money." The bubble burst, and over the next nine months Smith would be the target of at least thirteen lawsuits for outstanding debts, and he spent months in Missouri to avoid prosecution in Ohio courts.[42]

With the collapse of the Kirtland Bank, fractures opened over the legitimacy of Zion's Camp, the Fanny Alger incident, and progressive changes in theology. Dissenters began to denounce Smith in May 1837, and that June Smith sent his most loyal followers on a mission to England, protecting them from the contagion of dissent but leaving Kirtland in the control of his growing opposition.

By July David Whitmer, Oliver Cowdery, and Martin Harris, all witnesses to the Golden Plates who maintained a fervent belief in seer-stones, declared themselves the followers of a young girl who could read the future in a black stone and who would whirl in a Shaker-like trance until she fell to the floor, spouting revelation. Writing in the 1880s, David Whitmer was particularly concerned that Smith had moved "beyond the plain teachings of Christ" laid down in the *Book of Mormon*. He objected to the institutionalization of charisma bound up in the building of priesthoods and complained that, in the printing of the *Doctrine and Covenants* in 1835, revelations received "through the stone" had been changed. Indeed, it was only with the 1835 edition that the accounts of angelic

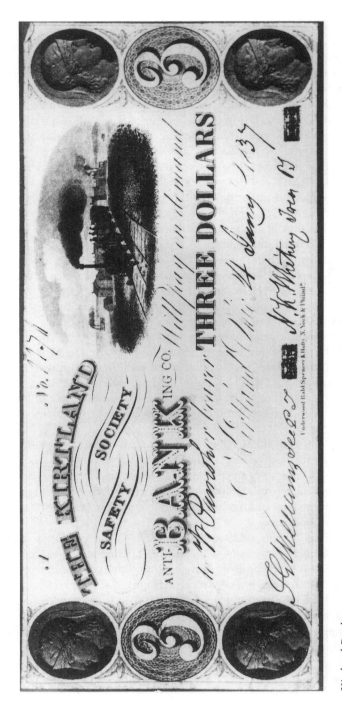

Kirtland Bank note.
Courtesy of the Utah State Historical Society.

ordinations of the priesthoods were included in the revelations. Whitmer was also aggrieved that the original name of the church had been changed in 1834 from the "Church of Christ" to the "Church of the Latter Day Saints."[43] The dissenters wanted to return to the church's original loose structure, which they felt had combined a traditional Christ-centered primitivism with a spontaneous magic charisma. In effect, they were reverting to the popular fusion of magical divining and religious revelation that first Smith and then Hiram Page and the Whitmers had essayed back in the Burned-over District in the 1820s. They opposed the entire direction that the church had taken since Joseph Smith had asserted his primary authority as seer and revelator in September 1830. In Warren Cowdery's words, the church had made Smith "a monarch, absolute and despotic, and ourselves abject slaves." The Cowderies, the Whitmers, their brother-in-law Hiram Page, the Johnsons, and Warren Parrish, once cashier of the bank, became the nucleus of the "Old Standard" dissenters, who continued to challenge the authority of Smith's hierarchy for the next several years until their excommunication. In some measure this group provided a model for future dissenters who, breaking away from the Mormon establishment over the next decade, coalesced into the core of the Reorganized Church of Jesus Christ of Latter Day Saints, opposed to polygamy, established in 1860.[44]

At the center of the Kirtland crisis lay the issue of authority and legitimacy. According to the dissenters, Smith had said that the bank was "instituted by the will of God and would never fail, let men do what they would." The bank had failed, and this proved that Smith was a false, or at least fallen, prophet. A loyal Heber C. Kimball wrote years later that in the summer of 1837 "there were not twenty people on earth that would declare that Joseph Smith was a prophet of God." Dissenter Warren Parrish wrote the next spring that Smith and Rigdon were "confirmed infidels" who "lie by revelation." In the minds of the dissenters, falsity was compounded by antinomian assurance. According to dissenter William McLellin, Joseph Smith and his associates in the Kirtland Bank "seemed to think that everything must bow at their nod – thus violating the laws of the land."[45]

The crisis was played out over the summer and fall months of 1837 in Kirtland's streets and even in the temple, where armed loyalist and dissenting leaders shouted at each other in public meetings from the Melchizedek and Aaronic Priesthood pulpits. It ended with a final confrontation in the temple in January 1838, when Sidney Rigdon attacked the dissenters as a "gang of liars, thieves, and drunkards," accusing them of adultery and of stealing from the Kirtland Bank to buy "bogus or counterfeit coin" from "the Tinker's Creek blacklegs."[46] The dissenters responded in kind. Three days later, one step ahead of another warrant for illegal banking, Joseph Smith fled Kirtland for Missouri, chased by a posse for two hundred miles to the Ohio border.[47]

Thus the theme of counterfeiting reemerges in Mormon history as the community in Kirtland collapsed into splintering factions. Suspicion fell on all parties. As another dissenter, Reed Peck, summed it up, "each of these contending parties . . . were, more or less, engaged in purchasing and circulating Bogas money or counterfeit coin."[48] For the next year, as civil war erupted between Mormons and gentiles in Missouri, the Mormon leadership in Missouri would continue to accuse dissenters – and be accused themselves – of counterfeiting money. Counterfeit money was a pervasive reality in the American frontier settlements, but for Mormons in the late 1830s it also became a powerful metaphor for the failure of authority and legitimacy and the collapse of the precarious boundary between purity and danger in the Mormon kingdom.

I have suggested that counterfeiting was one conduit of hermetic culture in the eighteenth-century colonies, and that it was bound in a symbiotic relationship with treasure-divining in postrevolutionary America. It seems to have taken on connotations of witchcraft; certainly it made up the dangerous element in a field of popular hermetic culture. In the 1820s Joseph Smith combined contemporary images of hermetic danger – counterfeiting gangs and spurious Masonry – in composing his picture of the Gadianton Bands and the Lamanites in the *Book of Mormon*, counterposed to the hermetic purity of the Nephites. Divining and counterfeiting, prophecy and sorcery, pure Masonry and spurious Masonry, Nephites and Lamanites–Gadiantons, the seed of Adam and the seed of Cain, God and Satan: these were the elements of a dichotomous system of truth and falsity upon which Smith built a Mormon cosmology.

As the logic of an embattled prophetic movement unfolded in Mormonism, the authority and legitimacy of the word of the prophet became the touchstone of truth. Within the Mormon worldview, dissent from the prophet's word was false; outside the Mormon worldview – especially among embittered dissenters – the prophet's word itself was false. Inasmuch as these contrary falsities were made to pass as truth, they were viewed as counterfeit by both parties.[49]

These contradictions, expressed in virulent conflict in Kirtland in 1837, lay at the root of the Mormon conundrum: convictions as to the prophet's powers and legitimacy led to the demonizing of contrary voices; belief in the marvelous brought a fear of the counterfeit. Reflecting but also focusing an anxiety widespread in a commercializing society where the means of exchange were multifarious and uncertain, loyal Mormons and their opponents in the late 1830s repeatedly accused each other of counterfeiting currency. The issue is complicated by the fact that there was some basis for the accusations: exaggerated rhetoric was at least partially based in the reality of the various forms that "money-making" could take. Setting aside this problem of "reality" for the moment, we need to briefly explore the rhetorical connotations of counterfeiting for Mormons in the 1830s, set against the broader canvas of authority and legitimacy of text, of revelation, and of spirit.

Religion and money in early-nineteenth-century America both depended upon faith in the legitimacy of printed paper. For a majority of Americans, the Bible was the revealed word of God, its authenticity clouded only by the question of translation from ancient languages. Similarly, behind the mass of printed money in circulation lay a constant questioning of its sources and the soundness (or even the existence) of the issuing institution. Parley Pratt, writing in the 1850s of a conversation with his brother in 1830, as he was leaving Ohio to search for a prophet, indicated how easily these systems of faith and print might be conflated. Asked why he was abandoning a prosperous farm built up over five years of hard labor, Pratt wrote that he replied, "I have bank bills enough, on the very best institutions in the world." Pointing to New Testament texts on the heavenly reward for preaching the gospel, he said, "[T]hey are true bills and founded on capital that will never fail, though heaven and earth shall pass away." Elaborating his metaphor, he continued, "If I sink, they are false. If I am sustained, they are true. I shall put them to the test."[50]

Pratt and other Mormons put equal faith in the *Book of Mormon* as a "true bill," but they had to face the ridicule of non-Mormons, who were equally convinced that it was counterfeit. From the start, critical commentary was laced with connotations of "bogus-making." Newspapers in New York connected the *Book of Mormon* with religious extremism, divining, and confidence tricks: it was "evidence of fraud, blasphemy and credulity"; it was "a new way of raising the wind." Joseph Smith had used "hocus-pocus" to induce Martin Harris to mortgage his farm to underwrite the translation and printing of the "Gold Bible."[51] Ohio newspapers picked up the stories of "peep-stones" and "money-digging," but they quickly moved on to the analogy of counterfeiting. The Painesville *Telegraph* called for an investigation: "if it be found to be a base counterfeit, like freemasonry, let it be nailed to the counter." The Ashtabula *Journal*, invoking the confidence games and counterfeit-based commerce of other bands of transients, warned the public that the early Mormon missionaries were the agents of a "newly invented money speculation." Stating that Oliver Cowdery was known to have been "a dabbler in the art of Printing" and "a pedestrian pedlar," the Cleveland *Herald* claimed that

Mormon missionary activity was simply advance work in a plan to make "money . . . by the sale of their books."[52] Imputations of fraud were central to the publication of *Mormonism Unvailed* in 1834, which claimed to expose a "singular imposition and delusion" by printing detailed affidavits of the money-digging origins. Three years later the counterfeiting accusation was taken up by Grandison Newell, a prominent opponent in Kirtland, who derided Joseph Smith as "the impious fabricator of gold bibles – the blasphemous forger of revelations with which he swindles ignorant people out of their hard-earned property."[53]

Mormon believers were deeply sensitive to such gentile contempt for Mormon texts and revelations. A Smith family outing could be spoiled by a mocking shout, "Do you get any revelations recently?"[54] But Mormon anxiety about external perceptions of counterfeited texts were easily matched by internal fears of false spirits. Ever since Smith drove the devil out of Newell Knight, Mormonism had claimed the power of supernatural connection between the visible and the invisible worlds. By early 1831, Smith was predicting that many among the faithful would be given gifts of the spirit: faith healing, working of miracles, prophecy, discerning of spirits, speaking in tongues, and the interpretation of tongues.[55] But if the devil could possess, the devil could deceive. Thus the Mormons soon were faced with the problem of "hypocrites." Whereas New England Calvinists were wary of counterfeit conversion, Mormons – as recent commentators have put it – were "wary of Satan's power and desire to counterfeit the works of God."[56]

Such fears were realized in Kirtland in the spring of 1831, when a host of spiritual manifestations among the newly converted Restorationists – what Parley Pratt called "a false and lying spirit" – threatened to undermine Mormon cohesion and reputation.[57] There followed a stream of revelations and instructions warning of "false spirits, which have gone forth in the earth, deceiving the world." Both the "adversary" Satan and "hypocrites among you" were attempting to deceive with false manifestations of spiritual gifts. Only the priesthood had the power to discern true spirits, and the people were repeatedly warned that "the Devil can speak in tongues" and to "not indulge too much in the exercise of the gift of tongues, or the devil will take advantage of the innocent and unwary."[58] Some, like the men in the Kirtland priesthood meeting of June 3, 1837, and a young woman at an Ohio meeting that same summer, had demonic spirits driven from them in grand public display.[59] Among others, as in the Missouri branch of the church, which was "enjoying more of the Spirit than elsewhere," the operation of the gifts was suspect. Here it was said that Sally Crandle's "gift of seeing was not of the Lord but it was of the Devil."[60]

Demonic possession could also be detected in doctrinal differences that were foreshadowings of dissent. In October 1830 Newell Knight's aunt Martha Peck (mother of dissenter Reed Peck) announced that "she must die for the redemption of this generation"; Knight declared that the devil had put "a lying spirit in her mouth" and "commanded Satan . . . to depart." Several years later, in Missouri, Martha Peck posed a more serious challenge when, as a new doctrine was being presented to the branch, she "arose and contradicted the revelation, saying it must be taken in a spiritual light." When Knight attempted "to rebuke her by the authority of the Priesthood," she divided the local Mormons with her message until Knight was able to reassert control. "I was able to make plain the cause of Sister Peck's illness – that she had risen up in opposition to the Priesthood . . . and had contradicted the revelations of God; [she] had fallen completely under the power of Satan, and could not extricate herself."[61]

Thus an ever-present Satan lay behind false spirits and false doctrines that threatened to discredit and disrupt the young church. In some cases, such as those of Sally Crandle and Martha Peck, many of the elements of seventeenth-century witchcraft accusations were repeated, including the suppression of strong women by a patriarchy.[62] Generally, the assumption was that of possession by the devil rather than a conscious compact. But Mormon doctrine made a place for such conscious compacts, and there was probably only a very shadowy divide between the two. Hypocrites would be "detected" and "cut off," and liars, sorcerers, adulterers, and whoremongers were consigned to the telestial kingdom, where they would suffer eternal fire. The Book of Moses placed liars into the dichotomous genealogy of the seed of Adam and the seed of Cain: Satan and then Cain were made "the father of all lies."[63]

Mormonism proposed a vision of reality radically different from that of mainstream America and was thus hypersensitive to questions of truth and falsehood. The entire fabric of the Mormon enterprise rested on the authority and legitimacy of the prophet; for the Mormon faithful anything that challenged that authority was false, lying, demonic. The defense of the kingdom against the world was founded on an almost impossible combination of faith in the supernatural and fear of the counterfeit.

These connotations of truth and falsity, certainty and indeterminacy, set the stage for the rhetoric of counterfeiting accusation in 1837 and 1838. The accusations began with the legal proceedings against the Kirtland Bank, moved to Rigdon's diatribe against the dissenters in the temple, and then contributed to the excommunication of Oliver Cowdery in Missouri in April 1838. Counterfeiting, or "being connected in the 'Bogus' business," was one in a long list of charges brought against Cowdery, but it was central to a letter written in June 1838 to several dissenters and signed by eighty-three Mormon militants. Oliver Cowdery, David Whitmer, and Lyman E. Johnson were accused of being "united with a gang of counterfeiters, thieves, liars, and blacklegs of the deepest dye." Sidney Rigdon used very similar language against the dissenters in his Salt Sermon of June 17, 1838. According to Reed Peck, he "accused them of counterfeiting, lying, cheating and numerous other crimes and called on the people to rise en masse and rid the county of such a nuisance . . . and hang them up as they did the gamblers at Vicksburg."64 In Fawn Brodie's estimate, by the winter of 1837 Rigdon had become a "witch-hunter."65

The narrative structure of the latter half of the *Book of Mormon* provided a useful framework for interpreting the collapse of Mormon consensus. Dissenter John Whitmer, one of the original New York witnesses, drew on language from the *Book of Mormon* to describe the chaos of the demise of the Kirtland settlement: behind the factions jockeying for position and monetary wealth he detected "Gadianton bands, in which they were bound with oaths, etc., that brought division and mistrust among those who were pure of heart, and desired the upbuilding of the Kingdom of God."66 In essence, gangs of witchlike, false Masonic counterfeiters were destroying the church, as the Gadiantons had threatened to destroy the Nephites. Joseph Smith similarly invoked an image of witchcraft and black magic when he condemned the dissenters in Missouri as a "Nicolaitaine band" practicing "secret abominations." Michael Quinn has argued that popular understanding linked the term "Nicolaitaines with the Gnostics and a threatening alien magic."67 Each side of the struggle could draw upon a sacred history of conspiracy and corruption, tinged with black magic, to tar their opponents.

The rhetoric of counterfeiting and Gadianton Bands would have powerful resonances in the Mormon experience in Missouri and at Nauvoo. But the reality, known and unknowable, of counterfeiting in the Mormon ranks in the late 1830s is equally important. It provides another perspective on a state-defying antinomianism inherited from a perfectionist tradition and increasingly potent in the Mormon story. Rhetorical exaggeration of the threats of danger to the Kingdom – hermetic and otherwise – may have concealed a partaking in those very same dangers.68

The accusations of counterfeiting have a powerfully rhetorical dimension, but their very specificity suggests that there was indeed some substance to them. Most obviously, the operation of the Kirtland Safety Society without a bank charter was a form of "money-making" that lay somewhere on a spectrum between legitimate wildcat banking and counterfeiting. But the charges against Oliver Cowdery contained quite specific language: Frederick G. Williams testified that Cowdery had told him that one of the Mormon followers "could compound metal and make dies, that he could make money so that it could not be detected." And, according to Joseph Smith, he and Rigdon had warned Cowdery to leave Kirtland when they learned of a warrant against him "for being engaged in making a purchase of Bogus money & dies." According to Williams's testimony, the skilled diemaker among the Mormons was named Davis; this man was probably Marvel C. Davis, a physician with metallurgical skills among the Kirtland Mormons.[69] For all its rhetorical excess, the Mormon letter of June 1838 accused the dissenters not only of "selling bogus money" but of selling "stones and sand for bogus," a charge with such prosaic specificity that it bears the ring of truth. Charges that Warren Parrish had looted the Kirtland Bank of hard currency in the summer of 1837 seem a bit farfetched, but it does seem likely that under his direction "runners" were sent out to buy livestock with worthless Kirtland notes. Smith eventually condemned Parrish and his associates as "speculators, renegades, and gamblers."[70] Similar counterfeit-based commerce endemic in the western states provided the model for either the reality or the accusation in both of these cases. The town of Boston in Portage County, a few miles west of the road often used by Mormons traveling between Kirtland and the Mormon outpost at New Portage, was in the 1830s the headquarters of a counterfeiting gang described as briefly "the most extensive banking establishment in Ohio, if not the Union." Although the gang was partially broken up in 1832 after the failure of a grandiose scheme to sail to China with a load of counterfeit notes on the Bank of the United States, some of its members were still active into the early 1840s. (They may well have been Rigdon's "Tinker's Creek blacklegs.") One of their number, William Ashley, began his career in Vermont and, not unlike Stephen Burroughs, fled Vermont via Slab City in Ontario before arriving in Ohio.[71]

Sorting out the rhetorical and the real in the Kirtland counterfeiting accusations might seem pointless. But the kernel of reality in these accusations leads to some intriguing hypotheses. Perhaps Oliver Cowdery and others among the dissenters, like John Finney eighty years earlier, lapsed into counterfeiting as their commitment to a perfectionist movement collapsed. Or, equally likely, perhaps Joseph Smith was beginning to take his prophetic mission to antinomian – and state building – extremes. The problem of the reality of counterfeiting among the Mormons must be posed, even if it can not be satisfactorily answered, because a Mormon challenge to secular laws of currency would fit into a broader pattern. Already Joseph Smith was defying the law in regard to marriage; currency would only be another step. And as the center of the Mormon story moved first to Missouri and then to Illinois, a third arena – military power – would reemerge as a point of Mormon appropriation of the monopoly powers of the state. In all of these areas, Smith's conviction of his prophetic authority in a new and ultimate dispensation allowed him to violate the conventional boundaries between purity and danger. More precisely, the prophet of the Mormon kingdom redefined those boundaries to suit his own purposes. The only legitimate boundary was now that between the kingdom and the world.

The Mormon communities in Missouri had been driven out of the area of Independence, the ancient seat of the Mormon Garden of Eden, in 1834. Settling in Clay County, by 1836 they were seen as threats to the non-Mormon inhabitants and were urged to depart, under threat of vigilante action. With the sponsorship of leading non-Mormons in the legislature, the Mormons were promised a county of their own, Caldwell County, northeast of Clay, on the south fork of the Grand River. Here the Missouri Mormons established a thriving town called Far West and a smaller settlement to the east at Haun's Mills, before the final collapse of the Kirtland stake sent thousands of Ohio Mormons west, to take up land in Zion.[72]

Joseph Smith and his family took two months to cover the eight hundred miles from Kirtland to the upper Missouri country, arriving at Far West on March 14, 1838. Seven and a half months later, he would be arrested for high treason by the state of Missouri. The spring, summer, and fall of 1838 would see the arrival of the Kirtland Mormons, the dispersal of Mormon dissenters, rising tensions, and then raging civil war between Missourians and Mormon loyalists.

During this period, Smith found time for a few of his established interests. Living at the house of the Harris family in Far West, he developed a plural relationship with Lucinda Morgan Harris, the remarried widow of the Antimasonic martyr William Morgan; later he made a similar connection with Prescindia Huntington Buell, who apparently bore him a child. Both of these women would be counted among his plural wives.[73] And several months after arriving in Missouri, Smith proclaimed that a bluff above Lyman Wight's ferry on the middle branch of the Grand River was the site of "Adam-Ondi-Ahman," the spot where Adam had settled after being driven from the Garden of Eden, located at Independence, roughly fifty miles to the south. Far West was designated the site where Cain killed Abel, but Adam-Ondi-Ahman had by far the more dramatic connotations, for here, Smith told his people, was "the place where Adam shall come to visit his people, or the Ancient of Days shall sit, as spoken of by Daniel the Prophet."[74]

Such a declaration had explosive implications, because Wight's ferry was located in Daviess County, outside the limits of Caldwell County, where the Missourians expected the Mormons to settle. Mormon expansionism – legitimated in some measure by Smith's Adamic decree – would have a central role in the troubles of the summer and fall of 1838 but so too would the dynamic of dissenters and loyalists, transplanted from Kirtland to the Missouri frontier.

As we have seen, Oliver Cowdery and other dissenters arrived in Far West in the spring of 1838, to be excommunicated and then threatened by the Mormon loyalists. Beyond the specificity of the counterfeiting accusations, the continuing confrontation between loyalists and dissenters brought an increasing ideological rigidity within the Mormon establishment. The Word of Wisdom – a strict temperance regime first announced in 1834 – and the Law of Consecration would be enforced. And a secret military order was created to achieve these ends, to drive out dissenters, and then to advance the Mormon Kingdom.

Rooted in the 1834 organization of the Army of Israel, the paramilitary Mormon forces of 1838 were variously called the Brothers of Gideon, the Daughters of Zion, or the Danites. Their exact structure is a matter of great historiographic dispute, but the consensus is that the terms were variously applied both to the overall Mormon forces in 1838 and to a secret brotherhood of officers drawn from the Army of Israel. Sworn by oaths to keep their business and identities secret, the Danite core was called by one member a "divine brotherly union."[75]

Their first mission was to expel the dissenters. Following Rigdon's violent Salt Sermon of June 17, which condemned the dissenters, and the threats by the Danites, the dissenters fled from Far West on June 19. Among the dissenters there were at least two men who had been ardent Antimasons a decade before: Martin Harris and William W. Phelps. These men and other early converts like Cowdery and the Whitmers included all of the surviving witnesses to the Golden Plates who were not among Smith's immediate family. They must have wondered about the parallels among the Gadianton Bands, Freemasonry, and the Danite militias. Even Joseph Smith, when he renounced the Danites in his *History*, called them a "secret combination." John Whitmer simply called them Smith's "new organized plan."[76] Clearly the spring and summer of 1838 brought a sharper articulation of the absolutist strain in Mormon thinking, which was totally antithetical to the almost anarchic magical populism – originally shaped in the Antimasonic and evangelical climate of the Burned-over District – that Smith had been battling against since he denounced Hiram Page's revelations in September 1830.

The new Mormonism would not emerge in full form in Missouri, because a short and brutal civil war lay just over the horizon. Emboldened by the success of his Salt Sermon and reacting to Missourians' hostility to Mormon expansionism, Sidney Rigdon delivered an inflammatory speech on July 4, promising "a war of extermination" against the Missourians. After an election-day riot on August 6 in Daviess County, tensions spiraled into all-out war in September and October. According to a Mormon eyewitness, Albert P. Rockwood, Mormon militias marched "without authority by the laws of the land, and are therefore considered as breakers of the peace." As Rockwood recalled, they were "called Danites because the Prophet Daniel has said they shall take the kingdom and possess it forever." Daniel's prophecies – and an ambiguous revelation of 1832 – were invoked to justify Mormon plundering. Sampson Avard was reported to have told his men that since it had been

> written, "the riches of the Gentiles shall be consecrated to my people, the house of Israel"; thus you shall waste away the Gentiles by robbing and plundering them of their property, and in this way we will build up the kingdom of God and roll forth the little stone that Daniel saw cut from the mountain without hands, until it shall fill the whole earth.

A new dispensation, a new Kingdom, justified an antinomian sinlessness.[77]

The Mormon dispensation was more than offset by the southern militia tradition. The Missourians, mostly migrants from border and southern states, fought with a viciousness that anticipated the Kansas troubles and the Civil War in Missouri. They plundered Mormon farms and villages, and on October 30 massacred in cold blood the Mormon defenders of Haun's Mills. The next day at Far West, surrounded by thousands of Missouri militia, Joseph Smith, Sidney Rigdon, and other leading Mormons surrendered on charges of high treason.[78] That winter, with Smith and five other leaders jailed in the village of Liberty, Missouri, and straggling Mormon families fleeing to the east to sanctuary in Illinois, the church seemed on the verge of total collapse.

10

The Keys to the Kingdom

I will show the world is wrong by showing what God is. . . . I will tell you & hear it O Earth! God who sits in yonder heavens is a *man like yourselves*[.] That God if you were to see him to day . . . you would see him like a man in form, like yourselves. Adam was made in his image and talked with him & walkd with him. . . . And you have got to learn how to make yourselves God, king and priest, by going from a small capacity to a large capacity to the resurrection of the dead to dwelling in everlasting burnings. . . . [You] will rise & dwell with everlasting burnings to be an heir of God & joint heir of with [*sic*] Jesus Christ enjoying the same rise exhaltation & glory untill you arive at the station of a God.

Joseph Smith funeral oration for King Follett, April 7, 1844, as recorded by Wilford Woodruff[1]

O N APRIL 22, 1839, Mormon Dimick Huntington noticed a haggard but familiar-looking passenger disembarking from the Missouri ferry at Quincy, Illinois. On close scrutiny he recognized the Mormon prophet, Joseph Smith, hidden under a long blue cloak and broad black hat.[2] A week before, Smith and four other Mormon prisoners had been allowed to escape confinement in Daviess County, ending a six-month imprisonment. The church had not collapsed in his absence. Under the leadership of Brigham Young and Heber C. Kimball, the defeated Mormons had gradually filtered east out of Missouri to the area around Quincy, where they were welcomed by local inhabitants. But the Mormon experiment was clearly in deep trouble. Their numbers depleted by dissent and war, the Mormon faithful had lost all of their property in western Missouri. These events, compounded by those that destroyed Kirtland, required that new and more secure arrangements be established to govern the political relationship between the church and its non-Mormon neighbors.

For the better part of the year following his escape from Missouri Smith was preoccupied with these immediate questions of property, people, and politics. But he also needed to attend to theology. Since 1830 Smith's authority as a prophet of a new dispensation and "the restoration of all things" had rested upon the miracles of the discovery, translation, and witnessing of the Golden Plates of the *Book of Mormon*. By 1839 only three of the eleven witnesses remained within the fold: Joseph's father and his brothers Hyrum and Samuel. Two of the five witnesses among the Whitmer family had died in 1835 and 1836, and the three others, with Martin Harris, Oliver Cowdery, and Hiram Page, either left the church or were excommunicated in 1838. Smith had been forced to flee Kirtland with a mob at his back, leaving the temple, the tabernacle of the Lord, in the hands of dissenters. For a second and shattering time, the Mormons had to abandon the sacred paradisial ground of western Missouri. Without strong measures and a new departure, the momentum of the church might well have evaporated.

Joseph Smith was well prepared for new departures. Within five years, in an interlude of relative stability like that of the early 1830s, a new Mormonism emerged from the ashes of the old. The *Book of Mormon* was still to be a central dimension of Mormon faith after Nauvoo, but it was overlain with a completely new ritual order in which the strands of hermetic culture running through the Mormon experience since the treasure-hunting of the 1820s were given a final centrality.

For years Smith had held out the promise of revealing to his people the keys to the mysteries of the Kingdom of God. When Smith and Cowdery had stood behind the veil in the Kirtland temple in April 1836, they were given the "keys to this dispensation" by the prophet Elijah in a "great and glorious vision."[3] But in the struggle and chaos of the ensuing years the content of these keys had never been revealed to the Mormon people. The Illinois interlude, conflicted and stressful as it was, provided the context where Smith could announce his understanding of the keys to the Kingdom of God. At Nauvoo he protected his church behind a wall of civil and military power that challenged both state and nation, more than hinting at revolutionary ambitions of theocratic empire.[4] Within his city-state, the prophet preached new doctrines to his people. The dead and the living would be sealed into an organic communion; men and women would be sealed in eternal celestial marriage; obedient to priesthoods and ordinances, endowed and anointed in temple ritual, they would rise in the afterlife to an ever-ascending divinity. Given form by the ritualism of a revitalized American Freemasonry, and with nostalgic references back to the culture of treasure-divining, the new Mormonism of Nauvoo was a powerful rearticulation of a literal restitutionism and a hermetic perfectionism deriving from the late Renaissance, the Radical Reformation, and the English revolutionary sects. And as the keys were revealed, a resolution was achieved in the unity of the new Kingdom that effectively erased conventional boundaries between purity and danger.

The first problem facing the Mormon community in April 1839 was finding land for a new start. Their welcome in Quincy was wearing thin, and the leadership was well aware that their church required open space and isolation from the gentile world. The Mormons' requirements had already been noticed by Isaac Galland, a speculator living up the Mississippi at a paper town called Commerce who had interests of varying legitimacy in lands on both sides of the river. Even before Smith was out of prison Galland had written to him about purchasing land, and three days after his arrival in Quincy, Smith and a committee traveled upriver to examine the possibilities.

Within weeks the Mormon church had contracted to buy land in both Illinois and Iowa. The townsite of Commerce, Illinois, promised to be both an important center of trade and easily defendable. Situated at the upper end of the Des Moines Rapids, from where an extensive river traffic on the Upper Mississippi might develop, it was a peninsula surrounded by water to the west and demarcated to the east by a line of bluffs. Despite the fact that the land below the bluffs was so wet that a team of horses could not be driven across it, Smith renamed the place Nauvoo, based on a Hebrew word suggesting "beauty and repose," and began to urge the Mormons in Quincy to "gather" at his new town. Here at Nauvoo a Mormon town rapidly took shape, centering on the Smith household and the red brick store where he would spend most of his remaining years.[5]

Those who took up land across the river in Iowa were not so lucky. Isaac Galland was a shady character. He had once run with a gang of counterfeiters and horse thieves operating out of a fort at the fork of the Ohio and Mississippi rivers, who were dispersed in 1831 by a band of "regulators" armed with artillery. In the 1830s Galland had acquired tenuous claims to land in Iowa called the Half-Breed Tract; the Mormon settlers found that their titles to this land were dubious or downright fraudulent. Galland was only the first of many dangerous adventurers to pass through the Mormon story at Nauvoo.[6]

The Mormon Kingdom at Nauvoo required a growing stream of converts, converts who would gather at the command of the prophet. Missions in the eastern states were still producing new believers, but the Mormon leadership had their eyes on another place. In July 1839 eight Mormon apostles, led by Young and Kimball, set out to preach the word in Great Britain to a doubly prepared people.

In the late 1830s Britain was wracked by depression and political strife. The economic downturn of 1837 had hardened into a seemingly permanent depression, idling thousands of industrial workers of all kinds while the Chartist demand for basic political rights was deflected by minimal reforms. The bleak conditions of British life set the stage for the conver-

sion of thousands of people, mostly operatives, artisans, and petty trades-
men, by a small band of common men from America.[7]

But the Mormon message also resonated with a centuries-old radical
religious culture. British converts to Mormonism were in great measure
already committed to millenarian, primitivist, and even magical religious
sensibilities that had been circulating through orbits of radical religion
ever since the seventeenth century. Revitalized in the decades following
the 1790s by prophets such as Richard Brothers and Joanna Southcott,
millenarianism and restorationism had persisted in odd corners of post-
Restoration England, entangled with the hermetic pietism of Jacob
Boehme, the Philadelphian Society, and Emmanuel Swedenborg and nour-
ished by the rise of Arminian Methodism and its various more radical
offshoots. Rooted in the pietism of the late-seventeenth-century "Second
Radical Reformation," these movements sustained the cause of restorationist and perfectionist radicalism in England long after its heyday in the
1650s.[8]

The Mormon missions to England were targeted at the heart of this
radical religious tradition. The first Mormon mission of 1837 had been
invited to preach in Preston, Lancashire, by the Reverend James Fielding
(a brother of a Canadian convert), who had left the Methodists to restore
his chapel to primitive Christianity. In a happy symmetry, this invitation
brought these missionaries, led by Heber C. Kimball, to the birthplace of
Lawrence Clarkson, who two centuries before had practiced Ranter free-
doms, divined for buried treasure, and speculated on hermetic preexistence before taking up the Muggletonian dispensation. Finding enthusiastic audiences among Fielding's primitivists and the followers of
independent Robert Aitken (called by some a "Ranter"), this first Mormon mission converted over a thousand in Preston and the surrounding
villages, establishing the first Mormon beachhead in the Old World.[9]

Leaving Nauvoo in September 1839 and arriving the following April,
the second Mormon mission to Britain found the faith had spread to
Manchester, Staffordshire, and Scotland. Most of the conversions, totaling over 50,000 by 1856, would come in the English Midlands, especially
Lancashire, fed by both industrial depression and religious preparation.
Lancashire was an ancient center of radical religion. In the seventeenth
century, besides Clarkson, Lancashire had produced Gerald Winstanley
and Samuel Gorton. The towns in the south, including Preston, were early
Puritan strongholds, and the northern reaches fell in the orbit of the early
emergence of Quakerism. Out of the intersection of Quakers and French
Camisards in the villages northeast of Manchester came the Shakers, most
notably the Wardleys and Mother Ann Lee of Bolton, where in 1780s
there was an active circle of Swedenborgians. Here and elsewhere this

radical tradition found new expression in the early nineteenth century in Methodist splinter groups and scattered millenarian sects. Mormon missionaries converted independent primitivists, Aitkenites, and United Brethren, who had split from the Methodists, and they attracted followers of John Wroe, a prophet of a Hebrew restoration who in turn had built upon Joanna Southcott's following.[10]

Mormons also converted many mainstream Methodists, Old Dissenters such as Independents and Baptists, and nominal attenders of the Church of England. Their millenarian and primitivist message resonated among a people who in many ways perpetuated the radical traditions of the seventeenth century. And as in the origins of American Mormonism, English hopes for a restoration were interwoven with reinforced beliefs in miracles and magic. One historian has found that British Mormon converts cited manifestations of the spirit almost as often as primitive restoration in their conversion accounts. The converts believed in the healing powers of holy oil, they had dreams and visions, they cast out the devil, and they practiced the "holy kiss," frowned on by the self-conscious American missionaries.[11] And when they came to America they brought with them artifacts from an earlier age of spiritual belief. Wandle Mace, a Utah Mormon, remembered that among the Mormon converts in the Staffordshire potteries there

> were some who had practiced Magic or Astrology. They had Books which had been handed down for many generations, they also had two stones, about the size of goose eggs, they were rough uncouth looking stones one end was flattened so they could be placed on a table. When they wished to gain information from this source, they would place these stones upon a table, and kneel down and pray to one who they addressed as Sameazer, which they called charging the stones, when upon looking into them they saw what they sought.

Given these items, one of the missionaries, George A. Smith, destroyed the books but was said to have carried the stones to Utah.[12] At least one such book of astrology survived the trip from England to Utah. A survey of older volumes in Utah found a commonplace book written in Warwickshire between 1690 and 1726, recording various observations on dyes, plants, and wine-making, as well as remedies and charms extracted from Culpeper's *Herbal* and the writings of Albert Magnus that noted the relationships between herbs and the planets. In a few instances, then, we can catch glimpses of the direct transmission of the seventeenth-century "Familistical-Levelling-Magical Temper" to the world of nineteenth-century American Mormonism.[13]

With the apostles on their way to England, Joseph Smith went on a mission of his own to the eastern states in October 1839, leading to a failure of great consequence. Carrying affidavits endorsed by the governors of Illinois and the Iowa Territory, Smith had a brief meeting with President Martin Van Buren to ask for a constitutional redress of the Mormon grievances against the state of Missouri. Van Buren is reported to have brushed him off with a plea of political expediency: "What can I do? I can do nothing for you! If I do anything, I shall come in contact with the whole state of Missouri." Smith and his associates similarly found no help among the congressmen they visited. Refused federal assistance, the Mormons would have to find their own protection against a hostile world.[14]

Returning to Nauvoo in March 1840, Smith was preoccupied for much of the rest of that year with building up his new city. By June, when Smith set aside his responsibility as the church's land agent to devote more time to theological matters, there were roughly two hundred and fifty houses built at Nauvoo. That month the first English Mormons set sail for America, and six months later they were among the 5,000 Mormons gathered at Nauvoo. By 1845 there would be about 15,000 Mormons in the city and in surrounding Hancock County. This explosive growth took place in the face of a constant toll taken by waterborne disease, most often an endemic malaria, which was especially deadly in the summers of 1839 and 1840. Many among the Smiths, especially the young and the old, died during these summers. In September 1840 the dead included the Patriarch of family and church, Joseph Smith Sr.[15]

On the same day that the old Vermont treasure-diviner was buried, Governor Lilburn Boggs of Missouri, who in 1838 had issued an "Extermination Order" against the Mormons, demanded that Illinois extradite Joseph Smith, Sidney Rigdon, Parley Pratt, and three others to face criminal charges. The authorities in Illinois made a show of cooperation, sending a sheriff, who could not find the accused, but by the end of the year they moved decisively to help the Mormons protect themselves. A very thinly populated state, Illinois could use all the population it could get, and the Mormon community at Nauvoo promised to grow at a rapid pace. Thus legislation to charter the city of Nauvoo, jokingly called a bill "for the Encouragement of the Importation of Mormons," quickly passed in the Illinois legislature that December. Modeled on the city charter for Springfield, the Nauvoo charter included several unusual features. Its municipal court was given powers of granting habeas corpus, which they would use in years to come to protect the Mormon leadership from state arrest. The city was granted the authority to raise "a body of independent militarymen," the Nauvoo Legion, which would be at the disposal of the mayor to enforce both city ordinance and state law. Nominally a unit of the state militia, the Legion was functionally autonomous and self-governing, its independence guaranteed by the powers of its "Court Martial" to "establish and execute" its own laws and regulations. Although unable to defend their Mormon county in Missouri in 1838, and without federal support in Washington, the Mormon leadership now had the framework for what would become a virtual city-state on the banks of the Mississippi.[16]

Within a few months the secular affairs of Nauvoo were redefined according to the new charter. The new city held its first elections on February 1, 1841, electing a slate of a mayor, aldermen, and city councilors overwhelmingly drawn from the Mormon leadership. On February 3 appointments were made to offices in a city university granted in the charter, and on February 4 the officers of the Nauvoo Legion were appointed, with Joseph Smith as lieutenant general commanding a force of six companies. By the time the missionaries returned from England in June, Nauvoo was firmly regulated by a web of civil, military, and religious ordinances woven by the Mormon leadership.[17]

Joseph Smith had already begun to elaborate Mormon religious ordinances by June 1841, and he would soon move toward a fundamental transformation, articulating in secret ritual and in public sermons the "keys of the mysteries of the kingdom," which he had been promising his followers for over a decade.[18] The roots of his new departure lay, in some part, in his six-month imprisonment.

In 1832 and 1833 Smith had announced revelations that radically challenged orthodox Christian doctrines of Creation and salvation. Matter and spirit had existed from eternity; they had not been created *ex nihilo* by an omnipotent God. The Mormon faithful would inhabit a celestial kingdom; the priesthood, endowed with powers of sealing on earth, would rule as gods in this heaven.[19]

If the rank and file of the Mormon movement knew of these doctrines, and most did not, their implications were unclear.[20] These ideas were partially elaborated in the Book of Abraham in 1835, but this manuscript was not published until 1842. The Mormons, however, were certainly a prepared people, anticipating a spiritual transformation and the restitution of all things through continuing revelation. Mormon preaching fueled these expectations. A Unitarian minister, observing a Mormon meeting in Quincy in January 1841, noted that an elder had spoken of revelation and of recovering sacred texts: "God's revelations are giving new light to the world. It is but [a] little while since the Book of Jasher was found in the East Indies – and another Sacred book has been found in

Ethiopia," the latter an apparent reference to the "Book of Enoch."[21] Ordinary Mormons had a strong belief that such mysteries would be reopened by their prophet, a man who had spoken with God.

Over the 1830s Smith occasionally mentioned the doctrines of divinization and plurality of gods, but his ideas about spirit and matter apparently lay fallow. During his imprisonment Smith's ideas about divinization were reinvigorated. Conversations among the Mormon prisoners, including Joseph and Hyrum Smith, Sidney Rigdon, and Parley P. Pratt, had worked to reinforce and clarify their beliefs. While in prison, Pratt wrote a long religious tract on the restoration, restating Smith's doctrine on matter and spirit to announce that an imminent Second Coming would bring "the renovation and regeneration of matter, and the restoration of the elements, to a state of eternal and unchangeable purity." Echoing a long tradition running back to the *Corpus Hermeticum,* Pratt was insistent that matter and spirit were eternal and uncreated.[22] In a letter written to the church from prison in March 1839, Smith referred once more to a plurality of gods.[23]

The definitive announcement of Mormon divinization would come in April 1844, in Smith's funeral sermon for one of his fellow prisoners in Missouri, King Follett. But on his release from prison, Smith preached on spirit and matter on a number of occasions. Willard Richards recorded a lecture in the summer of 1839 that moved from Adam as "the Ancient of Days," the "head of the human family," to the eternal, noncreated nature of the "Spirit of Man." Paraphrasing the unpublished Book of Abraham, Smith spoke of the organization of the preexistent spirits at Creation. In February 1840 Smith preached in Washington about the eternity of the soul; late the following August, commenting on a series of sermons Joseph was preaching to the Iowa Mormons, his cousin John noted that the prophet "continued his discourse on eternal Judgment and the eternal duration of matter."[24]

That same month Smith introduced a new doctrine that would become central to the definition of a new Mormonism: the ritual of baptism for the dead. Announced in a funeral sermon on August 15, 1840, the doctrine was grounded in both the disease environment on the Nauvoo flats and Smith's doctrines on spirit and eternity. Two weeks before, Smith had called a prayer meeting to ask the Lord "to pacify the Elements &c that health may be restored to the Saints." But in the funeral sermon Smith revealed that elders would have the authority to baptize the dead by living proxy into the Mormon church. The first baptisms began immediately in the Mississippi.[25] When he codified the doctrine two years later in a revelation, Smith made baptism for the dead a ritual binding together the visible and the invisible, the temporal and the eternal, matter and spirit.

His text came from the last verses of the Book of Malachi, in which it is prophesied that the prophet Elijah will return before judgment day to "turn the heart of the fathers to the children, and the heart of the children to the fathers." In Smith's vision, the living and the dead must be linked in a sacred and organic covenant:

> For we without them [the dead] cannot be made perfect; neither can they without us be made perfect . . . it is necessary in the ushering in of the dispensation of the fullness of times . . . that a whole and complete and perfect union, and welding together of dispensations, and keys, and powers, and glories should take place, and be revealed from the days of Adam even to the present time.[26]

The doctrine of baptism for the dead had been anticipated in a vision that Smith received in January 1836 at the charismatic meetings before the dedication of the Kirtland temple, during which he saw his long-dead brother Alvin in the celestial kingdom with his parents and Adam and Abraham. This sweeping revelation disclosed that all those who had "died without a knowledge of this gospel, who would have received it" were to be carried into the celestial kingdom. In the Kirtland temple vision Smith had also invoked the prophecy of Malachi that Elijah would come to seal the hearts of fathers and children. In the years to come it would be an increasingly important theme in the developing language of union and resolution of the coming Kingdom.[27]

This doctrine would be a comfort for those who so regularly lost family members in an increasingly sentimental nineteenth century. But baptism for the dead had a radical heritage. The German pietist mystics at Ephrata had, at the height of the Zionitic Brotherhood in the early 1740s, introduced baptism of the dead. And earlier, the extreme exponents of the Radical Reformation had espoused a broadly similar theme in their universalism, Christianizing the ancient prophets, as in Caspar Schwenkfeld's claim that "Adam, Abel, Enoch, Noah, and all the elect faithful fathers were members of the Church and were Christians."[28] Baptism for the dead would allow the Mormon church a similar selective appropriation of the past, all in the name of restoring the Kingdom of God.

The popular appeal of baptism for the dead allowed Smith to move forward with his doctrinal agenda. The church had abandoned a temple in Kirtland and two temple sites in Missouri, the sacred center of the Mormon restoration. But the Mormon gathering place required a "house of the Lord," so at a General Conference on October 3–5, 1840, Smith announced that a temple would be built at Nauvoo.

The Nauvoo temple, built of local gray limestone, was modeled on English church architecture rather than the American meetinghouse tradi-

The Nauvoo temple, photographed in the 1840s.
Courtesy of the Utah State Historical Society.

tions reflected in the Kirtland temple. It would have the same tiered ranks of pulpits assigned to the Melchizedek and Aaronic priesthoods on two main meeting floors, with small offices in the attic story, but other points distinguished the Nauvoo temple from Kirtland. Around its exterior, pilaster columns were ornamented at top and bottom with reliefs of a sun face and a moon face, the sunstone at the top representing the celestial kingdom, the moonstone at the bottom representing the second, terrestrial kingdom for pious nonbelievers. And in the basement of the temple there would be a baptismal font, eventually standing eleven feet high, supported by twelve carved oxen. The following January Smith announced in a revelation what he must have told the assembled elders in the October conference: a temple had to be built so that the baptisms of the dead could be accepted in heaven. If the temple was not built, the baptisms would have to stop, but once it was constructed there would be a sure reward, "for I design to reveal unto my church things which have been kept hid from before the foundation of the world, things that pertain to the dispensation of the fulness of times."[29]

The temple would not be completed until November 1845, a year and a half after Smith's assassination at Carthage. If the Lord could wait to reveal the secrets of his Kingdom, Joseph Smith could not. Harried by

Sunstone capital from the Nauvoo temple.
Courtesy of the National Museum of American History, Smithsonian Institution, Washington, D.C.

continued efforts by the Missouri authorities to secure his arrest, and increasingly unpopular in Illinois for his role in state politics, Smith may have anticipated that he would not survive very long. On May 4, 1842, he secretly gathered nine close associates in the second-floor room above his dry-goods store to initiate them into the temple endowment ceremony, which has been the central feature of Mormonism ever since. That summer he began sealing husbands and wives into eternal marriage. Over the next two years Smith initiated sixty-six men and women into these rituals. Starting in September 1843, an even more select company was given a second anointing to confirm their leading places in the celestial kingdom. And finally, two months before his death in June 1844, Smith used the funeral of his former fellow prisoner, King Follett, to deliver the most definitive and authoritative synthesis of his cosmology. These efforts constituted the core of Smith's new departure and remain crucial underpinnings of Mormon cosmology.

The adoption of these doctrines, however, was entangled with connections that modern Mormons would rather forget. The roots of the temple endowments were entangled with another encounter with Freemasonry, and the doctrine of eternal marriage was entangled with the secret principle of "a plurality of wives." Viewed together, all of these developments provide the critical and defining perspective on the Mormon restoration of a paradisial perfectionism forged in the hermetic tradition.

The January 1841 revelation commanding the construction of a temple also ordered that the Mormons build a hotel, a "house for boarding," which Joseph Smith was to manage. That October, as the cornerstone of this Nauvoo House was being dedicated, Joseph Smith ran to get the last surviving manuscript copy of the *Book of Mormon*. Muttering that "I have had enough trouble with this thing," he placed it in the cornerstone cavity. It would lie there until it was rediscovered forty-one years later, as the foundation walls of the hotel were being mined for salvage.[30]

With Martin Harris's "Antimasonick Bible" buried underground, Joseph Smith turned to Freemasonry, lately reemerging from an underground existence. Since the height of the Antimasonic movement in 1830, Freemasonry was shrunken to a shadow of its former splendor, with the few surviving lodges meeting quietly and secretly. But by 1841 the Antimasonic fervor had receded and the lodges once again were able to meet in public. They would provide the model for the proliferation of fraternal orders that became a central dimension of the lives of middle-class American men.[31]

Former Freemasons among the Nauvoo Mormons petitioned the Illinois Grand Lodge in the summer of 1841 that they be allowed to form a lodge, which was eventually granted under a "recess dispensation" dated October 15, 1841. With this temporary authority, given by a Grand Master who had hopes of Mormon support in an upcoming election, the Nauvoo Lodge began organization meetings that December. Its charter members, among them Hyrum and John Smith, had been Freemasons in lodges across New York and Ohio and a scattering of other states. Joseph Smith, Sidney Rigdon, and forty others petitioned for membership in December. Accepted the following February, Smith and Rigdon, by a special dispensation from the Grand Master, were advanced "at sight" through "the three several degrees of Ancient York Masonry" on March 15 and 16. Within a few months the Nauvoo Lodge had almost three hundred members, more than all of the other lodges in Illinois combined.[32]

Thus, with this departure, Joseph Smith turned his back on the Antimasonic culture that had shaped the *Book of Mormon* and that had been so important to many of his early followers, especially Martin Harris and William W. Phelps. In part, the founding of the Nauvoo Lodge was a means of forging political links across Illinois, where some of the leading men were also Freemasons. But the Mormon enthusiasm for Freemasonry rapidly alienated the Grand Lodge, which complained that the Nauvoo Lodge was departing from Masonry's "ancient landmarks" in admitting so many applicants so quickly.[33] Joseph Smith had his own uses for the fraternal oath taking, ritual drama, and religious mythology of Freemasonry, based on a Masonic model of a hermetic restorationism that ran back to his youth in the Burned-over District and his father's early life in the Green Mountains of Vermont.

These uses were revealed within the next six weeks. The day after Smith was made a Master Mason, he met with his wife Emma and nineteen other women to form a charitable association called the Female Relief Society. The manifest purposes of the society were to provide for the poor and the distressed, but Smith often used Masonic terminology when he spoke or wrote to the society; at one point he wrote that he hoped that they would be "sufficiently skill'd in Masonry to keep a secret." Emma Smith had long been called the "Elect Lady," a title in at least one branch of high-degree French Masonry that admitted women into special lodges. One important attack on Mormonism accused Smith of forming "a secret lodge of women," and the evidence suggests that this was indeed the case.[34]

Joseph Smith had been speaking of the keys to the kingdom for over a decade. As Seer, he held the keys of the gifts of translation and revelation; the priesthoods held keys to the ordinances and the mysteries. The nature of these mysteries had been sketched out in the early 1830s, but the keys of entering into those mysteries had been left unspecified, to be revealed in the "fulness of time." In the spring of 1842, when Smith was on the verge of explaining these keys to the kingdom to his closest followers, his language began to take on connotations that reflected both his renewed immersion in Freemasonry and his long-standing concern about authority and falsehood. On March 20 in a public sermon he spoke of "certain key words & signs belonging to the priesthood which must be observed in order to obtain the blessings." A month later he told the Relief Society that they would soon receive the "keys to the kingdom . . . that they may be able to detect every thing false." On May 1 he described "the keys of the Kingdom" as

> certain signs and words by which false spirits and personages may be detected from true, which cannot be revealed to the Elders till the Temple is completed. . . . The devil knows many signs but does not know the sign of the Son of Man, or Jesus. No one can truly say he knows God until he has handled something, and this can only be the Holiest of Holies.[35]

The keys to the kingdom were about to be specified, and they were being described in language that implied Masonic meanings. The key was a symbol of secrecy in Freemasonry, and Masonic ritual was filled with the signs, tokens, and handgrips that protected Masonic secrets.[36] So, too, would be Mormon temple ritual.

On May 4, 1842, Smith assembled nine leading Mormons in the second-floor room over his store to introduce them to the temple endowment. Exactly what happened that day is not clear; Brigham Young wrote in his journal that Smith "taught the ancient order of things for the first time in these last days, and [I] received my washings, anointings, and endowments." Years later Young recounted that at the end of the evening Smith had told him that "this is not arranged right but we have done the best we could under the circumstances. . . . I . . . wish you to take this matter in hand and organize and systematize all these ceremonies with the signs, tokens[,] penalties[,] and Key words." It probably never will be possible to dissect Smith's original plan for the ritual from Young's later elaboration.[37]

Various nineteenth- and twentieth-century accounts of the temple ritual as it developed after 1845, all roughly similar, divide it into four segments. First the initiates were washed and anointed with holy oil, cleaning off the sins of the world and signifying the promise of the celestial kingdom. Then they were clothed in ritual garments, given the new names they would bear in the celestial kingdom, and blessed. Identified as Adam throughout the ceremony, the initiates were taken through a dramatization of the history of the world and of redemption through the power of the Mormon priesthood. The second segment of the ritual was made up of miracle plays depicting Creation and the Fall of Adam and Eve from the Garden of Eden. The Creation scenes included three Creation gods: Elohim, Jehovah, and Michael. Originally, at Nauvoo, the initiates themselves acted out these roles under priestly instruction; later they were played by members of the hierarchy detailed to temple work. With the initiates-as-Adam reduced to a fallen condition, only the powers of the priesthood could save them. In the third segment the initiates were instructed in the First and Second Tokens of the two priesthoods – various handgrips, signs, and coded passwords – before they were allowed through the veil of the temple, hanging across the room, into the celestial kingdom. Along the way the initiates watched an encounter between Adam, the devil, and sectarian preachers, were clothed in priestly garments, chanted together in pure Adamic language, and prayed together in a prayer circle. This, then, was the "ancient order of things," opening the way to entry into the celestial kingdom.[38] By early 1846 more than five thousand Mormons had been initiated into the mysteries of the temple endowment.[39]

There is overwhelming evidence of the continuity between Masonic and Mormon symbolism. The sun, the moon, and the stars, the "lesser lights" of the Masonic symbology, had long been woven into the Mormon cosmology of three heavens, and the sun and the moon were to be prominently displayed on the Nauvoo temple. The Masonic beehive, All-Seeing Eye, and the phrase "Holiness to the Lord" would be ubiquitous symbols in Mormon Utah, where the temples would reflect the Mormon encounter with Freemasonry both in their sculpted ornamentation and in their east-facing orientation, following the tradition of Masonic temples, which Mormon Masons closely observed when they built a lodge building in Nauvoo. Planned before this immersion in Freemasonry, the temples at Kirtland and Nauvoo did not reflect the Masonic priority of the east. In the Kirtland temple, which opened onto the east, the pulpits of the Melchizedek, the senior priesthood, were at the west end of the temple; the Nauvoo temple faced the town and river, which were to the west of the bluff on which it was built. The Utah temples face east, and the east ends of the buildings are devoted to the Melchizedek, mirroring the eastward orientation of Masonic lodge buildings. Both were intended to be replications of Solomon's temple, a connection that Joseph Smith made when he began to call the Nauvoo temple the "Holiest of Holies."[40]

Throughout the temple rituals themselves there were striking similarities with Masonic symbolism, especially those of the York Rite, which was established at the Nauvoo Lodge. The temple garments, very similar to Masonic ceremonial garb, included an apron with the Masonic compass and square, which was also among the emblems on the temple veil. The language of the tokens and penalties of the Mormon priesthoods had exact parallels in Freemasonry, progressing from parallels with the first three degrees of Entered Apprentice, Fellow Craft, and Master Mason to parallels with the Royal Arch and the higher degrees. Among these parallels to the first three degrees were the signs of the "five points of fellowship," the penalties for disclosure of secrets, and priestly handgrips and bodily signing, including "the Sign of the Nail." Parallels with the Royal Arch included the use of the temple veil as the site of ritual discourses and catechisms and the role of a ritual actor representing God.[41]

There were also very specific parallels between the ritual drama of Creation and the Fall from the Garden of Eden. The initiation of the first Masonic degree, the Entered Apprentice, included a recitation of the first three verses of the Creation story in Genesis.[42] The ritual drama of Creation and the Garden was more fully developed in the higher degrees. According to one exposé of Freemasonry published in Cincinnati in 1827, the seventh Royal Arch degree included an address to the candidate on Creation and the Fall from the Garden in which a scroll, taken from a gold box, is given to Adam and passed down to Solomon and eventually buried in the arched vault, to be rediscovered at the rebuilding of the temple.⁴³ In the ritual of the twenty-eighth degree of the Scottish Rite, the Knight of the Sun, Father Adam, "vested in a robe of pale yellow," conveyed the candidate through the ritual, which included a discourse on the "Philosopher's Lodge" and a hermetic catechism on the "quintessence of the Elements," "the fire of the Philosophers," and "the Philosopher's Stone." Here Adam is served by seven cherubim, including Michael, reminiscent of the Seven Governors of the "Egyptian Genesis" of the hermetic "Pimander," anticipating the three Mormon Creation gods.⁴⁴ In the European Lodges of Adoption, established to provide a Freemasonry for women, the ritualized drama of the Garden of Eden was strikingly similar to the Mormon temple endowment ceremony. Here the initiate for the second degree played the role of Eve, taking an apple from a serpent coiled around the Tree of Life.⁴⁵

The symbolism of these higher degrees carries us back to the Masonic and hermetic connotations of the discovery of the Golden Plates in the Hill Cumorah. Ever since the formation of the church, Joseph Smith had been promising to reveal the specific details of the keys to immortal perfection. The temple endowment began to do that, establishing a ritual dramaturgy in which the Mormon-as-Adam could act out cosmic history and gain the specific "keys" that would admit him to the celestial kingdom. In April 1843, before rank-and-file Mormons were introduced to the secrets of the temple rituals, Smith referred back to his days as a treasure-seer in describing the keys: they were an Urim and Thummim, "a white stone . . . given to each of those who come into the celestial kingdom, whereon a new name is written." The earth itself, at the restoration, would "be like unto crystal" and become a vast Urim and Thummim to its inhabitants.⁴⁶ The framing of the temple rituals brought Smith through a full circle, back to his origins as a man of magic in the hills of western New York.

Apparently texts were available in Nauvoo that would have provided many of these details. Heber C. Kimball was reported to have kept a copy of William Morgan's *Masonry Exposed* locked away in a cupboard, and Morgan's widow, Lucinda, a plural wife of the prophet, had a copy of Stearns's *Inquiry into the Nature and Tendency of Speculative Freemasonry* in the summer of 1844. Brigham Young apparently owned a copy of Joshua Bradley's *Some Beauties of Freemasonry*.⁴⁷ Presumably other texts circulating in the wake of the Antimasonic furor were also available. Masonic knowledge also flowed from another source: John Cook Bennett.

A doctor with some militia experience, John C. Bennett was a powerful figure in Nauvoo in the early 1840s. Attracted to the Mormon community in 1840, he was instrumental in moving the Nauvoo City charter through the Illinois legislature. Basking in Smith's favor, he was elected the first mayor of the city, major general of the Nauvoo Legion, chancellor of Nauvoo University, chief justice of the municipal court, and a director of the cooperative Nauvoo Agricultural and Manufacturing Association. In April 1841 he was made "assistant president" of the church, replacing Sidney Rigdon as Smith's chief advisor.[48] Bennett had crossed the Mormon path at least once before, when he was briefly director of the medical college at Willoughby, Ohio, where Smith went to recruit Daniel Piexotto to teach Hebrew to the priesthood. Although his central role at Nauvoo was as vice-commander of the Nauvoo Legion, Bennett was a doctor by training. He had studied with his uncle Samuel P. Hildrith of Marietta and both before and after his tenure at Willoughby had promoted a series of ephemeral colleges, at one point peddling medical degrees for ten dollars apiece. He was known as a surgeon and as a "Professor of Midwifery," having written a pamphlet titled *The Accouchers Vade Mecum*. Bennett also had doctrinal experience that aligned him with the Mormons. During the 1820s he was a member of various Masonic lodges in Ohio, serving on a Grand Lodge committee of accounts in January 1831. For three years beginning in 1827 he was also a Methodist preacher, and in 1830 he became a Campbellite Restorationist. In this capacity he was elected Grand Chaplain of the Ohio Grand Lodge in 1831. Some Mormon leaders knew of him in 1833, but Bennett and Sidney Rigdon probably had known of each other by 1830.[49]

Bennett's early life, weaving together doctoring, Freemasonry, restorationist religion, and a touch of con artistry, fitted well with the broad picture of the early American occult. Indeed, Bennett had roots in the dissenting world of southeastern New England that had nurtured that tradition. Born in Fairhaven, Massachusetts, Bennett's family ran back to Quaker and Seventh-Day Baptist communities in nearby Newport and Tiverton, Rhode Island. Even in Ohio Bennett was in contact with individuals who came from the magical culture rooted in southeastern New England. In 1825 Bennett witnessed a land sale between his uncle Samuel Hildrith and Stephen Davis of Marietta, none other than the "Old Rodsman," who hailed originally from Westport, between Fairhaven and Tiverton. And ten years later a Ransford Rogers, perhaps some relation to the "Morristown Ghost" or perhaps a practical joker, signed an affidavit thanking Bennett for his lectures on midwifery at Willoughby College.[50]

These connections with the old axis of dissent and the occult may have inclined Bennett toward the higher degrees of Freemasonry, which were introduced into Ohio in 1827 by a "degree peddler" hailing from the

Scottish Rite Council in Charleston, South Carolina.[51] Bennett knew a lot about the higher degrees when, in 1846, he persuaded Mormon schismatic Jesse Strang to establish an "Order of the Illuminati," which made Strang "the actual Lord and King on Earth," supported by a "grand Council of Nobles of God's Kingdom." As his authority, Bennett claimed that Joseph Smith had a revelation in April 1841 that Bennett was to uphold the Kingdom after Smith's death by forming a "Halcyon Order," a term that forty years before had been connected with occult restorationism in Cincinnati and Marietta.[52] Bennett certainly played an important role in the founding of the Nauvoo Lodge in the summer and fall of 1841,[53] and it is likely that Smith discussed the ritual of the higher degrees with him while they were still close associates. By the spring of 1842, as we shall see, this was no longer the case.

There were other possible sources for the high hermetic tradition in Nauvoo. It has been suggested that Alexander Neibaur, a German Jew converted in 1837 in Preston, Lancashire, instructed Joseph Smith in the Cabala at Nauvoo, and there are other hints of influence from German traditions. One exposé claimed that Smith learned "all the strokes, and passes, and manipulations" of Mesmerism from "a German peddler, who, notwithstanding his reduced circumstances, was a man of distinguished intellect and extensive erudition." Smith was indeed studying German during the final months of his life, and in one account of his pivotal King Follett sermon Smith praised the Germans as "an exalted people" and "the old German translators" as "the most correct," for they corroborated his revelations on baptism by water, fire, and the Holy Ghost, and on the descent of the keys.[54]

But Mormon commentary made the link with Freemasonry firm and inescapable. Five weeks after the first temple endowment initiation Heber C. Kimball wrote to Parley Pratt about affairs at Nauvoo and about Freemasonry. Not mentioning the endowment, Kimball wrote that "thare is a similarity of preas Hood [priesthood] in Masonry. Bro. Joseph Ses Masonry was taken from preasthood but has become degenerated. But many things are perfect." According to Benjamin F. Johnson, Smith had told him that "Freemasonry, as at present, is the apostate endowment, as sectarian religion is the apostate religion." Joseph Fielding, the Canadian convert who had opened the door to the Preston mission, wrote in his journal that "Many have joined the Masonic Institution," which seemed "to be a Stepping Stone or Preparation for something else, the true Origin of Masonry." In 1858 Heber Kimball put it even more plainly. "We have the true Masonry. The Masonry of today is taken from the apostacy which took place in the days of Solomon and David. They have now and then a thing that is correct, but we have the real thing." Indeed, Brigham

Young, photographed in the early 1850s with a Masonic pin in his lapel, is reputed to have called the temple endowment ritual "Celestial Masonry."[55]

Since the 1820s, and probably earlier, the Smith family had seen in Masonic mythology a way to "the ancient order of things," a history of sacred continuities corrupted with the passage of time, yet still bearing fragmentary elements of the keys to divine perfection once held by Adam. The culture of Masonic millenarianism and restorationism had shaped the story of the discovery of the Golden Plates, the narrative structure of the *Book of Mormon,* and the formative revelations of the early 1830s. Now Mormonism was reaching behind the impurities of contemporary Freemasonry to recover the pure original.

Here, then, was the core of the new Mormonism of Nauvoo: Freemasonry and Mormon temple ritual shared a common ancestry in the secret hermetic keys to the mysteries handed down in priestly genealogies from the beginning of time. But the pure primitive Masonry of Adam, Seth, and Enoch had been corrupted by the spurious Cainite rituals; Joseph Smith's revelations restored the Adamic keys in their original and authoritative form. The Mormon priests, not the Freemasons, were the true inheritors of Adam's paradisial powers, a veritable hermetic theocracy. For Mormons, Masonic corruption was proven beyond a shadow of a doubt at the Carthage jail when Joseph Smith – attacked by a mob – jumped to the window shouting out the first words of the Masonic distress cry, "O Lord My God . . . ," only to fall riddled with bullets.[56]

During the early 1830s Joseph Smith had defined the mysteries of his restoration. The reward for the faithful would be a divinization in the highest of three heavens, in a cosmos where matter and spirit were integrally connected and where each had existed for eternity, before being organized at the Creation. For various reasons, however, most Mormons in the early 1840s probably did not understand the full dimensions of Smith's doctrinal innovation. Many of the early revelations were couched in obscure language, and many (as well as the Books of Moses and Abraham) were not published for many years. There had been considerable turnover in membership, and the new English converts were arriving with only a conviction of the gospel of restoration and the certainty of miraculous events. Only the inner circle of Smith's associates could have had a clear picture of the promised mysteries.[57]

With the King Follett discourse, a funeral sermon delivered in April 1844 for one of his compatriots in the Liberty jail, Joseph Smith incontrovertibly announced in public the nature of the mysteries of the kingdom, in language that reproduced the essence of the Renaissance hermetic tradition. In the theology announced in the sermon for King Follett, Creation was not out of nothing, *ex nihilo*, but from "chaotic matter," elements that had existed forever: "they can never have a beginning or an ending; they exist eternally." Similarly, human spirit, or "intelligence," was eternal, without "a beginning or an end." Preaching from his translation of the Hebrew Old Testament, Smith argued that God had put Adam's preexistent spirit into his body at the Creation. From this he concluded, "Man existed in spirit" before Creation; "the mind of man – the intelligent part – is as immortal as, and is coequal with God himself." This evidence proved Smith's dramatic opening announcement: "God Himself who sits enthroned in yonder heavens is a Man like unto one of yourselves – that is the great secret!" Taking "away the veil so you may see," Smith challenged his people: "you have got to learn how to make yourselves Gods in order to save yourselves and be kings and priests to God, the same as all Gods have done – by going from . . . a small degree to another, from grace to grace . . . , from exaltation to exaltation." This was the ideal of eternal progression, beginning on earth, where all spirits were "susceptible to enlargement and improvement," and continuing in heaven, where a tiered pantheon of gods progressed through infinite stages of divinity, powered by succeeding generations of saints-becoming-gods.[58] As a Mormon proverb later put it, capturing the doctrines of both eternity and divinization, "As man is now, so once was God; as God is now, man may become."[59]

This sermon, delivered twice to crowds of thousands gathered on successive days at the Nauvoo grove, is a critical benchmark in Mormon theology. What had been obscure and ill-defined was now part of the public record. But, if Smith urged his people to learn "how to make yourselves Gods," the ritual means to this godhood remained a closely guarded secret, and only the first of many secrets. By April 1844 the temple endowment ceremony had been given to only sixty-six people, and already this ritual was being elaborated with even more secret – and controversial – doctrines.

The first of these was the doctrine of eternal marriage. In the spring of 1843 Smith began to teach his inner circle that only through a special "sealing" ritual added to the temple endowment could a marriage on earth be guaranteed to last for eternity in heaven. On May 28, 1843, three weeks after the initial endowment ceremonies, Smith was sealed to his wife Emma Hale for "time and eternity." Ten days before, Smith had a revelation that there were "three heavens or degrees" in the celestial kingdom, and that only those who had been granted "this order of the priesthood" (i.e., eternal marriage) would be allowed into the "highest" degree.[60] That July he produced another revelation, extending and specifying his doctrine on eternal marriage, his last revelation to be canonized in the *Doctrine and Covenants*.

This revelation linked the three degrees of glory in the celestial kingdom with three categories of marriage. Only those Mormon faithful who had entered into "a new and everlasting covenant" of eternal, or celestial, marriage would have the potential for continuing exaltation in the celestial kingdom. Above and below them would be two other degrees of glory. Eternal marriage – and godhood – was guaranteed only by the marriage sealing added to the temple endowment; those who had only married in a secular marriage ceremony would have their marriages end at the end of their "time" on earth. In heaven, Mormons without sealed eternal marriages would occupy the lowest degree of glory in the celestial kingdom, where they would simply be ministering angels, servants to those in the higher degrees, and condemned to an unexalted existence, without prospect of progression toward and in divinity.[61]

Achieving higher degrees of glory would be the reward for those who fulfilled the command to restore the ancient "principle and practice of . . . having many wives and concubines." Celestial marriage would ensure Mormon exaltation; a plurality of wives, and their many children born on earth and in heaven, would increase the familial kingdom and thus elevate the Mormon patriarch to higher and higher degrees of glory. The prophet Abraham had "received promises concerning his seed and of the fruit of his loins," promises of eternal expansion: "both in and out of this world should they continue as innumerable as the stars; or if ye were to count the sand upon the seashore ye could not number them." All those who sought a "fulness" of glory were ordered to go and "do the works of Abraham." Their many wives and children would "multiply and replenish the earth," fulfill the divine promise made "before the foundation of the world," and ensure "their exaltation in the eternal worlds."[62] In Utah in the 1850s celestial marriage would be identified with plural marriage, only to be separated again after the Manifesto setting aside polygamy in 1890. Another important means to augment the celestial family kingdom was by the baptism of the dead, whose numbers in the lower rungs of the celestial kingdom would expand the glory of the familial patriarch as much as would his wives and children.

Finally, someone had to have the authority to bestow these privileges on the uninitiated and to receive the ultimate reward. In October 1831 Smith had announced at a conference in Kirtland that the high priesthood of the Melchizedek would receive the authority "to seal up the Saints to eternal life," and five years later, with Oliver Cowdery behind the veil in the Kirtland temple, he had had a vision of the prophet Elijah granting him certain unspecified "keys of this dispensation."[63] These keys were divulged to the inner circle in the summer and fall of 1843, with the inauguration of the ritual of the second anointing.[64]

On August 27 Smith lectured at the Nauvoo grove on three orders of priesthood. There was the Aaronic Priesthood, with the power to minister ordinances, and the "Patriarchal power" of Abraham, which was "the greatest yet experienced in this church." But yet to come was the "perfect law of Theocracy": the "kingly powers" of the Melchizedek Priesthood to "administer . . . endless lives to the sons and daughters of Adam." This "perfect law," "the Highest and Holiest Order," was realized in new washing and anointing rituals initiated that September when Joseph and Emma were given this final "fulness of the priesthood," or "second anointing," followed by others in the hierarchy in October, November, and June. By 1846 almost six hundred Mormons had been given a second anointing.[65]

The following March Smith described these ultimate priesthood powers as "the spirit power and calling of Elijah," the Old Testament prophet who had been bodily carried to heaven. These powers of Elijah, "the keys of the Kingdom of Jehovah," gave the priests of the Melchizedek the authority to "perform all the ordinances belonging to the Kingdom of God." As announced in Kirtland in 1836, when Smith had his vision of the prophet Elijah, and then reasserted in 1842 with the doctrine of baptism for the dead, the most potent of these ordinances was that of "sealing the hearts of the fathers unto the children & the hearts of the children unto the fathers[,] even those who are in heaven."[66]

The reward of the second anointing was a virtually unconditional guarantee of godhood in the highest degree of the celestial kingdom. The bearers of the "sealing powers of Elijah" were "sealed with the Holy Spirit of promise," and this seal was the key to godhood. Using predestinarian language in his March 1844 sermon, Smith told his people that the "power of Elijah is sufficient to make our calling & Election sure." According to his penultimate revelation, those who were endowed with the temple ordinance of marriage for time and eternity *and* were "sealed with the Holy Spirit of promise" – the "Second Anointing" – would be guaranteed divinity in the celestial kingdom.[67]

> [W]hen they are out of this world . . . they shall pass by the angels, and the gods, which are set there, to their exaltation and glory in all things, as hath been sealed upon their heads, which glory shall be a fulness and a continuation of the seeds forever and ever. Then

they shall be gods, because they have no end; therefore shall they be from everlasting to everlasting, because they continue; then shall they be above all, because all things are subject unto them. Then shall they be gods, because they have all power and the angels are subject to them.[68]

The second anointing made a favored few into gods and goddesses, kings and queens, while they were still here on earth. There were conditions. Divinity in the celestial kingdom would come to all who "abide in my [new and everlasting] covenant, and commit no murder whereby to shed innocent blood." Those who shed innocent blood and those who became apostates, the "Sons of Perdition," would be damned and "delivered up to the buffetings of Satan."[69] But among the faithful, there would be a pantheon of higher and lesser gods, the former guaranteed their place by the second anointing, the latter promised their place in the temple endowment and ritual of celestial marriage.

Here, then, Smith claimed the powers to unite the living and the dead in a single sacred universe of salvation and exaltation, fulfilling the apocalyptic prophecy of the final verses of the Books of Malachi and Revelation. But although Smith couched his theology in terms of restoration, his promise of divinity in these advanced temple rituals restated the central tenets of the hermetic tradition.

The Mormon doctrine of celestial marriage, either singular or plural, leading to exaltation to godhood, recaptured the hermetic concept of alchemical marriage. In the Egyptian Genesis of the "Pimander," the hermetic Adam had given up his divinity to mate with Nature. Alchemical theory posited a marriage of the elements of mercury and sulphur, the hermetic Sun King and Moon Queen, to regain Adamic perfection in the philosopher's stone. This concept of alchemical marriage, popularized in the early seventeenth century in the spurious Rosicrucian text *The Chemical Wedding of Christian Rosencreutz,* had encouraged various forms of sexual experimentation. Alchemists and hermetic philosophers, among them Paracelsus, John Dee, Simon Forman, John Milton, and Casanova, speculated upon or practiced forms of spiritual wifery or polygamy. During the English Revolution, Ranters were accused of sexual experimentation and may indeed have indulged in some "liberties." English Quakers and Shakers and German Ephratans and Rappites adopted doctrines of celibacy that had implicit and explicit roots in the hermetic ideal of Adam's androgynous perfection. Closer in time, Smith's concept of eternal, celestial marriage was extremely similar to that of Emmanuel Swedenborg, the eighteenth-century hermetic theologian who Smith once admitted "had a view of things to come."[70] A version of the alchemical theory of elemental marriage and reproduction was available in the 1840s in at least one Masonic text, the lecture on the philosophical lodge in the rite of the Knight of the Sun.[71]

Scattered evidence indicates that by the end of his life Joseph Smith had arrived at the ancient understanding of the dual-gendered divinity that lay at the heart of the hermetic theology. By 1839 he was reported to have spoken of an "eternal Mother, the wife of your Father in Heaven," and an oral tradition records that he, Sidney Rigdon, and Zebedee Coltrin had a vision of "the Father seated upon a throne" and "the Mother also." In 1844 Brigham Young preached on the Mormon relationship with "our Father in heaven and our Mother the Queen." One of Smith's plural wives, Eliza Snow, wrote a poem on "the Eternal Father and Mother," and in 1878 her cousin Erastus came the closest to formulating the hermetic ideal of an androgynous God in preaching "that the Deity consists of man and woman. . . . there can be no God except he is composed of the man and woman united."[72] Here was a position with which Paracelsus, Boehme, Beissel, Mother Ann Lee, and a host of other sectarians influenced by the hermetic tradition could agree. Coupled with the second anointing of Emma Hale Smith to the "sealing power of Elijah," the hermetic image of a dual-gendered divinity is today the basis for demands that Mormon women be granted the powers of the priesthood.[73]

If Mormon celestial marriage replicated alchemical marriage, and Mormon cosmology replicated hermetic cosmology, then we might suggest a broader parallel between the alchemical work of transmutation and the entire complex of Mormon temple ritual. Both were centered on the problems of Creation and Redemption. The Mormon ritual drama carried the initiate-as-Adam from Creation through the Fall to Redemption and entry into the celestial kingdom through the authority of the priesthood. The sealing to celestial marriage would follow in a separate ritual. Alchemy fused the language of Creation and Redemption; the alchemical work was intended to distill the *prima materia* from corrupted elements, simultaneously repeating the process of Creation and erasing the corruptions stemming from the Fall in a material Redemption.[74] In the basic alchemical sequence, the marriage of the King and the Queen would be followed by cohabitation. The two would merge in this cosmic sexual union, and then the product of the union, the seed, would die, putrefy, be washed or baptized, and then be resurrected in its final form. This would be the quintessence, the philosopher's stone, the material agency of immortal perfection, identified with the *prima materia*, the primal Adam, and Christ the Redeemer, the Second Adam.[75] In each case – Mormon and alchemic – the corrupting consequences of the Fall were overcome, with the outcome being divine perfection.

Finally, there was the ritual worker: the hermetic alchemist and the Mormon priest. Alchemists searched for procedures that would transmute the soul without the means of divine grace. As Carl Jung put it:

> The Christian earns the fruits of grace *ex opere operato*, but the alchemist creates for himself – *ex opere operantis* in the most literal sense – a "panacea of life" which he regards either as a substitute for the Church's means of grace or as the complement and parallel of the divine work of redemption that is continued in man.[76]

These alchemical powers of salvation without the means of grace were popularly ascribed to Freemasonry, at least in the spurious Locke–Leland letter appended to many Masonic manuals. Answering the question of what the Masons "conceal and hide," the letter stated that, in addition to "the art of wonder-working," the powers of prophecy, "the universal language," and the "way of winning the faculty of magic," the Masons "also conceal the art of transmutation of metals . . . [and] the skill of becoming good and perfect without the helpings of fear and hope."[77] "Fear and hope" meant the fears and hopes of the Christian, particularly the Puritan Protestant, about his or her election through divine grace and a limited atonement.

Some Mormons would eventually, in Utah, arrive at this extreme hermetic position, denying the necessity of grace and atonement in any form. The church itself, under the authority of the prophet, came very close to such a denial, and the issue is one of considerable debate. Clearly, by the 1840s, Mormon theology had long since qualified the classical Christian constructs of grace and atonement with the near-universal promise of salvation; Adam's fortunate Fall and immediate atonement erased any threat of original sin for humanity. An advocate of a Mormon doctrine of grace, Blake T. Ostler admits that "[a]fter 1835, Mormon thought turned from the role of grace in salvation and exaltation to the way persons appropriate grace."[78] The "Articles of Faith" adopted by the church in 1842 explicitly stated what had been implicit in the changing language of the revelations since the mid-1830s. Salvation would come "through the Atonement of Christ," but it would come "by obedience to the laws and ordinances of the Gospel." Rarely mentioning atonement and grace, Mormon doctrine in the 1840s spoke of the keys, of "fulness," of the ordinances, of sealing and binding, and of the ultimate goal of exaltation to godhood.[79]

Divine grace opened the door to salvation to almost everyone, but individual merit and obedience to law determined the degree of divine exaltation. Mormon priests, as the bearers of the authority of ordinance, held the final authority to grant entry into "eternal life" and to degrees of exaltation, the keys to the kingdom. In effect, they had the powers of ecclesiastical *magi,* powers that extended up from the visible world to the invisible world. In sealing souls to the celestial kingdom, they were commanding God to save and exalt the obedient Mormon faithful. Ostler suggests that this emphasis on "the efficacious power of ordinances" had brought Joseph Smith to the Catholic definition of grace, where the proper performance and acceptance of sacrament "cause" the appropriation of grace. David Buerger provides a more pointed position. He argues that the language of the *Book of Mormon* moved the locus of "sealing" from divine to human agency, a transformation, it should be added, that owed much to Joseph Smith's experience with magic. Then Smith in 1832 granted Mormon priests ritual powers "to seal up [the faithful] to eternal life"; the Nauvoo innovations simply specified these ordinances. "Thus," Buerger argues, "Mormon priesthood bearers themselves could perform a ritual . . . paralleling what strict Calvinists, for example, reserved solely to God." This human power was specified in Smith's final revelation of July 1843. God directed that the "power of Elijah," or "Holy Spirit of promise," could only be granted by

> him who is anointed . . . by revelation and commandment through the medium of mine anointed, whom I have appointed on the earth to hold this power (and I have appointed unto my servant Joseph to hold this power in the last days, and there is never but one on the earth at a time on whom this power and the keys of this priesthood are conferred).

Although the point is a matter of some debate, it seems clear that at Nauvoo, Mormon concepts of entry into eternal life included a generalized grace, individual obedience, and priestly powers of ordinance, in which – like the alchemist – a channel of spiritual power moved up from the visible to the invisible world. This power was divine in origin but it was only to be handled by a priest of the second anointing, in turn empowered through the Lord's appointed servant, Joseph Smith.[80]

Nineteenth-century Mormons did not lie under a fear of Adam's original sin; the consequences of Adam's Fall did not extend to his seed.[81] Rather, they were accountable for their own personal sins, and these – with the exception of apostasy and the murder of innocents – could be forgiven. The satirical "Buckeye's Lament for Want of more Wives," published by dissenter William Law in the Warsaw *Signal* in February 1844, summarized Mormon doctrine in this pointed verse:

> He'll seal you up, be damned you can't,
>   No matter what you do –
> If that you only stick to him,
>   He swears HE'LL take you through.[82]

In Smith's language, reported at the August 27, 1843, conference, the "sectarians" were all damned, because they did not have the Melchizedek powers to grant covenants of "endless lives." But, speaking of himself, "not all the powers of hell or earth combined can ever overthrow this boy," for he had "a promise from the eternal God."[83]

Mormons would be bound to Mormon law, to church ordinance, above all else. Salvation and then divinization would come not from grace alone but from the merit of obedience to sacred ordinance. The result was a new sin-free dispensation: Mormons were inherently perfectible, and beyond the bounds of human law. In essence, they were offered the promise of an antinomian perfectionism – if only they obeyed the authority of the prophet leader.

11

A Tangle of Strings
and the Kingdom of God

We've gotten into a jumble of late;
A deep intricate puzzle, a tangle of strings,
That no possible scheme can make straight.
Eliza Snow, Nauvoo, Illinois, August 1842[1]

THE HERMETIC RESTORATION forged by the Mormons at Nauvoo was in effect an institutionalized antinomianism, with a fundamentally radical notion of divinization contained and circumscribed by the absolute rule of Mormon ordinance, "the perfect law of Theocracy." The Mormon faithful were not to be held accountable to mere human law but to the higher law of the Kingdom of God. In writing the *Book of Mormon* Joseph Smith had reproduced and exaggerated conventional boundaries between good and evil, purity and danger. Now, with the institutional framing of the Kingdom, those boundaries were decisively set aside; the only boundary of any significance was that between the Mormon Kingdom and the corrupt world. The 1840s and 1850s, as the Mormons built their Kingdom on the Mississippi, only to pull up stakes and rebuild that Kingdom in the Great Basin, saw the most uninhibited expressions of hermetic divinity and antinomian innovation in American history. For a few years it seemed that the Mormons stood on the verge of a realized Kingdom, a Kingdom with political powers of organized violence and currency, a Kingdom of polygamous marriage and Adamic perfection. Then, once again their Kingdom was swallowed up in the American leviathan, and gradually and episodically, Mormons adjusted their culture to accommodate the American norm. The first story, running to the mid-1850s, is the subject of this chapter; the outline of the second story, running down to the present, is the subject of the final chapter.

Since the early days in Kirtland Joseph Smith had sought to restore the polygamous households of the ancient prophets. During the 1830s he had made a few hesitant steps toward this "principle" in his affairs with Fanny

Alger, Lucinda Morgan Harris, and Prescindia Huntington Buell. Finally, in the spring and summer of 1841, he began to quietly indoctrinate his closest followers into the principle, despite the growing unease among the leading women at Nauvoo following his public sermon on "the restoration of all things" on the model of the ancient prophets.[2] That year he secretly married two women, and by the time of his death he had married, by a conservative estimate, thirty-one wives in addition to Emma Hale Smith. At least twenty-one other Mormon men married plural wives at Nauvoo.[3]

The motives and impetus lying behind Smith's drive to establish plural marriage are complex and hotly debated. Lawrence Foster has ascribed it to Smith's intense "need for self-consistency"; Linda Newell and Valeen Avery bluntly point to his "insatiable sexual drive, fueled by a quest for power."[4] Both of these perspectives are compatible with Harold Bloom's description of Joseph Smith as a "libertine Gnostic," realizing in polygamous celestial marriage an ancient, mystical connection between sexuality and divinity.[5] And all of these perspectives are compatible with a hypothesis, following Carl Jung, that Smith's Nauvoo years saw the deep-running psychic tensions resolved on a grand scale, as Joseph Smith forged a road to divinity and ran a sexual marathon before accepting martyrdom at Carthage in the summer of 1844. Quite literally, celestial *coniunctio* led to divinity in the Mormon pantheon.

The road to this divinity was paved with rubble from the wall demarking the conventional boundary between purity and danger. Plural marriage required the abandonment of deeply rooted marital beliefs, and because this was impossible for so many people, it required deception on a massive scale. When he asked her to marry him, Smith could not convince Sidney Rigdon's daughter Nancy "that there was no sin in it whatever." Her father was enraged by Smith's explanation that followed in a letter: "That which is wrong under one circumstance, may be, and often is, right under another."[6] This episode alienated the already disenchanted Sidney Rigdon, pushing him, as the Fanny Alger affair had pushed Oliver Cowdery, into dissent and finally schism. Most importantly, Emma Smith rejected the practice entirely, and for at least two years Joseph's marital experimentation had to be carried out under a shroud of secrecy, complicated by the fact that he "married" a number of women living and working in his own household, women who were Emma's friends and close associates in the Relief Society. She would only reluctantly accept the doctrine in the summer of 1843, in part threatened by the command in Smith's last revelation that she "receive those that have been given unto my servant Joseph" or be "destroyed." But later that year it was suspected that she had attempted to poison him, and after his assassination, she left the church, refusing to accept that he had established plural marriage.[7]

Aligned with Emma against the idea of plural marriage were William Marks, Wilson Law, and a group of other new dissenters. Ultimately, their attack on plurality in a short-lived newspaper, the Nauvoo *Expositor,* in June 1844 would set the stage for Smith's final arrest and assassination at Carthage. But if Emma and these men opposed the principle, Smith was also threatened by those among the Mormons who accepted the principle too readily, most importantly John C. Bennett. Learning of plural marriage sometime in 1841, Bennett and several others apparently began to approach women with their own proposals of "spiritual wifery," claiming to have the prophet's sanction and arguing that "there was no sin where there was no accuser." Bennett and Smith were increasingly at odds in early 1842. After a complex effort to prevent the apostasy of a high-ranking member, who had access to much damaging information, Bennett was excommunicated that May.[8]

The complex cross-pressures created by the secret, yet rumored, adoption of plural marriage were one important element shaping the emergence of hermetic ritualism at Nauvoo in the spring of 1842. Plural marriage was illegal under Illinois bigamy statutes, and if Smith was to keep things under control he needed secrecy and loyalty. Thus in one of the first meetings of the Female Relief Society, Smith asked that the women keep his information that "some unprincipled men" were attempting to "deceive and debauch the innocent . . . a private matter in your Society." Their silence in the matter would determine, he added, "whether you are good masons." In the ensuing months Smith's references to the powers of the keys of the kingdom to detect the works of the devil must have been conditioned by his increasingly embattled situation. The secret tokens of the priesthoods that he taught that May were means to ritually identify a select priesthood – and to exclude the disloyal.[9]

Secrecy was interwoven with a multilayered campaign of deception, fueling stress felt particularly painfully in the Female Relief Society. Smith and the other leading men wanted the society to stifle rumors of plurality, but Emma aggressively pursued these rumors, establishing investigating committees and hounding women who had been heard to speak of Smith's plural wives. The cross-pressures became acute in April 1842, when Emma appointed to an investigating committee two older women who already had been secretly chosen by Joseph as "Mothers of Israel" and charged by the prophet with quietly indoctrinating younger women into the "principle." In the summer and fall of 1842 the situation became even more complex, as Emma announced that even those "in authority" had no legitimate claim to plural marriage, and John C. Bennett began to publish a lurid exposé of Nauvoo Mormonism.

In the face of these difficulties, Smith and his closest associates began a campaign to deny the reality of plural marriage while continuing to practice it. Men and women already living in secret plural marriages signed documents declaring that it did not exist and condemning Bennett's "secret wife system."[10] At the same time a deceptive code developed, allowing the leadership to condemn "polygamy, in the ordinary and Asiatic sense of the term," while defending "the Holy order of celestial marriage," "the true and divine order," and the "new and everlasting covenant." As a Salt Lake City newspaper put it in 1886, "Joseph and Hyrum were consistent in their action against the *false doctrines of polygamy* and *spiritual wifeism*," which were "altogether different to the order of *celestial marriage* including a *plurality of wives*." On these grounds, too, Smith could also claim to be free from the charge of adultery.[11]

That fall Smith apparently used the church press to test once again the climate of opinion regarding plurality. In December a pamphlet was published under the imprint of "J. Smith, Printer," called *The Peacemaker, or the Doctrines of the Millennium*. The essay provided a detailed justification of polygamy on restorationist grounds; Smith denied knowledge of its contents while defending the reputed author's right to publish his views.[12] Finally, beginning a year later, Smith may have begun a quiet campaign to make "his opponents *think* that he was abandoning" plural marriage, as part of a plan to protect his divine order.[13] In effect the circumstances of Mormon polygamy at Nauvoo created a situation reminiscent of the stories of "holy lying" among medieval Lollards and early modern Familists brought before the English courts. The sacred cause justified any means for its defense. Eliza Snow, Emma's close friend and one of Joseph's plural wives, was clearly troubled by this ethical quagmire when she described the situation in Nauvoo in the summer of 1842 as "a deep intricate puzzle, a tangle of strings."[14]

The only escape from this "tangle of strings" lay in an unfailing belief in the authority of the prophet. One use that Smith had for the new doctrine was to test the faith of his closest associates, including asking that he be married to their wives. Some, like Young and Kimball, only regretfully accepted plurality; Orson Pratt and his wife, Sarah, were excommunicated briefly for their adamant rejection of polygamy. Others, like William Clayton, seem to have indulged themselves.[15]

Once accepted, however, plural marriage became a bond among a people set apart. It simply was illegal in the state of Illinois, so following the prophet meant risking arrest.[16] Simultaneously, the Mormon inner circle was initiated into and defined by the secret endowment rituals, which set them apart from the rank-and-file Mormons. Those initiated into these rituals were known as the "Holy Order," the "Quorum of the Anointed," or the "Holy Order of the Holy Priesthood."[17] And marriage also brought kinship, reinforcing ritual secrecy and coconspiracy in violation of marital statutes with the traditional bonds of family. Business relationships in the antebellum decades were still profoundly structured by ties of family, and in this respect Mormon plurality was an extreme extension of a pattern of affiliation pervasively structuring antebellum society and economy.[18]

The "tangle of strings" was, in great measure, a tangle of family alliances, what would become, in Michael Quinn's analysis, a "Mormon dynasticism."[19] Kin connections among the Smiths, Whitmers, and Knights had accounted for a key body among the first converts to Mormonism in New York, and plural marriage worked to replace this kin connection at Nauvoo. Louisa Beaman, Smith's first plural wife at Nauvoo, was the daughter of Alva Beaman, an old New York diviner, recently dead, whom Smith had known since the 1820s, and the Partridge sisters were daughters of the late Mormon bishop Edward Partridge. But others among his plural wives connected him with leading families at Nauvoo. In July 1842 he married Newell K. Whitney's daughter Sarah Ann, and in 1843 he married Rhoda Richards, sister of Willard and Levi, and also Fanny Young Murray, a sister of Brigham, who could remember the unorthodox marital relations among the Hopkinton Immortalists. The benefits of kinship also worked in the other direction. Having a "great desire to be connected with the Prophet," Heber C. Kimball persuaded his daughter to marry Smith in 1843.[20] In a few cases where relatively obscure Mormons were elevated into the Quorum of the Anointed, one wonders whether a daughter's marriage was exchanged for the parents' divine exaltation.[21] This "tangle of strings" became even more complex after Joseph and Hyrum Smith were gunned down at the Carthage jail, and their plural wives needed new husbands. Brigham Young married three of Joseph's former wives, and Kimball married three of Joseph's and one of Hyrum's. Just as baptism for the dead and eternal marriage reinforced a sacred kinship, plural marriage worked to weld the Mormon elite into a familial, organic whole, irreconcilably setting them apart for their separate purpose.[22]

Ultimately, this purpose was to establish the Kingdom of God. Like the program of the Fifth Monarchists of the 1650s, this was to be an explicitly political process, the establishment of a theocratic world government. Certainly the germs of this idea went back to the origins of the church; Sidney Rigdon claimed that at one New York meeting they had talked "of whole nations being born in one day." In 1836 Parley Pratt published a pamphlet titled *A Voice of Warning*, predicting from the Book of Daniel the collapse of the United States and the rise of a political government by God's chosen saints. Thousands of copies of this book were sold, and it was particularly influential in the English missionary efforts.[23] Pratt's essay came out during the Missouri troubles, where the Danites likewise invoked the Book of Daniel. In the wake of the Missouri expulsion, this Mormon militance was given institutional expression in the peculiar powers of the city of Nauvoo, with its Nauvoo Legion and its quasi-autonomous legal system. But by 1842 Joseph Smith was thinking of a more ambitious program than merely defending his people from the gentiles.

It was in the eventful spring of 1842 that a specific revelation ordered the building of the political kingdom. On April 7, three weeks after Smith's initiation into Freemasonry and a month before the first endowment instructions, he recorded a revelation revealing the grandiose name of this government. It was to be called "The Kingdom of God and his Laws, with the Keys and power thereof, and judgment in the hands of his servants, Ahman Christ."[24] Like the sealing powers of the priesthood, this government combined divine power with human agency. It is possible that the first action by this new government was the attempted assassination of former Governor Lilburn Boggs of Missouri a month later on May 6. Former Danite Orrin Porter Rockwell was accused and he never explicitly denied his role, but he vehemently denied that the prophet, a friend since childhood, had paid him for the job.[25] In 1843 Smith wrote an open letter to the "Green Mountain Boys" of Vermont, asking for aid in the redress of Mormon grievances against Missouri, and he petitioned Congress that Nauvoo be set off from Illinois as a federal district, with the Nauvoo Legion enrolled as a federal unit under his authority.[26] Neither of these initiatives led anywhere. On September 28, 1843, the day on which he and Emma were anointed with the sealing power of Elijah, Smith convened a special council that apparently discussed the church's political future.[27] But Smith did not formally announce this revelation to his followers until March 1844, well after the secret systems of temple endowments and plural marriage had forged and tested a dependable inner circle.[28]

On March 10 and 11, 1844, Smith formed a Council of Fifty, sometimes known as the Council of the Gods. Of fifty-eight members appointed that spring, all but eleven either had been endowed or were members of the Nauvoo Lodge.[29] Their constitution was short, simple, and very comprehensive: "Ye are my Constitution and I am your God and ye are my spokesmen, therefore from henceforth keep my commandments."[30]

Thus the council itself was a "Living Constitution" of the Kingdom of

God, empowered by revelation to act on their reading of the word of God. Apparently one of these commandments was to ordain Smith "King on earth" by divine right. Another was to have him elected president of the United States, thus imposing the theocratic law of the Kingdom on the entire Republic. On April 8 Smith told the elders in conference that a limited concept of western Missouri as Zion was to be abandoned. Seeking to "cover a broader ground," Smith declared that "the whole of America is Zion itself from north to south," and that the temple should be situated "in the center of the land." The council in effect operated as an election committee for Smith, sending agents for his campaign to various locations. The council also attempted to function as a sovereign state, sending one delegate to negotiate with the autonomous Republic of Texas and another on a political mission to France, both regarding the possibility of establishing a Mormon state on the disputed border between Mexico and Texas. All of these efforts were forestalled on June 27, 1844, when Joseph and Hyrum Smith were killed by a mob in Carthage, where they had surrendered to state authorities. Under Brigham Young the authority of the Council of Fifty would be severely limited, as he asserted the right to succession and authority of the leadership of the Twelve Apostles. But Young would continue the council's plan to establish a Mormon state, independent of both state and federal authority.[31]

In many ways, the events of the spring of 1844 replicated those of 1837, when the Mormon community in Kirtland collapsed under the weight of economic stress and dissenting opinion. By 1843 the general economic depression was compounded for the Nauvoo Mormons by rising gentile hostility and the costs of building the temple. At the same time small groups of influential dissenters began to emerge, again concerned about the authoritarian quality of the church hierarchy, and this time with much more extensive evidence for their charges of adultery against Smith and now many other leaders. These charges became the focus of the newspaper campaign against Smith in the Nauvoo *Expositor,* put out by dissenters led by William Law, Wilson Law, and Robert Foster. The first issue of the *Expositor* came out on June 7, 1844, and three days later its office was destroyed by the legion on the orders of the city council.[32] The fundamental difference between the two crises lay in the fact that Joseph and Hyrum Smith allowed themselves to be arrested, rather than fleeing, setting the stage for their murder in Carthage.

One point of similarity linking 1837 and 1844 lay in the rhetorical cross fire between dissenters and the loyal hierarchy. When the Laws and Foster were excommunicated on April 18, one of the charges against Robert Foster was that he had branded Smith a "murderer, Bogus maker[,] counterfiter, [and] adulterer."[33] In return, at a city council meeting on June 8 assembled to deliberate on the fate of the *Expositor,* William Law and Robert Foster were similarly accused of "oppressing the poor, counterfeiting, theft, conspiracy to murder, seduction, and adultery."[34]

Once again, and not for the last time, the explosive issue of illicit money-making emerged at a point of crisis in the Mormon story. And as for the 1830s, the dissection of the rhetoric and the reality of the counterfeiting charges is not easy. There is no question, however, about the reality of counterfeiting. By April 1843 Hyrum Smith had been told of a counterfeiting ring operating in Nauvoo, and in April and June 1844 the Warsaw *Signal* reported that counterfeit coins called "Nauvoo Bogus" were in circulation. The troubled economy, the tensions between Mormons and gentiles escalating toward a state of civil war, and Nauvoo's relative legal autonomy from Illinois all contributed to the assembling of money-making rings in the Mormon city-state.[35] In light of the past history in Ohio and future developments in Utah, the critical question is the degree to which the Mormon hierarchy was implicated. Where was the boundary between hermetic purity and hermetic danger in the Mormon Kingdom at Nauvoo?

The accusation of counterfeiting brought against the dissenters rested on testimony given in the city council. Called by Joseph Smith as mayor, "Theodore Turley, a mechanic, . . . said that the Laws had brought bogus dies for him to fix."[36] A Canadian convert born in Birmingham, England, and a member of the second mission to England, Turley was a gunsmith at Nauvoo, and a trail of evidence suggests very strongly that he himself had a hand in the counterfeiting trade. In November 1845 he was arrested at Alton, Illinois, for counterfeiting, and that December he headed a list of twelve men from Nauvoo under federal indictment for counterfeiting, being cited as "the chief manufacturer of dies, &c." According to one Mormon apostate, "brother Turley shone conspicuous" in the counterfeit trade on the trek west to Utah: "at 'bogus' he could not be surpassed." Apparently Turley constructed a press from which coins, "composed of zinc, glass, etc., coated with silver, was executed in the best style." This press may have been one of two supposedly buried along the trail to Utah.[37] Another man indicted in December 1845, Peter Hawes, also a Canadian convert, was reputed to have carried a "bogus press" all the way to Utah. On the trail Brigham Young had to intervene in a conflict in Hawes's camp over livestock bought with counterfeit money, and he "reproved them for dealing in base coin."[38] A tangle of evidence ties four other men on the indictment to the counterfeit trade at Nauvoo. By one account Augustus Barton and Gilbert Eaton were recruited in Buffalo to set up a press at Nauvoo, an operation in which a certain Joseph H. Jackson had a hand. Edward Bonney, a bounty hunter who passed bogus on occasion, claimed to have been working to break up yet another gang operating on the Mississippi with a base at Nauvoo.[39]

Turley, Hawes, Jackson, Eaton, and Bonney were implicated in a complex series of alleged conspiracies, from murders in Iowa to a dissenters' plot to murder the Smith family in the spring of 1844, all of which defy disentanglement.[40] What can be determined, however, is that at least three of them were appointed to the Council of Fifty in the spring of 1844 and 1845. Peter Hawes and Edward Bonney (a non-Mormon) were appointed by Joseph Smith in 1844, and Theodore Turley was appointed by Brigham Young in March 1845.[41] All five were listed on the federal indictment of December 1845, along with names of men high in the Mormon hierarchy. Specifically, the indictment named Brigham Young, Willard Richards, John Taylor, Parley P. Pratt, and Orson Hyde as under suspicion of counterfeiting. Writs on charges of counterfeiting were also issued for various other leading Mormons, including Orson Pratt and Orrin P. Rockwell. When state and federal authorities attempted to arrest these Mormon leaders on these charges, they generally managed to escape, and "Whittling Societies," gangs of men and boys casually carving with long knives on scraps of lumber, were formed to discourage the presence of strangers in Nauvoo.[42]

The veracity of the charges in these writs and indictments is simply impossible to determine, and no reliable evidence from Nauvoo suggests that the Mormon leaders were involved in counterfeiting.[43] It appears that the presence of counterfeiters in Nauvoo provided the excuse for state and federal authorities to issue these warrants as a means of forcing the Mormons out of Nauvoo and into the territories sooner than they had planned.[44]

Of course the Mormon leadership was not unfamiliar with the culture of money-making. The Smiths had distant kinship ties among the counterfeiters operating in eighteenth-century New England, and they had brushed up against counterfeiters in 1807 and in the 1820s. Whatever the justification, Joseph Smith had been convicted of uttering spurious money in connection with the Kirtland Bank in 1837. If it is unlikely that the leaders were themselves directly involved in counterfeiting at Nauvoo, it also does not appear that they made a great deal of effort to root it out. In the final months at Nauvoo, Brigham Young knew of gangs of "consecrating thieves" operating out of Nauvoo on Avard's Danite principles. He planned eventually to excommunicate them, but for the time being was willing to overlook their activities.[45] In fact, Young did not condemn counterfeiting at Nauvoo until January 1846, after the Mormon leadership was indicted, apparently on the evidence of some of the non-Mormon counterfeiters.[46] On the trail west he and Orson Hyde did condemn the counterfeiters among the Mormon wagon trains, but the implication is that, once the Mormons were isolated among themselves, counterfeiting was no longer tolerated, as it apparently had been at Nauvoo.[47]

Counterfeiting and currency-making in general were bound up in a broader sense with governmental legitimacy. Two weeks after his indictment, Brigham Young came out of hiding to announce in the temple that the church would "leave this wicked nation," as everyone in it "from [President] Polk down to the nastiest Bogusmaker, or whiskey seller . . . [had] resolved to break up the Mormons." The church would leave a land of fraud and deceit to establish the Kingdom of God. Among the Mormons burying "bogus-presses" on the trail west there was, by one account, a related sentiment:

> They would want them on their return, as [the presses] would be available to press *good money*. The inference was, that when they returned, it would be as conquerors of the United States, and that then, having the political power in their hands, they would coin good money.[48]

Mormons would not return to conquer the United States for Zion, but they would establish the semiautonomous state of Deseret, and in this story the theme of money-making would reach its conclusion.

In February 1846 the Mormon leadership crossed the Mississippi into Iowa, and over the next six months most of the Mormon rank and file departed, after assembling wagon trains and after receiving the endowments in the soon-to-be-abandoned Nauvoo temple. In July 1847 Orson Pratt led the advance party of the Mormon exodus down Emigration Canyon into Salt Lake Valley, and in September 1848 Brigham Young brought a train of two thousand people into the valley.[49] Here, in the desolate Great Basin, the Mormon Kingdom would be forged under the authority of President Young and his apostles. Thousands of immigrants from the east and from Britain, and then Scandinavia, had to be accommodated in a desert environment. Mormon agricultural communities were established up and down the Wasatch front and into southern Utah, communities that had to administer scarce water resources and provide for the general welfare in a harsh frontier. And as the Mormon people framed their new economy, they also attended to the transcendent purposes of the Mormon Kingdom. If Mormon Utah was perhaps a "hydraulic society," it was also a monument-building society. The next half-century would be punctuated by the chronology of temple building, both at Salt Lake and in the outlying centers of St. George, Logan, and Manti. Once again, the Mormons would have tabernacles for the divinity to dwell in. Until those temples were built the Saints would receive their endowments in a long, low Endowment House, dedicated on Salt Lake City's Temple Square in 1855.[50]

As they had been throughout the early history of the church, and most recently at Nauvoo, gold and money were a diagnostic dimension of the story of the construction of a Mormon state in the Great Basin. A permanent and prospering settlement was now critical for the cause of the Mormon Kingdom and required a medium of commercial exchange. Such a medium was provided by the gold strikes in California.

In the interval between the beginning of the Mormon exodus from Nauvoo and their arrival at Salt Lake, on January 24, 1848, gold was discovered in California at John Sutter's millsite at Coloma on the south fork of the Sacramento River. Six of the ten people at the site were Mormons.[51] A battalion of Mormons had been recruited in 1847 to serve in the United States service during the Mexican War to capture and hold California, and it was a few of these demobilized soldiers who were at the Sutter's Mill discovery. They and hundreds of others from the Mormon battalion dominated the first wave of miners panning the California gold streams. They were joined that spring by other Mormons sent out from Salt Lake to get supplies. Among this group was Orrin P. Rockwell, who brought the first news of the gold strikes to Salt Lake City that June. Earlier that spring Rockwell had been arrested in California for passing counterfeit coins made from gold dust. Years later, coin-stamping machines were found at the fork of the Sacramento and San Joaquin rivers, near where the Mormons were panning for gold in 1848. According to Mormon historian Kenneth Davies, Mormon miners were using counterfeit coins to attempt to hide the fact that gold had been discovered. It would be Samuel Brannan, the renegade leader of a group of Mormons from Brooklyn, who broke the news of the gold discoveries in San Francisco. Well into 1850 Mormons formed a majority of the miners in the goldfields, and their relationship with the leadership in Salt Lake was complex. Although Brigham Young did not want his people infected with "California fever," he did want gold deposited at Salt Lake to provide the basis for a local economy. To this end, Davies has demonstrated, Young quietly organized "gold missions" to go into the goldfields to encourage the miners to continue their work and to bring their gold to Salt Lake, while he preached against the lure of gold to the Mormon emigrants arriving in Utah from the east.[52]

The first deposits at the Mormon "gold office" were made in November 1848, and immediately a "mint" began coining gold pieces. In January 1849, after the crucible broke, the newly formed "National Bank" began distributing signed and stamped notes, minimally backed with raw-gold deposits and inscribed with the initials "P.S.T.A.P.C.J.C.L.D.S.L.D. A.O.W.," standing for "Private Seal of the Twelve Apostles, Priests of the Church of Jesus Christ of Latter-day Saints in the Last Dispensation All Over the World." When these notes ran short, the high council put into circulation old bills from the Kirtland Safety Society Anti-Banking Company, which had survived all the Mormons' trials and tribulations since they were printed in Ohio twelve years previously. These paper notes were only a temporary measure, and by September 1849, with new crucibles, the mint again began to produce coins. At times, Brigham Young himself lent a hand in the mint, helping to turn out the currency. Apparently too much silver was alloyed with the gold to give more strength: to the east and to the west the Mormon currency was condemned as "debased," "spurious," and "vile falsehoods."[53]

This is a dramatic image: the Mormon prophet, once a neighborhood joiner, glazer, painter, and blacksmith in Mendon, New York, helping to stamp out these underweight coins at Salt Lake. Like the Kirtland Bank, the Mormon mint in Salt Lake – and Mormon coining in California – occupied an ill-defined hinterland between counterfeiting and lawful banking. Between 1848 and 1850 both regions lay in legal limbo, not yet under the control of the United States government. As Kenneth Davies stresses, the Mormon hierarchy at Salt Lake stopped their coinage in 1850, in no small measure to avoid being accused of counterfeiting.[54] Nonetheless, for a time they certainly were making a currency without any authority but their own. And if the Mormon leadership at Nauvoo had been falsely accused of counterfeiting in 1845, it is indeed interesting that those who escaped writs for counterfeiting in 1845 made up a majority of the men involved in the mint and the gold missions of 1848–50. These men also tended to be kin by marriage to either Joseph Smith or Brigham Young and to have been endowed, sealed, and anointed before Smith's death. One way or another, secret ritual, polygamous kinship, and unauthorized currency production linked these men.[55] Among the others accused in 1845, but not yet involved in the mint or the gold missions by 1850, Orson Hyde and Theodore Turley were assigned leadership roles in gold-mining areas in 1855. Another, Orson Pratt, was asked by the Salt Lake authorities in April 1849 to recruit "more mechanics or practical operators in smelting, assaying, mixing, compounding, dividing, subdividing, and proving all sorts of metals and minerals" on his mission to the east.[56]

Throughout the story of the Mormon emergence the quest for hermetic purities – the now ancient fusion of restoration and divinization – intersects with the hermetic dangers of extralegal money-making. A threatening evil force before the church was formed, money-making took

on different connotations as the church became progressively more alienated from American society. In effect, the boundary between hermetic
purity and hermetic danger was eroded as the Mormon leaders came to
see themselves as transcending the authority of a deceiving nation: the
achievement of purity negated the danger lurking on the other side of the
ancient hermetic equation. If it were not for the political reality of their
failure to escape that nation, the Mormons might well have completed the
translation of an antinomian disregard for "illegitimate" law into a
planned theocratic sovereignty.⁵⁷

California was very much on Brigham Young's mind when he preached at
a special church conference at Salt Lake's Temple Square in August 1853.
Indeed this discourse on "True and False Riches" echoed themes of hermetic purity and danger running deep into the history of the church. Faced
with the problem of the attraction of California gold, Young urged the
people to forsake the "false riches" of the world for the "true riches" of
the Kingdom. This rhetoric duplicated Joseph Smith's language in the
Book of Mormon, language driven by his immersion in the money-
digging culture. Young warned those pursuing gold and silver that God
might "say, as he did in the days of the Nephites, Let their substance
become slippery, let it disappear that they cannot find it." But the Saints
would be in possession of "true riches" when they achieved the Kingdom,
when they arrived at the powers of divinity, and

> when we can call gold and silver together from the eternity of
> matter in the immensity of space, and all the other precious met-
> als, and command them to remain or move at our pleasure; when
> we can say to the native element, "Be thou combined, and produce
> those commodities necessary for the use and sustenance of man."

Here a hermetic and counterfeiting analogy crept into Young's rhetoric.
The true riches were the "true coin" rather than "bogus." In Young's
words, in ancient times "the magicians of Egypt were instructed in things
pertaining to true riches, and had obtained keys and powers enough to
produce a bogus in opposition to the true coin."⁵⁸

   The lure of the "false riches" of California gold was certainly on Brigham Young's mind in the summer of 1853, but so was what he considered
the "bogus" of competing doctrine on the "mysteries." In his closing
remarks he spoke mockingly of having "had a kind of confab" with
"Professor Orson Pratt," who was arguing the "folly" that there was
"such a thing as empty space . . . *where God is not.*"⁵⁹ This was the
opening salvo in a conflict over the nature of divinity that would carry
through the 1850s. On one side stood Orson Pratt, who was becoming the

most important intellectual in Mormonism; on the other stood Brigham Young, the senior of the Twelve Apostles and the heir to Joseph Smith's prophethood. They were known respectively as "the Gauge of Philosophy" and "the Lion of the Lord" and they proposed sharply differing doctrines of divinity, which would constitute the final elaborations of hermetic theology among the Mormons.[60]

Orson Pratt's hermeticism was distant, muffled by his immersion in nineteenth-century science, but still unmistakable. In August 1852 Pratt had stayed within the bounds of Mormon orthodoxy when he was given the assignment to preach the first public lecture on plural marriage.[61] But over the next year, writing text for *The Seer,* a Mormon missionary publication put out in Washington, D.C., Pratt refined earlier writings into a theory of divinity infusing matter. Building on Smith's doctrine that "all spirit is matter" and echoing Andrew Michael Ramsay, mediated by Scottish Common Sense, Mesmerism, and theories of electrical current, Pratt argued that the Holy Spirit was "a diffused fluid substance," simultaneously inhabiting every particle of matter. God was not a specific being but a bundle of Platonic attributes:

> [T]he Unity, Eternity, and Omnipresence of God, consisting in the oneness, eternity of the attributes, such as *"the fulness of Truth,"* light, love, wisdom, & knowledge, dwelling in countless numbers of tabernacles in numberless worlds; and the oneness of the One God besides whom there is non other God neither before Him neither shall there be any after Him.[62]

These ideas influenced his brother, Parley, whose *Key to the Science of Theology,* published in 1855, described the Holy Spirit as a "spiritual fluid" communicating among all the particles of matter and mind in the universe.[63]

Though it evolved from Smith's revelation, Pratt's thesis of an absolute intelligence inhabiting matter as a holy fluid challenged the Mormon image of God as a specific and concrete being of matter – and the promise that the faithful would eventually become such beings. His interpretation of an absolute God also undermined the Mormon doctrine of precreated spirits coequal with God. Casting doubt on the idea of a continuing progression into divinity, his vision was shaped by scientific efforts to view the world as a steady state and by traditional Christian views of divinity.[64] But it was in his insistence on the fusion of spirit and matter that Pratt revealed his debt to both Smith and hermeticism. As Robert Paul has argued, Orson Pratt's philosophy of science was grounded "in the organic worldview rooted in the Hermetic tradition of the Renaissance" and revealed itself as "thoroughly occult precisely because the materiality of his world possessed self-volition."[65]

Brigham Young mocked Pratt in August 1853 and accused him of doctrinal deviation in a letter the next month, leading to a series of confrontations over the next decade. In some measure, Young's assault on Pratt derived from his own very different interpretation of the hermetic inheritance. Pratt's diffuse, absolute, and perfect divinity permeated matter, whereas Brigham Young's divinity was finite, grounded in a specific fusion of spirit and matter. Young's new doctrine, apparently suggested to him by his old friend Heber C. Kimball, had clear and unequivocal antecedents in the hermetic ideal of the divinity of Adam.[66] He first announced this doctrine in April 1852:

> Now hear it, O inhabitants of the earth, Jew and Gentile, Saint and sinner! When our Father Adam came into the garden of Eden, he came into it with a *celestial body,* and brought Eve, *one of his wives,* with him. He helped to make and organize this world. He is MICHAEL, *the Archangel,* the ANCIENT OF DAYS! about whom holy men have written and spoken – HE *is our* FATHER *and our* GOD, *and the only God with whom* WE *have to do.*[67]

Here Young was taking the hermetic ideal of the divine Adam to its logical conclusion. Adam was both a god and the progenitor of the human race, and as such was a sufficient divinity to head the Mormon pantheon. Following the logic of the Mormon deemphasis of Christ's atonement (the atonement leading to a near-universal salvation but not to exaltation to divinity), Young clearly suggested that Adam was the father of Christ: "Jesus our elder Brother, was begotten in the flesh by the same character that was in the garden of Eden, and who is our Father in Heaven." In later versions, Young suggested that Adam–Michael was the son and grandson of higher gods, Elohim and Jehovah, each presumably with many wives, or "queens."[68]

Young preached the Adam–God doctrine during the mid-1850s, but only occasionally in the years following, and it would be totally abandoned by the church after his death. But it was a perfect expression of a literal materialism springing from an artisan tradition. Young had been a blacksmith, and his old friend, brother-in-law, and Utah ally Heber C. Kimball had once been a potter. Like the Muggletonian conceptions of a century and a half earlier, the artisanal worldview of Young and Kimball rejected the dry scientific language of Orson Pratt for concrete metaphors transformed into believed reality. Young even proposed in a "chemical argument" that the temple in Salt Lake be built of adobe, which would progress to the perfect hardness of granite. As he had implied in the alchemical allusions of his 1853 discourse on "True and False Riches," Young told a Salt Lake congregation in 1872 that God himself was "the greatest chemist there is."[69]

In the late summer of 1860, a year of many transitions, the English adventurer Richard Francis Burton spent three weeks in Salt Lake City observing a people whose religion had taken such a "deep hold" in his native country. Fascinated by this newly formed polygamous society, Burton reveled in the natural wonders of the Great Basin while he assessed the Mormon opus of thirty years' gestation. He found it to be an "agglomeration of tenets" spontaneously assembled. Burton saw parallels in Gnosticism, in Judaic theocracy, in Islamic polygamy, in Masonry, in Swedenborg, and in Mesmer. He found "their belief in the Millennium . . . a completion of the dreams of the Apocalyptic sects." Joseph Smith's doctrine that "all spirit is matter," as elaborated by Orson Pratt, reminded him of "the astral spirit of the old alchymists."[70]

Burton spent many hours with Brigham Young, whose "appearance was that of a gentleman farmer in New England." It may have been Young, paraphrasing Joseph Smith, who accepted Burton's assessment of the eclectic construction of Mormon theology, simply stating that Mormons were "guided by the Spirit unto all truth . . . come whence it may."[71]

12

Let Mysteries Alone

Where are the true riches – the pearl of great price? They are here. How can we secure them? By being obedient, *for the willing and obedient will eat the good of the land by and by.* . . . What is a mystery? *We do not know, it is beyond our comprehension.* When we talk about mystery, we talk about eternal obscurity; for that which is known ceases to be a mystery.

Brigham Young, Salt Lake City, August 14, 1853

Some will come with great zeal and anxiety, saying "I want my endowments, I want my washings and anointings; I want my blessings; I wish to be sealed up to eternal lives. . . ." What good will all this do you, if you do not live up to your profession and practice your profession?

Heber C. Kimball, Salt Lake City, October 6, 1855

[I]t stands immutable, that all men shall be rewarded according to their works.

Jedediah M. Grant, Salt Lake City, October 6, 1855

Why say "We want to hear from the stand concerning the mysteries – the eternal mysteries of the kingdom of God. . . ." Allow me to inform you that you are in the midst of it all now.

Brigham Young, Salt Lake City, June 15, 1856

These are the mysteries of the kingdom of God upon the earth, to know how to purify and sanctify our affections, the earth upon which we stand, the air we breathe, the water we drink, the houses in which we dwell and the cities that we build, that when strangers come into our country they may feel a hallowed influence and acknowledge a power to which they are strangers.

Brigham Young, Salt Lake City, May 23, 1863[1]

THIS BOOK HAS FOCUSED ON THE PROPOSITION that the rise of the Church of Jesus Christ of Latter-day Saints can only be understood if it is placed in the context of the hermetic tradition. The distinctive doctrines of the church – preexistent spirits, material spirit, human divinization, celestial marriage – are opaque unless we explore their relationship to the evolving fusion of hermetic perfectionism and radical sectarianism occupying the extreme edge of the Christian tradition from the late Middle Ages into the early modern era. To this end I have given precedence to the content of culture over its sociological structure and function. I have placed specific texts and more diffuse beliefs and mentalities, the vehicles of memory, at center stage, with the intention of explaining the origin of seemingly unique and inexplicable belief.

But a hermetic interpretation of Mormonism does have its limits. By 1860, even as Richard Burton was detecting the influence of "the old alchymists" in the Mormon mysteries, the Mormon leadership had begun a long retreat from these hermetic origins. Now that the church was established in Utah, the central focus of attention was on the building of the Kingdom of God on earth. The prophet Joseph Smith had forged a mystery religion at Nauvoo, but Brigham Young and his apostles and successors at Salt Lake began a doctrinal shift toward works, the merits of individual obedience. The people were urged to "let mysteries alone" and to simply "live their religion."[2] They were to improve their condition and that of the Mormon Kingdom, and in that virtuous behavior find their exaltation. Increasingly, access to the mysteries of the temple was to be the emblem of, rather than the literal means to, Mormon divinity.

In spite of the hermetic elaborations emerging from the Young–Pratt controversies, Mormonism had turned a corner in its move to the Great Basin. Formerly a despised minority sect, they were now the majority church, and the next half-century would see dramatic movement along the classic continuum of religious routinization first identified by Max Weber. Having focused so intently on the hermetic content of the founding of Mormonism, it may be profitable, in conclusion, to reintroduce the functionalist sociological framework and briefly to explore the central points of my hermetic interpretation in its terms. This summary will provide a point of departure for situating the Mormon experience in its American context, both in the milieu of the antebellum era and in the longer chronology extending to the late twentieth century.

Among the various anthropological approaches to religious change informed by Weberian sociology and British social anthropology, those of Victor Turner and Anthony Wallace are probably the most comprehensive and flexible.[3] Turner's scheme of a social drama and Wallace's scheme of revitalization both posit a phased sequence in the creation of a new complex of cultural belief and social institutions. Taking some liberties, we can combine them into a unified model. First, a "steady state" is disrupted by a "breach," in which individuals feel the stress of discordant forces in their lives, eroding their relationship to existing structures of society and culture and leading to a point of crisis, when charismatic individuals can force a break in those structures, creating a liminal moment in a process of religious theater. This moment of transforming *"communitas"* then frames the terms for "redressive action" or "revitalization," which in turn will establish a new structure or "steady state."[4]

A host of problems arises in applying such a paradigm to a process as complex as the rise of the Mormon church. Nonetheless, such an exercise has its virtues. Very simply, the social stress school of Mormon history has identified a prior "steady state" in the culture of late colonial New England and an era of "breach" in the social dislocations of the American Revolution, the economic troubles of the 1780s, the experience of regional migration, and the erosion of traditional religious culture in postrevolutionary America. The liminal crisis can be identified as the years between 1823 and 1830, when Smith's visions, translation of the Golden Plates, and attendant miracles gathered an audience of converts who inaugurated the history of the church proper. Then, though the chronology is very problematic, the subsequent decade and a half of religious experimentation can be seen as the phase of "redressive action," leading to a new "steady state" in the framing of the new Mormonism at Nauvoo and in its successful relocation to the Great Basin of Utah.

Quite obviously, my analysis presents a very different view of the prior "steady state." Rather than the thesis of a prior stability in New England Puritan orthodoxy, I have proposed that the groups who would first respond to the Mormon dispensation had been living in an "unsteady state" for more than a century before 1830. They were a prepared people, prepared by a long history of marginality in the northern colonies, arriving late, inclined toward sectarian religion, and exposed to perfectionist traditions in southeastern New England that can only be seen as echoes of the hermetic sectarianism of revolutionary England and Reformation Germany.

Their experience of the "breach" in the eras of the Confederation and early Republic was formatively shaped by specific cultural content. The print-based reinvigoration of the hermetic tradition – manifested in the occult revival, the rise of Freemasonry, and the explosion of counterfeiting – intersecting with millenarian religious conviction, shaped popular culture in ways that historians have only occasionally glimpsed. I have tried to suggest that this experience was framed by an intensification of the conflict between conventional categories of purity and danger. The divining cults of the early Republic were rooted in multiple countervailing pressures and influences. Hopes of gain in the face of limited prospects, the temptations of counterfeiting, and the weight of corporate and familial injunctions to virtue all worked to draw particular people into these fantastic fusions of practical magic, millenarian inspiration, and simple avarice.

The religio-hermetic boundary between purity and danger was the critical ground for the "crisis" of the 1820s, as Joseph Smith experienced his visions and wrote his texts while he was immersed in divining, witnessing grand Masonic dramas of schism and corruption, driven by familial divisions, and tempted by money and sexuality. His immediate solution was to further exaggerate the conventional boundary, identifying the Kingdom of God with purity and the outside world with dangers and corruptions of all kinds, subject to imminent destruction in the millennial fire storm.

The years of "redressive action" from 1830 to 1844 saw Smith move from the ranks of the cunning folk to Christian prophet to Christian-hermetic *magus*. From the autumn of 1830 to the late 1830s Smith disguised an emergent hermetic theology under the coloring of traditional Christian restorationism. At Nauvoo he publicly and unequivocally announced his new theology of preexistent spirits, the unity of matter and spirit, and the divinization of the faithful, and he privately pursued the consummation of alchemical-celestial marriage as the ultimate vehicle to this divinity. The alchemical-hermetic term of *coniunctio* powerfully summarizes the resolution that Smith had achieved at Nauvoo by the summer of 1844. He had established a theology of the conjunction – the unification – of the living and the dead, of men and women, of material and spiritual, of secular and sacred, all united in a "new and everlasting covenant" over which he would preside as king and god. In these circumstances the conventional boundary between purity and danger, right and wrong, law and revolution, simply melted away. The Mormon Kingdom was to be the ultimate law, overturning all churches and nations. His life complete, Smith went almost voluntarily to martyrdom at Carthage. Led by the institution builder Brigham Young, the Mormon faithful carried their Kingdom to the Great Basin, a refuge where their dream of a hermetic restorationism could be realized far from the corruptions of the world.

At this juncture two points need to be stressed. In their relationship with the hermetic tradition, the Mormons were by no means unique in antebellum America. And the seeming resolution arrived at in Nauvoo and then Utah was by no means stable: Mormonism's revolution against nineteenth-century American society would be thwarted and truncated. As early as the 1850s the Mormon church began a long and slow retreat from a pinnacle of Kingdom autonomy and hermetic culture toward an accommodation with, if not an acceptance of, American culture. A new "steady state" would not emerge until after the Manifestos setting aside polygamy in 1890 and disassociating the church from politics in 1891. In this transformation, the hermetic fabric of Mormon theology was redisguised and partially abandoned, to the point that modern Mormonism may well soon become essentially indistinguishable from conservative Christian fundamentalism. In some measure, this disguising and elimination of hermetic connotations in Mormon theology stemmed, paradoxically, from its very lack of uniqueness in nineteenth-century American culture.

In focusing so intently on cultural tradition and memory, I have neglected situation and milieu, the commonalities that early Mormonism shared with parallel movements in antebellum America. One cannot help but be struck by the perhaps coincidental but nonetheless suggestive contemporary millenarian eruptions: the proud slave Nat Turner, driven by his reading of millennial signs to lead his bloody rebellion across Southampton County, Virginia, in August 1831, as Joseph Smith and Sidney Rigdon were dedicating a site for the temple in Zion, western Missouri; or William Miller, similarly driven by millennial signs, calculating the precise dates of the apocalypse in February 1843 and October 1844, as the Mormon drama at Nauvoo moved through its dramatic climax.[5]

If news of these movements would have fed the air of expectation among the Latter-day Saints, other contemporary movements fed their numbers. The emergence of the Cochranites in the Saco Valley of Maine provides a telling story in the years after the Cold Summer of 1816, when the Smiths emigrated from Vermont. Jacob Cochran, like Joseph Smith and the Wood family, who raised the New Israelites, borrowed from the Shakers, the Freewill Baptists, and the Universalists in framing a cult in which he claimed magical powers over his followers, attacked the Freemasons, reenacted scenes from the Garden of Eden, and engaged in spiritual wifery.[6]

In this brief summary of the Cochranites we can read elements of the hermetic tradition, and here there is a wide field awaiting comprehensive examination. Very simply, suggestions of hermetic influence run through most, if not all, of the perfectionist and spiritualist movements of nineteenth-century America. Occasionally this influence was explicit and direct, as in the alchemical experimentation among the celibate Rappites of New Harmony, German communitarians who followed the Boehmist traditions that also had shaped the hermeticism of the eighteenth-century Ephrata cloister. On the other hand, the Shaker doctrine of dual divinity has never been examined in terms of its possible hermetic implications, though at both ends of the Shaker experience, in Manchester in the 1780s and among the American Shakers of the late nineteenth century, there was a current of interest in Emmanuel Swedenborg's hermetic theology.[7]

Hermeticism had clear and decisive influences on a number of other antebellum perfectionists. Ralph Waldo Emerson wrestled with the writings of Swedenborg, Boehme, and Jan Baptista van Helmont in the 1820s and 1830s in framing his Transcendentalist vision; it was entirely in keeping that he would dismiss Swedenborg in his "Representative Men" after having absorbed central tenets of Swedenborg's doctrine of the harmony of mind and nature, spirit and matter.[8] Swedenborgian ideas fed into Transcendental communalism at Brook Farm and Fruitlands and they shaped the fascination with spiritual communication and healing beginning in the 1840s with Andrew Jackson Davis and Phineas P. Quimby, which led directly to Mary Baker Eddy's Christian Science in the 1870s. Davis, "the Poughkeepsie Seer," was briefly attracted to the Millerites and was also deeply involved in the mid-nineteenth-century revival of Mesmerism, which became synonymous with Spiritualism.[9] John Humphrey Noyes was similarly influenced by Mesmer's theories of electric fluids, which made possible "the most intimate connection" between humanity and divinity. Like the German communitarians and Shakers, Noyes posited an androgynous God; as among the Mormons, this vision became the basis for marital experimentation.[10] From the 1840s to the end of the century a popular Mesmerism, the hermetic cult of Theosophy, and, most importantly, a revived and wildly elaborated Freemasonry spread the elements of the hermetic culture into the far corners of American society, a diffusion whose implications have not yet been fully explored.[11]

All of these perfectionist movements might easily be assimilated into Harold Bloom's thesis of an "American religion" founded on Gnostic roots, though Bloom casts his net much more widely, drawing in Seventh-Day Adventists, the Jehovah's Witnesses, Pentecostals, New Agers, Southern Baptists, and the black church.[12] But with the Mormons we run into a paradox.

Mormonism, Bloom's prime example of a Gnostic "American religion," was certainly the most successful of the American perfectionisms shaped by the hermetic tradition, but this hermeticism has been disguised, denied, and significantly eroded in the century and a half since Joseph Smith announced human divinization at Nauvoo and since Brigham Young declared Adam to be God. Mormonism took the hermetic ideal to its fullest manifestation, but in the years after 1860 the church leaders began to move away from the implications and connotations of their hermetic roots. In some measure, this was an effort at boundary maintenance, an effort to distinguish the authority of a revealed dispensation from the luxurious growth of perfectionism in mid- to late-nineteenth-century America. Here the church hierarchy had two problems to contend with.

First, clearly, the Mormon revolution against the American nation-state was doomed to encapsulation and defeat. Nauvoo may have marked the emergence of "a new steady state" for Joseph Smith, as he announced the ritual keys that would give the Saints divinity and inaugurate the coming of the Kingdom. But even flight to the desert wilderness of the Great Basin could not guarantee the autonomy and stability of the Mormon Kingdom; the American Republic followed close behind. Eventually, the price of stability and reintegration would be accommodation, both political and doctrinal.

Second, and certainly connected with this accommodation, the church faced a potentially unruly and dissident membership. Despite its carefully structured hierarchy, Mormonism bore within it a great potential for divergence, dissent, and schism, as did the contemporary perfectionist movements, many of which have disappeared with barely a trace. Already, in the wake of the Nauvoo crisis, at least two dozen splinter groups had broken away from the church, many uniting in 1860 to form the Reorganized Church of Jesus Christ of Latter Day Saints.[13] Those who were nominally loyal to the church often had widely divergent conceptions of church doctrine, a condition that would persist down to the twentieth century. And the nature of the spiritual and millenarian beliefs that had brought them into the church made even the nonschismatic a volatile breed, ready to take the prophet's teachings to extreme and violent ends. The Mormon Reformation of 1856–7 marked a crucial juncture, when the church's efforts to restore piety and fervor backfired, leading to excesses that attracted intense hostility throughout the country and brought the United States Army into the Great Basin. After the Reformation and the Mormon War, the church authorities, though they fought fiercely to defend the autonomy of the Mormon Kingdom, began a process of doctrinal change that has in the late twentieth century radically diminished the boundary separating Mormons from fundamentalist Protestants.

The Mormon Reformation was an extension of the Mormon leadership's campaign to build up the Kingdom in Utah, and to turn the people's minds away from both the mysteries of the church and the attractions of the gentile world. Though the Mormon church had been founded in supernaturalism, Brigham Young and his apostles struggled in the early 1850s to deflate popular expectations. The faithful were not to expect miracles or visions, rely upon their endowments, or search out the mysteries.[14] Nor were they to neglect meeting, sell valuable grain to gentile wagon trains on the trail west while fellow Mormons suffered the effects of drought and grasshopper infestation, or themselves drift off to California. The Reformation was initiated on the premise that the Saints were to live their religion and serve the Kingdom. Here indeed is a remarkable parallel with the jeremiads of the Puritan ministry of seventeenth-century New England.

The Reformation was led by Jedediah M. Grant, who preached fiery sermons urging the Mormon people to "purify yourselves." Running from September 1856 to June 1857, the Reformation indeed purified the church. Throughout the Utah settlements people came forward to repent their sins and to be rebaptized. In hopes of demonstrating their loyalty to the church, men clamored both to be advanced from the Aaronic to the Melchizedek Priesthood and to be allowed to take more wives. The result was a wave of marriages involving teenage girls, and Wilford Woodruff wrote only partly in jest in April 1857 that "nearly all are trying to get wives, until there is hardly a girl 14 years old in Utah, but what is married, or just going to be."[15]

If there was a note of panic in the resumption of Mormon piety, it ran from the rhetorical extremes of the Reformation. Although they were deemphasizing the mysteries, the Mormon leadership nonetheless did preach on the mysteries as religious sanction, specifically the doctrines of "blood atonement" and the "second death." "Covenant-breakers" and "transgressors," the "Sons of Perdition," were said to be beyond the power of Christ's atonement; only death and their spilled blood would allow their salvation. The rhetoric of "blood atonement" mingled hermetic notions of condensing vapors, which carry us back to the "Old Rodsman" and to Ranter Lawrence Clarkson, with the Old Testament rituals of blood sacrifice, perhaps implicit in the Mormon restoration of the temple. Young presented the doctrine in full in September 1856:

> I do know that there are sins committed, of such a nature that if the people did understand the doctrine of salvation, they would tremble because of their situation. And furthermore I know that there are transgressors, who, if they knew themselves, and the only condition upon which they can obtain forgiveness, would beg of their brethren to shed their blood, that the smoke thereof might ascend to God as an offering to appease the wrath that is kindled against them, and that the law might have its course. . . . There are sins that can be atoned for by an offering upon the altar, as in ancient days; and there are sins that the blood of a lamb, of a calf, or turtle doves cannot remit, but they must be atoned for by the blood of man.[16]

The "second death" awaiting the unrepentant sinner also had alchemical connotations. As Heber C. Kimball put it in 1857, body and spirit would be denied eternal life, but in a "second death" would "go back into their native element, the same as the chemist can go to work and dissolve a five-dollar piece, and throw it into a liquid." Once a potter, Kimball often drew on the image of the potter's rejects, discarded and then ground up to make the rough forms for holding the finished ware in the kiln.[17]

A wave of violence ran through the Mormon settlements, aimed at apostates and gentiles, in beatings, house-burnings, and murder. An apostate family by the name of Parrish were murdered in the spring of 1857, on the terms of blood atonement, if not with the authority of the church.[18] The violence of the Reformation, Mormon harassment of federal territorial officials, and James Buchanan's own political calculus in the face of the rising Republican Party all led to the federal expedition into Utah in the summer and fall of 1857. The armed confrontation of the U.S. forces and Mormon defenders of the Kingdom never resulted in pitched battles, but it did lead to bloodshed at the hands of the old Danites. Various gentile traders and camp followers in Salt Lake met untimely ends, a party of gamblers coming up from California were wiped out, and at Mountain Meadows in south Utah a large party of emigrants from Arkansas and Missouri were massacred – men, women, and children – by Mormon militiamen and allied Indians. Among the Missourians were men who claimed to have killed Mormons at the Haun's Mill massacre of 1838, and they had rolled through Utah mocking the Mormons and predicting their destruction.[19] With the Reformation, the Mormon War, and the Mountain Meadows Massacre the boundary between the Kingdom and the world stood as absolute as it ever had, and, concomitantly, the conventional definitions of purity and danger were as ambiguous as they ever would be in the history of the Latter-day Saints.

The full story of the Mountain Meadows Massacre would not emerge for twenty years, but in the following decade the Mormon leaders began to pull back from the extremes of the late 1850s, in a cultural accommodation that would accelerate as the century closed. The federal invasion of Utah had led to the temporary abandonment of Salt Lake City, the establishment of a federal garrison, and the replacement of Brigham Young as governor by the first of a series of outside appointees. All of these were serious setbacks, and they were followed by yet another internal schism, in which the impoverished followers of a Joseph Morris blamed the hierarchy for the misfortunes of the Mormons. Emerging in 1859, this group was suppressed after a gun battle in 1862 that heightened American concerns about endemic violence in the Mormon Kingdom.[20] Millennial hopes were raised again when the Civil War broke out, and Mormons dreamed of the self-destruction of "Babylon." But, in the measured judgment of Leonard Arrington,

> the year 1857 had marked a high point of Mormon nationalism. [Young realized] that his rhetoric, and that of his associates, could have disastrous consequences. . . . The uncompromising lan-

guage, the militant stance, the violent imagery of his public "discourses" were abandoned . . . , [he began] to consider solutions, even if on a middle ground . . . [and] to neutralize some of his followers' least acceptable practices.[21]

Slowly but surely the Mormon boundary between the Kingdom and the world would be reduced, and the conventional boundary between purity and danger reestablished. In the process, the authority of the church hierarchy was extended and strengthened over the membership, just as its reach in civil affairs was diminished.

Some of the means to this end were institutional, as Young extended the scope of participation by reviving organizations abandoned since the days of Joseph Smith, such as the School for Prophets and the women's Relief Society in 1867. The Retrenchment Society for young women was established in 1869 and the Deseret Sunday School Union in 1872, roughly coinciding with a brief reemphasis of the Word of Wisdom.[22] Such groups would be the vehicle for spreading a single and consistent message to the membership, a message that would be developed within the innermost councils. Here Young worked "to see that correct doctrine is taught and to guard the church against error," guiding an 1860 council of the First Presidency and Apostles to a consensus that no one would preach or publish doctrine without collective council approval, so as to "keep as far away from the precipice" as possible.[23] Then he effectively abandoned his controversy with Orson Pratt over the nature of divinity. Pratt confessed error and agreed not to publicize his view of an absolute God running as an electric fluid through all matter, a target of hostile preaching during the Mormon Reformation. Young dropped his preaching that Adam was God and the father of Jesus Christ, a doctrine that he had been backing away from since the spring of 1857, when the fires of the Reformation had burned a little too fiercely.[24] If Young and the apostles were sometimes ambiguous – perhaps intentionally – on the mysteries in the 1850s, after 1860 they redoubled their efforts to ground Mormonism in the Saints' behavior in this world, "living their religion," rather than in their dreams of instant divinity, which the mysteries seemed to offer.

At the same time the hierarchy continued an effort to suppress countervailing voices, however benign. In March 1860 the council voted that novels were an evil influence, following the suppression of a literary and musical "Polysophical Society" during the Reformation.[25] Similarly, organizations advocating the occult were suppressed. When an Astrological Society was formed in Salt Lake City in 1855, Brigham Young "advised them to drop it altogether"; when they attempted to establish "a school to teach astrology" in 1861, Young told them "it would not do to favor Astrology."[26] Perhaps because Young and other church leaders had what

Michael Quinn calls "a general affinity for folk magic," no concerted campaign was inaugurated. In the scattered Utah settlements, beliefs in peep-stones, animal magnetism, the healing powers of lobelia, and the mystical three Nephites persisted among the Mormon rank and file to the end of the century, along with more sanctioned fears of evil spirits and belief in healing artifacts.[27]

The church also had bigger problems to contend with. The Morrisite schism of 1859 to 1862 was followed in 1868 by the New Movement, or Godbeites, centered on a group of Mormon merchants led by William Godbe, who decried the church's theocratic hegemony, demanding economic and political pluralism in Utah. Composed predominantly of English immigrants, the movement was also deeply involved in contemporary spiritualism, holding seances with mediums and speaking with dead relatives and church authorities. In 1869 they were excommunicated from the church and formed the Church of Zion. Though they lasted only fifteen years, the Godbeites formed the most potent internal dissension from the late-nineteenth-century church, in great part because they provided a haven for an apostate apostle, Amasa Lyman.[28]

Though the relationship has not been explored very deeply, Amasa Lyman's apostasy and excommunication seem to have been an important catalyst for a decisive shift in emphasis in Mormon doctrine. In the 1860s Young was content to call a truce with Orson Pratt, both men downplaying their hermetic interpretations of cosmic history. In the meantime another division within the ranks of the leadership demanded a reassertion of the traditional Christian doctrine of atonement.

After the Mormon Reformation Young stopped preaching not only the Adam–God doctrine but the doctrine of blood atonement, to the degree that later church historians would deny that he had even advocated them. Thus when Amasa Lyman similarly argued that atonement was not a requirement for salvation, he was touching a raw nerve. Involved in establishing a Mormon presence in southern California, Lyman by 1852 was reading the books of Andrew Jackson Davis and engaging in spiritualist seances. Lyman was sent to Britain in 1860, and in Scotland in 1862 he preached the universalist notion that "the Gospel is nowhere said to have been constituted of the death of Jesus." It was not the blood of the atonement but the active rejection of sin that led to salvation, an option open to the millions who had come before Christ's birth and death.[29] This doctrine was published in the *Millennial Star* in 1862, but it was not until December 1866 that a council met to consider Lyman's case. Though Lyman's doctrine seems to be a not unexpected extension of the church's growing emphasis on works, the council was amazed that an apostle "should get so far into the dark as to deny the Blood of Jesus Christ & say that it was unnecessary for the salvation of man." Appointing a committee to labor with him, the council extracted a confession of sorts. Three years later he joined the Godbeite New Movement and was excommunicated.[30]

Lyman's rejection of Christ's atonement, and probably a general continuing belief in the doctrine of blood atonement, seem to have impelled a general reconsideration of church doctrine. Certainly Brigham Young had mentioned the atonement in earlier sermons, but it was always conditioned in some way by blood atonement, the Kingdom, or even – in 1860 – the analogy between Christ's death and that of the Mormon faithful: "Some of our people have suffered unto death. Could a God do more?"[31] Then at the height of the Godbeite controversy between 1869 and 1871 Young preached at least four discourses that unambiguously emphasized that Christ's atonement was critical to salvation.[32] Others had already spoken out. In February 1863, perhaps in reaction to Lyman's original sermon, John Taylor preached a detailed sermon on the Christian themes of "Sacrament, Atonement, and Second Coming." Then, at a conference in the fall of 1867 Orson Pratt was asked to write an extended statement on the doctrine of atonement.[33]

But it would not be until 1882 that such a major work would appear. John Taylor, on the committee who had labored with Amasa Lyman in 1867, assumed the presidency in 1877, at the death of Brigham Young. In 1879 he began writing *The Mediation and Atonement,* which his modern biographer describes as "of great significance doctrinally, because it marked the rejection of the Adam–God concept . . . [and] restored Christianity to the church."[34] The book was written as an extended proof of the basic Christian principle that, Adam's fortunate Fall notwithstanding, "as in Adam all die, even so in Christ shall all be made alive." Again and again Taylor reaffirmed the principle of "the offering up of the Son of God, as a sacrifice and atonement and a propitiation for our sins." The proof texts were from the Bible, the *Book of Mormon,* and from Smith's Book of Moses of 1831 to 1832, but little was drawn from the Nauvoo theology, and Young's Adam–God thesis was totally ignored. Though Taylor stated that the "Priesthood on the earth [would] continue in the exercise of that Priesthood in the heavens," there was barely a reference to the makeup of those heavens, and no discussion of matter and spirit. And diagnostically, God is described as having a "comprehensive, intelligent, and infinite mind"; he "is unchangeable, so are his laws, in all their forms, and in all their applications." In saying that "in Him all animal life of every form has its being," Taylor came close to reversing Joseph Smith's assertions of the preexistence.[35]

Many of these ideas may reflect the influence of Orson Pratt's absolutism, and they would be powerfully restated in a new Mormon orthodoxy over the next forty years. John Taylor's "re-Christianizing" of Mormonism marked a fundamental departure from the explicit hermeticism of Joseph Smith at Nauvoo and Brigham Young in early Utah. But Taylor was not willing to jettison the entire classic Mormon theology. Although he reemphasized Christ's atonement he staunchly defended the ideal of the Mormon Kingdom of God and the practice of polygamy. His efforts were not sufficient to resist the full force of the United States government. A series of federal acts in 1882 and 1887 attacked plural marriage, imposing prison terms on polygamists, assuming more direct control over Utah's civil affairs, disenfranchising all Mormons, and confiscating the property of the church, including the Salt Lake temple.

John Taylor went underground from 1885 to his death in 1887. Wilford Woodruff assumed the presidency and ran the church from the underground until 1890, when a series of pronouncements paved the way for a fundamental accommodation of the Mormon Kingdom and the American Republic. An apostles' statement of December 1889 denied the church had ever advocated blood atonement, denied any church interference in civil affairs, denied any seditious, treasonous, or revolutionary statements or intentions, and argued that the Saints were not unique in their belief that "the kingdom of heaven is at hand."[36] In September 1890 the church issued its pivotal Manifesto agreeing to submit to the national laws against polygamy and advising the Saints "to refrain from contracting any marriage forbidden by the law of the land." The following May the church decided to dissolve the Mormon-controlled "People's Party" and to direct the Saints to join either of the two national parties, the Republicans or the Democrats.[37]

A decade previously, Wilford Woodruff had experienced an apocalyptic revelation in the mountains of southern Utah, predicting the destruction of a corrupt nation and the subsequent triumph of the Saints. Now he presided over the reintegration of the Saints into that corrupt nation. The barrier between the Kingdom and the world was decisively lowered, and the laws of that world superseded the laws of the Kingdom. Though secret plural marriages would continue to be performed on an extensive scale for at least a decade, the Manifesto publicly realigned the Mormons with the marital morality of the rest of the country. The adoption of the national parties quickly brought Utah into the Union, and – driven by the new mining economy – the new state was increasingly drawn into the national economy.[38]

These initiatives, rather than Smith's Nauvoo revelations, were the underpinnings of the redressive action that would bring Mormonism into a new steady state. In 1856 the new Republican Party had condemned the "twin relics of barbarism: Polygamy and Slavery"; during the Civil War Abraham Lincoln made it known that he was willing to simply "plow around" the Mormons while he dealt with the slaveholding South. But at the close of the century Mormon accommodations preserved the fabric of their society and culture. Here the circumstances of Mormon Utah bear comparison with those of both the American South and the South African Afrikaners, two other peoples in the greater Anglo-Atlantic world who in the second half of the nineteenth century also failed in their efforts at nation-building separatism.[39] Certainly the Mormons were eminently successful in forging a new relationship with the American nation-state, ironically in an alliance with their former persecutors, the Republican Party, building a platform for political power, economic strength, and conversionary impact unparalleled in American religious history.[40]

The 1890s, and especially the decades following Woodruff's death in 1898, brought a routinization of Mormonism far beyond anything Brigham Young had envisioned, a routinization that reminds one of that of the Quakers two centuries before. Starting in 1900, after Woodruff's death, the church began to approve an explicit rejection of the Adam–God doctrine, something that John Taylor had not really attempted in his *Mediation and Atonement.* In 1900 and 1901, church publications launched the first explicit attacks on folk magic, apparently part of a broader move to deemphasize the mystical dimension of Mormonism, especially a mystical dimension outside the control of the hierarchy. Historians studying this period have found a pervasive suppression of popular manifestations of the spirit. Slowly but surely the church discouraged spiritual healing, speaking in tongues, and other charismatic gifts, with the result that Mormon women lost an important role in the spiritual life of the church. Simultaneously the authorities reduced their use of the rhetoric of the Kingdom and the millennium. By 1912 language in the temple endowments that bound the Saints to pray for divine revenge for the deaths of Joseph and Hyrum Smith was being toned down, to be totally eliminated by 1927.[41]

Historians have argued recently that the church shifted the terms of boundary maintenance from the institution to the individual. Where the hierarchy had been the agent of explicit challenge to the world before 1890, now individual conformity to church authority would mark the Saints off from the world. Echoing the 1850s injunction to "live your religion," church rhetoric accentuated the themes of family, parenthood, and saintly behavior in the place of declining themes of the millennium and the Kingdom. The Word of Wisdom, doctrine forbidding tobacco, alcohol, coffee, and tea, had been only sporadically enforced in the last quarter of the nineteenth century, but starting in 1901 the church mounted a campaign of enforcement, culminating in 1921, when adherence to its code was required for attendance in the temple. Simultaneously, attendance at local ward meetings and at the temple began to increase, as traditional – if irregular – spiritual outlets were suppressed. Not unlike the rest of the country under the influence of Progressive reform, a routinized uniformity was sweeping away the last remnants of nineteenth-century eccentricities among the Mormons.[42]

The late nineteenth century saw a renewed attack on the Mormons by a rising Protestant fundamentalism, and certain doctrinal changes helped to mitigate that conflict. The enforcement of the Word of Wisdom, though uniquely Mormon doctrine, helped to reduce tensions with evangelical Protestants.[43] So, too, the church's abandonment of the Adam–God doctrine eliminated another point of evangelical critique. Young's Adam–God thesis was also at odds with the church's new focus on Christ's atonement, and it made the temple endowment ritual confusing. The temple ritual had always included three Creation gods, Elohim, Jehovah, and Michael. Smith and Young identified Michael as Adam, but if Adam was the "Father," who was Jehovah? Starting in the 1880s a resolution began to emerge. Jehovah, the Old Testament God, was declared to be a spirit version of Jesus Christ, and was thus superior to Adam–Michael. This resolution was worked out in its definitive form in 1915 in a tract by James E. Talmage titled *Jesus the Christ,* which identified Elohim as the "eternal Father" and Jehovah as "the Only Begotten in the flesh, Jesus Christ." In his 1899 *Articles of Faith,* Talmage had already arrived at an approved description of God and Christ as bodily but immortal beings, united by a third, spiritual personage in the Holy Spirit. Once a God, Adam was reduced to a mortal prophet.[44]

Talmage's work was in some measure an extension of Taylor's *Mediation and Atonement,* stressing the necessity of Christ's atonement for salvation. The next step would be canonization. Joseph Fielding Smith, admitted to the apostleship in 1870 in the place of Amasa Lyman, and church president since 1901, had a revelation in October 1918 that was accepted as the last of the "Doctrines and Covenants." Weeks away from his own death, Smith had been "reflecting upon the great atoning sacrifice that was made by the Son of God"; he then had a vision of a host of departed spirits who had died "firm in the hope of a glorious resurrection, through the grace of God the Father and his Only Begotten Son, Jesus, Christ." Only the dead who had died outside the faith explicitly required the saving powers of temple ordinance.[45]

Twentieth-century Mormonism is grounded in these significant departures from its nineteenth-century origins. The temporal Kingdom and polygamous plural marriage were set aside, and reemphasized doctrines of Christ's atonement and God's grace profoundly altered the hermetic theology of Joseph Smith and Brigham Young.[46] These measures drastically altered the relationship of Mormonism and the wider culture, as Mormons have learned to be in but not of the world. This has required a precarious balancing act, but so has the need to harmonize past and present. In some measure, in abandoning the radical separatism of the nineteenth century, the key problem for twentieth-century Mormons has become their relationship with their nineteenth-century origins, with their own history. The past for contemporary Mormons encompasses both purity and danger. Traditions running from the past define the distinctive claim of legitimacy and authority for the church, yet too close a connection with that past runs the risk of renewed dangers, renewed confrontations with the nation and the world.

The focal point of the twentieth-century Mormon inheritance from their nineteenth-century origins lies in the temple ordinances. The temples and their ritual were indeed the most central and visible departure that Joseph Smith made from his contemporary Protestant Christian culture. As Jan Shipps has suggested, the temples provide twentieth-century Mormons with "means of reentering sacred time and space," separating themselves unconditionally, if temporarily, in these secret places from the "profane and, in very many instances, Gentile world," recovering the absolute separatism of their past.[47] But even the temple ordinances have felt the impact of Mormonism's great transformation.

Two of these changes were direct consequences of the doctrinal shifts beginning in the 1880s and 1890s. First, the effective end of plural marriage in 1890 made the tradition of gathering family kingdoms in the celestial kingdom problematic. One solution was to have as unlimited fertility as possible, an injunction that remains in force to this day. A second solution was to expand the doctrinal emphasis on baptism for the dead, who would be counted in the family kingdom. This seems to have been the reason for the particular attention to the dead in Joseph Fielding Smith's revelation of 1918, which was followed by a heightened attention to temple work under the presidency of Heber J. Grant. A careful quantification has demonstrated that indeed baptisms for the dead increased by a factor of six, relative to membership, between 1912 and 1940, declined during World War II, and then more than doubled in the next forty years. At the same time, the church's involvement in genealogical study to facilitate the baptisms, beginning in the 1890s, accelerated in the 1920s, and in the 1980s has seen the application of very sophisticated computer technology in a Family History Center built on Salt Lake's Temple Square.[48]

A second consequence for the temple ordinances was of longer chronology and appears to be directly related to the growing emphasis placed by the Mormon hierarchy on Christ's atonement. The ritual of the second anointing established at Nauvoo in September 1843 had granted a virtually unconditional promise of divinity in the celestial kingdom, to be administered on the authority of God's human "medium" acting like a hermetic *magus*. Almost 600 people had received a second anointing at Nauvoo by early 1846, but the ritual was suspended in Utah, perhaps in anticipation of building a new temple. Twenty years later, in December 1866, at the council that met to consider the doctrines of self-atonement being advocated by Amasa Lyman, Young announced that the second anointing ritual would be given again. Over the next fifty years roughly 20,000 anointings were given (roughly a quarter of these were for the dead). But from the 1850s there were concerns about the unconditional nature of these promises of divinity, and by the time of Joseph Fielding Smith "the sealing power of Elijah" was being interpreted not as granted to a human agent but simply as the Holy Ghost itself, acting, in David Buerger's words, as a divine force "which both seals and *unseals* ordinances according to an ever-changing judgment of an individual's worthiness." The frequency of second anointings declined substantially after the turn of the century, and they were virtually eliminated under the authority of Heber J. Grant in the 1920s, to the point that modern Mormons are generally unaware of the ritual's existence, and the original meaning of the term "the fulness of the priesthood" has almost been forgotten. Buerger poses a "perplexing doctrinal question": can Mormons achieve the highest levels of divinity without the second anointing, or – as the church seems to argue – is it simply unnecessary?[49]

Finally, there are the temple endowments for the living, the introductions to the promise of the celestial kingdom and marriages for time and eternity. Buerger's quantification shows that not all is well here either. Since World War II there has been an ever-growing gap between the number of new converts and the annual frequency of temple endowments, from roughly two converts per endowment in the late 1940s to roughly five converts per endowment in the early 1980s. Two broad factors account for this change. First, as Mormon conversion expands outside the Utah hearth, and outside the United States, it is increasingly difficult for converts to get to temples, despite the growth in the number of temples from four in turn-of-the-century Utah to forty-four worldwide today. Second, Buerger identified in 1987 more subtle dissonances that have deterred contemporary Mormons from temple attendance. For many the symbols and secret signs derived from Freemasonry conflict with their sense of religious experience, the filmed Creation scenes that have replaced live actors are simply boring, and the racial boundaries and sexual hierarchies explicit in the temple experience are too much at odds with contemporary values.[50]

Church accommodation to these values began in 1978, when new doctrine overturned the restrictive language of the Book of Abraham, permitting men of African descent into the priesthoods, and thus into the temples.[51] In 1990 changes were made in the temple endowment ritual itself. Most importantly, the ritual was stripped of some of the language that enforced female inferiority: women are no longer required to promise to obey their husbands or to wear face veils during a part of the ritual. Elements derived from Freemasonry, including symbolic promises of throat-slitting and disembowelment for revealing the ritual secrets and the embrace of the "five points of fellowship," have been abandoned. And, in an effort to further diminish the boundary with traditional Christianity, a drama of Satan tempting Christian clergy into "false doctrine" has been eliminated.[52]

The alterations in the temple ritual highlight the central paradox in modern Mormonism: the fusion of structures of authoritarian control with the necessity of active popular participation. Without broad acceptance of and participation in the temple endowments, the authority and legitimacy of the hierarchy would begin to unravel. Here the theological retreat of the last century, some would say since the death of Joseph Smith, seems to be of central importance. Slowly but surely, since the 1860s, the Mormon church has been avoiding the human claim to divine power that Joseph Smith made at Nauvoo: like the alchemist, he held in his hand the power to grant divinity, to shape the invisible from the visible world. Clearly and emphatically, as it circumscribed its original mandate to forge the Kingdom of God on earth, the Mormon church turned back to the invisible world the determining powers in the cosmos that it once claimed. Some would argue that without the "fulness of the priesthood" and the second anointing, the linchpins of the system of spiritual power constructed by Joseph Smith, the church has little to offer its people except an elaborate orchestration of their inherent human nature.

Contemporary Mormonism's most fundamental inheritance from its origins is its essentially optimistic view of the human condition. Espousing concepts ultimately derived, I have argued, from the optimistic gnosis of the hermetic tradition – the Egyptian Genesis of precreated beings, a godlike Adam, and a fortunate Fall – most modern Mormons continue to believe that human nature is essentially good, that humans carry a seed of divinity and thus of free will, and that, although faith is necessary, it is not sufficient; good works will have their reward. The individual, potentially divine, bears the responsibility for her or his fate. Since the turn of the century the Mormon church has turned this emphasis on human works and endeavor into a central feature of the religion but has hedged it in with an increasingly authoritarian structure. Individuals are enjoined to seek their own salvation and exaltation, but only within the increasingly narrow channels of church-sanctioned diet, family order, gender relations, sexuality, and missionary activity. In effect, the priesthoods and churchly organizations are simply vast systems of social control, dispensing or denying "temple recommends" (slips allowing entrance into a temple) as rewards or punishments for individual behavior. Just as spiritual power and charisma are tightly contained within the presidency, Mormon free will and optimism about human nature are severely contained within the bureaucratic, corporate structure of the modern church.

There are at least four broad approaches to the modern Mormon condition. First, since the 1960s Mormons have distinguished between Iron Rod Saints and Liahona Saints. Referring to rods and compasslike "directors" given the Nephites in the *Book of Mormon*, by which God either pulled the rod holder to the Tree of Life or generally pointed the way by the director, these terms describe two broad tendencies, corresponding to the authoritarian and optimistic threads in Mormon culture. The Iron Rodders "follow the brethren," accepting the word of the authorities without question, whereas the Liahonas ask questions and attempt to reform the system.[53] Beyond these two broad tendencies there are two other diametrically opposed responses to the accommodations that the Mormon church has made in the last century. As they bear directly on the central themes of this book, they require more than passing attention.

The Mormon theological transformation since the 1890s reduced the rough edges of Mormonism's claims to spiritual powers and "re-Christianized" to the point of confirming the centrality of Christ's atonement. But in the last three decades a body of Mormon thinkers have been pressing for greater change in Mormon doctrine. Though there are variations on the theme, the central tenet of these "neo-orthodox" or "redemptionist" Mormons is the rejection of the traditional optimistic view of human nature.[54] They want to reemphasize the Fall of Adam and at least a variant of the theme of original sin, sin from which only Christ's atonement and God's grace can save humanity, rather than mere works. In "making a case for grace," the "neo-orthodox" posit a perfect and absolute divinity, against a finite immortal being progressing toward greater divinity. Concomitantly, their stress is on "redemption" and spiritual transformation, the new birth of sinful humanity, promising salvation, rather than the merit-based exaltation in the celestial kingdom. Clearly, this position builds on the developments of the last century, particularly the church's reemphasis of the atonement. In addition, the "neo-orthodox" are able to press their argument by using texts from the *Book of Mormon* and Joseph Smith's earliest revelations, while ignoring the doctrine developed in the late 1830s and at Nauvoo. With the resources of both the earliest (1827–32) and the transformative (1877–1918) periods of Mormonism at their disposal, the "neo-orthodox" are able to appeal to popular unease in arguing that "Mormon scripture teaches salvation by grace, while the ecclesiastical institution throws its weight behind self-reliance, self-help, self-atonement, and self-salvation."[55]

While a rising movement of "neo-orthodox" or "redemptionist" Mormons presses for further movement toward Christianity, a countervailing force of "fundamentalists" rejects the transformation of the last century, claiming to be the true Mormonism, complete with polygamy, the Adam–God doctrine, separatist kingdom-building, and suggestions of magical practice. Quite simply, Mormon fundamentalists seek to restore the structure of purity and danger that the church left behind after the Reformation of the 1850s.

Fundamentalist roots run back to people who maintained polygamy after the Manifesto and were excommunicated after hearings in the U.S. Senate in 1904 targeted continuing polygamy in the church. Beginning in the 1920s a series of connected fundamentalist Mormon sects began to emerge, claiming that President John Taylor had, while hiding from federal authorities in 1886, given them a revelation to continue the sacred practice of plural marriage after its public abandonment. They called themselves "Joseph Smith Mormons" or "Old Line Mormons." By the 1950s these groups were claiming to represent a restored kingdom, constructing competing hierarchies of key-holding priesthoods and the communal economy of the old United Order. They also revived the doctrine of blood atonement, which has led to several dozen murders in the last thirty years as internal feuds have broken out, some driven by revelations. They also revived Brigham Young's Adam–God doctrine, and through the 1960s and 1970s advanced it in a tract war carried on with the Mormon church. Most notorious among these groups have been the followers of the LeBaron family, who founded a scattering of competing "Churches of the First-Born," each claiming to be the true restoration of the priesthoods. The LeBaron sects engaged in polygamy, published Adam–God tracts, and were shattered in a string of killings and firebombings in the mid-1970s. Another fundamentalist family, the Laffertys, claimed that a "city of refuge" would be created at the site of an old mine where in the 1890s a Bishop John Koyle claimed to have found ore by angelic revelation, leading to his eventual excommunication. The Laffertys restored the

School of Prophets, the Council of Fifty, and plural marriage, and were broken up when they killed family members, following what they claimed were the commandments of revelation. From the late 1970s, a string of influences running from Adam–God ideas, seer-stones, and hostility to racial tolerance led to the separatism of the polygamous Singer family, who bombed a church and then were besieged in their cabin in 1988. Most recently, the siege of the Weaver family in Idaho has suggested that there are growing connections between the network of Mormon polygamous fundamentalists, some 50,000 in number, and the growing racist, survivalist, separatist groups in the Northwest.[56]

With their claims of restored authority and their sensational behavior, the fundamentalists constitute a dual threat to the Mormons, both in claiming to be the true restoration and in attracting the negative attention of the outside world. Once again sects claim to be separate from and above the rules of the mere world, immune from the moral and legal constraints of the nation-state. Once again the dualism of purity and danger has emerged among the Mormons. James Coates has recently suggested that

> it is not improper to ask whether there is something unique about Mormonism that creates a deadly fringe element along with a main body of admirable family-loving, civil-minded church goers. Is revelation something that, like alcohol, most people can handle without trouble, but which can drive certain vulnerable souls to wretched and dangerous excess?[57]

Yet another danger has emerged in a fear of satanic cults, alleged to be interwoven with polygamy and operating in the cities and suburbs of the Wasatch front and across the Mountain West. Supposedly, these cults have used wording from the temple endowments in the context of rituals of child molestation. These reports may well have forced the decision to drop the language and gestures of throat-cutting and disembowelment from the endowments. Some of those involved are said to be Mormons holding "temple recommends." Like the dangers confronting Joseph Smith in the 1820s and 1830s, the alleged satanic cults have been described as "secret combinations," the "Gadianton robbers" who preyed on the Nephites in the *Book of Mormon*.[58]

The church is apparently recognizing other such dangers within its ranks. It was reported in November 1992 that the church was engaged in the largest mass excommunication since the Reformation of 1856–7. Here the target is the ultraconservative, survivalist fringe, obsessed with the millennium, who have given up their jobs and taken refuge in mountain colonies. Like the alleged satanists, the survivalists have been accused of misusing the temple ceremonies, in this case being given access to temples after hours. Clearly concerned about a rising tide of Mormon fundamentalism, church authorities have recommended that Mormons "walking on the fringes of our faith . . . seek the safety of the center."[59]

Others are calling the entire Mormon community a danger to the nation at large, echoing the histories of the Kirtland and Salt Lake banks of 1837 and the late 1840s. The church's vast financial holdings, reported to stand at more than four billion dollars, and its control of over one hundred companies, have attracted considerable suspicion.[60] Certainly, the church holds a commanding economic influence in Utah and the Mountain West, but a recent assessment argues that its "holdings are conservatively run and free of financial fraud."[61] But around the edges some do see problems. It has been argued that high-ranking Mormons have worked to advance Utah as a center of high technology, leading to two of the most celebrated cases of scientific failure in the recent past. It has been argued that undue influence was exerted on NASA to steer the construction of the space shuttle to Utah's Morton-Thiokol Corporation, whose poor design and construction work allegedly led to the shuttle disaster of January 1986.[62] More recently, the efforts to bring scientific and economic advances to Utah led to the "cold fusion" episode, in which University of Utah researchers, aided by large sums steered to them by high officials, announced a new and cheap method of producing energy.[63] Both of these episodes are all the more interesting given Mormon doctrines on the nature of matter and the existence of planets "without number," inhabited by immortal beings progressing in divinity.[64]

More typically, allegations of fraud in contemporary Utah have focused on business scandals, to the degree that church leaders and law enforcement officials have called the state the "scam capital of the world," "the fraud capital of the world," and "the white collar crime capital." Apparently fraud is particularly easy in Utah because contemporary Mormons are so fixated on financial success and especially trusting of individuals endorsed by church leaders. In the early 1980s it became apparent that fraud was rampant in the Utah economy, mostly through Ponzi-style get-rich-quick schemes, latter-day alchemical projections, typically involving real estate or jewelry. According to the state attorney general's office, nine thousand people lost roughly two million dollars in 1980–3 alone. One of these scams in the early 1980s involved investments in a satellite system company, and most recently a massive fraud operating in Utah cost an Oregon utility company millions of dollars.[65]

Eight years ago there was a different danger, quite literally hermetic, lurking in Salt Lake City. Nominally a believing Mormon, Mark Hofmann spent five years building up a reputation as a document expert. He was, quite the contrary, a master counterfeiter, beginning his work as a boy, electroplating false mintmarks on American coins. His forged documents earned him money and, as he carefully worked the controversies of Mormon history, seemed to provide answers to question after question in the sacred past. Forging documents to meet the demand in the Utah market, Hofmann built up a pyramid of debt on the expectation that he would be able to sell a copy of "The Oath of a Freeman," one of the earliest items printed in Massachusetts, to an eastern archive. Then in October 1985, threatened with exposure, he set off three bombs, killing two people and severely injuring himself. Working his own version of the contemporary Ponzi scams, Hofmann also had a profile which echoed that of the fundamentalist fringe. His mother was born into a polygamous family once living in Mexico, and this secret was apparently the source of intense stress, as Hofmann blamed the church for seeming to encourage post-Manifesto plurality and then abandoning those "in the principle." Counterfeiting and fraud are a pervasive means to wealth in the modern violent separatist sects, as is the use of bombs. And his father, William Hofmann, the son of a German Mormon convert, wanted him to die by firing squad, to fulfill the doctrine of blood atonement.[66]

Mark Hofmann's infamous "White Salamander Letter," purporting to be written by Martin Harris to William W. Phelps, introduced a powerful alchemical symbol as the bait in a fraud worthy of any of the great eighteenth-century conning men. In the forged Harris letter, Hofmann changed a "toad" Smith was reported to have found in the stone-lined pit on the Hill Cumorah to a salamander that "transfigured" into a spirit that struck Smith and denied him the Golden Plates, challenging him to bring his dead brother Alvin the next year to gain the plates. Hofmann had already produced a number of examples of Martin Harris signatures, all forged, over the previous years. His ultimate intention, having established accepted examples of Harris's handwriting, was to produce a forgery of the original 116 pages of the *Book of Mormon,* the Book of Lehi, lost when Harris showed it to his wife. The church had already spent considerable money on controversial documents, the contents of which always seemed to leak out to the public. The "recovery" of a forged Book of Lehi – if all had gone as planned – would have served double duty. Sold to the church for a handsome sum, the contents would again have surfaced in an underground version. Writing in sordid details, and the implication that Smith was writing a novel, Hofmann hoped to embarrass – perhaps destroy – the Church of Jesus Christ of Latter-day Saints. Rather than by blood atonement, Hofmann is paying for his murders with a life sentence in the Utah state prison.[67]

Ironically, Mark Hofmann was riding a wave of interest in Mormon origins that already was generating a new, realistic view of the role of magic in Mormon origins. A "new Mormon history" had emerged in the 1970s, shaped both by currents running through the entire historical profession and by the opening of Mormon church archives to scholars. Mark Hofmann had literally been to school with the "new Mormon historians," attending their courses at Utah State. The year before the "White Salamander Letter" became public knowledge, Richard Bushman's excellent *Joseph Smith and the Beginnings of Mormonism* described Smith's involvement in magic and the money-digging culture in great detail. Hofmann's forgeries led to an explosion of interest in the connection between Mormonism and magical culture, unfortunately leading some, publishing before Hofmann's conviction, to use his forgeries as authentic documents.[68]

Paradoxically, authenticity may not matter for some. Hofmann's counterfeited image of the white salamander was carefully crafted to cut to the heart of the hermetic underpinnings of Mormonism. The salamander, in the high hermetic tradition, was an emblem of the philosopher's stone, the quintessence of perfection. In the words of Michael Maier, a seventeenth-century hermetic philosopher, "As the Salamander lives by fire, so does the Stone."[69] A figure basking in the fire of the Holy Spirit, the salamander was the stone, the figure in the furnace in Daniel's parable, the Christ figure. In Mormon context the salamander represents the Nephite prophets, indeed the Nephite–Mormon people, purified in the furnaces of affliction. Once again, in the late twentieth century, the Mormon people are confronted in Hofmann's counterfeited image of a pure white salamander with a summarizing emblem of their long entanglement on the boundary tenuously dividing hermetic purity and hermetic danger.

There are many who, either explicitly or implicitly, see the survival of Mormonism in the embracing of this hermetic tradition and its complex roots in the Gnostic mysteries of the ancient Mediterranean world. For nearly half a century Hugh W. Nibley has been exploring the analogues between Mormon doctrine and the mystery religions of ancient Egypt, Judaism, and early Christianity. In his own book, Michael Quinn follows Nibley's analysis, enumerating the parallels between Mormon doctrine and ritual and the ancient mysteries. Both Nibley and Quinn argue that the intervening hermetic traditions explored in this study were irrelevant, because Joseph Smith's revelations literally restored these ancient mysteries of deification.[70] Nibley's students have pursued the quest for ancient mysteries into the far corners of Egyptian and Coptic Christian Gnostic texts.[71] Most recently Harold Bloom, a self-described "Jewish Gnostic," has similarly described Mormonism as an "American Gnosticism," rooted in an imaginative reinvention of the Judaic Cabala and the deifying power of sexuality.[72]

In a very different part of the contemporary arena, feminist Mormons who hope to break down the doctrinal walls excluding women from the priesthood are advocating the central hermetic ideal of a dual divinity, comprising both male and female genders. Linda Wilcox first proposed this dual divinity, arguing that such a doctrine was preached by Joseph Smith at Nauvoo. Wilcox and Margaret and Paul Toscano have argued that Brigham Young rejected the thesis of a dual divinity and of women in the priesthood because of the threat that Emma Hale Smith posed to his leadership in the wake of Joseph Smith's assassination. They propose that an understanding of the Judaic and Gnostic sources of a theology of a dual divinity would legitimate the abandonment of Mormon patriarchy. Wilcox argues that the Gnostic "concept of a Mother in Heaven was a fitting expression of a larger movement that aimed at raising the status of women and expanding their rights and opportunities." The Toscanos have constructed a theology that interprets Eve's eating from the Tree of Knowledge of Good and Evil in the Garden of Eden as a sacrifice rather than a sin, a sacrifice opening the door to the fortunate Fall and the potential of all "preexistent spirits" to achieve divinity. Eve's sacrifice is equated with Christ's atonement. Following a Jungian model of stages from infantile unity through separation to reintegration, the Toscanos posit a cosmos governed by a "controlling deity . . . [that] is neither the Great Mother nor the Great Father, but the divine couple locked in erotic embrace" – the image of the alchemical *coniunctio*. With or without its hermetic connotations, the concept of a dual-gendered divinity has become a fundamental ideal for women seeking to transform the male-centered polity of the Mormon church.[73]

Finally, there is the opinion of Mormon artist Benson Whittle, who, in a review of Michael Quinn's book, asks what is to become "of our poor little salamander?" Now that Hofmann's image has been proved to be a counterfeit, "is he [the salamander] to be thanklessly cast off?" Whittle hopes not, and in a discussion of the magical undercurrents running through the Mormon imagination he proposes that a renewed understanding of Mormonism's origins in "Hermetic theology" might be a means of understanding its unique strengths. Whittle has great hopes for the "little salamander":

> A "scam" brought the salamander to our attention, but it may have been lurking in our history all along. Too much could be made of this, but evidently a decision is wanted whether to try to keep the little soft-skinned reptile. Where did he come from? Is he good? Have we the right to make him a part of our history? Are there advantages to keeping him? My answers are: He came from the collective unconscious, which craves renewed enthusiasm in

The hermetic salamander, depicted in Michael Maier, *Secretioris Naturae se-cretorum Scrutinium Chymicum* . . . (Frankfort, 1687).
Courtesy of the Department of Special Collections, Memorial Library, University of Wisconsin–Madison.

an aging charismatic sect threatened with blandness. Hence a fire-sprite for inspiration. Yes, he is good, especially since the sala-mander is replete with symbolic potential for poetry, theology, and the visual arts. What has the seagull or the ox to offer next to the salamander? There is no comparison. Use a seagull once or twice, and its imagistic potential is exhausted. But the salamander is, among other things, a god, an elemental, and sire to a race of giants. Yes, we have every right to incorporate it into our history.[74]

These are powerful symbols for a new Mormon departure: "the divine couple locked in erotic embrace," the salamander as "fire-sprite for in-spiration." If these emblems, their hermetic connotations, and their implications for gender relations were fully embraced, modern Mormonism would indeed constitute what Jan Shipps has called "a new religious tradition," differing "from traditional Christianity in much the same fashion that traditional Christianity . . . came to differ from Judaism."[75] Or better yet, Mormonism would return to its origins as a "new religious tradition," a tradition forged in nineteenth-century America from ancient elements, and a tradition increasingly attenuated in the last century of accommodation and assimilation to the American norm.[76] This need not be a return to the world of Joseph Smith and Brigham Young, but a new departure within the hermetic theme, building on its optimistic, spiritual, and equalitarian implications.

Such a new departure may yet unfold, but it is very unlikely. There are simply too many dangers for the Mormons to incorporate the salamander into their history. Embracing hermeticism would mean connecting a history of "fabrication," that of the hermetic texts themselves, backdated from the second century A.D to Mosaic times, and the salamander itself, counterfeited by Mark Hofmann, to the already shaky edifice of the *Book of Mormon,* a historical revelation far too accessible to the historian's prying eyes.

In great measure, the message of the new Mormon historians, Liahona Saints, seems to suggest that this would be the best course. Embrace the past with all its shadows, and the strengths in the Mormon tradition will survive, like the salamander–Nephites in the fire. But the church hierarchy has staunchly opposed this course, closing its archives and ordering the faithful to "follow the brethren" and grab the "iron rod" of doctrinal authority.[77] And one has to wonder whether the Mormon rank and file, either from long tradition or of recent conversion, are ready for such a departure. The host of real and apparent dangers to Mormon culture requires a statement of doctrinal purity and orthodoxy that will be clear and unequivocal, a statement that would be constructed more easily in a further accommodation with traditional Christian theology than from a revived hermeticism. Since 1890 (if not long before) Mormonism has been operating in a field where purity and danger are defined by a hostile force. Fundamentalist Protestantism and Mormonism, like the occult and sectarianism in seventeenth-century England, share a very similar audience, people attuned to revelation and the coming Kingdom of God. Defending their turf and their boundaries, the fundamentalist Protestants have demonized Mormon culture; in response Mormonism has accommodated its theology and values to those of its opponents. In particular, the magical connotations of its roots have been set aside and explicitly suppressed, in the interest of an externally defined respectability.[78] Given a century of "re-Christianization," the salience of traditional Mormon doctrines among ordinary Mormons, relative to a generalized Christ-centered salvation, is not altogether clear. Since the turn of the century the church itself has been deemphasizing the distinct doctrines of the church; since 1950 references to Joseph Smith have declined just as fast as references to Jesus Christ have grown.[79] O. Kendall White, the staunchest opponent of the growing influence of Christian fundamentalism in contemporary Mormonism, admits the probability that the church will continue to jettison traditional Mormon doctrine in an effort to attract converts and mollify uneasy members.[80]

The events of the autumn of 1993 clearly indicate that the church hierarchy will not tolerate dissident views tinged with the hermetic tradition. After excommunicating the right-wing survivalist fringe in 1992, the hierarchy in 1993 turned against a range of liberal dissenters. Among those excommunicated were Maxine Hanks, D. Michael Quinn, and Paul Toscano, each of whom had in some way advanced a hermetic interpretation of Mormon cosmology, most centrally the hermetic thesis of a dual-gendered divinity.[81]

Given the slippery and combustible qualities of the multiple hermetic dangers and purities running through Mormon history, reworking an explicit hermeticism into Mormon doctrine would be an extremely delicate passage in the best of circumstances. And the closing years of the twentieth century, with Mark Hofmann serving his life sentence at the Utah state prison at Point of the Mountain, are not the best of circumstances for a hermetic renaissance in Mormonism. Hofmann's counterfeiting may have guaranteed that neither the fiery salamander nor the divine couple in *coniunctio* are going to be embraced by the Mormon church any time soon. Forcing an increasingly rigid and conventional definition of Mormon purity, Mark Hofmann may well have closed doors both to the Mormon past and to potential Mormon futures. Perhaps Hofmann indeed has achieved his goal of doing irreparable harm to the Church of Jesus Christ of Latter-day Saints, if by his hermetic danger he has compromised a transforming renewal of Mormonism which yet might spring from a creative reinterpretation of its formative encounter with hermetic purities.

The Sectarian and Hermetic Circumstances of Mormon Origins in Vermont and New York

Divining and Counterfeiting in Vermont, 1780s–1830s

	Town sources of counterfeiting petitions		Towns adjacent to sources of counterfeiting petitions		All other towns		Total	
	N	%	N	%	N	%	N	%
Total towns in 1840	54	21	113	44	87	34	254	100
Towns with divining episodes	11	41	15	55	1	4	27	100
Towns adjacent to those with divining episodes	10	17	38	66	9	16	57	100
All other towns	33	19	60	35	77	45	170	100

Note: This table and the following include only those counterfeiting petitions that can be connected with a named town. An adjacent town is one sharing a boundary along at least a quarter of its perimeter with a town that is a counterfeiting-petition source or a location of a divining episode.

Relationship of Divining Episodes to Counterfeiting, Freemasonry, and Sectarian Meetings in Vermont Towns, 1780s–1830s

	Total towns	Towns with divining episodes	Percentage of divining total	Percentage of row total	P value
Total towns	254	27	100	11	–
Towns with:					
Counterfeiting petitions	54	11	41	20	.0115
Freemasonry	74	13	48	17	.0249
Universalist societies	85	12	44	14	.2046
Freewill Baptist societies	53	7	25	13	.4952
Methodist societies	71	9	33	13	.5110

Sectarian and Hermetic Influences in Vermont Towns where Mormon Converts Were Born

	Total towns	Towns producing Mormon converts			Mormon converts	
	N	N	% of total towns	P value	N	Ratio to total towns
Total towns	254	68	27	—	123	.48
Towns with:						
Methodist circuits	71	30	44	.0007	50	.70
Counterfeiting petitions	54	23	43	.0037	43	.80
Masonic societies	74	29	40	.0047	54	.73
Freewill Baptists	53	21	40	.0191	42	.79
Divining episodes	27	11	41	.0877	29	1.07
Universalist societies	85	28	33	.1167	53	.62
Masons and Methodists	38	20	52	.0002	32	.84
Counterfeiting and Freewill Baptists	19	12	63	.0007	22	1.16
Masons and Freewill Baptists	13	9	69	.0018	14	1.08
Counterfeiting and Methodists	24	13	54	.0025	16	.62
Both hermetic and sectarian presence	89	39	44	.0000	69	.77
Sectarian presence only	54	11	20	.2337	20	.37
Hermetic presence only	24	5	20	.4918	13	.54
Neither hermetic nor sectarian presence	87	13	15	—	21	.24

Localities of Mormon Conversion in New York State, 1830–3, Compared with Conversions among Persons Born in Vermont, 1830–40

	New York towns with converts	Converts			Vermont towns with converts	Converts		
	N	N	%	Ratio	N	N	%	Ratio
Total towns	25	144	100	5.8	68	123	100	1.8
Towns with:								
Methodist societies	9	48	33	5.3	30	50	41	1.7
Freewill Baptist churches	4	16	11	4.0	21	42	34	2.0
Universalist churches	7	39	27	5.6	28	53	43	1.9
Masonic lodges	14	63	44	4.5	29	54	44	1.9
Divining histories	5	64	44	12.8	11	29	24	2.6
Lodges or divining	16	81	56	5.1	36	68	55	1.9
Counterfeiting petitions	NA				23	43	35	1.9

Sources for Appendix

Divining: Stephen Greene, "Money Diggers," *Vermont Life* 24 (1969), 48; Alan
Taylor, "The Early Republic's Supernatural Economy: Treasure Seeking in the
American Northeast," *American Quarterly* 38 (1986), 26–7 (I am grateful to
Alan Taylor for allowing me to read and use an advance copy of this article).

Counterfeiting: Petitions for pardon, restoration of citizenship, and remission of
bonds recorded in the card file of the Vermont State Archives. I am very much
indebted to Greg Sanford and the staff of the Vermont State Archives for making
available this large body of information on counterfeiting in early Vermont.

Masonic towns: Lodges and chapters listed in *Records of the Grand Lodge of Free
and Accepted Masons of the State of Vermont, from 1794–1846 Inclusive* (Burlington, 1879), 82-3, 86-7; *Records of the Grand Chapter of the State of Vermont, from 1804–1850 Inclusive* (Burlington, 1878), 3, 441–3; *Extracts from
the Proceedings of the Right Worshipful Grand Lodge of the State of New York
. . .* (New York, 1836), 42, 46, 49–52, 54, 57, 58; *Extracts from the Proceedings
of the Grand Chapter of the State of New York, at its Annual Meeting, February,
5828* (Albany, 1828), 4–5; Eugene E. Hinman, Ray V. Denslow, and Charles C.
Hunt, *A History of the Cryptic Rite* (Tacoma, Wash., 1931), 1:441–3.

*Freewill Baptist, Methodist, and Universalist societies: The Free-Will Baptist Regi-
ster, for the Year of our Lord 1834* (Limerick, Me., 1834), 46–9, 58; *Minutes of
the Annual Conferences of the Methodist Episcopal Church, for the years 1829–
1939* (New York, 1840), 329–35; *Universalist Register and Almanac for 1836
. . .* (Utica, 1836), 28–30.

Mormon converts born in Vermont: All Vermont-born Mormons listed in Milton
V. Backman Jr., Keith Perkins, and Susan Easton, comps., *A Profile of the Latter-
day Saints of Kirtland, Ohio, and Members of Zion's Camp: Vital Statistics and
Sources* (Provo, 1983), 1–80, 101–15; in biographical notes in Lyndon W. Cook,
ed., *The Revelations of the Prophet Joseph Smith: A Historical and Biographical
Commentary of the Doctrine and Covenants* (Salt Lake City, 1981); and Lyndon
W. Cook and Milton C. Backman Jr., eds., *Kirtland Elders' Quorum Record,
1836–1841* (Provo, 1985), 69–109; and in various genealogical sources.

Mormon converts living in New York State, 1830-3: Larry C. Porter, "A Study of
the Origins of the Church of Jesus Christ of Latter-day Saints in the States of New
York and Pennsylvania, 1816–1831" (Ph.D. diss., Brigham Young University,
1971), 198–222, 253–68; Leonard J. Arrington, *Brigham Young: American
Moses* (Urbana, Ill., 1985), 20; George K. Collins, *Spafford, Onondaga County*
([Syracuse], 1917), 47–50.

Note: The P-value noted in some of these tables is a measure of the strength of the
relationship between two variables. In each case, the dependent and independent
variables were tested against each other in isolation from the effects of the other
variables, using the CATMOD routine in SAS. Any result of .1 or larger indicates
that the relationship is not significant. A backward elimination procedure (the
LOGISTIC routine in SAS), simultaneously testing a cluster of variables against a
given dependent variable, produced essentially the same results.

Abbreviations Used in Notes

Journals and Archival Sources

AFGS: American Family Group Sheets (produced by the LDS Family History Center, Salt Lake City).

Ambix: *Ambix: The Journal of the Society for the History of Alchemy and Chemistry.*

BYUS: *Brigham Young University Studies.*

CEA: Connecticut Ecclesiastical Archives. Connecticut State Archives, Hartford.

Dialogue: *Dialogue: A Journal of Mormon Thought.*

EIHC: *Essex Institute Historical Collections.*

HCTHS: *Historical Collections of the Topsfield Historical Society.*

JMH: *Journal of Mormon History.*

Mass. SJC Dockets: Massachusetts Supreme Judicial Court Docket Books. Judicial Archives, Massachusetts State Archives Building, Columbia Point, Boston.

MONH: Museum of Our National Heritage, Lexington, Massachusetts.

MsVtStP: "Manuscripts of the Vermont State Papers." Vermont State Archives, Montpelier.

NEHGS: New England Historic Genealogical Society.

NEQ: *New England Quarterly.*

PCSM: *Publications of the Colonial Society of Massachusetts.*

SJCWCVt Records: Supreme Judicial Court, Windsor County, Vermont, Records. Vermont State Archives, Montpelier.

Suffolk Files: Suffolk Files Collection. Judicial Archives, Massachusetts State Archives Building, Columbia Point, Boston.

WMQ: *William and Mary Quarterly,* 3d series.

Mormon Texts

Citations to *The Book of Mormon: An Account Written by the Hand of Mormon upon Plates Taken from the Plates of Nephi,* trans. Joseph Smith Jr. (originally published in Palmyra, N.Y., 1830; Salt Lake City, 1985), are to its various sections: 1 Nephi, 2 Nephi, Jacob, Enos, Jarom, Omni, Mosiah, Alma, Helaman, 3 Nephi, 4 Nephi, Mormon, Ether, and Moroni.

Cook, *The Revelations of the Prophet Joseph Smith:* Lyndon W. Cook, ed. *The Revelations of the Prophet Joseph Smith: A Historical and Biographical Commentary of the Doctrine and Covenants.* Salt Lake City, 1981.

DC: The Doctrine and Covenants of the Church of Jesus Christ of Latter-Day Saints, Containing Revelation Given to Joseph Smith, the Prophet, with Some Additions by His Successors in the Presidency of the Church. Salt Lake City, 1985.

Ehat and Cook, comps. and eds., *The Words of Joseph Smith:* Andrew F. Ehat and Lyndon W. Cook, comps. and eds. *The Words of Joseph Smith: The Contemporary Accounts of the Nauvoo Discourses of the Prophet Joseph.* Provo, 1980.

JD: Brigham Young et al. *Journal of Discourses.* 26 vols. Liverpool and London, 1854–86.

Jessee, ed., *The Papers of Joseph Smith:* Dean C. Jessee, ed. *The Papers of Joseph Smith.* Vol. 1, *Autobiographical and Historical Writings.* Salt Lake City, 1989.

Jessee, comp. and ed., *The Personal Writings of Joseph Smith:* Dean C. Jessee, comp. and ed. *The Personal Writings of Joseph Smith.* Salt Lake City, 1984.

Roberts, *Comprehensive History:* Brigham H. Roberts. *A Comprehensive History of the Church of Jesus Christ of Latter-day Saints: Century I.* 6 vols. Provo, 1965.

Smith, *Biographical Sketches:* Lucy Mack Smith. *Biographical Sketches of Joseph Smith, the Prophet, and His Progenitors for Many Generations.* London, 1853. Repr., New York, 1969.

Smith, *History of the Church:* Joseph Smith et al. *History of the Church of Jesus Christ of Latter-day Saints.* 7 vols. Ed. Brigham H. Roberts. Salt Lake City, 1932–53.

Secondary Sources

Andrew, *The Early Temples:* Laurel B. Andrew. *The Early Temples of the Mormons: The Architecture of the Millennial Kingdom in the American West.* Albany, 1978.

Arrington, *Brigham Young:* Leonard J. Arrington. *Brigham Young: American Moses.* Urbana, 1985.

Boyer and Nissenbaum, eds., *SWP:* Paul Boyer and Stephen Nissenbaum, eds. *The Salem Witchcraft Papers: Verbatim Transcripts of the Legal Documents of the Salem Witch Outbreak of 1692.* 3 vols. New York, 1977.

Brodie, *No Man Knows My History:* Fawn M. Brodie. *No Man Knows My History: The Life of Joseph Smith, the Mormon Prophet.* 1st ed., 1945. 2d ed., rev. and enl. New York, 1985.

Bushman, *Joseph Smith:* Richard L. Bushman. *Joseph Smith and the Beginnings of Mormonism.* Urbana, 1984.

Chronicon Ephratense: Brothers Lamech and Agrippa. *Chronicon Ephratense: A History of the Community of Seventh Day Baptists at Ephrata, Lancaster County, Penn'a.* Ed. J. Max Hark. Original German ed., Ephrata, 1786. Trans., Lancaster, 1889. Repr., New York, 1972.

Hansen, *Quest for Empire:* Klaus Hansen. *Quest for Empire: The Political Kingdom of God and the Council of Fifty in Mormon History.* East Lansing, 1977.

[Hildrith], "A History of the Divining Rod":   [Samuel Hildrith]. "A History of the Divining Rod; with the Adventures of an Old Rodsman." *United States Magazine and Democratic Review,* n.s. 26 (1850), 218–35, 317–27. (For attribution, see page 388, n. 50.)

Hill, *Joseph Smith:*   Donna Hill. *Joseph Smith: The First Mormon.* Midvale, Utah, 1977.

Hill, *Quest for Refuge:*   Marvin S. Hill. *Quest for Refuge: The Mormon Flight from American Pluralism.* Salt Lake City, 1989.

Kimball, *Heber C. Kimball:*   Stanley B. Kimball. *Heber C. Kimball: Mormon Patriarch and Pioneer.* Urbana, 1981.

Mackey, *An Encyclopedia of Freemasonry:*   Albert G. Mackey. *An Encyclopedia of Freemasonry and Its Kindred Sciences. . . .* 2 vols. Rev. ed., ed. William J. Hughan and Edward L. Hawkins. New York, 1924.

Newell and Avery, *Mormon Enigma:*   Linda King Newell and Valeen Tippits Avery. *Mormon Enigma: Emma Hale Smith – Prophet's Wife, "Elect Lady," Polygamy's Foe, 1804–1879.* New York, 1984.

Quinn, *Early Mormonism:*   D. Michael Quinn. *Early Mormonism and the Magic World View.* Salt Lake City, 1987.

Scott, *CCA:*   Kenneth Scott. *Counterfeiting in Colonial America.* New York, 1957.

Scott, *CCC:*   Kenneth Scott. *Counterfeiting in Colonial Connecticut.* New York, 1957.

Scott, "CCNH":   Kenneth Scott. "Counterfeiting in Colonial New Hampshire." *Historical New Hampshire* 13 (1957), 3–38.

Scott, *CCNY:*   Kenneth Scott. *Counterfeiting in Colonial New York.* New York, 1953.

Scott, *CCRI:*   Kenneth Scott. *Counterfeiting in Colonial Rhode Island.* Providence, 1960.

Shipps, *Mormonism:*   Jan Shipps. *Mormonism: The Story of a New Religious Tradition.* Urbana, 1985.

Vogel, *Religious Seekers:*   Dan Vogel. *Religious Seekers and the Advent of Mormonism.* Salt Lake City, 1988.

Yates, *Bruno:*   Frances A. Yates. *Giordano Bruno and the Hermetic Tradition.* Chicago, 1964.

Notes

Preface

1. Although I dissent from his notion of the essential "Americanness" of Mormonism, I have arrived at roughly the same interpretation of the theological origins of Mormonism as Harold Bloom in *The American Religion: The Emergence of the Post-Christian Nation* (New York, 1992), though he writes of Mormonism's cosmology in terms of gnosticism and the Cabala, and I discuss it in terms of hermeticism. A hermetic interpretation of Mormonism was earlier suggested by R. Laurence Moore, "The Occult Connection? Mormonism, Christian Science, and Spiritualism," in Howard Kerr and Charles L. Crow, eds., *The Occult in America: New Historical Perspectives* (Urbana, 1983), 137–43.

2. Brodie, *No Man Knows My History.* See also Bernard De Voto, "The Centennial of Mormonism: A Study in Utopia and Dictatorship," in *Forays and Rebuttals* (Boston, 1936), 71–137.

3. Max Weber, *The Sociology of Religion,* trans. Ephraim Fischoff (Boston, 1963); Ernst Troeltsch, *The Social Teachings of the Christian Churches,* 2 vols., trans. Olive Wyon (New York, 1931); and H. Richard Neibuhr, *The Social Sources of Denominationalism* (New York, 1929).

4. The studies emphasizing social stress in the origins of Mormonism include Alice Felt Tyler, *Freedom's Ferment: Phases of American Social History from the Colonial Period to the Outbreak of the Civil War* (Minneapolis, 1944), 86–107; Robert Kent Fielding, "The Growth of the Mormon Church in Kirtland, Ohio" (Ph.D. diss., Indiana University, 1957); Mario S. DePillis, "The Social Sources of Mormonism," *Church History* 37 (1968), 50–79; Gordon S. Wood, "Evangelical America and Early Mormonism," *New York History* 61 (1980), 359–86; Lawrence Foster, *Religion and Sexuality: Three American Communal Experiments of the Nineteenth Century* (New York, 1981); Bushman, *Joseph Smith,* 9–42; Nathan O. Hatch, *The Democratization of American Christianity* (New Haven, 1989); Hill, *Quest for Refuge,* 1–17; and Kenneth H. Winn, *Exiles in a Land of Liberty: Mormons in America, 1830–1846* (Chapel Hill, 1989).

5. Whitney R. Cross, *The Burned-over District: The Social and Intellectual History of Enthusiastic Religion in Western New York, 1800–1850* (Ithaca, 1950; repr., New York, 1965); and David Brion Davis, "The New England Origins of Mormonism," *NEQ* 26 (1953), 147–68.

6. This phrase is from Cross, *The Burned-over District,* 145.

7. The leading studies of the Mormon doctrine of the restoration of the King-dom of God include Mario S. DePillis, "The Development of Mormon Com-munitarianism, 1826–1846" (Ph.D. diss., Yale University, 1961); Mario S. DePillis, "The Quest for Religious Authority and the Rise of Mormonism," *Dialogue* 1 (1966), 68–88; Hansen, *Quest for Empire;* Gordon D. Pollock, "In Search of Security: The Mormons and the Kingdom of God on Earth, 1830–1844" (Ph.D. diss., Queen's University, Kingston, Ont., 1977); Shipps, *Mormonism,* 67–85; Jan Shipps, "The Reality of the Restoration and the Restoration Ideal in the Mormon Tradition," in Richard T. Hughes, ed., *The American Quest for the Primitive Church* (Urbana, 1988), 181–95; Richard T. Hughes and C. Leonard Allen, *Illusions of Innocence: Protestant Primitiv-ism in America, 1630–1875* (Chicago, 1988), 133–54; Vogel, *Religious Seekers;* and Hill, *Quest for Refuge.*

8. Important recent work that explores the cultural context and implications of Smith's magical practice and treasure-divining includes Jan Shipps, "The Prophet Puzzle: Suggestions Leading toward a More Comprehensive Interpre-tation of Joseph Smith," *JMH* 1 (1974), 3–20; Bushman, *Joseph Smith,* 69–78; Ronald Walker, "The Persisting Idea of American Treasure Hunting," *BYUS* 24 (1984, published 1986), 429–460; Marvin S. Hill, "Money-Digging Folklore and the Beginnings of Mormonism: An Interpretive Suggestion," *BYUS* 24 (1984), 473–89; Alan Taylor, "The Early Republic's Supernatural Economy: Treasure Seeking in the American North-East, 1780–1830," *American Quarterly* (1986), 6–34; Quinn, *Early Mormonism,* 1–52; and W. R. Jones, "'Hill-Diggers' and 'Hell-Raisers': Treasure-Hunting and the Super-natural," unpublished paper presented at "Wonders of the Invisible World, 1600–1900," Dublin Seminar for New England Folklife, June 30, 1992.

9. Many European historians, however, have serious doubts as to the necessary connection between social deprivation and religious extremism. See the sum-mary discussion in Clarke Garrett, *Respectable Folly: Millenarians and the French Revolution in France and England* (Baltimore, 1975), 6–9.

10. Yates, *Bruno;* Carlo Ginzburg, *The Cheese and the Worms: The Cosmos of a Sixteenth-Century Miller,* trans. John Tedeschi and Anne Tedeschi (Baltimore, 1976); Christopher Hill, *The World Turned Upside Down: Radical Ideas during the English Revolution* (London, 1972); Christopher Hill, *Milton and the English Revolution* (New York, 1977); and Jon Butler, *Awash in a Sea of Faith: Christianizing the American People* (Cambridge, Mass., 1990).

11. I write this in much the same spirit as Stephen Foster, *The Long Argument: English Puritanism and the Shaping of New England Culture, 1570–1700* (Chapel Hill, 1991), in which he argues that New England Puritanism must be viewed in terms of a continuing transatlantic culture – though here the focus is on the extreme elements of the Radical Reformation, rather than the Mag-isterial Reformation.

12. Among many others, see the substantive and methodological approaches defined in Jon Butler, "The Future of American Religious History: Prospectus, Agenda, and Transatlantic *Problématique,*" *WMQ* 42 (1985), 167–83; and

Edward Muir, "Introduction: Observing Trifles," in Edward Muir and Guido Ruggiero, eds., *Microhistory and the Lost People of Europe,* trans. Eren Branch (Baltimore, 1991), vii–xxviii.

1. Dreams of the Primal Adam

1. *DC* 132: 19–20.
2. A. D. Wright, *The Counter-Reformation: Catholic Europe and the Non-Christian World* (New York, 1982); Keith Thomas, *Religion and the Decline of Magic* (New York, 1971); Robert Muchembled, *Popular Culture and Elite Culture in France, 1400–1750,* trans. Lydia Cochrane (Baton Rouge, 1985).
3. George H. Williams, *The Radical Reformation* (Philadelphia, 1962), xxiii–xxxi, 234–41.
4. Norman Cohn, *Europe's Inner Demons: An Inquiry Inspired by Europe's Great Witch-Hunt* (New York, 1975); Richard Kieckhefer, *European Witch Trials: Their Foundations in Popular and Learned Culture, 1300–1500* (Berkeley, 1976); Brian P. Levack, *The Witch-Hunt in Early Modern Europe* (London, 1987); Julio Caro Baroja, "Witchcraft and Catholic Theology," and Stuart Clark, "Protestant Demonology: Sin, Superstition, and Society (c. 1520–c. 1630)," in Bengt Ankarloo and Gustav Henningsen, eds., *Early Modern European Witchcraft: Centres and Peripheries* (Oxford, 1990), 19–82.
5. Thomas, *Religion and the Decline of Magic,* 177–252; Muchembled, *Popular Culture and Elite Culture in France,* 61–93; David D. Hall, *Worlds of Wonder, Days of Judgement: Popular Religious Belief in Early New England* (New York, 1989), 98–100; Jon Butler, *Awash in a Sea of Faith: Christianizing the American People* (Cambridge, Mass., 1990), 20–5; Chadwick Hansen, *Witchcraft at Salem* (New York, 1969), 63–86.
6. Thomas, *Religion and the Decline of Magic,* 25–50; Richard Kieckhefer, *Magic in the Middle Ages* (Cambridge, 1989); Valerie I. J. Flint, *The Rise of Magic in Early Modern Europe* (Princeton, 1991).
7. Kieckhefer, *Magic in the Middle Ages,* 19–55; Flint, *The Rise of Magic,* 36–58 and passim; Ralph Merrifield, *The Archaeology of Ritual and Magic* (New York, 1987), 83–136.
8. Carlo Ginzburg, *The Cheese and the Worms: The Cosmos of a Sixteenth-Century Miller,* trans. John Tedeschi and Anne Tedeschi (Baltimore, 1976); Carlo Ginzburg, *The Night Battles: Witchcraft and Agrarian Cults in the Sixteenth and Seventeenth Centuries,* trans. John Tedeschi and Anne Tedeschi (Baltimore, 1983); Carlo Ginzburg, *Ecstacies: Deciphering the Witches' Sabbath,* trans. Raymond Rosenthal (New York, 1991); Robert Muchembled, "Satanic Myths and Cultural Reality," in Ankarloo and Henningsen, eds., *Early Modern European Witchcraft,* 139–60; Muchembled, *Popular Culture and Elite Culture in France,* 66–71; see also Carol F. Karlsen, *Devil in the Shape of a Woman: Witchcraft in Colonial New England* (New York, 1987), 9, 141–4.

9. Alan MacFarlane, *Witchcraft in Tudor and Stuart England: A Regional and Comparative Study* (New York, 1970), 103–30; Thomas, *Religion and the Decline of Magic,* 177–252, 535–60. Robert Whiting, *The Blind Devotion of the People: Popular Religion and the English Reformation* (New York, 1989), describes the collapse of traditional Catholicism by the 1540s and the failure of Protestantism to uniformly and immediately take its place.

10. Christina Larner, *Enemies of God: The Witch-Hunt in Scotland* (Baltimore, 1981), 170–1; Thomas, *Religion and the Decline of Magic,* 251–60; J. L. Teall, "Witchcraft and Calvinism in Elizabethan England: Divine Power and Human Agency," *Journal of the History of Ideas* 23 (1962), 31; Richard Weisman, *Witchcraft, Magic and Religion in 17th-Century Massachusetts* (Amherst, 1984), 54–7; Clark, "Protestant Demonology"; Muchembled, "Satanic Myths and Cultural Reality"; Clive Holmes, "Popular Culture? Witches, Magistrates, and Divines in Early Modern England," in Stephen L. Kaplan, ed., *Understanding Popular Culture: Europe from the Middle Ages to the Nineteenth Century* (Berlin, 1984), 85–112; John Putnam Demos, *Entertaining Satan: Witchcraft and the Culture of Early New England* (New York, 1984), 80–4; Richard Godbeer, *The Devil's Dominion: Magic and Religion in Early New England* (New York, 1992), 55–84.

11. Hermetic culture has been reviewed in luxurious and amusing detail in Umberto Eco, *Foucault's Pendulum,* trans. William Weaver (New York, 1989).

12. Garth Fowden, *The Egyptian Hermes: A Historical Approach to the Late Pagan Mind* (New York, 1986); Yates, *Bruno,* 1–19; E. J. Holmyard, *Alchemy* (Harmondsworth, 1957), 23–40, 58–101, 102ff.; Jack Lindsay, *The Origins of Alchemy in Graeco-Roman Egypt* (New York, 1970).

13. My understanding of alchemy has been informed by the studies cited in note 12 as well as the following: Carl G. Jung, *Psychology and Alchemy,* vol. 12 of *The Collected Works of C. G. Jung,* 2d ed., trans. R. F. C. Hull (New York, 1967); Carl G. Jung, *Alchemical Studies,* vol. 13 of *The Collected Works,* 2d ed., trans. R. F. C. Hull (New York, 1967); Carl G. Jung, *Mysterium Coniunctionis: An Inquiry into the Separation and Synthesis of Psychic Opposites in Alchemy,* vol. 14 of *The Collected Works,* 2d ed., trans. R. F. C. Hull (New York, 1963); Arthur E. Waite, *The Secret Tradition of Alchemy, Its Development and Records* (New York, 1926); John Read, *Prelude to Modern Chemistry: An Outline of Alchemy, Its Literature and Relationships* (New York, 1937), esp. 118ff.; F. Sherwood Taylor, *The Alchemists: Founders of Modern Chemistry* (New York, 1949), esp. 123–49; Mircea Eliade, *The Forge and the Crucible,* trans. Stephen Corran (New York, 1962); Gaston Bachelard, *The Psychoanalysis of Fire,* trans. Alan C. M. Ross (Boston, 1964); Jacques Soboul, *Alchemy and Gold* (London, 1972); Betty Jo T. Dobbs, *The Foundations of Newton's Alchemy: or "The Hunting of the Green Lyon"* (New York, 1975); and Walter Pagel, *Paracelsus: An Introduction to Philosophical Medicine in the Era of the Renaissance* 2d rev. ed. (Basel, 1982), 258–73.

14. Holmyard, *Alchemy,* 117.

15. See the excellent descriptions of fraudulent alchemy in Charles Nicholl, *The Chemical Theatre* (London, 1980), 7–10; Read, *Prelude,* 22, 28; Taylor, *The*

Alchemists, 106; and Gamini Salgado, *The Elizabethan Underworld* (London, 1977), 110, 114, 146–8.

16. Yates, *Bruno*, 20–129; D. P. Walker, *Spiritual and Demonic Magic from Ficino to Campanella* (London, 1958), 36–59; D. P. Walker, *The Ancient Theology: Studies in Christian Platonism from the Fifteenth to the Eighteenth Centuries* (London, 1972), 1–21.

17. Fowden, *The Egyptian Hermes*, 22–44, 57–74; Peter J. French, *John Dee: The World of an Elizabethan Magus* (London, 1972), 68; Yates, *Bruno*, 12–13, 398ff.; on Casaubon, see Anthony Grafton, *Forgers and Critics: Creativity and Duplicity in Western Scholarship* (Princeton, 1990), 76–98.

18. Fowden, *The Egyptian Hermes*, 77; Walter Scott, ed., *Hermetica* (London, 1968), 1:115–18; here I follow the summary of Christopher Hill, *Milton and the English Revolution* (New York, 1977), 325–6. On Mormon views about the relationship between spirit and matter, see Sterling M. McMurrin, *The Theological Foundations of the Mormon Religion* (Salt Lake City, 1965), 5–11.

19. Yates, *Bruno*, 22–8; Scott, ed., *Hermetica*, 1:121–7.

20. Taylor, *The Alchemists*, 145–61; Jung, *Psychology and Alchemy*, 392; French, *John Dee*, 76, 85 (emphasis in original).

21. Walker, *Spiritual and Demonic Magic*, 12–24; Yates, *Bruno*, 62–83.

22. Yates, *Bruno*, 84–116, 121–9; Frances A. Yates, *The Occult Philosophy in the Elizabethan Age* (London, 1979), 20–1, 29, 33–4, 63; French, *John Dee*, 30–1, 49, 87, 91, 115, 131.

23. There is an enormous literature advancing and qualifying the thesis of a hermetic role in the origins of the Scientific Revolution. Among many others see Paolo Rossi, *Francis Bacon: From Magic to Science*, trans. Sasha Rabinovitch (London, 1968); Charles Webster, *From Paracelsus to Newton: Magic and the Making of Modern Science* (Cambridge, 1982); and the studies by Pagel, Webster, Dobbs, French, Clulee, Margaret C. Jacob, and J. R. Jacob cited in notes 13, 43, 44, and 51. See also the essays in M. L. Righini Bonelli and W. R. Shea, eds., *Reason, Experiment, and Mysticism in the Scientific Revolution* (New York, 1975); Allen G. Debus, ed., *Science, Medicine and Society in the Renaissance: Essays to Honor Walter Pagel* (London, 1972); Mikulas Teich and Robert Young, eds., *Changing Perspectives in the History of Science: Essays in Honour of Joseph Needham* (Boston, 1973); Charles Webster, ed., *The Intellectual Revolution of the Seventeenth Century* (London, 1974); R. S. Westman and J. E. McGuire, eds., *Hermeticism and the Scientific Revolution* (Los Angeles, 1977); Brian Vickers, ed., *Occult and Scientific Mentalities in the Renaissance* (Cambridge, 1984); Ingred Merkel and Allen G. Debus, eds., *Hermeticism and the Renaissance: Intellectual History and the Occult in Early Modern Europe* (Washington, D.C., 1988).

24. Stephen E. Ozment, *The Age of Reform, 1250–1550: An Intellectual and Religious History of Late Medieval and Reformation Europe* (New Haven, 1980), 127–34; Bernard McGinn, "Meister Eckhart: An Introduction," in Paul E. Szarmach, ed., *An Introduction to the Medieval Mystics of Europe* (Albany, 1984), 237–58. Yates, in *Bruno*, 22–43, emphasizes the distinction

between optimistic and pessimistic gnosis. On the pessimistic dualism of the medieval mystics, see Evelyn Underhill, *Mysticism: A Study in the Nature and Development of Man's Spiritual Consciousness* (London, 1945), 44–50; Malcolm Lambert, *Medieval Heresy: Popular Movements from Bogomil to Hus* (New York, 1976), 121–31; R. I. Moore, *The Origins of European Dissent* (Oxford, 1985), 139–67; Jeffrey B. Russell, *Dissent and Reform in the Early Middle Ages* (Berkeley, 1965), 188–229.

25. *DC* 35:18.
26. *DC* 76:7, 50–117.
27. *DC* 27:11.
28. On free will, see Daniel P. Walker, *Decline of Hell: Seventeenth Century Discussions of Eternal Torment* (Chicago, 1964), 13–15, 236; McMurrin, *The Theological Foundations of the Mormon Religion*, x, suggests that "Mormon theology is a modern Pelagianism in a Puritan religion." For Mormon concepts of sin and grace, see McMurrin, 57–77 and passim, as well as O. Kendall White, *Mormon Neo-orthodoxy: A Crisis Theology* (Salt Lake City, 1987), 57–87; see also the essays in Gary James Bergera, ed., *Line upon Line: Essays on Mormon Doctrine* (Salt Lake City, 1989). On Pelagianism, see John Ferguson, *Pelagius* (Cambridge, 1956), esp. 159–84.
29. Donald Q. Cannon and Lyndon W. Cook, eds., *Far West Record: Minutes of the Church of Jesus Christ of Latter-Day Saints, 1830–1844* (Salt Lake City, 1983), 20–1.
30. Margorie Reeves, *The Influence of Prophesy in the Later Middle Ages: A Study in Joachimism* (Oxford, 1969), is the definitive work on Joachim (on Elias-Elijah, see 174, 176, 182, 252). See also Margorie Reeves, *Joachim of Fiore and the Prophetic Future* (London, 1976), 1–115; Gordon Leff, *Heresy in the Later Middle Ages: The Relation of Heterodoxy to Dissent, c. 1250–1450* (New York, 1967), 69–80, 124–32, 172–78; Lambert, *Medieval Heresy*, 182–216.
31. See Jarold K. Zeman, "Restitution and Dissent in the Late Medieval Renewal Movements: The Waldensians, the Hussites and the Bohemian Brethren," *Journal of the American Academy of Religion* 44 (1976), 17–20 and passim; Leff, *Heresy*, 411–14, 685–707; Lambert, *Medieval Heresy*, 217–34; Norman Cohn, *The Pursuit of the Millennium: Revolutionary Millenarians and Mystical Anarchists of the Middle Ages*, rev. and exp. ed. (New York, 1970), 209ff. The distinction between biblical restoration and dispensationalism is emphasized by Samuel S. Hill, Jr., "A Typology of American Restitutionism: From Frontier Revivalism and Mormonism to the Jesus Movement," *Journal of the American Academy of Religion* 44 (1976), 65–76; and by Vogel, *Religious Seekers*.
32. Lambert, *Medieval Heresy*, 49–91, 108–64.
33. D. Michael Quinn, "Socioreligious Radicalism of the Mormon Church: A Parallel to the Anabaptists," in Davis Bitton and Maureen U. Beecher, eds., *New Views of Mormon History* (Salt Lake City, 1987), 363–86; William E. Juhnke, "Anabaptism and Mormonism: A Study in Comparative History," *John Whitmer Historical Association Journal* 2 (1982), 38–46; John

Cairncross, *After Polygamy Was Made a Sin: The Social History of Christian Polygamy* (London, 1974).

34. Williams, *The Radical Reformation*, 259–65, 328–32, 839; Reeves, *Joachim of Fiore*, 143–4; Cohn, *Pursuit*, 258–60.

35. Cohn, *Pursuit*, 260–80; Franklin H. Littel, *The Anabaptist View of the Church: A Study in the Origins of Sectarian Protestantism* (Boston, 1958), 20–1, 29ff.; Williams, *The Radical Reformation*, xxviii, 362–86, 835.

36. James H. Overfield, *Humanism and Scholasticism in Late Medieval Germany* (Princeton, 1984), 159–63; Walker, *Spiritual and Demonic Magic*, 90–6; Yates, *Bruno*, 130–43.

37. Pagel, *Paracelsus*, 89–95, 119–20, 203–301, 315ff.; Allen G. Debus, *The English Paracelsians* (New York, 1965), 24–6; Yates, *Bruno*, 150–1; Rufus M. Jones, *Spiritual Reformers in the 16th and 17th Centuries* (Boston, 1914; repr., 1959), 138–9; William Newman, "Prophecy and Alchemy: The Origin of Eirenaeus Philalethes," *Ambix* 37 (1990), 97.

38. Williams, *The Radical Reformation*, 197, 458, 460–1, 836; Jones, *Spiritual Reformers*, 48, 53.

39. John Joseph Stoudt, *Sunrise to Eternity: A Study in Jacob Boehme's Life and Thought* (Philadelphia, 1957), 195–217, 241–57; Jones, *Spiritual Reformers*, 151–207; Desiree Hirst, *Hidden Riches: Traditional Symbolism from the Renaissance to Blake* (London, 1964), 83–94; Williams, *The Radical Reformation*, 813; Arlene A. Miller, "The Theologies of Luther and Boehme in the Light of the *Genesis* Commentaries," *Harvard Theological Review* 63 (1970), 261–303; Margaret L. Bailey, *Milton and Jakob Boehme: A Study of German Mysticism in Seventeenth Century England* (New York, 1964), 24–30; Nils Thune, *The Behmenists and Philadelphians: A Contribution to the Study of English Mysticism in the 17th and 18th Centuries* (Uppsala, 1948), 18–23.

40. Williams, *The Radical Reformation*, 477–82; Jean Dietz Moss, "'Godded with God': Henrick Niclaes and His Family of Love," *Transactions of the American Philosophical Society* 71, pt. 8 (1981), 5, 17–19, 22–30, 67–70; Alastair Hamilton, *The Family of Love* (Cambridge, 1981); J. W. Martin, "Elizabethan Familists and English Separatism," *Journal of British Studies* 20 (1980), 53–73; Herman de la Fontaine Verwey, "The Family of Love," *Quaerendo* 6 (1976), 219–71; Rufus M. Jones, *Studies in Mystical Religion* (London, 1909), 428–48.

41. Moss, "'Godded with God,'" 21; Hamilton, *The Family of Love*, 113; Frances A. Yates, *The Rosicrucian Enlightenment* (London, 1972), 72–3, 216.

42. French, *John Dee*, 173–87, 195–9; Nicholas H. Clulee, *John Dee's Natural Philosophy: Between Science and Religion* (London, 1988), 86–96, 166, 180–90, 220–28, 331; Yates, *The Rosicrucian Enlightenment*, 37–40.

43. Yates, *Rosicrucian Enlightenment*, 15–69, 72–3, 206–19; John W. Montgomery, *Cross and Crucible* (The Hague, 1973), 158–255; William R. Huffman, *Robert Fludd and the End of the Renaissance* (London, 1988), 36–49, 135–66; Newman, "Prophecy and Alchemy," 97–8; David Stevenson, *The Origins of Freemasonry: Scotland's Century, 1590–1710* (New York,

1988), 77–124, esp. 84–5; Margaret C. Jacob, *The Radical Enlightenment: Pantheists, Freemasons, and Republicans* (London, 1981), 108–81, esp. 160; Hamilton, *The Family of Love*, 142, 164 nn.1–2; Moss, "'Godded with God,'" 17.

44. Charles Webster, *The Great Instauration: Science, Medicine and Reform, 1626–1660* (New York, 1976), 8, 100, 246, 324–8, 264–6, 488–90, and passim (quotation from 8); J. R. Jacob, *Robert Boyle and the English Revolution: A Study in Social and Intellectual Change* (New York, 1977), 16–38; Thomas, *Religion and the Decline of Magic*, 288–9.

45. Christopher Hill, *The World Turned Upside Down: Radical Ideas during the English Revolution* (London, 1972), 234; Webster, *The Great Instauration*, 276–80; Hill, *Milton*, 328.

46. Jones, *Spiritual Reformers*, 208–20; Webster, *The Great Instauration*, 200, 28kA0, 330; Newman, "Prophecy and Alchemy," 110; Stanton J. Linden, "Alchemy and Eschatology in Seventeenth-Century Poetry," *Ambix* 31 (1984), 116–20.

47. Jones, *Spiritual Reformers*, 138, 148, 241–3, 255–61; Webster, *The Great Instauration*, 279; Jerome Friedman, *Blasphemy, Immorality, and Anarchy: The Ranters and the English Revolution* (Athens, Ohio, 1987), 72–4.

48. Rufus M. Jones, *Mysticism and Democracy in the English Commonwealth* (Cambridge, Mass., 1932; repr., New York, 1965), 64–5; Hamilton, *The Family of Love*, 139; Moss, "'Godded with God,'" 59–60.

49. Thomas, *Religion and the Decline of Magic*, 227, 288–9; Bernard Capp, *English Almanacs, 1500–1800: Astrology and the Popular Press* (Ithaca, 1979), 67–88; Patrick Curry, *Prophecy and Power: Astrology in Early Modern England* (Princeton, 1989), 19–44. See also A. L. Rowse, *Sex and Society in Shakespeare's Age: Simon Forman the Astrologer* (New York, 1974); and Patrick Curry, ed., *Astrology, Science and Society: Historical Essays* (Wolfboro, N.H., 1987).

50. Thomas, *Religion and the Decline of Magic*, 249, 296, 298–300, 304, 342–3, 375, 556; Capp, *English Almanacs*, 73–4; Curry, *Prophecy and Power*, 40–4; Hill, *The World Turned Upside Down*, 231–46; Christopher Hill, *The Collected Essays of Christopher Hill* (Amherst, 1985), 3:274–94; Webster, *The Great Instauration*, 311–14; P. M. Rattansi, "Paracelsus and the English Revolution," *Ambix* 11 (1963), 24–32; Michael MacDonald, *Mystical Bedlam: Madness, Anxiety, and Healing in Seventeenth-Century England* (New York, 1981).

51. Jacob, *Robert Boyle*; Margaret C. Jacob, *The Newtonians and the English Revolution, 1689–1720* (Ithaca, 1976).

52. Quotations from Thomas, *Religion and the Decline of Magic*, 270, 375. The following discussion assumes that there was a sharp and significant distinction between Calvinist Puritans and Spiritualist sectarians in the era of the English Revolution. This division obviously informs my discussion of the Radical Reformation, which is shaped by Williams, *The Radical Reformation*, and Jones, *Spiritual Reformers*. This issue in the context of the seventeenth century has been the subject of broad shifts in interpretation. The

mystical interpretation of Rufus Jones, established by the 1930s, came under a broad critique by those who wished to see Quakers in particular as closer to the Calvinist mainstream, and by those who wished to emphasize the role of the Holy Spirit in Puritan experience, correcting the intellectual focus of Perry Miller. The main exemplar of the former is Hugh Barbour, *The Quakers in Puritan England* (New Haven, 1964), and among the many examples of the latter are Geoffrey F. Nuttall, *The Holy Spirit in Puritan Faith and Experience* (Oxford, 1947), and Philip F. Gura, *A Glimpse of Sion's Glory: Puritan Radicalism in New England, 1620–1660* (Middletown, Conn., 1984). I am more convinced by those older and more recent studies that recognize the continuities of experience of individuals moving from Puritanism to Spiritualism but also posit a sharp doctrinal line dividing them. Here see Theodore Bozeman, *To Live Ancient Lives: The Primitivist Dimension in Puritanism* (Chapel Hill, 1988), 364–8; Melvin B. Endy Jr., "The Interpretation of Quakerism: Rufus Jones and His Critics," *Quaker History* 70 (1981), 3–21; Melvin B. Endy Jr., "Puritanism, Spiritualism, and Quakerism: An Historiographical Essay," in Richard S. Dunn and Mary Maples Dunn, eds., *The World of William Penn* (Philadelphia, 1986), 281–301; H. Larry Ingle, "From Mysticism to Radicalism: Recent Historiography of Quaker Beginnings," *Quaker History* 76 (1987), 79–94; and the various works of Christopher Hill cited above and below.

53. Hill, *Collected Essays*, 3:89–116; Barry Reay, *The Quakers and the English Revolution* (New York, 1985), 12–17.

54. Moss, "'Godded with God,'" 59–60, 63; Thomas, *Religion and the Decline of Magic,* 270–1; Hill, *Milton,* 328; Hill, *The World Turned Upside Down,* 233–4; Bailey, *Milton and Jakob Boehme,* 77–82; T. Wilson Hayes, "John Everard and the Familist Tradition," in Margaret Jacob and James Jacob, eds., *The Origins of Anglo-American Radicalism* (London, 1984), 60–9; Jones, *Spiritual Reformers,* 239–52; Jones, *Mysticism and Democracy,* 64ff.; Robert M. Schuler, "Some Spiritual Alchemies of Seventeenth-Century England," *Journal of the History of Ideas* 41 (1980), 308–18; Hamilton, *The Family of Love,* 137–8.

55. On the Seekers, I am indebted to Hill, *The World Turned Upside Down,* 118–19, 148–58; A. L. Morton, *The World of the Ranters: Religious Radicalism in the English Revolution* (London, 1970), esp. 127–30; George A. Johnson, "From Seeker to Finder: A Study in Seventeenth Century English Spiritualism before the Quakers," *Church History* 17 (1948), 299–315; Reay, *The Quakers and the English Revolution,* 10–17; Jones, *Mysticism and Democracy,* 58–104; and Vogel, *Religious Seekers.*

56. Saltmarsh quoted in Reeves, *Joachim of Fiore,* 161; see also Morton, *The World of the Ranters,* 127–9.

57. Morton, *The World of the Ranters,* 128.

58. T. Wilson Hayes, *Winstanley the Digger: A Literary Analysis of Radical Ideas in the English Revolution* (Cambridge, Mass., 1979), 23–4, 63–81, 102–6, 110–11, 117–19, 149–50, 177–81, and passim; Hill, *The World Turned*

Upside Down, 86–120, 236, 315; Christopher Hill, *The Religion of Gerald Winstanley* (Oxford, 1978), esp. 18–19; Hill, *Milton,* 324–31, 345–7; Hill, *Collected Essays,* 3:117–40; G. E. Aylmer, "The Religion of Gerald Winstanley," in McGregor and Reay, eds., *Radical Religion in the English Revolution,* 91–120; Brian Manning, "The Levelers and Religion," in McGregor and Reay, eds., *Radical Religion in the English Revolution,* 65–90.

59. There is considerable debate as to whether the Ranters and their antinomian ideology were real or were a construct of an embattled Presbyterian orthodoxy. The interpretations of the Ranters presented by A. L. Morton in *The World of the Ranters* and by Christopher Hill in *The World Turned Upside Down* have been challenged by J. C. Davis, *Fear, Myth, and History: The Ranters and the Historians* (Cambridge, 1986), and by J. F. McGregor, "Seekers and Ranters," in McGregor and Reay, eds., *Radical Religion in the English Revolution,* 121–40. There have been spirited rebuttals to the Davis thesis by G. E. Aylmer in "Review Article: Did the Ranters Exist?" *Past and Present* 117 (1987), 208–19; Edward Thompson, "On the Rant," in Geoff Ely and William Hunt, eds., *Reviving the English Revolution: Reflections on the Work of Christopher Hill* (London, 1988), 153–60; and Christopher Hill, *A Tinker and a Poor Man: John Bunyan and His Church, 1628–1688* (New York, 1989), 75–84, 380–1. Davis's most recent response is "Fear, Myth and Furore: Reappraising the 'Ranters,'" *Past and Present* 129 (1990), 79–103.

60. Clarkson quoted in Hill, *Collected Essays,* 3:170; see also Morton, *The World of the Ranters,* 70–92, 131–5; Hill, *The World Turned Upside Down,* 158–68; Barry Reay, "Lawrence Clarkson: An Artisan and the English Revolution," in Christopher Hill, Barry Reay, and William Lamont, eds., *The World of the Muggletonians* (London, 1983), 162–87; Friedman, *Blasphemy, Immorality, and Anarchy.*

61. Bernard S. Capp, *The Fifth Monarchy Men: A Study in English Seventeenth Century Millenarianism* (Totowa, N.J., 1972), 50–76, 143–4, 162–82. See also Louise Fargo Brown, *The Political Activities of the Baptists and Fifth Monarchy Men in England during the Interregnum* (London, 1911; repr., New York, 1964).

62. Capp, *Fifth Monarchy Men,* 112, 185–8; Thomas, *Religion and the Decline of Magic,* 377; Hill, *Milton,* 329; David S. Katz, *Sabbath and Sectarianism in Seventeenth-Century England* (Leiden, 1988), 36, 38, 69–133.

63. Christopher Hill, "Why Bother about the Muggletonians?" and "John Reeve and the Origins of Muggletonianism," in Hill, Reay, and Lamont, eds., *The World of the Muggletonians,* 23–33, 79–86; Morton, *The World of the Ranters,* 138–40; John F. C. Harrison, *The Second Coming: Popular Millenarianism, 1780–1850* (New Brunswick, 1979), 23–4.

64. Reay, *Quakers and the English Revolution,* 15–20.

65. Jones, *Spiritual Reformers,* 220–7; Rufus M. Jones, *Studies in Mystical Religion* (London, 1909), 494–5; Nuttall, *The Holy Spirit in Puritan Faith and Experience,* 16–19; William C. Braithwaite, *The Beginnings of Quakerism,* 2d ed., revised by Henry J. Cadbury (Cambridge, 1955), 34–42; Reay, *The*

Quakers and the English Revolution, 15–17; Henry J. Cadbury, "Early Quakerism and Uncanonical Lore," *Harvard Theological Review* 40 (1947), 192–4. For a different view, see Barbour, *The Quakers in Puritan England,* 27, 193. See discussion in note 52, and especially the important historiographical analysis in Endy, "Puritanism, Spiritualism, and Quakerism." For an important older essay emphasizing Quaker spiritualism, see James F. Maclear, "The Making of the Lay Tradition," *Journal of Religion* 33 (1953), esp. 127–33.

66. Reay, *The Quakers and the English Revolution,* 32–7, 53–5, 68–71; Thomas, *Religion and the Decline of Magic,* 486–92; MacDonald, *Mystical Bedlam,* 9–10, 170, 208, 228; G. F. Nuttall, "Unity with the Creation: George Fox and the Hermetic Philosophy," *Friend's Quarterly,* n.s., 1 (1947), 134–43.

67. Morton, *The World of the Ranters,* 116–39 (quotation from 136–7); Reay, "Lawrence Clarkson: An Artisan and the English Revolution," 162–82 (quotation from 171); Christopher Hill, *The Experience of Defeat: Milton and Some of His Contemporaries* (New York, 1984), 46–8. J. C. Davis has nothing to say about this phase of Clarkson's life in *Fear, Myth, and History.*

68. Thomas, *Religion and the Decline of Magic,* 377–8; Curry, *Prophecy and Power,* 29.

69. Reay, *Quakers and the English Revolution,* 81–100.

70. James R. Jacob and Margaret C. Jacob, "The Anglican Origins of Modern Science: The Metaphysical Foundations of the Whig Constitution," *Isis* 71 (1980), 251–67; Jacob, *Robert Boyle;* Jacob, *The Newtonians and the English Revolution;* Jacob, *The Radical Enlightenment;* Dobbs, *The Foundations of Newton's Alchemy;* Richard S. Westfall, "Newton and Alchemy," and Brian Vickers, "Analogy versus Identity: The Rejection of the Occult Symbolism, 1580–1680," in Vickers, ed., *Occult and Scientific Mentalities,* 95–164, 315–36; P. M. Rattansi, "The Social Interpretation of Science in the Seventeenth Century," in Peter Matthias, ed., *Science and Society, 1600–1900* (Cambridge, 1972), 27–32; Charles Webster, ed., *Samuel Hartlib and the Advancement of Learning* (London, 1970), 63–4; Webster, *The Great Instauration,* 98–9, 491–505; MacDonald, *Mystical Bedlam,* 32, 226–7. On the problem of the division of elite and popular culture, see James R. Jacob, " 'By an Orphean Charm': Science and the Two Cultures in Seventeenth-Century England," in Phyllis Mack and Margaret C. Jacob, eds., *Politics and Culture in Early Modern Europe* (Cambridge, 1987), 231–50. On conservatism, Calvinism, and radical magic, see Hill, *Collected Essays,* 3:282–93; and Webster, *The Great Instauration,* 506, 328–9, 332, 333, 498, 514.

71. The analogues between the English radical sects and Mormon cosmology have been noted in Hansen, *Quest for Empire,* 8–13; Vogel, *Religious Seekers;* Quinn, *Early Mormonism;* Quinn, "Socioreligious Radicalism"; Cairncross, *After Polygamy Was Made a Sin;* Harrison, *The Second Coming,* 7; Reay, "The Muggletonians: An Introductory Survey," in Hill, Reay, and Lamont, eds., *The World of the Muggletonians,* 30; and most recently, Thomas G. Alexander, *Things of Heaven and Earth: The Life and Times of Wilford Woodruff* (Salt Lake City, 1991), 17.

2. The True Spiritual Seed

1. Originally published in Eber D. Howe, *Mormonism Unvailed* (Painesville, Ohio, 1834), 259; reprinted in Rodger I. Anderson, *Joseph Smith's New York Reputation Reexamined* (Salt Lake City, 1990), 118. All subsequent references to the Howe affidavits will be to the Anderson volume.

2. For one of many accounts, see Bushman, *Joseph Smith*, 69–78.

3. See n. 8, Preface.

4. Peter Ingersoll and Joshua Stafford affidavits, in Anderson, *Joseph Smith's New York Reputation Reexamined*, 134–5, 142–3; Ronald Walker, "The Persisting Idea of American Treasure Hunting," *BYUS* 24 (1984), 430–4, 444; Brigham Young, Apr. 29, 1877, *JD* 19:37.

5. [Ransford Rogers], *A Collection of Essays on a Variety of Subjects . . .* (Newark, N.J., 1797), 9; "The Rodsmen," *Vermont American*, May 7, 1828, p. 2; [Hildrith], "A History of the Divining Rod," 218, 225.

6. Walker, "The Persisting Idea"; Marvin S. Hill, "Money-Digging Folklore and the Beginnings of Mormonism: An Interpretive Suggestion," *BYUS* 24 (1984), 473–89; and Alan Taylor, "Rediscovering the Context of Joseph Smith, Jr.'s Treasure Seeking," *Dialogue* 19 (Winter 1986), 18–28; all emphasize the religious and spiritual qualities of the divining cults.

7. [Hildrith], "A History of the Divining Rod," 318, 326–7.

8. See Chapter 3.

9. For the most recent effort to tie Mormonism to Puritanism, see Rex E. Cooper, *Promises Made to the Fathers: Mormon Covenant Organization* (Salt Lake City, 1990).

10. Jarold K. Zeman, "Restitution and Dissent in the Late Medieval Renewal Movements: The Waldensians, the Hussites and the Bohemian Brethren," *Journal of the American Academy of Religion* 44 (1976), 7–26; James C. Spalding, "Restitution as a Normative Factor for Puritan Dissent," *Journal of the American Academy of Religion* 44 (1976), 47–63; Gordon Leff, *Heresy in the Later Middle Ages* (New York, 1967), 411–605; George H. Williams, *The Radical Reformation* (Philadelphia, 1962), xxiv–v; and Theodore D. Bozeman, *To Live Ancient Lives: The Primitivist Dimension in Puritanism* (Chapel Hill, 1988). See also Richard T. Hughes, ed., *The American Quest for the Primitive Church* (Urbana, 1988); Richard T. Hughes and C. Leonard Allen, *Illusions of Innocence: Protestant Primitivism in America, 1630–1875* (Chicago, 1988).

11. Quotation from John Cotton, *Gods Promise to His Plantation* (London, 1630), in Hughes and Allen, *Illusions of Innocence*, 25.

12. See Robert G. Pope, *The Half-Way Covenant: Church Membership in Puritan New England* (Princeton, 1969); and David D. Hall, *Worlds of Wonder, Days of Judgement: Popular Religious Belief in Early New England* (New York, 1989), 117–212.

13. This is the substance of Bozeman, *To Live Ancient Lives*, 287–343.

14. William G. McLoughlin, *New England Dissent, 1630–1833: The Baptists and the Separation of Church and State*, 2 vols. (Cambridge, Mass., 1971); for

Biblicism in the Great Awakening, see C. C. Goen, *Revivalism and Separatism in New England, 1740–1800: Strict Congregationalists and Separate Baptists in the Great Awakening* (New Haven, 1962), 211–12, 259–60, 284. For primitivism in the Second Great Awakening, see Nathan Hatch, *The Democratization of American Christianity* (New Haven, 1989), 82–3, 167–70, 179; and Samuel S. Hill, Jr., "A Typology of American Restitutionism: From Frontier Revivalism and Mormonism to the Jesus Movement," *Journal of the American Academy of Religion* 44 (1976), 65–76.

15. Philip F. Gura, *A Glimpse of Sion's Glory: Puritan Radicalism in New England, 1620–1660* (Middletown, Conn., 1984), 133–6; James F. Maclear, "New England and the Fifth Monarchy: The Quest for the Millennium in Early American Puritanism," *WMQ* 32 (1975), 223–48; Bozeman, *To Live Ancient Lives*, 237–86. For the implications of Thorowgood and Eliot for Mormon concepts of Indians as the Lost Tribes, see Dan Vogel, *Indian Origins and the Book of Mormon* (Salt Lake City, 1986), 22, 41, 43.

16. Maclear, "New England and the Fifth Monarchy," 225, 235–6; see also Bozeman, *To Live Ancient Lives*, 198–236, 264–5.

17. Hall, *Worlds of Wonder*, 71–116, 199–204.

18. Keith Thomas, *Religion and the Decline of Magic* (New York, 1971); Paul Boyer and Stephen Nissenbaum, *Salem Possessed: The Social Origins of Witchcraft* (Cambridge, Mass., 1974); Richard Weisman, *Witchcraft, Magic and Religion in 17th-Century Massachusetts* (Amherst, 1984); Hall, *Worlds of Wonders*, 71–116; Richard Godbeer, *The Devil's Dominion: Magic and Religion in Early New England* (New York, 1992), esp. 179–222.

19. Richard Dunn, *Puritans and Yankees: The Winthrop Dynasty of New England, 1630–1717* (Princeton, 1962), 65, 80–96; Robert C. Black, *The Younger John Winthrop* (New York, 1966), 55, 87–8, 155–7, 192; Ronald S. Wilkinson, "'Hermes Christianus': John Winthrop, Jr. and Chemical Medicine in Seventeenth Century New England," in Allen G. Debus, ed., *Science, Medicine and Society in the Renaissance: Essays to Honor Walter Pagel* (London, 1972), 221–42.

20. Ronald S. Wilkinson, "The Alchemical Library of John Winthrop, Jr. (1606–1676)," *Ambix* 11 (1963), 39, 42–3, 45–7; Raymond P. Stearns, *Science in the British Colonies of America* (Urbana, 1970), 119–21; G. L. Turnbull, "George Stirk, Philosopher by Fire (1626?–1665)," *PCSM* 38 (1947–51), 224–5, 231; Ronald S. Wilkinson, "George Starkey, Physician and Chemist," *Ambix* 11 (1963), 127–9, 133–4, 151; Ronald S. Wilkinson, "Further Thoughts on the Identity of 'Eirenaeus Philalethes,'" *Ambix* 19 (1972), 204–8.

21. Wilkinson, "The Alchemical Library," 39, 42–3, 45; Frances A. Yates, *The Occult Philosophy in the Elizabethan Age* (London, 1979), 88; G. L. Kittredge, "Robert Child the Remonstrant," *Transactions of the Colonial Society of Massachusetts* 21 (1919), 123–46; G. H. Turnbull, "Robert Child," *PCSM* 38 (1947–51, publ. 1959), 21–50.

22. Kittredge, "Robert Child," 129; Wilkinson, "The Alchemical Library," 2, 37–8; William Newman, "Prophecy and Alchemy: The Origins of Eirenaeus

Philalethes," *Ambix* 37 (1990), 109; Ronald S. Wilkinson, "New England's Last Alchemists," *Ambix* 10 (1962), 133; Frances A. Yates, *The Rosicrucian Enlightenment* (London, 1972), 70–90, 206–19; Herbert Leventhal, *In the Shadow of the Enlightenment: Occultism and Renaissance Science in Eighteenth-Century America* (New York, 1976), 126–36.

23. I am indebted to Rosamund Rosenmeier for sharing with me her manuscript on Anne Bradstreet, which explores the hermetic dimension of Bradstreet's work. See also Gura, *A Glimpse of Sion's Glory,* 24; Laurel Thatcher Ulrich, *Goodwives: Images and Reality in the Lives of Women in Northern New England, 1650–1750* (New York, 1980), 110–13; Elizabeth W. White, *Anne Bradstreet: "The Tenth Muse"* (New York, 1971), 174–6.

24. Leventhal, *In the Shadow of the Enlightenment,* 128–9. On Taylor's use of Bradstreet, I am obliged to Rosamund Rosenmeier.

25. Kenneth Silverman, *The Life and Times of Cotton Mather* (New York, 1984), 32, 36, 41–2, 231–2, 299–303, 330–2, 414; Weisman, *Witchcraft, Magic and Religion,* 29–34, 170–5; Jon Butler, *Awash in a Sea of Faith: Christianizing the American People* (Cambridge, Mass., 1990), 72–3, 176; Stearns, *Science in the British Colonies of America,* 405–26; Leventhal, *In the Shadow of the Enlightenment,* 17–18, 29–30, 41–2, 215–16, 268.

26. Weisman, *Witchcraft, Magic and Religion,* 33.

27. For an excellent description of the separate intellectual orbit of elites in late-seventeenth-century New England, see Richard D. Brown, *Knowledge Is Power: The Diffusion of Information in Early America, 1700–1865* (New York, 1989), 16–41. For an English manuscript suggesting how Calvinism and alchemy could be reconciled, see Robert M. Schuler, "Some Spiritual Alchemies of Seventeenth-Century England," *Journal of the History of Ideas* 41 (1980), 303–8.

28. Leventhal, *In the Shadow of the Enlightenment,* 14–16, 18, 67, 126–7; Butler, *Awash in a Sea of Faith,* 76; Stearns, *Science in the British Colonies of America,* 446–55.

29. Gura, *A Glimpse of Sion's Glory,* 23, 72.

30. Stephen Foster, "English Puritanism and the Progress of New England Institutions, 1630–1660," in David Hall, John M. Murrin, and Thad W. Tate, eds., *Saints and Revolutionaries: Essays on Early American History* (New York, 1984), 3–37; Hall, *Worlds of Wonder,* 7; Jon Butler, "Magic, Astrology, and the Early American Religious Heritage, 1600–1760," *American Historical Review* 84 (1979), 323–5; and Carla Pestana, *Quakers and Baptists in Colonial Massachusetts* (New York, 1991), 8–11.

31. Robert Paul Thomas and Terry L. Anderson, "White Population, Labor Force, and Extensive Growth of the New England Economy in the Seventeenth Century," *Journal of Economic History* 33 (1973), 641; David W. Galenson, *White Servitude in Colonial America: An Economic Analysis* (New York, 1981), 120, 167.

32. Other than in his discussions of Gorton's parallels with Dell and Saltmarsh, Philip Gura nowhere in his encyclopedic *A Glimpse of Sion's Glory* mentions hermeticism directly. In a discussion, he has agreed that the migrants of the

1630s could not have had a systematic exposure to the hermetic tradition. See also Jon Butler's assessment in "Magic, Astrology, and the Early American Religious Heritage," 323–5.

33. Gura, *A Glimpse of Sion's Glory*; Arthur J. Worrall, *Quakers in the Colonial Northeast* (Hanover, N.H., 1980); Rufus M. Jones, *Quakers in the American Colonies* (New York, 1911; repr., New York, 1966); Ned C. Landsman, *Scotland and Its First American Colony, 1683–1765* (Princeton, 1985).

34. See summary accounts in David S. Lovejoy, *Religious Enthusiasm in the New World: Heresy to Revolution* (Cambridge, Mass., 1985), 154–60, 162–8; Sidney E. Ahlstrom, *A Religious History of the American People* (New Haven, 1972), 230–6, 241–4.

35. This account of Continental Pietism draws upon F. Ernest Stoeffler, *The Rise of Evangelical Pietism* (Leiden, 1965), 109–21, 187–242; F. Ernest Stoeffler, *German Pietism during the Eighteenth Century* (Leiden, 1973), 1–88, 131–216; Mary Fulbrook, *Piety and Politics: Religion and the Rise of Absolutism in England, Wurttemberg, and Prussia* (Cambridge, 1983), 23–7, 130–73; Ahstrom, *A Religious History*, 236–41; Elizabeth W. Fisher, "'Prophesies and Revelations': German Cabalists in Early Pennsylvania," *Pennsylvania Magazine of History and Biography* 109 (1985), 302–6, 311; Donald F. Durnbaugh, "The Brethren in Early American Church Life," in F. Ernest Stoeffler, ed., *Continental Pietism and Early American Christianity* (Grand Rapids, 1976), 222–65.

36. Milton J. Coalter, *Gilbert Tennent, Son of Thunder: A Case Study of Continental Pietism's Impact on the First Great Awakening in the Middle Colonies* (New York, 1986); F. Ernest Stoeffler, "Pietism, the Wesleys, and Methodist Beginnings in America," in Stoeffler, ed., *Continental Pietism and Early American Christianity*, 184–221; Bernard Simmel, *The Methodist Revolution* (New York, 1973), 30–41; Martin Schmidt, *John Wesley: A Theological Biography* (New York, 1962); W. R. Ward, "The Relations of Enlightenment and Religious Revival in Central Europe and the English-Speaking World," in *Reform and Reformation: England and the Continent, c. 1500–c. 1750*, Studies in Church History, vol. 2, ed. Derek Baker (Oxford, 1979), 281–305.

37. Butler, *Awash in a Sea of Faith*, 74–5, 82–3, 118; Leventhal, *In the Shadow of the Enlightenment*, 109–10; Henry J. Cadbury, "Early Quakerism and Uncanonical Lore," *Harvard Theological Review* 40 (1947), 203–5.

38. David Stephenson, *The Origins of Freemasonry: Scotland's Century, 1590–1710* (New York, 1988), 203–4; Fisher, "'Prophesies and Revelations,'" 311–15, 325–8; Alison Coudert, "A Quaker–Kabbalist Controversy: George Fox's Reaction to Francis Mercury Van Helmont," *Journal of the Warburg and Courtauld Institutes* 39 (1976), 171–89.

39. Julius F. Sachse, *The German Pietists of Provincial Pennsylvania* (Philadelphia, 1895), 37–40, 69–72, 83, 109–19, 148, 180–91; Fisher, "'Prophesies and Revelations,'" 299–302, 321–33.

40. Sachse, *The German Pietists*, 85–92.

41. *Chronicon Ephratense*, 16–18; Julius F. Sachse, *The German Sectarians of Pennsylvania, 1708–1742: A Critical and Legendary History of the Ephrata*

Cloister and the Dunkers, 2 vols. (Philadelphia, 1899), 1:72–5; E. Gordon Alderfer, *The Ephrata Commune: An Early American Counterculture* (Pittsburgh, 1985), 32, 35–6; Lovejoy, *Religious Enthusiasm in the New World,* 162.

42. Alderfer, *The Ephrata Commune,* 14–51; Sachse, *The German Sectarians,* 1:32–48, 71–83, 111–40; Peter C. Erb, "Introduction," in Erb, ed., *Johann Conrad Beissel and the Ephrata Community: Mystical and Historical Texts* (Lewiston, N.Y., 1985), 3–14.

43. The best account is in Erb's "Introduction" to Erb, ed., *Johann Conrad Beissel,* 15–20. Quotation from [Johann Conrad Beissel], *A Dissertation on Man's Fall, Translated from the High-German Original* (Ephrata, 1765), 4–5.

44. Alderfer, *Ephrata,* 58–60; *Chronicon Ephratense,* 165; Sachse, *The German Sectarians,* 2:172–5.

45. Sachse, *The German Sectarians,* 1:386; [Beissel], *A Dissertation,* 4; *Chronicon Ephratense,* 173–4. Citing a manuscript since lost, Sachse described a ritual of alchemical regeneration supposedly performed among the Zionitic Brethren, involving fasting, bloodletting, and the ingestion of a mysterious white elixir and then grains of the *prima materia,* the alchemical quintessence, with the purpose of gaining 5,777 years of immortality. See Sachse, *The German Sectarians,* 1:350–65; Alderfer, *The Ephrata Commune,* 70–1; and Erb, "Introduction," in Erb, ed., *Johann Conrad Beissel,* 31–2.

46. Sachse, *The German Sectarians,* 1:385–6; see also Leventhal, *In the Shadow of the Enlightenment,* 107–9, 118–20; Henry W. Shoemaker, *The Origins and Language of Central Pennsylvania Witchcraft* (Reading, 1927); A. Monroe Aurand, *The "Pow-Wow" Book* (Harrisburg, 1929); Frederick Klees, *The Pennsylvania Dutch* (New York, 1961), 298–311. On Ephrata's more limited success in reproducing culture on its own terms, see A. G. Roeber, "'The Origin of Whatever Is Not English among Us,' The Dutch-speaking and German-speaking Peoples of Colonial British America," in Bernard Bailyn and Philip D. Morgan, eds., *Strangers within the Realm: Cultural Margins of the First British Empire* (Chapel Hill, 1991), 250–2.

47. Sachse, *The German Sectarians,* 1:366, 2:290.

48. W. Clark Gilpin, *The Millenarian Piety of Roger Williams* (Chicago, 1979), 30–62; C. Leonard Allen, "Roger Williams and 'the Restauration of Zion,'" in Hughes, ed., *The American Quest,* 33–49; Hughes and Allen, *Illusions of Innocence,* 53–78; Jesper Rosenmeier, "The Teacher and the Witness: John Cotton and Roger Williams," *WMQ* 25 (1968), 411–31; Bozeman, *To Live Ancient Lives,* 129, 137–8, 156, 263–4; Gura, *A Glimpse of Sion's Glory,* 41–3, 76–7; Vogel, *Religious Seekers,* 5, 13–15, 57–8, 142, 183–4; Quotations from Williams, *George Foxe Digged,* and *Bloudy Tenent,* are taken from Allen, "Roger Williams," 35, 46–7.

49. Gura, *A Glimpse of Sion's Glory,* 61, 260.

50. Ibid., 264.

51. Quotations from ibid., 63, 84, 292; see in general, 62–3, 80–6, 291–2. See also Lovejoy, *Religious Enthusiasm in the New World,* 93–9.

52. Gura, *A Glimpse of Sion's Glory,* 277–303, esp. 293; see also Gura, "The

Radical Ideology of Samuel Gorton: New Light on the Relation of English to American Puritanism," *WMQ* 36 (1979), 78–100; Gura, "Samuel Gorton and Religious Radicalism in England, 1644–1648," *WMQ* 40 (1983), 121–4; Barbara R. Dailey, "Root and Branch: New England's Religious Radicals and Their Transatlantic Community, 1600–1660" (Ph.D. diss., Boston University, 1988), 174–251; Kenneth W. Porter, "Samuel Gorton: New England Firebrand," *NEQ* 7 (1934), 442–4.

53. Arthur J. Worrall, *Quakers in the Colonial Northeast* (Hanover, N.H., 1980), 3–42; McLoughlin, *New England Dissent*, 1:3–78; Gura, *A Glimpse of Sion's Glory*, 105–6, 120–5; Dailey, "Root and Branch"; Pestana, *Baptists and Quakers in Colonial Massachusetts*.

54. McLoughlin, *New England Dissent*, 1:10–11; Worrall, *Quakers in the Colonial Northeast*, 18–20; Gura, *A Glimpse of Sion's Glory*, 98–105, 108–13, 148–9.

55.
Dissenters and New England Population in 1740: An Estimate

	Quaker Monthly Meetings in 1743[a]	Baptist churches in 1740[b]	Estimated population in 1740[c]	Population per meeting or church[c]
Maine and New Hampshire	2	0	36,000	18,000
Old Plymouth Colony	5	4	40,000	4,444
Rhode Island	4	13	30,000	1,764
Southeast Connecticut[d]	0	4	20,000	5,000
Other areas in Massachusetts Bay and Connecticut	1	7	154,000	19,250

[a]Jones, *Quakers in the American Colonies*, 142.

[b]McLoughlin, *New England Dissent*, 1:261, 279–80.

[c]Population estimates based on data in Jackson T. Main, *Society and Economy in Colonial Connecticut* (Princeton, 1985), 13–4, Bruce C. Daniels, *The Connecticut Town: Growth and Development, 1635–1790* (Middletown, Conn., 1979), 45–52; Douglas R. McManis, *Colonial New England: A Historical Geography* (New York, 1975), 69. Evarts B. Greene and Virginia D. Harrington, *American Population before the Federal Census of 1790* (New York, 1922; repr., Gloucester, Mass., 1966), 21–30; 58–60, 66.

[d]Southeast Connecticut includes New London County plus Lebanon, Colchester, and East Haddam, towns influenced by the Rogerenes in various ways. See McLoughlin, *New England Dissent*, 1:261; and John R. Bolles and Anna B. Williams, *The Rogerenes* (Boston, 1904), 276.

56. David S. Katz, *Sabbath and Sectarianism in Seventeenth-Century England* (Leiden, 1988), 135–64; *Seventh Day Baptists in Europe and America* (Plainfield, N.J., 1910), 122–33; *The Seventh Day Baptist Memorial: A Quarterly*

Magazine Devoted to Biography, History, and Statistics (New York, 1852–4), 1:22–89, 120.

57. Christopher Hill, "Radical Pirates," in Margaret Jacob and James Jacob, eds., *The Origins of Anglo-American Radicalism* (London, 1984), 17–28; Christopher Hill, "From Lollards to Levelers," in Hill, *The Collected Essays of Christopher Hill* (Amherst, 1985), 3:89–116, esp. 107; on these points and in general, see Peter Linebaugh, "All the Atlantic Mountains Shook," and Marcus Rediker, "Good Hands, Stout Heart and Fast Feet: The History and Culture of Working People in Early America," in Geoff Eley and William Hunt, eds., *Reviving the English Revolution: Reflections and Elaborations on the Work of Christopher Hill* (London, 1988), 193–249, esp. 202–6, 221, 226.

58. Lovejoy, *Religious Enthusiasm in the New World*, 140–3; Lyle Koehler, *A Search for Power: The "Weaker Sex" in Seventeenth Century New England* (Urbana, 1980), 367. On the migration of freed servants from Barbados to the northern colonies, see Richard S. Dunn, *The Rise of the Planter Class in the English West Indies, 1624–1713* (Chapel Hill, 1972), 111–16. While rich planters began settling South Carolina, poorer sorts tended to go further north. In 1679, 130 of 233 individuals departing Barbados were bound for New England and New York.

59. Carla G. Pestana, *Liberty of Conscience and the Growth of Religious Diversity in Early America, 1636–1786* (Providence, 1986), 56–7.

60. Francis M. Caulkins, *History of New London, Connecticut* (New London, 1895), 201–21; McLoughlin, *New England Dissent* 1:250–1; James S. Rogers, *James Rogers of New London, Ct. and His Descendants* (Boston, 1902), 16–22; Charles Stark, *Groton, Conn., 1705–1905* (Stonington, Conn., 1922), 213–40.

61. John Rogers, *A Midnight Cry from the Temple of God to the Ten Virgins Slumbering and Sleeping* . . . (New York, 1705), 31–4, 36, 43, 45–6, 103; John Rogers, *A Midnight Cry* . . . (*with an epistle to the Church of Christ, called Quakers, & to the Seventh-Day Baptists*), 2d ed. (New London: Joseph Bolles, 1722), 207, 209, 211; Peter Pratt, *The Prey Taken from the Strong* . . . (New London: T. Green, 1725), 40–1, 46–7, 51–3. For Continental and English parallels, see George H. Williams, *The Radical Reformation* (Philadelphia, 1962), 839; A. L. Morton, *The World of the Ranters: Religious Radicalism in the English Revolution* (London, 1970), 129, 138; Barry Reay, "The Muggletonians: An Introductory Survey," in Christopher Hill, Barry Reay, and William Lamont, eds., *The World of the Muggletonians* (London, 1983), 28.

62. Koehler, *A Search for Power*, 288, 474–7, 480–1; Carol F. Karlsen, *Devil in the Shape of a Woman: Witchcraft in Colonial New England* (New York, 1987), 122–5; Hall, *Worlds of Wonder*, 100–2; John Putnam Demos, *Entertaining Satan: Witchcraft and the Culture of Early New England* (New York, 1984), 113, 380; Christine L. Heyrman, "Specters of Subversion, Societies of Friends: Dissent and the Devil in Provincial Essex County, Massachusetts," in Hall, Murrin, and Tate, eds., *Saints and Revolutionaries*, 39–75.

63. Thomas Harmon Jobe, "The Devil in Restoration Science: The Glanvill–Webster Witchcraft Debate," *Isis* 72 (1981), 343–56; Christopher Hill, "John Reeve and the Origins of Muggletonianism," in Hill et al., *The World of the Muggletonians,* 89.

64. Christine Heyrman found accused witches from ten Quaker and Quaker-affiliated families in Salem, Lynn, Beverley, and Andover (Nurse, Proctor, Farrar, Hood, DeRich, Bassett, Hawkes, Hart, Wardwell, and Tookey). Comparing lists of Quakers with the court records, I have found another ten Quaker families whose members accused or provided evidence against accused witches (Ruck, Pope, Shattuck, Maule, Wilkins, Trask, Bacon, Hill, Gray, Small). Members of three other Quaker-affiliated families signed petitions for the pardon of accused witches (Gaskin, Smith, Stone). See Heyrman, "Specters of Subversion," 51–3; Quaker lists in Jonathan Chu, *Neighbors, Friends, or Madmen: The Puritan Adjustment to Quakerism in Seventeenth-Century Massachusetts Bay* (Westport, 1985), 169–74; accused witches and petitioners in Boyer and Nissenbaum, eds., *SWP.*

65. Chadwick Hansen, *Witchcraft at Salem* (New York, 1969), 66, 79–80; Koehler, *A Search for Power,* 421. It might be argued that I am making too close an identification of the cunning folk and the dissenters, especially in light of the evidence from the Salem witch trials, where considerable evidence for occult practice was heard. It ought to be pointed out that many of those people who admitted to occult practices were outsiders of some sort or another. Of the ten individuals discussed in Hansen, *Witchcraft at Salem,* 63–86, Samuel Shattuck and Thomas Maule were Quakers, Bridget Bishop was connected to the Oliver family, known for their dissent in early Salem, Tituba and Candy were slaves from the West Indies (one Indian, one African), George Burroughs had lived in Maine, and Wilmot Redd was from Marblehead, a fishing community long marginal to Puritan orthodoxy (others: Thomas Andrews, Boxford, Dorcas Hoar, Beverly, Roger Toothaker, Salem Village). Similarly, Richard Godbeer's evidence in *The Devil's Dominion* suggests that dissenters were an important element among those knowledgeable in magic, that many of the latter "were clearly not Puritans," and that only a minority of the "godly layfolk used magic" (46–54).

66. Godbeer, *The Devil's Dominion,* 158; Thomas, *Religion and the Decline of Magic,* 442–3.

67. Demos, *Entertaining Satan,* 387–94; Leventhal, *In the Shadow of the Enlightenment,* 66–125; Butler, *Awash in a Sea of Faith,* 83–97.

68. In a survey of all evidence for occult practitioners available for early New England, data collected by Peter Benes indicates that, of eleven known conjurers working between 1700 and 1775, five were located in Rhode Island. See Peter Benes, "Fortunetellers, Wise-Men, and Transient 'Witches' in New England, 1644–1850," paper presented at "Wonders of the Invisible World, 1600–1900," Dublin Seminar for New England Folklife, June 30, 1992.

69. *Diary of Ebenezer Parkman, 1703–1782, First Part,* ed. Francis G. Walett (Worcester, 1974), 288; *Literary Diary of Ezra Stiles,* ed. Franklin B. Dexter (New York, 1910), 1:385–6.

70. F. M. Angellotti, "Sylvester Stover of York, Me., and Some of His Descendants," *New England Historic Genealogical Register* 85 (1931), 300–5; Don Charles Nearpass, "Materials for a Genealogy of Josiah Stover, Who Became Josiah Stafford of Tiverton, R.I.," data filed at LDS Family History Center; Lenore Evans et al., *A Patchwork History of Tiverton, Rhode Island* (Tiverton, 1976), 41; *Peleg Burrough's Journal, 1778–1798: The Tiverton, R.I. Years of the Humbly Bold Baptist Minister*, ed. Ruth W. Sherman (Warwick, 1981), xv, 5, 31; McLoughlin, *New England Dissent*, 1:582 n. 34.

71. James Franklin, Joseph Stafford, and Anne Franklin, *The Rhode Island Almanack . . .* (Newport, 1735, 1737, 1738, 1739); Joseph Stafford, *An Almanack for the Year . . .* (Boston, 1739, 1740, 1744). None of the Stafford almanacs survive for 1741–3 and 1745.

72. Joseph Stafford's books, manuscript fragments, and some articles of furniture were passed down through the Stafford family to Marie Stafford Stokoe and her son, William Stokoe. At Professor Stokoe's invitation, I examined this material at his home in May 1988. The Joseph Stafford collection has since been donated to the Rhode Island Historical Society.

73. See Otho T. Bealls Jr., "*Aristotle's Master Piece* in America: A Landmark in the Folklore of Medicine," *WMQ* 20 (1963), 207–22.

74. [Hildrith], "A History of the Divining Rod," 221.

75. I am grateful to Thomas L. Revere for the use of his research on Stephen Davis. Working back from a Stephen Davis in the 1850 and 1860 census in Marietta, born in Maine around 1813, Revere found Stephen Davises in Westport in 1790, in Kennebec County in 1800, in Sydney in 1810, in Marietta in 1820 and 1830, and elsewhere in Washington County, Ohio, in 1840. The Stephen born in 1813 presumably was the Rodsman's son; his occupation in 1850 and 1860 was listed as "pilot." These references can be found using the U.S. census indexes, with the exception of the 1820 reference, which is in vol. 10 of the Ohio 1820 manuscripts (roll 95), p. 191, U.S. Census manuscripts, National Archives. The Rodsman's alchemist "B. Devoe" was probably a misprint of "B. Devol," a common name in Westport, Tiverton, and Marietta. Joseph Stafford's children married Devols as had his brother David. Various Davises and Devols were Freemasons in Marietta as early as 1790. *History of the American Union Lodge No. 1, Free and Accepted Masons of Ohio, 1776 to 1833* (Marietta, Ohio, 1934), 118–20, 162. On the Welsh Davises among the Seventh Day Baptists, see *The Seventh Day Baptist Memorial* (1853), 2:101–61; Richard M. Baylies, *History of Newport County, Rhode Island* (New York, 1888), 924; Dartmouth Vital Records, 2:154; Westport Vital Records, 39. On Stafford Road, see Bushman, *Joseph Smith*, 48, 70–4.

76. For Ransford Rogers and the Rogers family, see New London Probate District Document 4467, Apr. 7, 1763, Connecticut State Archives ("Mrs Charity Rogers is apointed Guardian to her Son Joseph Rogers on his Choice – & to Benjamin & Ransford in Minority"); and Rogers, comp., *James Rogers of New London*, 56.

77. I am indebted to Thomas L. Revere for locating Rogers in the U.S. census, and

in *Rolls and Lists of Connecticut Men in the Revolution, 1775–1783* (Hartford, 1901), 50. See also Alan Taylor, "The Early Republic's Supernatural Economy: Treasure Seeking in the American Northeast, 1780–1830," *American Quarterly* 38 (1986), 26; [Rogers], *A Collection of Essays,* 22–4; Charles H. Bell, *The History of Exeter, New Hampshire* (Exeter, 1888), 412–14; Andrew M. Sherman, *Historic Morristown, New Jersey: The Story of Its First Century* (Morristown, 1905), 406–30; W. C. Carter, *History of York County from Its Erection to the Present Time [1729–1834],* new ed., ed. A. Monroe Aurand Jr. (Harrisburg, 1930), 126–30.

78. Clark Jillson, *Green Leaves from Whittingham, Vermont* (Worcester, Mass., 1894), 119; [Hildrith], "A History of the Divining Rod," 225; Washington Irving, "The Money-Diggers," in *Tales of a Traveller,* vol. 2 (London, 1825), cited in Walker, "The Persisting Idea," 446; J. E. A. Smith, *The History of Pittsfield (Berkshire County), Massachusetts, from the Year 1734 to the Year 1800* (Boston, 1869), 304. I am indebted to Mark Mastromarini for this last reference.

79. I would like to thank Wayne Bodle for sharing draft copies of his manuscript titled "'The Humour That Now Prevails': Mines and *Mentalité* in Early America," and his paper "'Such a Great Noise in the World': Schuyler's Mine and the Response in the Middle Colonies, 1719–1729," presented at the Transformation of Philadelphia Project, Philadelphia Center for Early American Studies, Mar. 20, 1989. See also Collamer M. Abbott, "Colonial Copper Mines," *WMQ* 27 (1970), 293; Leventhal, *In the Shadow of the Enlightenment,* 224–5.

80. James Steel to Isaac Taylor, Sept. 8, 1722, Taylor Papers, vol. 14, #2980, Historical Society of Pennsylvania, cited in Bodle, "'Such a Great Noise,'" 21.

81. Louis B. Wright, ed., *The Prose Works of William Byrd of Westover . . .* (Cambridge, Mass., 1966), 408.

82. Bodle, "'Such a Great Noise,'" 55, 57, 47.

83. William Lincoln, *The History of Worcester, Massachusetts . . .* (Worcester, 1837), 353–4.

84. Bodle, "'Such a Great Noise,'" 47–8.

85. Sachse, *The German Pietists,* 161–6. Printing formed another link between New London and the Delaware Valley. John Rogers had some of his tracts published in Philadelphia, which was the center for the republication of the writings of the English Seekers before they began to be published in New London late in the eighteenth century.

86. *Chronicon Ephratense,* 176–7; Sachse, *The German Sectarians,* 2:95–113; Alderfer, *The Ephrata Commune,* 100–1.

87. Goen, *Revivalism and Separatism,* 150–1.

88. William G. McLoughlin, "Free Love, Immortalism, and Perfectionism in Cumberland, Rhode Island, 1748–1768," *Rhode Island History* 33 (1974), 67–85; *Extracts from the Itineraries of Ezra Stiles and Other Miscellanies of Ezra Stiles,* ed. Franklin B. Dexter (New Haven, 1916), 418; Clarke Garrett,

Spirit Possession and Popular Religion: From the Camisards to the Shakers (Baltimore, 1987), 134–9; Goen, *Revivalism and Separatism*, 200–2; Howard Finney, *Finney–Phinney Families in America* (Richmond, 1957), 9, 17, 18, 19, 38, 85.

89. Stiles, *Itineraries*, 418; see Garrett, *Spirit Possession*, 137.
90. Genealogical letter written by Fanny Young Murray, sister of Brigham Young, to her brother Phinehas Howe Young, Jan. 1, 1845, loaned to the Genealogical Association for microfilming by Mildred A. Clark, 1962, Film 0281261, LDS Family History Center, Salt Lake City. Quote from p. 16. Hereafter cited as Fanny Young Murray letter. This letter is also cited in Rebecca Cornwall and Richard F. Palmer, "The Religious and Family Background of Brigham Young," *BYUS* 18 (1978), 286–310.
91. Clifford S. Shipton, ed., *Sibley's Harvard Graduates* (Cambridge, Mass., 1951), 8:257; Stiles, *Itineraries*, 418; C. J. F. Binney, *The History and Genealogy of the Prentice or Prentiss Family . . .* (Boston, 1852), 22–4, 33; Caleb Butler, *History of the Town of Groton* (Boston, 1848), 256n.
92. Henry F. Bishop, *Historical Sketch of Lisbon, Connecticut, from 1786 to 1900* (New York, 1903), 16–17; Garrett, *Spirit Possession*, 134–5.
93. John S. Wood, *The Wood Family Index* (Germantown, Md., 1966), 114, 261, 354, 411; Francis M. Caulkins, *History of Norwich, Connecticut* (New London[?], 1874), 441; Goen, *Revivalism and Separatism*, 84; Barnes Frisbie, *The History of Middletown, Vermont . . .* (Rutland, Vt., 1867), 44–6.
94. Frisbie, *Middletown*, 44–6, 52–3, 56; *Vermont American*, May 7, 1828; Quinn, *Early Mormonism*, 30–2, 84–90; J. H. French, *Gazetteer of the State of New York . . .* (New York, 1860), 357–8.

3. Something of Our Ancestors

1. "A Family Meeting in Nauvoo: Minutes of a Meeting of the Richards and Young Families Held in Nauvoo, Ill., Jan. 8, 1845," *Utah Genealogical and Historical Magazine* 11 (1920), 105.
2. See works cited in note 4, Preface.
3. Formative works on Mormonism that stress history and cultural continuity rather than environment include Whitney R. Cross, *The Burned-over District* (New York, 1950), 138–50; David B. Davis, "The New England Origins of Mormonism," *NEQ* 26 (1953), 147–68; and Hansen, *Quest for Empire*, 3–24. For historical interpretations that emphasize the broader circumstances of familial memory and continuity, see Natalie Z. Davis, "Ghosts, Kin, and Progeny: Some Features of Family Life in Early Modern France," *Daedelus* 106 (1977), 87–114; Bertram Wyatt-Brown, "The 'Family Arrow in Time': An Evangelical Case History," in *Yankee Saints and Southern Sinners* (Baton Rouge, 1985); and Ronald Hoffman, "The Carrolls: Princes of Eli, Planters of Maryland," manuscript in preparation.

4. Daniel Scott Smith, "'All in Some Degree Related to Each Other': A Demographic and Comparative Resolution of the Anomaly of New England Kinship," *American Historical Review* 94 (1989), 44–79; David H. Fischer, *Albion's Seed: Four British Folkways in America* (New York, 1989).

5. Quotation from Robert Gross, *The Minutemen and Their World* (New York, 1976), 71. See also Fred Anderson, *A People's Army: Massachusetts Soldiers in the Seven Years' War* (Chapel Hill, 1984), 42–4; Barbara R. Dailey, "Root and Branch: New England's Religious Radicals and Their Transatlantic Community, 1600–1660" (Ph.D. diss., Boston University, 1988); Gerald F. Moran, "Religious Renewal, Puritan Tribalism, and the Family in Seventeenth-Century Milford, Connecticut," *WMQ* 36 (1979), 236–54; and especially David Cressy, *Coming Over: Migration and Communication between England and New England in the Seventeenth Century* (New York, 1987), 178–90, 213–34, 263–91; and David Cressy, "Kinship and Kin Interaction in Early Modern England," *Past and Present* 113 (1986), 38–70.

6. Here it must be emphasized that much of what follows is speculative. The early Mormon families emerged from very obscure backgrounds, and it is striking how much we do know about them. What we know, however, is often situational and circumstantial: whom they married, something of their religious affiliations, a few fragmentary pieces of life history, and a certain amount about the communities in which they lived. The reconstruction from this evidence presented in this chapter often required some speculation and inference. In cases such as these the historian can only present an interpretation of recurring patterns. For a discussion of this problem, and of a family in circumstances not far from that of many of the early Mormons, see Paul E. Johnson, "The Modernization of Mayo Greenleaf Patch: Land, Family, and Marginality in New England, 1766–1818," *NEQ* 55 (1982), 488–516, esp. 489–90.

7. Joseph Bill [Packer], *A Journal of the Life and Travels of Joseph Bill Packer* (Hartford and Albany, 1773), 6.

8. This point was first made by Marvin S. Hill, in "The Shaping of the Mormon Mind in New England and New York," *BYUS* 9 (1969), 351–72; most recently it has been developed in Vogel, *Religious Seekers*. For the new denominations, see Stephen S. Marini, *The Radical Sects of Revolutionary New England* (Cambridge, Mass., 1982); and Nathan O. Hatch, *The Democratization of American Christianity* (New Haven, 1989).

9. Hill, "The Shaping of the Mormon Mind," 354–7; Hill, *Quest for Refuge*, 13–14; Arrington, *Brigham Young*, 21–2; Rebecca Cornwall and Richard F. Palmer, "The Religious and Family Background of Brigham Young," *BYUS* 18 (1978), 296–310; Hill, *Joseph Smith*, 62, 101, 152; Joseph Smith, "History," 1:8, an extract published with the *Book of Mormon*.

10. Leonard A. Morrison and Stephen P. Sharples, *History of the Kimball Family in America . . .* (Boston, 1897), 90, 166, 313; Kimball, *Heber C. Kimball*, 13–15.

11. Breck England, *The Life and Thought of Orson Pratt* (Salt Lake City, 1985),

21–3; Parley P. Pratt, *Autobiography of Parley P. Pratt* . . . (Salt Lake City, 1938; repr., 1985), 30–1; Vogel, *Religious Seekers*, 37–9; Hill, *Quest for Refuge*, 1–17; Thomas G. Alexander, *Things of Heaven and Earth: The Life and Times of Wilford Woodruff* (Salt Lake City, 1991), 18; Cook, *The Revelations of the Prophet Joseph Smith*, 80–2, 102.

12. This point is made in different ways in Cross, *The Burned-over District*, 145; Davis, "The New England Origins of Mormonism"; and Kenneth Winn, *Exiles in a Land of Liberty* (Chapel Hill, 1989), esp. 40–62.

13. Here I rely upon Theodore D. Bozeman, *To Live Ancient Lives* (Chapel Hill, 1988).

14. Vogel, *Religious Seekers*, 37, quoting Alexander Campbell, *Memoirs of Alexander Campbell Embracing a View of the Origin, Progress and Principles of the Religious Reformation Which He Advocated* (Philadelphia, 1880), 2:346. Vogel's book is an extended analysis of the distinction between biblical primitivism and literal restorationism (Seekerism). See also Shipps, *Mormonism*, 67–84; Richard T. Hughes and C. Leonard Allan, *Illusions of Innocence* (Chicago, 1988), 133–53, 170–87; Jan Shipps, "The Reality of the Restoration and the Restoration Ideal in the Mormon Tradition," in Richard T. Hughes, ed., *The American Quest for the Primitive Church* (Urbana, 1988), 181–95.

15. The discussion that follows is based upon an effort to trace several hundred Mormon patrinomial family lines back from the 1830s and 1840s to their date and point of immigration into the colonies or the United States. The genealogical resources used were the LDS American Family Group Sheets (AFGS) on deposit at the New England Historic Genealogical Society (NEHGS), the computerized Family History Files at the LDS Family History Center in Salt Lake City, and various other resources available at the NEHGS. The names checked were those listed in three contexts: persons baptized in 1830 (Larry C. Porter, "A Study of the Origins of the Church of Jesus Christ of Latter-day Saints in the States of New York and Pennsylvania, 1816–1831" [Ph.D. diss., Brigham Young University, 1971], 96–103, 198–222, 253–68), persons involved at the General Conferences in Ohio between June 6 and October 25, 1831 (Donald Q. Cannon and Lyndon W. Cook, eds., *Far West Record: Minutes of The Church of Jesus Christ of Latter-day Saints, 1830–1844* [Salt Lake City, 1983], 6–19), those persons given offices in the church in 1841 (DC 124:123–42), and those persons known to have been given temple endowments, sealings, and second anointing before Joseph Smith's assassination (David J. Buerger, " 'The Fulness of the Priesthood': The Second Anointing in Latter-day Saint Theology and Practice," *Dialogue* 16 [Spring 1983], 23). This sample apparently captures all of the most important early Mormon leadership, but it barely scratches the surface of the overall Mormon membership during these years. I only attempted to trace the patrinomial lines systematically for these names, an effort that produced complete information for only fifty-three families.

16.   *Proto-Mormon Families Arriving during the Great Migration*

	Proto-Mormon families arrived by 1650	Estimated population in 1650	Ratio of population per family
Orthodox Massachusetts and Connecticut	20[a]	17,070	856
Southeastern New England	7	3,230	461

[a]Includes the Cowderies, who moved from Reading, Massachusetts, through Connecticut Valley to East Haddam, Connecticut, by the 1730s.
Sources: Populations from Douglas R. McManis, *Colonial New England: A Historical Geography* (New York, 1975), 68 (Sutherland estimates), with an estimated total population of 930 in the New London area in 1650, based on evidence cited in Jackson T. Main, *Society and Economy in Colonial Connecticut* (Princeton, 1985), 13n.

17.   Philip F. Gura, *A Glimpse of Sion's Glory* (Middletown, Conn., 1984), 35; Ronald W. Walker, "Martin Harris: Mormonism's Early Convert," *Dialogue* 19 (Winter 1986), 29–43.

18.   On the Hoosac Valley, see Grace Greylock Niles, *The Hoosac Valley: Its History and Legends* (New York, 1912), 184–270, 442; Stephen Wright, *History of the Shaftsbury Baptist Association, from 1781 to 1853* (Troy, 1853), 371, 382, 394–6, 412–13, 422, 424, 432–3, 438, 453, 457–64; on Farmington, see R. P. Smith, *Historical and Statistic Gazetteer of New York State* (Syracuse, 1860), 496; on Eliot Ward, see Vogel, *Religious Seekers*, 15. John and Tyla Stafford, son and grandson of David Stafford, were living in the towns of Hoosick and Cambridge respectively in 1790 and 1800. As of the 1810 census there were five Stafford families in Farmington and one in Palmyra.

19.   Valerie Dyer Giorgi, *Colver–Culver Genealogy as Descended from Edward Colver of Groton, Connecticut, to the Thirteen Generations in America* (Santa Maria, Calif., 1984), 16–18, 36–9, 62, 97–9; Charles R. Stark, *Groton, Connecticut, 1705–1905* (Stonington, 1922), 126–7, 219–20; *Chronicon Ephratense*, 176; Nathan Culver, *A Very Remarkable Account of the Vision of Nathan Culver. Late of New Town (New York) . . .* (Boston, 1795), 7. At least four other early Mormons, including William W. Phelps, were born in Morris County, New Jersey. For Aaron Culver see Porter, "A Study of the Origins of the Church of Latter-day Saints in the States of New York and Pennsylvania," 202.

20.   Mitchell J. Hunt, *The Mysterious Beebe Families of Beebe, Vermont–Quebec . . .* (Willow Grove, Pa., 1979); and Orval O. Calhoun, *800 Years of Colquhoun, Colhoun, Calhoun, and Cahoon Family History in Ireland, Scotland, England, United States of America, Australia, and Canada* (Baltimore, 1982), 2:124–30, 3:65–7.

21. Mabel Young Sanborn, "The Ancestry of President Brigham Young," *Utah Genealogical and Historical Magazine* 20 (1929), 99–105; Cornwall and Palmer, "The Religious and Family Background of Brigham Young," 288–9. On religious culture in the seventeenth-century fishing communities north of Boston, see Christine L. Heyrman, *Commerce and Culture: The Maritime Communities of Colonial Massachusetts, 1690–1750* (New York, 1984), 29–51, 207–30.

22. Pulsipher information from AFGS. On Mack, see Sylvanus Hayward, *History of the Town of Gilsum, New Hampshire, from 1752 to 1879* (Manchester, 1881), 357; on Goddard, see Josiah H. Temple, *History of Framingham, Massachusetts, early known as Danforth's Farms, 1640–1880, with a Genealogical Register* (Framingham, 1887), 195–6, 211–12, 566. Because they were matrilineal forebears of the Smiths and Youngs, the Macks and Goddards were excluded from the sample discussed above.

23. Quinn, *Early Mormonism*, 193; information on the Rich family from AFGS. See also David S. Lovejoy, *Religious Enthusiasm in the New World* (Cambridge, Mass., 1985), 157; *Seventh Day Baptists in Europe and America* (Plainfield, N.J., 1910), 1:129–30.

24. James B. Allen, *Trials of Discipleship: The Story of William Clayton, a Mormon* (Urbana, 1987), 16–18.

25. D. Michael Quinn, ed., "The First Months of Mormonism: A Contemporary View by Rev. Diedrich Willers [Letter, 18 June 1830]," *New York History* 54 (1973), 331.

26. John H. Evans, *Joseph Smith: An American Prophet* (New York, 1946), 20–1; Sidney Perley, *History of Boxford, Essex County, Massachusetts* (Boxford, 1880), 32–5; George F. Dow, "Records of the Congregational Church in Topsfield," *HCTHS* 14 (1909), 6. Probate documents in the Essex County, Massachusetts, Probate Records: Robert Smith Probate, docket no. 25729; Samuel Smith Probate, docket no. 25744. Samuel was born in Boxford on January 26, 1666; he would have been twenty-six in September of 1692, when he was identified as "Samuell Smith of Boxford about 25 yers" in the records of the Mary Easty case (Boyer and Nissenbaum, eds., *SWP*, 301–2). See also Joseph F. Smith, "Asahel Smith of Topsfield, with some Account of the Smith Family," *HCTHS* 8 (1902), 87–8; Mary A. S. Anderson, *The Ancestry and Posterity of Joseph Smith and Emma Hale* (Independence, Mo., 1929), 55; *Vital Records of Topsfield*, 193.

27. Boyer and Nissenbaum, eds., *SWP*, 301–2. The original manuscript of the Asael Smith letter to Jacob Towne is in the Towne Family Papers, at the Essex Institute, Salem, Massachusetts, and is reproduced in Richard L. Anderson, *Joseph Smith's New England Heritage* (Salt Lake City, 1971), 118–23.

28. Anderson, *Ancestry and Posterity*, 54.

29. Boyer and Nissenbaum, eds., *SWP*, 287–304. Samuel's sister Amy married Joseph Towne, a nephew of Mary Easty, on August 10, 1687.

30. In Robert's words, Thomas Smith had left home "as soone as he was abel to doe any thing . . . [and had gone to live] with his grandfather Frainch and never came to mee to help mee in my old age" (Robert Smith will, Essex

County Probate Records, docket no. 25729). It may also have been significant that the French family of Ipswich had been prominent signers of a statement of character for Mary Bradbury, an accused witch in Salisbury (Boyer and Nissenbaum, eds., *SWP*, 119–20).

31. Location of land determined from George F. Dow, *History of Topsfield, Massachusetts* (Topsfield, 1940), 69, 70, 116–17. Samuel Smith I will, Essex County Probate Records, docket no. 25744; *Vital Records of Topsfield*.

32. These controversies can be followed in George F. Dow, comp., "Court Records Relating to Topsfield," *HCTHS* 23 (1918), 67–71; Benjamin A. Gould, *The Family of Zaccheus Gould of Topsfield* (Lynn, 1895), 30–1, 34, 40–2, 44–5; Dow, *History of Topsfield*, 25, 30–1, 54–5, 61–3, 320–42; Perley, *The History of Boxford*, 49; Boyer and Nissenbaum, eds., *SWP*, 221–3, 287–304, 583–608, 814; Suffolk Files, files 45498, 47335, 49137; George F. Dow, "Records of the Congregational Church in Topsfield," *HCTHS* 14 (1909), 15–16; Edward S. Towne, comp., "Towne Family Papers," *HCTHS* 18 (1913), 64–96; *Vital Records of Topsfield;* and Edwin E. Towne, comp., *The Descendants of William Towne . . .* (Newtonville, Mass., 1901).

33. Temple, *Framingham*, 195–6, 208–15, 565–7, 580; Edward Goddard, *A Brief Account of the Formation and Settlement of the 2nd Church and Congregation in Framingham* (Boston, 1750).

34. *Extracts from the Itineraries of Ezra Stiles and Other Miscellanies of Ezra Stiles,* ed. Franklin B. Dexter (New Haven, 1916), 418.

35. The Smith–Singletary connection was reconstructed from Lou Singletary-Bedford, *Genealogy of the Singletary–Curtis Families* (New York, 1907), 5–11; Temple, *Framingham*, 700–1; Abraham Hammatt, "The Early Inhabitants of Ipswich, Mass., 1633–1700," in *The Hammatt Papers* (Ipswich, 1880), 1:333–4; and the *Vital Records* for Ipswich and Hopkinton. Nathaniel Smith was apparently no relation to the Topsfield Smiths.

36. Fanny Young Murray letter, 17; for full citation, see Chapter 2, note 90.

37. Ibid., 18–22.

38. Ibid., 22.

39. This episode can be dated because the twins mentioned, Samuel and Edward, were born April 16, 1759, and Edward Goddard sold his property in Framingham on February 18, 1760. For these points, see Temple, *Framingham*, 213, 566–7.

40. John P. Demos, *Entertaining Satan* (New York, 1984), 43–4.

41. "A Family Meeting in Nauvoo," 105. Eight pages are missing from the Fanny Young Murray letter (32–9). They may have included details about Susannah, which appear to start on p. 30.

42. Demos, *Entertaining Satan*, 387–94; Charles Upham, *Salem Witchcraft*, 2 vols. (Boston, 1867), 2:513; Dow, *History of Topsfield*, 326; Clark Jillson, *Green Leaves from Whitingham, Vermont: A History of the Town* (Worcester, 1894), 111–12; Hayward, *Gilsum*, 162–3; George F. Willey, *Willey's Book of Nutfield* (Derry Depot, N.H., 1895), 284–5; Charles H. Bell, *The History of the Town of Exeter, New Hampshire* (Exeter, 1888), 411ff.; Barnes Frisbie, *The History of Middletown, Vermont . . .* (Rutland, Vt., 1867), 43–

64; Alan Taylor, "The Early Republic's Supernatural Economy," *American Quarterly* 38 (1986), 6–34.

43. Pomeroy Tucker, *The Origin, Rise, and Progess of Mormonism* (New York, 1867), 50 (quoted in Walker, "Martin Harris," 34–5); Quinn, ed., "The First Months of Mormonism," 333; Fayette Lapham, "The Mormons," *Historical Magazine*, 2d ser., 2 (1870), 308. See Quinn, *Early Mormonism*, 27–52, 193–200, for extensive detail; and Bushman, *Joseph Smith*, 70–7.

44. Newell and Avery, *Mormon Enigma*, 2; Bushman, *Joseph Smith*, 54; Hill, *Joseph Smith*, 109; Brodie, *No Man Knows My History*, 86; Mormon 1:19, 2:10; 3 Nephi 21:16; DC 63:17, 76:103, 84:65–72.

45. See, e.g., Mark 16:17–18, Acts 28:3. I am obliged to Jan Shipps for this point.

46. *The Literary Diary of Ezra Stiles*, ed. Franklin B. Dexter, 3 vols. (New York, 1901), 3:345, 348; Ronald S. Wilkinson, "New England's Last Alchemists," *Ambix* 10 (1962), 136; Calhoun, *800 Years of . . . Cahoon Family History*, 2:129; Susan Woodruff Abbott, *Woodruff Genealogy: Descendants of Mathew Woodruff of Farmington, Connecticut* (Milford, 1963), 9, 19, 215.

47. Kimball, *Heber C. Kimball*, 179–80; Arrington, *Brigham Young*, 311.

48. Sidney Perley, "Mining and Quarrying, and Smelting of Ores, In Boxford," *EIHC* 25 (1888), 295–305; Paul Boyer and Stephen Nissenbaum, *Salem Possessed* (Cambridge, Mass., 1974), 123–6, 196; Boyer and Nissenbaum, eds., *SWP*, 437–9, 451–3, 805–18. Simon Bradstreet's son Dudley was suspected of witchcraft in 1692 but never accused. See Sarah L. Bailey, *Historical Sketches of Andover* (Boston, 1880), 130–1, 199.

49. Perley, *History of Boxford*, 49–50, 63–5, 70; Perley, "Mining and Quarrying," 298–9; Dow, *History of Topsfield*, 300.

50. Evans, *Joseph Smith*, 20–1; Anderson, *Joseph Smith's New England Heritage*, 92–5, 193 n. 136; Dow, *History of Topsfield*, 363; Samuel Smith I will, Essex County Probate Records, docket no. 25744.

51. Herbert Leventhal, *In the Shadow of the Enlightenment* (New York, 1976), 223–30; James Thacher, "Observations on the Natural Production of Iron Ores . . . ," *Collections of the Massachusetts Historical Society*, 1st ser., 9 (1804), 253–7; on bog iron in Boxford, see Perley, "Mining and Quarrying," 297.

52.

Topsfield Church Admissions: 1729–1744

Family	Date	Owned covenant	Full membership	Total
Smith	1729–40	3	2 (40.0%)	5
	1741–4	0	0	0
Towne	1729–40	10	6 (37.5%)	16
	1741–4	4	4 (50.0%)	8
Gould	1729–40	6	6 (50.0%)	12
	1741–4	2	9 (81.8%)	11

Source: Dow, "Records of the Congregational Church in Topsfield," 34–45.

53. Brodie, *No Man Knows My History,* 27–8; David D. Hall, *Worlds of Wonder, Days of Judgment* (New York, 1989), 15–16.

54. Samuel Smith II wrote the Reverend John Emerson's will in 1772, and in turn one Gould witnessed Smith's will in 1785.

55. Smith, "Asahel Smith," 88; Perley, *History of Boxford,* 34–5; Anderson, *Joseph Smith's New England Heritage,* 91.

56. Samuel's company at Lake George was commanded by Israel Herrick, a distant cousin of the Herrick who would witness Samuel's father's will nine years later (Dow, *History of Topsfield,* 157–62, 363). The other early cooper-ing families in Topsfield were Easty, Knight, Wilde, and Cummings.

57. Perley, *History of Boxford,* 59–61; Perley, "Mining and Quarrying," 295–311; Richard Dunn, *Puritans and Yankees: The Winthrop Dynasty of New England, 1630–1717* (Princeton, 1962), 80–96.

58. G. Warren Towne, "The Topsfield Copper Mines," *HCTHS* 2 (1896), 73–81; Dow, *History of Topsfield,* 157–62, 378–86; Gould, *Family of Zaccheus Gould,* 35; Samuel Smith II will, Essex County Probate Records, docket no. 25750; Anderson, *Joseph Smith's New England Heritage,* 91.

59. Marini, *Radical Sects,* 67, 107–9; Bushman, *Joseph Smith,* 26–9. Charlotte Irwin, "Pietist Origins of American Universalism" (M.A. thesis, Tufts Univer-sity, 1966), provides a very detailed analysis of the Pietist roots of American Universalism through 1805.

60. D. A. Massey, ed. and comp., *History of Freemasonry in Danvers, Mass., from September, 1778, to July, 1896* (Peabody, Mass., 1896), 11–20, 29–30, 32, 34, 41, 49, 54; E. J. V. Huiginn, *Freemasonry in Beverley, 1779–1924* (Beverley, Mass., 1924), 11.

61. Anderson, *Joseph Smith's New England Heritage,* 91–101; Towne, "The Topsfield Copper Mines," 76–9 (quotation from 77); Hamilton Child, *Ga-zetteer of Orange County, Vt., 1762–1888* (Syracuse, N.Y., 1888), 13ff.; the Smith mining covenant of 1825, originally published in the Susquehanna *Journal,* Mar. 20, 1880, is reprinted in John P. Walker, ed., *Dale Morgan on Early Mormonism* (Salt Lake City, 1986), 323–6. Another roughly contem-porary mining covenant, signed by fourteen men from Groton and Pepperell, Massachusetts, and dated November 6, 1783, is located in the Lawrence Family Papers, Lyman Robbins Collection, Lawrence Library, Pepperell, Massachusetts.

62. Towne, "The Topsfield Copper Mines," 76–8; Towne, comp., "Towne Fam-ily Papers," 20–1; Leventhal, *In the Shadow of the Enlightenment,* 223–30; F. Sherwood Taylor, *The Alchemists* (New York, 1949), 11–16.

63. The language Asael Smith used in his 1799 "will" written for the guidance of his wife and children was again suggestive: they were to "hold union and order a precious jewel." See Anderson, *Joseph Smith's New England Heri-tage,* 119, 128. The language about the "stone cut out of the mountain" is from Daniel 2:31–45; T. Wilson Hayes, *Winstanley the Digger* (Cambridge, Mass., 1979), 241, discusses its alchemical connotations.

64. Gura, *A Glimpse of Sion's Glory,* 4, 14; Arthur J. Worrall, *Quakers in the Colonial Northeast* (Hanover, N.H., 1980), 28–9, 69.

65. Anderson, *Ancestry and Posterity,* 57–9.

66. On soil quality in Lyme, with comparative data for all of Connecticut, see Bruce C. Daniels, *The Connecticut Town* (Middletown, Conn., 1979), 186–9. On population, land distribution, and class in Lyme, see Christopher Collier, "Saybrook and Lyme: Secular Settlements in a Puritan Commonwealth," and Jackson T. Main, "The Economic and Social Structure of Early Lyme," in George J. Willauer, Jr., ed., *A Lyme Miscellany, 1776–1976* (Middletown, Conn.), 9–47.

67. Jean C. Burr, *Lyme Records, 1667–1730: A Literal Transcription* (Stonington, Conn., 1968), 95, 103.

68. Anderson, *Joseph Smith's New England Heritage,* 5–12; Solomon Mack, *A Narrative of the Life of Solomon Mack . . .* (Windsor, Vt., [1811]), in Anderson, ibid., 34–40. Solomon Mack reported his date of birth as 1735, but the Lyme Vital Records give 1732.

69. Collier, "Saybrook and Lyme," 13–15.

70. William G. McLoughlin, *New England Dissent* (Cambridge, Mass., 1971), 1:279.

71. C. C. Goen, *Revivalism and Separatism in New England* (New Haven, 1962), 17–31, 68–90, 302–9; Peter S. Onuf, "New Lights in New London: A Group Portrait of the Separatists," *WMQ* 37 (1980), 627–43; Harry S. Stout and Peter Onuf, "James Davenport and the Great Awakening in New London," *Journal of American History* 71 (1983), 556–78.

72. On Rogers, see James S. Rogers, comp., *James Rogers of New London* (Boston, 1902), 14–16, 45; *The First Hundred Years: Pawtucket Seventh-Day Baptist Church, Westerly, Rhode Island, 1840–1940* (Westerly, 1940), 283. On Wightman, see Stark, *Groton,* 127. On Gorton, see Apelos Gorton, *The Life and Times of Samuel Gorton . . .* (Philadelphia, 1907), 186–7; and McLoughlin, *New England Dissent,* 1:260–1.

73. *The Literary Diary of Ezra Stiles,* 3:266–7.

74. Reported in the New London *Weekly Oracle,* Aug. 12, 1797, and recorded in Charles Evans, *American Bibliography,* 13 vols. (Chicago and Worcester, 1903–55), 11:277; there are apparently no surviving copies of this reprint of Reeve's *Spiritual Treatise.* On Walden's earlier life, see *A Narrative of the Travels of Isaac Walden, at the Time he was in the King's Services . . .* ([New London], 1773), 6–12.

75. Burr, *Lyme Records,* 119, 131–2.

76. Anderson, *Joseph Smith's New England Heritage,* 31.

77. Will of John Mack, Feb. 13, 1721, Colchester Probate District Records, docket no. 3349. On pious clauses, see Margaret Spufford, *Contrasting Communities: English Villagers in the Sixteenth and Seventeenth Centuries* (New York, 1974), 320–44.

78. 1721 North Lyme Petition, CEA 3:42, 44. Petitions regarding HadLyme Parish, 1723–42: CEA 2:269, 270, 273, 280, 282, 283, 285, 291; 3:47; 6:367, 370. Samuel Selden, guardian of Ebenezer Mack (son of John Jr.), had shifted from the north Lyme group to the HadLyme petitioners, as did John Comstock, one of the witnesses to John Mack Sr.'s will. Of the witnesses to John

Mack Jr.'s will in 1734, George Beckwith was the minister of the north Lyme church, and Peter Pearson signed one of the north Lyme petitions (CEA 3:47). See John Mack Jr.'s will, 1734, New London Probate District Records, docket no. 3350.

79. East Lyme Petition, 1718, CEA 3:25a. Chesterfield Parish Petition, 1764, CEA 13:140–1, 146. On the rise of dissent in this region in general, see Richard L. Bushman, *From Puritan to Yankee: Character and the Social Order in Connecticut, 1690–1765* (Cambridge, 1967), 54–72, 165.

80. Clara J. Stone, *Genealogy of the Descendants of Jasper Griffing* (Guilford, Conn., 1981), 5–7; Burr, *Lyme Records*, 103.

81. 1743 North Lyme Separate Petition, CEA 3:43. With John Mack Jr. dead, and Ebenezer Mack "incompetent," the only Mack signer was Jonathan Mack, Solomon Mack's uncle. On New London, see Stout and Onuf, "James Davenport and the Great Awakening in New London." I am grateful to Peter Onuf for his loan of the manuscripts relating to the New London Separates.

82. Petition of Solomon Paine and 331 others, May 2, 1748, CEA 10:29a–c. See McLoughlin, *New England Dissent*, 1:390; Goen, *Revivalism and Separatism*, 197.

83. Goen, *Revivalism and Separatism*, 78, 252, 264–5; 303–4; Stiles, *Itineraries*, 265–7; Silas L. Blake, *The Separates, or Strict Congregationalists of New England* (Boston, 1902), 182; D. Hamilton Hurd, *History of New London County* (Philadelphia, 1882), 562–3; McLoughlin, *New England Dissent*, 1:448–50.

84. Mack, *Narrative*, in Anderson, *Joseph Smith's New England Heritage*, 35.

85. Mack, *Narrative*, in Anderson, *Joseph Smith's New England Heritage*, 36–40; see also Bushman, *Joseph Smith*, 12–13.

86. Anderson, *Ancestry and Posterity*, 197–202; *History of Middlesex County, Connecticut, with Biographical Sketches of Its Prominent Men* (New York, 1884), 282–4, 296–8; Anderson, *Joseph Smith's New England Heritage*, 26, 177–8.

87. Anderson, *Ancestry and Posterity*, 239–44; William H. Fuller, *Genealogy of some of the Descendants of Edward Fuller . . .* (Palmer, Mass., 1908), 1:24–37, 43; William H. Fuller, *Genealogy of some of the Descendants of Capt. Matthew Fuller . . .* (Palmer, Mass., 1914), 3:12–17, 26, 63.

88. Clifford K. Shipton, ed., *Sibley's Harvard Graduates* (Boston, 1956), 9:338–40; *History of Middlesex County*, 296, 298; Franklin B. Dexter, *Biographical Sketches of the Graduates of Yale College . . .* (New York, 1885), 1:559–60; Louise Beebe Wilder, *Lucius Beebe of Wakefield and Sylenda Morris Beebe, His Wife, and Their Forbears and Descendants* (New York, 1930), 41–6. See also Dexter, *Biographical Sketches*, 2:573–4.

89. East Haddam, Connecticut, 2nd Congregational Church and Ecclesiastical Society, known as Millington Church and Society, Records, 1733–1931, Connecticut State Archives, Hartford, 1:19, 2:13. A Benjamin Fuller added to the church membership after 1767 and made deacon in 1778 was a very distant relation.

90. This interpretation is drawn from Bushman, *Joseph Smith*, 25; see Smith,

Biographical Sketches, 25; and Anderson, *Joseph Smith's New England Heritage,* 26–7.

91. Smith, *Biographical Sketches,* 21, 53; Bushman, *Joseph Smith,* 18; Vogel, *Religious Seekers,* 28–9.

92. Smith, *Biographical Sketches,* 25–6; see Anderson, *Joseph Smith's New England Heritage,* 63–87, for an extended discussion and different versions of Lovisa's healing vision.

93. Mack, *Narrative,* in Anderson, *Joseph Smith's New England Heritage,* 54–5; Smith, *Biographical Sketches,* 54–9, 70–1.

94. John R. Bolles and Anna B. Williams, *The Rogerenes* (Boston, 1904), 276; McLoughlin, *New England Dissent,* 1:260–1; Rogers, comp., *James Rogers of New London,* 41–2; John C. Cooley, *Rathbone Genealogy* (Syracuse, 1898), 708; Stone, *Jasper Griffing,* 9, 17. For Abigail Fox, see Smith, *Ancestry and Posterity,* 58; and Diane D. Ivins and Aileen S. Freeman, *The Fox Genealogy* (n.p., 1982), 208–10.

95. Wilder, *Lucius Beebe,* 30–2, 34, 41–4.

96. Rogers, comp., *James Rogers of New London,* 16–23, 42. Sarah Cole is identified as a Singing Quaker in Peter Pratt, *The Prey Taken by the Strong, or an Historical Account, of the Recovery of One from the Dangerous Errors of Quakerism* (New London, 1725), 59; see Francis M. Caulkins, *History of New London,* 2d ed. (New London, 1895), 216–18.

97. Pratt, *Prey Taken by the Strong,* 53–61; F. W. Chapman, *The Pratt Family: or the Descendants of Lieut. William Pratt . . .* (Hartford, 1864), 332–4; Paul Beckwith, *The Beckwiths* (Albany, 1891), 73–6, 78, 80; Willauer, ed., *A Lyme Miscellany,* 34–5.

98. East Lyme Baptist Petition, 1766, CEA 15:281a; Dumas Malone, ed., *Dictionary of American Biography* (New York, 1935), 17:258–9; Hatch, *The Democratization of American Christianity,* 68–70, 167, 169; Brodie, *No Man Knows My History,* 22.

99. On the Gee family, see East Lyme Baptist Petition, 1766, CEA 15:281a; Hunt, *The Mysterious Beebe Families,* 17; and Lyme Vital Records. On the Pratt family see England, *Orson Pratt,* 2–4. On the Spencer family see AFGS data at NEHGS; and Edna B. Garnett, *West Stockbridge, Massachusetts* (West Stockbridge, 1974), 69.

4. A Urim Spiritual

1. Quotations from Parley P. Pratt Papers and Manuscript History of Brigham Young, Church Archives, Historical Department of the Church of Jesus Christ of Latter-day Saints, Salt Lake City, Utah, quoted in Kimball, *Heber C. Kimball,* 85.

2. Here I borrow language, with considerable license, from Mary Douglas, *Purity and Danger: An Analysis of Concepts of Pollution and Taboo* (New York, 1966), and Victor Turner, *Dramas, Fields, and Metaphors: Symbolic Action in Human Society* (Ithaca, 1974).

3. *Literary Diary of Ezra Stiles,* ed. Franklin B. Dexter (New York, 1901), 2:216.

4. Ibid., 2:173–4, 216, 3:266; Ronald Wilkinson, "New England's Last Alchemists," *Ambix* 10 (1962), 132–8.

5. Ibid., 1:56, 3:105–6, 240, 326–7, 512, 550.

6. Frances A. Yates, *The Rosicrucian Enlightenment* (London, 1972), 206–19; David Stephenson, *The Origins of Freemasonry: Scotland's Century, 1590–1710* (New York, 1988); Margaret C. Jacob, *The Radical Enlightenment: Pantheists, Freemasons, and Republicans* (London, 1981), 109–37; Marsha K. M. Schuchard, "Freemasonry, Secret Societies, and the Continuities of Occult Traditions in English Literature" (Ph.D. diss., University of Texas at Austin, 1975).

7. Jacob, *The Radical Enlightenment,* 116–25; Schuchard, "Freemasonry, Secret Societies, and the Continuities of Occult Traditions," 166ff.

8. Margaret C. Jacob, *The Newtonians and the English Revolution, 1689–1720* (Ithaca, 1976); Margaret C. Jacob, *Living the Enlightenment: Freemasons and Politics in Eighteenth-Century Europe* (New York, 1991).

9. Daniel P. Walker, *The Ancient Theology: Studies in Christian Platonism from the Fifteenth to the Eighteenth Century* (Ithaca, 1972), 231–63; Hillel Schwartz, *The French Prophets: The History of a Millenarian Group in Eighteenth-Century England* (Berkeley, 1980), 156, 280, 320; Schuchard, "Freemasonry, Secret Societies, and the Continuities of Occult Traditions," 183–7; Jacob, *The Radical Enlightenment,* 129; H. L. Haywood and James E. Craig, *A History of Freemasonry* (New York, 1927), 291.

10. John M. Roberts, *The Mythology of the Secret Societies* (New York, 1972), 31–57, 90–117; Heinrich Scheider, *Quest for Mysteries: The Masonic Background for Literature in Eighteenth-Century Germany* (Ithaca, 1947), 78–94.

11. Mary Ann Meyers, *A New World Jerusalem: The Swedenborgian Experience in Community Construction* (Westport, Conn., 1983), 21–34.

12. Robert Darnton, *Mesmerism and the End of the Enlightenment in France* (Cambridge, Mass., 1968), 3–45; Clarke Garrett, "Swedenborg and the Mystical Enlightenment in Late Eighteenth-Century England," *Journal of the History of Ideas* 45 (1984), 77–81.

13. Mackey, *An Encyclopedia of Freemasonry,* 1:68–9, 2:555–6; A. C. F. Jackson, *Rose Croix: The History of the Ancient and Accepted Rite for England and Wales* (London, 1980), 31–62; Samuel H. Baynard, *History of the Supreme Council, 33° Ancient and Accepted Scottish Rite of Freemasonry, Northern Masonic Jurisdiction of the United States of America and Its Antecedents* (Boston, 1938), 1:18–25, 129–31.

14. Clark Garrett, *Respectable Folly: Millenarians and the French Revolution in France and England* (Baltimore, 1975), 97–120, 171–223; John F. C. Harrison, *The Second Coming: Popular Millenarianism, 1780–1850* (New Brunswick, 1979), 57–85; Schuchard, "Freemasonry, Secret Societies, and the Continuities of Occult Traditions," 402–17.

15. Abigail Stickney Lyon, *Observations on Freemasonry, with a Masonic Vision.*

Addressed by a Lady in Worcester to her Female Friend (Worcester, 1798); John Stanford, *Urim and Thummim: A Discourse delivered before Hiram Lodge, No. 72 on St. John's Day, Dec. 27, 1800, at Mount Pleasant, Westchester County, New York State* (Mount Pleasant, 1800); Mouradgea d'Ohsson Ignatius, *Oriental Antiquities, and General View of the Othoman Customs, Laws, and Ceremonies . . . with the various Rites and Mysteries of the Oriental Freemasons* (Philadelphia, 1788).

16. Stephen C. Bullock, "The Ancient and Honorable Society: Freemasonry in America, 1730–1830" (Ph.D. diss., Brown University, 1986); Stephen C. Bullock, "The Revolutionary Transformation of Freemasonry, 1752–1792," *WMQ* 47 (1990), 347–69; and Stephen C. Bullock, "A Pure and Sublime System: The Appeal of Post-revolutionary Freemasonry," *Journal of the Early Republic* 9 (1989), 335–58; Thomas S. Webb, *The Freemason's Monitor; or Illustrations of Masonry: in Two Parts* (New York, 1802), 288–93.

17. See Quinn, *Early Mormonism*, 11–21.

18. Clifford K. Shipton and James E. Mooney, eds., *National Index of American Imprints through 1800*, 2 vols. (Worcester, 1969), 2:713, 815.

19. Jackson, *Rose Croix*, 104–8; Schuchard, "Freemasonry, Secret Societies, and the Continuities of Occult Traditions," 256–67; Garrett, "Swedenborg and the Mystical Enlightenment," 74–7.

20. Darnton, *Mesmerism*, 10, 62, 64, 65–6, 88–9; Robert C. Fuller, "Mesmerism and the Birth of Psychology," in Arthur Wrobel, ed., *Pseudo-science in Nineteenth-Century America* (Lexington, Ky., 1987), 205–22; *Recollections of Samuel Breck; with passages from his notebooks, 1771–1862*, ed. Henry E. Scudder (Philadelphia, 1877), 70–2, 303–4.

21. Meyers, *A New World Jerusalem*, 6–7; Schomer S. Zwelling, "Robert Carter's Journey: From Colonial Patriarch to New Nation Mystic," *American Quarterly* 38 (1986), 613–36; Gay Wilson Allen, *Waldo Emerson: A Biography* (New York, 1981), 90–1, 452–7, 576–7.

22. In general, for these themes, see Ruth Bloch, *Visionary Republic: Millennial Themes in American Thought, 1756–1800* (New York, 1985), 150–68; David Austin, *Masonry in Its Glory, or Solomon's Temple Illuminated* (East Windsor, Conn., 1799).

23. See Bloch, *Visionary Republic*, 161–8; Harrison, *The Second Coming*, 71. See also Shipton and Mooney, eds., *National Index of American Imprints*, 1:39–40, 115, 432–3, 2:719–20; *Remarkable Prophecy* (Exeter, N.H., 1794), 11; *The Whole, Genuine, and Complete Works of Flavius Josephus . . .* (New York, 1792), 9.

24. Thomas S. Webb, *The Freemason's Monitor, or Illustrations of Masonry . . .* (New York, 1802), 245–60; Yates, *The Rosicrucian Enlightenment*, 44–50; Haywood and Craig, *A History of Freemasonry*, 246–7; Bernard Fay, *Revolution and Freemasonry, 1680–1800* (Boston, 1925), 202–3. [William Morgan], *Illustrations of Masonry . . .* (Cincinnati, 1827), 120–2, has a somewhat different account of the legend of Enoch.

25. Webb, *The Freemason's Monitor*, 199; Jeremy Cross, *The True Masonic Chart, or Hieroglyphic Monitor . . .* (New Haven, 1824), 125.

26. The parallels between the story of the recovery of the *Book of Mormon* and the Royal Arch mythology were first discussed by L. H. Adamson, "The Treasure of the Widow's Son," unpublished paper, n.d., University of Utah, and then by Reed Durham, "Is There No Help for the Widow's Son?" unpublished presidential address presented at the Mormon History Association, April 20, 1974. See also Robert N. Hullinger, *Mormon Answer to Skepticism: Why Joseph Smith Wrote the Book of Mormon* (St. Louis, 1980), 100–19.

27. Albany Grand Lodge of Perfection, Transcribed Minute Book, 1767–74, 1821–5, and 1841–5, at MONH; Baynard, *History of the Supreme Council, 33°*, 1:25–31; Jackson, *Rose Croix*, 46–62; Mackey, *An Encyclopedia of Freemasonry*, 1:278, 2:492.

28. Vernon Stauffer, *New England and the Bavarian Illuminati* (New York, 1918).

29. Baynard, *History of the Supreme Council, 33°*, 1:56–67, 80–97, 97–101, 183–6; Albert G. Mackey, *The History of Freemasonry in South Carolina* (1861; repr., Charleston, 1936), 505–30; *The Supreme Council, 33°: Mother Council of the World, Ancient and Accepted Scottish Rite of Freemasonry, Southern Jurisdiction, U.S.A.* (Louisville, Ky., 1931), 49–58, 132–48.

30. David Bernard, *Light on Masonry: A Collection of all of the Most Important Documents on the Subject of Speculative Freemasonry . . .* (Utica, 1829).

31. William Hutchinson, *The Spirit of Freemasonry* (London, 1775; repr., Wellingborough, N.H., 1987), 3–9.

32. Webb, *Freemason's Monitor*, 39–40.

33. Hutchinson, *The Spirit of Freemasonry*, appendix, 6–7; Webb, *Freemason's Monitor*, 260.

34. *The Voice of the Midnight Cry. The Little Book The Arcanum Opened, containing the Fundamentals of the Most Pure and Ancient Theology* (Cincinnati, 1801), 2, 3, 5, 24. The text includes an internal date of September 1799 and is dedicated to a John Baily of Kentucky. See also *The Urim or Halcyon Cabala; Containing the Fundamental Principles of the Halcyon Church of Christ in Columbia; Otherwise known as the Columbian Church, In Defense of Genuine Christianity and in Opposition to "Lo Here and Lo There"; consisting of one Supreme Object and Seven Leading Topics* (Cincinnati, 1801). I am grateful to Jon Butler for these references. Drew Cayton has suggested to me that a Christian minister named Abel M. Sargent, who published *The Halcyon Itinerary and True Millenium* in Marietta in 1807, was probably the leader of the Cincinnati Halcyon church. On Sargent, see Nathan Hatch, *The Democratization of American Christianity* (New Haven, 1989), 75–6.

35. Vermont *American*, May 7, 1828, p. 2.

36. Charles H. Bell, *The History of the Town of Exeter, New Hampshire* (Exeter, 1888), 412–14.

37. Brigham Young, July 19, 1857, JD 5:55; Quinn, *Early Mormonism*, 82–4, 89–97; Brodie, *No Man Knows My History*, 430–1.

38. Barnes Frisbie, *The History of Middletown, Vermont . . .* (Rutland, Vt., 1867), 56–9. There are several competing theories as to the identity of this

counterfeiter. In Frisbie's account the counterfeiter is identified as a man named Wingate or Winchell. Payne Wingate, accused of counterfeiting in the Connecticut Valley town of Bradford in 1797, was the son of a prominent Federalist family in New Hampshire. There were no Wingates in the Vermont censuses for 1790 and 1800. Given that a Justis Winchell was warned out from Middletown on September 7, 1802, the consensus is for a Winchell counterfeiter. There were, however, two Justis Winchells, both living across the New York border in Washington County in the 1790s. Michael Quinn accepts the "American Justis"; I opt for the "German Justis." Children of "American Justis" were born in Sandy Hill, Kingsbury, and Argyle in Washington County but some distance from Middletown, between 1778 and 1795; in 1797 his last child was born in Cattaraugus County in extreme western New York, placing him hundreds of miles from Middletown. "German Justis" lived in Hebron, New York, south of Middletown, where his children were born between 1789 and 1801. The Winchell genealogies describe him as having been born in Hesse-Cassell in 1759 and pressed into service for the American war. He married Eva, or Aphiah, Savage in Westfield, Massachusetts, in 1787, where they both seem to have been living as servants. Winchell served in the Third Massachusetts Regiment from 1780 to 1783, and his pension record includes an affidavit from Major William Shepherd, who stated that he had been "acquainted with him from the year 1777." It is at least possible that Winchell had been a German soldier captured with Burgoyne's troops; alternatively the German connection may have been a subsequent fabrication. Winchell died in Rose, New York, east of Palmyra in Wayne County, a town where there was a divining episode in the 1830s. For Payne Wingate, see Charles E. L. Wingate, comp., *History of the Wingate Family* . . . (Exeter, N.H., 1886), 152–70. For "American Justis," see Alexander Winchell, *Genealogy of the Family of Winchell in America* . . . (Ann Arbor, 1869), 57; and Quinn, *Early Mormonism*, 85–90. For "German Justis," see Winchell, *Genealogy of the Family of Winchell*, 229–30; and Application of Justis and Aphiah Winchel (W 16971), Revolutionary War Pension Files, National Archives. Thomas Revere has provided me with extensive information on the Winchell debate, including the Winchel pension file and a copy of the warning-out notice (from Middletown, Vermont, Town Records, 1801–35, 15). On Rose, see Laurence A. Johnson, "The 'Money-Diggers' of Rose," *New York Folklore Quarterly* 13 (1957), 215–17. On alchemy in Hesse-Cassel, see Bruce T. Moran, "Privilege, Communication, and Chemiatry: The Hermetic-Alchemical Circle of Moritz of Hessen-Kassel," *Ambix* 32 (1985), 110–26.

5. Alchymical Experiments

1. Reed Peck, "The Reed Peck Manuscript" (Modern Microfilm, Salt Lake City, n.d., typescript), 5.
2. Quotation from [George Starkey], *Secrets Revealed: or an Open Entrance*

onto the Shut-Palace of the King . . . (London, 1669), 48, quoted in Christopher Hill, *The World Turned Upside Down: Radical Ideas during the English Revolution* (London, 1972), 233. See also William Newman, "Prophecy and Alchemy," *Ambix* 37 (1990), 99.

3. Andrew M. Davis, *Currency and Banking in the Province of Massachusetts Bay* (1901; repr., New York, 1970), 2:16–19, 63–71; Joyce Appleby, *Economic Thought and Ideology in Seventeenth Century England* (Princeton, 1978), 212–15, on Hartlib, 158–279, in general, on the commodity and intrinsic theories of money.

4. Appleby, *Economic Thought and Ideology,* 199–241, 252–9; Joyce Appleby, "Locke, Liberalism, and the Natural Law of Money," *Past and Present* 71 (1976), 43–69; on the land bank tradition, see E. James Ferguson, "Currency Finance: An Interpretation of Colonial Monetary Policies, *WMQ* 10 (1953), 153–80; Theodore Thayer, "The Land-Bank System in the American Colonies," *Journal of Economic History* 13 (1953), 145–59; Janet Riesman, "The Origins of American Political Economy, 1690–1781" (Ph.D. diss., Brown University, 1983).

5. Andrew M. Davis, ed., *Colonial Currency Reprints, 1682–1751* (1911; repr., New York, 1964), 1:241, 249–50, 2:209; William Pencak, *War, Politics, and Revolution in Provincial Massachusetts* (Boston, 1981), 142 n. 49, citing *The Advertizer,* Mar. 27, Apr. 11, 1748.

6. Any examination of early American counterfeiting is indebted to the meticulous work of Kenneth Scott. His *Counterfeiting in Colonial America* (New York, 1957) (hereafter Scott, *CCA*) provides a summary of his copious investigations into counterfeiting, which are detailed in a series of colony-focused articles and monographs.

7. Scott, *CCA,* 138, 140, 157, 168, 171, 173–85, 220–2; Scott, *CCNY,* 151–73; Scott, *CCC,* 103, 105, 150, 209–10, 216, 220 (quotation from 216). Bill was a more distant relative of the Smiths (through a 1703 marriage with the French family); see Ledyard Bill, ed., *History of the Bill Family* (New York, 1867), 81–4, 88, 116, 151–2, 154–5; Richard L. Anderson, *Joseph Smith's New England Heritage* (Salt Lake City, 1971), 21, 29.

8. Joseph Bill Packer, *A Journal of the Life and Travels of Joseph Bill Packer . . .* (Hartford and Albany, 1773).

9. Packer, *A Journal,* 3–5; Louis B. Wright, ed., *The Prose Works of William Byrd of Westover . . .* (Cambridge, Mass., 1966), 408. Between the Dan River and the New River lay Pittsylvania County, where a band of counterfeiters, whose money "put a stop to all business" in the province, was broken up in 1773 (Scott, *CCA,* 236–7).

10. Packer, *A Journal,* 5–14, esp. 7; Scott, *CCA,* 140, 168, 171, 175–6, 178–9, 215–18, 220–1; Scott, *CCNY,* 169.

11. Scott, *CCC,* 162–3; Franklin B. Dexter, ed., *The Literary Diary of Ezra Stiles* (New Haven, 1901), 3:472, quoted in Ronald Sterne Wilkinson, "New England's Last Alchemists," *Ambix* 10 (1962), 136–7. On cropping, see *Acts and Resolves, Public and Private, of the Province of Massachusetts Bay . . .* (Boston, 1869), 1:53–4, 556–7, 673; *Acts and Laws of His Majesty's English*

Colony of Connecticut in New England in America (New London, 1750), 24; Scott, *CCA*, 40, 43, 47, 56, 57; Benjamin H. Hall, *History of Eastern Vermont* (New York, 1858), 576.

12. Suffolk Files 47734, 47829, 49055.

13. John Jubeart, *The Confession and Dying Statement of John Jubeart, who was Executed at New York . . .* (New York, 1769; broadside); Scott, *CCA*, 229–31; Scott, *CCC*, 163; Scott, *CCNY*, 68–9, 99; Scott, "CCNH," 3; Abby Maria Hemenway, ed., *Vermont Historical Gazetteer: A Magazine Embracing a History of Each Town, Civil, Ecclesiastical, Biographical and Military*, 5 vols. (Burlington, 1867–91), 1:228; Alan McFarlane, with Sarah Harrison, *Justice and the Mare's Ale: Law and Disorder in Seventeenth Century England* (New York, 1981), 214–15; Case of Stephen Gates of Chatham, Superior Court Files, Hartford County, Connecticut, Sept. 1772, RG 3, Box 6, Connecticut State Archives; E. J. Holmyard, *Alchemy* (Harmondsworth, 1957), 215; F. Sherwood Taylor, *The Alchemists* (New York, 1949), 92.

14. For the various "doctors" among the counterfeiters besides Bill, see Scott, *CCA* 140, 158–72, 176, 241–8, 258; Scott, *CCC*, 82–92, 97; Scott, *CCRI*, 18; Samuel Stearns, *Dr. Stearns Petition to His Excellency* (Worcester, 1785); Marion B. Stowell, *Early American Almanacks: The Colonial Weekday Bible* (New York, 1977), 168–9; MsVtStP, 55:186.

15. Charles Nicholl, *The Chemical Theatre* (London, 1980), 10–13; George L. Kittredge, *Witchcraft in Old and New England* (Cambridge, Mass., 1929), 185–203; John L. McMullan, *The Canting Crew: London's Criminal Underworld, 1550–1700* (New Brunswick, 1984), passim, 104; Gamini Salgado, *The Elizabethan Underworld* (London, 1977), 109–16, 146–8; Taylor, *The Alchemists*, 106–8; Jacques Soboul, *Alchemists and Gold* (London, 1972), 109; Peter French, *John Dee* (London, 1972), 113n; for horses and oxen, see Herman Rosencrantz, *The Life and Confession of Herman Rosencrantz; executed in the City of Philadelphia, on the 7th of May, 1770, for Counterfeiting and Uttering Bills of Credit of the Province of Pennsylvania . . .* (Philadelphia, 1770), 5–9; Ellen D. Larned, *History of Windham County, Connecticut*, 2 vols. (Worcester, 1874–80), 2:360; Scott, *CCNY*, 62; Scott, "CCNH," 20–1; [Hildrith], "A History of the Divining Rod," 322; Marsha K. M. Schuchard, "Freemasonry, Secret Societies, and the Continuities of the Occult Traditions in English Literature" (Ph.D. diss., University of Texas at Austin, 1975), 292–7.

16. Stephen Burroughs, *Memoirs of the Notorious Stephen Burroughs of New Hampshire*, with a preface by Robert Frost (New York, 1924; reprint of the Albany edition, 1811), 60–3. In general, the local details in Burroughs's *Memoirs* are quite accurate. For other companies and covenants see Clark Jillson, *Green Leaves from Whitingham, Vermont* (Worcester, 1984), 115–19; John P. Walker, ed., *Dale Morgan on Early Mormonism: Correspondence and a New History* (Salt Lake City, 1986), 323–6; "Mining Covenant," signed Nov. 26, 1783, in Groton or Pepperell, Mass., in Lawrence Family Papers, Lyman Robbins Collection, Lawrence Library, Pepperell, Mass.

17. Burroughs, *Memoirs*, 62, 77ff. See Taylor, *The Alchemists*, 106–8.

18. Burroughs, *Memoirs,* 81, 84–9; Mass. SJC Dockets, 1785: 178–80, 184, 1786: 201–2, 206–7.

19. Christina Larner, *Enemies of God* (Baltimore, 1981), 196. For a suggestion of how witchcraft had other echoes in the eighteenth century, see Robert Darnton, *The Great Cat Massacre and Other Episodes in French Cultural History* (New York, 1984), 92–100.

20. [Owen Sullivan], *A Short Account of the Life of John ********, Alias Owen Sullivan . . .* (New York, 1756), unpaginated; John Smith, *The Last Speech, Confession, and Dying Words of John Smith, who was Executed at Albany . . .* (Albany, 1773), 7; Scott, CCC, 91–2.

21. Burroughs, *Memoirs,* 120–7.

22. Scott, CCA, 244–5; Burroughs, *Memoirs,* 62–3.

23. Burroughs, *Memoirs,* 47ff.; Stephen Burroughs, *Sermon Delivered in Rutland, On a Haymow* (Hanover, N.H., 1798), 7.

24. Burroughs, *Memoirs,* 47ff.; Petition of John Niles, Oct. 17, 1810, MsVtStP, 48:245; introduction to Burroughs, *Memoirs,* xi (notes from the 1858 Amherst edition); Hemenway, ed., *Vermont Historical Gazetteer,* 2:832n.

25. Scott, CCNY, 141; Rosencrantz, *Life and Confession,* 4; John Cartwright, *The Last Speech and Dying Words of John Cartwright, who was executed at Poughkeepsie on Friday, the 20th of July Instant, for Horse-Stealing . . .* (New York, 1770); Mass. SJC Dockets, 1787: 86.

26. Clay Perry, *New England's Buried Treasure* (New York, 1946), 33–54, 342–3; Scott, CCC, 138–9; Anne S. Warner, *A Bicentennial History: Goshen, Massachusetts, 1781–1981* (Goshen, 1981), 275–82; in eighteenth-century Montague, Massachusetts, gangs of counterfeiters operated in shops hidden in the deep woods, which the constables on occasion spotted by their "smoaks." See Edward P. Pressey, *History of Montague: A Typical Puritan Town* (Montague, 1940), 143.

27. John Demos, "Witchcraft and Local Culture in Hampton, New Hampshire," in Richard Bushman et al., *Uprooted Americans: Essays to Honor Oscar Handlin* (Boston, 1979), 29–31; Scott, CCA, 10, 41, 205, 226; Scott, CCC, 92; Pressey, *Montague,* 143; Larned, *History of Windham County,* 2:360; Chadwick Hansen, *Witchcraft at Salem* (New York, 1969), 77ff.; Scott, "CCNH," 27–8; William Little, *History of Weare, New Hampshire, 1735–1888* (Lowell, 1888), 415.

28. Chauncy Graham, *God Will Trouble the Troublers of his People. A Sermon Preached at Poughkeepsie, in Dutchess County, in the Province of New York, July 14th, 1758. Being the Day of Execution of Hugh Gillaspie . . .* (New York, 1759), 8–9. For discussions of fears of demonic conspiracy in Essex County see Paul Boyer and Stephen Nissenbaum, *Salem Possessed* (Cambridge, Mass., 1974), 153–78; Christine Heyrman, "Specters of Subversion, Societies of Friends," in David D. Hall et al., eds., *Saints and Revolutionaries* (New York, 1938), 38–74; Richard Weisman, *Witchcraft, Magic, and Religion in 17th Century Massachusetts* (Amherst, 1984), 120–3; Sarah L. Bailey, *Historical Sketches of Andover, Massachusetts* (Boston, 1880), 198;

James E. Kences, "Some Unexpected Relationships of Essex County Witch-craft to the Indian Wars of 1675 and 1689," *EIHC* 120 (1984), 179–212.

29. Appendix to *Life of the Notorious Stephen Burroughs, son of Rev. Eden Burroughs, Hanover* (Greenfield, Mass., 1812); Scott, CCC, 199; Scott, CCA, 253–63.

30. On heresy and witchcraft, see Normon Cohn, *Europe's Inner Demons* (New York, 1975); David D. Hall, *Worlds of Wonder, Days of Judgement* (New York, 1989), 100–2; Carol F. Karlsen, *Devil in the Shape of a Woman* (New York, 1987), 122–5; Larner, *Enemies of God*, 138–43; Heyrman, "Specters of Subversion"; on Quaker punishment, see Sidney Perley, *The History of Salem*, 3 vols. (Salem, 1924–8), 2:245.

31. Thomas H. Jobe, "The Devil in Restoration Science: The Glanvill–Webster Witchcraft Debate," *Isis* 72 (1981), 343–56; Charles Webster, *From Para-celsus to Newton: Magic and the Making of Modern Science* (New York, 1982), 93–9; P. M. Rattansi, "The Helmontian–Galenist Controversy in Res-toration England," *Ambix* 12 (1964), 1–23; Frances Yates, *The Occult Phi-losophy in the Elizabethan Age* (London, 1979), 64–71; Frances Yates, *The Rosicrucian Enlightenment* (London, 1972), 103–6; Cotton Mather, *Re-markable Providences*, quoted in Weisman, *Witchcraft, Magic, and Religion*, 33–4. See also Leland L. Estes, "Good Witches, Wise Men, Astrologers, and Scientists: William Perkins and the Limits of European Witch-Hunts," in Ingrid Merkel and Allen G. Debus, eds., *Hermeticism and the Renaissance: Intellectual History and the Occult in Early Modern Europe* (Washington, 1988), 154–65, for a somewhat different view.

32. Scott, CCA, 84–5, 106–20, 232; Scott, CCC, 72–5; Scott, CCNY, 59–67, 71, 81; James Smith, *History of Dutchess County, New York* (Syracuse, 1882), 63; Perley, *Salem*, 2:22–3, 76, 122–3, 143, 385, 3:2–5; Alonzo Lewis, *His-tory of Lynn* (Boston, 1865), 125, 183–6, 305; Amesbury Vital Records; Salem Vital Records; Lynn Vital Records; and Suffolk Files cited in note 39.

33. C. C. Goen, *Revivalism and Separatism in New England, 1740–1800: Strict Congregationalists and Separate Baptists in the Great Awakening* (New Haven, 1962), 307; Bill, ed., *Bill Family*, 151–2; Scott, CCC, 96, 162–3; Charles R. Stark, *Groton, Connecticut, 1705–1905* (Stonington, 1922), 161; George Colesworthy, *Historical Sketches of the Baptist Church in Shutesbury, Mass.* (n.p., n.d.), 5; Erastus Andrews, *A Historical Discourse delivered at the Baptist Meeting-House at N. Leverett . . .* (Amherst, 1847), 10; Suffolk Files 155431; William G. McLoughlin, *New England Dissent*, 2 vols. (Cambridge, Mass., 1971), 1:546; Henry S. Nourse, *History of the Town of Harvard, Massachusetts, 1732–1893* (Harvard, 1894), 222–3.

34. Samuel Orcutt, *A History of the Old Town of Stratford and the City of Bridgeport, Connecticut*, 2 vols. (Bridgeport, 1896), 2:1167; Frederick Chase, *History of Dartmouth College and Hanover, New Hampshire, up to 1815*, 2 vols. (Cambridge, Mass., 1891), 1:195, 205, 206, 215–6; Anson Titus, "Reminiscences of Early American Universalism," *Universalist Quar-terly and General Review* (1881), 438–9; Burroughs, *Memoirs*, 181ff.

35. Scott, *CCC,* 67; Diane D. Ivins and Aileen S. Freeman, *The Fox Genealogy* (n.p., 1982), 5–7; James S. Rogers, comp. *James Rogers of New London* (Boston, 1902), 44; SJCWCVt Records, 2:20 (Mar. 1797); for Finney, see William G. McLoughlin, "Free Love, Immortalism, and Perfectionism in Cumberland, Rhode Island, 1748–1768," *Rhode Island History* 33 (1974), passim and 77; Howard Finney, *Finney–Phinney Families in America* (Richmond, 1957), 9, 17, 18, 38, 85; for Solomon Prentice, see Clifford S. Shipton, *Sibley's Harvard Graduates* (Cambridge, Mass., 1951), 8:249–57; on Jemima Wilkinson, see Herbert A. Wisbey, *Pioneer Prophetess: Jemima Wilkinson, the Public Universal Friend* (Ithaca, 1964), 41–6, 82–94; Charles E. Potter, *Genealogies of the Potter Families and their Descendants in America* (Boston, 1888), 1–2, 27–8; Israel Wilkinson, *Memoirs of the Wilkinson Family in America* (Jacksonville, Ill., 1869), 114; Scott, *CCRI,* 17–22, 55–6; Scott, *Counterfeiting in Colonial Pennsylvania* (New York, 1955), 78–9.

36. Grant Powers, *Historical Sketches of the Discovery, Settlement, and Progress of Events in the Coos Country . . .* (Haverhill, N.H., 1841), 43, 62–5; John Q. Bittinger, *History of Haverhill, N.H.* (Haverhill, 1888), 104; Scott, *CCA,* 222–31; Scott, *CCRI,* 55; Scott, "CCNH," 29ff.; Burroughs, *Memoirs,* 94–5.

37. Kenneth Scott, "Counterfeiting in Early Vermont," *Vermont History* 33 (1965), 298.

38. David W. Galenson, *White Servitude in Colonial America: An Economic Analysis* (New York, 1981); Abbott E. Smith, *Colonists in Bondage: White Servitude and Convict Labor in America, 1607–1776* (Chapel Hill, 1947), 116–19; Scott, *CCNY,* 77, 92, 168–9 (quotation from 168); Smith, *The Last Speech, Confession, and Dying Words of John Smith,* 7 (quotation); Scott, *CCC,* 199; Scott, *CCA,* 5–6, 253–63.

39. The Essex County gangs are described in Scott, *CCA,* 84–5, 121, 126; Scott, *CCRI,* 10–12, 22, 24, 26, 64; Scott, *CCC,* 68. See also Mellen Chamberlain, *A Documentary History of Chelsea* (Boston, 1908), 2:386–7. The records of the cases can be found in Suffolk Files 47566, 47590, 47734, 47741, 47829, 48664, 48699, 48708, 49055, 49132, 49251, 49733, 50294, 50359, 50363, 50365, 50389, 50443, 50485, 51526, 51529, 53326, 54930, 54932, 55292, 55304, 55800, 55801, 55807, 55809, 55932, 56278, 56417, 59608, 59609, 60741, 60890, 60967, 64692, 68447.

40. Of forty-one accused counterfeiters, occupation can be determined for thirty-three. Of these, six were laborers; nineteen were from various trades, including cordwainers, innkeepers, a clockmaker, an iron-bloomer, and various sorts of carpenters; two were physicians; one was a gentleman; only five were husbandmen or yeomen.

41. This summary is based on an analysis of the names of accused counterfeiters in the Suffolk Files (see note 39); the accused witches, their sureties, and their accusers in Boyer and Nissenbaum, eds., *SWP;* and the kinship information in Little, *History of Weare,* 415, 825; Perley, *Salem;* Jame R. Newhall, *History of Lynn, Essex County, Massachusetts* (Lynn, 1883); Bailey, *Andover;* and the Vital Records of Amesbury, Andover, Lynn, and Salem.

42. Rosamund Rosenmeier, "Anne Bradsteet Revisited" (manuscript); Lyle

Koehler, *A Search for Power: The "Weaker Sex" in Seventeenth Century New England* (Urbana, 1980), 480–1.

43. Rosencrantz, *Life and Confession,* 9; Scott, *CCNY,* 153; on social banditry, see Eric J. Hobsbawm, *Bandits* (London, 1969); Eric J. Hobsbawm, *Primitive Rebels: Studies in Archaic Forms of Social Movement in the 19th and 20th Centuries* (New York, 1965); and Marcus Rediker, *Between the Devil and the Deep Blue Sea: Merchant Seamen, Pirates, and the Anglo-American Maritime World, 1700–1750* (New York, 1987), 254–87.

44. Scott, "CCNH," 35; Burroughs, *Memoirs,* 83–4.

45. Christopher Hill, *The Experience of Defeat: Milton and Some Contemporaries* (New York, 1984), esp. 290–6; Hobsbawm, *Bandits,* 31; Christopher Hill, "Radical Pirates," in Margaret Jacob and James Jacob, eds., *The Origins of Anglo-American Radicalism* (London, 1984), 17–32.

46. Edward A. Kendall, *Travels through the Northern Parts of the United States, in the Years 1807 and 1808* (New York, 1809), 3:84–104. For a recent account, see Alan Taylor, *Liberty Men and Great Proprietors: The Revolutionary Settlement on the Maine Frontier, 1760–1820* (Chapel Hill, 1990), 81, 178–80, 344.

47. Jillson, *Green Leaves from Whitingham,* 59, 111–19; MsVtStP, 20:72; Scott, "CCNH," 28ff.; Scott, *CCA,* 223ff.; SJCWCVt Records, 3:169; Burroughs, *Memoirs;* Mass. SJC Dockets, 1785: 178–84, 1786: 201–2, 206–7.

48. John P. Demos, *Entertaining Satan* (New York, 1982), 99–103; Mining Covenant, Nov. 26, 1783, Lawrence Family Papers, Lyman Robbins Collection, Lawrence Library, Pepperell, Mass.; Nourse, *History of the Town of Harvard,* 71–2, 104, 267–8; Caleb Butler, *History of the Town of Groton* (Boston, 1848), 256–7; C. J. F. Binney, *The History and Genealogy of the Prentice or Prentiss Family . . .* (Boston, 1852), 32–3, 37; Mass. SJC Dockets, 1785: 156, 1787: 231–3, 290, 1788: 365, 367, 377, 1790: 79; MsVtStP, 74:14 (pp. 5–6), 55:188. For Morristown, see note 53.

49. See Appendix.

50. Barnes Frisbie, *The History of Middletown, Vermont . . .* (Rutland, Vt., 1867), 57.

51. Burroughs, *Memoirs,* 77ff.; George Sheldon, *A History of Deerfield, Mass.* (Deerfield, 1895–6), 2:767; SJCWCVt Records, 2:200; Hamilton's journal in Jillson, *Green Leaves from Whitingham,* 117; Cooperstown *Federalist,* Dec. 14, 1811. I am obliged to Alan Taylor for this last reference.

52. Hemenway, *Vermont Historical Gazetteer,* 3:1087–90; MsVtStP, 48:45, 171.

53. [Ransford Rogers], "The Morristown Ghost Deliniated," in *A Collection of Essays on a Variety of Subjects in Prose and Verse* (Newark, N.J., 1797), 8–9, 14–15, 20, 23–4; Andrew M. Sherman, *Historic Morristown, New Jersey: The Story of Its First Century* (Morristown, 1905), 401–30. A similar coining mint may have contributed to the rise of the New Israelites. In Rupert, two towns south of Middletown, the independent republic of Vermont had chartered a coining mint in 1785 to produce copper currency, complete with furnace, rolling mill, and cutting and stamping machinery. Although there do not seem to have been any divining episodes in Rupert, the abandoned mint

machinery was being used in 1800 to counterfeit silver coins (Hemenway, *Vermont Historical Gazetteer,* 1:227–8; Scott, "Counterfeiting in Early Vermont," 298–9). One of those involved in operating this early mint was William Buel, son of Abel Buel, a mechanic who had at various times counterfeited and had operated a state coinage for the colony of Connecticut (Scott, *CCC,* 160–2). See also MsVtStP, 48:66, 51:224, 53:185, for counterfeiters from Rupert in 1810 and 1816.

54. Alan Taylor, "The Early Republic's Supernatural Economy," *American Quarterly* 38 (1986), 6–34, develops this latter argument with relation to divining, and William Rorabaugh, *The Alcoholic Republic: An American Tradition* (New York, 1979), provides a useful collateral interpretation of the questions of expectations and opportunities of the early national period. For a discussion of "arena," see Victor Turner, *Dramas, Fields, and Metaphors: Symbolic Action in Human Society* (Ithaca, 1974).

55. Scott, *CCA,* 215–18; Scott, *Counterfeiting in Colonial Pennsylvania,* 97–8.

56. Paul A. W. Wallace, *Conrad Weiser: 1696–1760, Friend of Colonist and Mohawk* (New York, 1945; repr., 1971), 50–64, 102–11; J. F. Sachse, *The German Pietists of Provincial Pennsylvania, 1694–1708* (Philadelphia, 1895), 5, 57–8, 109–12, 129–38, 161–6; J. F. Sachse, *The German Sectarians of Pennsylvania, 1708–1742* (Philadelphia, 1899), 1:350–63, 2:290.

57. W. C. Carter and A. J. Glossbrenner, *History of York County, from Its Erection to the Present Time (1729–1834),* rev. ed. (Harrisburg, Pa., 1930), 126–30.

58. Sachse, *The German Pietists,* 161ff.; Sachse, *The German Sectarians,* 2:95–113, 331–59; Walter Klein, *Johann Conrad Beissel: Mystic and Martinet, 1690–1768* (Philadelphia, 1942), 154–63; Elmer L. Smith, John G. Stewart, and M. Ellsworth Kyger, *The Pennsylvania Germans of the Shenandoah Valley,* Publications of the Pennsylvania Folklore Society, vol. 26 (Allentown, Pa., 1964), 154–63; Klaus G. Wust, *The Saint Adventurers of the Virginia Frontier: Southern Outposts of Ephrata* (Edinburgh, Va., 1977), 9–53; *Chronicon Ephratense,* 184–6.

59. *Chronicon Ephratense,* 262–77; Klein, *Beissel,* 166; Sachse, *The German Sectarians,* 2:172–5, 261–5, 381–6; Wust, *The Saint Adventurers,* 82–101.

60. Wust, *The Saint-Adventurers,* 61.

6. I Was Born in Sharon

1. Smith, *History of the Church,* 6:88–94.

2. Bushman, *Joseph Smith,* 17–19, 22–3; Richard L. Anderson, *Joseph Smith's New England Heritage* (Salt Lake City, 1971), 18–21, 100–2.

3. Abby Maria Hemenway, ed., *Vermont Historical Gazetteer: A Magazine Embracing a History of Each Town, Civil, Ecclesiastical, Biographical and Military,* 5 vols. (Burlington, 1867–91), 2:1085–8, 1137–8; *Acts and Laws, passed by the Legislature of the State of Vermont . . .* (Randolph, 1809), 32–4; Collamer M. Abbott, "Early Copper Smelting in Vermont," *Vermont His-*

tory 33 (1965), 233–4; Collamer M. Abbott, *Green Mountain Copper: The Story of Vermont's Red Metal* (Randolph, 1973), 1–3.

4. Tunbridge, Vermont, Town Records, Dec. 6, 1797, p. 188, provided by Ruth E. Durkee, assistant town clerk.

5. Stephen A. Marini, *Radical Sects of Revolutionary New England* (Cambridge, Mass., 1982), 40–8, 63–81; Randolph A. Roth, *The Democratic Dilemma: Religion, Reform, and the Social Order in the Connecticut River Valley, 1791–1850* (New York, 1987), 62–7; *The Free-Will Baptist Register, for the Year of our Lord 1834* (Limerick, Me., 1834), 46–9, 58;, *Minutes of the Annual Conferences of the Methodist Episcopal Church, for the years 1829–1939* (New York, 1840), 329–35; *Universalist Register and Almanac for 1836 . . .* (Utica, 1836), 28–30.

6. Brodie, *No Man Knows My History*, 12, 22; Nathan O. Hatch, *The Democratization of American Christianity* (New Haven, 1989), 68–70; *Herald of Gospel Liberty*, Aug. 18, 1809.

7. Marini, *Radical Sects*, 49–59, 94; Louis J. Kern, *An Ordered Love: Sex Roles and Sexuality in Victorian Utopias – The Shakers, the Mormons, and the Oneida Community* (Chapel Hill, 1981), 207–10; Wayne R. Judd, "William Miller: The Disappointed Prophet," in Ronald L. Numbers and Jonathan M. Butler, eds., *The Disappointed: Millerism and Millenarianism in the Nineteenth Century* (Bloomington, 1987), 17–35. On Leman Copley, see Cook, ed., *The Revelations of the Prophet Joseph Smith*, 67.

8. Asael Smith Address to His Family, Apr. 10, 1799, in Anderson, *Joseph Smith's New England Heritage*, 104–9, 125–6.

9. Asael Smith's letter to Jacob Towne, Jan. 14, 1796, in Anderson, *Joseph Smith's New England Heritage*, 119; Richard Brothers, *Revealed Knowledge* (Philadelphia, 1795), 51.

10. "Brothers' Prophesies" was one item listed in a *Catalogue of Books, for Sale at the Bookstore in Hanover . . .* (Hanover, N.H., 1799), 6.

11. Quinn, *Early Mormonism*, 22, 31–2; Hill, *Joseph Smith*, 67, Ronald W. Walker, "The Persisting Idea of American Treasure Hunting," *BYUS* 24 (1984), 444; Stephen Green, "The Money-Diggers," *Vermont Life* 24 (1969), 48; Hemenway, ed., *Vermont Historical Gazetteer*, 3:1089.

12. On the role of William Cowdery and Joseph Smith Sr. in the New Israelite movement, see Barnes Frisbie, *The History of Middletown, Vermont* (Rutland, Vt., 1867), 46, 56–61; Marini, *Radical Sects*, 54–5; David Persuitte, *Joseph Smith and the Origins of the Book of Mormon* (Jefferson, N.C., 1985), 234–8; Quinn, *Early Mormonism*, 31–2, 84–90. For the revelation about the rod, see *A Book of Commandments, for the Government of the Church of Christ, organized according to Law, on the 6th of April, 1830* (Zion [Independence, Mo.], 1833), 19. There may have been a distant connection to the Cumberland, Rhode Island, perfectionists in the New Israelite cult, because an Ephraim Wood, possibly the grandson of Nathaniel Wood, was arrested with Appollus Finney for counterfeiting in Shrewsbury, Vermont, in 1795. Wood was acquitted but Finney was convicted. Finney was the nephew

of John Finney Jr., the perfectionist counterfeiter. See Kenneth Scott, "Counterfeiting in Early Vermont," *Vermont History* 33 (1965), 299; Howard Finney, *Finney–Phinney Families in America* (Richmond, 1957), 9, 18, 38, 85; William G. McLoughlin, "Free Love, Immortalism, and Perfectionism in Cumberland, Rhode Island, 1748–1768," *Rhode Island History* 13 (1974), 77–8.

13. Hill, *Joseph Smith,* 85–7.

14. Mary B. A. Mehling, *Cowdrey–Cowdery–Cowdray Genealogy: William Cowdery of Lynn, Massachusetts, 1630, and His Descendants* (New York, 1911), 37, 67–8, 77–85, 95–6; William H. Fuller, *Genealogy of Some of the Descendants of Edward Fuller* (Palmer, Mass., 1908), 1:199; Millington Church and Society, Records, 1733–1931 CEA, 47–8; Millington Meetinghouse documents, 1761, CEA, 13:37–8, 40–1; U.S. census manuscripts for 1810, 1820, 1830, National Archives. In 1810 William Cowdery was listed as living in the town of Ontario; his daughter Rebecca was born in 1810 in Williamson, adjacent to the east.

15. Mehling, *Cowdrey–Cowdery–Cowdray Genealogy,* 83–4.

16. Bushman, *Joseph Smith,* 29–30.

17. *DC* 19:35, 42:40–52, 64:27.

18. Bushman, *Joseph Smith,* 30–42; see also Richard L. Bushman, "Family Security in the Transition from Farm to City, 1750–1850," *Journal of Family History* 6 (1981), 238–56.

19. Anderson, *Joseph Smith's New England Heritage,* 9–15; Solomon Mack, *Narrative* (Windsor, 1811), 9–17, in Anderson, *Joseph Smith's New England Heritage,* 40–7; Bushman, *Joseph Smith,* 16; Smith, *Biographical Sketches,* 22.

20. Bushman, *Joseph Smith,* 19; Anderson, *Joseph Smith's New England Heritage,* 21; Mack, *Narrative,* 17–18, in Anderson, 49–50.

21. Anderson, *Joseph Smith's New England Heritage,* 94–101; Bushman, *Joseph Smith,* 21.

22. Mack, *Narrative,* 3–8, in Anderson, *Joseph Smith's New England Heritage,* 34–9; Fred Anderson, *A People's Army: Massachusetts Soldiers in the Seven Years' War* (New York, 1985); Scott, "CCNH," 21–2; C. E. Potter, *The History of Manchester, Formerly Derryfield, in New Hampshire* (Manchester, 1856), 489; C. E. Potter, *The Military History of the State of New Hampshire* (Concord, 1866), 155–9. There are a number of places where Mack did indeed confuse details of his long and adventurous life; see Anderson, *Joseph Smith's New England Heritage,* 31–2.

23. Scott, CCC, 200; Fuller, *Genealogy of Some of the Descendants of Edward Fuller,* 1:46.

24. Stephen Burroughs, *Memoirs* (New York, 1924), 62, 91; Anderson, *Joseph Smith's New England Heritage,* 9–12; Mack, *Narrative,* 9–10, in Anderson, 40–1; Scott, CCA, 223–7, 257–61.

25. Potter, *History of Manchester,* 484; William Little, *History of Weare, New Hampshire* (Lowell, 1888), 230–2; Scott, CCA, 257–61.

26. SJCWCVt Records, 1:105, 2:19, 22; Supreme Judical Court, Orange County, Vermont, Records, 1:7; MsVtStP, 11:196, 249, 17:365.

27. Burroughs, *Memoirs*, 365–6; SJCWCVt Records, 2:19, 20, 22, 23, 157, 171, 200.

28. Mitchell J. Hunt, *The Mysterious Beebe Families of Beebe, Vermont–Quebec.* . . (Willow Grove, Pa., 1979), 15–17, 25–6; "Statement of Services rendered by Oliver Barker in Compton in the Province of Lower Canada in detecting and prosecuting counterfeiters of Bank Bills," MsVtStP, 14:14 (pp. 2–4).

29. SJCWCVt Records, 2:512, 525.

30. SJCWCVt Records, 2:19–20, 22–3, 157, 171, 200, 512, 516, 525, 611, 622–4; 3:15, 17, 19, 21, 23, 25, 76, 78, 80, 84–6, 88, 92, 108–12, 115, 124, 151–2, 156–7, 159, 165–6, 169, 172, 175.

31. Brodie, *No Man Knows My History,* 7; John P. Walker, ed., *Dale Morgan on Early Mormonism: Correspondence and a New History* (Salt Lake City, 1986), 367n; *Historical Magazine,* 2d ser., 8 (1870), 316; SJCWCVt Records, 3:78–9; Kenneth Scott, "Counterfeiting in Early Vermont," *Vermont History* 33 (1965), 307. There were other connections to counterfeiting among the early Mormons. John Woodruff, another distant cousin of Wilford Woodruff, was caught up in a counterfeiting scheme in Farmington in 1710, and quickly confessed. Several of the Culvers of Groton were similarly accused in 1724. In the intervening years, between 1716 and 1723, four members of the Peck family of Rehobeth, close cousins of the Mormon Peck family, operated an extensive counterfeiting ring that was broken up by the Rhode Island authorities. In 1742 Benoni Benson of Mendon, forebear of a noted Mormon family, was implicated in the extensive counterfeiting operations of Joseph Boyce of Salem. Mormon Peter Dustin was a great-nephew of the notorious Dr. Samuel Dustin, who had worked with Joseph Bill in the 1740s and 1750s; he was also related to several others arrested with the Haverhill gang in 1745. Thus counterfeiting, broadly associated with the sectarian orbit in New England, intersected with the trajectories of certain proto-Mormon families. On Woodruff see Scott, CCC, 4–7; Susan W. Abbott, *Woodruff Genealogy* . . . (Milford, Conn., 1963), 1–9. On Culver see Valerie D. Giorgi, *Colver–Culver Family Genealogy* . . . (Santa Maria, Calif., 1984), 39. On Peck see Scott, CCA, 64–6; Scott, CCRI, 7–8; Ira B. Peck, *A Genealogical History of the Descendants of Joseph Peck* . . . (Boston, 1868), 131–3. On Benson see Mendon Vital Records; and Scott, CCA, 123. On Dustin see Suffolk Files 49132, 60741, 60890; C. E. Dustin et al., comps., "A History of the Dustin Family in America" (NEHGS, 1933, Typescript), 1:31–2, 69–70, 167, 4:73a; Scott, CCA, 178–80; Scott, CCC, 97, 104, 126–7, 147.

32. Hill, *Quest for Refuge,* 1.

33. Bushman, *Joseph Smith,* 37–8, quotation from p. 38, where Bushman cites Lucy Mack Smith, "Preliminary Manuscript"; see also Hill, *Joseph Smith,* 33–4. (On the "Preliminary Manuscript," see page 366, note 47.)

34. Frisbie, *The History of Middletown,* 42–64; Willard Chase affidavit in

Rodger I. Anderson, *Joseph Smith's New York Reputation Reexamined* (Salt Lake City, 1990); E. D. Howe, *Mormonism Unvailed* . . . (Painesville, Ohio, 1834), 123.

35. Mary A. S. Anderson, *The Ancestry and Posterity of Joseph Smith and Emma Hale* (Independence, Mo.), 301–2. Yet another connection with Rutland County may have been Beniah Woodward, convicted of passing counterfeit money to Joseph Smith Sr. in 1807. In 1802 Beniah Woodward signed a petition to the state from the town of Benson, and in 1809 he mentioned in a petition for clemency that in 1807 he had "moved his family from Royalton to his father's in Orwell," just north of Benson. Benson and Orwell lie just northwest of Poultney, and one wonders whether Woodward also might have been involved with the New Israelites (MsVtStP, 43:106, 48:222).

36. *Records of the Grand Lodge of Free and Accepted Masons of the State of Vermont, from 1794 to 1846 Inclusive* (Burlington, 1879), 99, 154, 420; Returns of the Ontario Lodge, Dec. 1817 to Dec. 1818, and the Mount Moriah Lodge, June 1827 to June 1828, in the files of the Grand Lodge of New York State. John Smith may have already moved to St. Lawrence County with his father, Asael, by 1813 (Anderson, *Joseph Smith's New England Heritage*, 213 n. 209).

37. New York lodges before 1800 are listed in Charles T. McClenachan, *History of the Most Ancient and Honorable Fraternity of Freemasonry in New York*, 2 vols. (New York, 1892), 2:133–5. Vermont lodges are listed in *Records of the Grand Lodge of* . . . *Vermont*, 82–3, 86–7. For Royal Arch lodges and chapters, see *Extracts from the Proceedings of the Grand Chapter of the State of New York, at its Annual Meeting, February, 5828* (Albany, 1828), 4–5; *Records of the Grand Chapter of the State of Vermont, from 1804–1850 Inclusive* (Burlington, 1878), 3; Thomas S. Webb, *The Freemason's Monitor, or, Illustrations of Masonry; in two parts* (New York, 1802), 290–1. On Hibbard, see John Spargo, *The Rise and Progress of Freemasonry in Vermont* . . . (Burlington, 1944), 51. On Ethan Smith, see William B. Sprague, *Annals of the American Pulpit* . . . , 9 vols. (New York, 1857–69), 2:296–8; *A Brief Report of the Debates in the Anti-Masonic State Convention of the Commonwealth of Massachusetts, Held in Faneuil Hall, Boston, December 30, 31, 1829, and January 1, 1830* (Boston, 1830), 45.

38. *Records of the Grand Lodge of* . . . *Vermont*, 194, 216; *Records of the Grand Chapter of* . . . *Vermont*, 17, 30, 46, 63, 124; James R. Sace, *Jeremy Ladd Cross: Renowned Author and Lecturer* (Bethel, Conn., 1958); Eugene E. Hinman, Ray V. Denslow, and Charles C. Hunt, *A History of the Cryptic Rite* (Tacoma, Wash., 1931), 1:441–3. Jan Shipps pointed out the significance of Jeremy Cross.

39. See *A Book of Commandments* . . . (Zion, 1833), 19.

40. Quotations from James White, *Sketches of the Christian Life and Public Labors of William Miller, gathered from his Memoir* . . . (Battle Creek, 1875), 25–6, 31, 43–6. Miller's Royal Arch membership is listed in *Records of the Grand Chapter of* . . . *Vermont*, 80, 110. See also Judd, "William Miller," in Numbers and Butler, eds., *The Disappointed*.

41. Persuitte, *Joseph Smith and the Origins of the Book of Mormon,* esp. 5–8; Brigham H. Roberts, *Studies of the Book of Mormon,* ed. Brigham D. Madsen (Urbana, 1985); Robert N. Hullinger, *Mormon Answer to Skepticism: Why Joseph Smith Wrote the Book of Mormon* (St. Louis, 1980), 55–61, 66–7; Dan Vogel, *Indian Origins and the Book of Mormon* (Salt Lake City, 1986), 18–19, 29, 42, 48. It is possible that Oliver Cowdery helped to print Ethan Smith's *View of the Hebrews.* This text was printed on a press in Poultney, and Cowdery had had experience as a printer. In 1830, when he led a mission into Ohio, the Cleveland *Herald* wrote: "We had known Cowdry some seven or 8 years ago, when he was a dabbler in the art of Printing, and principally occupied in writing and printing pamphlets, with which as a pedestrian ped-lar, he visited the towns and villages of eastern N. York, and Canada" (quoted in Max Parkin, "Conflict at Kirtland: The Nature and Cause of Internal and External Conflict of the Mormons in Ohio between 1830 and 1838" [M.A. thesis, Brigham Young University, 1966], 41).

42. Here it may be very cautiously noted that researchers interested in the possibility of ancient European migrations to the New World have found "an uncanny number of standing stones situated along the hillsides of Tunbridge, South Royalton, and South Woodstock, usually found in the vicinity of stone chambers and rock-cut inscriptions." Specifically, near a stone chamber "in a field adjoining the farmhouse where the Mormon prophet Joseph Smith was born, is a series of [ten] small, saucer-shaped standing stones . . . placed into the ground at intervals of 50–100 yards" in parallel lines. Rather than megalith-building prehistoric Europeans (latter-day Nephites!), an equally interesting, if perhaps less exotic, explanation of these stone configurations (if they indeed exist) may lie in the fusion of millenarian Freemasonry and treasure-divining, which the Smiths and many of their peers were involved in. Quotation from Salvatore Michael Trento, *The Search for Lost America: Mysteries of the Stone Ruins in the United States* (New York, 1978), 169. I am obliged to Stephen Turner for bringing this citation to my attention.

43. William H. H. Stowell, *The Stowell Genealogy: A Record of the Descendants of Samuel Stowell of Hingham, Mass.* (Rutland, 1970), 112–13, 225ff.; Clark Jillson, *Green Leaves from Whitingham, Vermont* (Worcester, 1894), 115–18; Arrington, *Brigham Young,* 7–18; Kimball, *Heber C. Kimball,* 248, 249, 256n.

44. Kimball, *Heber C. Kimball,* 85.

45. Mervin B. Hogan, "The Official Minutes of Nauvoo Lodge" (Scottish Rite Library, MONH, n.d., Typescript); Kimball, *Heber C. Kimball,* 12–13, 85; Parley P. Pratt, *Autobiography of Parley P. Pratt* (Salt Lake City, 1970), 44.

46. Timothy L. Smith, "The Book of Mormon in a Biblical Culture," *JMH* 7 (1980), 9–10; Hill, *Joseph Smith,* 62, 101, 152; Vogel, *Religious Seekers,* 29–30; Malcolm R. Thorp, "The Religious Backgrounds of Mormon Converts in Britain, 1837–52," *JMH* 4 (1977), 60.

47. Bushman, *Joseph Smith,* 38–9; Mack, *Narrative,* 20–1, in Anderson, *Joseph Smith's New England Heritage,* 52–3.

48. Smith, *Biographical Sketches,* 60–1. It should be noted that these words do

not appear in the original manuscript draft ("Preliminary Manuscript") narrated by Lucy Mack Smith but only in the subsequent Martha Corey manuscript. (See Chapter 7, note 47.)

49. Arthur M. Schlesinger Jr., *A Pilgrim's Progress: Orestes A. Brownson* (Boston, 1939), 7.

50. Bushman, *Joseph Smith*, 40–2; Smith, *Biographical Sketches*, 66.

7. Secret Combinations and Slippery Treasures in the Land of Zarahemla

1. Mormon 1:2–6. (See Abbreviations.)

2. The consensus regarding the Smith decision to settle in Palmyra revolves around the apparently chance encounter with a Caleb Howard, who traveled with Joseph Sr. and then – generating some controversy – drove the family's team the following winter. See Bushman, *Joseph Smith*, 41. But the real question remains of why the Smiths did not join Asael Smith and several of the Smith brothers who had already emigrated to St. Lawrence County, roughly one hundred and fifty miles northeast of Palmyra. Several points may be significant: Dr. Jacob Cowdery had lived in Palmyra in the 1790s, and the offspring of his bigamous relationship apparently were still in the town in the 1820s; William Cowdery (Oliver's father) had moved his family to Ontario County temporarily around 1810 and would return in the late 1820s; and Luman Walter, the diviner who would influence Joseph Smith Jr. in Manchester, married a Harriet Howard in Andover, Vermont, in 1819. Was Harriet a relative of Caleb Howard? Michael Quinn has also noted that an Anna Walter (perhaps a relative of Luman) lived in Royalton in 1810. These scraps of evidence suggest that the Smiths' move to Palmyra was determined in part by their connections with a hypothetical network of divining families stretching from Tunbridge to Poultney to Andover. I am indebted to Thomas L. Revere for this insight and for much of the reconstruction of the divining network discussed below. See also Mary B. A. Mehling, *Cowdrey–Cowdery–Cowdray Genealogy* (New York, 1911), 83–4, 95–6; June S. Parfitt, *A Genealogy of the Walter Family* (Manchester, N.H., 1986), 128; Quinn, *Early Mormonism*, 95.

3. Smith, *Biographical Sketches*, 67–70; Pomeroy Tucker, *Origin, Rise, and Progress of Mormonism: Biography of Its Founders and History of Its Church* (New York, 1867), 12–13; Bushman, *Joseph Smith*, 47; John P. Walker, ed., *Dale Morgan on Early Mormonism* (Salt Lake City, 1986), 221–2.

4. Hill, *Joseph Smith*, 59–60; Brodie, *No Man Knows My History*, 414–15; Smith, *Biographical Sketches*, 73, 88–90; Bushman, *Joseph Smith*, 64–6.

5. Bushman, *Joseph Smith*, 144; Smith, *Biographical Sketches*, 72; Hill, *Joseph Smith*, 59–60; Brodie, *No Man Knows My History*, 27–8.

6. Wesley P. Walters, "New Light on Mormon Origins from the Palmyra (N.Y.) Revival," *Dialogue* 4 (Spring 1969), 60–81, dated this revival to 1824, but has been challenged by Milton V. Backman Jr., in "Awakenings in the Burned-

over District: New Light on the Historical Setting of the First Vision," *BYUS* 9 (Spring 1969), 301–20. Marvin Hill reviewed the evidence and sides with Walters on the dating of the revival, in "The First Vision Controversy: A Critique and Reconciliation," *Dialogue* 15 (Summer 1982), 31–46, although he dissents from Walters's conclusions on the implications about the prophetic visions. Quotations from Orasmus Turner, *History of the Pioneer Settlement of Phelps and Gorham Purchase and Morris' Reserve* (Rochester, 1851), 214; and from "Alexander Neibaur Report, 1844," in Jessee, ed., *The Papers of Joseph Smith,* 1:460 (see also Hill, "First Vision Controversy," 41–2). The importance of gender relations in the Smith family religious culture was stressed by Paul Johnson, "Patriarchy and Plebeian Revivals, 1790–1850," commentary delivered at the Annual Meeting of the Organization of American Historians, Louisville, Ky., Apr. 11, 1991.

7. "1832 History," in Jessee, ed., *The Papers of Joseph Smith,* 1:5–7; in Jessee, comp. and ed., *The Personal Writings of Joseph Smith,* 4–6; and in Dean C. Jessee, "The Early Accounts of Joseph Smith's First Vision," *BYUS* 9 (Spring 1969), 275–94.

8. The accounts of Joshua McKune and Michael Morse, published in 1879, state that Joseph Smith Jr. himself considered joining the Methodist church in Harmony, Pennsylvania, in 1828, casting further doubt on the First Vision story. See Jerald Tanner and Sandra Tanner, *Mormonism: Shadow or Reality?* 4th ed. (Salt Lake City, 1982), 156–62a; and the discussion in Hill, "First Vision Controversy," 37–44. See Jan Shipps, "The Prophet Puzzle," *JMH* 1 (1974), for an extended analysis of the debate over the First Vision.

9. Joseph Ketts, *Rites of Passage: Adolescence in America, 1790–Present* (New York, 1977); Bushman, *Joseph Smith,* 59, 82, 84; Larry Porter, "The Church in New York and Pennsylvania, 1816–1831," in F. Mark McKiernan et al., eds., *The Restoration Movement: Essays in Mormon History* (Lawrence, Kans., 1973), 31; Willard Chase affidavit, in Rodger Anderson, *Joseph Smith's New York Reputation Reexamined* (Salt Lake City, 1990), 120–6.

10. Bushman, *Joseph Smith,* 70–1; Stafford Family AFGS prepared by Don Charles Nearpass.

11. Bushman, *Joseph Smith,* 70; Oliver Chase, *Genealogy of the Ancestors and Descendants of Joseph Chase, who died in Swanzey* (Fall River, 1874), 9–11, 13, 18; William F. Reed, *The Descendants of Thomas Durfee of Portsmouth, R.I.,* 2 vols. (Washington, D.C., 1902), 1:213–14; Lenore Evans, *A Patchwork History of Tiverton, Rhode Island* (Tiverton, 1976), 41; AFGS.

12. Notices of Walter's jail escape were printed in the *New Hampshire Patriot,* Sept. 1, 1818, and the *Concord Gazette,* Sept. 1, 1818. I am obliged to Peter Benes for this reference. See also Parfitt, *Walter Family,* 3–10, 62, 71, 109–10, 128, 246. Michael Quinn, in *Early Mormonism,* 53–111, presents an extremely detailed discussion of possible magical influences on the Smith family that differs somewhat from the short discussion I have presented here. Quinn discounts the Masonic influence that I develop throughout this chapter and focuses on a series of artifacts apparently passed down from Hyrum Smith, including parchments, a dagger, and a "jupiter talisman" thought to have been

in Joseph's possession at his death. The interpretation of these artifacts is highly complex and controversial, and without direct access to these materials, I must reserve judgment. The interested reader is referred to Quinn's study. If Quinn is correct, then the story is significantly more complex, but not essentially different, from the one presented here.

13. On the seer-stones, see Quinn, *Early Mormonism*, 38–41.

14. Quotations from Martin Harris interview, originally published in *Tiffany's Monthly* V (May 1859), reprinted in Francis W. Kirkham, ed., *A New Witness for Christ in America: The Book of Mormon*, rev. ed. (Salt Lake City, 1959), 2:377; and from William Stafford affidavit, in Anderson, *Joseph Smith's New York Reputation Reexamined*, 144. Also see W. D. Purple's reminiscences, Norwich *Chenango Union*, May 3, 1877, republished in Walker, ed., *Dale Morgan on Early Mormonism*, 333–4; Tucker, *Mormonism*, 20; and Walker, ed., *Dale Morgan on Early Mormonism*, 233.

15. Lists of the money-diggers are given in the Harris interview, in Kirkham, ed., *New Witness*, 2:377, and Tucker, *Mormonism*, 38–9. For Peter Ingersoll, see affidavit, in Anderson, *Joseph Smith's New York Reputation Reexamined*, 134–8.

16. Shipps, "The Prophet Puzzle," is the most important non-Mormon discussion of the relationship between the occult and religion in this critical period in Joseph Smith's life. See also Bushman, *Joseph Smith*, 64ff., for a Mormon perspective. Quotations from Jonathan Lapham and Rosewell Nicholls affidavits, in Anderson, *Joseph Smith's New York Reputation Reexamined*, 131, 139.

17. Willard Chase affidavit, in Anderson, *Joseph Smith's New York Reputation Reexamined*, 120–6; Smith, "1832 History," in Jessee, ed., *The Personal Writings of Joseph Smith*, 7. The celebrated "White Salamander" letter, a forgery crafted by Mark Hofmann in the early 1980s, is a description of this episode, supposedly written by Martin Harris.

18. Smith, *Biographical Sketches*, 91–8; Bushman, *Joseph Smith*, 66–8; Reed, *The Descendants of Thomas Durfee*, 1:127, 318–19; Evans, *Patchwork History of Tiverton*, 41.

19. The most direct evidence on the Bainbridge court trials is developed in Wesley P. Walters, "Joseph Smith's Bainbridge, N.Y., Court Trials," *Westminster Theological Journal* 36 (1974), 123–55. See also Walker, ed., *Dale Morgan on Early Mormonism*, 239–43, 331–9; Bushman, *Joseph Smith*, 64–9, 74–5; and Marvin S. Hill, "Joseph Smith and the 1826 Trial: New Evidence and New Difficulties," *BYUS* 12 (Summer 1972), 223–33.

20. The discovery of the plates has been described in detail most recently by Bushman, *Joseph Smith*, 79–84, and Quinn, *Early Mormonism*, 112–49.

21. Brodie, *No Man Knows My History*, 413–17. The Book of Ether, a fragment set at roughly 2500 B.C., describes a band called the Jaredites as the first settlers of the Americas; one of the first settlers in Manchester was a man named Stephen Jared. See David Persuitte, *Joseph Smith and the Book of Mormon* (Jefferson, N.C., 1985), 207.

22. Mormon 1:6–16, 4:23, 6:6.

23. Harris interview, in Kirkham, ed., *New Witness*, 2:379–83; see also Bushman, *Joseph Smith*, 80–5.
24. Bushman, *Joseph Smith*, 85–113, 143ff.
25. *Extracts from the Proceedings of the Right Worshipful Grand Lodge of the State of New York* . . . (New York, 1836), 47–9, 52, 58–9; *Extracts from the Proceedings of the Grand Chapter of the State of New York, at its Annual Meeting, February, 1828* (Albany, 1828), 4–9.
26. For several decades scholars have been exploring Masonic influences on early Mormonism, and my discussion owes a lot to their analyses. The seminal essay on this relationship is C. M. Adamson, "The Treasure of the Widow's Son" (University of Utah, n.d., unpublished paper); followed by Reed Durham, "Is There No Help for the Widow's Son?" (unpublished presidential address to the Mormon Historical Association, 1974); and Robert N. Hullinger, *Mormon Answer to Skepticism: Why Joseph Smith Wrote the Book of Mormon* (St. Louis, 1980), 100–19. Earlier accounts that suggested this line of analysis include Samuel H. Godwin, *Mormonism and Masonry: A Utah Point of View* (Salt Lake City, 1925); and Kenneth W. Godfrey, "Joseph Smith and the Masons," *Journal of the Illinois State Historical Society* 64 (1971), 79–81. I use the version of the Royal Arch Enoch tale transcribed in Webb, *Freemason's Monitor* (1802), 246–60. I am very grateful to Jan Shipps and Thomas L. Revere for providing much of this material.
27. This information is derived from Hullinger, *Mormon Answer to Skepticism*, 105–10. See also *DC* 17:1; and Oliver Cowdery's Letter VIII, *Messenger and Advocate*, Oct. 1835, pp. 196–7.
28. D. Booth interview with William R. Kelley, in Anderson, *Joseph Smith's New York Reputation Reexamined*, 170.
29. William Hutchinson, *The Spirit of Masonry* (London, 1775; repr., 1987), appendix, 6; John E. Thompson, " 'The Facultie of Abrac': Masonic Claims and Mormon Beginnings," *The Philalethes* 35, 6 (1982), 9, 15. Bushman, *Joseph Smith*, 72, contains a full quotation of this passage from Lucy Mack Smith's manuscript. A note in George Oliver, *The Antiquities of Free-Masonry* . . . (London, 1823), 122–4, contains an extended discussion of "Abraxas," described as an ancient heathen mystery.
30. *Proceedings of the Grand Chapter of Royal Arch Masons of the State of New York, From its Organization in 1798, to 1867, Inclusive* (Buffalo, 1871), 1:231.
31. *Catalogue of Books, for Sale at the Bookstore in Hanover* . . . (Hanover, N.H., 1799), 8, 15; Clay Perry, *New England's Buried Treasure* (New York, 1946), 13, 34–47, 107, 116, 123–5, 133–5, 274, 374–5.
32. Genesis 23:49–50; Joshua 10; 1 Samuel 24; 1 Kings 19:18.
33. See affidavits of Peter Ingersoll, Christopher M. Stafford, and Sylvia Walker, in Anderson, *Joseph Smith's New York Reputation Reexamined*, 136, 166, 179; Brigham Young, Apr. 29, 1877, in *JD* 19: 38. This cave was rediscovered in 1974, with fragments of a wooden door (Rochester *Democrat and Chronicle*, Apr. 24, 1974; Palmyra *Courier Journal*, May 1, 1974).
34. 1 Nephi 1:1–5, 17:9–11, 16, 18:25, 19:1; 2 Nephi 5:15–21; Ether 10:23;

Helaman 6:11. See also Jacob 2:12; Jarom 1:8; Mosiah 11:10; Alma 1:29, 4:6; Ether 7:9, 9:16–17; Helaman 6:9; Moses 5:46. (For the Book of Moses, see below, note 55.)

35. Ether 10:7; Alma 34:29.
36. 3 Nephi 24:2–3; see also *DC* 128:24; Malachi 3:2–3.
37. 3 Nephi 28:21; 4 Nephi 1:32; Mormon 8:24; Mosiah 12:3; Helaman 5:23.
38. Hill, *Joseph Smith*, 113; Jessee, comp. and ed., *The Personal Writings of Joseph Smith*, 75; Matthew 3:11; Luke 3:16; *DC* 33:11.
39. Austin Fife and Alta Fife, *Saints of the Sage and Saddle: Folklore among the Mormons* (Bloomington, 1956), 233–49.
40. Daniel, 3:19–26; Carl G. Jung, *Psychology and Alchemy*, vol. 12 of *The Collected Works of C. G. Jung*, 2d ed., trans. R. F. C. Hull (New York, 1967), 343–4; Carl G. Jung, *Alchemical Studies*, vol. 13 of *The Collected Works*, 2d ed., trans. R. F. C. Hull (New York, 1967), 95, 346–7, 357.
41. Jung, *Alchemical Studies*, 357–431; F. Sherwood Taylor, *The Alchemists: Founders of Modern Chemistry* (New York, 1949), 148–53, 222, 241; Hans Jonas, *The Gnostic Religion: The Message of the Alien God and the Beginnings of Christianity*, 2d ed., rev. (Boston, 1958), 125; Matthew 13:46; *DC* 50:144.
42. Jung, *Alchemical Studies*, 419–20.
43. Smith, *Biographical Sketches*, 55; Bushman, *Joseph Smith*, 37.
44. Genesis 2:9.
45. Smith, *Biographical Sketches*, 57–9.
46. 1 Nephi 8:10–30, 11:25, 15:21–30; see also Alma 12:21, 14:2–6.
47. It should be noted that when it was published, Lucy Smith's *Biographical Sketches* incorporated these dreams into the family's history in Vermont. However, her original account of the Vermont years in her "Preliminary Manuscript" did not include these dreams. They were written out on separate sheets and later included in the revised transcription by Martha Coray. In the manuscript file of "Lucy Mack Smith. History" in the collections of the LDS Historical Department ("Preliminary Manuscript"), the original text (unpaginated), with no reference to dreams, is in folder 2, and accounts of some of the dreams are in folder 5. I am obliged to Jan Shipps for pointing this out. For the tangled history of the text of the Lucy Mack Smith manuscript, see Shipps, *Mormonism*, 87–108.
48. Kenneth Silverman, *The Life and Times of Cotton Mather* (New York, 1984), 108; Theodore D. Bozeman, *To Live Ancient Lives* (Chapel Hill, 1988), 271, 272n; Dan Vogel, *Indian Origins and the Book of Mormon* (Salt Lake City, 1986), 35–43.
49. See illustrations of the Whitmers' seer-stones, in Quinn, *Early Mormonism*, figs. 11–13, following p. 228. Compare with the polished and drilled gorgets and pendants illustrated in William A. Ritchie, *The Archaeology of New York State* (Garden City, N.Y., 1965), 181, 192, 224, 249, and 256.
50. David Levin, "Giants in the Earth: Science and the Occult in Cotton Mather's Letters to the Royal Society," *WMQ* 45 (1988), 751–70.
51. The contemporary sources are detailed in Hullinger, *Mormon Answer to*

Skepticism, 48–64; and Vogel, *Indian Origins and the Book of Mormon*, 22–69; Peter Ingersoll testimony in Anderson, *Joseph Smith's New England Reputation Reexamined*, 136; Rochester story in George H. Harris, "Myths of Ononda" (c. 1887), George H. Harris Collection, Rochester Historical Society, Rochester, New York; and Dorothy Dengler, "Tales of Buried Treasure in Rochester," *New York Folklore Quarterly* 2 (1946), 174–81. For the "Book of Enoch" see James H. Charlesworth, ed., *The Old Testament Pseudepigrapha*, vol. 1: *Apocalyptic Literature and Testaments* (Garden City, N.Y., 1983), 8, 16. For the Seneca, see Anthony F. C. Wallace, *The Death and Rebirth of the Seneca* (New York, 1969), 291–2.

52. George Oliver, *The Antiquities of Freemasonry; Comprising the Three Grand Periods of Masonry from the Creation of the World to the Dedication of King Solomon's Temple* (London, 1823), chapters 2, 4, 6, 8, 10 (quotations from pp. 41–5). The theme of primitive and spurious Masonry is summarized in Mackey, *An Encyclopedia of Freemasonry*, 2:584–5, 706–8.

53. Andrew Michael Ramsay, *The Philosophical Principles of Natural and Revealed Religion. Part Second.* (Glasgow, 1749), 8–15, 215–99; Mary Ann Meyers, *A New World Jerusalem* (Westport, Conn., 1983), 23–5.

54. Mackey, *An Encyclopedia of Freemasonry*, 2:584; A. L. Morton, *The World of the Ranters* (London, 1970), 138–40; Christopher Hill et al., *The World of the Muggletonians* (London, 1983), 28–30, 79–80, 85; Rufus M. Jones, *Spiritual Reformers in the 16th and 17th Centuries* (Boston, 1914; repr., 1959), 225–6; John Rogers, *A Midnight Cry from the Temple of God to the Ten Virgins* (New York, 1705), 32–6, 43–6; Peter Pratt, *The Prey Taken by the Strong* (New London, 1725), 51–3. See also Quinn, *Early Mormonism*, 166–8.

55. Moses 6:6–7, 7:22. The Book of Moses is a section of *The Pearl of Great Price: A Selection from the Revelations, Translations, and Narrations of Joseph Smith, First Prophet, Seer, and Revelator of the Church of Jesus Christ of Latter-day Saints* (Liverpool, England, 1851); all citations are to the 1985 Salt Lake City edition. Compare with Genesis 4–5.

56. DC 76:7, 84:5–19, 107:18. See below, Chapter 8.

57. For a sketch of this division, see H. L. Haywood and James E. Craig, *A History of Freemasonry* (New York, 1927), 235–69.

58. On the schism, see Samuel H. Baynard, *History of the Supreme Council, 33°* (Boston, 1938), 182–9; Ossian Lang, *History of Freemasonry in New York State* (New York, 1922), 96–107; Charles T. McClenachan, *History of the Most Ancient and Honorable Fraternity of Freemasonry in New York*, 2 vols. (New York, 1892), 2:351–9, 370, 414, 443; Peter Ross, *A Standard History of Freemasonry in the State of New York* (New York, 1899), 1:259–301. I am indebted to Jules Garfunkel for the suggestion that corruption in the Country Grand Lodge might explain Masonic violence against Morgan.

59. The idea of alienated Masons, or "anti-Masonic Masons," was first developed by Rick Grunder, in "More Parallels: A Survey of Little-known Sources of Mormon History," a paper delivered at the 1987 Sunstone Conference. See *Transactions of the Grand Lodge of Free and Accepted Masons of*

.the State of New York. 1816–1827 (New York, 1880), 337–40; *Proceedings of the (Country) Grand Lodge of Free and Accepted Masons in the State of New York. 1823–1827* (New York, 1880), 22–4, 42–51. On the Nauvoo lodge, see Mervin B. Hogan, ed., *The Founding Minutes of the Nauvoo Lodge* (Des Moines, Iowa, 1971), 8; and the tables appended to Mervin B. Hogan, "The Rise and Fall of the Nauvoo Lodge," unpublished paper on file at MONH Library. On Phelps, see David Bernard, *Light on Masonry . . .* (Utica, 1829), 455; Cook, *The Revelations of the Prophet Joseph Smith*, 87.

60. On Antimasonry and the general climate of political culture in the 1820s, see Ronald P. Formisano and Kathleen S. Kutolowski, "Antimasonry and Masonry: The Genesis of Protest, 1826–1827," *American Quarterly* 29 (1977), 139–65; Kathleen S. Kutolowski, "Freemasonry and Community in the Early Republic: The Case for Antimasonic Anxieties," *American Quarterly* 34 (1982), 543–61; and Kathleen S. Kutolowski, "Antimasonry Reexamined: Social Bases of the Grass-Roots Party," *Journal of American History* 71 (1984), 269–93; Persuitte, *Joseph Smith and the Book of Mormon*, 174–80; Dan Vogel, "Mormonism's Anti-Masonick Bible," *John Whitmer Historical Association Journal* 9 (1989), 17–29; Helaman 7:4. See also 3 Nephi 6:27–30; Brodie, *No Man Knows My History*, 64n, 459–60; Walter F. Prince, "Psychological Tests for the Authorship of the Book of Mormon," *American Journal of Psychology* 28 (1917), 373–89. Looking for word parallels between Antimasonic culture and the *Book of Mormon*, Prince counted forty proper names in the *Book of Mormon* beginning with "Mor," twenty-eight with the letters "ant" or "anti," and various other parallels. On Martin Harris, see Wayne *Sentinel*, Oct. 5, 1827; *Geauga Gazette* (Painesville), Mar. 15, 1831. These Masonic influences are most recently and thoroughly discussed in David John Buerger, "The Development of the Mormon Temple Endowment Ceremony," *Dialogue* 20 (Winter 1987), 39–41.

61. Bushman, *Joseph Smith*, 129–31; Richard L. Bushman, "The Book of Mormon and the American Revolution," *BYUS* 17 (Fall 1976), 3–20.

62. Geneva *Gazette*, Jan. 10, 1827, p. 3; Geneva *Palladium*, Jan. 10, 1827, p. 3.

63. *Ontario Repository and Freeman*, Feb. 11, 1824, p. 3.

64. *Proceedings of a Convention of Delegates, from the Different Counties in the State of New York, Opposed to Free-Masonry, Held at the Capitol in the City of Albany, on the 19th, 20th and 21st Days of February, 1829* (Rochester, 1829), 9. First cited in Rick Grunder, "Mormon List Twenty-eight, April, 1988."

65. Helaman 2:11, 3:23, 7:5; Geneva *Palladium*, Sept. 8, 1824, p. 3.

66. All convictions for counterfeiting had a mandatory sentence in the state prison. The following discussion is based on an analysis of the "Auburn Prison Register of Convicts, [1817–1848]," #500m, vol. 12, New York State Archives, Albany. I am grateful to Dr. James Folts of the New York State Archives for making this material available. The Auburn State Prison drew its prisoners from throughout the state; this analysis involves those convicted in or west of Oneida, Madison, and Chenango counties.

67. Geneva *Palladium*, Feb. 4, 1824, p. 3; *Ontario Repository and Freeman,* Jan. 28, 1824, p. 3. I am grateful to Gary Thompson, Elaine Morie, and Michael Hunter of Hobart/William Smith Colleges for sharing material from their index of Geneva, New York, newspapers.

68. Geneva *Gazette*, Feb. 25, 1824, p. 2. Also reported in Wayne *Sentinel,* Feb. 18, 1824.

69. Wayne *Sentinel,* copied in both the Geneva *Gazette* and the *Ontario Repository and Freeman,* Apr. 6, 1825. Turner, *Phelps and Gorham Purchase,* 217–23; Mass. SJC Dockets, 1785: 177, 1787: 58.

70. John G. Forbes Jr. is identified in the Auburn Prison records as having been born in Manlius in 1803. According to the U.S. census, John G. Forbes Sr. lived in a succession of towns around Syracuse: Manlius in 1820 and Salina in 1830; by 1840 he had moved to Syracuse, where he had law offices and was on the executive committee of a library association. John G. Forbes Sr. rose in the militia from lieutenant in 1809 to colonel in 1817; he was the town attorney for Salina at its incorporation in 1824 and was elected as a Democrat to the Assembly in 1825. He was involved in a number of railroad and turnpike projects and by the late 1830s was a Whig. See Carroll E. Smith, *Pioneer Times in the Onandaga Country* (Syracuse, 1904), 295, 350; Dwight H. Bruce, ed., *Onondaga's First Centennial: Gleanings of a Century* (Boston, 1896), 1:276–7, 430, 2:947–8; indictments, Livingston County Clerk's Office; Wayne County Court of Oyer and Terminer, *Minutes,* vol. 1; Monroe County Court of Oyer and Terminer, *Minutes;* Ontario County Court of Oyer and Terminer, *Minutes, 1793–1847,* 167, 170, 171. I am particularly obliged to Dr. Ann Filiaci at the Ontario County Clerk's Office, Kathy Muzdakis at the Monroe County Clerk's Office, and Margaret McCaughey at the Livingston County Clerk's Office for locating and copying this material for me.

71. Tucker, *Mormonism,* 14, 17. Oliver P. Alderman, *Autobiography of O. P. Alderman . . .* (Merchantville, N.Y., 1874), 55–66, provides a detailed account of the dimensions and mechanics of the trade in bad money in central New York in the 1830s. Burroughs's *Memoirs* was republished in abbreviated form in Albany, Hudson, Otsego, and Canandaigua between 1810 and 1813; the 1811 Albany edition was available at the lending library in Manchester village. See Robert Paul, "Joseph Smith and the Manchester (New York) Library," *BYUS* 22 (Summer 1982), 347. Abigail Harris affidavit in Anderson, *Joseph Smith's New York Reputation Reexamined,* 130.

72. Another four witnesses were located to the east: two near Syracuse in Salina and Cazanovia, one to the northeast in Whitestown, and one to the west at Brutus. These Syracuse area witnesses suggest that the gang operated along the Erie Canal and add credence to the connection between the Butlers and John G. Forbes Jr., the Salina lawyer's son convicted in Livingston County. Ontario County Court of Oyer and Terminer, *Minutes, 1793–1847,* 167, 170, 171; indexes of the U.S. census for 1820 and 1830.

73. Among those enumerated by Pomeroy Tucker as followers of Joseph Smith in

money-digging who never became Mormons are Peter Ingersoll of Palmyra and William, Joshua, and Gad Stafford of Manchester (Tucker, *Mormonism,* 38–9). A "Tile Stafford" in Palmyra in the 1820 census is apparently Stiles, listed in Ontario County in 1810. A "Tilor" Stafford, the son or grandson of David Stafford, was listed in Washington County in 1800. For the connection to David Stafford, see Nearpass, "Materials for a Genealogy of Josiah Stover who became Josiah Stafford." Census data from Thomas L. Revere.

74. The Ingersolls were living in both Ontario and Onondaga counties. Peter Ingersoll was a teamster who – according to his statement in 1833 – lived in the Smith neighborhood "until about 1830." This must have been a relatively short residence, because the 1810 census lists a Peter in Williamson, north of Palmyra, the 1820 census put him in Tompkins County, and the 1830 census recorded two, one in Onondaga County in the town of Pompey and a second far to the west in Chautauqua County. Similarly, there was a Thomas Ingersoll in Bloomfield in 1810 and in Victor in 1820 (adjacent towns just west of Farmington), in Salina in 1820, and in Onondaga in 1830. All of these Ingersolls were part of a large family originally located in Westfield and Great Barrington, Massachusetts. Peter Ingersoll, the teamster and Smith family neighbor, seems to have moved between Ontario and Tompkins counties before settling in Onondaga County, dying in 1863. Both his wife and his father, Thomas, died in Liverpool, the postal village of Salina township, where John G. Forbes Sr. was located prior to his move to Syracuse. Either his father or an older brother named Thomas could have been the witness for George Butler in 1823. The other possibility is that the Thomas Ingersoll located in Victor, west of Farmington, was the witness for Butler. If that was the case, the connection between Thomas the witness and Peter the teamster is more distant, third cousin rather than brother, but there is still an interesting connection. Thomas of Victor was the father of Dorus Ingersoll, born in Ontario County in 1808 according to the Auburn Prison records and convicted at Canandaigua of grand larceny in May 1826. The information in the U.S. census for 1810, 1820, and 1830 for New York State on the Ingersolls fits well with the data in Lillian D. Avery, *A Genealogy of the Ingersoll Family in America, 1629–1925* (New York, 1926), 151–2, 173–4, 178. For witnesses for Carr and Butler see Ontario County Court of Oyer and Terminer, *Minutes,* 167, 170, 171. Convictions are listed in alphabetical and chronological order in "Auburn Prison Register of Convicts." A Charles Butler who testified on behalf of George Butler in 1823 probably was the same Charles Butler who was convicted of passing counterfeit money in Steuben County in 1827. There is always the chance that the indictments of Forbes as well as of Carr and Butler were part of an elaborate political game, with Clintonians trying to discredit Bucktails. But the important question is not the reality of counterfeiting but the *public perception* of counterfeiting, particularly the Smiths' perception of it as an all-pervading force. I have chosen to accept these court and prison records at face value.

75. Harris interview, in Kirkham, ed., *New Witness,* 2:381. Harris was referring

to the fall of 1827, but at this point in the interview "Mr. Harris seemed to wander from the subject," so I feel free to make this a general statement.

76. W. D. Purple's account, quoted in Bushman, *Joseph Smith*, 75.
77. Helaman 2:4, 5:8, 23–4, 43–4.
78. Helaman 6:9, 8:25, 11:31, 13:17–22, 31–4.
79. 3 Nephi 1:27, 13:19–20, 21:16, 19; Alma 1:32; 3 Nephi 25:5, 26:3, 28:21.
80. This is not the final narrative cycle in the *Book of Mormon,* for the Book of Ether describes the fortunes of a previous people, the Jaredites, who had ventured across the Atlantic after the fall of the Tower of Babel. Although miracles and interpreter-stones played central roles in this story, and eventually the Jaredites are destroyed after they ignore prophecy, there is no reference to furnaces. Rather, alchemical references are limited to the accumulation of gold and treasure before the Jaredite downfall.
81. Mormon 1:6, 15–17.
82. Mormon 1:18–19, 2:10.
83. Rosewell Nichols affidavit, in Anderson, *Joseph Smith's New York Reputation Reexamined,* 140.
84. Tucker, *Mormonism,* 20; Alma 37:21–7.
85. Solomon Mack's final exhortation to the readers of his *Narrative* was as follows: "remember your unfortunate friend Solomon Mack, who worried and toiled until an old age to try to lay up treasures in this world, but the Lord would not suffer me to have it, but now I trust I have treasures laid up that no man can take away, but by the goodness of God through the blood of a bleeding Saviour" (Mack, *Narrative,* 44, cited in Anderson, *Joseph Smith's New England Heritage,* 31).
86. Smith's move toward prophetic stature was not without hesitation. As late as the fall of 1829 and the spring of 1830 he and his family clearly had hopes that the sale of the *Book of Mormon* would provide a way out of debt and into competency. See Hill, *Quest for Refuge,* 19–20.
87. See below, Chapter 9.
88. DC 6:7, 11, 8:11, 11:7, 28:7.
89. Shipps, "The Prophet Puzzle," 6 and passim.
90. Brodie, *No Man Knows My History,* 18, 26–7, 84, 127. Most recently, see Harold Bloom, *The American Religion,* 96–111; or Bloom, "The Religion-making Imagination of Joseph Smith," *Yale Review* 80 (1992), 26–43.
91. Brodie, *No Man Knows My History,* 412–21. Brodie's interpretation was grounded in her reading of Phyllis Greenacre, "The Impostor," *Psychoanalytic Quarterly* 27 (1958), 359–82. Klaus J. Hansen, *Mormonism and the American Experience* (Chicago, 1981), 14, notes that "it is quite possible to fit Smith into [the] pattern" identified by Brodie. But Hansen is more concerned with the problem of explaining *how* Smith received his visions and presents an important argument suggesting that "voices" and "visions" are seen and heard in the right brain (see 18–24). He draws on Julian Jaynes, *The Origin of Consciousness in the Breakdown of the Bicameral Mind* (Toronto, 1978).

92. For a variety of perspectives on the question of mystical or prophetic religion and psychosis, see Clark Garrett, *Spirit Possession and Popular Religion* (Baltimore, 1987), 1–12; Silvano Arieti, *The Intra-psychic Self: Feeling, Cognition, and Creativity in Health and Mental Illness* (New York, 1967), 417–35; W. W. Meissner, *The Psychology of a Saint: Ignatius of Loyola* (New Haven, 1992), 311–58; I. M. Lewis, *Ecstatic Religion: A Study in Shamanism and Spirit Possession*, 2d ed. (London, 1989), 160–84; Bryan R. Wilson, *Magic and the Millenniun: A Sociological Study of the Religious Movements of Protest among Tribal and Third-World Peoples* (New York, 1973); Wallace, *The Death and Rebirth of the Seneca*, 239–54; J. Kroll and B. Bachrach, "Visions and Psychopathology in the Middle Ages," *Journal of Nervous and Mental Disease* 170 (1982), 41–9; Peter Buckley, "Mystical Experience and Schizophrenia," *Schizophrenia Bulletin* 7 (1981), 516–21; and David Lukoff, "The Diagnosis of Mystical Experiences with Psychotic Features," *Journal of Transpersonal Psychology* 17 (1985), 155–81. On the interactive relationship of the prophet and an audience, I have been particularly influenced by Thomas W. Overholt, "Prophecy: The Problem of Cross-cultural Comparison," in Bernard Lang, *Anthropological Approaches to the Old Testament* (Philadelphia, 1985), 60–82; Thomas W. Overholt, "The Ghost Dance of 1890 and the Nature of the Prophetic Process," *Ethnohistory* 21 (1974), 37–63; and Garrett, *Spirit Possession and Popular Religion*.

93. Stephen Burroughs, *Sermon Delivered in Rutland, On a Haymow* (Hanover, N.H., 1798), 7.

94. Carl G. Jung, *Mysterium Coniunctionis: An Inquiry into the Separation and Synthesis of Psychic Opposites in Alchemy*, vol. 14 of *The Collected Works*, 2d ed., trans. R. F. C. Hull (New York, 1963), 3 and passim; Curtis D. Smith, *Jung's Quest for Wholeness: A Religious and Historical Perspective* (Albany, 1990), 99–115, provides an excellent introductory summary. See also Ann Belford Ulanov, *The Feminine in Jungian Psychology and in Christian Theology* (Evanston, 1971), 26–95, esp. 63, 74–5.

95. I find that a Jungian approach to Mormonism is not new. It was originally developed in T. L. Brink, "Joseph Smith: The Verdict of Depth Psychology," *JMH* 3 (1976), 73–83, in which Brink made the connection between divining, alchemy, and the Jungian search for psychic perfection. Brink does not connect the Jungian alchemical-psychological model to the oppositions outlined by Brodie (see 79–80). See discussion in Hansen, *Mormonism and the American Experience*, 25. Most recently, a Jungian approach to Mormon theology has been developed in Margaret Toscano and Paul Toscano, *Strangers in Paradox: Explorations in Mormon Cosmology* (Salt Lake City, 1990), 75–9.

96. Such a resolution is discussed in terms of conversionary religion in William James, *The Varieties of Religious Experience: A Study in Human Nature* (London, 1910), 166–88 ("The Divided Self, and the Process of Its Unification").

97. Steven L. Olsen, "Joseph Smith and the Structure of Mormon Identity," *Dialogue* 14 (Autumn 1981), 89–99.

98. DC 128:18.

8. The Mysteries Defined

1. *DC* 76:54–8.
2. 3 Nephi 24:2–3.
3. Mormon 8:24, 9:2, 11, 17–25; Mark 16:17–18.
4. Wayne *Sentinel*, Mar. 26, 1830, p. 3.
5. Accounts of the witnesses include Bushman, *Joseph Smith*, 102–6; Roberts, *Comprehensive History*, 1:134–49; Smith, *Biographical Sketches*, 138–41.
6. Larry C. Porter, "A Study of the Origins of the Church of Latter-day Saints in the States of New York and Pennsylvania, 1816–1831" (Ph.D. diss., Brigham Young University, 1971), 259–61; Bushman, *Joseph Smith*, 142–9.
7. "Newell Knight's Journal," in *Classic Experiences and Adventures: Scraps of Biography* (Salt Lake City, 1969), 50–1, 59–60; Bushman, *Joseph Smith*, 154; Roberts, *Comprehensive History*, 1:200–3, 208–10; Porter, "A Study of the Origins of the Church," 181–6, 195–222.
8. Early Mormon faith healing and speaking in tongues are described in Eber D. Howe, *Mormonism Unvailed* (Painesville, Ohio, 1834), 124–47; Max C. Parkin, "Conflict at Kirtland: The Nature and Cause of Internal and External Conflict of the Mormons in Ohio between 1830 and 1838" (M.A. thesis, Brigham Young University, 1966), 55–88; Breck England, *The Life and Thought of Orson Pratt* (Salt Lake City, 1985), 30–4; Hill, *Joseph Smith*, 268–9.
9. See Appendix.
10. *Manual of the Churches of Seneca County with Sketches of their Pastors* (Seneca Falls, 1896), 98, 101–2, 103, 123; Porter, "A Study of the Origins of the Church," 227–9.
11. D. Michael Quinn, ed., "The First Months of Mormonism: A Contemporary View by Rev. Diedrich Willers," *New York History* 54 (1973), 331–3.
12. See above, Chapter 3, and Vogel, *Religious Seekers*, 25–41; Hill, *Quest for Refuge*, 11–17. On the populist appeal of Mormonism, see Nathan O. Hatch, *The Democratization of American Christianity* (New Haven, 1989), 122–3, 134–5.
13. Among other studies see Mario S. DePillis, "The Quest for Religious Authority and the Rise of Mormonism," *Dialogue* 1 (Spring 1966), 68–88.
14. Marvin S. Hill, "The Shaping of the Mormon Mind in New England and New York," *BYUS* 9 (Spring 1969), 363–5; Timothy L. Smith, "The Book of Mormon in a Biblical Culture," *JMH* 7 (1980), 3–21.
15. Thomas F. O'Dea, *The Mormons* (Chicago, 1957), 156–60.
16. Bushman, *Joseph Smith*, 166–8; Hill, *Joseph Smith*, 116–18; *DC* 28:7. Quinn, *Early Mormonism*, 192–210, discusses the persisting conflict between popular religious belief and the church hierarchy in the nineteenth century.
17. *DC* 29:46–7; Hill, *Quest for Refuge*, 22; Sterling M. McMurrin, *The Theological Foundations of the Mormon Religion* (Salt Lake City, 1965), 67–8.
18. Grant Underwood, "Seminal versus Sesquicentennial Saints: A Look at Mormon Millennialism," *Dialogue* 14 (Spring 1981), 32–44; Grant Underwood, "Early Mormon Millennialism: Another Look," *Church History* 54 (1985), 215–29.

19. DC 28:1, 8–11; Bushman, *Joseph Smith,* 168–71. The eventual group of missionaries was composed of Oliver Cowdery, Peter Whitmer Jr., Parley Pratt, and Ziba Peterson.

20. Vogel, *Religious Seekers,* 37; F. Mark McKiernan, *The Voice of One Crying in the Wilderness: Sidney Rigdon, Religious Reformer, 1793–1876* (Lawrence, Kans., 1971), 25–30; Parley P. Pratt Jr., ed., *Autobiography of Parley P. Pratt* (1873; Salt Lake City, 1985), 24–48; Milton V. Backman, "The Quest for a Restoration: The Birth of Mormonism in Ohio," *BYUS* 12 (Summer 1972), 346–64; Hans Rollman, "The Early Baptist Career of Sidney Rigdon in Warren, Ohio," *BYUS* 21 (Winter 1981), 37–50. I write this assuming that Smith and Rigdon first met in December of 1830. However, it should be noted that Rodger I. Anderson, in his *Joseph Smith's New York Reputation Reexamined* (Salt Lake City, 1990), 87–8, suggests that the testimony placing Rigdon at the Smith farm as early as March 1827 ought to be taken seriously.

21. Parkin, "Conflict at Kirtland," 66–89; Robert Kent Fielding, "The Growth of the Mormon Church in Kirtland, Ohio" (Ph.D. diss., Indiana University, 1957), 33–43; McKiernan, *The Voice of One Crying,* 50–1; DC 50:1–9.

22. DC 44–8, 102; see O'Dea, *The Mormons,* 160–1, 174–9; D. Michael Quinn, "The Mormon Hierarchy, 1832–1932: An American Elite" (Ph.D. diss., Yale University, 1976), 6–7, 9, 23, 32.

23. See E. Gordon Alderfer, *The Ephrata Commune* (Pittsburgh, 1985), 47, 74–6, 99–106; Edward D. Andrews, *The People Called Shakers: The Search for the Perfect Society* (New York, 1953), 57–60. See J. F. C. Harrison, *The Second Coming: Popular Millenarianism, 1780–1850* (New Brunswick, 1979), 148–50, for similar hierarchies among the English Wroeites, many of whom converted to Mormonism in the 1840s. On the Anabaptists, see William E. Juhnke, "Anabaptism and Mormonism: A Study in Comparative History," *John Whitmer Historical Journal* 2 (1982), 38–46; D. Michael Quinn, "Socioreligious Radicalism of the Mormon Church: A Parallel to the Anabaptists," in Davis Bitton and Maureen U. Beecher, eds., *New Views of Mormon History: A Collection of Essays in Honor of Leonard J. Arrington* (Salt Lake City, 1987), 363–86.

24. Jean Dietz Moss, "'Godded With God': Henrick Niclaes and His Family of Love," *Transactions of the American Philosophical Society* 71, pt. 8 (1981), 17.

25. DC 13, 20:38–66; Bushman, *Joseph Smith,* 147–8; O'Dea, *The Mormons,* 174–6.

26. Smith, *History of the Church,* 1:72; Fielding, "The Growth of the Mormon Church," 111–13; Vogel, *Religious Seekers,* 115–19; Hill, *Quest for Refuge,* 25–6.

27. Quotations from DC 6:7, 38:32; see also DC 6:11, 8:11, 10:64, 11:7, 19:8–10, 28:7, 35:18, 38:13, 42:61, 65, 43:13. On the continuing "bait" of further revelations of "mysteries" during Smith's lifetime, see David John Buerger, "'The Fulness of the Priesthood': The Second Anointing in Latter-day Saint Theology and Practice," *Dialogue* 16 (Spring 1983), 22–4.

28. Donald Q. Cannon and Lyndon W. Cook, eds., *Far West Record: Minutes of the Church of Jesus Christ of Latter-day Saints, 1830–1844* (Salt Lake City, 1983), 6–7; *DC* 84:19, 107:8, 14.

29. Cannon and Cook, eds., *Far West Record,* 6–7; Smith, *History of the Church,* 1:175–6; Fielding, "The Growth of the Mormon Church," 41–2; Brodie, *No Man Knows My History,* 111–12; Ezra Booth's "Letter IV," in Howe, *Mormonism Unvailed,* 188–90.

30. *DC* 84:66–72; "Newell Knight's Journal," 66–7, 69, 74–5; England, *The Life and Thought of Orson Pratt,* 30–3; Jon Butler, *Awash in a Sea of Faith: Christianizing the American People* (Cambridge, Mass., 1990), 245–6.

31. Mark 16:17–18.

32. *DC* 68:12; Cannon and Cook, eds., *Far West Record,* 20–1. For the best analysis of the powers of the high priesthood, see Buerger, " 'The Fulness of the Priesthood,' " 12–16.

33. Helaman 10:7.

34. *Chronicon Ephratense,* 165; Benjamin S. Youngs, *The Testimony of Christ's Second Coming . . .* (Lebanon, Ohio, 1808), 387, quoted in Robley E. Whitson, ed., *The Shakers: Two Centuries of Spiritual Reflection* (New York, 1983), 227; Karl J. R. Arndt, *George Rapp's Harmony Society, 1785–1847* (Rutherford, N.J., 1965), 309; Orestes A. Brownson, *Defense of the Article on the Laboring Classes* (Boston, 1840), 24; Arthur M. Schlesinger, *Orestes A. Brownson: A Pilgrim's Progress* (Boston, 1939), 187.

35. Thomas S. Webb, *The Freemason's Monitor, or Illustrations of Freemasonry: in Two Parts* (New York, 1802), 199–200; Jeremy L. Cross, *The True Masonic Chart, or Hieroglyphic Monitor* (New York, 1824), 125.

36. The Royal Arch register for 1829 lists a John Rigdon in the Norwalk chapter and a Thomas Rigdon in the Columbus chapter. In 1820 and 1830 Thomas was living near Columbus in Knox County, but in 1830 John was living over a hundred miles from Norwalk. See *Proceedings of the Grand Chapter of Royal Arch Masons, of the State of Ohio . . .* (Columbus, 1872), 122. On their Campbellism and connection to Sidney Rigdon, see A. S. Hayden, *Early History of the Disciples in the Western Reserve, Ohio . . .* (Cincinnati, 1875), 92. On Sidney Rigdon's later Masonic membership, see Thomas J. Gregory, "Sidney Rigdon: Post Nauvoo," *BYUS* 21 (Winter 1981), 59.

37. David Whitmer, *An Address to All Believers in Christ* (Richmond, Mo., 1887; repr., 1938), 35; Alma 13:1–18.

38. Moses 6:67, 7:22.

39. Moses 6:5–7.

40. *DC* 84:5–16; Max H. Parkin, "Kirtland: Stronghold for the Kingdom," in F. Mark McKiernan et al., *The Restoration Movement: Essays in Mormon History* (Lawrence, Kans., 1979), 70–1; Smith, *History of the Church,* 1:297.

41. Genesis 2:19–20; Moses 3:19–20.

42. There is an extensive literature on the early modern search for a universal Adamic language and its relationship to hermetic belief and the origins of scientific and linguistic thought. See Nicholas H. Clulee, *John Dee's Natural*

Philosophy: Between Science and Religion (London, 1988), 82–96; Thomas C. Singer, "Hieroglyphics, Real Characters, and the Idea of Natural Language in Seventeenth-Century Thought," *Journal of the History of Ideas* 50 (1989), 49–70; James Knowlson, *Universal Language Schemes in England and France, 1600–1800* (Toronto, 1975); Russell Fraser, *The Language of Adam: On the Limits and Systems of Discourse* (New York, 1977); M. M. Slaughter, *Universal Languages and Scientific Taxonomy in the Seventeenth Century* (New York, 1982); Paul Cornelius, *Languages in Seventeenth- and Early Eighteenth-Century Voyages* (Geneva, 1965). On the suggestion of a "Masonic universal language," see the spurious Leland letter in William Hutchinson, *The Spirit of Masonry* (London, 1775; repr., 1987), appendix, 7. On the rock carvings, see Robert N. Hullinger, *Mormon Answer to Skepticism: Why Joseph Smith Wrote the Book of Mormon* (St. Louis, 1980), 81.

43. Mormon 9:32–3.
44. Hullinger, *Mormon Answer to Skepticism*, 72–93. Elements of this story were woven into Smith's revision of Isaiah. See Brodie, *No Man Knows My History*, 117.
45. Mormon 9:34.
46. Ether 1:33–5, 3:24.
47. Wayne *Sentinel*, Mar. 26, 1830; Fielding, "The Growth of the Mormon Church," 35.
48. *DC* 84:5; compare with 1 Kings 8.
49. For Solomon's temple in Freemasonry, see George Oliver, *The Antiquities of Free-Masonry . . .* (London, 1823), 131–72; Mackey, *Encyclopedia of Freemasonry*, 2:767–9. On the original temple as the "house of God," see Baruch A. Levine, "On the Presence of the Lord in Biblical Religion," in Jacob Neusner, ed., *Religion in Antiquity: Essays in Memory of Erwin Ramsdell Goodenough* (Leiden, 1970), 71–87; and F. E. Peters, *Jerusalem and Mecca: The Typology of the Holy City in the Near East* (New York, 1986). For a description of the biblical tabernacle and temple probably available to Smith, see *The Genuine Works of Flavius Josephus . . .* (New York, 1821), 1:202–14, 2:124–32, 141–55.
50. 2 Nephi 5:16; 3 Nephi 11:1, 24:1.
51. *DC* 36:8, 42:36; Moses 7:19, 21. See discussion in Bushman, *Joseph Smith*, 186–8.
52. Mormon temple-building theology and architecture has been described in Andrew, *The Early Temples*.
53. "Newell Knight's Journal," 70–1; Hill, *Joseph Smith*, 136; Andrew, *The Early Temples*, 29–30.
54. Andrew, *The Early Temples*, 30–3; Hullinger, *Mormon Answer to Skepticism*, 112; David J. Whittaker, "Substituted Names in the Published Revelations of Joseph Smith," *BYUS* 23 (Winter 1983), 103–12.
55. Andrew, *The Early Temples*, 8; Brodie, *No Man Knows My History*, 211; Klaus J. Hansen, *Mormonism and the American Experience* (Chicago, 1981), 69–70; *DC* 107:53–7, 116:1, 117:8.

56. Andrew, *The Early Temples,* 32.
57. Cook, *The Revelations of the Prophet Joseph Smith,* 157–8.
58. 1 Corinthians 15:41.
59. Brodie, *No Man Knows My History,* 118; DC 76:31–49, 81–6, 102–6, 88:24–31.
60. DC 76:71–9.
61. DC 76:54–60, 96–112.
62. Hill, *Joseph Smith,* 142–7; Brodie, *No Man Knows My History,* 118–20; Cook, *The Revelations of the Prophet Joseph Smith,* 157–66, 311–12 n. 4.
63. Psalms 82:6; John 10:34.
64. Fielding, "The Growth of the Mormon Church," 64–73.
65. DC 76:54, 57, 93:15, 21.
66. DC 93:21–3.
67. DC 93:29–30.
68. DC 93:33–6.
69. DC 131:7–8.
70. Moses 3:5, 9.
71. For discussions of the Mormon doctrines of preexistence, creation, and materialism, see McMurrin, *Theological Foundations,* 3–8, 19–26, 49–57; Van Hale, "The Origin of the Human Spirit in Early Mormon Thought," in Gary James Bergera, ed., *Line upon Line: Essays on Mormon Thought* (Salt Lake City, 1989), 115–17; Blake T. Ostler, "The Idea of Preexistence in Mormon Thought," in Bergera, ed., *Line upon Line,* 127–31; O. Kendall White Jr., *Mormon Neo-orthodoxy: A Crisis Theology* (Salt Lake City, 1987), 59–70; Charles R. Harrell, "The Development of the Doctrine of Preexistence, 1830–1844," *BYUS* 28 (Spring 1988), 77–84; John S. Tanner, "Making a Mormon of Milton," *BYUS* 24 (Spring 1984), 200–1.
72. DC 27:11.
73. See summary in Yates, *Bruno,* 27–8.
74. Moses 5:5–11.
75. Moses 6:53–4, 59–68.
76. Moses 5:10–11, 6:53; DC 93:38. Mormon doctrinal abandonment of original sin is discussed in McMurrin, *Theological Foundations,* 57–68; and White, *Mormon Neo-orthodoxy,* 68–80.
77. McMurrin, *Theological Foundations,* 68–77; Articles of Faith 2–4.
78. Cannon and Cook, eds., *Far West Record,* 20–1; Buerger, " 'The Fulness of the Priesthood,' " 12–16.
79. DC 93:12–14, 20. There were two other references to grace before Smith's death in 1844: one in 1834 in reference to Warren Cowdery, soon to be a dissenter (DC 106:8) and one in 1841 in reference to the president and governors of the United States, seen to be oppressing the Mormon church (DC 124:9).
80. For two views on these changes, see White, *Mormon Neo-orthodoxy,* 68–80; and Blake T. Ostler, "The Development of the Mormon Concept of Grace," *Dialogue* 24 (Spring 1991), 57–87.

Changing Usage of Critical Theological Terms in the Doctrine and Covenants

	1828–9	1830–3	1834–9	1841–4
"Sections" of the *DC* attributed to each period	16	85	24	10
Theological terms used:[a]				
Atonement	1	6	—	1
Justification	—	4	—	—
Elect or election	—	7	—	—
Grace	2	14	1	1
Sanctification	—	21	3	1
Mysteries	5	18	1	—
Key	3	17	8	12
Fulness	—	22	4	5
Ordinances	—	6	3	4
Seal	—	8	—	7
Bind	—	11	3	4
Pure/purity	—	12	3	5
Exaltation to godhood	—	—	—	5

[a]Figures refer to the frequency of a given word in the *Doctrine and Covenants* (rather than the appearance of a theme in a "section" of the *DC*).

81. Stephen A. Marini, *The Radical Sects of Revolutionary New England* (Cambridge, Mass., 1982), 136–55; Charlotte Irwin, "Pietist Origins of American Universalism" (M.A. thesis, Tufts University, 1966); George H. Williams, *The Radical Reformation* (Philadelphia, 1962), 834–44.

82. John L. Peters, *Christian Perfection and American Methodism* (New York, 1956), 42–3; Robert N. Flew, *The Idea of Perfection in Christian Theology: An Historical Study of the Christian Ideal in the Present Life* (Oxford, 1934), 332–6; Robert E. Chiles, *Theological Transition in American Methodism: 1790–1935* (New York, 1965), 115–23.

83. See Harrell, "The Development of the Doctrine of Preexistence," 76.

84. E. Robert Paul, "Joseph Smith and the Plurality of Worlds Idea," *Dialogue* 19 (Summer 1986), 15–36; E. Robert Paul, "Joseph Smith and the Manchester (New York) Library," *BYUS* 22 (Summer 1982), 333–56; Thomas Dick, *The Philosophy of a Future State* (Brookfield, Mass., 1829); E. Robert Paul, *Science, Religion, and Mormon Cosmology* (Urbana, 1992), 76–8.

85. Quinn, *Early Mormonism*, 174–5. See also Mary Ann Meyers, "Death in Swedenborgian and Mormon Eschatology," *Dialogue* 14 (Spring 1981), 58–64, an essay that points out the close parallels between Mormon and Swedenborgian thought; "Sermon on 1 Corinthians 15:41–42," *The Churchman's Magazine* 4 (July 1825), 101–6; Mary Ann Meyers, *A New World Jerusalem* (Westport, Conn., 1983), 23–7; Marguerite Beck Block, *The New Church in*

the New World: A Study of Swedenborgianism in America (New York, 1932; repr., 1968), 19–51.

86. Andrew Michael Ramsay, *The Travels of Cyrus* (Boston, 1795), xi–xii, xv, 79–80, 100, 219, 221; Andrew Michael Ramsay, *The Philosophical Principles of Natural and Revealed Religion. Part Second.* (Glasgow, 1749), 215–18, 225, 235–6, 372.

87. Paul, "Joseph Smith and the Manchester Library," 340.

88. Leonard J. Arrington et al., *Building the City of God: Community and Cooperation among the Mormons* (Salt Lake City, 1976), 19; Arndt, *George Rapp's Harmony Society,* 430, 497, 531–2; Brodie, *No Man Knows My History,* 171n. Smith certainly read the work of Thomas Dick, for in January 1844, at the establishment of the Nauvoo Library, he was credited for one copy of "Dick's Philosophy" (Nauvoo Library and Literary Institute, Amount of Stock, Historian's Office Library, LDS Church).

89. See Hill, *Quest for Refuge,* 21–2; Fielding, "The Growth of the Mormon Church," 134–46.

90. Angelic alphabets ("taken from the Kabbalistic Tree") were an element of the Fourth, or Secret Master's, degree in the Masonic sequence, suggesting that there may have been some Masonic influence at Kirtland (Mackey, *An Encyclopedia of Freemasonry,* 1:49).

91. Parley P. Pratt, *Key to the Science of Theology . . .* (Liverpool, 1855), 97–107; Pratt, ed., *Autobiography of Parley P. Pratt,* 32; Parley P. Pratt, *A Voice of Warning* (1837; repr., Salt Lake City, 1978), 12–14. On popular Mesmerism, see John L. Greenway, "'Nervous Disease' and Electric Medicine," and Robert C. Fuller, "Mesmerism and the Birth of Psychology," in Arthur Wrobel, ed., *Pseudo-science and Society in Nineteenth-Century America* (Lexington, Ky., 1987), 46–73, 205–22.

92. DC 35:18; Whitmer, *An Address to All Believers,* 35.

9. Temples, Wives, Bogus-Making, and War

1. DC 110:13–16.

2. I am in fundamental agreement with the thrust of the interpretation in Hill, *Quest for Refuge.*

3. Kenneth Winn, *Exiles in a Land of Liberty* (Chapel Hill, 1989), 87–98; Hill, *Quest for Refuge,* 39–41.

4. Max H. Parkin, "Kirtland: Stronghold for the Kingdom," in F. Mark McKiernan et al., *The Restoration Movement* (Lawrence, Kans., 1979), 82–4; Max H. Parkin, "Conflict at Kirtland: The Nature and Cause of Internal and External Conflict of the Mormons in Ohio between 1830 and 1838" (M.A. thesis, Brigham Young University, 1966), 120–8. For a discussion of Hurlburt's possible connections to the divining culture, see Quinn, *Early Mormonism,* 84–6.

5. Hill, *Quest for Refuge,* 42–7; Brodie, *No Man Knows My History,* 143–58.

6. Hill, *Quest for Refuge,* 57.

7. Hill, *Quest for Refuge,* 47, 51–3; Hansen, *Quest for Empire,* 49; Brodie, *No Man Knows My History,* 159–65.

8. Newell and Avery, *Mormon Enigma,* 54; Hill, *Joseph Smith,* 192–3; Brodie, *No Man Knows My History,* 170–1.

9. Joseph Smith Diary, 1835–6, in Jessee, comp. and ed., *The Personal Writings of Joseph Smith,* 60, 62, 90–2.

10. Abraham 1:27, 3:1–28, 4:1–31; Yates, *Bruno,* 23–4. These documents were shown to be standard funerary inscriptions from the "Book of Breathings," dating from roughly 100 B.C. to A.D. 100. See Jerald Tanner and Sandra Tanner, *Mormonism: Shadow or Reality?* 4th ed. (Salt Lake City, 1982), 262–369.

11. Louis C. Zucker, "Joseph Smith as a Student of Hebrew," *Dialogue* 3 (Summer 1968), 41–55; Brodie, *No Man Knows My History,* 170–1; Jacob R. Marcus, *United States Jewry, 1776–1985* (Detroit, 1989), 1:277–81, 375, 429–30; Joseph Smith Diary, 1835–6, and Joseph Smith Jr. to William W. Phelps, Jan. 11, 1833, in Jessee, comp. and ed., *The Personal Writings of Joseph Smith,* 70, 91–3, 96–8, 108–9, 117–18, 123–4, 150–71, 262; James Knowlson, *Universal Language Schemes in England and France, 1600–1800* (Toronto, 1975), 12, 14.

12. "Newell Knight's Journal," quoted in Brodie, *No Man Knows My History,* 183–4; "Lydia Knight's History," quoted in Richard S. Van Wagoner, *Mormon Polygamy: A History* (Salt Lake City, 1985), 7–8.

13. Van Wagoner, *Mormon Polygamy,* 8; Brodie, *No Man Knows My History,* 183–4; Lawrence Foster, *Religion and Sexuality: Three American Communal Experiments of the Nineteenth Century* (New York, 1981), 138; Joseph Smith Diary, 1835–6, in Jessee, comp. and ed., *The Personal Writings of Joseph Smith,* 92.

14. Joseph Smith Diary, 1835–6, in Jessee, comp. and ed., *The Personal Writings of Joseph Smith,* 90–2.

15. Van Wagoner, *Mormon Polygamy,* 9–10; Joseph Smith Diary, 1835–6, in Jessee, comp. and ed., *The Personal Writings of Joseph Smith,* 74–9.

16. Danel W. Bachman, "New Light on an Old Hypothesis: The Ohio Origins of the Revelation on Eternal Marriage," *JMH* 5 (1978), 22–5, 30–1.

17. Here I follow the excellent discussion in Rex E. Cooper, *Promises Made to the Fathers: Mormon Covenant Organization* (Salt Lake City, 1990), 72–8. See also Milton V. Backman Jr., *The Heavens Resound: A History of the Latter-day Saints in Ohio* (Salt Lake City, 1983), 242–4.

18. Bushman, *Joseph Smith,* 77, 81, 91; Newell and Avery, *Mormon Enigma,* 27, 39; Sophia Lewis affidavit, in Rodger I. Anderson, *Joseph Smith's New York Reputation Reexamined* (Salt Lake City, 1990), 151.

19. James J. Tyler, "John Cook Bennett, Colorful Freemason of the Early Nineteenth Century," in *Proceedings of the . . . Grand Lodge . . . of the State of Ohio [1947]* (Cincinnati, 1948), 141–3; Brodie, *No Man Knows My History,* 311–12, 346.

20. Otho T. Beall Jr., "*Aristotle's Masterpiece* in America: A Landmark in the Folklore of Medicine," *WMQ* 20 (1963), 219–20.

21. To say nothing of the alchemical implications of the Thompsonian regime itself. On Mormons and Thompsonian medicine see Arrington, *Brigham Young,* 310–11; Kimball, *Heber C. Kimball,* 179–80; and Robert T. Divett, "Medicine and the Mormons: A Historical Perspective," *Dialogue* 12 (Fall 1979), 18–21.

22. Beall, "*Aristotle's Masterpiece,*" 207–22; Nicholas Culpeper, *Pharmacopoeia Londinensis: or the London Dispensatory further Adorned . . .* (London, 1653; repr., Boston, 1720), i, 253; *Aristotle's Complete Masterpiece . . .* (New York[?], 1796), 3, 41, 113; *Aristotle's Book of Problems* (Philadelphia, 1792), 38–9; Louis A. Montrose, "Shaping Fantasies: Figurations of Gender and Power in Elizabethan Culture," *Representations* 2 (1983), 73.

23. Austin Fife and Alta Fife, *Saints of the Sages and the Saddle: Folklore among the Mormons* (Bloomington, 1956), 358; Louis Kern, *An Ordered Love: Sex Roles and Sexuality in Victorian Utopias* (Chapel Hill, 1981), 155, 184.

24. Sophia Lewis affidavit, in Anderson, *Joseph Smith's New York Reputation Reexamined,* 151.

25. Newell and Avery, *Mormon Enigma,* 64–5.

26. Levi Lewis affidavit, in Anderson, *Joseph Smith's New York Reputation Reexamined,* 149; Newell and Avery, *Mormon Enigma,* 64–6; Brodie, *No Man Knows My History,* 181–2; Van Wagoner, *Mormon Polygamy,* 9; Danel W. Bachman, "A Study of the Mormon Practice of Plural Marriage before the Death of Joseph Smith" (M.A. thesis, Purdue University, 1975), 113.

27. Benjamin Winchester, "Primitive Mormonism," *Salt Lake Tribune,* Sept. 22, 1889, quoted in Bachman, "New Light," 31.

28. William G. McLoughlin, "Free Love, Immortalism, and Perfectionism in Cumberland, Rhode Island, 1748–1768," *Rhode Island History* 33 (1974), 77–8; Christopher Hill, *The World Turned Upside Down* (London, 1972), 306–23; Kern, *An Ordered Love,* 213, 373n; Van Wagoner, *Mormon Polygamy,* 9–10; Joyce Butler, "Cochranism Delineated: A Twentieth Century Study," in Charles E. Clark, James S. Leamon, and Karen Bowden, eds., *Maine in the Early Republic: From Revolution to Statehood* (Hanover, 1988), 146–64.

29. Donald Q. Cannon and Lyndon W. Cook, eds., *The Far West Record* (Salt Lake City, 1983), 163; Foster, *Religion and Sexuality,* 148.

30. McLoughlin, "Free Love," 77–8; Mary Ann Meyers, *A New World Jerusalem* (Westport, Conn., 1983), 29–30; Leo Miller, *John Milton among the Polygamophiles* (New York, 1974); John Cairncross, *After Polygamy Was Made a Sin: The Social History of Christian Polygamy* (London, 1974).

31. Jacob 1:15, 2:23–7, 3:5; Mosiah 11:2–4, 14; Ether 10:5; DC 76:103.

32. Newell and Avery, *Mormon Enigma,* 65.

33. Quotation from Hansen, *Quest for Empire,* 49. See also Hill, *Quest for Refuge,* 53, 75; Jessee, and comp. and ed., *The Personal Writings of Joseph Smith,* 59.

34. On Mormonism as a revolutionary movement, see the useful comments of Samuel S. Hill Jr., "A Typology of American Restitutionism: From Frontier Revivalism to the Jesus Movement," *Journal of the American Academy of Religion* 46 (1976), 69–70; and Hansen, *Quest for Empire*.

35. Parkin, "Kirtland: Stronghold for the Kingdom," 79; Andrew, *The Early Temples*, 46–50; Mackey, *An Encyclopedia of Freemasonry*, 2:824–35.

36. Smith, *History of the Church*, 2:379–92; Brodie, *No Man Knows My History*, 177–8.

37. Hill, *Joseph Smith*, 196–7; Brodie, *No Man Knows My History*, 178–80; Andrew, *The Early Temples*, 51–2; Vogel, *Religious Seekers*, 120–1; DC 110.

38. Parkin, "Conflict at Kirtland," 200–13.

39. David R. Proper, "Joseph Smith and Salem," *EIHC* 100 (1964), 88–97; DC 111; Brodie, *No Man Knows My History*, 192–4; Quinn, *Early Mormonism*, 206–11. There is an interesting parallel here in the writing of Nathaniel Hawthorne. In 1838, Hawthorne published "Peter Goldthwaite's Treasure," the first version of a story revised into *The House of the Seven Gables*. Writing about a house on the corner of Essex and North streets in Salem, Hawthorne told the story of a man who tore apart his family's house looking for alchemical gold distilled by a distant ancestor, only to find a chest filled only with the "worthless paper money of colonial days." In all probability, stories circulating in Salem about ancient treasure provided the common source both for Smith's divining and for Hawthorne's literature. See *Visitor's Guide to Salem*, rev. ed. (Salem, 1939), 68. I am grateful to John Engstrom for this reference.

40. Parkin, "Conflict at Kirtland," 295–308, provides the most detailed description of the Kirtland Bank; on the question of a bank revelation, see 296–300; on boxes of lead shot, see 307n. For a revisionist view of the Kirtland Bank, see Marvin S. Hill, C. Keith Rooker, and Larry T. Wimmer, *The Kirtland Economy Revisited: A Market Critique of Sectarian Economics* (Provo, 1977). See also Cale W. Adams, "Chartering the Kirtland Bank," *BYUS* 23 (1983), 467–82; Brodie, *No Man Knows My History*, 194–204; Hill, *Joseph Smith*, 205–17.

41. [Hildreth], "A History of the Divining Rod," 322–6; Karl J. R. Arndt, *George Rapp's Harmony Society, 1785–1847* (Rutherford, N.J., 1965), 532–5, 541–2.

42. Brodie, *No Man Knows My History*, 194–204; Hill, *Joseph Smith*, 205–15.

43. David Whitmer, *An Address to All Believers in Christ . . .* (Richmond, Mo., 1887; repr., 1938), 30–73; Vogel, *Religious Seekers*, 106, 218. Compare *A Book of Commandments, for the Government of the Church of Christ . . .* (Zion [Independence, Mo.], 1833), chapter 28, p. 60, with DC 27.

44. Brodie, *No Man Knows My History*, 194–206; Hill, *Quest for Refuge*, 57–61; Hill, *Joseph Smith*, 205–17; Marvin S. Hill, "Cultural Crisis in the Mormon Kingdom: A Reconsideration of the Causes of Kirtland Dissent," *Church History* 49 (1980), 291–7; Smith, *Biographical Sketches*, 211–13.

45. Roberts, *A Comprehensive History*, 1:402–3; Brodie, *No Man Knows My History*, 203, 207; Hill, *Joseph Smith*, 206.

46. *Elder's Journal,* Aug. 1838 [Far West, Mo.], 56–8, 60; see also Brodie, *No Man Knows My History,* 207.

47. Parkin, "Conflict at Kirtland," 315–18.

48. Reed Peck, "The Reed Peck Manuscript" (Modern Microfilm, Salt Lake City, n.d., Typescript), 5.

49. For a complementary but somewhat different approach to this problem, see R. Laurence Moore, *Religious Outsiders and the Making of Americans* (New York, 1986), 25–47.

50. Parley P. Pratt Jr., ed., *Autobiography of Parley P. Pratt* (1873; Salt Lake City, 1985), 16–17.

51. Francis W. Kirkham, *A New Witness for Christ in America,* rev. ed. (Salt Lake City, 1959), 2:40–1.

52. Kirkham, *A New Witness,* 2:98–9; Parkin, "Conflict at Kirtland," 41–2.

53. Eber D. Howe, *Mormonism Unvailed . . .* (Painesville, Ohio, 1834); Parkin, "Conflict at Kirtland," 269.

54. Newell and Avery, *Mormon Enigma,* 55.

55. *DC* 46:17–26.

56. Cannon and Cook, eds., *Far West Record,* 63–4 n. 2.

57. Pratt, *Autobiography,* 61.

58. Quotations from *DC* 50:1–3, 7; Cannon and Cook, eds., *Far West Record,* 63 n. 2. See also *DC* 46:7; Parkin, "Conflict at Kirtland," 66–89; Smith, *History of the Church,* 2:162; Lyndon W. Cook and Milton V. Backman Jr., eds., *Kirtland Elders' Quorum Record: 1836–1841* (Provo, 1985), 49; Ehat and Cook, comps. and eds., *The Words of Joseph Smith,* 12.

59. Parkin, "Conflict at Kirtland," 75, 79–80.

60. Cannon and Cook, eds., *Far West Record,* 79–83, 89–91 (quotation from 80 and 91).

61. "Newell Knight's Journal," 66–7, 74–5.

62. Carol F. Karlsen, *The Devil in the Shape of a Woman: Witchcraft in Colonial New England* (New York, 1987).

63. Moses 4:4, 5:24–5.

64. Cannon and Cook, eds., *Far West Record,* 162–3; *Document Containing the Correspondence, Orders, &c. in relation to the Disturbances with the Mormons . . .* (Fayette, Mo., 1841), 104; Peck, "The Reed Peck Manuscript," 6–7.

65. Brodie, *No Man Knows My History,* 206.

66. "The Book of John Whitmer Kept by Commandment" (Modern Microfilm, Salt Lake City, n.d., Typescript), 21.

67. *DC* 117:11; Quinn, *Early Mormonism,* 160.

68. See Moore, *Religious Outsiders,* 32–40.

69. Cannon and Cook, eds., *Far West Record,* 169; Parkin, "Conflict at Kirtland," 256–7; Milton V. Backman et al., comps., *A Profile of the Latter-day Saints of Kirtland, Ohio, and Members of Zion's Camp: Vital Statistics and Sources* (Provo, 1983), 20; Jessee, ed., *The Papers of Joseph Smith,* 483. Davis might also have been one of the two men, Solomon H. Denton and a "Mr.

Davis," indicted for an alleged plot to assassinate Grandison Newell in May 1837; see Parkin, "Conflict at Kirtland," 270–7.

70. *Document Containing the Correspondence,* 105; Parkin, "Conflict at Kirtland," 304–8. According to a suspect source, a counterfeiter and bounty hunter named Joseph H. Jackson who operated in Nauvoo in the 1840s, Joseph Smith was directly involved in counterfeiting in Ohio. Jackson claimed that Smith told him that he, Oliver Cowdery, and several others "were engaged in a bogus establishment on Licking Creek, but that their operations were cut short by the bursting of the Kirtland Bank" (*Adventures and Experiences of Joseph H. Jackson* [Warsaw, Ill., 1844; repr., 1960], 14).

71. P. P. Cherry, *The Western Reserve and Early Ohio* (Akron, 1921), 293–302, quotation from 293; Samuel A. Lane, *Fifty Years and Over of Akron and Summit County* (Akron, 1892), 57–9, 666–8, 876–91. For a recent discussion of these counterfeiters and of a later gang in Geauga County, see Gerald W. McFarland, *The Counterfeit Man: The True Story of the Boorn-Colvin Murder Case* (New York, 1990), 178–84. For Rigdon's comment, see *Elder's Journal,* Aug. 1838 [Far West, Mo.], 58.

72. Stephen C. LeSueur, *The 1838 Mormon War in Missouri* (Columbia, Mo., 1987), 16–27.

73. Brodie, *No Man Knows My History,* 459–62; Bachman, "A Study of the Mormon Practice of Plural Marriage," 113.

74. Smith, *History of the Church,* 3:35; Brodie, *No Man Knows My History,* 211.

75. Hill, *Quest for Refuge,* 75–6. The historiographical debate has pitted Mormon defenders against their critics, one side denying the existence of the Danites, or at least Smith's knowledge of their affairs, the other arguing the opposite. Three recent studies accept the view that Smith was fully aware of the Danites' operations: Hill, *Quest for Refuge,* 75–7; Winn, *Exiles in a Land of Liberty,* 123; and LeSueur, *The 1838 Mormon War,* 40–4, 114–15. For a recent defensive position, see Dean C. Jessee and David J. Whittaker, eds., "The Last Months of Mormonism in Missouri: The Albert Perry Rockwood Journal," *BYUS* 28 (Winter 1988), 5–15. For a useful older view, see Leland H. Gentry, "The Danite Band of 1838," *BYUS* 14 (Summer 1974), 421–50.

76. Smith, *History of the Church,* 3:179; "The Book of John Whitmer," 22.

77. Jessee and Whittaker, eds., "The Last Months of Mormonism in Missouri," 19, 23; Smith, *History of the Church,* 3:180. Also see *DC* 42:39; Gentry, "The Danite Band of 1838," 428–9.

78. LeSueur, *The 1838 Mormon War.*

10. The Keys to the Kingdom

1. Ehat and Cook, comps. and eds., *The Words of Joseph Smith,* 344–5.

2. Hill, *Joseph Smith,* 255, 263.

3. *DC* 110:12, 16.

4. The political history of the Nauvoo period of Mormon history has been very carefully analyzed by a number of scholars, and it will receive only passing treatment here. See Robert Bruce Flanders, *Nauvoo: Kingdom on the Mis-*

sissippi (Urbana, 1965), 92–178, 211–341; Robert Bruce Flanders, "Politics in Utopia: The Kingdom of God in Illinois," *Dialogue* 5 (Spring 1970), 26–36; Hansen, *Quest for Empire,* 49–120; Hill, *Quest for Refuge,* 99–182; Kenneth Winn, *Exiles in a Land of Liberty* (Chapel Hill, 1989), 152–238; and D. Michael Quinn, "The Mormon Succession Crisis of 1844," *BYUS* 16 (Winter 1976), 187–233.

5. Flanders, *Nauvoo,* 27–45, 161–3.

6. Flanders, *Nauvoo,* 55; Thomas Ford, *A History of Illinois* (Chicago, 1854), 232–3, 406–7.

7. M. Hamlin Cannon, "Migration of English Mormons to America," *American Historical Review* 52 (1947), 436–55; Dorothy Thompson, *The Chartists: Popular Politics in the Industrial Revolution* (New York, 1984).

8. J. F. C. Harrison, *The Second Coming* (New Brunswick, 1979); Clarke Garrett, *Respectable Folly* (Baltimore, 1975); W. H. G. Armytage, *Heavens Below: Utopian Experiments in England, 1560–1960* (London, 1961), 32–73, 259–71; William H. Oliver, *Prophets and Millennialists: The Uses of Biblical Prophecy from the 1790s to the 1840s* (Auckland, 1978); Richard H. Popkin, *Millenarianism and Messianism in English Literature and Thought, 1650–1800: Clark Library Lectures, 1981–1982* (Leiden, 1988); Clarke Garrett, "Swedenborg and the Mystical Enlightenment in Late Eighteenth-Century England," *Journal of the History of Ideas* 45 (1984), 67–81; Deborah M. Valenze, *Prophetic Sons and Daughters: Female Preaching and Popular Religion in Industrial England* (Princeton, 1985); Paul J. Korshin, "Queuing and Waiting: The Apocalypse in England, 1660–1750," in C. A. Patrides and Joseph Wittreich, eds., *The Apocalypse in English Renaissance Thought and Literature* (Ithaca, 1985).

9. The first Mormon mission is described in detail in Kimball, *Heber C. Kimball,* 44–53.

10. Kimball, *Heber C. Kimball,* 70–8; Grant Underwood, "The Religious Milieu of English Mormonism," in Richard L. Jensen and Malcolm R. Thorp, eds., *Mormons in Early Victorian Britain* (Salt Lake City, 1989), 21–48; Harrison, *Second Coming,* 188–90; Garrett, "Swedenborg and the Mystical Enlightenment," 77–81; Armytage, *Heavens Below,* 259–71.

11. Malcolm R. Thorp, "The Religious Backgrounds of Mormon Converts in Britain, 1837–52," *JMH* 4 (1977), 60, 63; Harrison, *Second Coming,* 191; James B. Allen, *Trials of Discipleship: The Story of William Clayton, a Mormon* (Urbana, 1987), 25–6.

12. Journal of Wandle Mace, 1809–90, typescript, pp. 63–6, Harold B. Lee Library, Brigham Young University; see also Quinn, *Early Mormonism,* 202; and Richard L. Anderson, "The Mature Joseph Smith and Treasure Searching," *BYUS* 24 (Fall 1984), 536.

13. "Thomas Dunsbee Common Place Book, 1690–1726," described in "Mormon Biographies," Film P–F (Reel 2), Bancroft Library, University of California, Berkeley. Michael Quinn devotes considerable attention to an analysis of certain artifacts associated with magical belief that have apparently passed down in Mormon hands. See *Early Mormonism,* 53–111. The provenance

and source of these items are uncertain, and they are not available for direct examination. Just as Quinn found that a Masonic badge associated with Joseph Smith and Brigham Young had an English origin (73), I suspect that much of the other material is also English, brought in by the first wave of English Mormons.

14. Hill, *Joseph Smith,* 270–4.

15. Dean May, "A Demographic Portrait of the Mormons, 1830–1980," in D. Michael Quinn, ed., *The New Mormon History: Revisionist Essays on the Past* (Salt Lake City, 1992), 122–3; Flanders, *Nauvoo,* 51–6; J. Christopher Conkling, *A Joseph Smith Chronology* (Salt Lake City, 1979), 144.

16. Flanders, *Nauvoo,* 94–102; Winn, *Exiles in a Land of Liberty,* 157–9.

17. Flanders, *Nauvoo,* 101–4; Roberts, *Comprehensive History,* 2:53–60.

18. Quotation from Ehat and Cook, comps. and eds., *The Words of Joseph Smith,* 413.

19. See Chapter 8.

20. Van Hale, "The Doctrinal Impact of the King Follett Discourse," *BYUS* 18 (Winter 1978), 212–16, 224; Charles R. Harrell, "The Development of the Doctrine of Preexistence, 1830–1844," *BYUS* 28 (Spring 1988), 77–88.

21. Diary of George Moore, Quincy, Illinois, Jan. 10, 1841, in Kenneth W. Cameron, ed., *Transcendental Epilogue,* 3 vols. (Hartford, 1965), 1:325.

22. Parley P. Pratt, *The Millennium and Other Poems: To which is annexed a Treatise on the Regeneration and Eternal Duration of Matter* (New York, 1840), 127; see Breck England, *The Life and Thought of Orson Pratt* (Salt Lake City, 1985), 55–6.

23. DC 121:28, 32; see Hale, "The Doctrinal Impact," 216 n. 36.

24. Ehat and Cook, comps. and eds., *The Words of Joseph Smith,* 9, 33, 37, see also 60, 68; and Harrell, "The Development of the Doctrine of Preexistence," 85–6.

25. See Ehat and Cook, comps. and eds., *The Words of Joseph Smith,* 36–8, 49n; Conkling, *A Joseph Smith Chronology,* 146.

26. DC 128:17–18; Malachi 4:5–6.

27. DC 137:1–10, 110:15.

28. George H. Williams, *The Radical Reformation* (Philadelphia, 1962), 837; J. S. Sachse, *The German Sectarians* (Philadelphia, 1899), 1:365.

29. Andrew, *The Early Temples,* 55–83; Flanders, *Nauvoo,* 191–210; DC 124:27–55.

30. DC 124:23; Brodie, *No Man Knows My History,* 275–6; Dean C. Jessee, "The Original Book of Mormon Manuscript," *BYUS* 10 (Spring 1970), 264–5.

31. See Mark C. Carnes, *Secret Ritual and Manhood in Victorian America* (New Haven, 1989); Mary Ann Clawson, *Constructing Brotherhood: Class, Gender, and Fraternalism* (Princeton, 1989); and Lynn Dumenil, *Freemasonry and American Culture, 1880–1930* (Princeton, 1984).

32. Kenneth W. Godfrey, "Joseph Smith and the Masons," *Journal of the Illinois State Historical Society* 64 (1971), 79–90; E. Cecil McGavin, *Mormonism and Masonry* (Salt Lake City, 1956), 88–121; Mervin B. Hogan, *The Found-*

ing Minutes of Nauvoo Lodge (Des Moines, 1971), 3–13; Mervin B. Hogan, "Nauvoo Lodge Founding Roster," Scottish Rite Library, MONH, Typescript; Brodie, *No Man Knows My History,* 279–83; Andrew, *The Early Temples,* 83–4.

33. Godfrey, "Joseph Smith and the Masons," 87–9.
34. Newell and Avery, *Mormon Enigma,* 105–7, 111; John C. Bennett, *The History of the Saints, or an Exposé of Joe Smith and Mormonism* (Boston, 1842), 217; Mackey, *An Encyclopedia of Freemasonry,* 1:235.
35. Ehat and Cook, comps. and eds., *The Words of Joseph Smith,* 108, 117, 119–20. See also Flanders, *Nauvoo,* 248.
36. Mackey, *An Encyclopedia of Freemasonry,* 1:380.
37. Arrington, *Brigham Young,* 102. Arrington notes that Young mentions a second temple endowment meeting on May 26, 1843. Latter quotation from L. John Nuttall Diary, quoted in David J. Buerger, "The Development of the Mormon Temple Endowment Ceremony," *Dialogue* 20 (Winter 1987), 47.
38. Various sources describe the temple ritual. Though they are always in some way hostile to Mormonism, these accounts are generally similar. On this point see Buerger, "The Development of the Mormon Temple Endowment Ceremony," 48 n. 15. The accounts consulted include (in chronological order) Increase McGee Van Dusen, *The Sublime and Ridiculous Blended, called the Endowment: As was Acted by upwards of Twelve Thousand, in secret, in the Nauvoo Temple* . . . (New York, 1848), 6–11; John Hyde Jr., *Mormonism: Its Leaders and Designs* (New York, 1857), 89–101; William Jarman, "Temple Endowment Ritual and Ceremonies [1869]," typescript from *Hell upon Earth* (1885), ed. Wesley M. Jones, Oakland, 1965, Bancroft Library, University of California, Berkeley; Mrs. S. G. R., "Mysteries of the Endowment House," *Salt Lake City Tribune,* Sept. 24, 1879 (pamphlet on file at the Bancroft Library); William J. Whalen, *The Latter-day Saints in the Modern Day World: An Account of Contemporary Mormonism* (New York, 1964), 159–94; Gerald Tanner and Sandra Tanner, *Mormonism: Shadow or Reality?* 4th ed. (Salt Lake City, 1982), 462–73. See also Brodie, *No Man Knows My History,* 278–82; Buerger, "The Development of the Mormon Temple Endowment Ceremony," 44–9; Boyd Kirkland, "The Development of the Mormon Doctrine of God," in Gary J. Bergera, ed., *Line upon Line: Essays on Mormon Doctrine* (Salt Lake City, 1989), 38–9; and Carnes, *Secret Ritual and Manhood,* 6–7.
39. Buerger, "The Development of the Mormon Temple Endowment Ceremony," 49.
40. Andrew, *The Early Temples,* 85–91; Ehat and Cook, comps. and eds., *The Words of Joseph Smith,* 120.
41. See comparison of rituals in Tanner and Tanner, *Mormonism,* 486–9; Whalen, *The Latter-day Saints in the Modern Day World,* 182–3, 187–8. In 1990 many or all of these Masonic symbols were cut from the Mormon endowment ritual. See Chapter 12.
42. Malcolm C. Duncan, *Duncan's Masonic Ritual and Monitor* . . . 3d ed. (New York, 1866), 35.

43. *Illustrations of Masonry, By One of the Fraternity, Who has devoted Thirty Years to the Subject: with an Appendix, containing a Key to the Higher Degrees of Freemasonry; By a member of the Craft* (Cincinnati, [1827]), 118–22.

44. David Bernard, *Light on Masonry: A Collection of all of the Most Important Documents on the Subject of Speculative Freemasonry . . .* (Utica, 1829), 253–4, 264, 268; typescript of 1785 manuscript of regulations for the Massachusetts Lodge of Perfection, on file at MONH, 248–53; see also Yates, *Bruno,* 23–5.

45. Mackey, *An Encyclopedia of Freemasonry,* 1:26–7; John T. Thorp, "Lodges of Adoption," *Masonic Papers V* (Leicester, 1915), 16–23.

46. DC 130:9–11.

47. Buerger, "The Development of the Mormon Temple Endowment Ceremony," 42 n. 10; *Deseret News,* Nov. 27, 1875, p. 3.

48. Flanders, *Nauvoo,* 93–6, 101, 110; Brodie, *No Man Knows My History,* 266–8; Hill, *Joseph Smith,* 279–86.

49. James J. Tyler, "John Cook Bennett, Colorful Freemason of the Early Nineteenth Century," *Proceedings of the . . . Grand Lodge . . . of the State of Ohio . . .* (Cincinnati, 1947), 140–4; Richard S. Van Wagoner, *Mormon Polygamy: A History* (Salt Lake City, 1986), 16–18; *Proceedings of the Grand Lodge of . . . Ohio . . . From 1808–1847 Inclusive* (Columbus, 1857), 222–7.

50. The Bennett family is described in Charles P. Bennett, *Yankee Clippers, Golden Slippers and More: A Bennett Family History and Genealogy* (Mount Ayr, Iowa, 1987), 10–35. Land-sale record discovered by historian George Mitten in Washington County, Ohio, Recorder's Office, Deed Records, vol. 19, pp. 70–1, dated Apr. 22, 1825. Samuel Hildrith was a noted local historian of early Ohio, and given this connection with Stephen Davis, it seems highly likely that he was the author of "A History of the Divining Rod." The Ransford Rogers signature is in Bennett, *The History of the Saints,* 13.

51. Eugene E. Hinman et al., *A History of the Cryptic Rite . . .* (Tacoma, 1931), 1:426–7. This Masonic-degree peddler may have been kin to Bennett's wife. His name was John G. Barker and her name was Mary Ann Barker. According to Van Wagoner, *Mormon Polygamy,* 16, Bennett was a thirty-third degree Mason.

52. Roger Van Noord, *King of Beaver Island: The Life and Assassination of James Jesse Strang* (Urbana, 1988), 49–50; Milo M. Quiafe, *The Kingdom of St. James: A Narrative of the Mormons* (New Haven, 1930), 48–50; Hansen, *Quest for Empire,* 55, 98. On the Halcyon church in Cincinnati and Marietta, see page 102.

53. Flanders, *Nauvoo,* 247, 260–1; Hansen, *Quest for Empire,* 55.

54. Newell and Avery, *Mormon Enigma,* 325 n. 36; Jessee, ed., *The Papers of Joseph Smith,* 459; Maria Ward, *Female Life Among the Mormons* (New York, 1856), 417; Ehat and Cook, comps. and eds., *The Words of Joseph Smith,* 342–3, 366.

55. Kimball, *Heber C. Kimball,* 84–5; Godfrey, "Joseph Smith and the Masons,"

86; Andrew F. Ehat, ed., "'They Might Have Known That He Was Not a Fallen Prophet' – The Nauvoo Journal of Joseph Fielding," *BYUS* 19 (Winter 1979), 145; Buerger, "The Development of the Mormon Temple Endowment Ceremony," 45–6; Arrington, *Brigham Young,* 452 n. 7.

56. For Mormon perspectives on a hermetic restoration, see Quinn, *Early Mormonism,* 185–91; and Hugh W. Nibley, *The Message of the Joseph Smith Papyri: An Egyptian Endowment* (Salt Lake City, 1975). On the assassination, see Newell and Avery, *Mormon Enigma,* 195; M. H. Adamson, "The Treasure of the Widow's Son" (University of Utah, n.d., unpublished paper), 11; McGavin, *Mormonism and Masonry,* 15–31.

57. Hale, "The Doctrinal Impact of the King Follett Discourse," 220–2.

58. Quotations from Stan Larson, ed., "The King Follett Discourse: A Newly Amalgamated Text," *BYUS* 18 (Winter 1978), 200–1, 203–4. See also Hale, "The Doctrinal Impact of the King Follett Discourse," 212–20; and Donald Q. Cannon, "The King Follett Discourse: Joseph Smith's Greatest Sermon in Historical Perspective," *BYUS* 18 (Winter 1978), 179–92.

59. Thomas F. O'Dea, *The Mormons* (Chicago, 1957), 128.

60. Newell and Avery, *Mormon Enigma,* 140; DC 131:1–4. In an addendum to this revelation, Smith announced that "all spirit is matter," anticipating a theme of his King Follett discourse, as did his April 1, 1842, editorial on "body and spirit" in the *Times and Season,* reprinted in Smith, *History of the Church,* 4:571–81.

61. DC 132:15–18.

62. DC 132:1, 6, 30–9, 63; Lawrence Foster, *Religion and Sexuality* (New York, 1981), 144–5; Louis J. Kern, *An Ordered Love* (Chapel Hill, 1981), 144–57.

63. Donald Q. Cannon and Lyndon W. Cook, eds., *The Far West Record* (Salt Lake City, 1983), 20–1; DC 110:13–16.

64. David J. Buerger has summarized the evolution of Mormon ritual in a passage which beautifully captures the process. "[T]he constant reshuffling and recombining of theological and scriptural images during these early years could easily be termed 'the fulness that was never full.' At each step of the way, Joseph Smith proclaimed that he had 'completed the organization of the Church,' and 'passed through all of the necessary ceremonies,' or restored 'the highest order of the Melchizedek Priesthood,' only to introduce more revelations and theological innovations creating yet new layers of ritual, deposited on or integrated with the old. . . . As the ritual evolved, lay Mormons advanced into the 'inner circle,' receiving ordinances and symbols formerly only held by Joseph Smith and his immediate circle, while Joseph and his associates moved on to higher kingdoms, more sure promises, and more secret rituals" (David J. Buerger, "'The Fulness of the Priesthood,' The Second Anointing in Latter-day Saint Theology and Practice," *Dialogue* 16 [Spring 1983], 23–4).

65. Ehat and Cook, comps. and eds., *The Words of Joseph Smith,* 244–5; Buerger, "'The Fulness of the Priesthood,'" 20–1; Buerger, "The Development of the Mormon Temple Endowment Ceremony," 49.

66. Ehat and Cook, comps. and eds., *The Words of Joseph Smith,* 329–30; see also Buerger, "'The Fulness of the Priesthood,'" 21–2. For the 1836 and 1842

revelations, see *DC* 110:15 and 128:17. References to Elijah's prophecy (Malachi 4:5–6) in New York revelations (*DC* 2:2, 27:9) are attributed to 1823 and 1830, but no record of these revelations exists before their publication in 1842 and 1835 respectively. A reference in an 1833 revelation (*DC* 98:16) regarding the Missouri troubles suggests that Smith began thinking about the Elijah prophecy in the early years in Kirtland. See Cook, *The Revelations of the Prophet Joseph Smith*, 6–8, 38–9, and 201.

67. *DC* 132:7, 18, 19, 26; Ehat and Cook, comps. and eds., *The Words of Joseph Smith*, 330, 335. Here I am very much indebted to Buerger, " 'The Fulness of the Priesthood,' " 36–7.

68. *DC* 132:19–20.

69. *DC* 132:19, 26–7.

70. Frances A. Yates, *The Rosicrucian Enlightenment* (London, 1972), 30, 59ff., 206ff.; Peter French, *John Dee* (London, 1972), 120–1; Gamini Salgado, *The Elizabethan Underworld* (London, 1977), 112ff.; A. L. Rowse, *Sex and Society in Shakespeare's Age: Simon Forman the Astrologer* (New York, 1974); Leo Miller, *John Milton among the Polygamophiles* (New York, 1974), 39–44; Arthur Worrall, *Quakers in the Colonial Northeast* (Hanover, N.H., 1980), 14, 30, 51; Kern, *An Ordered Love*, 76–90; Foster, *Religion and Sexuality*, 46–8; Peter C. Erb, "Introduction," in Erb, ed., *Johann Conrad Beissel and the Ephrata Community* (Lewiston, N.Y., 1985), 15–20; Karl J. R. Arndt, *George Rapp's Harmony Society, 1785–1847* (Philadelphia, 1965), 98–9; Christopher Hill, *The World Turned Upside Down* (London, 1972), 314–23; Quinn, *Early Mormonism*, 175. Harold Bloom has arrived at the same conclusion about the relationships among Mormon celestial marriage, divinization, and mystery traditions, through the perspective of the Cabala (*The American Religion: The Emergence of the Post-Christian Nation* [New York, 1992], 104–6). See also Harrell, "The Development of the Doctrine of Preexistence," 90.

71. The text of this passage is as follows: "Conception in the moon: The conception or woman, rising in the moon, demonstrates the purity that matter subsists of, in order to remain in its pure state unmixed with any other body, from which must come a new king, and a revolution or fullness of time, filled with glory, whose name is ALBRA-EST." This quotation from Bernard, *Light on Masonry*, 265, is almost exactly the same as the text in the 1785 Lodge of Perfection manual (typescript, p. 249, MONH).

72. Linda P. Wilcox, "The Mormon Concept of a Mother in Heaven," in Maureen U. Beecher and Lavina F. Anderson, eds., *Sisters in Spirit: Mormon Women in Historical and Cultural Perspective* (Urbana, 1987), 64–7; Rex E. Cooper, *Promises Made to the Fathers: Mormon Covenant Organization* (Salt Lake City, 1990), 104.

73. See Wilcox, "The Mormon Concept," and Carol Cornwall Madsen, "Mormon Women and the Temple: Toward a New Understanding," in Beecher and Anderson, eds., *Sisters in Spirit*, 80–110; Margaret Toscano and Paul Toscano, *Strangers in Paradox: Explorations in Mormon Theology* (Salt Lake City, 1990), 47–59, 71–97.

74. Carl G. Jung, *Psychology and Alchemy*, vol. 12 of *The Collected Works of C.*

G. *Jung,* 2d ed., trans. R. F. C. Hull (New York, 1967), 317–431. Carl G. Jung, *Alchemical Studies,* vol. 13 of *The Collected Works,* 2d ed., trans. R. F. C. Hull (New York, 1967), 197: "the alchemist, in his small way, competes with the creator insofar as he strives to do work analogous to the work of creation; and therefore he likens his microscopic *opus* to the work of the world creator."

75. F. Sherwood Taylor, *The Alchemists* (New York, 1949), 123–49; Jung, *Psychology and Alchemy,* 228–30; John Read, *Prelude to Chemistry: An Outline of Alchemy, Its Literature and Relationships* (New York, 1937), 118ff.

76. Jung, *Psychology and Alchemy,* 477.

77. William Hutchinson, *The Spirit of Masonry* (London, 1775; repr., 1987), appendix, 6–7; quotation from Henry Dana Ward, *Free Masonry: Its Pretensions Exposed in Faithful Extracts from Standard Authors . . .* (New York, 1828), 7.

78. Blake T. Ostler, "The Development of the Mormon Concept of Grace," *Dialogue* 24 (Spring 1991), 76.

79. See note 80, Chapter 8.

80. Ostler, "The Mormon Concept of Grace," 77; Buerger, " 'The Fulness of the Priesthood,' " 13–14, 36–7; *DC* 132:7. Ostler and Buerger represent extremes in the contemporary Mormon debate over grace: the "neo-orthodox" attempting to build bridges to Christianity, and the traditionalists defending distinctive Mormon doctrines. For traditional views of the Mormon doctrine of grace, see Sterling M. McMurrin, *The Theological Foundations of the Mormon Religion* (Salt Lake City, 1985), 68–77; and O. Kendall White, *Mormon Neo-orthodoxy: A Crisis Theology* (Salt Lake City, 1987), 80–5. It should be stressed that not only strict Calvinists but nineteenth-century Methodists would have rested salvation on grace and atonement alone (Robert E. Chiles, *Theological Transition in American Methodism: 1790–1935* [New York, 1965], 145–8). For an analysis of the Mormon doctrine into the twentieth century, see Chapter 12.

81. White, *Mormon Neo-orthodoxy,* 68–80; McMurrin, *The Theological Foundations,* 57–68.

82. Quoted in Danel W. Bachman, "A Study of the Mormon Practice of Plural Marriage before the Death of Joseph Smith" (M.A. thesis, Purdue University, 1975), 339. William Law is identified as the author in David J. Buerger, "The Adam-God Doctrine," *Dialogue* 15 (Spring 1982), 27.

83. Ehat and Cook, comps. and eds., *The Words of Joseph Smith,* 247.

11. A Tangle of Strings and the Kingdom of God

1. Nauvoo *Wasp,* Aug. 20, 1842, quoted in Newell and Avery, *Mormon Enigma,* 120.

2. Newell and Avery, *Mormon Enigma,* 95–6.

3. Danel W. Bachman, "A Study of the Mormon Practice of Plural Marriage before the Death of Joseph Smith" (M.A. thesis, Purdue University, 1975), 104–15, established the conservative estimate of thirty-one wives. For other, more extensive lists of Smith's wives, see Andrew Jenson, "Plural Marriage,"

Historical Record 5 (May 1887), 219–40; Brodie, *No Man Knows My History*, 434–65; and Jerald Tanner and Sandra Tanner, *Joseph Smith and Polygamy* (Salt Lake City, n.d.), 41–7. For an important synthetic discussion, see Lawrence Foster, *Religion and Sexuality* (New York, 1981), 151–8. Kimball (*Heber C. Kimball*, 95) provides a list of men known to have married plural wives at Nauvoo.

4. Foster, *Religion and Sexuality*, 125–49; Newell and Avery, *Mormon Enigma*, 97.

5. Harold Bloom, *The American Religion: The Emergence of the Post-Christian Nation* (New York, 1992), 69, 96–111.

6. Quoted in Richard S. Van Wagoner, *Mormon Polygamy* (Salt Lake City, 1986), 30.

7. See Newell and Avery, *Mormon Enigma*, 95–120, 130–68; Foster, *Religion and Sexuality*, 149–50; *DC* 132:52, 54.

8. Newell and Avery, *Mormon Enigma*, 111–12; Van Wagoner, *Mormon Polygamy*, 15–25; Brodie, *No Man Knows My History*, 309–14.

9. Newell and Avery, *Mormon Enigma*, 111.

10. Newell and Avery, *Mormon Enigma*, 106–18, 128–9; Van Wagoner, *Mormon Polygamy*, 27–35; Foster, *Religion and Sexuality*, 169–74; Brodie, *No Man Knows My History*, 314–22.

11. Newell and Avery (*Mormon Enigma*, 112–13) detail this code.

12. Foster (*Religion and Sexuality*, 174–7) discusses *The Peacemaker* in detail.

13. Newell and Avery, *Mormon Enigma*, 179–80 (emphasis in original).

14. Nauvoo *Wasp*, Aug. 20, 1842, quoted in Newell and Avery, *Mormon Enigma*, 120.

15. Arrington, *Brigham Young*, 100–1; Kimball, *Heber C. Kimball*, 93–103; Van Wagoner, *Mormon Polygamy*, 27–35. See George D. Smith, ed., *An Intimate Chronicle: The Journals of William Clayton* (Salt Lake City, 1991), 99, 108–9, 111–13, 115, 118, 150, and 156, for Clayton's struggle with one of his wives who was in love with someone else, his efforts to sleep with two of his wives in the same bed, and his dream about marrying another young woman.

16. The antinomian circumstances of the Nauvoo leadership were not fundamentally dissimilar to those of the restorationist Anabaptists at Münster in 1534–5. See John Cairncross, *After Polygamy Was Made a Sin: The Social History of Christian Polygamy* (London, 1974), 1–28, 166–200; D. Michael Quinn, "Socioreligious Radicalism of the Mormon Church: A Parallel to the Anabaptists," in Davis Bitton and Maureen U. Beecher, eds., *New Views of Mormon History* (Salt Lake City, 1987), 363–86; William E. Juhnke, "Anabaptism and Mormonism: A Study in Comparative History," *John Whitmer Historical Association Journal* 2 (1982), 38–46.

17. D. Michael Quinn, "Latter-day Saint Prayer Circles," *BYUS* 19 (Fall 1978), 85. It should be noted that plurality was a secret even within the endowed inner circle, because a few members had not accepted the principle.

18. Bernard Farber, *Guardians of Virtue: Salem Families in m1800* (New York, 1972), 66–155; Naomi Lameroux, "Banks, Kinship, and Economic Development: The New England Case," *Journal of Economic History* 46 (1986), 647–67.

19. D. Michael Quinn, "The Mormon Hierarchy, 1832–1932: An American Elite" (Ph.D. diss., Yale University, 1976).

20. Kimball, *Heber C. Kimball,* 97.

21. William Law made this argument in the "Buckeye's Lamentation for Want of More Wives." See Bachman, "Plural Marriage," 339.

22. Smith's, Young's, and Kimball's marriages are enumerated in Bachman, "Plural Marriage," 333–6; Arrington, *Brigham Young,* 420–1; Brodie, *No Man Knows My History,* 457–88; Kimball, *Heber C. Kimball,* 307–16. Michael Quinn's conclusions, looking at marriage data from nineteenth-century Nauvoo and Utah, are that the Mormon elite was, "in effect, an extended family," and that the "practice of polygamy by the General Authorities multiplied the possibility of in-law relationships within the hierarchy" (Quinn, "The Mormon Hierarchy," 33, 62). See also Leonard J. Arrington and Davis Bitton, *The Mormon Experience: A History of the Latter-day Saints* (New York, 1979), 204–5; Foster, *Religion and Sexuality,* 166–9; and Louis J. Kern, *An Ordered Love* (Chapel Hill, 1981), 142–3.

23. Jan Shipps, "Mormon Restorationism," in Richard T. Hughes, ed., *The American Quest for the Primitive Church* (Urbana, 1988), 186; Hill, *Quest for Refuge,* xviii–xix.

24. Andrew F. Ehat, " 'It Seems Like Heaven Began on Earth': Joseph Smith and the Constitution of the Kingdom of God," *BYUS* 20 (Spring 1980), 254.

25. Harold Schindler, *Orrin Porter Rockwell: Man of God, Son of Thunder* (Salt Lake City, 1983), 67–73.

26. Hill, *Quest for Refuge,* 136–7.

27. Hansen, *Quest for Empire,* 59.

28. This point is stressed in Hansen, *Quest for Empire,* 56–7; and Ehat, " 'It Seems Like Heaven Began on Earth,' " 254–7.

29. Council membership is from Hansen, *Quest for Empire,* 223, and D. Michael Quinn, "The Council of Fifty and Its Members, 1844 to 1945," *BYUS* 20 (Winter 1980), 193–7. Endowments are from David J. Buerger, " 'The Fulness of the Priesthood': The Second Anointing in Latter-day Saint Theology and Practice," *Dialogue* 16 (Spring 1983), 23; Masonic members from Mervin B. Hogan, *The Official Minutes of Nauvoo Lodge, U.D.* (Des Moines, Iowa, n.d.).

30. Ehat, " 'It Seems Like Heaven Began on Earth,' " 259.

31. Hansen, *Quest for Empire,* 72–89; Robert Bruce Flanders, *Nauvoo: Kingdom on the Mississippi* (Urbana, 1965), 292–305, quotation from 298; Hill, *Quest for Refuge,* 138–41; Kenneth Winn, *Exiles in a Land of Liberty* (Chapel Hill, 1989), 194–202; see also Quinn, "The Council of Fifty and Its Members," 163–97.

32. Flanders, *Nauvoo,* 306–10; Newell and Avery, *Mormon Enigma,* 180–98; Van Wagoner, *Mormon Polygamy,* 61–9.

33. Minutes of the Council of the Twelve Apostles, Apr. 18, 1844, quoted in Hill, *Quest for Refuge,* 143.

34. Nauvoo City Council minutes, June 10, 1844, quoted in Van Wagoner, *Mormon Polygamy,* 66.

35. Hill, *Quest for Refuge,* 128, 250 nn. 19–20; *Warsaw Signal,* Apr. 24, June 5,

June 12, 1844, quoted in Gerald Tanner and Sandra Tanner, *Mormonism – Shadow or Reality?* 4th ed. (Salt Lake City, 1982), 536–7; Edward Bonney, *The Banditti of the Prairies, or, the Murderer Doom!! A Tale of the Mississippi Valley* (Chicago, 1850; repr., Norman, Okla., 1963), viii–ix.

36. Smith, *History of the Church*, 6:434–5.

37. On Turley's background, see Milton V. Backman et al., comps., *A Profile of the Latter-day Saints of Kirtland, Ohio, and Members of Zion's Camp: Vital Statistics and Sources* (Provo, 1983), 72; Ehat and Cook, comps. and eds., *The Words of Joseph Smith*, 295 n. 7; James B. Allen, *Trials of Discipleship: The Story of William Clayton, a Mormon* (Urbana, 1987), 28, 48, 50–1. For the counterfeiting evidence, see Smith, *History of the Church*, 7:525; "Report of Suits Pending in the Circuit Court of the United States for the District of Illinois at its December Term 1845," in Reports of the U.S. District Attorneys, 1845–50, National Archives, Washington, D.C.; William Hall, *The Abominations of Mormonism Exposed* (Cincinnati, 1852), 20, 80–1.

38. "Report of Suits Pending"; "Manuscript History of Brigham Young," Apr. 5, May 12, 1846; quoted in Tanner and Tanner, *Mormonism – Shadow or Reality?* 540, 542; N. W. Green, *Mormonism: Its Rise, Progress, and Present Condition. Embracing the Narrative of Mrs. Mary Ettie V. Smith . . .* (Hartford, 1870), 107. For Hawes's biography, see Cook, *The Revelations of the Prophet Joseph Smith*, 260–1.

39. "Report of Suits Pending"; Joseph H. Jackson, *A Narrative of the Adventures and Experience of Joseph H. Jackson, in Nauvoo* (Warsaw, 1844; repr., Morrison, Ill., 1960), 13–14; Bonney, *Banditti*, viii–xvii, 257–8.

40. See Bonney, *Banditti*; Jackson, *Narrative*; Allen, *Trials of Discipleship*, 85–6.

41. Quinn, "The Council of Fifty and Its Members," 193–7. A fourth man, Gilbert Eaton, may have been Marenus G. Eaton, another non-Mormon, who was appointed by Smith in March of 1844. Marenus G. Eaton exposed the alleged plot by Jackson and the dissenters against the Smiths and was apparently the man described by Lucy Mack Smith as "a man named Eaton, who was our friend" (Smith, *Biographical Sketches*, 276). He was a friend of old acquaintance if he was the "Miruans Eaton" born in Tunbridge, Vermont, in 1797 according to the Tunbridge Vital Records.

42. Smith, *History of the Church*, 7:395–6, 408, 428, 485, 549–51, 553–4; Breck England, *The Life and Thought of Orson Pratt* (Salt Lake City, 1985), 108; Schindler, *Orrin Porter Rockwell*, 136. On the Whittling Societies, see Tanner and Tanner, *Mormonism – Shadow or Reality?* 538–9.

43. Whereas accounts of counterfeiting by the other indicted men can be found in a number of sources, there appears to be only one such account mentioning the Mormon inner circle. Joseph H. Jackson's *Narrative* states that Joseph Smith had recruited him as well as Barton and Eaton for the Nauvoo "Bogus establishment," and a press had been set up in a meeting room where the "holy order" had met. According to Jackson all of the Twelve Apostles except Orson Pratt and Heber C. Kimball were involved and actually "took turns working" the press (Jackson, *Narrative*, 13–14). See Allen, *Trials of Discipleship*, 85–6, for an account of the relationship between Jackson and Smith.

44. Roberts, *Comprehensive History*, 2:532–6.
45. Hill, *Quest for Refuge*, 172–3.
46. Bonney was indicted on the word of A. B. Williams, who was accused by Bonney's acquitting jury of running a counterfeiting operation at Nauvoo. It is possible that Williams also accused the Mormon hierarchy. See Bonney, *Banditti*, 243–4, 251–8.
47. For Young's Jan. 24, 1846, condemnation of counterfeiting see Smith, *History of the Church*, 7:574. The post-Nauvoo evidence is from April 6 and 12 and May 12, 1846 ("Manuscript History of Brigham Young," quoted in Tanner and Tanner, *Mormonism – Shadow or Reality?* 540–1), and from June 20, 1847 (Hosea Stout, *On the Frontier: The Diary of Hosea Stout*, ed. Juanita Brooks [Salt Lake City, 1964], 1:261–2).
48. Journal of Heber C. Kimball, Jan. 2, 1846, quoted in Hill, *Quest for Refuge*, 179; Hall, *The Abominations*, 81.
49. England, *Orson Pratt*, 131–2; Arrington, *Brigham Young*, 143–66.
50. Mark P. Leone, *The Roots of Modern Mormonism* (Cambridge, Mass., 1979), 86–110; Andrew, *The Early Temples*.
51. J. Kenneth Davies, *Mormon Gold: The Story of California's Mormon Argonauts* (Salt Lake City, 1984), 19–20.
52. Davies, *Mormon Gold*, 77–91.
53. Davies, *Mormon Gold*, 78–83, 90–1; Tanner and Tanner, *Mormonism – Shadow or Reality?* 543.
54. Davies, *Mormon Gold*, 78–9, 95. On Young's early life as an artisan, see Arrington, *Brigham Young*, 14–18; J. Sheldon Fisher, "Brigham Young as a Mendon Craftsman: A Study in Historical Archaeology," *New York History* 61 (1980), 431–48.
55. *Counterfeiting Accusations (1845–6) against and Role in Salt Lake Bank and Gold Missions (1848–50) of the Thirty-three Members of the 1844 Council of Fifty Settling in Utah*

	Indicted or escaped arrest (1845–6)	Others	Total
Salt Lake Bank and Gold missions (1848–50)	6 (4) [4]	3 (1) [1]	9 (5) [5]
Others	4 (3) [2]	20 (5) [6]	24 (8) [8]
Total	10 (7) [6]	23 (6) [7]	33 (13) [13]

Note: Numbers in parentheses indicate individuals related to Joseph Smith or Brigham Young. Numbers in brackets indicate individuals endowed, sealed, and anointed by June 1844.
Sources: Council of Fifty: Quinn, "The Council of Fifty and Its Members," 193–7. (Thirty-three members of the council appointed in 1844 emigrated to Utah and were still in good standing in 1850.) 1845–6: "Report of Suits Pending"; Smith, *History of the Church*, 7:395–6, 408, 428, 485, 549–1,

553–4. 1848–50: Davies, *Mormon Gold,* 77–95. Kinship: Bachman, "A Study of the Mormon Practice of Plural Marriage," 113–15, 333–6; Arrington, *Brigham Young,* 418–21; and various sources. Ritual: Buerger, "'The Fulness of the Priesthood,'" 23.

56. Davies, *Mormon Gold,* 87, 295–301, 309.

57. One instance of magical belief led to yet another encounter with hermetic danger. Despite Young's dictum, William Clayton, once Joseph Smith's secretary, was fascinated by high magic during the 1860s. From a borrowed copy of an English almanac titled *Zadkiel's Astronomical Ephemeris,* Clayton developed a passion for astrology in 1862, writing impatiently to various booksellers for later issues and demonstrating a familiarity with the work of William Lilly, the English Civil War astrologer. In 1864 Clayton began to communicate with Dr. William Freeman in New York City, who that March sold him a copy of his *Guide to the Cabala,* two "Mysterious Electrical and Weird Rings, or Secret Talisman of the Ancient Hebrews and Egyptians," and a membership in a society called the British Mutual Metallic Association. Eventually recruiting another twenty-five members for the association, Clayton ordered a variety of items from Freeman, including secret "fish bait," metal insoles with healing properties, and a number of expensive "outfits" for experiment by the members. Nothing worked as advertised. On July 22 he wrote to Freeman much discouraged: "Bro. Wm. Walker, one of the members of this branch is, by trade and occupation, a cutler and worker in metals. He has built a small furnace at his residence (which is very quiet and retired) for the purpose of transmuting and working up the outfits for the members to the best possible advantage. . . . everything worked to a charm with one very important exception, and that is the growing properties after melting. He tells me the instructions were followed literally during the three days heat, as well as during the whole process; the metal was never suffered to chill, and it was attended to during the three days heat with the greatest punctuality; yet the metal is no heavier at the end of three days than it was immediately after melting, neither will the metal stand the test of acids." A week later Clayton complained to a friend that none of the outfits had "exhibited the 'growing' principle"; he was certain that "Dr. Freeman has withheld some important ingredient until he assures himself of the purity and integrity of our intentions." Later that fall the members of the association gave up, resigned to the loss of their considerable investment. In the same tradition of alchemical puffery that Phillips the transmuter had used to trick Burroughs and "Lysander" eighty years before in the Quabbin Hills of central Massachusetts, Dr. Freeman had promised these Utah Mormons the philosopher's stone. Heirs to a theology of transformation to divinity, they were easy targets for the con man's hermetic promise that they could grow metals in a furnace. See William Clayton to William Freeman, Mar. 2, May 18, May 25, June 6, July 22, 1864, and William Clayton to D. M. Thomas, July 28, 1864, in the William Clayton Letterbooks, Bancroft Library, University of California, Berkeley. For a full account, see Allen, *Trials of Discipleship,* 323–37.

58. Brigham Young, Aug. 14, 1853, *JD* 1:264–71.

59. Young, Aug. 14, 1853, *JD* 1:276.
60. England, *Orson Pratt*, 100.
61. England, *Orson Pratt*, 175–6; Orson Pratt, Aug. 29, 1852, *JD* 1:53–66.
62. Quotation from *The Seer* (Aug. 1853), 1:117, cited in Gary James Bergera, "The Orson Pratt–Brigham Young Controversies: Conflict within the Quorums, 1853–1868," *Dialogue* 13 (Summer 1980), 11. See in general, Bergera, 9–11; and England, *Orson Pratt*, 197–9.
63. Parley P. Pratt, *Key to the Science of Theology* . . . (Liverpool, 1855), 97–107.
64. England, *Orson Pratt*, 200; Bergera, "The Orson Pratt–Brigham Young Controversies," 11–13.
65. E. Robert Paul, *Science, Religion, and Mormon Cosmology* (Urbana, 1992), 129–30. See also Robert C. Fuller, "Mesmerism and the Birth of Psychology," in Arthur Wrobel, ed., *Pseudo-science and Society in Nineteenth-Century America* (Lexington, Ky., 1987), 205–20.
66. On Kimball's role see T. B. H. Stenhouse, *The Rocky Mountain Saints* (New York, 1873), 561n; and Bergera, "The Orson Pratt–Brigham Young Controversies," 30, 46 n. 53.
67. Brigham Young, Apr. 9, 1852, *JD* 1:50 (emphasis in original).
68. Young, Apr. 9, 1852, *JD* 1:50–1; David J. Buerger, "The Adam–God Doctrine," *Dialogue* 15 (Spring 1982), 18–22.
69. Buerger, "The Adam–God Doctrine"; Kimball, *Heber C. Kimball*, 208–10; Andrew, *The Early Temples*, 99–100; Brigham Young, Oct. 7, 1852, Aug. 11, 1872, *JD* 1:218, 15:127.
70. Richard F. Burton, *The City of the Saints, and Across the Rocky Mountains to California* (New York, 1862; repr., Niwot, Colo., 1990), 385, 397–8. See Fawn Brodie, *The Devil Drives: A Life of Sir Richard Burton* (New York, 1967), 179–89.
71. Burton, *City of the Saints*, 237, 398.

12. Let Mysteries Alone

1. *JD* 1:273, 274; 3:124, 126, 336; 10:176.
2. Brigham Young, Apr. 9, 1852, Mar. 16, 1856, *JD* 1:46, 3:254.
3. Max Weber, *The Sociology of Religion*, trans. Ephraim Fischoff (Boston, 1963); A. F. C. Wallace, "Revitalization Movements," *American Anthropologist* 58 (1956), 264–81; Victor Turner, *The Ritual Process: Structure and Antistructure* (Chicago, 1969); Victor Turner, *Dramas, Fields, and Metaphors: Symbolic Action in Human Society* (Ithaca, 1974). Here my understanding is also informed by the sect–church literature, but – for reasons developed in this chapter – I find its linearity problematic. See H. Richard Niebuhr, *The Social Sources of Denominationalism* (New York, 1929); Ernst Troeltsch, *The Social Teachings of the Christian Churches*, 2 vols., trans. Olive Wyon (New York, 1931); and Benton Johnson, "On Sect and Church," *American Sociological Review* 28 (1963), 539–49.
4. Wallace, "Revitalization Movements"; Turner, *Dramas, Fields, and Metaphors*, 37–42.

5. Stephen B. Oates, *The Fires of Jubilee: Nat Turner's Fierce Rebellion* (New York, 1975); Eric Anderson, "The Millerite Use of Prophecy: A Case Study of a 'Striking Fulfilment,'" in Ronald L. Numbers and Jonathan M. Butler, eds., *The Disappointed: Millerism and Millenarianism in the Nineteenth Century* (Bloomington, 1987), 78–91. For Joseph Smith's reaction to William Miller, see Ehat and Cook, comps. and eds., *The Words of Joseph Smith*, 332.

6. Joyce Butler, "Cochranism Delineated: A Twentieth Century Study," in Charles E. Clark et al., eds., *Maine in the Early Republic: From Revolution to Statehood* (Hanover, 1988), 146–64.

7. Clarke Garrett, "Swedenborg and the Mystical Enlightenment in Late Eighteenth-Century England," *Journal of the History of Ideas* 45 (1984), 67–81; Stephen A. Marini, *Radical Sects of Revolutionary New England* (Cambridge, Mass., 1982), 148–53; Stephen J. Stein, *The Shaker Experience in America: A History of the United Order of Believers* (New Haven, 1992), on dual divinity, see 72–3, 174, 195, 206, 258, 259, 267, 310–11, 324–6; on Shakers and Swedenborg, see 227, 322, 324.

8. Susan Sutton Smith, ed., *The Topical Notebooks of Ralph Waldo Emerson* (Columbia, Mo., 1990), 1:28, 35, 50, 53, 69, 81, 83, 90, 91, 112, 133, 135, 138, 147, 154, 157, 172, 176, 178, 185, 301, 310, 312; Gay Wilson Allen, *Waldo Emerson: A Biography* (New York, 1981), 89–92, 454–7; John S. McAleer, *Ralph Waldo Emerson: Days of Encounter* (Boston, 1984), 84–5, 92–3, 168–9.

9. R. Laurence Moore, "Mormonism, Christian Science, and Spiritualism," in Howard Kerr and Charles L. Crow, eds., *The Occult in America: New Historical Perspectives* (Urbana, 1983), 143–56; Ann Braude, *Radical Spirits: Spiritualism and Women's Rights in Nineteenth-Century America* (Boston, 1989), 32–43; Robert W. Delp, "Andrew Jackson Davis: Prophet of American Spiritualism," *Journal of American History* 54 (1967), 43–56; J. Stillson Judah, *The History and Philosophy of the Metaphysical Movements in America* (Philadelphia, 1967), 11–12, 33–49, 51–6, 148–54, 272–6.

10. Frank Littel, "Radical Pietism in American History," in F. Ernest Stoeffler, ed., *Continental Pietism and Early American Christianity* (Grand Rapids, 1976), 172; John H. Noyes, *The Berean: A Manual for the Help of those who seek the Faith of the Primitive Church* (Putney, Vt., 1847; repr., New York, 1969), 58–9, 487–8, cited in Gillian G. Fuqua, "The Origins of Oneida Perfectionism: A Reassessment" (senior honors thesis, Tufts University, 1989), 24–7, 34; Louis J. Kern, *An Ordered Love* (Chapel Hill, 1981), 219–34.

11. See Judah, *The History and Philosophy of the Metaphysical Movements*, 92–145; R. Laurence Moore, *In Search of White Crows, Spiritualism, Parapsychology, and American Culture* (New York, 1977); Kerr and Crow, eds., *The Occult in America*; Arthur Wrobel, ed., *Pseudo-science and Society in Nineteenth-Century America* (Lexington, Ky., 1987); Mark C. Carnes, *Secret Ritual and Manhood in Victorian America* (New Haven, 1989).

12. Harold Bloom, *The American Religion: The Emergence of the Post-Christian Nation* (New York, 1992).

13. Steven L. Shields, *Divergent Paths of the Restoration: A History of the Latter-day Saint Movement,* 3d ed. (Bountiful, Utah, 1982), 28–73.

14. On these points, see Brigham Young, Dec. 3, 1854, *JD* 3:144; Oct. 6, 1855, *JD* 3:44–5; Feb. 17, 1856, *JD* 3:205–11; Apr. 20, 1856, *JD* 3:318; Oct. 25, 1857, *JD* 5:352; Apr. 8, 1860, *JD* 8:42; and note 1 above.

15. Eugene E. Campbell, *Establishing Zion: The Mormon Church in the American West, 1847–1869* (Salt Lake City, 1988), 181–98; Thomas G. Alexander, "Wilford Woodruff and the Mormon Reformation of 1855–57," *Dialogue* 25 (Summer 1992), 25–39. See also Paul H. Peterson, "The Mormon Reformation of 1856–1857: The Rhetoric and the Reality," *JMH* 15 (1989), 59–87.

16. Brigham Young, Sept. 21, 1856, *JD* 4:53–4. See also Campbell, *Establishing Zion,* 198–9; Alexander, "Wilford Woodruff and the Mormon Reformation," 27–8; T. B. H. Stenhouse, *The Rocky Mountain Saints: A Full and Complete History of the Mormons . . .* (New York, 1873), 298–300.

17. Heber C. Kimball, Apr. 19, 1857, *JD* 4:363; July 26, 1857, *JD* 5:95; Sept. 27, 1857, *JD* 5:271–3. See also Brigham Young, Aug. 14, 1853, *JD* 1:275; Sept. 21, 1856, *JD* 4:54.

18. Norman F. Furniss, *The Mormon Conflict, 1850–1859* (New Haven, 1960), 88–9.

19. Juanita Brooks, *The Mountain Meadows Massacre* (Stanford, 1950), 21–37, 161; Campbell, *Establishing Zion,* 233–52; Furniss, *Mormon Conflict,* passim; Harold Schindler, *Orrin Porter Rockwell: Man of God, Son of Thunder* (Salt Lake City, 1983), 268–81.

20. Campbell, *Establishing Zion,* 296–9.

21. Arrington, *Brigham Young,* 300–1.

22. Arrington, *Brigham Young,* 305–6, 348; Campbell, *Establishing Zion,* 160–1; Thomas G. Alexander, *Mormonism in Transition: A History of the Latter-day Saints, 1890–1930* (Urbana, 1986), 259.

23. Arrington, *Brigham Young,* 302–5.

24. Breck England, *The Life and Thought of Orson Pratt* (Salt Lake City, 1985), 200–2, 213–17; Gary James Bergera, "The Orson Pratt–Brigham Young Controversies: Conflict within the Quorums, 1853–1868," *Dialogue* 13 (Summer 1980), 17–35; David J. Buerger, "The Adam–God Doctrine," *Dialogue* 15 (Spring 1982), 23–4, 28–31.

25. England, *Orson Pratt,* 214; Alexander, "Wilford Woodruff and the Mormon Reformation," 29; Stenhouse, *Rocky Mountain Saints,* 300–1.

26. Quinn, *Early Mormonism,* 215–16.

27. Priddy Meeks, *Journal* (Dugway, Utah, [1970?]); Quinn, *Early Mormonism,* 195–211, 215.

28. For the Godbeites and Amasa Lyman, see Ronald W. Walker, "The Commencement of the Godbeite Protest: Another View," *Utah Historical Quarterly* 42 (1974), 217–44; Davis Bitton, "Mormonism's Encounter with Spiritualism," *JMH* 1 (1974), 39–50; Loretta L. Hefner, "Amasa Mason Lyman: The Spiritualist," *JMH* 6 (1979), 75–88; Loretta L. Hefner, "From Apostle to

Apostate: The Personal Struggle of Amasa Mason Lyman," *Dialogue* 16 (Spring 1983), 91–104; Stenhouse, *Rocky Mountain Saints,* 630–45. For the contemporary rise of Spiritualism in England, see Logie Barrow, *Independent Spirits: Spiritualism and English Plebeians, 1850–1910* (London, 1986).

29. Amasa M. Lyman, "Nature of the Mission of Jesus," *The Latter-day Saints' Millennial Star* 24 (Apr. 5, 1862), 209–17, esp. 211, 213, 215; Hefner, "From Apostle to Apostate," 92–93.

30. Thomas G. Alexander, *Things of Heaven and Earth: The Life and Times of Wilford G. Woodruff* (Salt Lake City, 1991), 204–5; quotation is from Woodruff's journal.

31. Brigham Young, Aug. 15, 1852, *JD* 6:296–7; Mar. 16, 1856, *JD* 3:247; Sept. 21, 1856, *JD* 4:53–4; May 22, 1859, *JD* 7:144; July 8, 1860, *JD* 8:114.

32. Brigham Young, July 18, 1869, *JD* 13:59; May 8, 1870, *JD* 14:41; July 10, 1870, *JD* 14:70–3; May 21, 1871, *JD* 14:130. This summary is based on a review of the titles of Young's discourses and on an analysis of those discourses cited as discussing atonement in John A. Widstoe, ed., *The Discourses of Brigham Young . . .* (Salt Lake City, 1926), 27, 388.

33. John Taylor, Feb. 22, 1863, *JD* 10:113–20; England, *Orson Pratt,* 234.

34. Samuel W. Taylor, *The Kingdom or Nothing: The Life of John Taylor, Militant Mormon* (New York, 1976), 278; see also Buerger, "The Adam–God Doctrine," 35.

35. John Taylor, *An Examination in and an Elucidation of the Great Principle of the Mediation and Atonement of Our Lord and Savior Jesus Christ* (Salt Lake City, 1882), 9, 128, 167–8.

36. Alexander, *Things of Heaven and Earth,* 235, 258–9.

37. Alexander, *Things of Heaven and Earth,* 266–76.

38. Alexander, *Things of Heaven and Earth,* 239–40, 266–87; Richard S. Van Wagoner, *Mormon Polygamy: A History* (Salt Lake City, 1986), 141–56; Edward L. Lyman, *Political Deliverance: The Mormon Quest for Utah Statehood* (Urbana, 1986).

39. Arrington, *Brigham Young,* 251, 295; Drew Gilpin Faust, *The Creation of Confederate Nationalism: Ideology and Identity in the Civil War South* (Baton Rouge, 1988); Steven Hahn, "Class and State in Post-emancipation Societies," *American Historical Review* 95 (1990), 75–98; F. A. van Jaarsveld, *The Awakening of Afrikaner Nationalism, 1868–1881* (Cape Town, 1961); Hermann Giliomee, "The Beginnings of Afrikaner Ethnic Consciousness, 1850–1915," in Leroy Vail, ed., *The Creation of Tribalism in Southern Africa* (Berkeley, 1989).

40. Robert Gottlieb and Peter Wiley, *America's Saints: The Rise of Mormon Power* (New York, 1984); John Heinerman and Anson Shupe, *The Mormon Corporate Empire* (Boston, 1985).

41. Buerger, "The Adam–God Doctrine," 38–43; Quinn, *Early Mormonism,* 204, 213, 218; Linda K. Newell, "Gifts of the Spirit: Women's Share," in Maureen U. Beecher and Lavina F. Anderson, eds., *Sisters in Spirit: Mormon Women in Historical and Cultural Perspective* (Urbana, 1987), 111–50; Alexander, *Mormonism in Transition,* 290–8; Gordon Shepherd and Gary

Shepherd, *A Kingdom Transformed: Themes in the Development of Mormonism* (Salt Lake City, 1984), 194–6; David J. Buerger, "The Development of the Mormon Temple Endowment Ceremony," *Dialogue* 20 (Winter 1987), 52–5.

42. Shipps, *Mormonism,* 109–29; Alexander, *Mormonism in Transition,* 258–71, 297–302; Shepherd and Shepherd, *A Kingdom Transformed,* 73–102, 147–77.

43. Alexander, *Mormonism in Transition,* 258.

44. James E. Talmage, *A Study of the Articles of Faith* . . . (Salt Lake City, 1899; repr., 1952), 41–2; James E. Talmage, *Jesus the Christ: A Study of the Messiah and His Mission according to Holy Scriptures both Ancient and Modern* (Salt Lake City, 1915; repr., 1972), 38, 43–4; Boyd Kirkland, "The Development of the Mormon Doctrine of God," in Gary J. Bergera, ed., *Line upon Line: Essays on Mormon Doctrine* (Salt Lake City, 1989), 43–7; Thomas G. Alexander, "The Reconstruction of Mormon Doctrine," in Bergera, ed., *Line upon Line,* 60–1.

45. DC 138:2–4, 14, 58. See Shipps, *Mormonism,* 131–49.

46. The theological and intellectual course of this transformation was shaped in great measure by a debate within the Mormon hierarchy about science and religion (specifically regarding the question of evolution) involving Brigham Roberts, James Talmage, John Widstoe, and Joseph Fielding Smith Jr. See Richard Sherlock, "'We Can See No Advantage to a Continuation of the Discussion': The Roberts/Smith/Talmage Affair," *Dialogue* 13 (Fall 1980), 63–78; Jeffery E. Keller, "Discussion Continued: The Sequel to the Roberts/Smith/Talmage Affair," *Dialogue* 15 (Spring 1982), 79–98; and E. Robert Paul, *Science, Religion, and Mormon Cosmology* (Urbana, 1992), 146–91.

47. Shipps, *Mormonism,* 129.

48. Buerger, "The Development of the Mormon Temple Endowment Ceremony," 56–61; Alexander, *Mormonism in Transition,* 298–9; Alex Shoumatoff, "The Mountain of Names," *New Yorker,* May 13, 1985, pp. 51–101.

49. Buerger, "The Development of the Mormon Temple Endowment Ceremony," 57; David J. Buerger, "'The Fulness of the Priesthood': The Second Anointing in Latter-day Saint Theology and Practice," *Dialogue* 16 (Spring 1983), 27–44, quotation from 39; Alexander, *Things of Heaven and Earth,* 204; Margaret Toscano and Paul Toscano, *Strangers in Paradox: Explorations in Mormon Theology* (Salt Lake City, 1990), 144, 153, 179–96.

50. Buerger, "The Development of the Mormon Temple Endowment Ceremony," 63–8. For a contemporary, and controversial, critique of Mormon temple ritual, and Mormon culture in general, see Deborah Laake, *Secret Ceremonies: A Mormon Woman's Intimate Diary of Marriage and Beyond* (New York, 1993).

51. Armand L. Mauss, "The Fading of the Pharaoh's Curse: The Decline and Fall of the Priesthood Ban against Blacks in the Mormon Church," *Dialogue* 14 (Fall 1981), 10–45.

52. Peter Steinfels, "Mormons Drop Rite Opposed by Women," *New York*

Times, May 3, 1990, section A1, p. 22; John Dart, "Mormons Modify Temple Rites," *Los Angeles Times,* May 5, 1990, p. F20.

53. Richard D. Poll, "What the Church Means to People Like Me," *Dialogue* 2 (Winter 1967), 107–17; see most recently Jeffrey C. Jacob, "Explorations in Mormon Social Character: Beyond the Liahona and Iron Rod," *Dialogue* 22 (Summer 1989), 44–74.

54. The term "neo-orthodox" is problematical, because the orthodoxy referred to is Christian, not Mormon. This term emerged because the more appropriate term "fundamentalist" had already been assigned to the Mormon schismatic sects emerging since the 1920s. See paragraphs below.

55. O. Kendall White, *Mormon Neo-orthodoxy: A Crisis Theology* (Salt Lake City, 1987), 89–157. Quotation from Toscano and Toscano, *Strangers in Paradox,* 119.

56. Van Wagoner, *Mormon Polygamy,* 183–222; James Coates, *In Mormon Circles: Gentiles, Jack Mormons, and Latter-day Saints* (Reading, Mass., 1991), 152–66, 175–97; Hans A. Baer, *Recreating Utopia in the Desert: A Sectarian Challenge to Modern Mormonism* (Albany, 1988), 31–42; Quinn, *Early Mormonism,* 210–11; Ogden Kraut, *Seerstones* (Dugway, Utah, n.d.); Ogden Kraut, "Adam: He Is God! A Letter to Mark E. Petersen, November 13, 1980," typescript pamphlet, Utah State Historical Society files; Joseph W. Musser, *Michael Our Father and Our God: The Mormon Conception of Deity,* 4th ed. (Salt Lake City, 1963). For the broader context of right-wing sectarian violence in the Mountain West, see James Coates, *Armed and Dangerous: The Rise of the Survivalist Right* (New York, 1987).

57. Coates, *In Mormon Circles,* 165. At this writing, April 1993, it is apparent from the siege of the Branch Davidian sect in Waco, Texas, that the Mormons are not unique in this regard.

58. Gerald Tanner and Sandra Tanner, "Ritualist Child Abuse and the Mormon Church" [printing a memorandum by Bishop Glenn L. Pace, July 19, 1990], *Salt Lake City Messenger* 80 (Nov. 1991); James Coates, "Mormon-affiliated Group Linked to Rituals of Devil-Worship, Occult," *Chicago Tribune,* Nov. 3, 1991, section 1, p. 9.

59. Chris Jorgensen and Peggy Fletcher Stack, "It's Judgement Day for Far Right: LDS Church Purges Survivalists," *Salt Lake Tribune,* Nov. 29, 1992, pp. A1–2; Dirk Johnson, "Seeking a Moderate Image, Mormons Expel Extremists," *New York Times,* Dec. 21, 1992, p. A14.

60. Gottlieb and Wiley, *America's Saints;* Heinerman and Shupe, *The Mormon Corporate Empire.*

61. "Render unto Smith," *Economist,* July 13, 1991, pp. 27–9.

62. Anson Shupe, *The Darker Side of Virtue: Corruption, Scandal, and the Mormon Empire* (Buffalo, 1991), 141–60.

63. Robert Pool, "How Cold Fusion Happened – Twice!" *Science* 244 (1989), 420–3; Mark Crawford, "Utah Looks to Congress for Cold Fusion Cash," *Science* 244 (1989), 522–3; Frank Close, *Too Hot to Handle: The Race for Cold Fusion* (Princeton, 1991).

64. On the latter point, see the concluding chapter, "Extraterrestrial Intelligence and Mormon Cosmology," in Paul, *Science, Religion, and Mormon Cosmology,* 192–228.

65. Shupe, *The Darker Side of Virtue,* 44–75; Jaye Scholl, "Snookered in Salt Lake City: How a Major West Coast Utility Was Fleeced Out of Millions," *Barron's,* Jan. 11, 1993, pp. 8–9, 20–4. See "Church Leader Decries Mormon Fraud," *Sunstone Review* 2 (Sept. 1982), 10; Linda Sillitoe, "The Successful Marketing of the Holy Grail," *Dialogue* 20 (Winter 1987), 97; Jacob, "Explorations in Mormon Social Character," 55. On recent bank failures in Utah, see Jeff Gerth, "U.S. Accused of Easing Pursuit of S.&L. Cases," *New York Times,* Aug. 12, 1992, p. D1; Jeff Gerth, "Two Regulators Say Testimony Led to Demotions," *New York Times,* Aug. 13, 1992, p. D1; "A Second S.&L. Scandal," *Harper's Magazine,* Nov. 1992, 17–24.

66. Linda Sillitoe and Allen Roberts, *Salamander: The Story of the Mormon Forgery Murders* (Salt Lake City, 1988), 200–10, 472; Robert Lindsey, *A Gathering of Saints: A True Story of Money, Murder, and Deceit* (New York, 1988), 41, 349–50; Steven Naifeh and Gregory White Smith, *The Mormon Murders: A True Story of Greed, Forgery, and Death* (New York, 1988), 73, 478. See also Sillitoe, "The Successful Marketing of the Holy Grail"; and Allen D. Roberts, " 'The Truth Is the Most Important Thing': The New Mormon History according to Mark Hofmann," *Dialogue* 20 (Winter 1987), 87–96; and Richard E. Turley Jr., *Victims: The LDS Church and the Mark Hofmann Case* (Urbana, 1992).

67. Lindsey, *A Gathering of Saints,* 380–1; Naifeh and Smith, *The Mormon Murders,* 386–7. A "forensic analysis" by George J. Throckmorton, appended to Sillitoe and Roberts, *Salamander,* 531–52, provides a list of twenty-one documents proven to be forged by Mark Hofmann.

68. See Dean C. Jessee, "New Documents and Mormon Beginnings," and Marvin S. Hill, "Money-digging Folklore and the Beginnings of Mormonism: An Interpretive Suggestion," both in *BYUS* 24 (Fall 1984 [released May 1986]), 397–428, 473–88; and Alan Taylor, "The Early Republic's Supernatural Economy," *American Quarterly* 38 (1986), 10–11, 13–14.

69. John Read, *Prelude to Modern Chemistry: An Outline of Alchemy, Its Literature and Relationships* (New York, 1937), 128. See also Michael Quinn's efforts to salvage the salamander image in *Early Mormonism,* 128–33.

70. Hugh Nibley, *The Message of the Joseph Smith Papyri: An Egyptian Endowment* (Salt Lake City, 1975); Hugh Nibley, "The Early Christian Prayer Circle," *BYUS* 19 (Fall 1978), 41–78; Quinn, *Early Mormonism,* 186–91.

71. Stephen E. Robinson, "The Apocalypse of Adam," *BYUS* 17 (Winter 1977), 131–53; John M. Lundquist and Steven D. Ricks, eds., *By Study and Also by Faith: Essays in Honor of Hugh W. Nibley on the Occasion of His Eightieth Birthday, 27 March 1990,* 2 vols. (Salt Lake City, 1990).

72. Bloom, *The American Religion.*

73. Linda Wilcox, "The Mormon Concept of a Mother in Heaven," in Beecher and Anderson, *Sisters in Spirit,* 66, 71; Toscano and Toscano, *Strangers in*

Paradox, 50–3, 71–97. See also Melodie Moench Charles, "The Need for a New Mormon Heaven," *Dialogue* 21 (Fall 1988), 73–88; Lavina Fielding Anderson, "Landmarks for LDS Women: A Contemporary Chronology," *Mormon Women's Forum* 3 (Dec. 1992), 1–20; the essays in Maxine Hanks, ed., *Women and Authority: Re-emerging Mormon Feminism* (Salt Lake City, 1992); Suzanne Gordon, "Challenging the Mormon Church," *Boston Globe,* Mar. 26, 1993, p. 53; Dirk Johnson, "As Mormon Church Grows, So Does Dissent from Feminists and Scholars," *New York Times,* Oct. 2, 1993, p. 7.

74. Benson Whittle, "Review of D. Michael Quinn, *Early Mormonism and the Magic World View* (Salt Lake City, 1987)," *BYUS* 27 (Fall 1987), 105–21.

75. Shipps, *Mormonism,* 148.

76. White, *Mormon Neo-orthodoxy;* Shepherd and Shepherd, *A Kingdom Transformed;* Philip L. Barlow, *Mormons and the Bible: The Place of the Latter-day Saints in American Religion* (New York, 1991).

77. Compare Thomas G. Alexander, "Historiography and the New Mormon History: A Historian's Perspective," *Dialogue* 19 (Fall 1986), 25–49; and Boyd Packer, "The Mantle Is Far, Far Greater than the Intellect," *BYUS* 21 (Summer 1981), 259–78.

78. Quinn, *Early Mormonism,* 218.

79. Shepherd and Shepherd, *A Kingdom Transformed,* 97–98, 101–2, 192.

80. White, *Mormon Neo-orthodoxy,* 174–5. The hermetic interpretation of Mormon origins proposed here creates problems for recent suggestions that Mormonism, having moved from sect to church, is now moving back along this continuum toward sect. Rather, the Mormon church is clearly moving into a position parallel to the Protestant fundamentalists and is by no means returning to the past. See Armand L. Mauss, "Assimilation and Ambivalence: The Mormon Reaction to Americanization," *Dialogue* 22 (Spring 1989), 30–67; and Armand L. Mauss and Philip L. Barlow, "Church, Sect, and Scripture: The Protestant Bible and Mormon Sectarian Retrenchment," *Sociological Analysis* 52 (1991), 397–414.

81. "Mormons Penalize Dissident Members," *New York Times,* Sept. 19, 1993, p. 13; Johnson, "As Mormon Church Grows, So Does Dissent from Feminists and Scholars."

Index